Nathan Crosby

Annual obituary notices of eminent persons who have died in the United States

Vol. 3

Nathan Crosby

Annual obituary notices of eminent persons who have died in the United States
Vol. 3

ISBN/EAN: 9783337723705

Printed in Europe, USA, Canada, Australia, Japan

Cover: Foto ©ninafisch / pixelio.de

More available books at **www.hansebooks.com**

ANNUAL OBITUARY NOTICES

OF

EMINENT PERSONS

Who have Died in the United States.

FOR

1858.

BY HON. NATHAN CROSBY.

For behold the Lord, the Lord of Hosts, doth take away from Jerusalem and from Judah the stay and the staff. * * * The mighty man and the man of war; the judge and the prophet, and the prudent and the ancient; the captain of fifty and the honorable man, and the counsellor, and the cunning artificer, and the eloquent orator. — ISAIAH iii. 1-3.

BOSTON:
JOHN P. JEWETT AND COMPANY.
1859.

TO THE

PRESIDENT

OF THE

MASSACHUSETTS HISTORICAL SOCIETY,

HON. ROBERT C. WINTHROP,

AND TO THE MEMBERS,

WHOSE HISTORICAL GATHERINGS EMBRACE CURRENT DATA AS WELL AS
SUCH AS ARE OBSCURED BY TIME,
IN THE HOPE
THAT SUCH ANNUAL COLLECTIONS AS ARE FOUND IN THIS WORK
WILL MEET WITH YOUR FAVORABLE REGARD,

To You, this Volume,

BEING THE SECOND OF THE SERIES,

IS MOST RESPECTFULLY DEDICATED.

N. CROSBY.

Entered, according to Act of Congress, in the year 1860, by
NATHAN CROSBY,
In the Clerk's Office of the District Court of the District of Massachusetts.

STEREOTYPED AT THE
BOSTON STEREOTYPE FOUNDRY.

PREFACE.

WITH much labor and anxiety I have finished the compilation of my volume of "Obituary Notices" for 1858 — the second of the proposed annual series. I presume I have failed to find notices of many persons who had equal claims for remembrance, and in whom society had equal interest. Until the work becomes more generally known, and friends of deceased persons more careful to furnish notices, I fear my omissions and imperfections will occasion disappointments.

This work is an endeavor to save from forgetfulness those whose virtues are our inheritance, and whose lives are our worthiest models — an effort, by permanent record, to embalm precious memories, and preserve biographical and historical data, as individual elements of our national and social character. "Good men are the stars of the ages in which they live — they illustrate their times." By grouping the dead of single years together, we form interesting pictures of the generations as they pass away, and save from oblivion the men and women who have been most useful in sustaining and perfecting institutions which so well merit the praise and excite the admiration of the nations. It is a grateful tribute we ought to pay, and a benefit to future generations which should not be lost.

In my volume for 1857, I announced my purpose to be to publish annually such Obituary Notices as I could obtain of the "men who have originated and developed our institutions — of those whose names should be remembered by the generations'to come as the statesmen, the soldiers, the men of science and skill, the sagacious merchants, the eminent clergymen and philanthropists — those who have brought our country to the prosperity and distinction it now enjoys." I have been gratified at the kind opinions of the Press, and of many individuals, in favor of my work. In this volume I have introduced a less number of persons whose names, age, and residence were the only data of interest I had of them. As far as I can, I am desirous to give genealogical facts, family alliances, and social relations in connection with the marked traits of character which make men eminent in any of the departments of life.

PREFACE.

The last edition of Dr. Allen's American Biographical Dictionary has brief notices of the eminent dead down to 1857, where my first volume commences its more general and more extended notices of those who annually pass away.

I owe an apology to my numerous correspondents, who had reason to expect this volume much earlier. The delay was occasioned, in part, by want of the necessary subscriptions for the work to encourage me to proceed, and in part by delay in preparing the plates at the Stereotype Foundry. I owe a still further apology to those who have expected in an Appendix to find notices of persons who died before 1858. Upon further reflection, it has been thought best not to go back of 1857, except by gathering enough for one or two preliminary volumes hereafter.

I shall be most grateful for the aid of any person in collecting and preparing notices for my subsequent volumes, who has an interest in this particular field of labor — whose friends and acquaintances are proper persons for notice, or whose judgment and taste harmonize with my plan and effort — by correspondence, and by transmission of eulogies, obituaries, funeral sermons, *in memoriams*, newspapers, or unpublished family memorials.

To the kindred and friends of those whose names appear in this volume I may be allowed to say that I have taken great interest and received much satisfaction in this service. The name, the life, the influence of every man make a part of the history of the times; and I am sure this contribution to our annals will be of service to the future historian, and a present consolation to the surviving relatives.

I am greatly indebted to the many gentlemen who have contributed individual obituaries; but I am most especially obliged to Messrs. James C. and Frederick Ayer, distinguished chemists and druggists in this city, for the use of their newspaper exchanges, and for the uniform courtesy and assistance of those gentlemen and their clerks in my almost daily visits to their office since I commenced this work.

NATHAN CROSBY.

LOWELL, MASS., December, 1859.

OBITUARY NOTICES FOR 1858.

A.

ABBOTT   [1858.]   ABBOTT

HON. JAMES ABBOTT, Detroit, Mich., Mar. 12, æ. 83. Judge A. was a native of Detroit; for many years he and Joseph Campan were the only surviving inhabitants who were heads of families there in 1810. His father, also named James Abbott, was an Irishman, who came to this country at an early day, and, settling at Detroit, became agent of the American Fur Co., of which John Jacob Astor was a prominent stockholder. The father dying, his son James, who had long been in partnership with him, succeeded him as agent, and carried on the great and lucrative business of the company with success. The agency being removed, he continued till his death connected with the steadily diminishing fur trade at that point.

Judge A. was postmaster of Detroit in the territorial existence of Mich., his term of service commencing about 1808. While the British troops held the city in 1812, and to the end of the war, he, of course, was out of office; but, when the Americans regained possession on the declaration of peace, he was reinstated, and continued to be postmaster until 1827, when he was succeeded by John Norvall. During the greater part of the above period, he was also receiver of the U. S. land office. He was succeeded by Maj. Kearsley.

He was appointed by Gov. Hull a major in the Mich. militia in 1805, and, during the war of 1812, he was quartermaster general of the army. He derived his title of judge from the fact that he was an associate or side judge in the old Court of Common Pleas, which exercised pretty extended powers as a court for the limited business which it was called upon to transact. The number of inhabitants, however, was small; and not much other than ordinary police matters were transacted.

His wife, who survives him, is an estimable lady, the daughter of Maj. John Whistler, of the U. S. army, and sister to the famous engineer who constructed the railway from Boston to Stonington, and was afterwards, till his lamented death, employed by the Czar Nicholas on the magnificent railway from St. Petersburg to Moscow.

Judge A.'s mother was a noble woman, one of the true-hearted matrons of the revolutionary era. She was obliged to remain in Detroit during the British occupation. At the close of the war she was in very feeble health, and frequently remarked that she had but two earthly wishes, viz., to live to see the stars and stripes again wave over Detroit, and to see her exiled son (the judge) once more at home. When the American vanguard crossed the river and raised the flag, she was supported in her bed, that she might gratify her wish to once more behold its radiant folds. Her other wish was also granted; for her son hastened to his home, and reached it just in time to receive the blessing of his dying mother.

Judge A. leaves behind him only one child — a son, bearing his own name.

ABBOTT, Capt. John, Monroe Co., Miss., July 2, æ. 59. He was a native

1 *

of Ga., emigrating to Ala. above 20 years ago. While there he raised a company of volunteers, and commanded it in the Florida war. In 1838 he removed to Monroe Co.; in 1841 and in 1843 he was elected therefrom to the Miss. legislature.

ABBOTT, Mrs. Robert, Detroit, Mich., March —, æ. —. She had resided there 73 years; she was daughter of M. Audrain, one of the original settlers of what was then the trading post of Detroit.

ABBOTT, Dr. William, Fairlee, Vt., July 30, æ. 78 years, 6 mos., formerly of Salem, Mass.

ADAMS, Mrs. Abigail B., Gilsum, N. H., Feb. 23, æ. 43, wife of Rev. Ezra Adams. She was one of the earliest scholars at Mt. Holyoke Female Seminary, and bore through life the impress of the moral and intellectual power of Miss Lyon. She was deeply interested in her husband's work; a faithful mother, and a humble and steadfast Christian.

ADAMS, Benjamin, Boston, Mass., Nov. 13, æ. 77. He was born in Exeter, N. H., Mar. 13, 1781; was a grandson of Rev. Joseph Adams, settled in Stratham, N. H., (H. U. 1742.) His father removed to B. while he was a child, and at a proper age placed him as an apprentice to mercantile business. In 1801 he commenced business under the firm of B. Adams & Co., (afterwards Adams, Homer, & Co.) He spent 40 years in the dry-goods business.

HON. CHESTER ADAMS,

Natick, Mass., March 15, æ. 72. He was born in Bristol, Conn., in 1785, removed to Dedham, Mass., in 1799, thence to Needham and Natick in 1808. He was one of the finest specimens of a New England self-made man. Punctual, exact, faithful, and strictly honest in the several relations of life; shrewd, intelligent, and careful in his business, — he won the confidence and respect of all who knew him, gained a high position in society, and acquired a handsome fortune. He did much more than any other man in his neighborhood for the promotion of taste and skill in the culture of ornamental and fruit trees. He was well read in English literature, and especially in the constitution and laws of the state of his adoption; and few lawyers had so large a list of confiding clients, though he never entered the profession, and had no advantages of education, except such as are afforded by a common New England district school. He met with heavy losses and severe afflictions in the course of his life; but he never lost his courage, energy, and industry, his habits of rigid temperance and frugality, and incessant activity; and he always cherished a religious faith, which was founded on the old, severe, uncompromising Puritanism of his ancestors.

He was a minute-man during the war of 1812, though always in politics a consistent Federalist; and in 1820, having resigned his commission as colonel of the first regiment of the Mass. militia, he received an honorable discharge from military service. For about 30 years he was town clerk and treasurer of Natick, and during all that time was never absent from a town meeting; and a neater, more accurate set of books than that which he kept cannot be found in the commonwealth. He was representative to the legislature in the years 1833, '34, '35, '37, and '38. When first chosen representative, instead of *treating*, as had before been the custom, he gave $60 to the school fund. He was in the state Senate in 1842 and '49, and was one year in the Governor's Council. He was also for seven years postmaster. For about 40 years he was a justice of the peace in constant business; and his ability and integrity in that office were never called in question. When he died, all who knew him felt that a good, faithful, and most useful man had passed away.

ADAMS, Christopher, Kittery, Me., Oct. 25, æ. 82. He was the last of the fourth generation who lived in his house, which was built in 1668 by his great-grandfather, Christopher Adams.

ADAMS, Dr. F. W., at the Union House, Montpelier, Vt., Dec. 17, æ. 71, interred at Barton. He was a well-known physician of that region, and was highly respected for his skill, and beloved for his devotion and tenderness to the suffering who came under his care. He had many peculiarities and caprices; yet he was a man of large heart, giving half his practice to the poor; and his grave was surrounded by many sincere mourners.

ADAMS, Henry, Springfield, Mass., April 29, æ. 62. In 1851 he was a member of the Mass. legislature, and took part in the protracted and memorable contest which resulted in the election of Charles Sumner to the U. S. Senate by one majority. Mr. Adams was on a sick bed, but receiving advices by telegraph, he five times disobeyed the commands of his physician, and leaving his couch went to Boston, (100 miles distant,) and having voted for his favorite, returned to his chamber at home.

ADAMS, Mrs. Jennette Root, at her father's house, Brooklyn, N. Y., Oct. 3, æ. 28. She was wife of William H. Adams, and only daughter of Rev. Seth Bliss, late Secretary of the American Tract Society, at Boston.

ADAMS, John, Middlesex, Yates Co., N. Y., æ. 66. He was a native of Pawlet, Vt., and came to M. at the age of 13; he amassed a large fortune, but retained a high reputation for integrity and social worth.

ADAMS, Hon. Samuel, at Townsend, Mass., April 5, æ. 52. He held several local offices of trust and honor, and was, at his death, senator from the fourth district of Middlesex. His death was caused by aconite, which he had been using externally for rheumatism, and through some mistake was led to take internally.

ADDAMS, Judge Wm., Spring Township, Berks Co., Pa., May 28, æ. 82. He was a member of Congress from that section from 1825 to 1829, and more recently associate judge of the county.

JAMES ADGER,

Charleston, S. C., at the St. Nicholas Hotel, New York city, of pneumonia, Sept. 24, æ. 81. He was born near Randalstown, County Antrim, Ireland, in the year 1777. At the age of 16 years he emigrated to this country, arriving in New York in Jan. 1794. He was apprenticed to a carpenter, but, after an experience of some four or five months, abandoned the trade, and obtained a situation as clerk in Mr. John Bailey's hardware store, in Maiden Lane. In the year 1802, he came to Charleston, on his way to visit his brother William, of Fairfield District, where he first saw the destined partner of his life, to whom he was married in the year 1806. In the autumn of 1803, the stage being full, he walked, with a friend, from Columbia to Charleston, arriving in advance of the stage, and with that friend, Mr. John Bones, commenced business in King Street, at the corner of Blackbird's Alley. His trade was mainly with the wagoners, who sold their cotton and purchased supplies. He was without any capital of consequence, but had already established a character, and by it obtained credit sufficient for his business, which rapidly grew and prospered. From this time until his death, he continued in active business, having never failed, through all that period of more than half a century, to pay in every instance the full amount of every one of his commercial and legal obligations.

It is well known that he never adventured into any speculations in the great staples of our produce. His settled policy was to pursue the path of patient, systematic labor. From the foot of the ladder he ascended, climbing step by step, slowly but surely; and the success of his whole career was not owing to any luck or fortune, but must be attributed under Providence to the qualities he possessed in a remarkable degree of economy, integrity, judgment, decision of character, punctuality, and unbounded energy and industry.

This eminent merchant, this architect of his own fortune, this bright example to our youth of the success attending well-directed energies, has now passed away. In his death society has lost a pillar of strength; our community a wise and public-spirited citizen; obscure and struggling merit a head to advise, and a hand to help; and the distressed and needy a generous friend, whose pity extended to the most forlorn.

He was a strong character, not always understood, prompt in action, but often slow to speak, thinking much and biding his time; not forward to volunteer or obtrude his counsel, but giving his opinion, when sought or when needed, in few words, clear, sententious, comprehensive. Underneath the blunt outside man were to be found a loving human heart, sensibilities of unfathomed depth, a soul devising the most generous deeds, and capable of the sublimest of all virtues—justice and impartiality. An occasional abruptness or sharpness of manner might be seen on a transient acquaintance; but it was for those who knew the man to appreciate him in the justice of his nature, in the unassuming simplicity of his character, in the patience of his labor, in the quiet, unostentatious streams of his charity, in his good will to man, and his submission to God.

When success crowned his labors, he did not become enslaved by money; but the man was, at every stage of his progress, superior to his acquisitions. This was true success. The mere accumulation of large property is a failure of life's end, unless with that increase the individual grows into a larger manfulness of soul. His success was that his property did not own him, but he was owner of his property, and could cheerfully part with it for wise and beneficent uses, or when taken from him by the stroke of Providence. His losses were many and heavy, at various epochs in the convulsions of trade and in the ruins of conflagration. After such blows of fortune, he was found always serene, and even cheerful—never looking back vainly upon yesterday, but forward to the morrow, and abating not a jot from the fortitude and energy of his continued labor in the present. Many of his deeds of charity are known to the community; more are known to his family and friends; but probably the greater part were seen only by the omniscient eye. In inspiring young men with the right spirit; in stimulating them, by his advice and example, to pursue a career of useful and honorable industry; in the judicious and generous employment of his capital for the establishment of others in advantageous business, he exerted a wide and salutary influence, and was thus a benefactor to his country. It is well known that the present generation of young men of our community take more correct views of a life of energetic labor, than those that preceded them; and it cannot be denied that the life and career of this self-made man contributed largely to this happy change. By his example as well as words, he spake through his long life, and, being dead, he yet speaketh.

Among the sterling qualities that gave him success in life we name prominently decision of character. The first element in decision of character is reliance on our own judgment; and the second is that energy of will and enthusiasm of the passions which, when a wise plan is selected, immediately spring into active powers of execution. These were conspicuous elements of his character. He had confidence in his own judgment, and did his own thinking in all practical affairs. No sooner was his plan determined than he commenced action. He had been through life an early riser. Not more certain was the sun to climb the eastern sky, than was this man to be early at his post; his purpose standing out clear to his view, and the energy of his will and the enthusiasm of his nature driving him from day to day onward to deserve, if not to attain, success. As a consequence of this concentration of mind, punctuality was a kindred virtue in his character worthy of universal imitation. To him may be truly applied the remark made by the celebrated Lord Nelson, when he said he owed every thing to being always a quarter of an hour before time.

Another and a chief virtue in his character was integrity. The basis of the gigantic operations of commerce are laid in confidence. A man in Europe stakes his property, his faith, his name, with perfect reliance on the character of another man whom he has never seen, thousands of miles distant in America. Parties at a distance know whether or not their correspondents are faithful to their trust. All, therefore, who knew the strict attention to details, and the system of rigid justice to the interest of absent owners, on which this man conducted all his affairs, are at no loss to know why business flowed in upon him; and his name was known far and near as an agent in whom the largest confidence might be reposed. Integrity was as conspicuous in his character as decision and sound judgment; and it was, doubtless, owing to the fact that he, as an agent, was intrusted with the property of others, that his far-sighted and just mind laid it down as an axiom that in his business he must never speculate. The temptation might be very great, but it never moved his firm resolve. "*Justum ac tenacem propositi virum.*"

Were we to select for imitation the most conspicuous moral quality in his character, we would name the clement *Intrinsic*. Beneath all the factitious distinctions of the world; through all sects, and parties, and conditions; in whatever form suffering and sorrow may be found, — the electric chord of genuine love finds its way. It seeks no reward; its language is, "I am a man." He esteemed others not according to outside show, but according to their real worth. He did nothing for effect or mere appearance. He had no wish to be valued for qualities he did not possess. He never acted a part. "*Esse, non videri*," was not formally chosen by him as a motto. He did better. He acted it out in his life, and it may now be chosen for him by others as briefly expressing the mould of his manly nature and the form of his intrinsic character. Unassuming, honest, and humble himself, he had for all pomp and ostentatious parade the most profound contempt; and the stream of his beneficence was not directed to conciliate the rich and great, but it flowed where his kind heart prompted, to the obscure and neglected, to the stranger and the friendless, to the widow and the fatherless.

It would be an omission not to notice also his fortitude under affliction. It is not yet five years since his son, William, died suddenly in New York, under the most painful circumstances. In the expression of public sympathy, many said the sudden and cruel death of such a son would kill the aged father. When the heavy tidings came, it was like the tornado bearing down on the old oak tree, or the earthquake moving beneath the solid rock; but the granite rock stood firm, and the old oak tree, bending for the moment, soon stood erect again, and defied the fury of the storm. His heart bled, but the solid, fixed mind never quailed. He fully appreciated the dimensions of his loss, but he saw that it was done — it was inevitable — it was past and gone forever. He saw the hand of God, and bowed in submission to his will. After a proper season of bitter tears — nature's inexorable claim — he said, it is enough; and, thenceforth, instead of leaning upon others, he, the aged, but the strong, stood, the bulwark and support of his family around him. His conduct in that dark hour illustrated his iron strength of mind and his heroic trust in God.

He was eminently social in his feelings, enjoying with the greatest zest the companionship of old, tried, and trusty friends, to whom he always opened his hand and his heart, whatever might be their station in life. Favors done to him were never forgotten, but always repaid, if opportunity offered, with interest. At the friendly fireside and the festive board he presided an acknowledged chief. The old and the young alike owned the spell of a soul so brimful of social glee and gladness. It would be a task to find in any circle his peer for the combination of those qualities of head and heart that shone out in every feature, and found vent in every expression, diffusing around him the good will and happiness of his genial nature. His life is his best eulogy. His last act was a visit to some of the friends of his early days; a visit and generous relief of the fatherless and the widow in their affliction. God saw that his work was done, and called him home.

Having filled up his long life to the end with untiring usefulness, — having raised a large family in respectability and honor, and left to them and to his countrymen a brilliant example in all the affairs of practical life of a virtuous energizer, — he has fallen asleep. He died after a brief illness of only five days. He who never lingered through life in performing his duty, was not kept lingering on the bed of death. He retained his faculties to the last, and died as he had lived — a hearty and an earnest man. His only desire for life was that he might still longer be useful to his family; but he expressed submission to God's will, and implicit reliance on his love and mercy through the great Redeemer.

AGATE, William, Pittsford, Monroe Co., April 10, æ. 88. Mr. A. was a native of England. In 1795, after a boisterous voyage, he landed in New York, with his life-long friend, Rev. Thos. Billinghurst, one of the pioneer preachers of the Universalists. The friends, who had brought their families with them, first settled at Sparta, on the Hudson. Soon after, Mr. B. moved into the wilderness, where Pittsford now stands, and in 1798, Mr. A. joined him, taking an adjoining tract of land. Four hundred miles from New York city, with no road for a considerable part of the way, they suffered many long-continued privations. The two families continued closely united till death. In 1848, Mr. Billinghurst died, and soon after his wife, at the age of 79. In 1854, Mr. A. followed his own wife to the grave, after a companionship of 58 years, her age being 85. It is noteworthy that all these victims of so much hardship and privation enjoyed "length of days." Mr. A. was temperate, industrious, cheerful, and active in every good word and work, — a course of life that will help account for his continuance in the community he had helped to found for almost a score of years beyond the allotted threescore and ten.

REV. LABAN AINSWORTH,

Jaffrey, N. H., March 17, æ. 100 yrs. 7 mos. and 28 days, son of Capt. William Ainsworth. He was born at Woodstock, Ct., July 19, 1757, and was ordained pastor of the church at Jaffrey, in pursuance of a call and vote of the town, Dec. 10, 1782, being the first settled minister of the place — the church having been organized May 13, 1780. He continued pastor 49 years, when, Jan. 11, 1832, Rev. Giles Lyman was ordained colleague. Mr. Lyman was dismissed May 3, 1837. Rev. Josiah D. Crosby was ordained colleague, Oct. 4, 1837, and dismissed April 19, 1844. Rev. Leonard Tenney was ordained colleague, April 19, 1845, and dismissed Aug., 1857, making the entire pastorate of Mr. A., over the same people, 76 years.

He fitted for college with Rev. Abiel Leonard, of Woodstock, and entered the Sophomore class of Dartmouth College at the age of 19 — the class which graduated in 1778. His father contemplated sending him to Harvard, but on account of the war then raging — the college buildings being used as barracks — sent him to Dartmouth, fitting him out with a horse and equipments, which were sold for his expenses the first year. It was at the commencement of 1781 that the committee from Jaffrey met him at Hanover, and gave him the call to preach as a candidate, which resulted in his settlement. Where he studied theology does not appear; but probably with Mr. Leonard, at Woodstock. He was always an evangelical preacher of more than ordinary ability, a man of great humor in his social intercourse, but earnestly intent in his great calling. He retained the respect and affection of his people to the last. His powers of body and mind held out remarkably, so that he was able to attend the public services in the church, celebrating his one hundredth birthday. In person he was of medium stature, thick set, good features, every way well formed, except one hand, which was disabled by an early sickness. He had two children; Sarah, who married Isaac Parker, of Boston, and died May 29, 1857; and William, who died at Concord, June 14, 1842, while member of the legislature for New Ipswich. The year 1858 is remarkable for the death of four aged clergymen, all graduates of Dartmouth College, and nearly contemporary, whose united age exceeds four hundred years, viz: Laban Ainsworth, Zach. Green, Ethan Osborn, John Sawyer.

Mr. A. was a man of vigorous health and sound constitution. He had a pleasant aspect, voice, and manner, was gifted with a good judgment and a genial humor, and knew how to make his home agreeable to children, grandchildren, and guests. He had the respect of his contemporaries, and the veneration of the younger generations who grew up around him. He loved the Bible, and took delight in its strong Calvinistic doctrines.

AINSWORTH, Nathan, Newport, N. Y., May 31, æ. 87. When he was five years old the revolutionary war broke out; his father died in the army, and his brother perished of small pox in the infamous prison-ship Jersey, where he was confined as prisoner of war. Nathan was then bound out to a farmer by his destitute mother. At the age of 31 he removed to Herkimer Co., where he was till death active in every religious, educational, reformatory, and other philanthropic work.

ALBERTSON, Hon. Joseph C., San Francisco, Cal., Dec. 8, æ. 41, son of Joseph C. Albertson, Esq., of Southold,

N. Y. After a thorough preparatory course at Clinton Academy, and with the late lamented Rev. Jonathan Hunting, he entered Yale College, and graduated in 1837. The three ensuing years he spent in the law offices of George Miller, Riverhead, N. Y., and Charles B. Moore, New York. In 1840, he commenced the practice of law in the city of New York, and he represented the city in the state legislature during the session of 1846; was assistant alderman of the second ward, and subsequently city judge. In 1854, in the strong hope of a quicker attainment of his object, he left his northern home, and settled in San Francisco. Rich in mental endowments, cultivated in taste, noble, generous, and confiding in disposition, a large circle of friends will long lament his early death in a far-off land.

ALDEN, Henry, South Abington, Ms., April 4, æ. 41.

ALDEN, Timothy, at New York, —— 4, æ. —. He was a native of Barnstable Co., Mass. He devoted his life to the invention of a machine that should set and distribute type. After many years of toil and anxiety, he succeeded in producing an invention that performed both operations some three or four times faster than human fingers; but before its merits became generally known to printers he died. If the expense does not prevent, this machine will probably come into general use among book printers.

ALLAN, Hon. Chilton, Winchester, Ky., Sept. 3, æ. 73. He was a native of Winchester Co., Va., removing to Kentucky in 1786. He was elected to the State Assembly in 1811, and continued in one or the other branch of the legislature till 1830. From the latter year until 1837, when he declined further service, he was a representative in Congress. In 1837–8, he was president of the State Board of Internal Improvement. In 1842, in the financial crisis, he served another term in the legislature, but refused all subsequent political honors. Mr. Allan was a fine specimen of a self-made man. Removing to Kentucky when a mere lad, he for many years worked at his trade, that of a wheelwright; and when the hours of toil were over, spent the evening in patient study, that he might give himself that education to which no friend had assisted him. After a time he became a teacher in the public schools, and while yet a young man began the successful practice of the law, proving that his self-instruction had been patient and faithful. His official course was ever marked with prudence, faithfulness, and a considerable degree of conservatism; the latter quality was of especial value to the councils of a new state surrounded by communities disposed to innovation and rash political experiments. His death was felt to be a great public loss.

ALLEN, Dr. Alfred S., Vicksburg, Miss., Feb. 4, æ. 45. He was a native of New Jersey, emigrating in 1837 to Texas, where he served for a time as surgeon in the army. He was mayor of Vicksburg at his death.

ALLEN, Anson H., Keeseville, N. Y., Nov. 16, æ. 53. He was the pioneer editor of that region. Some 30 years ago, when Keeseville was little more than a wilderness, he established there the Herald; afterwards he published a very popular biographical paper, called — The Old Settler. He held many local offices, and was for some years collector of customs at Whitehall.

ALLEN, Dr. Frederick, Hallowell, Me., Mar. 17, æ. 46. Formerly of Martha's Vineyard.

ALLEN, Lieut. J. K., of the 9th Infantry, U. S. Army, on the Yakima River, Aug. 15. He was in command of a detachment in pursuit of some Indian murderers; his party of 15 captured 21 warriors, and some 70 other prisoners. In the engagement, Lieut. A. received a mortal wound. He was a brave and talented officer from Illinois, graduating at West Point in 1853.

ALLEN, Hon. J. J., Mt. Jackson, Shenandoah Co., Va., Aug. 6, æ. 55, for several years presiding justice of the County Court.

ALLEN, James, son of Judge Charles Allen, Worcester, Oct. 28, from bursting a blood-vessel. A young man of great worth and promise.

ALLEN, Dr. James H., Irvington, N. Y., Aug. 8, æ. 41.

ALLEN, Deacon Jonathan, Sedgwick, Me., æ. 90. He was for about 50 years deacon in the Baptist church of that place. His father, Nathaniel, removed to S. from Beverly, Mass.

ALLINSON, David, near Pemberton, N. J., Sept. 14, æ. 85. He was a member of the Society of Friends, and was for many years a publisher in New York city. In establishing the Apprentices' Library, he rendered an invaluable service to the community.

ALLISON, Mrs. Mary, Louisiana City, Mo., Aug. 24, æ. 84, wife of James. She was the daughter of Samuel Carroll, of York district, S. C., and well remembered many of the fearful incidents of the partisan warfare of the revolution, her father being closely allied with Marion's patriotic troop. She was among the pioneer settlers of Pike Co., Mo.

ALLSTON, Col. John Ashe, Sullivan's Island, S. C., ———, æ. 42. He was a nephew of Washington Allston, the great artist, and employed his talents and wealth in the promotion of literature, the fine arts, and scientific agriculture. He was a legislator of experience.

AMES, Capt. Ambrose, at Greenfield, Aug. 29, æ. 96, a native of Bridgewater, Mass., where the Ames family settled in the days of the Pilgrims. He lived in Greenfield more than 70 years, representing the town in the General Court several times. He was appointed postmaster by Jefferson in 1804, and continued in office until 1841. He was a man of strong constitution and very regular habits.

AMES, Dr. Silas, Montgomery, Ala., Dec. 7, æ. 55. He was one of the oldest and most esteemed physicians of that place, and a valued citizen.

AMMIDON, Otis, Philadelphia, Dec. 23, æ. 87. He was born in Mendon, Mass., before the struggles of the colonies for freedom. At the time of his decease he was treasurer of the Lehigh Coal and Navigation Co., an office he had filled with exemplary fidelity for a period of years. In early life Mr. A. was engaged in commercial pursuits, as agent of Thos. H. Perkins, in St. Domingo, until those troubles which terminated in the frightful massacre and expulsion of the whites. After his return, he engaged in business with the Hon. Jona. Russell, his brother-in-law. Subsequently he resided in Paris, at the period when Napoleon was declared first consul, and also for some time in Norway. His commercial enterprises were not successful; and in 1827 he was appointed to the post which he occupied at the time of his death, and which was peculiarly adapted to his habits. Mr. A. was appointed a ruling elder in the Seventh Presbyterian Church, Philadelphia, in 1818, and was the last surviving member of the Board of Elders as it then existed. The character of the deceased was highly appreciated in the church and the community. Of retiring habits, he was, nevertheless, a man of most genial, guileless, and cheerful spirit. His countenance was usually lighted with a smile, and his soul was the seat of benevolence. None doubted the sincerity of his friendship, and his character for more than fourscore years was Christian consistency. Few men, perhaps, have lived for so many years, and under so many circumstances of temptation, with so few faults.

AMORY, Mrs. Elizabeth, Roxbury, Mass., ———, æ. 82, widow of Thomas Amory, Esq., and daughter of the late Dr. Wm. Bowen, of Providence, R. I.

ANDERSON, Cornelius V., New York city, Nov. 21, æ. 49. In 1837, when only 28 years of age, he was appointed to the responsible position of chief engineer of that city. At that time the department was in a state of disorganization, caused by an unpopular change in its management; but Mr. A. soon restored order, and the department reached its highest state of efficiency during his administration. He found the annual expenses of the department $72,000; but, before the close of his term, he had, while adding to its force and equipment, reduced them to about $30,000. In 1848 Mr. A., whose health had suffered by the arduous duties of his office, resigned the chief-engineership, and was elected register of the city and county by a vote which testified to the esteem in which he was held by his fellow-citizens. In 1851 he was nominated for reëlection, but, owing to party changes, he was defeated. About that time the Lorillard Insurance Co. was organized, and Mr. A. was chosen as its president — an office which he held until death. In 1856 he was appointed a governor of the almshouse for the unexpired term of Mr. Duke, and in 1858 was nominated by the republicans for reëlection; but, as his health was failing rapidly, he declined the nomination. Mr. A.'s chief traits of character were a sound judgment, combined with decision and energy in the discharge of his duties, and uncompromising integrity.

ANDERSON, Dr. James, Richmond, June 1, æ. 77.

ANDERSON, John, Boonsboro', Md., May 23, æ. 87. He was a soldier in the war of 1812, and helped repel the British at Baltimore.

ANDERSON, Dr. Richard, Aberdeen, Pike Co., Mo., Nov. 14, æ. 51. He was a native of Va., but for 25 years had been a devoted and beloved physician in Pike Co. He was a man of great skill, and greater benevolence and tenderness.

ANDERSON, Maj. W. C., Marion Co., Mo., April 23, æ. 77. He was a native of Ky., and was the last of six brothers, all of whom bore arms in the war of 1812. Maj. A. was private secretary to Com. Bainbridge, and was taken prisoner with that officer at the time the frigate Philadelphia fell into the hands of the Tripolitans. The ship's company all remained in captivity 22 months. Maj. A. served in both the Ohio and Mo. legislatures, and for 21 years had been pension agent in Mo., resigning within six months of his death, on account of infirmity.

ANDERSON, William B., Aaronsburg, Pa., June 2, æ. 58, for several years a member of the legislature, in both branches.

ANDREWS, David, Providence, R. I., April 20, æ. —, for 25 years cashier of the Commercial Bank, from its foundation to his death, and a philanthropic, Christian man.

ETHAN ALLEN ANDREWS, LL.D.,

New Britain, Ct., March 25, æ. 71. He graduated at Yale in 1810, and for some years practised law. In 1822 he became Professor of Ancient Languages in the University of North Carolina. After six years' service, he returned to the north, and taught a select school in New Haven for five years, and for six years longer in Boston. In 1839 he retired to his native town, and spent the most of his time in the preparation of Latin text-books. In connection with the late Prof. Solomon Stoddard, he had several years before issued the Latin Grammar bearing their joint names; this Prof. A. now revised; it became a standard, and no less than 65 editions of it have already been required. His Latin text-books number 13, of which the principal are the Grammar and his great Lexicon. Prof. A. was an ardent friend of popular education, a man of great moral worth, and a life-long consistent Christian.

ANDREWS, Dr. Simeon J., Glastenbury, Ct., Nov. 15, æ. 56, for several years a very widely practising physician in that region.

ANDREWS, Rev. Samuel R., New Haven, Ct., June 2, æ. 71. He was, for about a quarter of a century, the esteemed and successful pastor of the Congregational church in South Woodbury, Ct. He was affectionate and agreeable in his intercourse with his people, and one of the ablest men in the state. He was an excellent writer, and a frequent and able contributor to the Quarterly Christian Spectator in its best days. He was obliged to give up his pastoral charge some 10 years before his death, on account of failing health. Thereafter he resided in New Haven, preaching occasionally, and filling the office of secretary to the corporation of Yale College.

ANDREWS, Capt. William R., Little Rock, Ark., Aug. 2, æ. 39. He belonged in Buffalo, N. Y. During the Mexican war he was appointed a captain in the 10th U. S. Infantry, a position which he afterwards resigned, but was subsequently reappointed. Until May, 1858, he held command of Fort Vergennes, Vt., when he was ordered to take command of the fort at Little Rock, where he died.

ANGELL, Oliver, Providence, R. I., Nov. 11, æ. 71. He was descended from one of the five companions of Roger Williams at his landing at that place in 1636. He graduated at Brown in 1807, and became a teacher first in a private and then in a public school. He also published a series of school books some 25 years ago, which became quite popular. After long and successful service, he left teaching, and gave his attention to agricultural pursuits, of which he was very fond, and became one of the most useful members of the "R. I. Society for the Encouragement of Domestic Industry."

ARCHER, Mrs. Elizabeth, Vernon,

N. Y., Oct. 16, æ. 107 years, 4 mos. Her health was excellent to the last, when, without sickness, she "fell asleep."

ARMSTEAD, William, in Franklin Co., O., —— 15, æ. 74. He was commissary of Gen. Harrison's army while in that vicinity in the war of 1812.

ARMSTRONG, Maj. Horatio Gates, near Baltimore, Md., April 6, æ. 68.

ARMSTRONG, Robert Livingston, Esq., Garrison, Putnam Co., N. Y., —— 17, æ. 30, a promising lawyer.

ARMSTRONG, W. G., at Jeffersonville, Ky., July 29, æ. 62, a member of the legislature of that state for 11 successive years.

ARNOLD, Maj. A., Westport, Mo., Sept. —, æ. —. He was recently Indian agent for the Pawnees, and was the first representative from Washington Co. to the Nebraska legislature. His family residence was Fort Calhoun, N. T.

ASHBY, Mrs. Temperance, Troy, N.Y., ———, æ. 79. She was the oldest inhabitant of Troy, having resided on the spot 73 years, during which time the place had become first a small village, then a city. At her death there was only one building in that whole county that was erected before she came to reside at Troy. She was a lady of much sense, and for many years had been the great source of information as to local history.

ASHMORE, Mrs., off the Cape of Good Hope, May 19, æ. —, wife of Rev. Wm. A., of the Siam mission. She was the daughter of Dea. Sanderson, Brookline, Mass., whom she was coming with her two children to visit, parting from her husband at Hong Kong.

ASHTON, Mrs. Anna Maria, White Creek, N. Y., Sept. 11, æ. 60. She was the youngest daughter of the late Rev. Thos. Beveridge, and sister of Rev. Dr. Thos. Beveridge, of Xenia, O.

ATKINS, Rev. J. W., Saco, Me., May 27, æ. 50. A popular preacher of the Methodists.

ATKINSON, Col. B., Lucas Co., O., Aug. 2, w. —. He was one of the heroes of Fort Stephenson, under Croghan, and died on the anniversary of that victory, which was then being celebrated in the neighboring town of Fremont.

ATKINSON, Thomas Chalkley, Alexandria, Va., Dec. 6, w. —. He was appointed a civil engineer on the Baltimore and Ohio Railway in 1836, and from 1849 to the time of his death was chief engineer of the Orange and Alexandria (Va.) road. He was eminent in his profession, and was learned in the cognate sciences as well as in general literature.

REV. JEREMIAH ATWATER, D.D.,

New Haven, July 29, æ. 84. The first president of Middlebury College, and afterwards president of Dickinson College, at Carlisle, Pa. He was a native of New Haven, and a graduate of Yale College, class of 1793; was tutor in that college from 1795 to 1799; president at Middlebury from 1800 to 1809, and president at Carlisle from 1810 to 1818, when he resigned, and was succeeded by the distinguished Dr. John M. Mason, of New York. Since that time he has lived a very retired life on the patrimony left him by his father — the later years almost as a recluse. His house stood on the site once occupied by Col. John Dixwell, famous as one of the judges by whom King Charles I. was sentenced to execution as a traitor.

Dr. A. was a man of great reading, and of a retentive memory, especially of historical events and the lives and characters of men he had known, but had not a fondness for writing, and has left, it is believed, but few literary remains of his life. He was descended from David Atwater, who came to New Haven in the year 1639. Three children survive him — two sons, who graduated at Yale, class of 1827 and 1834, and a daughter, who married the late Rev. Oliver B. Hart, of South Britain.

SAMUEL AUSTIN,

Boston, Ms., Sept. 15, æ. 65. He was son of Samuel A., and was born (1794) in Boston, where he spent the whole of his life. From 1812 to 1816 he was a clerk in the State Bank. In 1818 he entered mercantile life as partner of Nathan Bridge. After two years he went into business by himself, and so continued to the end of his life. He was extensively engaged in the Calcutta trade, which rewarded his industry with a liberal fortune. He was very highly esteemed as a merchant and as a man of the greatest integrity and moral excellence. He was elected as a representative to the legislature in 1827, and received six successive reëlections; he was chosen to the city council of Boston in 1829 and in 1830, and was annually re-elected a director in the State Bank from 1824 to his death. He was a gentleman of much refinement of manners and a high literary taste. Never marrying, he devoted nearly all the moments spared him by business to the cultivation of his mind; his favorite authors were the metaphysicians, psychologists, and political economists, on whose speculations he was very fond of arguing with his chosen friends, and his arguments were always good-tempered.* By his demise the community has parted with a merchant of remarkable business talent, a profound student and thinker, and a man of such intelligence and uprightness that it can ill afford to lose the influence of his example.

REV. CHARLES AVERY,

Alleghany City, Pa., Jan. 17, æ. 73. He was born in Westchester Co., N. Y. Leaving home without a dollar, he became apprentice to an apothecary. In time he gathered a small capital, all of which he lost by the wrecking of a vessel in which it was adventured, between New York and Philadelphia. In 1813 he established himself at Pittsburg, Pa., as a druggist and a manufacturer of white lead. He soon found that he could not compete with his rivals in the white-lead trade unless he followed the common practice of adulterating the article. This he indignantly refused to do, and at once gave up that part of his business. In all his career he was ever honest, open, liberal, and strictly truthful. The estate of nearly a million dollars that he left showed that these qualities were no hinderance to success in business. His money was ever freely expended for philanthropic purposes. Many years ago, when steamboat explosions were of almost daily occurrence on the western rivers, Mr. A., happening to be on the Hudson, saw a boat intended to protect the passengers from such disasters. It consisted of a forward boat, containing the machinery, and a cabin-boat, separated by a little interval from the first. Immediately on his return to Pittsburg he liberally advanced the money for building a costly steamer on this plan. The craft sailed to Cincinnati, but found the crookedness and currents of the Ohio fatal to her success. The cabin-boat soon after became a produce flat-boat, and the engine portion, having started for New Orleans during a flood, was, by a careless pilot, stranded in the woods, half a mile from the channel of the river, and left there to rot, not the monument of a visionary speculation, but of a truly philanthropic attempt to protect the lives of the travelling public. Mr. A. built many churches in Virginia, Ohio, and Pennsylvania. He was especially interested in the improvement of the colored race, often purchasing the freedom of well-deserving slaves, and aiding poor negroes in acquiring comfortable homes. He also founded a college for colored youth, the first established in the country, and at his death a touching eulogy was pronounced at "Avery College" by a colored speaker. Having no children, Mr. A. bequeathed liberal sums to various "Methodist Protestant" churches, to a fund for the support of disabled clergy of that sect, to Avery College, the Insane Asylum of Western Pennsylvania, and similar institutions, and to various relatives. He then provided that the balance, from a quarter to half a million dollars, should be invested in two equal perpetual funds, one for the education of the colored population of the United States and Canada, and the other for the conversion and civilizing of the black races in Africa. Hon. Thos. M. Howe, Wm. M. Shinn, and Josiah King, Esqs., his executors, seem wisely selected to be the almoners of this good man's bounty. The biography of Mr. A. seems remarkable, and worthy of study by the youth of our land.

AYERS, Dr. Jessie, Brownville, N. Y., æ. 57. He was a native of Vt., an excellent physician, and a beloved citizen.

* Hon. William Appleton said of him, "I have been his neighbor and have had business relations with him for the past 30 years, and during that long period I have always found him on the side of broad, comprehensive views. Nothing mean found favor with him; of strict integrity, and in his intercourse with the world kind and conciliatory."

B.

BACHMAN, John F., Easton, Pa., April 29, æ. 27. When a mere boy of 16 summers, while an apprentice at the Argus office, he joined Capt. Miller's corps of Stockton Artillerists, and went with this company to Mexico. He was engaged in the bombardment of Vera Cruz, in the battle of Cerro Gordo, and in the taking of Chapultepec, where he took four prisoners himself, marching three of them to safe quarters. While in the city of Mexico, he helped to print a paper there called the North American. After the war he returned to Easton, and remained there until the breaking out of the California gold fever in the latter part of Jan., 1849, when he went to California, but soon returned to Easton. Three years ago he was elected clerk of the Quarter Sessions; and last fall was reëlected for three years more. He was faithful in the performance of the duties of his office, and was liked by all who had business transactions with him.

BACKUS, Dr. Frederick, Rochester, N. Y., Nov. 4, æ. 64. Dr. B. was a son of the Rev. Dr. Azel Backus, a distinguished divine of New England, and at his death, which occurred in 1817, the president of Hamilton College. He was born at Bethlem, Conn., June 15, 1794. Dr. B. was one of a family of eight children, of whom only one, Theodore, survives. He graduated at Yale College, in 1814, in the same class with Prof. Olmsted, and a number of other distinguished men. In 1815, having obtained a license to practise medicine, Dr. B. took up his residence in Rochester, where he continued till his death. In 1818 he married Miss Fitzhugh, of Maryland, a sister of the wives of Gerrit Smith and James G. Birney. Mr. Smith's first wife was also a sister of Dr. B. In 1842, Dr. B. was elected senator from the old eighth district, and served four years, with great ability. In 1846 he was a member of the convention which gave the present state constitution. These are the only elective offices he ever filled, though he was often called to trusts of great importance in the management of public institutions. As a physician, he had but few superiors, and he enjoyed for many years a large and lucrative practice. In the cholera seasons of 1832 and '33, when general panic pervaded the city, Dr. B. was the efficient and calm health officer, from whose wise counsels the timid took courage, and whose prudent plans did much to check alarm and stay the progress of the scourge. As a man, he was possessed of a genial, happy temperament, which not only gave assurance to those whom he met professionally, but which made him a general favorite. His wit was quiet but keen, and he looked down upon life with a vision quick to discern and take advantage of that which was pleasant, and which ignored and avoided that which was repulsive. All who knew him bear testimony to his uniform good nature, and the ready and sympathetic kindness of heart which attached the poor and the sorrowing to him. In the Senate of New York he originated the movement in behalf of the education of idiots; and when, years after, that movement had taken shape, in the present Asylum at Syracuse, his name received no tardy or unwilling recognition of the fact, and the able report from his pen was quoted with approbation. In this institution, and the kindred one in Massachusetts, Dr. B. always took great interest. Thousands of unfortunates, the windows of whose soul are darkened, will have occasion to thank Dr. B. for his earnest and successful advocacy of their cause.

BACKUS, Mrs. Sarah, Binghampton, N. Y., æ. 82, daughter of Col. Eleazar Lindsley, an officer of the revolutionary war. She was born at Morristown, N. Y., in 1776. When quite a young woman, she travelled on horseback from the Hudson River, her path marked with blazed trees, to the site where Binghampton now stands, then almost a wilderness. The deceased was endowed with a constitution naturally strong and robust, which was hardened in the stern school of her early endurances and experiences. She possessed a mind well harmonized with her body—fresh, original, and vigorous.

BACKUS, Hon. Thomas, West Killingly, Ct., Dec. 9, æ. 58. Mr. B. was a graduate of Brown University; studied the legal profession in Woonsocket, and entered upon its practice in Windham Co., Ct., where he soon acquired an eminent position as a lawyer and as a man. He was elected lieutenant governor of the state, and for a number of years was judge of the County Court.

BACON, Amos, Esq., Ogdensburg, N. Y., May 24, æ. 72. Mr. B. was born at Canterbury, Ct. His father was a soldier of the revolution, and served under Washington, in the vicinity of Boston, until the British evacuated that city. Mr. B. served as a volunteer several months in the war of 1812, on the eastern shore of Maryland. He came to O. immediately after the close of the war, and established himself as a merchant. In the comparative infancy of O., Mr. B. became one of its most distinguished citizens. As a merchant he was prompt in business, punctual in the fulfilment of every obligation, and by his skill and industry accumulated a handsome estate. In all the enterprises for the advancement of education, religion, and other village interests, none were more liberal, or devoted more of their time and energies. He was a most affectionate husband and father, and in all his domestic relations most exemplary.

BACON, Mrs. Hannah Eliza, Warrenton, Va., Dec. 3, æ. 46, wife of Rev. Joel S. Bacon, D. D., late president of Columbia College, in the District of Columbia.

BAER, John, Lancaster, Pa., Nov. 6, æ. 61, senior editor and publisher of the Lancaster Volksfreund. He was born in Lancaster Co., Jan. 31, 1797. He became connected with the publication of the Volksfreund in 1817, and in 1818 became sole editor and proprietor. Many books of a religious and miscellaneous character, both English and German, have been published by him at various times and in large editions. The first of these was a folio German Bible, which appeared in 1819, the publication of which, at that period of his life, was an undertaking peculiarly difficult and hazardous. It is the largest German Bible ever published in America.

HON. ARTHUR P. BAGBY.

Mobile, Ala., Sept. 21, æ. 59. "Gov. B.," says the Mobile Register, "was a native of Virginia, but removed to Alabama at an early age, when, under the inspiration of an ardent and emulous nature, he devoted his solid sense and brilliant talents to the active and practical exercise of the profession of law. He came to Alabama, if we are not mistaken, in 1818, established a residence at Claiborne, and took at once an elevated position as a criminal lawyer, which soon conferred popular confidence, and enabled him to acquire a more extended reputation as a safe general counsellor and jurist. But it was not in the law, only, that his genius and ability commanded attention. In the course of a successful career in his personal pursuits, he was called upon to assume the station and duties of a legislator and statesman. He was returned as a member of the state legislature from the County of Monroe, was afterwards elected speaker of the House of Representatives of that body, and signalized his services not only by a rigidly equitable discharge of the duties of that office, but by the singular ability with which he maintained his elevated views and statesmanlike positions. The reputation so honorably gained by these important services led to further and more distinguished consequences. He was afterwards elected governor of Alabama, and filled that office with the approbation of his fellow-citizens as long as the constitution of the state permitted, when he was transferred to a wider field of political labor as a general counsellor of the entire republic, and as one of the immediate representatives of his adopted state in the Senate of the United States. To this honorable position he was twice commended; and, while he yet served in that elevated station, he was still further distinguished by being selected from the ranks of his compeers to represent the dignity of the whole country at the court of Russia, under President Polk. This is but a rapid outline of the career of Gov. Bagby. On his return from Russia, he retired to private life and to the practice of his early profession. During the calm which succeeded his voyage of public life, he received other tokens of the confidence and respect of Alabama. He was appointed as one of the commissioners to modify the laws of the state, and the present 'Code of Alabama' was the joint work of Gov. Bagby, Judge Ormond, and Judge Goldthwaite. For the few past years of his life he has been a resident of our city, where, as every where, he has drawn around him the most affectionate and respectful regard of all who have enjoyed his acquaintance.

As an individual, Gov. Bagby was a man of large mental endowment, great intelligence, high moral worth, strict integrity and honor, and liberal public spirit. The usefulness of his life, his Christian charities, his lofty tone, and his exalted manly nature, stamped him with a nobility of character that bespoke and commanded at once the respect and admiration of the world.

As a member of the bar he was respectful to the court, courteous to his professional brethren, and kind to all with whom he had intercourse. He had many warm personal friends, and, in the conflicts and collisions of party strife, he had no doubt made some political enemies.

In private life he was no less remarkable than in public duty. He was an affectionate husband and father, a devoted friend, and a magnanimous foe, an agreeable companion, and an excellent citizen. His virtues will long survive in the memory of his associates, whilst his acts as a statesman will be recorded in the history of his age.

BAILEY, Adams, Esq., Boston, Mass., Nov. 20, æ. 68, a gentleman widely known to the business public from his long connection with the Boston custom house. The deceased was first appointed to an office in the custom house, in 1815, and continued through all the political changes until the appointment of the Hon. Levi Lincoln, as collector of the port, in 1841. When the late Hon. Robert Rantoul, Jr., was collector, in 1843, he reinstated Mr. Bailey in his former place of deputy collector, which station he filled until last year. His last removal occasioned much feeling among the elder classes of the mercantile community, who remembered his forty years' service. For many years Mr. B. was the recorder of the Massachusetts Society of Cincinnati, and took deep interest in those who were aided by that benevolent and honored organization. Mr. Bailey was one of the most genial, popular, and efficient public officers. In his habits of promptness, impartiality, and politeness, he was a model for persons in official station.

BAKER, Alpheus, Columbus, Ga., Feb. —, æ. 86, a graduate of Dartmouth College in the class of Daniel Webster.

BALCH, Dr. Israel, Amesbury, Mass., July 7, æ. 70.

BALCH, Perley, Topsfield, Mass., May 9, æ. 75, "a devout Christian, a kind neighbor, and true friend," father of Perley Balch, teacher of the Edson Grammar School in Lowell, Mass.

BALDWIN, Cyrus W., Esq., Lisbon, N. Y., May 5, æ. 48, at the residence of James North, his brother-in-law. For several years a practising lawyer, and for a number of the last years of his life a justice of the peace, he had come to be quite extensively known and respected for his legal knowledge, the accuracy of his decisions, and the undeviating integrity of his character. He was an honest man; and the innate devotion of the man to the principle of exact justice to all men, and of equal rights to all, was not a dormant or inert principle: it shone out conspicuously in his every act, and won the confidence and respect of every man with whom he was brought into connection in the varied affairs and pursuits of life. The bar say of him, "That we receive the announcement of the death of our departed brother with sentiments of unfeigned sorrow; that in his decease the bar of St. Lawrence Co. has lost a member estimable alike for his accurate knowledge of his profession, his unblemished integrity, his kindly disposition, and many amiable qualities; and our community, a citizen, who, in his private and official relations, was entitled to our unqualified respect."

BALDWIN, Judge ———, St. Paul, Min., July 15, æ. —, an old and respected citizen.

BALESTIER, Joseph, Esq., York, Pa., Nov. 13, æ. 70. He had been for a number of years United States consul at Singapore, and was a resident of New York city in the years 1856, 1857.

BALFOUR, Mrs. Mary D., Charlestown, Mass., May 29, æ. 71, widow of Rev. Walter Balfour. She was born in Charlestown, and descended from the ancient and honored Devens family. She lived a good and useful life, and died a calm and happy death.

BALL, Rev. Thomas H., A. M., Huntsville, Texas, Oct. 30, æ. 39, a member of the Texas Annual Conference. He was born in Northumberland Co., Va. He embraced religion when about 19 years of age, and shortly afterwards received license to preach in the Methodist Episcopal church. In the fall of 1855 he was called to the presidency of Andrew Female College, which responsible position he occupied until the day of his death. He always maintained an unblemished reputation, as a high-toned, Christian gentleman.

BALLARD, Joseph A., Esq., Boston, Mass., Oct. 1, æ. 53. Mr. B. was for 25 years the marine reporter of the Boston Daily Advertiser. He was born in Boston, Aug. 15, 1805. In early life he entered as an apprentice in the counting room of Messrs. Winslow and Channing, auctioneers, in Kilby Street, where he remained about two years, when he left, and was employed in the Patriot and Chronicle newspaper office, Mr. Davis C. Ballard, of the firm of Ballard & Wright, the proprietors of that paper, being his uncle. Here he served as a local reporter until 1832, when that paper was merged in the Daily Advertiser, after which he acted in the same capacity until Sept., 1834, when he took charge of the ship-news department, which he held until his death. It is not often that we see a man whose talents and attainments make him eminent in a special department of duty, who is at the same time so pure, so unselfish, so modest, as was Mr. B. No temptation of any sort could swerve him from the direct path of his duty, could chill his zeal, or interrupt his progress.

BALLINGALL, Patrick, Esq., Chicago, Nov. 21, æ. 47. Mr. B. was a native of Scotland, and was born in the town of Ayr, in the year 1811, a place rendered famous for being the birthplace of the Scottish poet Robert Burns. He came to Chicago in 1834, and soon after commenced the study of law in the office of Messrs. Spring & Goodrich. In 1839 he was appointed clerk of the Circuit Court of Du Page Co. In 1842 he resigned, and opened a law office in Chicago. In 1848 he was elected a member of the convention of the state to form a new constitution. In 1852 he was elected district attorney, and in 1854 city attorney. The bar of Chicago say,

"*Resolved*, That, as a member of the bar of Chicago for a period of 20 years, Patrick Ballingall displayed a deep knowledge and clear perception of the principles of the profession; that in his practice he was ever actuated and guided by sentiments of high honor and justice; in his intercourse with the brethren of the bar, his conduct was uniformly marked with kindness, courtesy, and genuine liberality; and as a pleader, an advocate, and a man, he occupied a high and merited position, both socially and professionally."

BARBER, George W., M. D., De Peyster, St. Lawrence Co., N. Y., March 23, æ. 64. Dr. B. was a native of Windham Co., Vt., whence in 1823 he emigrated to De Peyster before its organization into a township, where he ever after resided, practising his arduous profession with unusual success, and for more than 20 years discharged the duties of magistrate as an impartial minister of the law. In him were centred those qualities of head and heart which distinguish the upright man in whatever circumstances or condition of life he may be placed. His character, adorned by the Christian graces of humanity, charity, and love, is a priceless legacy to his children; and his memory will long be cherished in the affections and respect of the community in which he labored. The town of De Peyster, as a mark of their appreciation of his worth, have erected over his grave a beautiful marble monument, as a testimonial of their respect to his memory. Mrs. Ellen M. Chandler, wife of John B. Chandler, Esq., and daughter of Dr. B., died in De Peyster, March 19, 1858, æ. 25.

BARBER, Jessie, Chicago, Ill., April 22, æ. 4. This is the last surviving member of the family of the late Jabez Barber, of Chicago, who, with his wife and daughter, perished in the Collins steamer Pacific in 1856. At the time of his death his property was estimated at about $250,000, and has increased in value to $400,000. After leaving sensible provisions for the family during the settlement of the will, and $250 per annum to his four sisters in England during their lives; also to his wife's sister, Matilda Wilde, of Chicago, $1000; to the American and Foreign Missionary Society, $1000; to the American Home

Missionary Society, $1000; to the American Bible Society, $1000; to the Third Presbyterian Church, Chicago, $3000,— the balance of the property was left for the benefit of the family; and, as the child whose death is recorded above was the only surviving member, she was the sole heir. In case of her death, it was to revert to the next of kin. The nearest of kin are Mary Ann, Harriet, and Lucy Barber, of Birmingham, England, and Eliza Bell, of Simcoe, C. E. These ladies, who are, we understand, in somewhat straitened circumstances, will receive something over $100,000 each.

BARCLAY, David, Richmond, Va., Nov. 18, æ. 76. Mr. B. was a native of Ayrshire, North Britain, and one of the few remaining tobacco merchants who inaugurated the trade in that valuable staple in Richmond, after 1806. He realized an ample fortune in the trade, which he freely expended for the benefit of those whom he thought deserving, and, after a laborious life, impoverished himself by acts of benevolence. He had been a citizen of Richmond for 52 years at the time of his death. It may be truly said that Richmond never had a more honest man in its borders, or one who more sedulously sought to advance its interest, than David Barclay.

BARCLAY, Dr. M. W., Richmond, Ky., Oct. 23, æ. 33, at the residence of Gen. Miller. He was born in Lexington, Rockbridge Co., Va., Dec. 2, 1824; graduated at Washington College, Va., in 1844; received the degree of medicine from Jefferson College, Philadelphia, in 1847; removed to Kentucky in 1849; was married in 1851 to the eldest daughter of Gen. John Miller; practised medicine in Bourbon Co. until 1854, when he removed to St. Francis Co., Ark., where, after enjoying a lucrative practice of his profession until 1857, he was attacked with consumption. Endowed by nature with superior intellect, the life, which under all circumstances would have been marked with interest, was especially so with the superadded advantages of refined and scholastic education. Who can but lament that one so gifted should have been cut down in the meridian of manhood? that the tree which promised so abundant a harvest of usefulness should in a few months lie low with earth?

BARKER, Maj. James N., Washington, D. C., March 9, æ. —. He was born in Philadelphia, was an efficient and brave officer in the war of 1812, in which he gained the rank of major; in 1820 was elected mayor of Philadelphia; in 1829 was appointed collector of that port by President Jackson, which office he held until 1838, when he was appointed first comptroller of the treasury, which office he held some years; and afterwards, until his death, he remained in the treasury department. He was from early life a contributor to dramatic and poetical literature, and was a well-known play writer, and a contributor to the public journals in Philadelphia and Washington.

BARKER, Philip Porcher, Sept. 26, æ. 18; Mary Elizabeth, Oct. 9, æ. 16; Sanford William, Jr., Oct. 12, æ. 21,— children of S. W. Barker, M. D., Charleston, S. C., of yellow fever. Philip was a member of the Sophomore class in the S. C. College, and is spoken of as a young man of "gentlemanly deportment, endearing and winning manners, and whose fine talents gave promise of a bright and prosperous future." It is said of Mary that "she had thrown off the heedless waywardness of girlhood, and was daily developing the thoughtfulness and grace of womanhood; above all, that best grace of womanhood which habitually preferred the wishes and comfort of those around her to her own ease and gratification. Her loving heart knew no speech earnest enough to utter her devotion to her mother; and her friendship with her father rose into a mystery, undefined, and conceived only by their suggestive dependence upon each other's tenderness. The real treasure which her household of kindred cherished in her was her most affectionate temper to them all. She died young, and yet had lived to good purpose." Sanford had attained his manhood, "had chosen the profession of the law; his tastes were cultivated, his intellectual resources various, his moral nature informed, his self-training advanced; and he was characterized by his companions for his filial piety and sense of religious responsibility. Only those who witness the indiscriminate ravages of yellow fever can imagine the sorrows and desolations it produces. In a common calamity, here is an instance of uncommon desolation, of most piteous grief. The pride, beauty, youth, and opening manhood, and promise of a family, are swept away in a day as it were, affections blasted, hopes cut off, and resignation demanded in the deepest sorrow and sublimest mystery. He who gave has taken away. He only who thus wounds can heal."

BARLOW, Rev. Joseph, Franklin, Pa., May 22, æ. 60. He was a Presbyterian clergyman, an Englishman, and lost his life at the conflagration of his own house by inhaling the flame.

BARLOW, Hon. Alanson, Aug. 28, æ. 77, Ashland, N. Y., (father of Allen Barlow, of Binghampton,) and Mrs. MARY ANN BARLOW, wife of Hon. A. B., May 11, æ. 70. Mr. Barlow belonged to a family whose members have done the state some service. He was a nephew of Joel Barlow, of revolutionary memory, who deserves honorable mention among the statesmen and men of letters of that period. His "Columbiad" is still the only American national epic, the only example of a poet daring to celebrate in heroic verse contemporary or recent historic events. As a politician he ranked among the leading men of the organizing epoch of this government. He was the friend and coadjutor of Madison and Jefferson, to whose school of politics he belonged, or rather helped to found. His death was occasioned by the fatigue of a forced journey to join Napoleon, in council at Wilna, in Poland. In personal appearance Alanson Barlow much resembled his uncle, judging by the portrait in the Cyclopedia of American Literature. There was inherited, also, the diplomatist's inflexibility of purpose, his profound reserve of manner and of expression — a man of more thought than speech, giving one the impression of a plain, solid cast of character, in keeping with his robust and iron frame ; a man whose word was a bond ; trespassing a hair's breadth upon no man's rights ; not wearing his heart upon his sleeve — a friendly but deep-seated heart. Though rarely expressing personal interest in spiritual truth, unless drawn to it by others, yet his manual of devotion was found in many places literally worn away, though it had not been long in use. The biography of Mrs. B., in its main features, would be that of the early inhabitants of this region, a generation of energetic men and women, exchanging the refinement and culture of New England for lonely homes in this then wilderness. They derived from their frugal and simple habits a hardiness of constitution, an elastic vigor of frame, a power of enduring the rigors and changes of this austere climate — nature's compensations to the pioneers of civilization. They are gone. The husband, the father, venerable judge — the friend, the wife, the mother, the Christian — have bowed to the common lot. The torn fibres of the disturbed soil have knit together again above their place of rest. Thus the links that bind us to the past are broken. The outlook is toward the future, and the future is eternity.

BARNARD, Abner L., South Boston, Ms., Sept. 2, æ. 26. An officer in the house of correction, and a native of Enfield, N. H.; a young man of great purity of character and benevolent influence.

BARNARD, John D., Esq., Thomaston, Me., Sept. 12, æ. 57, cashier of Thomaston Bank.

BARNES, Mrs. Almira, Troy, N. Y., Mar. 29, æ. 72, at the residence of her son-in-law, the Hon. John D. Willard.

BARNES, Maj. Samuel B., Baltimore, Md., Dec. 14, æ. 72, one of the defenders. Maj. Barnes went to Baltimore city from his native county, Queen Anne's, at an early age, and learned the printing business. After the conclusion of his apprenticeship he moved to Frederick City, and there conducted the Examiner for several years. During his residence there he participated in the defence of Baltimore, and held the rank of major in the battle of North Point. He was four times elected to represent the County of Frederick in the state legislature. He then returned to Baltimore, and in 1841 assumed the editorial department of the Baltimore Clipper, of which he continued to be editor for 16 years. For some time past he had lived in retirement at his late residence. He was a whig in principle, and an earnest advocate of the principles of the American party — a consistent politician, fearless in the defence of right or in the condemnation of wrong.

BARNES, Dr. S. H., San Jacinto, Ts., Oct. 16, æ. 29, formerly of Cleveland, O. Dr. B. practised medicine for a length of time in Louisville, and by his assiduity and kindness for his patients, united with fine medical abilities, acquired friends who truly sympathize with the bereaved in their irreparable loss. Fond affection for his truly amiable partner has cost him his life. She was laboring with pulmonary disease, and, with the hope that a warmer and more genial clime would add to her health and comfort, the doctor removed, a year since, in fine health and spirits, to the sunny south; but alas! the fell destroyer, death, by yellow fever, cut short hope, health, life.

BARNEY, Jonathan, Esq., Barneysville, Swansey, Ms., Dec. 3, æ. 45, son of Mason Barney, Esq. He was highly esteemed, and his death brings unfeigned sorrow to a large circle of acquaintance. He was twice elected to the legislature, and he possessed a merited influence in his town, where his presence and counsel will be greatly missed.

BARR, Col. John Gorham, May 18, æ. 35, on board the royal mail steamer Emeu, between Suez and Melbourne, Australia, as U. S. consul to M. Col. B. was born at Milton, Caswell Co., N. C., Nov. 22, 1823. His father, Thos. Barr, died three years afterwards, and his mother, Mrs. Mary Jane Barr, moved with her family to Raleigh, where she lived seven years, and then removed to this city, where she resided till her death, not long afterwards, leaving the subject of this notice without father or mother to provide for or advise him. John Gorham having received the mental culture which the limited means of his widowed mother and his tender age permitted, was bound as an apprentice in a printing office, and by his industry and sprightliness attracted the attention and regard of David M. Boyd, (now of California,) who took him from the printing office, and generously afforded him means for the completion of his education. Having been prepared in the primary schools, he entered the freshman class in the University of Alabama in 1838, where he graduated in 1841, with the highest distinction — a result reflecting credit alike upon the sagacity and kindness of the benefactor and the talents and energy of the beneficiary. He immediately applied himself to the study of law; and being qualified and admitted a member of the bar, about twelve months afterwards he established an office in Tuscaloosa for the purpose of practising his profession. He was elected tutor in mathematics in the University of Alabama in 1844. He resigned at the expiration of two years, and returned again to his profession. In 1847 he was a candidate for the representative branch of the legislature, and conducted the canvass, though very young, with much tact and ability, and with entire satisfaction to his own party, and won for himself an enviable reputation as a public speaker. His uniform courtesy and signal ability displayed in debate gained him also the good will and highest esteem even of his political opponents. In the fall of the same year, the United States and Mexico being at war, and a call made upon Alabama for soldiers, a warm, ardent temperament, a laudable ambition, and a patriotic love of his country soon found Col. Barr actively engaged in a canvass for volunteers. He drew together large assemblages of people in Tuscaloosa and some of the adjacent counties, and by his fervent, stirring, eloquent, and patriotic appeals, a company of more than a hundred men, most of them young, gallant, and chivalrous like himself, speedily enlisted to "do or die" for their country on the crimson field of battle. He was unanimously elected their captain, and his was the first company from Alabama that landed in the city of Mobile and was received for the war. After his return from Mexico he resumed his profession, but turned his thoughts mainly to the political questions of the day, and was elected for his congressional district in 1856. He contributed to various literary periodicals, exhibiting the richest humor and wit. In social life he was eminently entertaining and attractive.

BARR, Dr. William, Abingdon, Va., June 14, æ. 75, at the residence of his son, Dr. W. F. Barr. He was born in Greenbrier Co., Va., on the 19th of Nov., 1782. His father afterwards settled in Halifax Co., Va., from whence Dr. B. moved to Germantown, N. C., in which place he resided for some years, and where, as a merchant and high sheriff, he exerted his highest energies in promoting the interests of his fellow-citizens. He was of patriotic ancestry, being a relative to the brave Col. Barré, of whom history makes honorable mention as having defended the American colonies in the British Parliament, and his father, at the early age of 16 years, entered the revolutionary army, in which he continued until the termination of the war. The deceased moved to Abingdon in 1823, upwards of 34 years ago, where he has since resided, living to see, what he ardently desired, his children grown up, all of whom — one a minister of the gospel — are members of the church of Christ. He was kind-hearted, warm in his attachments, and devoted to his friends. His feelings were of a liberal and elevated character. In his opinions he was honest and decided, and never failed to express them. His wife, Mrs. Rebecca Barr, died Aug. 16, 1857, æ. 72, a lady singularly mild and gentle in her disposition, a devoted member of the Methodist Protestant church in Abingdon.

BARRETT, Hon. Benj. Franklin, (of Rock Island, Ill.,) Carlisle, Mass., Sept. 28, æ. 56, while on a visit to his native place. Mr. B. was born in Carlisle, Mass., Feb. 24, 1802. He sought a new home in the west in 1836. He first resided in Northern Illinois, at Chicago. In 1839 he removed to Port Byron, where he lived till 1842, when he came to Rock Island, where he had long designed to make his permanent home. During his residence there he was an active business man, having been engaged extensively in the lumber and milling business, besides being the proprietor for some years of the Rock Island House, one of our most popular hotels. He was generous and noble-hearted, and possessed of a cheerful and pleasant disposition that endeared him to a large circle of friends and acquaintances. His purse was always open to assist the needy, and no one appealed to him in vain when in suffering circumstances. His fellow-citizens evinced their appreciation of Mr. B.'s manly integrity and business capacity by many marks of confidence in them. When Rock Island received a city charter all eyes turned instinctively to him as the fittest and worthiest man for the honorable office of her first mayor. Again, in 1854, during his absence at the east, he was a second time elected to that office. For a full third of a century Mr. B. was a Mason. He was made a Mason in 1825, in the lodge at Concord, Mass. Through all the vicissitudes and trials of life Mr. B. showed to the world a bright example of the true and pure life which is led by those who are faithful to Masonic precepts and teachings. He leaves a widow and three adopted daughters, children taken from the humblest walks in life.

BARROWS, Mrs. Asenath, Foxborough, Mass., July 17, æ. 81, relict of the late Wm. Barrows, of Templeton. Mrs. B. leaves three sons in the gospel ministry, Rev. Simon Barrows and Rev. Lewis Barrows, of Iowa, and Rev. W. Barrows, of Reading, Mass.

BARRY, William F., Esq., Nashville, Tenn., Dec. 20, æ. —. Mr. B. was for some time president of the Bank of Memphis, and alderman of the city for one term, and in all the relations of life, as an officer or as a gentleman, he was beloved by all who knew him.

BARTHOLOMEW, Edward S., Naples, Italy, May 1, a native of Colchester, Ct., æ. 32. In early life he turned his attention to painting, and subsequently adopted, as his profession, sculpture, which he followed with the greatest enthusiasm for the last eight years, in Rome. We give the following extract from a letter just received from Mr. W. C. Bryant, now in Italy: "You have heard of the death of poor Bartholomew, the sculptor. He came to the hotel at Naples, where I was, the evening before I went with my family to Castellamare. I was absent a week, and when I came back he was dead, and in his grave. He had fought a hard battle with poverty, and had just won it; orders were beginning to come in upon him from all quarters, and his great grief, when he breathed his last, was, that he could not place his mother in that state of comfort which he would easily have secured to her if a brief respite from death had been allowed him. I have been to his studio since my arrival in Rome, and there I saw the last work of his hand — a fine statue, justifying the reputation he has lately acquired — Eve, after the fall, in an attitude of dejection, and wearing an expression of profound sorrow. I could scarcely help fancying that the marble figure mourned the death of the artist to whom it owed its being." Among his most celebrated finished works we may mention Paradise Lost, Shepherd Boy, Sappho, Youth and Old Age, monument to Charles Carroll of Carrollton, greatly admired, Belisarius at the Porta Pincinia, and a group recently completed, and now being engraved for the London Art Journal, representing Ganymede and the Eagle of Jupiter.

BARTIME, Hon. Stephen Noah, Bensalem. Pa., Oct. 1, æ. 59. He was the son of David W. and Louisa Bartime, and was born at Cherry Hill, near Princeton, N. J. He had a large family of children, having three wives, the last surviving him. He was for many years a magistrate; and in 1851 he was elected to the associate judgeship on the democratic ticket, and reëlected in 1856. His courtesy and patient attention to counsel, the dignity of his demeanor, and the uprightness of his conduct on the bench and in private life, gained the entire confidence of his judicial district. His children looked up to him with affectionate reverence; and his friends regarded him as a beautiful exponent of the charities of life.

BARTLETT, Frederick Kinloch, St. Croix Falls, Wis., Dec. 1, æ. 39. Mr. B. was an old resident of the St. Croix Valley. He settled at Stillwater, Min., some ten years ago, and distinguished himself as a jurist. His eminent abilities and many virtues endeared him to all who knew him, and render his decease a severe loss to the community in which he lived. Full of hope and enterprise, he had lately entered an extensive undertaking at St. Croix Falls. He was for some time a resident of Milwaukie, and during the winter of 1856-7 he represented that city in the legislature of the state. Mr. B. leaves a wife and two children.

BARTLETT, Rev. Horace, New Haven, Ct., Feb. 5, æ. 65, member of the N. Y. East Conference.

BARTLETT, Mrs. Jane M., Dover, N. H., June 21, æ. —, widow of James Bartlett, Esq., for many years register of probate at D. He was brother of the late Hon. Ichabod Bartlett, the distinguished lawyer and member of Congress of Portsmouth, N. H. Mrs. B. was daughter of George Andrews, for many years a very honorable merchant in Dover.

BARTLETT, Mrs. Mary S., Lowell, Mass., Oct. 3, æ. —, wife of Hon. Homer Bartlett. She was daughter of William Starkweather, of Williamstown, Mass.; and, as might have been expected from the character of the college and the people of Williamstown, she was intellectual, polished, and pious. Educational advantages of a college are not confined to the students, but affect most happily society around it. Sons are educated under the very best advantages in preparation by the wholesome exhibition of rewarded ambition among college students; and daughters receive intellectual culture and strength from a literary atmosphere, as plants derive vigor from the dew-drops of the evening. Mr. Starkweather gave a public education to two of his three sons, and married four of his five daughters to graduates of the college. One daughter, the wife of Rev. Parsons Cooke, D. D., of Lynn, Mass., and another, the wife of Rev. Mr. Woodbridge, for many years pastor of the church in Ware, Mass., were called before Mrs. B. to the tomb. They were indeed *helpmeets* to their husbands in their Master's service, were faithful to their high trusts, honorable among women, and loved by Christians. Their praise is in the churches. Mrs. B., called to a more quiet, but by no means retired, post of duty and obligation on earth, has followed them. In the language of one of the public journals, " Sadly and tearfully do we chronicle the death of this dear friend, conscious as we are of the sorrow it must bring to all our hearts. Gifted with intellectual powers of unusual keenness and discrimination, and manifesting, on all occasions, the warmest interest in the pursuits and welfare of her friends, she was ever a cherished and animated companion; and those who knew her most intimately ever found her twining herself more closely about their affections, and rendering herself more essential to their happiness. Truly sincere and constant in her regard, all felt that they might trust and confide in her with full confidence that they should receive a friendly response. Yet more beautiful and true, if possible, were the traits she manifested in her own home, where she presided with so much wisdom and womanly dignity, together with an amiable solicitude for the comfort and happiness of the loved ones around her own hearthstone. As a wife and mother, she was most exemplary and devoted, and constantly sought to render her home attractive by all those domestic excellences which a true woman knows so well how to adopt. A liberal hospitality, too, was ever dispensed to strangers and friends beyond the home circle; and the mistress of the mansion never seemed happier than when others were sharing the bounty which Providence had granted to her in so large a measure. But more and better than all this was the simple beauty of her Christian life. Long devoted by profession and practice to the cause of her Redeemer, she moved in her appointed sphere in a humble, childlike spirit, ever distrusting her own religious experience, yet treasuring deeply in her heart the sacred principles of truth, which are the Christian's surest guide in death as in life."

BARTLETT, Mrs. Rebecca, Marblehead, Mass., Dec. 23, æ. 80, widow of Rev. John Bartlett.

BARTLETT, Rev. Jonathan, Redding, Ct., Feb. 22, æ. 93, formerly pastor of the Congregational church in that place.

BARTLETT, Miss Sarah, Newburyport, Mass., July 6, æ. 56, daughter of the late Capt. Josiah Bartlett.

BARTON, Mrs. Agnes, Lewiston, N. Y., April 6, æ. 85. Mrs. B. was one of the pioneers of Western N. Y. She came to that frontier in 1807, when the surrounding country was little more than a dense forest, inhabited, with few exceptions, by vagrants, savages, and wild animals. She lived to see the wilderness superseded by the progressive energy of civilization, wealth, and refinement. On the busy stage of life she acted well her part. Long will her acts of charity and benevolence, her social qualities, and parental affections, remain engraven upon the hearts of those who shared them.

BATTLE, Dr. Joel, Chapel Hill, N. C., Nov. 22, æ. —, at the house of his father, Hon. William H. Battle, judge of the Supreme Court. Like his father and three brothers, he graduated with the highest honors of the university, and took his diploma in 1847. He commenced the practice of medicine in Wayne Co., where he soon found himself surrounded with a lucrative practice, having gained the confidence and esteem of all who knew him, being alike distinguished for piety and talent.

BEAN, Dr. Edward, Bradford, Me., Dec. 16, æ. 50. Dr. B. occupied the position of one of the best physicians in this section for many years, and had an extensive practice until within a year or two, which practice ceased with his failing health.

BEATTY, John, Mount Holly, N. J., Oct. 2, cashier of the Mount Holly Bank, having served as cashier for the past 40 years.

BEATY, Hon. Adam, Mason Co., Ky., June 9, æ. 82. Mr. B. was well known to the church as a lay delegate of the diocese of Kentucky to the General Convention, of several years' standing. He was a man of superior legal ability, having occupied the highest judicial trusts in that state, and was universally esteemed for his wisdom and probity. From the year 1841 he took part in the affairs of the diocese of Kentucky as a trustee of Shelby College, delegate to diocesan as well as general conventions, and warden of the parish to which he belonged. As an agriculturist, he attracted attention, having written several important papers, particularly on the cultivation of tobacco and hemp, and also on the renovation of exhausted land. The commonwealth and the church have cause to lament his loss, and their deprivation of his wise and prudent counsels; yet he went to his rest in peace and well-founded hopes of a happy resurrection.

BECK, Preston, Jr., Santa Fe, N. M., April 8, æ. —, senior partner of the firm of Beck & Johnston, Santa Fe. The intelligence of his death occasioned profound sorrow in Philadelphia, and especially in the commercial community, by whom he was held in the highest estimation, as a gentleman and a merchant. At a meeting at the court house in Santa Fe, the citizens gave expression to their sorrow as follows, John B. Grayson presiding. "Although a native of Ind., he had resided in Mo. for many years, and from thence he removed to New Mexico in 1845, where he has spent most of the days of his manhood. We have not met here to eulogize the dead, but to manifest in this public manner the position occupied by the deceased here, where he was best known. He came here one of the early pioneers of the west, to seek his fortune in a then foreign land. By his enterprise, industry, and liberal, enlightened views, he had acquired a fortune; by his virtues, his social qualities, his public spirit, and high-toned sentiments, he had endeared himself to all who knew him; by his upright, manly course, he has left an impress upon this community that he died as he had lived — an honest man, the noblest work of God. In every patriotic, public-spirited work, Preston Beck, Jr., was always foremost; his hand was never shut to the needy and meritorious; and the young and enterprising always found in him a fast friend. He has left a blight upon New Mexico that will be felt throughout its entire extent. Finally, we feel that his place here can never be filled; for he occupied, as a merchant, as a man, and as a friend, all that any man can occupy in any community. He merited and had acquired the confidence, esteem, and friendship of all. Be it therefore

"*Resolved*, that in the death of Preston Beck, Jr., this community has lost one of its most useful, worthy, and highly esteemed citizens, which has left a void in our midst which can never be filled.

"*Resolved further*, that by his death at this time, in the prime and vigor of manhood and usefulness, a blight has been cast over this community from which it will not soon recover."

BECKER, Hiram, St. Paul, Min., Sept. 22, æ. —, a resident of Ann Arbor, Mich., and father of the Hon. G. L. Becker, of St. Paul, to whom he was paying a short visit. Mr. B. was U. S. marshal for Mich. under President Fillmore, and was elected to Congress from Minnesota, but, through some irregularity, did not get his seat.

BECKER, Rev. Dr., Bethlehem, Pa., Aug. 18, æ. 75.

BECKHAM, Maj. Armistead, Alleghany City, Pa., Nov. 24, æ. 69, warden of the Western Penitentiary. The inspectors, in their annual report, say of him, in the language and enforcing sentiment of his talented and estimable friend, Mr. Fleeson, "Maj. B. was a remarkable man, peculiarly qualified for the position he has filled so long and well. Rigid and systematic in discipline; studiously careful and economical in management; commanding in figure, and enforcing respect and obedience by his powerful nerve and iron will; lion-hearted in courage, cool in emergency or trial; yet discriminating in judgment, a rare judge of character, knowing when to place confidence in the professions of men, when to be lenient, or watchful, or strict, — he was a model officer, whose like the inspectors of that prison may long seek for in vain. As he lived, so he died — a hero to the last. But in the patient suffering of his closing days of life, the meek bowing of the strong man to the chastening of his God, his friends and relatives gladly saw another and a nobler heroism — that of the humble Christian, brought to bow calmly down to the will of the King of kings, the Lord of life; to say, in real sincerity of belief, 'Thou doest all things well.' Maj. B. had been the warden nearly 22 years, having been appointed in Feb., 1837. He was a native of Orange Co., Va.; had been master armorer at Harper's Ferry, and was transferred to the Alleghany Arsenal somewhere between 1828 and 1830, where he remained in the position of master armorer till appointed to the wardenship. He continued to interest himself in the affairs of the prison during all his illness, summoning the managers to his bedside to hear their reports with the precision and care of all his life. It is stated, as a creditable trait in human nature, that the convicts, although aware of his illness and infirmity, maintained most exemplary order during his confinement and last hours of life."

HON. HENRY BEDINGER,

Shepherdstown, Va., Nov. 26, æ. 48. He was naturally amiable, and blessed with many noble endowments. His native wit, happy humor, and affability made him numerous friends, and indeed a general favorite. He truly possessed social qualities of rare attraction. Few men have had as devoted friends. Indeed, the admiration of his particular associates knew no bounds. They almost idolized him. His opportunities of education were but limited. His father, the late Daniel Bedinger, of revolutionary memory, died when Henry was young, — only about 10 or 12 years of age, — leaving him in the care of a devoted mother, a daughter of the late Robert Rutherford, the first representative in Congress from the lower end of the Valley. Not many years after, his mother, too, was called to that better world.

At the age of about 18 he had been

placed, by the advice and means of the elder brother and a friend, much to the satisfaction of his mother, in the clerk's office in Romney, Hampshire Co., under the auspices of Col. J. Baker White, preparatory to the study of the law, the profession of his choice. He was then invited by his brother-in-law, Wm. Lucas, to become an inmate of his family in Charlestown, and then commenced reading law with him in 1835 or '36.

He obtained a license to practise law in 1837 or '38, at the age of 22, and opened a law office in Shepherdstown, in sight of which place he was born and raised on the banks of the Potomac, and which he called his native place, and loved so dearly, and where he breathed his last. In the mean time he married a daughter of the lamented Gen. George Rust, and entered into a partnership with his brother-in-law, and removed to Charlestown; and in 1845 succeeded his as representative in Congress from this district.

In that capacity he served two terms. He belonged to the democratic party, of which, in his day, his father had been the acknowledged head in the lower end of the Valley, and a distinguished leader. It was while his brother-in-law was in Congress, leaving him in charge of the law office, that the subject of this notice was first invited by his political friends to attempt a display of those oratorical powers which he possessed in so high a degree, and that were so often afterwards called into requisition. So telling and thrilling were his very first efforts that he was at once, by common consent, regarded as the most popular and effective speaker in this part of the state, and, indeed, within its entire limits. He became a "star," and one of the first magnitude, in the "Old Dominion."

He was always ready and at hand, and with his electrifying eloquence ever aroused the democratic party in the darkest and gloomiest hours, and enkindled that burning enthusiasm which gave the triumph that else had been lost.

His wit, his fancy, poured forth in incessant sallies; his withering sarcasm, his deep pathos, and his originality, with a ridicule, all resistless when indulged, constituted him the most formidable of speakers in political contests, and the most admired of popular orators.

It was his misfortune to lose his first wife soon after his removal to Charlestown — a lovely woman, and with whom he lived about six years most happily — amiable, gentle, and a devoted wife. She was the object, as she deserved to be, of the most ardent affections of a noble mind and heart, and was held in high estimation by all. She left behind a son and two daughters, one of whom soon followed her to the grave.

During his service in Congress, Mr. B. married his second wife, Miss Lawrence, a daughter of the Hon. ——— Lawrence, of New York, then also a member of the House of Representatives. Her he has left behind with three little children — a son and two daughters — the children, as were those of his first wife, of too tender years to feel how great is their bereavement.

Not long after the end of his second congressional term, President Pierce appointed him a *chargé d'affaires* to Denmark, in which position he was subsequently commissioned minister there, the office having been raised to that dignity during his service as *chargé*, and he well performed his part in the discharge of the honorable and responsible trust. The question of the Sound Dues was most advantageously settled for his country by a treaty which he wrote with his own hand — itself a monument to his name and to his fame.

Rarely has a public man passed from the stage of life having fewer enemies and a larger body of admiring and enthusiastic friends.

At the session of the County Court for Berkley, Dec. 13, a public meeting was held at which Col. J. B. A. Nadenboush presided, and the following resolutions were passed by the citizens: —

1. That they bear willing testimony to the great patriotism, ability, and fidelity with which Hon. Henry Bedinger fulfilled the high public trusts confided to him; and that in his death Virginia has lost a true and loyal son, and her dearest rights and interests a bold and eloquent defender.

2. That while painfully lamenting this, the memory of his many virtues now alone remains to them: they will ever recall, with mournful pleasure, the frank and genial nature, high-toned character, and gallant and chivalric bearing, which made Henry Bedinger always wel-

come to every heart and home in their midst.

BEEBEE, Mrs. Elenor F., Henrietta, O., —— 15, æ. 41. She was the daughter of Daniel Beebee, of West Hartwick, Otsego Co., ——, sister of the Rev. Albert Beebee, missionary to the Armenians in Turkey, and granddaughter of the late Rev. Dr. Chauncey Lee, of Colebrook, Ct. The same feeling of devotion which led her brother to abandon home, seemed to actuate her in all her conduct, and wherever the spiritual or temporal good of those around her demanded that the Christian should go, there she was found. Quiet, gentle, and unostentatious, yet firm and decided, her whole character was like the genial warmth of spring mingled with the grave aspect of autumn.

BEECHER, Rev. J. W., Vernon Centre, N. Y., Jan. 26, æ. 54. He was a descendant of John Beecher, who, after the Pequot war, with seven others, spent the winter upon the present site of New Haven, Ct., before Davenport preached under the oak. He was born at Southbury, Ct., Nov. 2, 1803. His early education was in strict accordance with the Puritan tendencies of the times — attended to classical studies under the tuition of the late President Tyler, his pastor, and Mr. Pitman, at Hanover, N. H. He entered the Southwest Theological Seminary, at Marysville, Tenn., in 1826; and in 1830 was licensed to preach, and received a commission under the American Sunday School Union to labor in East Tenn., where he labored one year. In 1832 he preached with great success in Bridgewater, Ct.; but subsequently for several years was the agent of the Presbyterian Education Society and the Home Missionary Society. From 1841 to 1846 he was pastor of a church in Ellsworth, Ct.; but, upon his failing health, he removed to Central New York, preaching at Sangerfield and Stockbridge; but ultimately fixed his residence in Vernon Centre, where he waited his change from his earthly to his heavenly home. Humble fidelity and endurance in missionary and pastoral duties — death hastened by privation and exposure in doing good — compose the lights which the grave cannot darken.

BEERS, Hon. Jacob, Newtown, Conn., June 28, æ. 76. The deceased had been through a long life one of the most prominent citizens of the town. He was a representative for many years in the popular branch of the legislature, and several times represented the eleventh district in the state Senate. He was also, during the former organization of the courts in the state, one of the associate judges of the Fairfield Co. Court; and in all the public stations he occupied he discharged the duties of the same honorably to himself and acceptably to the community at large. Perhaps few men have lived more respected, or died more regretted.

BEERS, Philo, Esq., Chicago, Ill., March 9, æ. 66. He was one among the first settlers of Illinois, and was much respected by his large acquaintance as an honest, upright, kind-hearted man. He in an early day represented, with much credit, the County of Clinton in the state legislature, then held at Vandalia. Thus are passing away the noble pioneers of our now flourishing state.

BEERS, Dr. Timothy Phelps, New Haven, Conn., Sept., 22, æ. 68. He was born in New Haven, Christmas day, 1789, was graduated in Yale College in 1808, studied his profession with Eli Ives, M. D., subsequently attended the medical lectures in Philadelphia, and licensed to practise in 1811. During the "late war," he was appointed surgeon of a regiment of Connecticut militia, commanded by the late Gen. Hezekiah Howe, and performed the duties of his appointment during the summer of 1812, with his regiment at New London. In 1830 he was elected Professor of Obstetrics in the medical institution of Yale College, the duties of which office he discharged for more than a quarter of a century.

BELDEN, Capt. Clifford, Cleveland, Ohio, —— æ. 74. Capt. B. was a native of the State of Connecticut. He was a ship carpenter by trade, and sailed in an American vessel from Portland, Me., in that capacity during the last war with Great Britain, and was captured by the British. He was confined on the Island of Bermuda over 11 months, and suffered severely from rigorous treatment at the hands of his captors during that time. On his release, in the autumn of 1814, Capt. Belden came to C. Since then he has been captain of vessels upon the lakes, and was the compeer of Capts. Stannard, Blake, and others.

BELKNAP, Andrew Eliot, Boston, Ms., Jan. 25, æ. 78. He was a son of the late Rev. Dr. Belknap, and was for many years a reputable merchant in that city. He took much interest in historical matters, especially in such as related to Boston, and was a frequent contributor to the newspapers under the signature of "A Boston Boy."

BELKNAP, Mrs. Anne Clark, Keokuk, Iowa, Dec. 7, æ. 57, the wife of a gallant and distinguished soldier, — the late Brig. Gen. William G. Belknap, — with whom she united her fortunes ere he had yet attained high rank and distinction. Mrs. B. came with her husband to the then far west, more than the third of a century ago, to lead a frontier life at what were, at that time, the outposts of our little army. Crossing from Green Bay, one of those outposts, to the Mississippi, and proceeding down the latter to St. Louis, she passed this point over thirty years ago, when there was not yet a human habitation here, save, perhaps, the wigwam of the Sacs and Foxes, old Black Hawk, Keokuk, and their associates; long, in fact, ere even the territory of Iowa was ushered into existence, and while it still formed a part, not of Wisconsin, but of Michigan! Of what now constitutes the Territory of Kansas, Mrs. B. was, perhaps, the first white woman that ever became an inhabitant. Her husband, then Capt. Belknap, was ordered to establish a military post on the Missouri, which he did accordingly, probably in 1827 or '28, with the name of Fort Leavenworth, near where the present city of the same name stands. While the buildings for this post were being erected, Mrs. B., like a true soldier's wife, ate and slept under a tent, until they were ready to be occupied. Subsequently she followed her husband to Florida, where he had been ordered during the campaign with the Seminoles; and, later still, she accompanied him to the posts on the Arkansas, Forts Smith and Gibson, where this devoted and noble wife, always of a frail constitution, and never of robust health, spent several years more, far removed from those thousand comforts and refinements to which she had been accustomed in early life. She possessed a most cheerful and happy temperament, and it was under her own hospitable roof that her beautiful traits of character were most strikingly developed. It was there that she ever appeared a true model for her sex, not only in all her domestic relations, but in its *avocations* as well. Home — that home where so much of the last few years of her life were spent — was to her evidently one of calm and true rational enjoyment, while to her friends one of never-failing attractions. But it was as a sincere and genuine, though wholly unpretentious, Christian, that the character of Mrs. B. shone forth in its greatest beauty and loveliness. It was clearly mirrored upon her ever calm and serene countenance, and evidenced in the daily acts of her life. After Gen. B.'s death, which occurred in 1851, in Texas, where he was on duty with his troops, Mrs. B., accompanied by her daughters, came to Keokuk to join her only son, and make it her home.

In connection with the notice of Mrs. B. it is thought proper to notice briefly the life of her gallant husband. Brevet Brig. Gen. W. G. BELKNAP, Lieut. Col. of the Fifth U. S. infantry, died near Preston, Texas, Nov. 10, 1851, æ. 57. He entered the service as a third lieutenant of the twenty-third regiment of infantry, U. S. army, in April, 1813, and accompanied the expedition of that year down the St. Lawrence, under Gen. Wilkinson. He served, during the campaign of 1814, on the Niagara frontier, with great distinction, and especially on the occasion of the attack of the British army on Fort Erie, on the 15th of Aug. of that year. Lieut. Belknap commanded a picket guard of 100 men on that night, which was thrown out one mile or more in the direction of the enemy. He was met at that point with a heavy assaulting column of 2000 men, under the command of Lieut. Gen. Drummond, and, although obliged to retreat before this large force, kept up a constant and unremitted fire, until they arrived at the defences of Fort Erie. Lieut. Belknap received a severe wound on this occasion. At the peace establishment, in 1815, he was retained in the second regiment U. S. infantry, (Col. Brady,) where he continued till the reduction of the army in 1821, when he was transferred as senior first lieutenant of the third U. S. infantry, in which regiment he continued as lieutenant and captain more than 20 years, and until promoted to a majority in the eighth infantry, in 1842. He was breveted a lieutenant colonel in 1842, for his services in Florida. In the battle of Palo Alto and Resaca de la Palma he commanded a brigade with much gallantry and distinction, and received the brevet of colonel. At the siege and capture of Monterey, he was acting inspector general of Gen. Taylor's army, and at the battle of Buena Vista was breveted a brigadier general, having served under Gen. Taylor in every battle fought by him during the Mexican war.

BELKNAP, Zedekiah, Weathersfield, Vt., June 8, æ. 77, a graduate of Dartmouth College in the class of 1807.

BELL, Wm A., Boston, Mass., May 28, æ. —. Mr. B. came to Boston at the age of 15, from Portsmouth, N. H., of which place he was a native, and found employment in a hardware store in Dock Square. Mr. B. had been long identified with Odd Fellowship, and had passed through the various official grades of the order, having filled the chair of grand master. He was a very active and efficient member of that institution, and was in high estimation. He also served in the Common Council, and was elected president of the council in place of Mr. Story, when that gentleman went to Europe. He was much respected, and his sudden death will cause painful emotions in a wide circle of friends and acquaintances.

BELLOWS, Aaron, Fulton, N. Y., April 28, æ. 90, descended from John Bellows, who emigrated from England in the ship Hopewell, 1635. His mother was Mary Parker, of New Hampshire, a relative of the ancestors of Hon. J. P. Hale. She was a faithful mother, training her children in "wisdom's ways." Mr. Bellows was born in Worcester Co., Mass., Feb. 22, 1768. His youth was passed amid the privations and disturbances of the revolution. At the age of 21 he emigrated to Central New York. All his possessions consisted of a rifle and a knapsack, in which were provisions for his journey and a change of raiment. The city of Utica consisted, at the time of his arrival, of one log tavern, a barn, and a frame for a small dwelling. He proceeded to Clinton, and thence following marked trees westward, he came to Salina; and afterwards established himself at Onondaga, where he spent the most active and apparently the most useful part of his life. He married Miss Azuba Patterson, about the year 1794. He was public spirited, was active in constructing roads and bridges, and was connected in matters of public improvement with Col. Danforth, whose name is associated with the early history of Onondaga Co. In 1809, at the death of a daughter, he and his wife were hopefully converted. The same year the religious society of Onondaga Hollow was formed. Under its first pastor, Rev. Dirck C. Lansing, afterwards D. D., they united with the church. He was chosen trustee of the society, and afterwards became a ruling elder. He was a devoted Christian, and was given to hospitality. His house was the place for prayer meetings, and for Sabbath gatherings of the youth and children, that he might instruct them from the Bible and the Catechism. Is is worthy of notice that he lived on terms of friendship with the Indians, who were troublesome, and with whom many of his neighbors had difficulty. As a mark of respect for him they gave him the name of "Onnocoonas" or Full Moon. He resided 26 years in Oneida Co., and subsequently removed to Fulton, Oswego Co. Here he was called upon to part with his wife in 1851, who had been the sharer of his toils and his faithful companion for more than half a century. His remaining days were passed in retirement, in reading his Bible, the newspapers, and in pious contemplation; and, though he suffered from infirmities of the body, he preserved the exercise of his mental faculties. To the close of life his interest in public affairs was unabated. He voted at every presidential election except the first.

BELT, Capt. William J., Calvert Co., Ind., April 2, æ. 64, for many years an officer in the U. S. navy. He was appointed a midshipman by Mr. Madison, then president of the United States, Sept. 11, 1811; served through the war of 1812; was twice taken prisoner: the last time taken he was carried to the Cape of Good Hope, where he remained two years; from thence to England; sailed from England for the United States in the Cartell, Sept. 4, 1815. He afterwards served his country faithfully for many years. His last cruise was in command of the Marion.

BEMAN, Rev. Jehiel C., New York, Dec. 27, æ. 68, father of Rev. Amos G. Beman.

BEMIS, Mrs. Hannah H., Weathersfield, Vt., March 9, æ. 68, wife of Jeremiah Bemis, Esq., and daughter of the late Ebenezer Herrick, of Marlboro', N. H. At the early age of ten years Mrs. B. became a subject of renewing grace, and a year after publicly put on Christ by uniting with the Methodist Episcopal church; and from that time religion with her was a living, active, and propelling principle, giving to her neighbors and all who knew her an evidence of its power upon the life of its possessor. In the church she was regarded as a very worthy and consistent member. But in her own family especially was seen and exemplified, in the clearest manner, the beauty of that influence which is only exerted by a loved companion and Christian mother.

BENDER, Charles W., Philadelphia, Pa., Oct. 6, a prominent and well-known citizen of P. Mr. B. at one time took an active part in municipal and state politics, being identified with the old whig party. The announcement of his death was received with extreme regret.

BENNETT, Hon. Thomas, New Haven, Conn., April 5, æ. —. Mr. B. was a faithful and considerate public officer, and an amiable and honest man. Without an enemy, his death will be universally mourned. He leaves a large family to regret their loss.

BENNETT, Mrs. Martha, Green Co., N. Y., Aug. —, æ. 76, widow of P. W. Bennett, mother of T. R. Bennett, inspector of the 18th precinct police, New York city. Mrs. B. was a noble-minded woman, and much beloved by a large circle of friends. She was born in Newark, N. J. At the commencement of the revolutionary war her father, John Chesters, was seized by a gang of bandits in England, and brought to New York city against his will, for the purpose of fighting the Americans. His father, William Chesters, despatched a man to America with $200 to ransom the captive; but the British officer to whom the application was made detained both money and agent, and gave John 25 lashes on the bare back for asking to be set at liberty. Young Chesters then deserted, taking with him his horse and such things as he could conveniently carry; and, sympathizing with the Americans in their struggle for liberty, lost no time in joining the American army. He was one of Gen. Washington's main men, and, after faithfully serving his adopted country for seven years, received an honorable discharge, with a medal. During the struggle for liberty by the Americans, young Chesters, then only 19 years of age, with four others, was watching one night for smugglers on the banks of the Passaic River, when they were surprised by a body of British soldiers, who had landed with the intention of taking Newark. Chesters and his companions, seeing that resistance against such powerful odds was useless, fled for their lives; but three of them were overtaken and murdered. John succeeded in gaining the court house, and, while entering the door, three bullets were fired at him; but, fortunately, they lodged in the door without doing further damage. Chesters sounded the alarm to Generals Ray, Knox, and Cummings, then asleep in a hotel near by, who instantly marshalled their forces, and saved the town. Incensed at their defeat, the British offered a large reward for young Chesters's head, which, however, they did not get. He died in Newark, when only 30 years of age.

BENJAMIN, Mrs. Sarah, Mount Pleasant township, Pa., April 20, æ. 114. Her maiden name was Sarah Matthews; and she was born in Goshen, Orange Co., N. Y., Nov. 17, 1743. She was thrice married. Her first husband was Mr. William Reed. He served in the revolutionary army in the early part of the struggle, and died of a wound received in Va. Her second husband was Mr. Aaron Osburne, of Goshen, N. Y. He also was in the army of the revolution, but survived the war. Her last husband was Mr. John Benjamin, with whom she settled in Mount Pleasant in 1812. He died four years afterwards. She had five children, the youngest of whom is 70 years old. She has left four generations of descendants. From her youth, until past 40 years of age, she was in the midst of the rough and stirring scenes of border warfare or of the revolutionary struggle. Her temperament was such that she could not be an idle spectator of events. She entered very deeply in all these vicissitudes.

Up to the latest period of her life she distinctly recollected the family of Mr. Broadhead, whose sons in 1755 boldly resisted a party of 200 Indians, making a fort of their house. She was in the vicinity of Minisink when Brant, the Indian chief, led a party of Indians and tories through that settlement, scalping the inhabitants and burning the houses. After the second marriage she accompanied her husband in the army. During marches she made herself useful in preparing food, and, when in quarters, engaged in sewing for the officers and men. When the army was engaged in embarking some heavy ordnance at Kingsbridge, on the Hudson, ostensibly to attack New York, then in the hands of the enemy, it was necessary to do it in the night, and to place sentries around, lest they should be observed, or taken by surprise. Her husband having been placed as a sentinel, she took his station, with overcoat and gun, that he might help to load the heavy artillery. Soon Washington came round to examine the outposts, and, detecting something unusual in her appearance, asked, "Who placed you here?" She promptly replied, in her characteristic way, "Them who had a right to, sir." He, apparently pleased with her independent and patriotic spirit, passed on. She accompanied the army, with her husband, to the south, and was present at the seizure of Yorktown and the surrender of Cornwallis. During the battle she was busy in carrying water to the thirsty, and relieving the wants of the suffering. When passing where the bullets of the enemy were flying, she met Washington, who said, "Young woman, are you not afraid of the bullets?" She instantly answered, "The bullets will never cheat the gallows." She possessed extraordinary energy, even in her extreme age, and would relate the events of her early days with all the vivacity of youth. Up almost to the period of her death she exercised herself in carding and spinning. The fineness and uniformity of her yarn was a wonder and an admiration. She visited her friends on foot, making long walks, and, when she used a carriage, disdained to be helped to enter it. Two or three years ago she remarked that she had never been sick but once. She then sent for a physician, who left her some medicine. After he had gone, she, not liking the smell of it, "threw the dirty stuff in the fire, and then had to pay for it." The simplicity of her life was peculiar. For some years past she has been regarded as a sort of curiosity on account of her great age and vivid recollection of events long past. Many visitors called upon her, and were always received with cheerfulness, and went away surprised and delighted with her flow of genial humor, combined with rare physical activity. She was, indeed, a link connecting the present age with ages past and gone. For a long period she was ready and cheerfully waiting to depart; her end was calm and peaceful.

BENSON, Dr. Cyrus, Bridgewater, Mass., July 16, æ. 74. Dr. B. was a native and resident of Bridgewater. He was born May 15, 1784. He practised medicine between 20 and 30 years with good success, when his health became infirm; and he has since cared for his farm only. He was one of the first receivers of the doctrines of the New Jerusalem church in Bridgewater, and has ever maintained high moral deportment. He has left a widow in Bridgewater, and two married daughters in Leeds, Me. Two lovely sons have passed into the spiritual world.

BENSON, Mrs. Maria, Smyrna, Del., Oct. 30, æ. 67, wife of Benjamin Benson, and daughter of Capt. Robert Shewell, of Philadelphia. She was the niece of Elizabeth Shewell, who became the wife of the celebrated painter Benjamin West under circumstances of difficulty and opposition from her friends that made their marriage one of romantic interest, and the theme of writers who have rendered it familiar to most readers. But not to any connection with the names of the great or renowned did the subject of this memoir look. In her own home and amid its endearments she found her appropriate sphere, possessing in an eminent degree all the elements that constitute female excellence.

BENTLEY, Gideon, Constantia. Oswego Co., N. Y., Feb. 27, æ. 107. He was a soldier of the revolution, and the father of 13 children, who are all living. The eldest is 77 years old. Thomas Bentley, the third son, lives at Columbus, is 73 years old, in the enjoyment of unimpaired health, and bids fair to outlive many younger men.

HON. THOMAS HART BENTON.

Washington, D. C., April 10, æ. 76. "Mr. B. for more than 40 years has been a prominent man in the councils and politics of our nation. With Adams, Webster, Clay, Calhoun, and others of our great men of the 19th century, he has gone beyond the struggles here for promotion, or the sincere action of patriotism, both of which motives enter so largely into the lives of statesmen, the latter, we trust, largely predominating. Mr. B. may have been for a moment swerved from the straight path by the desire of a presidential term, which has obtained more or less influence over all of our great men; but few have escaped as unscathed as Thomas H. Benton. That he lived and died a true patriot and lover of liberty, none can question; and it is a fact which our young men ought to lay to heart, that the great man died thanking God that he had lived to see that great wrong, the Lecompton measure, which the disunion democracy were trying to force upon the people of Kansas, defeated in the House of Representatives." — *Adrian Evening Express*.

"The dart of death was aimed at a high place yesterday. Thomas H. Benton fell before it, not unexpectedly, nevertheless to the deep grief of his countrymen, and to the manifest loss of the world. His ardent wish, through the last weeks of his bodily suffering, was to be spared for such time, and with such measure of strength, as would enable him to finish his Abridgment of the Debates of Congress, which he had brought down to the year 1850. It has not pleased God to grant his wish.

"Dying full of years, having lived for three quarters of a century, Col. B. has left behind few riper scholars, few greater statesmen, and, without doubt, no more striking evidence of that power of industry, system, and observation. He was a wonder of assiduity, of painful toil, of intense thought, of iron memory, and of indomitable will. His virtues, as well as his failings, have been throughout life such as belong to a strong character; and, whenever he has been deemed to have erred, his most strenuous opponents have yielded to him the praise of sincerity and of patriotism; but, inasmuch as he was a bitter politician in early and middle life, his judgment, and sometimes his motives, have been arraigned, not without cause. His courage, high ambition, talents, and impetuosity, combined in him to make a powerful competitor, and not seldom, in the struggle of professional and political life, a bitter enemy.

"In his relations to his country, Col. B. has been a signally useful man, though candor compels the admission that his measure of usefulness was at times impaired, and that seriously, by private animosities, as well as by partisan acerbity. He worked well and faithfully; he struck fearlessly and strongly; but he made his blow tell first for himself, next for his party, and then for his country.

"His evening of life was a mellow, genial close after a tempestuous day. During that hour his feelings have toned down and mollified, and his aim has been more for his God and his country than for his party or himself. In that hour he has stood up well and faithfully by the principles of human freedom, and has frowned steadfastly upon the attempts of the president to overawe Congress into bad measures.

"Col. B. was born in North Carolina, in 1782. He was educated at Chapel Hill, and read law at William and Mary College, Va., and commenced practice at Nashville, Tenn. He was elected to the legislature, and advocated the passage of a law giving slaves trial by jury. He became a judge of the Supreme Court of Tennessee, but took a commission in the army at the age of 23, and raised a regiment of volunteers in the war of 1812, and became a lieutenant colonel. After the war he removed to St. Louis, Mo., edited the Missouri Argus, and advocated the admission of Missouri into the Union. He advocated the settlement of Oregon, the protective system, and preëmption laws, but was opposed to nullification, and the U. S. Bank, and the compromise of 1850. He supported Mr. Buchanan, who defeated Col. Fremont, Mr. Benton's son-in-law. He was elected a senator from Missouri, provisionally, before the long-contested admission of that state, and took his seat in the Senate in 1821, where he remained until 1851, when he failed of a reëlection. Col. B. sustained the administration of Jackson and Van

Buren most ardently, and was recognized as the leader of the party who elected them. For the greater part of his life Col. B. was the idol of the State of Missouri. The people clung to him as their political adviser; and after his defeat in the Senate they called upon him again and again to run him in the House of Representatives. He never was an effective speaker, for he lacked eloquence, flow of words, imagination, warmth, and fertility, but he was clear, accurate, logical, and practical; but, never addressing a popular audience except after the most careful preparations, it may be readily understood that his efforts appeared better to the reason than in the delivery.

"Col. B. was an accomplished linguist, and, in respect to general information out of range of political study, was by no means wanting." — *Detroit Advertiser.*

He married Elizabeth McDowell, of Virginia, who died in 1854. He leaves four daughters — Mrs. Jones, Mrs. Fremont, Mrs. Jacob, and Mrs. Boileau.

The following eloquent tribute to Col. B. is taken from the St. Louis Democrat: —

"'Greatness is ended,
An unsubstantial pageant all:
Droop o'er the scene the funeral pall.'

"Weave the cypress for the bier of the departed. Gather the burial cortege to lay his body within the final home. Summon fitting words of elegy to voice the sorrow of those who knew him in life, and mourn him in death. For this day, amid the drooping of banners, the low wail of martial music, and the multitudinous concourse of our citizens, the solemn words, 'Dust to dust, and earth to earth,' will be spoken over the remains of Thomas H. Benton — a statesman without fear, a patriot without price. Let us deal gently with his errors, remember his labors, and embalm his virtues. In the fierce contentions of public life, his stern energy was not of a kind to conciliate rivals, or turn away the wrath of opposing parties; but all must concede that in every passage he bore himself with manly fortitude and daring openness of purpose. In the domestic circle he evinced what few who saw only his outward bearing would have penetrated — a heart overflowing with kindness and love; and from the tender solicitude with which he watched over the decline of the gentle companion of his way, not less than from the infinite pathos in which, when summoned forth again to his country's service, he told of his occupation in planting assembled graves on the sunset side of the Father of Floods, we have assurance that his nature was warm with the pulses of a soft and genuine sympathy. In his solicitude for the preservation of a cordial unity of feeling, and a generous forbearance of hostility, between different sections of the republic, he manifested ever a consistency of aim and a purity of ambition that will model forth one of the brightest examples in history to those who may hereafter be intrusted with the care of a nation's honor and peace. In his closing hour, when all the vanities of earth had passed from his thought; when his hand had dropped, released from the work at which he toiled; when his faint utterance had transmitted a dying wish that no unseemly action of Congress should mark his departure into the silent land, — he gathered his robes around him with more than senatorial dignity, and marched into the great presence as calmly, as solemnly, as consciously, as though he had sounded the depths of eternity, and had measured the spaces of the infinite. And thus — in his public services and in his private attachments, in his arduous life and in his majestic death — he has earned an abiding place in the memory of the American people, whilst his name will be emblazoned more in the future than in the present, as one of the most illustrious of those who gave so much of renown to the deliberations of our national councils."

BERRY, Rev. L. W., Cincinnati, O., July 23, æ. 43. Dr. B. was born in Alburgh, Vt., in 1815. He entered the travelling connection, in the Ohio Conference, at the age of 18. He succeeded Dr. Simpson in the presidency of the Indiana Asbury University in 1848. After remaining for about six years in charge of this institution, he accepted the presidency of the Iowa Wesleyan University at Mount Pleasant. He remained in connection with this institution for about three years. In the summer of 1857 he resigned his place at Mount Pleasant, and took charge of a new college enterprise in Missouri. He labored with all that zeal and energy for which he has always been noted to build up the Jefferson City University.

BETHUNE, Mrs. Frances, Columbus, Ga., May 20, æ. —, wife of Gen. Bethune, of the Corner Stone. Mrs. B. died of a pulmonary disease, after a lingering illness. She was a consistent member of the Methodist church, and an exemplary wife and mother. The Superior Court, being in session, took a recess, and the judge and members of the bar, in a body, attended her funeral.

BINN, Robert S., Rankin Co., Miss., July 7, æ. 39. Mr. B. was a native of Alabama, a son of the late Gov. Bibb, of that state, and was connected with a large and influential circle of relatives and friends in Mississippi and Alabama. For the last six years Mr. B. had been a citizen of Rankin Co., and by his gentlemanly manners and generous disposition won many friends, who will long lament his early death. Receiving a liberal education, he engaged in the business of planting, and by his success afforded another instance proving that a practical success in the business of life is not incompatible with scholastic attainments, which, added to refined enjoyments, in no degree detracts from the usefulness of the citizen.

BILLINGS, Dr. James A., Batavia, N. Y., Aug. 2, æ. 63.

BILLINGS, Dr. John, Rochester, N. Y., June 29, æ. 75.

BIRD, George L., M. D., Crawfordville, Ga., ——— 5, æ. 47. He was a man of great respectability and integrity of character, and stood high in the respect and esteem of a wide circle of friends and acquaintances. His intercourse with the world was marked by the utmost simplicity of manners, attended with modesty, candor, frankness, and truth, in all he said or did. As a physician, he was attentive, kind, and sympathizing with his patients. Long will he be remembered by many whose pains he has relieved, and whose hours of suffering he has kept watch with. He has fallen, if not in the very prime of his life and his manhood, at least in the meridian of his usefulness, good name, and all those excellences and virtues which won the confidence and love of those who knew him. He has left a widow and several children, upon whom the affliction is peculiarly severe.

BIRD, George, New York, June 20, æ. —, a native of Greenfield, Mass. Mr. B. went into business in New York as a merchant in early life; his chief capital — integrity, energy, and superior business capacity. To him may be applied the oft-used designation, "architect of his own fortune." He was a man of great forecast, of sound judgment, and unswerving integrity and honor. These were marked elements in his course of enterprise, and of the success he achieved — an ample fortune and unusual respect and confidence. Another trait of character and habit of life — and we refer to these for lights to the young men of the times — was this: In the midst of his severe occupations, while in active business, he ever found time to give attention to the improvement of his mind and the acquisition of knowledge. Thus it was from his early years; his reading was extensive and well directed, and his stock of knowledge thus acquired was enlarged and improved by foreign travel. But a sketch of his character would be quite imperfect which should not set out other traits of his life, for which he was known, loved, and honored. We have alluded to his fortune, acquired as we have indicated, with which he was enabled to retire from active business. He employed a due share of it in acts of judicious liberality and active charities. The poor found in him a ready friend and helper. New York, the great metropolis of trade, wealth, and foreign immigration, may be denominated also the metropolis of suffering, poverty, and abject wretchedness. For some relief, or mitigation of these frightful evils, his hand and influence were promptly offered. A favorite object of his bounty was the institution of the "Five Points House of Industry," of which he was a trustee. To this object he contributed liberally, and had the joy to know of thousands of homeless, helpless, outcast children sent to safe and happy homes and occupations in the west, by him and his associates in that heavenly charity. In religion — Mr. B. was of the Episcopal communion — a vestryman and communicant in Rev. Dr. Hawks's church, and of a decided Christian character. He was blessed in all his domestic relations; was married, rather late in life, to the daughter of the late honored Le Grand Cannon, Esq., of Troy. By her many virtues, and intelligence, and affection, his home was made a precious rest and joy. From that scene of peace, hospitality, and happiness, he has been suddenly removed. He has been separated, too, from a widowed mother, living in G.; and no mother was ever blessed with a more affectionate and devoted son. And herein was seen one of the crowning graces of a beautiful life.

BIRDSONG, Elijah Perry, M. D., Bellaire, Ohio, March 1, æ. 39. Dr. B. was a native of Virginia. He received the degree of doctor in medicine in 1852, and commenced the practice of his profession in Bellaire the same year. He was an intelligent gentleman, a sincere friend, and an honor to his profession. In him the poor have lost a liberal benefactor.

BISSELL, Harry H., M. D., Buffalo, N. Y., Sept. 16, æ. 62. Dr. B. was born in Randolph, Vt., June 21, 1796. His mother was of the family of Leavitt, from Suffield, Ct. In 1826, and after pursuing a thorough preparatory course, he graduated at the New Haven Medical School, and commenced the practice of medicine at Lancaster, in Western New York. During his course of study at New Haven he was honored by the warm friendship of the lamented Dr. Nathan Smith, in whose office he was for some time a student; and it is but just to say, that in after life he endeavored to mould his character as a physician and surgeon after that distinguished teacher and practitioner, to whom he always felt he was indebted in a great measure for his success in practice. After seven years of successful and laborious practice, Dr. B. visited and spent six months at the medical institution and hospitals at Cincinnati, Ohio. This visit was to him of great interest, and he returned to his labors with renewed health and courage. In 1838, worn down by his professional duties in the country, he spent the fall and winter at the medical institutions and hospitals of New York and Philadelphia, and in June, 1839, removed to Buffalo, and assumed the office and practice of his former preceptor, Dr. J. E. Marshall, who had just died. This was hardly a new field, and he was enabled to enter immediately upon a full practice, which he maintained with success and honor to the last. At the time of his death he was the oldest practising physician in Buffalo. For forty years he had been a professor of religion, and in his practice love for mankind was ever the ruling principle. Possessed of a sound judgment and indomitable energy, he never faltered in the discharge of his whole duty through fear of consequences. To the calls of the suffering poor, from whom he could expect no remuneration, he answered as readily and cheerfully as to those of the affluent. As a citizen he commanded the love and respect of all who knew him. To his family he has left a legacy more precious than gold — the memory of a devoted husband, an indulgent father, and a true Christian physician.

BLACK, Rev. Andrew W., Sewickly, Pa., Sept. 10, æ. 51, of the Reformed Presbyterian church. He was well and favorably known as an eminent divine, and useful member of society, devoting his time to the spiritual and temporal interests of his fellow-men.

BLACK, Dr. William Lowndes, Glenn's Springs, S. C., July 8, æ. 32.

BLACKBURN, Gen. William, Allen Co., Ohio, May 7, æ. 69. Gen. B. was born in the State of Maryland, June 23, 1787, coexistent with the constitution of the United States. His father removed to the State of Pennsylvania when William was quite young; from thence he removed to Ohio among the early pioneers of that state, and settled in Columbiana Co. In 1813, after Hull had surrendered the American army at Detroit, and our frontier was laid open to the tomahawk and scalping-knife of the savages, the call of his country found young Blackburn ready to gird himself for the contest. He raised a company of volunteers, at the head of which he took the field in that ever-memorable winter campaign of the north-west. Through the mud and rain, snows and storms, of that terrible winter, he was ever at his post, and ready for duty. He arrived, with the command to which he was attached, on that field of blood and carnage where Winchester was defeated at Frenchtown, on the River Raisin, after a forced march of many hours, in time to rescue a few of the flying fugitives from the merciless foes that pursued them; after which they returned to the Maumee, and built

Fort Meigs. At the expiration of his term of enlistment, with his company he returned to Columbiana Co., where he married, and engaged in agricultural pursuits. In 1817 he was elected a member of the legislature from Columbiana Co., and was continued without intermission a member of that body until 1835 — a rare instance of continued confidence in a public servant. In the spring of 1835, he was appointed by Andrew Jackson, receiver of public money at the land office at Lima, Ohio; and in that year he removed with his family to Allen Co. In 1839 he was reappointed by Martin Van Buren to the same office. In 1843, at the expiration of his second term, he retired to private life on his farm. In 1851 he was again returned to the legislature of Ohio, since which time he has quietly resided on his farm.

BLACKBURNE, William, Philadelphia, Pa., March —, æ. —. He was a well-known citizen of P. At one time he was engaged in cotton manufacture, and claimed to have spun at Huntsville, Ala., the first cotton yarn ever made in the United States.

BLAKE, Benjamin, Columbus, Ohio, March 27, æ. 45. For many years Mr. B. served his fellow-citizens in the town council, wherein he was distinguished for great zeal in furthering measures calculated to benefit and improve the city. Sound and deliberate in his judgment, his opinions in all matters were generally received by his associates, and to him are the citizens of Columbus chiefly indebted for very many of our most wholesome and valuable municipal laws. As a father, neighbor, and friend, a severe loss has been sustained — one which time alone can heal.

BLAKE, Mrs. Jemima, Newport, N. H., Dec. 28, æ. 95, widow of Abel Blake, formerly of Keene, N. H. The deceased was the daughter of Samuel Warren, of Milford, Mass., a captain in the revolutionary army, and first cousin to Dr. Joseph Warren, who fell at the battle of Bunker Hill.

BLAKSLEE, Judge Thomas, Colesville, N. Y., July 19, æ. 76.

BLANEY, Benj., Boston, Mass., Oct. 10, æ. 63. The deceased was born in Boston, Sept. 20, 1794. He was a mason by trade, and worked on many of the most substantial structures built in the city from 1815 to 1835. He was a representative from Boston to the legislature in 1853 and 1854, and has served in other public trusts. He was for many years a prominent member of the fire department, and received a handsome testimonial from the insurance companies for his efficiency at the famous Beacon Street fire. His integrity and stability of character won for him the respect and regard of a wide circle of friends.

BLEVINS, George P., Selma, Ala., Aug., æ. —. He was a member of the bar, and a graceful and energetic orator. He was educated at Yale College, and was a promising contributor to the College Magazine. Subsequently he was a contributor to the Knickerbocker Magazine and other periodicals. Mr. B. was a classical scholar, and the south, by his demise, has lost one of its brightest ornaments.

BLEWEND, Prof. Adolph, A. M., St. Louis, Mo., April 10, æ. 41, director and professor in Concordia College.

BLISS, Dr. John, Brunswick, Me., Jan. 27, æ. 42.

BLODGET, Almond, Esq., Lyme, N. Y., Mar. 25, æ. 72. Mr. B. was well known at home, and commanded the highest respect and esteem of his neighbors, as well as his acquaintances abroad. He enjoyed the confidence of all, as an honest and an upright man. He was a volunteer in the war of 1812, and was one of the brave soldiers of Gen. Brown at the battle of Sacketts Harbor. He volunteered, he said, " not for the love of war, but for the love of liberty, and to vindicate the cause of freedom." After the war was terminated he located on a farm lying on Chaumont Bay, where he quietly remained until he finished his labors.

BLODGETT, Augustus C., Concord, N. H., Sept. 23, æ. 48, formerly publisher of the New Hampshire Courier.

BLOOD, Dr. Oliver Hunter, Worcester, Mass., April 8, æ. 57. He was son of Thomas Howard and Polly (Sawyer) Blood, and was born in Sterling, Mass., May 31, 1800. He was fitted for college by Rev. Lemuel Capen, of Sterling, (H. U. 1810.) On leaving college he determined to become a physician, and pursued his professional studies under the instruction of Dr. John Green, of Worcester, (B. U., 1804.) Having received his degree of M. D. in 1826, he began the practice of his profession in Brookfield, Mass., where he remained two years. He then removed to Worcester, where he resided during the remainder of his life. He married Ellen Blake, daughter of Hon. Francis Blake, of Worcester, (Il. U. 1789,) and had eight children, four sons and four daughters. Dr. B. was a man of social and genial disposition. With a fund of ready wit always at command, he was ever a welcome guest at the festive board. Possessed of the kindest feelings, and of a most obliging disposition, he was greatly beloved, not only by his family, but by the community among whom he had so long lived.

BLOOMER, Rev. Joseph, McGregor, Iowa, Feb. 21, æ. 30. Mr. B. graduated at Amherst, in 1856. In the autumn of that year he entered the Theological Seminary at Andover. In Nov. last he was married to Miss Caroline M. Backus, of Norwich, and was soon after installed pastor of the Congregational church at McGregor, a flourishing town on the Mississippi, opposite to Prairie du Chien. He was a man of ardent piety and active zeal, and gave promise of great goodness in his chosen field.

BOATNER, General Mark, Greenwell Springs, Caldwell Par., La., July 30, æ. —, a distinguished citizen of North La. He had filled many posts of honor and distinction, and was called away at a time when his state could ill afford to spare him.

BOHANNON, Dr. R. B., Versailles, Ky., April 23, æ. 71. Dr. B. located in Versailles as a physician in 1808, after graduating with some distinction in the Philadelphia School of Medicine. He soon, by his great energy and industry, got into fine practice, and at that early day the life of a physician was a life of great self-sacrifice. The roads were bad, distances long, with scarcely needful rest, day or night. Truly it was a life of labor. He continued to practise until 1846, when declining health obliged him to give it up.

BOKER, Charles S., Philadelphia, Feb. 10, æ. —, the well-known president of the Girard Bank. His death has perhaps caused deeper grief in a wider circle of personal friends than often happens, even in a metropolis like Philadelphia. It is generally the lot of warm-hearted and intelligent men, who occupy leading positions in the active world of finance or politics, to attract to themselves many friends; but it is not once in a thousand times that such men are so closely bound to so many as was the deceased by the active exercise of the noblest and most generous virtues. There are many leading men who conceal their kindness of heart under an austere deportment which they deem exemplary. Mr. B. was not one of these. He was genial and pleasant to all, and eminently gifted with that affability which attracts not only the young, but those most experienced in life. Familiar with human nature in many forms, and especially with the most varied arcana of business life, he never made a misanthropic reflection, nor ceased his generous exertions to do good. There are, however, even tenderer traits of the deceased, which we might hesitate to sketch were they not also deeply characteristic of a noble nature. Scarcely a month has elapsed since the death of Mr. B.'s wife occurred; and now the death of the husband, within so short a time, is painfully mournful. A bond which had endured even to the silvering of the hairs — to the first sight of the last limit of life — was broken, and with it the heart and happiness of the remaining one. No wonder that after the loss of one whose whole life was gentleness and goodness, the survivor should be heart-broken; and yet we may call it a wonder, for it is seldom indeed that we meet in life a couple so intimately allied by the most beautiful and noblest traits of character, and bound so closely together by heart ties, after long years of union, that death should call unto death. We pass over the talents, the position, the influence of the deceased, and speak of him only as the possessor of the noblest and tenderest qual ties which form the father, the husband, the friend, the benefactor — the qualities which render the individual best deserving the love of all the world.

BOLLES, Frederick D., Cambridge, Mass., Nov. 7, æ. 67, printer, formerly of Hartford, Ct. He had been a resident of Cambridge the past ten years, most of the time connected with the printing office of his brother, the late Charles Bolles. Mr. B. commenced the publication of the Hartford Weekly Times on the 1st of January, 1817, when the toleration struggle was rousing the attention and enlisting the feelings of the people. Shortly after he associated with him his brother-in-law, Mr. Francis, and during the same spring he announced that he had employed "a young lawyer from Windsor, a talented writer, by the name of John M. Niles," to assist him in the editorial department. Mr. B. continued the publication of the Times for several years, when he sold out his interest, and the establishment passed into the hands of Norton & Russell. Mr. B. was a man of pleasant disposition and affable address, and he had many warm friends in Connecticut, as well as in Cambridge, his more recent home, who will most truly sympathize with the family in their bereavement.

BOLLES, George W., M. D., Hartford, Ct., May 21, æ. 72.

BOLTON, Nathaniel, Esq., Indianapolis, Ind., Nov. 26, æ. 55. Mr. B. was a native of Chillicothe, O. At a very early age he was left an orphan, dependent for means in life upon his own inherent energies of character. When but a mere child he learned the art of printing in the office of his step-father, Judge Smith. At the age of 15 he was able to earn journeyman's wages as a printer. In 1822, when but 19 years of age, he came with his step-father to Indianapolis, and associated himself in the editorial department of the Indianapolis Gazette, the pioneer newspaper of the city. He continued editor of this paper for several years, until it gave place to the Indiana Democrat, of which Mr. B. was editor and publisher, in connection with the late A. F. Morrison and others, until, in 1841, it, in its turn, gave place to the Indiana State Sentinel. After the discontinuance of the Democrat, Mr. B. continued as a writer and correspondent for the press, though no longer personally engaged in any publication. Whenever any hard editorial work was required by the political organization, of which he was ever a reliable member, Mr. B. was called on to do it. It was — and there only — in the select circle of friends, and by the domestic hearth, that Nathaniel Bolton became really known. In public he was always reserved, and sometimes he appeared distant and cold. At home he was himself, as nature made him, kind, sympathetic, and affectionate. In the conflicts of life he had been taught many a severe lesson. He was retiring and unassuming. His moral sentiments were of a high order of excellence. He knew not guile. Honesty of purpose, and inflexible adherence to the right, marked all his acts. He was tenacious of the right, but he was no fanatic. He was religious, but he never could become a bigot. He is gone; gone from among us, to be no more of us. He has departed on the journey which so many of his early associates have travelled before him — Noble and Quarles, and Morris and Maguire, and many another of the race of worthy men of whom Indiana's city and Indiana herself have reason to be proud.

BONSALL, Dr. Jesse R., Chester, Pa., Nov. 7, æ. —. Dr. B. was one of those good-humored, whole-souled, and generous men who cast around them a genial glow of friendship and good feeling wherever they move. As a physician he has stood among the first for many years, and has been one of the most successful practitioners in the community.

BOON, Rev. William E., Aiken, S. C., Oct. 30, æ. —. Mr. B. was a member of the South Carolina Conference of the Methodist Episcopal Church South, and filled the pastorate of St. James's Church two years. That tasteful structure, at the corner of Coming and Spring Streets, was erected mainly by his assiduity and perseverance. At the time of his death he was pastor of the Methodist church in Aiken, where he had been engaged with untiring energy in the construction of a new house of worship for his charge. His death will fill many hearts with sorrow.

BOOTH, Chauncey, M. D., Somerville, Mass., Jan. 12, æ. 41, physician and superintendent of the McLean Asylum for the Insane. Dr. B. was a native of Coventry, Ct., the eldest son of the late Rev. Chauncey Booth, for many years pastor of the South Parish in that town. After two years at Amherst College, having turned his thoughts towards the medical profession, he accepted an invitation from a relative to reside as an assistant at the Vermont Institution for the Insane. This providentially gave that special direction to his life for which he proved to have been so eminently fitted by his intellectual and social characteristics. From the institution at Brattleboro', he went to the state institution for the insane at Augusta, Me., and thence, about 14 years since, he came to the McLean Asylum at Somerville, (then Charlestown,) as assistant physician to Dr. Bell. On the resignation of Dr. Bell, Dr. Booth was elected to supply his place as superintendent, which highly responsible and useful position he has occupied, with credit to himself and honor to the asylum, until by his lamented death, in the early ripeness and distinguished promise of his attainments, the institution is now deprived of his professional skill and administrative ability, in a department always most difficult to be well supplied. The numerous patients who have received benefit from his professional and personal attentions at the asylum, with their grateful friends, will unite with the immediate connections of Dr. B. in a more intimate sympathy of sorrow at his death than is often shared by those beyond the sacred enclosure of the domestic circle.

BOOTH, Brigadier Gen., Barbour, Va., Mar. 13, æ. —. He was buried with military honors by the Barbour Blues. Gen. B. represented Randolph Co. in the legislature for 21 years.

BOTTOM, Col. Thomas, St. Joseph, Dec. 27, æ. —. Col. Bottom had been a resident of St. Joseph for over four years, during which time he established a very enviable reputation. He was a gentleman of elegant literary attainments, a lawyer learned in his profession, a man of the highest sense of honor and of sterling worth. Col. B. emigrated to St. Joseph from Amelia Co., Va., where he had been a prominent and honored citizen, having represented his district in the legislature, rendering services alike honorable to himself and to the commonwealth.

BOWEN, Rev. Geo., Davenport, Iowa, May 26, æ. 34. Just one year ago Mr. B., in company with his now bereaved family, bid farewell to his many friends of the Philadelphia Conference, where, for the space of thirteen years, he had labored with honor and great success, to renew his labors in this more destitute field, and, as himself expressed it, "to grow up with this young conference." From June to Sept. he supplied a vacancy at Cedar Rapids with great acceptance. He was appointed to Davenport, one of the most responsible and important charges within our bounds, and entered upon his duties with high hopes of success and extended usefulness. He was an able minister of the New Testament, and an arduous laborer in the vineyard of the Lord. In December he commenced holding a series of meetings, in which he labored alone for five weeks with great success, until, indeed, his declining strength convinced him that he must have help, or the meetings must cease. His urgent calls for help were heeded. His meetings continued for three months, and resulted in the accession of between 100 and 200 to the fellowship of the saints; but his extraordinary labors for the good of others seem to have resulted fatally to him.

BOWEN, Capt. Isaac, U. S. A., Pass Christian, Miss., Sept. 30, æ. 36, and Mrs. CATHARINE, his wife, Oct. 5, æ. 27. Capt. B., although attached to the commissary department at the time of his death, belonged to the artillery, and in that arm of the service won distinction for gallant services at Monterey and Buena Vista during the Mexican war. He was a brave and gallant officer, a reliable friend, and beloved by all who knew him for his many excellent qualities of mind and heart.

BOWMAN, Isaac, Jackson, O., April 20, æ. 84, a member of the Society of Friends, and one of the first settlers of the township in which he resided. He became a resident of Stark Co. in 1811, before the township which he selected as a home was organized, and before much had been done in the way of a settlement west of the now city of Canton. The township of Perry, in which Massillon is situate, and containing a population of near 6000, was not organized until 1813, and Jackson not until a still later period. He was, with Thomas and Charity Rotch, (the latter the founder of the Charity School of Kendal,) Mayhew and Mary Folger, Joseph and Rebecca Hobson, Micajah and Sarah Macy, Daniel and Elizabeth Richmond, Richard and Sarah Williams, Charles and Mary Coffin, Aaron Chapman, William Mott, and Zacheus Stanton, among the earliest settlers on the east side of the Tuscarawas River, and west of the then little village now so justly proud of its right to be ranked among the cities of Ohio. The persons we have named, with our deceased friend, comprising but seven or eight families, were active in establishing "Kendal Preparation Meeting of the Society of Friends," which existed for many years, the monthly meeting being held at Marlborough. By birth an Englishman, he inherited the sturdy integrity of his English ancestry, and which strongly marked his life and character in all his intercourse with his fellow-men. Believing in and faithfully following the admonitions of "the inward voice uncreated by schools," and disowning allegiance to creeds, he found a sure pathway to immortal truth in the faith of the people called Quakers — a faith which was not only, like his unyielding honesty, the inheritance of his English ancestry, but the result of his matured and ripened judgment, and which he never forsook nor even questioned in all the mutations which have marked the history of Friends for the past 30 years. With the Holy Scriptures as "the rule and guide of his faith," he found in George Fox, William Penn, and Robert Barclay, in his earlier years, and Joseph John Gurney, in later life, exponents of the Scriptures upon whom he could rely, superadded to what was the "inner light, the Son of God in the soul," and which was to him the highest revelation of truth. His Christian character was exhibited in all his conduct towards his fellow-man, and was that which endeared him particularly to the members of his own society, and secured him the esteem of all who knew him.

BOWMAN, Mrs. Sarah J., Bath, Me., May 8, æ. 90, a native of Andover, Mass, and widow of the late Dr. Nathaniel J. Bowman, of Gorham, Me.

BOYKIN, Dr. Anthony Godwin, Isle of Wight Co., Va., Oct. 17, æ. 46. Dr. B. was one of the old school of gentlemen, now so rare, whose intelligence, chivalry, courteous manners, and high sense of honor have given so much distinction to the title of a Virginia gentleman. Amiable in disposition, generous in feeling, kind and hospitable, he won and maintained the respect and affection of all who knew him. He was a Christian, and his life was a beautiful and consistent illustration of all the virtues of that holy profession. As a practitioner of medicine, Dr. Boykin was bold, energetic, and eminently successful. In his death the community has suffered an irreparable loss; and long will his memory be endearingly cherished by neighbors, friends, and all who knew him. Never was there a more tender and affectionate husband, a more devoted father, or a fonder brother. He leaves a widow and six children.

BOYNTON, Rev. Alden, Wiscasset, Me., Dec. 25, æ. 53.

BRADFORD, Rev. James, Sheffield, Mass., Dec. 16, æ. 72, for about 40 years pastor of the Congregational church in Sheffield. A very impressive sermon was preached on the occasion by Rev. Dr. Todd, of Pittsfield.

BRADLEY, Dr. Crœsus, Monmouth, Iowa, April 23, æ. —. Dr. B. was born in Dover, Cuyahoga Co., O. In early life he commenced the study of medicine under the tuition of his father. After studying for several years with him, he attended three courses of lectures at the Cleveland Medical College, from which he graduated with superior honors. In the summer of 1856 moved to Monmouth, and established himself as a physician and surgeon. During his residence in that vicinity he had most emphatically shown himself to be a well-read and skilful physician. As a surgeon, he was an ornament to his profession.

BRADLEY, Dr. William, Philadelphia, Pa., Oct. 16, æ. 79.

BRADY, Walter K., St. Louis, Mo., March 5, æ. —. "The deceased was a native of Tennessee, a lawyer by profession, of high order of talent, a man of great goodness of heart, and justly endeared to a large circle of friends and acquaintances. He settled in Farmington, Mo., about seven years ago, where he engaged in the practice of his profession, which he continued until about three months before his death, when, from indisposition, he was removed to St. Louis, where he died.

BRAGG, Dr. John, Petersburg, Va., Sept. 25, æ. —. He leaves behind him the reputation of a scholar, and a refined and true-hearted man. He was eminently worthy of the esteem and confidence of our community. In all the relations of life he was exemplary, and in the line of his profession he deservedly occupied a high place in public favor. Up to the summer of 1856 his health was good, and, though advanced in years, he was enabled to attend to the arduous calls of an extensive practice. Dr. B., in a remarkable degree, enjoyed the confidence of his patients, and, by his kind and assiduous attention to them, merited it.

BRAMAN, Rev. Isaac, Georgetown, Mass., Dec. 26, æ. 88. He was son of Sylvanus and Experience (Blanchard) Braman, and was born in Norton, Mass., July 5, 1770. He graduated at Harvard College, with high honors, in 1794, and for several years has been the only survivor of his class. After leaving college, he studied for the ministry with Rev. Jason Haven, of Dedham, (H. U. 1754,) and Rev. Pitt Clark, of Norton, (H. U. 1790.) He was ordained, June 7, 1797, pastor of the second parish in Rowley, then called New Rowley, and since incorporated into a town by the name of Georgetown. He was successor of Rev. James Chandler, (H. U. 1728,) who died April 19, 1789, at the age of 83 years, and in the 58th year of his ministry. The parish was destitute of a settled minister nine years; and Mr. B. was the last of 64 candidates who preached there on probation. He continued pastor of this society until his death, — a period of more than 61 years, — discharging the duties of his profession with great fidelity, and to the entire acceptance of his people, until within a few years, when, on account of the infirmities of age, he was obliged to relinquish his arduous duties, and the Rev. Charles Beecher was ordained as colleague pastor with him. Mr. Braman was a man of great originality of mind, and his sermons evince deep thought and profound reflection. He was famous for his keen wit, and was a prominent figure in Sawney Bigelow's celebrated classology. He married, Aug., 1797, Hannah Palmer, youngest daughter of Rev. Joseph Palmer, of Norton, (H. U. 1747,) born June 12, 1773. They had five children; viz., — 1. Harriet, born July 17, 1798, married Rev. John Boardman, (D. C. 1817,) minister in Douglas, Mass.; 2. Milton Palmer, born Aug. 6, 1799, (H. U. 1819,) now minister of the First Church in Danvers, Mass.; 3. James Chandler, born Sept. 29, 1801, died at sea, (on his passage from Calcutta for Salem, 75 days out,) Dec. 5, 1820; 4. Adeline, born July 10, 1805, died Sept. 10, 1830; 5. Isaac Gordon, born March 12, 1813, is a physician in Brighton, Mass. Mr. B.'s wife died Aug. 14, 1835, æ. 62; and he married for his second wife, in 1837, Sarah Balch, daughter of John Balch, Esq., of Newburyport. She survives him.

BRASS, A. J., M. D., Philadelphia, Pa., March 17, æ. 33, of Berwick, Pa. Dr. B., although but 33 years of age, had acquired an eminent professional reputation. During the last three years his health had been extremely precarious, and his worldly business experienced frequent interruptions by spells of severe sickness. He left a widow and three little children to mourn what is their loss, but his gain.

BRAUD, J. A., Parish St. James, New Orleans, La., Nov. 23, æ. 48. Mr. B. was a native of Southern Louisiana, and from early age was engaged in commercial pursuits, for a number of years past as the senior partner in the highly respectable domestic commission house of J. A. Braud & Landry. Mr. B. had filled several important public trusts with ability, intelligence, and great integrity; had been an alderman of the city, and also a senator of the state, and was, at the time of his decease, an administrator of the Charity Hospital, and a director of the Citizens' Bank, enjoying in the latter institution a position only second in public estimation to that of its able and accomplished president. J. A. Braud was a noble specimen of the native sons of Louisiana, honorable in all his dealings, truthful, sincere, and always disposed to touch lightly and kindly upon the weaknesses of others. His loss is a public calamity; and to those endeared to him by friendship or the ties of blood it is an irreparable bereavement.

BRAYTON, Mrs. Anna, Apponaug, R. I., May 12, wife of Hon. William D. Brayton, representative in Congress from that state.

BRECKENRIDGE, Mrs. Mary Hopkins, Louisville, Ky., Mar. 26, æ. 89, relict of Hon. John Breckenridge, one of the most eminent citizens Kentucky has ever had. She was the daughter of Joseph Cabell and Mary Hopkins, and was born in the colony of Virginia, Feb. 22, 1769. On the afternoon of Sabbath, March 28, appropriate religious services, occasioned by her decease, were held in the First Presbyterian Church in Louisville, of which her son, Dr. William L. Breckenridge, is pastor; and on the 29th her remains were carried to the county of Fayette, and deposited, according to her special request, in the same grave in which those of her husband had been laid more than 51 years before, in the cemetery of her family at Cabell's Dale, where her home had been since 1793. Previous to the interment appropriate religious services were held in the Horeb church, of which she had been a member since its organization, about 30 years ago. Few persons have been more remarkably dealt with by divine Providence than this lady. She was born in affluence; both her parents were members of large connections of the greatest respectability. At a very early age she married a man whose career was one of remarkable success and distinction. In her 38th year she was left a widow with seven children, all but one daughter then minors. She survived by many years all those children but two, (Dr. Robert J. Breckenridge and Dr. William L. Breckenridge.) Born a subject of the King of England; a spectator of the revolutionary war, and a daughter of one of its heroes; an emigrant to Kentucky when the greater part of it was a wilderness, and liable to constant invasion by hostile savages; living to an extraordinary age, with every advantage which independent fortune and the friendship of the excellent of the earth could bestow, — she saw her children's great-grandchildren; she saw descendants through those generations acquitting themselves to her praise and joy; she saw the country whose birth, and progress, and glory she had witnessed, in the first rank of nations; she saw the church, which in her youth was a reproach, covering the whole land with blessings; and then she fell asleep in Jesus, leaving behind her no human being, who knew aught of her, who did not know that she had done what she could, always and under all circumstances, in her place and in her degree, to promote all good and to resist all evil. Nor was her character less remarkable than the destiny through which God conducted her. With so much to lift her above the common lot, nothing distinguished her nature more than her tender care of the humble and the poor. With every temper to make conformity with the weakness of refined society almost excusable in her, she shunned even the smallest approach to ostentation with a resolute aversion. Well knowing the use of riches, she valued them so little that at the decease of her husband she refused to accept more than half of the provision which appertained to her from his estate, and, practising the most rigid personal economy thenceforward for more than 50 years, practised at the same time a generosity deserving, both in the motive and the amount, to be called princely. She was endowed by nature with a true, loving, gentle, and heroic spirit. Her intellectual powers were bright, quick, clear, and just in the highest degree, and remained unclouded until she had passed, considerably, her 80th year. And her physical endowments were said by those who knew her before the middle of life to have been singularly prepossessing. In stature she was rather under than above the middle size, with features a little oval, and remarkable eyes and hair, of very dark color. Her son, the late Dr. John Breckenridge, is thought to have resembled her in appearance most of all her children who lived to adult years. During the last 20 years increasing infirmities, and especially her failure of sight, and at length total blindness, prevented her from going much into promiscuous society; but nearly to the end of her long life she took great delight in the society of those she knew well, and kept up her interest in all that passed. Her family, like most Virginia colonial families east of the mountains, belonged to the Protestant Episcopal church of the colony. Her husband's family, from the west side of the mountains, were Presbyterians; and with that church she connected herself after her husband's death, uniting herself with the Presbyterian church in Lexington, Ky., at its first organization. Her eldest son, the late Joseph Cabell Breckenridge, (whose only son is the present Vice President of the United States,) was one of the first elders of that church; and its first pastor, the late Rev. James McChord, was loved by her, and in his many sorrows cherished by her, as a son. Few Christian lives have been more tried by severe and protracted bodily sufferings, and by sore and repeated domestic bereavements, than that of this mother in Israel. For more than 50 years she never put off the habiliments of mourning; and during as many years she was the victim of acute bodily suffering. Yet she neglected no duty, uttered no murmur, never distrusted God! Full of the sense of her own unworthiness, simple and perfectly sincere in her religious faith, she believed in Jesus, she denied herself, she took up her cross, and she followed him, through good report and ill. No human being ever loved or reverenced the word of God more than she did; nor is it known that it ever entered into her heart to stagger at one of its precious truths, no matter how much she might think it condemned her, or how much her deeply sensitive heart might be wrung thereby.

BRENNAN, Dr. Thomas, Dayton, Ohio, June 10, æ. 35. Dr. B. was a native of Ireland; emigrated to this country in 1848; received the degree of M. D. from the Cincinnati Medical College in 1855. He commenced the practice of his profession in D., and discharged the duties of his office in a manner which not only elicited the warmest approval of his numerous friends and acquaintances, but alike honorable to himself and to the profession to which he belonged. He was a man of more than ordinary ability, without ostentation; of noble and generous parts, courteous and gentlemanly in his deportment, with a due appreciation of his spiritual as well as temporal welfare.

BREWER, J. N. M., Robbinstown, Me., April 4, æ. —. For 30 years a shipbuilder on the St. Croix River, he had during his life built upwards of 100 vessels.

BREWSTER, Rev. Benjamin D., Dalton, N. H., May 11, æ. 50. He was born in Claremont, N. H., Aug., 1808. In a glorious revival on Unity Circuit he was converted, and united with the M. E. church, A. D. 1828. He soon felt that it was his duty to preach, and commenced his labors under the presiding elder, Rev. J. G. Dow, and in 1835 united with the N. H. Conference, which relation he retained for 15 years, filling his appointments, in each of which he was blessed with some ingatherings to the church of God. He was a true friend of the church of his choice, standing firm amid great agitations; and, though his appointments were not among those which afforded as much pecuniary benefit as many others, yet he always went to his work cheerfully, and labored faithfully, and consequently with success. In 1850, his health failing, he chose to locate, and since then has cultivated a small farm in Dalton, N. H. As his health recruited, he commenced laboring in destitute places, and continued to do so, preaching regularly till God called him from labor to rest.

BRIDGE, Miss Nancy, Beverly, Mass., July 11, æ. 74. For more than forty years she was actively engaged in the Sunday school, and possessed a peculiar faculty of attracting and influencing the pupils. Of her church and parish she was a consistent, earnest, faithful member. The daughter of an eminent physician, and daughter-in-law of one more widely known, Dr. Joshua Fisher, she improved the opportunities thus afforded for most intelligently and efficiently ministering to the sick, for whom, as for all the afflicted, she had a never-failing sympathy. As a relative and friend none could be more true and self-sacrificing, and none in the large circle of friends to whom she was devoted will be more respectfully and tenderly remembered.

BRIDGES, Col. Moody, North Andover, Mass., April 16, æ. 73. For nearly 45 years he had been a deputy sheriff of Essex Co. He was an excellent officer, and in private life was a most amiable and worthy gentleman of the old school.

BRIGGS, Mrs. Cornelia C., Cleveland, Ohio, June 8, æ. 23, wife of George P. Briggs, Esq., of Lawrence, Mass., and daughter of Dr. Erastus Cushing, of C.

BRIGGS, Mrs. Betsey, East Bridgewater, Mass., June 22, æ. 79, widow of Rev. Wm. Briggs, and daughter of the late Nathl. Hudson, Esq. Mrs. B. was a resident of Kittery, Me., 50 years ago. Her husband was the minister at Kittery Point, and was also teacher of the north school in Portsmouth, N. H.

BRIGHAM, Isaac, Milford, Mass., March 13, æ. 65. He was born in Holliston, Mass., Aug. 30, 1793, and was a son of Dr. Isaac Brigham, who lived and died in Milford, a physician of some note, and who served his country in the revolutionary war, probably as a surgeon. The deceased was also grandson of Rev. Amariah Frost, the first settled minister of Milford, a man of eminent piety and patriotism, who served as chaplain some years in the revolutionary war, and who returned to spend his last days in Milford. He died in the pastoral office of the first parish and church in Milford, preaching the Sabbath before his death. He was known personally to Gen. Washington, and had the pleasure of meeting him in Milford on his presidential tour to New England in 1790. Their interview was one of many affectionate embraces and tears, at the only public house of the then small village of M., and now a place of 10,000 inhabitants. That house was then kept by Col. Nelson, who had also been in the army, and stood where the dwelling house of Mr. Leonard Chapin now stands, on Main Street. One gray-headed man still lives in M. who witnessed the interesting scene, then a member of Mr. Frost's family. They had labored and prayed together to establish the liberties of their country, and this was their first interview after the grand achievement. Mr. Frost died on the same spot where Mr. Brigham has now gone to his rest. Mr. B. left a widow, but no children. His only son and two daughters had gone down to the grave before him, in the faith of the Christian.

BRIGHAM, Hon. Benjamin G., Fairfax, Vt., March 16, æ. 53. Mr. B. was well known in the state as a successful business man; as a man of sound practical judgment, sterling integrity, and especial large-heartedness; one of Vermont's noble sons. In the love of his family, in the esteem of his neighbors, in the respect and confidence of those who knew him best, he was rich, and never richer than at the day of his death. He had been familiarly known for many years for his extensive operations in farming, and had been in the legislature of his state several times.

BROCKENBROUGH, Dr. Austin, Tappahannock, Essex Co., Va., Dec. 31, æ. —. He was the brother of Dr. John Brockenbrough, former president of the Bank of Virginia, and was the last of a number of brothers, beloved and esteemed for strength of mind and many heightened virtues. He had represented the county of Essex in the House of Delegates for several years, and had served his fellow-citizens up to the time of his death as magistrate and as presiding justice.

BROCKENBROUGH, Dr. Wm. A., Tappahannock, Essex Co., Va., Nov. 3, æ. 49, eldest son of Dr. Austin Brockenbrough. His was a blameless life. Possessed of great excellence, combining in his character firmness, amiability, and the attributes of the gentleman, he was esteemed by those who knew him. He was a communicant in the Episcopal church.

BRONSON, Rev. Thomas, Wyoming, Iowa, Dec. 30, æ. 65.

BROOKS, Lieut. Henry, U. S. N., June 24, æ. 45. Mr. B. was one of the most reliable and distinguished officers of the expeditions to the arctic regions, and was justly held in high esteem by all who were fortunate enough to know him. At the time of his death he was acting as boatswain in the navy yard, though his real position was that of lieutenant. He wore medals from Queen Victoria, President Buchanan, and Lady Franklin, all awarded him for the distinguished services which he had rendered in the humane undertaking of searching for the remains of Sir John Franklin. He has not been to sea since the arctic voyage, because he lost part of both feet by the frost on that expedition.

BROOKS, Deacon Lebbeus, Saco, Me., July 25, æ. 38. Dea. B. was born in Wells, Me., Aug. 31, 1819. At an early age he gave evidence of the inventive faculty, and was never satisfied in any pursuit in which this faculty was unemployed. The fertility of his mind in this respect is seen in the following record. He secured copyrights as follows: In 1849, on a 6 per ct. interest table and perpetual almanac; in 1851, on an average table and a 7 per cent. interest table. He also obtained patents, in 1854, on an improved spirit level; in 1856, on a machine for sawing marble, and a saw-set. At the time of his death he had ready for application for patents, a mill saw-set, a straw cutter, and a spring bed rest; and for copyright, an improved decimal interest table.

BROOKSHIRE, Mrs. Elizabeth, New Castle, Ind., June —, æ. 40.

BROOM, Daniel L., M.D., Oak Hall, Ala., Sept. 24, æ. 46, son of the late James M. Broom, Esq., of Philadelphia, Pa.

BROTHERTON, Capt. T. W., Jr., San Andreas, Cal., Nov. 21, æ. 66. Capt. B. was born in Baltimore, Md., in 1792. Early in life he entered the merchant service of our country, and became a successful and popular navigator. When the spirit of liberty and independence manifested itself among the South American republics, under the leadership of Bolivar, fired by that honorable zeal which ever animates the true American heart, he sought and obtained a position as captain in the Colombian navy, in which service he continued with honor to himself and to the advantage of the cause in which he fought, for several years. After the achievement of the independence of Colombia, he again betook himself to the merchant service, under the flag of his native country. In 1849 he emigrated to California, and since that time has, for the most part, resided in Georgetown, El Dorado Co., Cal. His life has been bustling, eventful, and adventurous — signalized by probity, courage, and an unusual amount of fortitude and intelligence.

BROWN, Alexander, Clarion Co., Pa., æ. 105. He was considered the oldest man in the county. He settled on Piney Creek when the surrounding country was a howling wilderness.

BROWN, Charles H., Boston, Mass., April 1, president of the Atlas Bank.

BROWN, Hon. George W., Shelbyville, Ind., May 24, brother of the late Wm. J. Brown, of Indianapolis. He had been a member both of the Senate and House of Representatives of the legislature.

BROWN, Harry, Southbury, Ct., Sept. 4, æ. 73. He had during his long life been one of the most prominent and useful citizens of the town, and died retaining the respect and esteem of all who knew him.

BROWN, Major H. B., Cincinnati, O., Nov. 7, æ. 40. Major B. was born in Kentucky, of a respectable family, received a good education, studied law, and was admitted to the bar early, was afterwards for many years connected with the press, and went to Cincinnati some ten years ago, when he became connected with one of the journals, but subsequently practised his profession. In 1853 he was sent to the Ohio legislature, was elected prosecuting attorney of the Police Court in 1855, and re-elected in 1857. He was a man of warm affections, and bore the sufferings of his long illness with patience.

BROWN, Dr. Henry T., Brunswick, Va., Nov. 14, æ. 26, son of R. Ruffin Brown.

BROWN, Rev. J. Holland, (of Painesville, O.,) Hamilton, N. Y., June 27, æ. 30, at the residence of his father-in-law, David Osgood, Esq. Mr. B. was born in Franklin, N. Y., June 27, 1828. In 1851 he entered the Sophomore class of Madison University; and, having successfully completed the full course of instruction, graduated from the Theological Seminary in Aug. 1856. In Sept. of the same year he accepted a call from the Baptist church in Painesville, O., of which he continued pastor to his death. Entering upon his ministry with earnestness, and a deep love for souls, his labors were signally marked with tokens of divine approbation.

BROWN, Hon. Jeremiah, Fulton township, Pa., March 2, æ. 74, late one of the associate judges of his county, and formerly member of Congress, and a member of the constitutional convention. His wife was buried on the 1st of March, having preceded her husband to the grave but two or three days.

BROWN, John B., Esq., Hampton Falls, N. H., March 31, æ. 59. Mr. B. was president of the Weare Bank, and a man of extensive business, being a very efficient financier, a warm and firm friend of the Christian Society at Hampton Falls, and of the cause of the Christian denomination.

BROWN, Rev. Joshua R., East Longmeadow, Mass., Sept. 7, æ. 46. He was born at Stonington, Ct., June 14, 1812; was hopefully converted in the revival of 1831, and united with the church in his native place. From his conversion his heart was set on preaching the gospel, and he soon commenced a preparatory course of study. In 1845 he was ordained over the Second Congregational Church in Lebanon, Ct., where he remained 8 years, preaching the gospel with great acceptance. In 1855 he was installed over the Congregational Church in East Longmeadow, Mass., where he remained until his death, enjoying the confidence and esteem of all. As a husband, father, brother, son, he was affectionate and faithful, and greatly beloved. As a preacher he was lucid, instructive, earnest, fearless. As a pastor he had few equals, was eminently kind, sympathizing, prudent, studious; was instant in season and out of season, and went about doing good.

BROWN, Hon. Jeremiah, Lancaster,

Pa., Feb. —, late associate judge of the Lancaster (Pa.) District, and a member of Congress from 1841 to 1845. His wife was buried a few days before. During a long life, more or less connected with public affairs, he enjoyed the respect and confidence of his fellow-citizens of all parties.

BROWN, Mrs. Mary L., Hallowell, Me., Oct. 30, æ. 91, granddaughter of the late Rev. Jonathan Parsons of Newburyport.

BROWN, Samuel, Esq., Adrian, O., July 28, æ. 46. Mr. B. was a native of Brownsville, Jefferson Co., N. Y., a nephew of the late Gen. Jacob Brown, and a brother of the late Thompson Brown, who died abroad, a year or two since, when on his return from Russia, where he had been in the employ of Nicholas I., as chief engineer on a railroad from St. Petersburg to Moscow. Mr. S. Brown for a number of years was engaged on the New York and Erie Railroad, — of which road, it will be remembered, Thompson Brown was one of the first engineers, — and ultimately became the superintendent of the freight department, a position of great trust and responsibility, and in which office the deceased displayed remarkable business talent, energy, and decision, and where he undermined a constitution naturally robust and strong. From the New York and Erie Road Mr. B. went to the superintendency of the Canandaigua and Niagara Falls Road, and afterwards to the position on the Michigan Southern Road, which he occupied until near the close of his life. Mr. B. wore himself out in the exhausting toils of that species of mental and physical labor so inseparable — as it would seem — from railroad management. His nervous system became prostrated, and the constant strain upon his faculties, and the unremitting excitement, broke him down. Mr. B. married the daughter of Gen. Joseph Brown, of Toledo, and the sister of Mrs. Samuel F. Lester, of Cleveland, O. A prominent trait in the deceased — and a jewel in any man's character — was his devotion to the interests and happiness of his friends; and a host who have been recipients of the kindness and assistance of the deceased will mourn him as a good friend gone.

BROWNE, Dr. William, Fredericksburg, Va., Dec. — æ. —. At a meeting of the medical faculty of Fredericksburg and Falmouth, held at the residence of Dr. John H. Wallace, on the 6th inst., Dr. J. H. Wallace was appointed chairman, and Dr. Scott secretary. The chair offered the following resolutions, which were unanimously adopted: —

"The physicians of Fredericksburg and Falmouth, having received the painful intelligence of the death of Dr. William Browne, deem it a privilege and a duty to offer the following tribute to his memory:

"*Resolved*, That while we bow in submission to this decree of an all-wise Providence, under a deep sense of our loss, we truly mourn the death of our highly-esteemed friend, Dr. William Browne.

"*Resolved*, That in his death we have been bereaved of a brother of the highest merit, and the community of a most valued, beloved, and useful citizen.

BUBIER, Capt. John, Jamaica Plain, Mass., Sept. 18, æ. 66. Capt. B. was a native of Marblehead. He was an officer in the U. S. N. for nearly 40 years, but resigned his commission as commander a few years since. He was taken prisoner in the U. S. brig Syren, by the English, in the war of 1812, and incarcerated in Dartmoor prison. He performed much active service in early life.

BUCAUT, Rev. Francis, Baltimore, Md., April 23, priest of the Most Holy Redeemer. He was a native of Canada, and was ordained in 1854. For the space of three years he was stationed over the French congregation at Rochester, N. Y.

BUCKLEY, William F., Poughkeepsie, N. Y., Sept. —, æ. 53. Mr. B. was a son of Gershom Buckley, late of Williamstown. Many years since he left his native town with no capital other than his own energy and a capacity for business of no ordinary measure. Having first commenced business in Albany, he afterwards removed to New York, where the success foreshadowed in small beginnings elsewhere was fully realized; and a few years since he retired from business in affluence, at the head of the great house of Buckley & Claflin, (now Claflin, Miller, & Co.) About a year since he removed to

Poughkeepsie. Brought up upon his father's farm, he never lost his taste for agricultural pursuits, and his residence at Poughkeepsie was but a realization of a long-cherished desire to end his days in a country seat where the luxuries of labor and of wealth could be happily blended and rationally enjoyed.

BUCKLEY, William S., M. D., Petersburg, Rensselaer Co., N. Y., Nov. 6, æ. 31., at the residence of M. G. Phillips, his father-in-law. The deceased, though an invalid, and coming but recently to these parts, had become extensively known and highly respected, and his death is greatly lamented by all. He was, from his mental powers and the culture he had given them, and from his indomitable energy and activity, a man of more than ordinary promise in his profession.

BUCKLIN, Joseph, Providence, R. I., Dec. 11., æ. 82. Mr. B. was a native of Pawtucket, Mass. In 1813 he removed to the town of Ludlow, where he embarked in the cotton manufacturing business, and continued its prosecution there until about 1843, when he retired from business with a competence, and removed to this city, where he has ever since resided. He was a man of respectability and character, and held offices of trust and honor in the town where his active years were passed.

BULL, Ann Jacobs, Chester Co., Pa., July 10, æ. 70, wife of the Rev. Levi Bull, D. D., and daughter of the late Cyrus Jacobs, Esq., of Lancaster Co.

BULLARD, Samuel P., New Orleans, La., Feb. 7, æ. 58. Mr. B. was born in Providence, and in early life was assistant in one of the public schools in that city. He also resided in Ware, Mass., in 1824–5. He was, for many years, a citizen of Mobile, and for a good portion of the time assisted in the editorial conduct of a paper. He was a man of quick perceptions, of genial temper, of ready wit, and a fluent and graceful writer. He was also a remarkably skilful accountant, and in this capacity rendered the city great service in the settlement of her foreign indebtedness.

BULLARD, Sampson, Boston, Mass., July 10, æ. 73. Mr. B. formerly resided in Boston, whence, a few years since, he removed to Littleton, where his home remained up to the time of his death. He was a man of large wealth, a public-spirited citizen, and a genuinely honest man.

BULLIONS, Henry L., M. D., Troy, N. Y., Oct. 19, æ. 23. Dr. B. was a son of Rev. Peter Bullions, D. D., an eminent divine and scholar. (See Obit., 1857.) He graduated with honor at Union College, and commenced the study of medicine in the office of Dr. Blatchford, of Troy. He took his degree at the Albany Medical College in 1853, and was afterwards house surgeon at the Troy Hospital, where he enjoyed the confidence and respect of all connected with that institution. Always of delicate constitution, Dr. B. went to the Sandwich Islands, in the year 1855, to benefit his health, and practised his profession at Honolulu, but soon returned.

BULLOCK, Col. John O., Columbus, Ky., Sept. —, æ. 29. Col. B. graduated at Bloomington College, Ind., in 1847. In 1848 he entered the law department of the University of Louisville, where he graduated in 1850. He entered upon the practice of his profession at Louisville, and continued until 1854, when he became the editor and proprietor of the Times. In 1857 he resumed his profession, but moved to Columbus, Ky., at the beginning of 1858. Here disease came upon him in his new home, in the midst of full joy and bright hopes, and ended his career. Young, generous, gifted with more than ordinary abilities, eminent in every social quality, a thorough scholar, a plighted gentleman, and a devoted friend, he was an object of singular regard and esteem.

BULLOCK, Hon. Rufus, Royalston, Mass., Jan. 10, æ. 78. He had been a member of the state Senate, and of the conventions for the revision of the state constitution. He was a successful manufacturer, and a conscientious, liberal, and honorable man.

BUNDY, David S. B., Otego, N. Y., April 4, æ. 67. In the death of Mr. B., community has lost one of its most valuable citizens. In all the relations of life he was a true man, a warm friend, honorable, high-minded, and always energetic in promoting the best interests of the public. As a farmer, he practically has done as much as any other citizen for

BURCH   [1858.]   BURT   49

the promotion of agriculture. He was for 20 years an active member of an agricultural society, and contributed largely to its success.

BURCH, Rev. James, Chicago, Ill., July 28, æ. 74. Mr. B., soon after an afflictive bereavement, had but recently closed his ministerial labors at Washington, Va. His previous ministry, we believe, was chiefly spent in Kentucky, where he was distinguished for usefulness as a pastor, soundness in doctrine, and wisdom in counsel. The testimony both of his life and death is a rich legacy of comfort to his bereaved children.

BURCH, Hon. Thomas, Little Falls, N. Y., æ. 59. He was formerly state senator, and was one of the foremost business men of Herkimer Co.

BURKE, Col. Nicholas, Baltimore, Md., æ. 77. He commanded a company in the war of 1812.

BURNETT, Rev. J., Rossville, Staten Island, March 3, æ. 36, late pastor of the Baptist church in Rossville. He was born in London, England; emigrated to America some eight years since; had been pastor of the Baptist church in East Marion, L. I., from whence he removed to Staten Island in the fall of 1854.

BURNS, Thomas, Morrisville, Pa., March 24, æ. 72. He served in the war of 1812-15; was in the battle of Fort George, &c.

BURNS, Capt. W. Oliver, Austin, Texas, March 18, æ. 34, a member of the bar of the 17th judicial district.

BURROUGHS, Henry J., Providence, R. I., Aug. 25, æ. 42.

BURROWS, Rev. Daniel, Mystic River, Ct., Jan. 23, æ. 92. He represented Connecticut in Congress during the last term of Mr. Monroe's administration, 1821 to 1823; was one of the commissioners to define the boundaries between Massachusetts and Connecticut, and surveyor of the port of Middletown for 20 years. His last days were eminently characteristic of his life. He died triumphantly in the faith which he so faithfully advocated.

BURRUS, Dr. Joseph C., Napoleon, Ark., April 12, æ. 37.

BURT, Mrs. Jane Ann, Auburn, N. Y., May 20, æ. 48, wife of Alexander Hamilton Burt, Esq. She was the daughter of Morse Ingersol, Esq., and was born in Ridgefield, Ct., Jan. 22, 1810. In 1829 Mr. Ingersol removed with his family to Cayuga Co., N. Y., where he died in 1834. Mrs. B. was married in St. Peter's Church, Auburn, by the Rev. Dr. Rudd, rector, Sept. 14, 1830. In 1837 she was confirmed and admitted to the communion of the church. It is little to say of her that she was an affectionate wife and mother. She was more than this. She was a humble and devout Christian, and faithful in all the relations of life. Modest, retiring, and domestic in her habits, she always endeavored to make her home pleasant and agreeable, and to train up her children in the ways of virtue and Christian living; and in all this she was eminently successful.

BURT, Dr. Joel M., Benton, Ala., Nov. 28, æ. 62, formerly of Westhampton, Mass., and a graduate of Williams College.

BURT, William A., Hamtramck, N. Y., Aug. 18, æ. 67, widely and favorably known as the inventor of "Burt's Solar Compass," at the residence of his son. Mr. B. was born in Massachusetts, but removed at an early day to Northern New York, and located in Saratoga Co., from whence he removed to Buffalo, where he married; and from that place he came to Michigan in 1823, and located at Vernon, Macomb Co., which was then a wilderness, but is now a populous and thriving district. Mr. B.'s original occupation was a millwright; but, shortly after removing to Michigan, he was appointed government surveyor, which office he held until about five years since. The event of Mr. B.'s life, which chiefly distinguished him, was the invention of the "Solar Compass," which is invaluable to surveyors, and is used in preference to all similar instruments where its merits are known.

BURT, William S., Ithaca, N. Y., Nov. 22, æ. 64. Mr. B. was formerly from Hampden Co., Mass., where the family name was familiar from its settlement. He was a graduate of Union College, of the class of 1818, and, from the time he graduated till his death, was entirely given up to literary and scientific pursuits. Among his classmates were Bishop Potter, of Pennsylvania, Bishop Drew, of New Jersey, and Rev. Dr. Waterbury, formerly of Boston. He was one of the Board of Instruction at Amherst College at the time of its or-

5

ganization, and was connected with the Hon. Horace Mann and the Hon. Wm. B. Calhoun while a member of the state legislature, in behalf of the common schools, and in initiating the present common-school system of Massachusetts. He was the last of his family, his brother, the Rev. Enoch Burt, who graduated at Princeton in 1812, having died a short time since in Manchester, Ct. (Obit., 1857.) He left two daughters and one son, the only surviving male member of the family for three generations.

BURTON, Miss Sarah Warren, Cambridge, Mass., Aug. 17, æ. 23, only child of Rev. Warren Burton. In the character of Miss B. there was a rare union of the qualities which engage affection and inspire respect, blended together in beautiful and just proportion. The moral and religious elements of her nature were early developed and assiduously cultivated. At school she was remarkable for sweetness of temper, docility, cheerful compliance with the requisitions of her teachers, and the singular energy, fidelity, thoroughness, and success with which she prosecuted her various studies — in no small degree the fruit of judicious moral and religious training at home, the importance of which has, for a series of years, been so strongly and so widely urged in the public teachings of her father.

BURTON, Rev. Wm., Austenburg, O., March 12, æ. 69. Mr. B. was a native of Vermont, graduated from Dartmouth College in 1815, and studied theology with his eminent relative, the Rev. Asa Burton, D. D., of Thetford, Vt. In 1821 he became pastor of the Presbyterian church at Circleville, O., and in 1840 was settled at Piketon, O., whence in 1849 he removed his family to Northern Ohio, with the hope of finding a climate more favorable to his impaired constitution. Here he took charge of a farm for the benefit of his sons, and preached but occasionally. He was, however, an extensive reader, and, for his own amusement, was in the habit of poetical composition. As a preacher and divine, Mr. B. will always be remembered with respect. His discourses were delivered with great deliberation and simplicity of manner, and he spoke usually without notes; and it may with truth be averred that no minister of Christ on the Western Reserve regarded with greater aversion, or combated with more firmness or ability, the errors of doctrine and practice infecting man of its churches than did this venerable man. In his character humility and unpretending simplicity were conspicuous traits. He has left a widow and several children to mourn his loss and cherish his memory.

BUSH, William, Coventry, Chenango Co., N. Y., Nov. 15, æ. 73. Mr. B. was born in Sheffield, Berkshire Co., Mass., April 15, 1785, and in the same fall came to what is now Chenango Co., where he has ever since resided. He was the first white boy brought into Chenango Co. He may well have been called the "oldest inhabitant." He lived to a good and honorable old age, and died respected and lamented by a large circle of relatives and friends. He was the father of Riley Bush, Esq., of Mineveh, present supervisor of Colesville.

BUSHNELL, James, Bennington, Vt., Dec. 3, æ. 96, a revolutionary soldier.

BUTLER, Dr. Albert W., Hartford, Ct., March 11, æ. —. He was a prominent citizen of Hartford, exemplary in all his relations, active, efficient, and benevolent in his efforts to do good.

BUTLER, Elder Asa, Worcester, Otsego Co., N. Y., Aug. 26, æ. 80. He was a doctrinal, experimental, and practical Christian. His statements of divine truth were unflinching. He held and declared it with simplicity, sincerity, and affection. He did not change with the changing policy of the times, but bore one uniform testimony to the gospel. He was a zealous promoter of every Christian and benevolent institution. The cause of evangelical missions was dear to his heart.

HON. B. F. BUTLER,

Paris, France, Nov. 8, æ. 63. He was born at Stuyvesant, near Kinderhook, N. Y., Dec. 14, 1795. He was a lineal descendant of Oliver Cromwell, on the mother's side; and he exhibited through life characteristic traits of that greatest of England's great men. From his earliest age Mr. B. was passionately fond of reading; and he greedily devoured the contents of his father's small library, and all the books to be found in the neighborhood, which, combined with the village school, were all the advantages he had for obtaining an education, until, in 1811, he entered the office and family of Hon. Martin Van Buren, as a student at law, in which capacity he remained until he was admitted to the bar in 1817, when he became the partner of Mr. Van Buren, then the attorney general of the state, which connection subsisted until the appointment of Mr. Van Buren to the U. S. Senate in Dec., 1821. Mr. B. made his first appearance before the Supreme Court as counsel in 1821, when he argued and won a cause against the celebrated John B. Henry, of Albany, one of the most distinguished members of the bar at that time; and in Feb. of the same year he was appointed district attorney of the city and county of Albany, which office he held with great honor until March, 1825, when he resigned. In Nov., 1824, Mr. B. was appointed one of the commissioners charged with the revision of the statutes of the state, which occupied the greatest part of his time for five years. He was elected to the Assembly in 1827, with special reference to the work of revision. In 1829 he was appointed one of the regents of the University, but resigned the office in 1832. In 1833 he acted as commissioner on the part of New York to settle the boundary-line question with New Jersey. In Nov. of the same year he accepted, at the urgent request of Gen. Jackson, then president, the office of attorney general of the United States, which office he held under Jackson and Van Buren, until Sept., 1838, when he resigned, at the same time refusing to accept the head of one of the departments under his distinguished friend, the then president, Martin Van Buren. For about five months, from Oct., 1836, to March, 1837, Mr. B. added to his gigantic labors of attorney general that of secretary of war, under Gen. Jackson, filling both offices with distinguished ability. He was U. S. district attorney of the southern district of New York from 1838 to 1841.

In 1845 he was offered the position of secretary of war by President Polk, but declined it, and accepted the office of district attorney for New York, which he held until 1848, when he was removed for supporting Mr. Van Buren for the presidency. Mr. B. was an ardent and active politician, adhering to what proclaimed itself the regular democratic organization until 1848, when he fought the battle of free soil under the banner of Van Buren and Adams. He returned with the Van Burens to the national democratic fold, and supported Gen. Pierce; but the Nebraska bill revolted him again, and he joined the republican party, and voted for Fremont and Dayton.

After leaving public life, Mr. B. entered upon the practice of his profession, and also attended to the duties of principal professor of the law faculty of the New York University, which institution he was instrumental in establishing.

Mr. B.'s last great effort was on the great trust case of Curtiss vs. Leavitt, reported in the 15th volume of the New York Reports. In argument he was "calm, clear, strong, with no passionate appeals, no vehemence of voice or gesture, no wordy declamation. His argument made its way directly to the understanding, and showed a speaker who felt himself above all the arts of the rhetorician, and all desire of display. His doctrines were such as became an American jurist, equally remote from the wild speculations of the latitudinarian, and the narrow and impracticable limitations of the close construer of words."

He was equally distinguished in private as in public life, and, by his kind, courteous demeanor, drew round him large numbers of firm friends, and commanded the respect and admiration of his enemies.

He was, in the language of another, "as a patriot, lofty and pure; as a statesman, philosophical and sagacious; as a politician, liberal and disinterested; as an advocate, eloquent, calm, persuasive, and forcible; and as a man, in a general sense, possessing one of those admirably-organized minds so rarely met with, in which different qualities of excellence are so harmoniously blended and tempered, without an undue excess of any, so as to produce, on the whole, one of the best and finest characters we can possibly conceive — piety without bigotry, philanthropy without fanaticism, enthusiasm without quixotism, boldness without rashness, firmness without obstinacy, sagacity without cunning, all the dignity of self-respect without any of the hauteur of pride, and the expansive wisdom of the man of study, reflection, and practical experience of life, with the single-hearted simplicity of the child."

Of late years he had withdrawn from public affairs, and devoted himself assiduously to his profession — too assiduously, doubtless, for his health, which, though a good constitution enabled him long to resist the effect of excessive application, yielded at last, and he determined to try the effect of a voyage to Europe and a residence abroad. He sailed in the steamer Arago for Havre on the 16th Oct., 1858.

He arrived at Havre on the 30th, and, after visiting some of the places in its neighborhood, went to Rouen, and thence to Paris, which he reached on the 3d of Nov. The excitement and fatigue of seeing the marvellous monuments of antiquity which meet the eye of the stranger on entering France, and which make so strong an impression on the traveller from our own young country, proved too rude a trial for his health. A violent attack of diabetes was the consequence — a disease to which he had been somewhat subject, and which now resisted all remedies.

He was not unaware of the danger he was in, and for 48 hours before his death expected that event. At 9 o'clock on the evening of the 8th of Nov. he expired, passing to another state of existence as one might be expected to pass who had lived so well and so holily in this.

Mr. B. took a deep interest in all benevolent undertakings, which will hereafter greatly miss the useful assistance he was so ready to give them. His cheerful and kindly presence will also be missed from our courts of justice, where he set the example of a graceful, unstudied urbanity, which was simply the natural expression of his character, and which won the regard of all who saw him.

BUTLER, Rev. Geo. W., Berlin Heights, Lake Co., O., Oct. 15, æ. —, pastor of the Baptist church in that place.

BUTLER, Colonel John Lord, Wilkesbarre, Pa., Aug. 4, æ. 62. Col. B. was the son of Gen. Lord Butler, who, in early life, removed from Lyme, Ct., to W., in company with his father, Col. Zebulon Butler, of revolutionary memory. He was from his earliest manhood identified with all the interests of society and business in his region. To develop the riches of the coal, and open channels for its transport to market, has been the object of his untiring efforts; and he has lived to see these efforts crowned with a greater degree of success than often falls to the lot of men engaged in similar undertakings. In his death the business public have sustained a loss. But a heavier loss and a more heartfelt regret will be experienced in the social relations of the deceased, to the very large circle in which he moved. Multitudes have been the subjects of his daily kindnesses in imparting substantial aid, and greater multitudes will testify to the uniform urbanity of his manners, and the tried integrity of his life. It was the habit of his life to consult the interest of others, either individuals or the public, first, and for himself last. In grateful and respectful testimony of this feature of his character, we doubt not, was the extraordinary attendance at the funeral of the deceased. He married the sister of Rev. John Richards, D. D., of Hanover, N. H. He died in the full expression of his faith in Christ, and hope of salvation through him, and him alone.

BUTLER, Samuel, New York, Feb. 1, æ. 75. He was gunner on board the U. S. ship Hornet at the capture of the Penguin, and was severely wounded in the face in that action.

BUTTERFIELD, Charles, Tyngsboro', Mass., July 26, æ. 62. He was the son of Capt. Asa and Abiah (Colburn) Butterfield, and was born in T. Dec. 21, 1795. He was fitted for college at Westford Academy. Having chosen the profession of law, he pursued his legal studies under the tuition of Hon. Daniel Richardson, of T. On the completion of his professional studies, having been admitted to the bar, he opened an office in his native town, but left the profession in a few years, and devoted himself to agriculture. He was never married. He was a man of a most amiable and genial disposition, with a fund of wit ever at command. He was universally esteemed by the inhabitants of his native town. He represented the town in the state legislature in 1834 and '35. In 1857 he was appointed librarian of the Middlesex Mechanic Association in Lowell, and took up his residence in that city. It was a quiet place, among books, and, with the changes contemplated, was just the situation where he hoped to pass, in a manner suited to his tastes, among pleasant companions, ·many long years of a healthy and vigorous old age. He was in perfect health, was careful of himself, and was of a long-lived race, — his father having lived in robust health to the age of 94 years. But, in the midst of the happiness he was enjoying in his new position, sickness came, and he returned home to die. He was one of the most beloved and respected of the people among whom he passed nearly the whole of his life, and who in his death mourn the loss of a worthy, good man.

BUZZELL, Elder Hezekiah D., Alton, N. H., Sept. 6, æ. 80. Mr. B. commenced in the ministry in 1799, and received ordination Jan. 25, 1803. As an itinerant preacher, he has been very useful in the ministry, and his labors have been crowned with success. Hundreds have been converted under him who will be as stars in his crown at the coming of Christ. He was a firm democrat of the old Jefferson school; was a member of the House of Representatives for several years; also a member of the Senate.

BYERLY, Jacob, Westmoreland Co., Pa., ———, æ. 99. Mr. B. was at one time a resident of the only cabin between Fort Pitt and Ligonier. In the revolution he was active, and his scouting expedition extended throughout Western Virginia and Pennsylvania, and into Ohio. He went with a party to bury 21 settlers who had been killed at Wheeling; went to the relief of Fort Lawrence and Wallace's station; was on a scout to Punxutawney, and joined in pursuit of the party who killed the Willards; was on the expedition against the Tuscaroras in Ohio, and served under Gen. Broadhead in the destruction of the towns of the Cornplanter Indians. In this expedition, while following a trail, in company with Jacob Smith and another scout, he killed an Indian chief in a hand-to-hand conflict.

C.

CAIN, Dr. Levi, near Springfield, Va., Oct. 30, at an advanced age. He was a useful and an esteemed citizen.

CAIN, Dr. V. T., near Greenwood, S. C., Jan. 6, æ. —.

CALDCLEUGH, Robert A., Philadelphia, June —, æ. —. Mr. C. was born at Annapolis, Md., but came to Philadelphia in early manhood, and for years was an active and enterprising merchant of strict and uncompromising integrity and unwearied industry. As the fruits, in the meridian of life he had acquired a large and ample estate, which, surrounded by his children and grandchildren, he fully enjoyed until the close of his long and well-spent life. Freed from the cares of business, from which he had retired many years since, his home was the place of his true enjoyment. His mind, cultivated in retirement, was filled with a vast amount of information upon almost every subject, and especially upon the past history of his country. His reminiscences of times long since were vivid and strong; and his references to the distinguished men, his contemporaries in early life, were very interesting and instructive. To strangers his manners were somewhat reserved, but to those who knew him well his courtesy and politeness were remarkable, and his hospitality to all unbounded.

CALDWELL, Rev. David, Leesburg, Va., Nov. 24, æ. 43. He was a native of Bennington, Vt., but removed in very early life to Virginia, and was ordained in Alexandria in 1841 by the venerable Bishop Moore. Few clergymen have been so successful in so short a period (17 years) in building up the congregation in which they have ministered as he. Frail and delicate as was his frame, his spirit was strong; his zeal knew no abatement in his Master's cause; his vigorous intellect was manifest in his pulpit ministrations, while the cross of Christ ever constituted with him a peculiar source of rejoicing. A little more than two years since he succeeded in the rectorship of St. James's Church, Leesburg, Rev. George Adie, who, the preceding spring, had been called to his rest. He was an able and eloquent divine, who, out of the pulpit as well as in it, earnestly labored for the spiritual good of those under his charge. He had scarcely attained the meridian of his life, and was cut down in the midst of his usefulness.

CALHOON, Mrs. Mary Ripley, July 18, æ. 54, wife of Hon. George C. Calhoon, daughter of Hon. Nicholas Baylies, formerly of Montpelier, granddaughter of Rev. Sylvanus Ripley, a professor of divinity in Dartmouth College, and great-granddaughter of Rev. Eleazar Wheelock, D. D., first president of that institution.

CALHOUN, Maj. Patrick, Pendleton, S. C., June 1, æ. 37, at the residence of his mother. He was son of the late Hon. John C. Calhoun, and a gallant officer of the U. S. army.

CALHOUN, Col. William Lowndes, Abbeville District, S. C., Sept. 19, æ. 28, brother of Maj. Patrick Calhoun. He won distinguished literary honors in the S. C. College, but after graduation devoted himself to planting, having no ambitious aims beyond that of being a good citizen. Had not wealth and high position by birth removed the usual incentive to ambition, his talents would have insured distinction. He was a dutiful son, an affectionate and devoted husband, a constant and unswerving friend, manifesting in every relation of life a kind heart, filled with noble and generous impulses. Of prepossessing manners, lively and engaging in his conversation, his loss will long be lamented by all who knew him, and his grave long bedewed with the tears of mourning kindred. Since the death of Mr. C., three sons and a daughter have followed him to the tomb.

CALLARD, Rev. Joseph, fell dead in the street at Grayville, Wabash Co., Ill., ———, æ. —. He had been a resident of the county nearly 30 years.

CAMP, Dr. J. B., Jefferson, Ala., June 20, æ. 22, a graduate of the medical college of the University of Louisiana in the course for 1856-57. His untimely fall is fraught with many sad bereavements. In quick succession he follows an affectionate brother, leaving a disconsolate mother, a doting father, and weeping brothers and sisters to mourn his untimely end.

CAMPBELL, Colin, drowned in the Hudson River, opposite Castleton, May 19, æ. 20, son of Hon. William W. Campbell, of Cooperstown, N. Y. He was a senior in Union College, and a young man of much promise.

CAMPBELL, Harvey W., Lockport, N. Y., Sept. 5, æ. 71. He was one of the pioneers of the village, having removed from Rochester to Lockport in 1823. He was one of the earliest merchants, and was identified with all the important enterprises of the day. He was a contractor on the public works in New York and other states, and always enjoyed the confidence of those with whom he had business connections. He also filled several important civil offices. Among them was the office of justice of the peace, which he held for several years, the duties of which he discharged with honor to himself and satisfaction of the public. We may truly say that during his whole life he was in walk and conversation a shining example of the good man, and consistent and unwavering Mason.

CAMPBELL, James, Upper Lisle, N. Y., July 4, æ. 93. He was one of the oldest settlers of the town, and served in the war of 1812.

CANBY, James, Wilmington, Del., May 24, æ. 77. He was of an old Quaker family who came in about the time of William Penn, and probably with Penn. They settled in or near the banks of Brandywine; and his father, Samuel Canby, Esq., owned and operated one of the celebrated Brandywine mills, and was one of those who assisted in building up the reputation of the Brandywine brand of flour, known and appreciated throughout the world. His father having retired, James conducted the same business until within 15 or 20 years, when he sold his mills, and retired from business. He was one of the main founders and originators of the Philadelphia, Wilmington, and Baltimore Railroad Co., and the most active, energetic, and able in its construction and completion. He was the first president of the Union Bank of Delaware, as well as one of its principal founders and patrons. He was a man of sound and enlarged views in every sense of the word; a close observer of men and things; possessed great self-control, and the power also of controlling others; was very courteous in his intercourse with others, and scrupulously punctual in all his transactions; and had great liberality and consideration for the opinions of others. He transacted a large amount of public business, and was esteemed by all as one of the most intelligent, far-seeing, and reliable members of society. He has left a very large circle of relatives and friends, who are among the most prominent and influential citizens, and his family connections are very widely extended. But three of his children survive him, viz., William Canby, Esq., who resides in Wilmington, and Samuel Canby, Esq., who resides on his splendid farm, near by. Both of these are most estimable gentlemen, and among the first citizens. A married daughter, the wife of the Rev. Mr. McCullough, resides in Baltimore, where her husband is the much-esteemed pastor of one of the most important churches in that city.

CANNON, Col. William R., Columbus, Miss., April 15, æ. —. The news of his death produced a profound sensation throughout the state. Wherever he was known, he was highly esteemed for the noble properties of his character, manifested in all the relations of life. A native of South Carolina, he removed to Mississippi many years since, and successively served in both branches of her legislature from the counties of Oktibbeha and Lowndes. As a legislator, he held the highest position for solidity of judgment, enlightened knowledge of public interests, faithful devotion to duty, and dignity and urbanity of demeanor. The esteem of his associates was manifested in his elevation to the presidency of the Senate, which he held for a number of years. In the social sphere of life Col. C.'s character shone with its brightest lustre. As a neighbor, a parent, a friend, he held the hearts of all about him, and, by deeds of pure benevolence and constant acts of usefulness, contributed to the welfare of the community. Such a character, so nicely adjusted and evenly balanced, could but exist under the influence of the Christian virtues; and this was the secret of the unbroken esteem in which he was held by all who knew him. Purity of life, unbending probity, and kindness of heart, set forth his fine talents and attainments in their most attractive garb, and caused his death to be lamented as a public as well as private bereavement. The religion that had pervaded his life sustained and brightened its close.

CAPEN, Benjamin, Stoughton, Mass., June 22, æ. 86. Few men have passed through a long life more universally respected, or held in higher estimation. He was possessed of a well-balanced, discriminating mind, sound judgment, and good sense, combined with the most stern and inflexible integrity. He was the fifth son of Edward Capen, of Stoughton, who died in 1819, æ. 88. James Capen, brother of Benjamin, died at Stoughton in 1853, æ. 97. Benjamin was probably the last surviving original member of Rising Star Lodge of Freemasons. That lodge was chartered in the year 1799. In 1800 it was constituted, and its officers publicly installed, in the meeting house in Stoughton. The following, among other officers of the Grand Lodge, we are informed, were present on that occasion : Paul Revere, Isaiah Thomas, Benjamin Russell, Thaddeus Mason Harris, Samuel Dunn, and Josiah Bartlett. Mr. C. was buried with the ceremonies of the order.

CAPEN, Rev. Lemuel, South Boston, Mass., Aug. 28, æ. 69, a descendant from Barnard and Joan (Purchis) Capen, who were among the early settlers of Dorchester. He was the son of John, Jr., and Patience (Davis) Capen ; was born in Dorchester, Nov. 25, 1788 ; graduated at Harvard College in 1810 ; was ordained pastor of the Unitarian church in Sterling, Mass., March 22, 1815, and resigned his pastoral charge June 21, 1819. His farewell sermon delivered on this occasion has been twice printed. Oct. 31, 1827, he was installed over the Hawes Place Church in South Boston, until 1839, when he resigned. He was afterwards a minister at large in Baltimore. For the last few years, before his health failed, he preached occasionally, supplying vacant pulpits. Although quite feeble in body, he attended the commencement at Cambridge in July, 1858, being anxious to be present, as he remarked that he had attended every commencement at Harvard since he graduated. In 1836 he wrote, "Attended commencement for the 35th time, the 33d in succession." He was a gentleman of a most amiable disposition, and was greatly beloved and respected ; a worthy man, and devout Christian. He was the father of nine children, six of whom are living. Of these is Edward Capen, Esq., librarian of the Public Library at Boston.

CAPRON, Rev. John A., Morristown, Vt., Nov. 23, æ. 86.

CARD, Rev. Nathan, Rochester, N. Y., Feb. 27, æ. 74, at the residence of his son. He was born in Pownall, Vt., and removed at an early age to Madison Co., N. Y. He united with that "nursery of ministers," the Baptist church at Woodstock, under the pastoral care of Rev. John Peck, and was ordained to the ministry in July, 1826. His first pastorate was that of the church at Otselic and Lincklaen, Chenango Co., and his last at Newark, Ill., having removed to the latter state in 1846. He went to reside with a son, a few months since, and has now peacefully passed away, yielding to the accumulated infirmities of age. His aged consort still survives.

CARLISLE, Dr. Samuel, Misspillion Hundred, Del., Feb. 5, æ. —.

CARLTON, Rev. Isaac, Oxford, Me., Jan. 5, æ. 51. Mr. C. was born at Shelburne, N. H., Aug. 27, 1807. At ten years of age, he was indentured to John Burbank, Esq., of Gorham, N. H., and remained with him ten years. Desiring earnestly to procure an education, he removed to Bethel, and studied with Dr. Grover, purposing to be a physician. Becoming a Christian, he resolved to devote himself to the work of the ministry. He devoted himself to teaching in Westminster, Vt., Oakham, Mass., and Hallowell, Me., until he entered the Theological Seminary at Bangor, where he graduated in 1836. While at Bangor, he was active in forming and sustaining Sabbath schools in the vicinity, and for a time was employed as city missionary. After leaving Bangor, Mr. C. was located two and a half years at Lubec. In 1838 he was installed over the Congregational church in Oxford, and continued its pastor 14 years. In 1853 he removed to Falmouth, and labored as long as his health permitted him. In 1854 he returned to Oxford, where he remained until his death. His confidence and humble trust in Christ, was his support during three years of intense suffering.

CARNEY, Edward L., Esq., Fiflin, O., May 22, æ. 39. Mr. C. was a printer, and graduated as such in the Citizen office, in the fall of 1838. He afterwards studied law, and edited a democratic newspaper at Canton and in Wooster. He was a young man of fine abilities as a writer and a lawyer.

CARPENTER, Mrs. Sarah, Saratoga, N. Y., Dec. 30, æ. 81, relict of the late Dr. Cyrel Carpenter.

CARPENTER, Marcus T., Esq., Jackson, Miss., Aug. 24, æ. —. He was a native of N. Y. He was a fine writer. Under the circumstances in which he wrote and published, his success as a poet evinced genuine ability. His book of poems published in 1851, entitled the Memories of the Past, was not only received with the unusual commendation of his friends, but the Literary World, a New York journal of critical merit, pronounced most favorably upon it, and predicted eminence for the author.

CARPENTER, Dr. William, So. Wilbraham, Mass., May 17, æ. 42. Dr. C. was an intelligent, liberal-minded, upright man — a man of refined sensibility and generous impulses, a devoted seeker after truth, a friend of progress, a lover of his race, diligent in solid usefulness, just, honorable and kind in the intercourse of life, a dutiful son, a tender and faithful husband, an affectionate and careful father, — in fine, a man most deservedly beloved in the domestic circle, and universally esteemed in the much wider sphere of personal friendship.

CARPENTER, Wm. Alison, Esq., Buffalo, N. Y., Dec. 25, æ. 78. Mr. C. leaves but few of his contemporaries behind him, who shared in the early scenes of the history of Buffalo. He was born in the town of Warwick, Orange Co., N. Y., April 5, 1781. Having learned the occupation of a printer, he commenced, in early life, the publication of a weekly newspaper, in the village of Goshen; but the office having unfortunately been destroyed by fire, he removed to Buffalo in 1810, where he has continued to reside for most of the long interval of nearly fifty years which have elapsed since his settlement here, nearly thirty years of which were passed in the house where he died. He was the oldest printer and editor among us, having "worked off," with his own hands, the first number of the Buffalo Gazette, the publication of which was commenced in 1811, by the late Smith H. and Hezekiah A. Salisbury. In 1816 he removed to the village of Fredonia, Chautauque Co., where he published, for a short time, the first paper issued in that county, with the title of the Chautauque Gazette. Returning to Buffalo, he was for a while associated with H. A. Salisbury in the publication of the Buffalo Patriot, under which title the former Buffalo Gazette was then published. During the memorable period of the anti-masonic excitement, which was intensely prevalent throughout the western portion of New York in 1827-8, &c., he had the editorship of the Patriot, which paper, under his direction, took a leading part in the organization of that anti-masonic party which changed, for the time, the politics of this county, and for many years afterwards exercised a controlling influence over its political character. The deceased was no ordinary man. Few, indeed, possess a more intimate and thorough acquaintance with the theory and formation of our government, or have equal knowledge of the details of its early history. Frugal in his expenditure, plain in his exterior, faithful in his friendships, and of remarkable integrity in all business affairs, he was a good citizen of the old school, whose venerable form we shall truly miss from the accustomed haunts he was wont to frequent, and which shall know him no more forever.

CARROLL, Rev. Lawrence, East Cambridge, Nov. 23, æ. —, pastor of the Roman Catholic church. He was buried with the usual ceremonies of the Catholic church, and his remains were followed to the grave by a vast procession of his friends and parishioners, by whom he was much esteemed.

CARRUTHERS, Rev. James, Portland, Me., Nov. 28, æ. 86, and the thirty-first year of his varied and most successful ministry. Mr. C. was born at Ecclefechan, Dumfriesshire, Scotland, Nov. 21, 1772; emigrated to Nova Scotia in 1817; removed to the vicinity of Boston in 1818, and afterwards to the city itself, devoting his leisure time to the visitation of prisons, attendance on district meetings, the circulation of tracts, &c. In Sept., 1823, he removed to Portland. In 1826 he received a license to preach. For seventeen years he labored assiduously, either in the service of the Maine Missionary Society, or under the supervision of a local committee. As a man, Mr. C. possessed a naturally energetic mind, warm affections, great firmness of purpose, and ever-unfailing ur-

banity of manners. As a Christian, he adorned his profession; as a Christian minister, his praise is in all the state, and in many of its churches.

CARSON, David, Esq., Pittsfield, Mass., Sept. 20, æ. 75, one of the oldest and most esteemed citizens of Berkshire. Mr. C. was a native of Albany, and served his apprenticeship to the paper-making business at Newburg, on the Hudson, from which place he removed to Dalton, in 1806, and entered the mills of Messrs. Wiswell & Crane. In 1811 he set up business for himself in the same town, founding the famous house now known as Carson, Brothers, & Co., the founder having retired in 1846 with an ample fortune. After relinquishing the business, Mr. C. removed to Pittsfield, and became the first president of the Pittsfield Bank, whose affairs he managed with distinguished ability and fidelity, until, to the great regret of all connected with the bank, he was compelled by declining health to resign. In all the relations of social and domestic life, Mr. C. was as kind and estimable as he was enterprising and skilful in business, and his death is deeply lamented by a wide circle of friends and relatives. He expired at the residence of his son-in-law, Samuel L. Parker, Esq., with whom he has for some years resided.

CARTER, Rev. James, Indian Springs, Ga., Aug. 25, æ. 66. He was pastor of the Mandonia Church near thirty years, and, to use his own words, baptized, at that church, " above one thousand souls ;" meantime his labors were signally blessed in other churches within the bounds of the Flint River and Central Associations, in which there are many living witnesses of his great zeal, usefulness, and efficiency as a chosen vessel of the Redeemer. The church, by resolution, say, " In him we have lost a good citizen, a zealous and faithful minister, and a consistent and accepted disciple of our Lord Jesus Christ."

CARTER, Elder J. W., Dyer Co., Tenn., March 15, æ. 41. He was born Feb. 6, 1817; was married to Ann Jane Hart, July 6, 1836; joined the Baptist church, and was licensed to preach, April, 1843. He then moved to Madison Co., and united with the Cane Creek church, where he was ordained by the laying on of the hands of the presbytery, consisting of Elders Allen Hill, A. Wade, Allen Thompson, and Reuben Day, Sept. 21,

1845. He served several churches as pastor with great acceptance.

CARTER, Dr. Seneca, San Andreas, Texas, Aug. 15, æ. —, formerly of Weston, Vt.

CARTLAND, Mrs. M. Jane, Lee, N. H., April 16, æ. 38, wife of Jonathan Cartland, Esq., and granddaughter of the late Hon. Jeremiah Smith, of Exeter, N. H., who died Sept. 21, 1843.

CARY, Alfred, Esq., Oakfield, O., Sept. 17, æ. 78, founder of the Cary Collegiate Seminary, and brother of Trumbull Cary, of Batavia, N. Y.

CASE, Rev. Lyman, Coventry, Vt., Feb. 27, æ. 66. He was the fourth child and second son of Abijah and Thankful (Cowles) Case, and was born in Connecticut, April 13, 1792. His early advantages for education were such only as the common schools afforded. He read theology with the Rev. Josiah Hopkins, of New Haven, and the Rev. Benjamin Wooster, of Fairfield. He was licensed to preach by the Winooski Association; preached at Montgomery, Lowell, and other towns in Vermont, and on the 19th day of March, 1823, was ordained the first pastor of the Congregational church and society in Coventry. In this pastorate he remained until Oct. 8, 1828, when he was dismissed. He preached after this in a number of towns in Vermont and Canada, but was never again settled as a pastor. During the latter years of his life, he was in the service of the American Tract Society as a colporteur. He married, Sept. 12, 1819, Phebe (Hollister) Montague, widow of Samuel Montague, of Cambridge, Vt., by whom he had five sons and one daughter. She and the sons survived him.

CASSEL, Amos H., Norritonville, Pa., March 2, æ. 27, son of Joseph and Rebecca Cassel, of Worcester township, Montgomery Co., Pa. He was a member of the class of 1857 in Dartmouth College, and graduated with high distinction. In his relations of life he was sprightly and cheerful, and his varied attainments, his fine conversational powers, his evident desire to please, and, above all, his exceeding kindness of heart, made him the idol of all who knew him.

CASTON, W. Thurlow, Esq., Camden, S. C., July 5. Mr. C. was a native of Lancaster, but for the past ten years a resident of Camden, where, by strict attention to his profession and a faithful discharge of duty, he gained the confidence and respect of the community, and enjoyed at the time of his death a large and lucrative practice at the bar. He was a conscientious, good man, and whether in public or private, in his relations and dealings with others, he followed the golden rule. His life as a Christian was above reproach — ever zealous in doing good, and warmly interested in every moral and religious enterprise which looked to the social and religious improvement of the community.

CHAMPION, Rev. J. Porter, Chatham Four Corners, N. Y., Aug. 2, æ. 22. He had been for nearly five years a member of the Methodist Episcopal church, and for about two years a preacher of the gospel. He was born in Saratoga Co., Jun. 26, 1836.

CHAPIN, Rev. Alonzo Bowen, D. D., Hartford, Ct., July 9, æ. 50. Dr. C. was born at Somers, March 10, 1808. His education was first directed with reference to his entering the ministry of the Congregational church; but owing to ill health, his plans were changed, and he studied law. He was admitted to practice in 1831, and immediately established himself at Wallingford. While there, he became an Episcopalian; and as he was somewhat known as a contributor to various church periodicals, the convention of the diocese, in 1836, elected him to edit a church paper to be established in New Haven. The paper was called the Chronicle of the Church, and was edited by Dr. C. for eight years. During this time, he resumed his theological studies, and was ordained in 1838. He was rector of Christ Church, West Haven, until 1850, at which time he removed to Glastenbury, and was rector of St. Luke's Church until 1855, when, owing to infirmities, he was obliged to relinquish active pastoral duties. He removed to Hartford, and has since been engaged in editing the Calendar. His editorial duties were commenced, however, over a year previous to his removal from Glastenbury. Besides numerous contributions to magazines and reviews, Dr. C. was frequently before the public as the author of books and pamphlets. Among the former may be mentioned A View of the Organization and Order of the Primitive Church, Views of Gospel Truth, Glastenbury for Two Hundred Years, and a Classical Spelling

Book. His pamphlets are quite numerous. — *Hartford Press.*

CHAPIN, David, Havana, N. Y., Jan. 5, æ. 95, was an old revolutionary soldier, born in New Hartford, Conn., in Aug., 1762. At the age of sixteen he entered the revolutionary army, and served in it for five years, until the close of the war in 1783. He was present at the execution of Andre, the evacuation of New York, Nov. 25, 1782, and at the farewell of Washington to his army. His widow, who is ninety years of age, and three out of eight children, survive him. Mr. and Mrs. C. were married seventy-two years ago.

CHAPIN, Mrs. Sarah Orr, Waverley, Ill., Aug. 29, æ. 64, widow of Rev. William A. Chapin, of Greensboro', Vt.

CHAPMAN, Mrs. Evalina Clara, Asheville, N. C., Aug. 13, æ. 46, wife of Rev. Robert Hett Chapman, D. D. As wife, mother, mistress, friend, she well fulfilled all of life's duties, shedding upon them the richest offerings of Christian affection. Her piety was humble, unpretending, distrustful of self, and ever retiring, but burned with a steady flame, and grew clearer and brighter to the last. Her sick chamber, though the scene of intense suffering, was cheered by hallowed influences, and even joyous; and her dying bed, through divine grace, was made the place of richest Christian triumph.

CHAPMAN, Rev. Nathaniel, Pittston, Me., April 1, æ. 69. He was a native of Exeter, and had supplied the Congregational Church in P. about two years.

CHAPPOTIN, Mrs. Bridget Coleman, Providence, R. I., Feb. 4, æ. 83, at the residence of her son-in-law, S. B. Wheaton, wife of Levi Chappotin, and daughter of the late Col. Dudley Coleman, of Newbury, Mass.

CHASE, Mrs. Charlotte H., Hampton, N. H., Aug. 20, æ. 42, wife of Rev. N. L. Chase, of the same place. She was the daughter of Oliver Atherton, of Middlesex, Vt., who died Sept. 8, 1838, aged 76, and his wife Olive, died May 2, 1843, æ. 67. She became pious very early in life, and joined the Methodist Episcopal church, and for twelve years faithfully and affectionately performed the duties incident to an itinerancy. She made friends every where, labored for souls, loved holiness, and lived by faith. Her dying charge to her husband was, "Preach holiness."

CHASE, Enoch, Esq., Rollinsford, N. H., —— 19, æ. 66. We cannot suffer the above formal record to pass without adding a few words in commemoration of him who is the subject of it. Mr. C. was born in the neighborhood where the last hours of his life were passed, and continued to reside there till 1819, when he entered the counting house of Messrs. Waterston, Pray, & Co., in Boston, in which service he remained as confidential clerk for nearly forty years.

There were few persons in our community connected with the department of mercantile business pursued by that house who did not know him; and he became, as it were, a link uniting the past generation with the present. It is something to say, that during all this period of time he was a faithful, conscientious, and intelligent clerk; unremitting in his endeavors to serve his employers in the duties pertaining to that office. For these duties he had a peculiar fitness. In the use of figures he was remarkable, giving results almost instantaneously, which are arrived at by most persons only through a long and tedious process.

His "Advance Book," so well known to our merchants, and his "Tables of Interest," were composed by him as mere recreations. But this was not all. Although too timid himself to embark on the uncertain sea of a mercantile career, he yet possessed many qualities which adorn the character of the merchant. To a nice sense of honor, and of mercantile integrity, he united a knowledge, in a remarkable degree, of the principles, maxims, and usages which go to make up a part of our commercial law; and possessing a sound judgment, and viewing every question in the light of the principles which underlaid it, his opinions were often sought, and never disregarded by his employers.

Indeed, he was treated more as a member of the house than as a surbordinate; and well did he deserve the trust and confidence reposed in him. He had a strong taste for legal questions, and if he had chosen the professson of law, would have attained a respectability, if not eminence, in it. With great fondness for books, and with a very retentive memory, his mind became a great storehouse of facts. But few persons were better informed on matters of history. His tastes were pure and simple. His wants were few, and he pursued a system of economy, as a matter of principle, which may well be commended to others in like situations; and the result is before us. He has not only brought up and educated a large family, now well settled in life, but has left them a respectable property to be divided among them — a good illustration of what small yearly savings, with interest, will produce in a series of years. But few merchants, compared with the whole number who have passed off the stage under his eye, can show so good a pecuniary result. On a memorandum found among his papers, giving a list of his effects, were these significant words: "I owe nothing." But the best inheritance he has left to his children is his good name.

Our old friend has made his last entry, his books are balanced, and he has gone to render up his final account. We doubt not he will receive the welcome of, "Well done, good and faithful servant." — *Boston Transcript.*

CHASE, Henry, Esq., Detroit, Mich., Oct. 2, æ. 32, only brother of T. R. Chase, of the late firm of Chase & Slade. He was formerly editor of the Lake Superior Journal, and at the time of his death a member of the Detroit bar.

CHASE, Capt. Moses, Newburyport, Mass., Dec. 19, æ. 74.

CHASE, Mrs. Sally Adams, Haverhill, Mass., Oct. 28, æ. 66. She was the wife of the late Samuel A. Chase, of Haverhill, and daughter of the late David Gile, of Hopkinton, N. H. Bereft by death, at the early age of 11 years, of a beloved and excellent mother, Mrs. C. was deprived of the priceless blessing of maternal influence and love, and, many of the endearments of home; yet, by her native force of character and strength of intellect, she acquired a position in the respect and veneration of those who knew her, of which the best cultivated mind might well be proud. Her early afflictions, together with her natural thoughtfulness, gave to her manners an aspect of unusual seriousness and solemnity, and it would be difficult to point to a single occasion in which she indulged in a trifling act, or turned aside, for the sake of pleasure, from the rugged path of duty. In woman's true sphere, the education of her family, she employed the highest energies of her strong mind and the best affections of her fond and earnest heart. Two of her sons secured a liberal education at Dartmouth College — C. C. Chase, principal of the High School, Lowell, and Leverett M. Chase, principal of the Adams School, Dorchester, Mass.; three of them are now principals of high and grammar schools in Mass., and all her eight surviving children have been, at some time, employed in the business of teaching. For more than twenty years, Mrs. C. has been a consistent member of the Baptist church in East Haverhill.

CHENAULT, Hon. William, Madison Co., Ky., Jan. 5, æ. 52. He was the second son of William Chenault, Sen., who emigrated to Kentucky from Virginia, at an early period in the history of the commonwealth. Those noble traits of character, untiring energy and honesty of purpose, which won for him success in every theatre of action in which he was a participant, were strongly evidenced in his boyhood and early manhood. In 1840 he was elected to the lower house of the legislature of Kentucky, proved himself a faithful representative, and a man of fine business qualifications. In 1842 he was elected to serve as a senator from the counties of Madison and Garrard; and in 1849 he was member of the constitutional convention of Kentucky.

CHESEBROUGH, Henry H., Webster, N. Y., Nov. 8, æ. 52, principal of the academy at that place. He was an exemplary Christian, a sincere and upright citizen, and a valuable educator of youth.

CHEVERS, Mrs. Sarah P., Portsmouth, R. I., Dec. 10, æ. 42, wife of Rev. Geo. W. Chevers. Notwithstanding her many family duties, she gave much time to missionary and charitable purposes. She often had the care of the church music, vocal and instrumental, and sometimes led in both. She was a tender, affectionate, and self-sacrificing wife and mother. The faith of the deceased in her blessed Redeemer was firm and sustaining, and having finished her work on earth, she was ready, yea, desirous, "to depart and be with the Lord."

CHILD, Hon. Asa, Norwich, Ct., May 11, æ. 60, counsellor at law, and brother of Hon. Linus Child, of Lowell, Mass. Mr. C. was born in Woodstock, Ct., and graduated at Yale College in the class of 1821; studied law at the New Haven law school, and in the office of Hon.

Ebenezer Stoddard, of Woodstock; was admitted to the bar in 1823, and opened an office in Norwich, Ct. During the administration of Gen. Jackson he was U. S. district attorney of Connecticut, and kept his office in Hartford. In 1842 he removed to New York, but returned to Norwich just before his death to connect himself with a son who had opened an office there. He confined himself laboriously to his profession, and proved himself an able and successful lawyer and advocate. He never engaged in political life, and held no public political office, except that of U. S. district attorney, and that was a matter of professional importance and interest with him.

CHIVERS, Dr. Thomas Holly, Decatur, Ga., Dec. 19. He was an author, an able classical scholar, and remarkable for many eccentricities.

CHOATE, Mrs. Rebecca, Salem, Mass., Aug. 6, æ. 25, wife of Hon. George F. Choate, and daughter of George Greenleaf, Esq., of Newburyport, Mass.

CHURCH, John P., Esq., Albion, N. Y., Dec. 23, æ. 46, clerk of Orleans Co., and brother of Comptroller Church. He was a faithful and capable officer, a kind husband and father, a warm friend, and in every sense a true and noble man.

CILLEY, Mrs. Martha, Aug. 26, æ. 86, and PETER CILLEY, Sept. 29, æ. 84, Brooks, Me. They were among the first settlers of Brooks, and had been married 66 years.

CLAGGETT, William, Esq., Nashua, N. H., May 5, æ. 82. Mr. C. was born in Litchfield, June 10, 1776, and was a son of Hon. Wiseman Claggett, the king's attorney at Portsmouth before the revolution, and the U. S. attorney after. Judge Clifton Claggett, formerly of Amherst, was another son. William lived, until about ten years ago, in Londonderry. Since that time he has resided in Nashua. He was a magistrate in Londonderry for several years, and was considered one of the best in the state. Some of the eminent lawyers of a past generation have appeared before him, such as Mason, Samuel Bell, Gov. Plumer, &c. His judgment was excellent, and through life he maintained an unexceptionable respectability. He was a firm and unyielding democrat, having voted for all the democratic presidents from Jefferson to Buchanan.

CLAPP, Charles, Esq., Bath, Me., June 3, æ. 84. He came to Bath in 1790, and has ever since been a permanent resident. For a long series of years he stood prominent in the mercantile community, and was very extensively engaged in ship building and commercial enterprise. He was the last survivor of the original North (Congregational) Church, now known as the "Winter Street," which was organized in 1795. He was a man of sterling integrity, deeply imbued with Christian philanthropy, and zealous for the cause of religious truth, unwavering in his attachment to the church, and always ready to sympathize with suffering humanity.

CLARDY, Dr. Erasmus S., Parkville, Mo., Sept. 14, æ. 33. As a skilful and accomplished physician, as a warmhearted and generous friend, he will long be missed in the community.

CLARK, Dr. John J., Salem, O., Aug. 18, æ. 24, at the residence of his father. To talents of a fine order and an enterprising spirit was added every trait that could adorn the character of a gentleman and a scholar.

CLARK, Joseph W., Esq., Albany, N. Y., Dec. 28, æ. 28, civil engineer, and late U. S. consul at Arica, Peru, S. A.

CLARK, Mrs. Mary, May 8, æ. 82, and EZRA, May 24, æ. 79, Sidney Plains, N. Y. They had lived together over half a century, and are nearly the last of the early settlers of that town. The father of Mrs. C, was in the army of the revolution, and on such terms of intimacy with Gen. Washington, that Mrs. C., then a child and motherless, was fondly played with by the general in his leisure hours while at West Point, and for some years after. She distinctly remembered the personal appearance of Washington, Lafayette, and others of the great men of that time.

CLARK, Dea. Royal, Bangor, Me., Dec. 15, æ. 75. He came to Bangor in 1816. He was once the sheriff of this county, and during the administrations of Presidents Monroe and Adams he was postmaster of Bangor. He was one of the original members, and first deacon of the First Baptist Church; and, having faithfully performed the service of youthful labor in the church, he continued to be the honored and much-respected counsellor and officer in the church till his death.

CLARK, Stanford R., West Brattleboro', Vt., April 2, æ. 46, graduate of Amherst, son of Hon. Samuel Clark, of West Brattleboro', Vt.

CLARK, Dr. W. F., Dansville, N. Y., Oct. 5, æ. 72, father of Francis B. and Willis G. Clark, of Mobile, Ala.

CLARKE, Edward, Esq., Northampton, Mass., July 21, æ. 67. Mr. C. was born in Northampton, April 25, 1791. At the age of 14 he left that place for Boston, where, after several years of preparation in one of the first importing houses in that city, he established himself as a dry-goods merchant, which business he prosecuted successfully until 1835, when, having accumulated a fortune sufficiently large to justify his retiring, he did so, cheerfully resigning the field, as he said, to younger men. Mr. C. then returned to his native town, where he erected a delightful house on Round Hill, and where he continued to reside until his death. Mr. C. was in early life a Unitarian; but, having devoted much time and serious and prayerful consideration to the study of the Holy Scriptures, he, at an advanced period of life, boldly declared himself in favor of the Orthodox doctrines of the Protestant Episcopal church, of which church he was for 15 years an earnest, devoted, and truly consistent member. Mr. C. was eminently a benevolent man, never indiscriminate in his charities, but ever ready to aid the deserving poor, to comfort and relieve the sick and sorrowing, and to counsel and encourage the weak and erring; and many for whom his efforts were, while he lived, unknown, now mourn his loss, as that of their best earthly friend. Mr. C. was twice married. His first wife was the niece, and his second, who survives him, the daughter, of the late honored and lamented Joshua Blake, Esq., of Boston. Mr. C. let three adopted daughters, but no own children.

CLARKE, Michael N., Esq., Columbus, Ga., Sept. 25, æ. 63. He has resided in this city since its first settlement, and held positions in the county, which he filled with credit. He was a lieutenant in the Cadet Riflemen commanded by Capt. T. C. Evans in the Florida war in 1836, and bore himself as a soldier during that campaign.

CLARKE, Dr. William, Staunton, Va., Jan. 20, æ. —, formerly of Bloomington.

CLARKSON, William, Columbia, S. C., Aug. 8, æ. 50. Mr. C. was the eldest surviving son of William Clarkson, a native of England, who in early youth removed to Charleston, where he lived a merchant, and won the character of a good citizen. Maternally, the subject of this notice was the grandson of Dr. Tucker Harris, and, through the wife of that eminent Charleston physician, a descendant of the Scotch divine, the Rev. Thomas Boston, so well known as the author of "The Fourfold State of Man." He was thus of pious parentage, and singularly illustrated in his own career, not in a general way only, but in his every thought, word, and action, the pious fruits which such an influence, continued through more than one generation, may be supposed to produce. Born to fortune, and tenderly and delicately bred as such persons usually are, his personal habits were of the simplest, the least exacting character proper to the condition of a Christian gentleman, with the readiest service and the amplest means at his command. Ever alive to the responsibilities of his position, he devoted much time and personal attention to the moral and religious culture of his slaves.

CLAYTON, Joseph, Trenton, N. J., April 23, æ. 107. He enjoyed good health up to a few days before his death.

CLEAR, Michael, Greenwich, Ct., April —, æ. —, a native of Queen Anne's Co., Md. In 1810 he was a sailor before the mast; but during the war of 1812 he was captain of the foretop on board the old U. S. ship Constitution. He aided at the taking of the British frigate Guerriere, under Com. Hull, at the taking of the British frigate Java, under Com. Bainbridge, and at the taking of the Cyane and Levant, under Com. Stewart. He subsequently returned to the merchant service, where he continued for many years, when he reëntered the U. S. service on the sloop-of-war Erie, and subsequently on the frigate Congress. His last position was that of sailing master at the Brooklyn navy yard.

PROF. PARKER CLEAVELAND,

Brunswick, Me., Oct. 15, æ. 78. He was son of Dr. Parker and Elizabeth (Jackman) Cleaveland, and was born in

Rowley, (Byfield Parish,) Mass., Jan. 15, 1780. His father was son of Rev. John Cleaveland, and was born in Chebacco, parish of Ipswich, which is now the town of Essex, Mass. Rev. John Cleaveland entered Yale College, and when in his senior year, he was, with another, expelled for embracing the doctrine of the "New Lights." Prof. C.'s father was fitted for college, but the war broke out, and he relinquished his intention of obtaining a collegiate education, studied medicine, became a surgeon in the revolutionary army, and was stationed at Cambridge. Prof. C. was fitted for college at Dummer Academy, in Newbury, Mass., under Rev. Isaac Smith, (H. U., 1767.) He taught school in Boxford, Mass., in his Sophomore, and in Burlington or Wilmington, Mass., in his Junior year. Immediately after his graduation, he entered, as a law student, the office of Ichabod Tucker, of Haverhill, Mass.), H. U. 1791,) where he remained one year. In the middle of the year 1800, he began teaching a school at York, Me., and at the same time was clerk in the office of Daniel Sewall, Esq., the clerk of the Supreme Court; accompanied him at the courts, and continued the study of the law. Here he remained until the autumn of 1803, when he was appointed tutor in mathematics at Harvard College, which office he held until commencement in 1805, when he resigned it in consequence of having received an invitation to fill a professorship in Bowdoin College, which he accepted, and he was installed Oct. 23, 1805, as professor of mathematics and natural philosophy, the college then having been in operation but a single year. The duties of this professorship, together with those of lecturer on chemistry and mineralogy, he discharged with distinguished ability until 1828, when it was deemed expedient to separate the departments of mathematics and natural philosophy, and establish a distinct professorship of chemistry and mineralogy. Mr. William Smyth, the distinguished professor of mathematics, was raised to that department, and Mr. Cleaveland was installed in the new professorship of chemistry, mineralogy, and natural philosophy. This position he occupied until his death, having acquired a world-wide reputation, and a success seldom attained by a scientific instructor. He was thus connected with the college for a period of fifty-three years, during which he devoted the whole powers of his mind and the energy of his body to the advancement of his favorite studies; and no man in the country has done more to inspire a passion and create an interest and knowledge of the details of the sciences which he taught. The pupils of no college have taken a greater interest in mineralogy and chemistry, or are more frequently met in scientific explorations, than those of the institution whose usefulness and reputation he has done so much to promote. The more than 1000 pupils living, of the 1300 graduates of the college, will rise up with one accord and bless his name and memory.

He spent six hours a day in his laboratory, recitation and lecture room, and was frequently engaged sixteen of the twenty-four hours. The college never bought any minerals. James Bowdoin gave about five hundred specimens; the rest have been collected either by Prof. C.'s personal labor, or by the exchange of specimens which he obtained, and they now amount to upwards of seven thousand. He became widely known in the United States, in Great Britain, and on the continent of Europe, by his great work on mineralogy and geology, which he published in 1816, in one volume, and a second edition in 1822, in two volumes. It gained for him the title of "Father of American Mineralogy," and was unhesitatingly pronounced, by the Edinburgh Review, "the most useful work on the subject in the English language." The author was engaged on the third edition for nearly thirty-five years, making large additions, to keep up with the advancement of the science.

On the publication of this work, correspondence with Prof. C. was sought by many scientific men throughout the world, and soon his correspondents embraced the greatest names in science. Honors crowded thick and fast upon him. He was in the prime of life. Diplomas from over sixteen scientific societies of Europe were sent him; and among other institutions he received offers of professorships, with much higher salaries than that he had at Bowdoin, at Harvard repeatedly, at Dartmouth, at William and Mary's College, at the University of Pennsylvania, Princeton College, and at the College of Physicians and Surgeons in New York. But he refused them all, and adhered to his resolve to remain at Bowdoin. President Woods substantially said his mind was practical rather than speculative; clear in its perceptions rather than profound in its investigations; strong in its grasp of great principles rather than acute and discriminating in analysis; better adapted to the orderly arrangement of facts, and to the safe deduction and clear enunciation of laws, than to the deeper intuitions and the higher generalizations of science — a condition of mind better adapted than any other to make a good teacher. Another quality indicated by the president, was Prof. C.'s conscientious official fidelity, a matter in which he never failed. The president said that the day before his death he had been prevented from attending his recitation for the third time only since the term began. On Thursday, the day before he died, the president met him riding out, and implored him to relieve himself of all further duty until he should recover. He replied, with great feeling, that there had not been an absence in his class since he had been sick, and that he should not be absent himself if he could help it; and accordingly, the next morning he was getting ready to go to his recitation, when he died. In private life, Prof. C. was universally respected for his unblemished moral character, his genial and affable disposition as a husband, a father, and a friend, and as a public spirited and generous citizen. In 1825 he was chosen captain of the first fire company in Brunswick, in the formation of which he greatly assisted, and for twenty years he fulfilled, with his accustomed punctuality, all the duties belonging to his situation; was forward in danger and prompt to duty.

The president adverted to his religious character, and declared that none who knew him could doubt that he was a devout man and a sincere Christian, making, it is true, his religion, to a singular and excessive degree, an affair between himself and his Maker.

Prof. C.'s wife was Martha Bush, of Cambridge, Mass., by whom he had two sons and three daughters; Martha, one of the daughters, married the Hon. Peleg W. Chandler, of Boston. Mrs. Cleaveland died about five years ago.

Prof. C. received the degree of LL. D. from Bowdoin in 1824, was elected a member of the American Academy of Arts and Sciences, was also chosen a fellow of the Wernerian Society of Edinburg, the Mineralogical Societies of Dresden and St. Petersburg, and the Geological Society of London. He was also many years corresponding secretary of the Maine Historical Society.

Prof. C. was always an earnest supporter of the Medical School of Maine, which was founded at Bowdoin in 1820, and was connected with it as a lecturer in chemistry, dean, and librarian. From 1831 to 1834, after the removal of President Allen by the legislature, Prof. C. acted as president; and on the resignation of President Allen in 1839, at the close of his second term of office, refused to accept the situation of the permanent president, which was offered him; conscious as he was of his peculiar fitness for the position he had so long occupied, and with love and enthusiasm for those sciences in which he was so deeply engaged. By the testimony of all who have enjoyed his instruction, and of the many others who have known his daily walk, or whom his fame has reached, he stands wholly unrivalled as a teacher.

At the time of the succession of honored President Leonard Woods to President Allen in 1839, Prof. C. had nearly completed his threescore years; and from this period he gradually withdrew from all labors, except those immediately connected with his professorship. But he lost none of his energy and activity until, for a short period, a few years since, his strength seemed to fail him. But he quickly recovered, and with such increased vigor, that he seemed "to have taken a new lease of life," and to have entered upon a second career of usefulness and active exertion for others' good.

The death of this learned man will create a vacancy in the institution which his long life has so ably illustrated, which it will not be easy to supply. His familiar form his pleasant and affable address, and his fluent and winning conversation, will still linger in the memory of those who have had the pleasure of enjoying them; while his pupils and the scientific world will long cherish his name and his instructions in kind and fond remembrances.

CLELAND, Hon. Jonas, Warren, N. Y., April 24, æ. 78. He was born in 1780, in Massachusetts. The republic being then in its infancy, disruptive forces were yet active; and new institutions were encountering the difficulties of a recent formation, of the prestige of an ancient monarchy, and of the prejudices of royalists. Born at such a period, current events and necessities were well calculated to produce that self-reliance and force of character for which he was so justly distinguished. The scarcity and defectiveness of educational institutions left him very much to his own efforts to acquire knowledge and a fitness for future usefulness and success. The degree of energy with which he encountered these early disadvantages is best seen in the light of his long and honorable career. Perceiving that he must be the architect of his own fortunes, he went manfully to work, gained knowledge and character, so that, when he had just reached his majority, he was admitted to the seat of magistracy in Herkimer Co., which seat he occupied for 40 years in succession. For several years he sat in the New York state legislature, to which he was elected as early as 1814, and warmly supported the Erie Canal, and filled the office of judge in Herkimer Co. In all his public offices, as in his private relations, he was distinguished for suavity and firmness, for sagacity and purity. He leaves a widow, a daughter, and two sons.

CLELAND, Mrs. Lucretia, Natchez, Miss., Oct. 24, æ. —, wife of Rev. T. H. Cleland, pastor of the Second Presbyterian Church. Mrs. C., though in delicate health, had been active in visiting the sufferers from the prevailing epidemic in her neighborhood. She was still more severely taxed by her devotion to sick members of her own family. When seized at last by the disease, she was ill prepared to meet so powerful an enemy, and the result, as feared by her friends from the first, was fatal. She was the daughter of Rev. Thomas Savage, of Bedford, New Hampshire.

CLELAND, Rev. Thomas, D. D., New Providence, Ind., Jan. 31, æ. 80. Dr. C. was born in Fairfax, Virginia, May 22, 1778. After some removals, his father finally located in Marion Co., where, amid the perils and hardships of pioneer life, by hard labor he acquired the vigorous and elastic constitution that so well sustained him in his after life. Being designed for the bar, his father allowed him, as he neared manhood, such facilities for a classical education as the state afforded. He entered Transylvania University under very encouraging circumstances; but these advantages were cut short by the quickly succeeding deaths of his father and mother, these events rendering it incumbent on him to take charge of the family. Meanwhile, though surrounded by no religious influences, Dr. C. had united himself with the Presbyterian church, under the care of Dr. Blythe, of Lexington, Ky.; and, though the burden of his father's and his own family required his daily labor, he resolved to dedicate his services to the church, and under many disadvantages accomplished this end. He was licensed in 1803. From that period until 1813 he had care of three churches in Washington Co., separated by many miles of wilderness. He also missionated extensively through Southern Kentucky and Indiana. In 1803 he took charge of the Harrodsburg and New Providence churches. With the first he dissolved his connection in 1838. With the last his pastoral relation was dissolved by death. In all events of importance in the church he took a prominent and decided part; and none who differed from him doubted that he followed his strong convictions of duty. Dr. C. labored diligently also with his pen. He kept up for many years a spirited controversy on the "divinity of Christ," issued a volume of hymns, contributed largely to the religious periodicals of the day, and leaves many sermons in circulation. Besides these labors, and the education of a large family of children, including a thorough collegiate and theological course for two sons, he gave the use of his library and instructions free to many students of divinity. Seventeen young men went out from under his roof into the ranks of the Presbyterian ministry.

CLEMENT, Jacob B., M. D., West Point, N. Y., Sept. 23, æ. —.

CLEMENT, Mrs. Mary Elizabeth, Dubuque, Iowa, May 23, æ. 38, wife of the editor of the Daily Times.

CLEMENTS, Rev. Manning E., Greene Co., Ark., May 12, æ. 56, formerly of Tuscaloosa Co., Ala., much beloved for his many virtues.

CLEVELAND, Gen. Benjamin, Clarksville, Ga., June 27, æ. —. He was a soldier of 1814, and had held high political positions. In the wars with the Creeks, Seminoles, and Cherokees, he had seen service.

CLEVELAND, Dr. Hiram, Pawtucket, R. I., —— 7, æ. 59.

CLOUTIER, Dr. Rene, Cloutierville, La., May 23, æ. 23. In Dr. C. were combined and beautifully blended all the elements of the true man. Noble, generous, honorable, and magnanimous almost to fastidiousness, he was a model of gentlemanly urbanity, and the breathing impersonation of the high-toned and honorable gentleman. Clear, practical ability, a highly cultivated intellect, the noblest physical proportions, and a stern grandeur of spirit were combined in his personal and mental constitution.

COBB, Col. Joseph B., Columbus, Miss., Sept. 15, æ. 40. The deceased was born in Oglethorpe Co., Ga., April 11, 1819, being the second son of the late Hon. Thos. W. Cobb, who was distinguished as one of the first intellects of his state, and who was especially memorable for his able, eloquent, and fearless attack in the Senate of the United States, upon the policy of Gen. Jackson in his Florida campaign. His early education was commenced at Wilmington, S. C., in a school rendered famous as the nursery of Calhoun, McDuffie, Longstreet, and others, then taught by a son of the venerable preceptor of such sages and statesmen; whence he was transfered to the University of Georgia. He married the eldest daughter of the late Hon. A. S. Clayton, and removed to Mississippi in the fall of 1838. Although but 21 years of age, the people of Noxubee Co., where he had settled, elected him as their representative to the state legislature, from which time he became ardently interested in the political controversies of the day. In 1851, however, after a heated canvass, in which he represented the policy of the Union party of the state, and made one of the most eloquent and effective appeals in its behalf, delivered during the eventful struggle, he was triumphantly elected a member of the state convention, the call of which gave rise to the controversy. At the next state election, he was chosen senator for Lowndes Co., after a hard-contested campaign. He was a graceful, fluent speaker, and a sprightly, vigorous writer. A large portion of his leisure hours he devoted to writing essays, sketches, stories, and critiques for the magazines and reviews, many of which were much read and admired. As a man, Col. C. was universally respected and esteemed for the many excellent qualities, both of his head and his heart, and his memory will long be cherished by hosts of admiring friends.

COCHRAN, Dr. William S., Darlington, Pa., Sept. 19, æ. 30. He had already taken rank among the most judicious and skilful physicians, and bid fair to be eminent in his profession had his life been spared. His innate modesty and high sense of honor endeared him to a large circle of acquaintances, and particularly to his medical brethren, with all of whom he was on the most friendly terms. Dr. C. had opinions carefully formed on all public questions, and expressed them on all suitable occasions. While he devoted himself to the profession of his choice, he was not a mere physician, but had thoughts, words, and efforts for other subjects and other interests.

COCHRAN, W. D., Lansing, Mich., Sept. 29, æ. —, late principal of Detroit Commercial College. He was well known as its founder, and won for himself, in this branch of business, the universal esteem of his fellow-citizens. His memory will ever be fondly cherished by his numerous students, and his influence, exerted through them, remembered with pleasure, as having raised the standard of mercantile knowledge to an honorable point. It has been Mr. C.'s privilege to send forth into the commercial world very many of the best business men of the state, and of other states. Not only in a business point of view, but also as a private citizen, he was a firm maintainer of the right, a defender and aider of the poor, a counsellor and guide.

COE, Rev. Truman, Kirtland, O., May 22, æ. 60. Mr. C. was a native of Derby, Conn., and removed to K. in 1832. He was, for many years, the useful and beloved pastor of the church in K., an active, earnest, and devoted friend of education, and deeply interested in every thing affecting the well-being of his fellow-men.

COFFEE, Hon. Edward, Rabun Co., Ga., May 30, æ. 65. He was born on Changee Creek, Parker District, S. C.

He commenced his public career by serving as a bailiff in his native state, after which he emigrated to Rabun Co., Ga., while that portion of the state was inhabited by the Cherokee Indians. In 1818, soon after the county was organized, he served as a justice of the peace, then as sheriff of the county, and for more than 20 years as one of the judges of the Inferior Court. In 1831 or '32 he was elected to the lower house of the state legislature, where he served for several years, and after that was elected senator, in which capacity he served for many years, and was the senator of the county when he died. In 1851 and '52 he introduced in the Senate the Blue Ridge railroad bill. He also was elected senator of the 43d senatorial district when the state was divided into districts. He filled all the stations he has occupied with untiring industry, scrupulous fidelity, and with distinguished ability. He married, in 1820, Miss Elizabeth Nevill, daughter of Jesse Nevill, (a revolutionary soldier,) and then settled permanently in Rabun. The fruits of this union were three daughters, who are all married, and settled near his former residence. He had a fond and doting family, had accumulated an ample fortune, and few enjoyed life better.

COFFEE, Gen. T. J., Oyster Creek, Brazoria Co., Texas, Nov. 2, æ. —. Gen. Coffee was one of the best of citizens, and was held in the highest estimation by all who knew him. He came to Texas, some years since, from Mississippi, where he had held several offices of trust, and had been for several years a member of the state legislature. In Texas he did not aspire to public office, but devoted his time to his family and domestic affairs. He was one of our best planters, and left a large fortune.

COFFIN, Mrs. Betsey, New Bedford, Nov. 24, æ. 58, widow of the late Hon. Timothy G. Coffin.

COGSWELL, Rev. Frederick, Memphis, Tenn., Aug. 4, æ. 65. He was a minister of the N. H. Christian Conference. His last moments were peaceful and happy; and he expired in the full hope of a glorious immortality.

COLCORD, Rev. David, Bucksport, Me., Feb. 21, æ. 57.

COLEGROVE, Mrs. Theodora, Ellicottville, N. Y., Dec. 30, æ. 25, wife of Dr. James B. Colegrove, and daughter of the Hon. Stanley N. Clark, of E.

COLEMAN, Hon. Daniel, Dayton, Ala., May 18, æ. 65. He was one of the earliest settlers in the state, and was for many years judge of Washington Co.

COLEMAN, Rev. William P., Northampton Co., Va., Sept. 9, æ. —.

COLES, Mrs. Sarah, M. D., Syracuse, N. Y., April 22, æ. 58, widow of Dr. L. B. Coles, of Boston, Mass., and mother of Mrs. S. F. Smith, of Syracuse. The prominent traits in Mrs. C.'s character were her strength of mind, and her piety, benevolence, and liberality. The cause of her Redeemer was always before her. Her mind was constantly looking heavenward. Her liberal hand was ever reaching to aid the poor and oppressed. Her heart was alive to every good work.

COLLINS, Rev. Wellington H., Pontiac, Mich., Aug. 11, æ. —, presiding elder of the Methodist Episcopal church. The church at Pontiac say of him that "the church has lost a self-sacrificing, faithful, and efficient minister, the Detroit conference one of its brightest ornaments, the state one of her truest sons, and the world a consistent and exemplary Christian.

COLLINS, Dr. W. F., Deer Isle, Me., June 15, æ. 38.

HON. AMOS MORRIS COLLINS,

Hartford, Ct., Nov. 10, æ. 70. He was born in Litchfield, Ct., March 30, 1788. Descended from the old Puritan stock, with an ancestry distinguished for their piety and active benevolence, he was, from his first days, surrounded by such examples and influences as were calculated to form and develop a decided character, both as a man and Christian. Educated at a time and place when and where every pursuit and calling tasked the strength and nerve of men, he early acquired those habits of industry, self-denial, and earnest application, which marked his life, and contributed so greatly to his success. In later years he was called to fill public positions in the church of Christ and in the community where he lived, for which, by his uncompromising integrity, rare business ability, and strong demonstrative character, he was found to be eminently qualified. In 1810 he went from Goshen,

Ct., where he first engaged in mercantile life, to Blandford, Mass., and there at once inaugurated a business which has ever since distinguished the town. In 1811 he was married to Mary, only daughter of the late Col. Moses Lyman, of the former place. In 1819 he removed with his family to Hartford, Ct., and there retired from the mercantile business in 1842. He was a member of the Common Council of Hartford for several years; was elected mayor in 1843 and 1845. After establishing himself in Hartford, he united with the First Congregational Church, under the pastorate of the Rev. Dr. Hawes. He, however, withdrew his relationship in 1824, in order to assist in the formation of the North Congregational Church, (Rev. Dr. Bushnell's,) where he was from the first a deacon, also an active supporter of the Sabbath school, even retaining his Bible class till within a few weeks of his death.

The Hartford Evening Press said of him, "Positively, it is precisely true, and no unmeaning eulogy, if we say that the symmetry and strength of his physical man harmonized with his fine proportions as a Christian merchant, citizen, friend, and neighbor. He was such an outgrowth of New England hills, schools, and churches, as we can point to with pride."

The New York Evangelist also remarks, in an article entitled "A Model Church Officer," "It has been our privilege to know Dea. Collins, and we can add our testimony to his rare excellence. While inflexible in principle, his disposition was kind and gentle; and those who have shared the hospitality of his home know how welcome was the stranger, and how cordial and generous was his reception."

Rev. Dr. Bushnell, in an article bearing the title "A True Man," speaks of him as follows: —

"Dea. Collins was one of the few men or Christians who require to be noted as specialities. He was among the landmark characters of our city, and a man so positive, in every sphere of action or council, that the void which is made by his death will be deeply felt, and for a long time to come.

"His birth and education were distinctly and rigidly Puritan; and the perfectly unaccommodating, undeviating, and square fidelity of his life to first principles and convictions of duty was the spinal column, so to speak, of his character from first to last. His temperament was sanguine, athletic, forceful, and positive, and yet as genial and playful as, with so much of really foredoomed enterprise, efficiency, and progressiveness, it could be. The exactness, the perfect reliableness, and the fine business talent of his clerkship put him at once in full character and credit for any kind of business; and he made his beginning for himself, most characteristically, in creating a business that was not, and that required him to harness and guide the industrial methods of a whole agricultural community; becoming himself the purchaser and factor of their products, and holding them in connection, at his trading establishment, with all the best markets in the country. He was successful, for every thing he took hold of was bound to succeed; but the labor of so much travel, transportation, trade, and the multifarious cares of a business so complex, were too much for him, and he broke, after a time, under the load. He came to Hartford to find an easier business, and, as he supposed, to finish the few years that were left to him. Here his health rallied, and his former energies returned. Here, accordingly, has been the principal sphere of his life; and there is almost nothing here that has not somehow felt his power, nothing good that has not somehow profited by his beneficence. Banks, savings institutions, railroads, the singular anomaly of a large wholesale dry-goods trade which distinguishes Hartford as an inland city, the city improvements, the city missions and Sunday schools, the Asylum for the Dumb, the Retreat for the Insane, the high school, the almshouse, three at least of the churches, — almost every thing public, in fact, has his counsel, impulse, character, beneficence, and, what is more if possible, his real work incorporated in it. All the great societies of Christian beneficence were supported also by his bounty. He went to the last line of what he believed to be the true principles in respect to the wrongs of intemperance and slavery, and there held firm, taking no counsel with popularity; and what he held firm he advocated and thrust on with such energy as justified his convictions.

"In his business, from the first, he

had never any thought of nice fetches and adventures that would make him rich in a day. All gains of trade but such as are proportionate with industries employed, and services actually rendered in the transfer and distribution of products, were entirely out of his ken. His plan was to get his increase by earning it, as truly as if he had gotten it by the wages of toil. Hence there was never any gate open through which gusts of sudden expectation could break in, to fan his eagerness, or to unsettle his principles, and loosen the methods of his life. All trade became, in this manner, a drill in righteousness. He did not even allow his beneficence to mix with his business; that was squared by his rights and by the laws of exact arithmetic; and he must first know what he had to give or bestow before he began to loosen himself in deeds of allowance or charity.

"He lived up to the line of bounty without show, and squared all his expenditures by a rational and worthy economy. He trained his sons to industry, and to the expectation of being what they might become for themselves, and not what he might make them; only giving them such assistance as would stimulate their industry and enterprise. And he had the satisfaction, as every Christian man should, of seeing all his family early enrolled in the Christian church, and living in a way of repute to shed honor on his example.

"To the church of which he was one of the founders he was a pillar from the first, and, as he advanced in age, was more and more distinctly a father. He was habitually responsible for it as truly as for his family. Every appointment was a law to him, and found him promptly in his place. If there was any thing to be done for recovering a falling member, or restoring a general decline of duty, or remodelling the church, or lifting a debt, he was ready, not to encourage a little, and set on somebody else, but to work, taking always the heavy end himself, and that with such heartiness that every body saw the work was to be done.

"There was never a better man to support and steady a Christian pastor. If he saw defects, he covered them up with a mantle of wise forbearance. If there were parties on foot, he stood by his principles calmly, and let time work at them. He had no flatteries to bestow when he was pleased, and yet found a way to encourage by kind intimations. His counsel was never thrust upon a pastor, but, when sought, it was given impartially, and was never dishonored by the event.

"He resolved, some 20 years before his death, to lay up no more property, not even with a design to expend it in charities after his death. Since that time he has expended all his income carefully, allowing no deviation from the rule, except when he has drawn, as he is known more than once to have done, on his future income. In this manner, instead of cheating himself, as many do, with promises hereafter, but in fact never, to be fulfilled, he has made himself responsible, day by day, for true judgments of occasions, schooled himself thus into a sanctification of his judgments, kept his heart open, and taught his love to flow in the continuous flood of a river. In this manner he took the rewards of his beneficence into his own life, and grew by the Christly measures of his beneficence. No matter how much he dispensed in these 20 years, — be it $60,000, be it more, or be it less, — it is not in his will; it is in his own expanded life and person; and he has it with him still before God. That is the principal thing, and there his wisdom lay."

COLMAN, William, M. D., Pittsfield, Mass., April 27, æ. 92.

COLTON, Rev. George, Wethersfield, Ct., Feb. 12, æ. 79. He was born in West Hartford, son of Dea. Abijah Colton, who lived to 85 years of age. His grandfather was Rev. Benjamin Colton, the first minister of West Hartford, who was ordained Feb. 24, 1713. His uncle was Rev. George Colton, minister of Bolton, Ct., where he died about 80 years old. His own sons were three or four of them ministers. One of them, Rev. John Owen Colton, died a minister in New Haven, Ct. One is now the pastor of the First Church in Wethersfield. He was said to be one of the best scholars in the district school, and was especially elegant in his handwriting. He had great acquaintance with books before he entered college. He loved Latin and Greek. He undertook to read the whole college library, and especially those folios of the Latin fathers. He was less anxious to shine as a scholar than to be largely qualified for the Christian ministry. Jonathan Edwards, of Northampton, Dr. Bellamy, of Bethlem, Dr. Smalley, of New Britain, and Dr. Strong, of Hartford, were favorite authors with him. In that great attention in 1802, under Dr. Dwight's presidency, which produced a whole college of ministers, he was a mature Christian, able to be a counsellor and helper to the inquiring students. He labored as a minister near Cherry Valley, N. Y., many years; then in the military tract at Camillus, Pompey, De Ruyter, &c.; then near Niagara Falls; after which he lived in Ware, Mass., and in New Haven, Ct., and finished his course suddenly at Wethersfield. He was a great lover of Christ, a good minister, an experienced guide to anxious souls, a sound theologian, but not a popular preacher. His life and services were all employed in the work of the great Redeemer. His brother, Rev. Chester Colton, was a very good and acceptable minister, first at Brentwood, N. H., then at Lyme, Ct., then at Colebrook, Ct., then at North Bend, O., where he died, at the age of about sixty.

COMSTOCK, Dr. J. L., Hartford, Ct., Nov. 21, æ. 71. For nearly forty years he had lived in Hartford. He was born in East Lyme, Ct., and was a self-educated man. During the last war with Great Britain he was appointed to the post of a surgeon in the army, and was, it is believed, stationed near Lake Erie. He first went to Hartford when the recruiting office was opened there, near the stone bridge, and subsequently made it his place of residence. Here he wrote his book of Natural Philosophy, and the numerous other works which have contributed to make his name famous. Of these, we may mention his work on Chemistry, the one on Natural History, his Physical Geography, his work on Mineralogy, and his History of Gold and Silver. Of all his works, however, none have had such a wide sale as Comstock's Natural Philosophy, which has become a standard school book, and has gone through very numerous editions. It is supposed the sale of this book in the United States has reached nearly a million of copies. It has also met with marked success in Europe. Mr. C. was a man of decided opinions, and accustomed at all times to feel confidence in his own positions. He enjoyed the respect and esteem of the community in which he lived, and was a very worthy citizen.

CONDICT, Rev. Edward W., Morristown, N. J., Nov. 28, æ. 24. He was a recent graduate of Princeton Theological Seminary. A short period before his decease he went to Maryland to labor as a missionary; but upon the active duties of this work he was not permitted to enter.

CONDY, Col. Thomas D., Charleston, S. C., May 12, æ. —. For many years U. S. marshal in that city.

CONE, Elias De Long, Walworth, N. Y., Dec. 4, æ. 34. He had established a reputation as an able physician and surgeon. He was nearly five years in Mexico, in the army under Gen. Taylor, and served in the capacity of assistant surgeon. He held a professorship in Geneva College for two years. His residence for a few years past had been in Hinsdale, Mich., but his health failing, he came back to his former residence in Walworth. For years past he had been an acceptable member of the M. E. Church.

CONRAD, Hon. Robert T., West Philadelphia, Pa., June 27, æ. 48. He was born in Philadelphia, June 10, 1810. His father was John Conrad, for many years the most extensive publisher and bookseller in the United States, and at one time mayor of the Northern Liberties. Young Conrad studied law in the office of his uncle, Thomas Kittera, and was admitted to the bar in 1830. About the time of young Conrad's admission to the bar, he became connected with the press, and began a long series of elegant and forcible contributions to journalism. In 1832 he commenced the publication of the Daily Intelligencer, which was afterwards united with the ancient Philadelphia Gazette. In 1835 Conrad was called to the bench in one of the inferior courts. At that time he was the youngest judge, save one, in Pennsylvania. In March, 1838, he was appointed to a court of a higher jurisdiction, and in 1840 he was still further promoted. Subsequently, the constitution of the court was changed, and the judge returned to the practice of his profession as a counsellor and advocate. He mingled in politics, and won distinction as an orator and writer in defence of the doctrines of the whig party. He wrote leading articles for the North American, and also edited Graham's Magazine. In the mean time, he had achieved a great success in dramatic literature by the production of the tragedy of Jack Cade, which still keeps the stage, and is one of the most popular of plays. He contributed a number of minor poems to the periodicals of the day, a few of which have been highly commended. Upon the dissolution of the whig party, Judge Conrad connected himself with the American movement, and after the consolidation of the old city and the adjacent districts, he was elected mayor by a large majority. At this time he was also acting as president of the Hempfield Railroad. After the expiration of his term of office as mayor in 1856, he resumed the practice of the law. Shortly afterwards, Judge Kelley, of the Court of Common Pleas, having resigned, Gov. Pollock appointed the ex-mayor to fill the vacancy, and during the brief period that elapsed before the election, Judge Conrad discharged his duties with vigor, ability, and success. He was a candidate at the election for the same position, but was defeated by James R. Ludlow, the present judge. Judge Conrad then resumed the practice of his profession, which he continued up to the time of his sudden demise. He was the last of a circle of literary men who once shed lustre upon Philadelphia. He was a frequent orator before literary and political assemblages; and his command of language, his vivid fancy, and his peculiarly agreeable manner gave him great success on such occasions. Of a fine, commanding presence, with a voice of rare tenderness, which was at the same time capable of the most vehement expression and the most graceful gesticulation, whether he strove to persuade or arouse, he was equally successful, and many an audience has surged and swayed with the motion of his eloquence, both from the platform and the hustings. He was a man of undoubted genius, — impulsive, ardent, perhaps undisciplined and erratic, — but yet genius of a high order, which, under better control and united with greater earnestness and stability, would have won for him a high position among the great minds of the age. As a journalist, a political orator, a magistrate, and a poet, he exhibited very considerable ability, and he will also be remembered by many friends as a delightful conversationist and a very fascinating gentleman. At a meeting of the Philadelphia bar, it was said, they had heard, with sentiments of deep regret, of the sudden and unexpected death of the Hon. R. T. Conrad, their old associate and cherished friend, and now award to him superiority of intellect, with the reputation of a learned, wise, and urbane judge, a fearless and independent magistrate, an orator of consummate skill, and a writer of the highest attainments.

CONVERSE, Theron, Pamelia, N. Y., Nov. 28, æ. 85. He was a son of Col. Thomas Converse, an officer in the regular army of the revolution, and was born in Litchfield, Ct. Early in life he removed to the State of New York, and was settled in business at Watertown, from which place he retired to his farm in Pamelia, many years since. He had a family of fourteen children, who lived to mature years before death entered their circle. He had long been a consistent member of the Presbyterian church.

COOK, Byron F., Esq., New Orleans, La., Sept. 18, æ. 32. He was born in Jefferson Co., N. Y., 1826, and was the only son of Rev. E. P. Cook. He graduated at Hamilton College at the age of 22. He had for the last five years resided in Louisiana, and commenced the practice of law in New Orleans some four years since. At the time of his decease he was a member of the Young Men's Christian Association of that city. He was a young man of sterling integrity, and possessed energy of character which had gained for him an enviable reputation. As a son, brother, and friend, he was firm and devoted.

COOK, J. D., Esq., Sacramento, Cal., Nov. 29, æ. —. He had been lately a practising lawyer in Yreka, where he was well known.

COOKE, Dr. Wm. T. B., Philadelphia, Pa., March 6, æ. 29, son of Col. Giles B. Cooke.

COOLEY, Dr. Abiel A., Hartford, Ct., Aug. 18, æ. 76. He was the inventor of the "lucifer" or "locofoco" friction match; an article insignificant in itself, it is true, yet one that has become a material item in commerce, and a necessity in every household. He was also the inventor of one of the first power presses in use, as well as of an ingenious shingle machine, and was the first to apply the cam movement to pumps.

COON, Elder Daniel, Hopkinton, R.I., May 27, æ. 66, son of Elder Abram Coon, a former pastor of the First Hopkinton Church, and predecessor of Elder Matthew Stillman. He was called to the work of the ministry in the First Hopkinton Church, and received ordination April 4, 1819. The season is memorable in the history of that church, as at the same time four of her young men, viz., W. B. Maxson, Daniel Coon, Thomas Varnum Wells, and Amos Russel Wells, were called by the church to be ordained to the work of the gospel ministry. He preached some time in Brookfield, N. Y., but returned to his native town and preached for a number of years in the church of which his venerable father had been pastor. For some years past he preached in the Second Church in Hopkinton, where the closing labors of his life were devoted. He was arrested by the sickness which terminated his life while preaching in Westerly the ordination discourse of Elder Christopher C. Stillman.

COOPER, Rev. Preston, Holmes Co., Miss., Sept. —, æ. —. He was well known to have been one of the most useful men in the Mississippi conference for the last twenty years and more. He was a man of most extraordinary faith and piety. His confidence in the immediate presence and superintending providence of God, in all the details of practical life, was most extraordinary. He was well known and greatly beloved in all the territory of the conference where he lived and labored so faithfully, he having filled successfully all the most prominent appointments of that field. There is probably no man in this conference the living fruits of whose ministry are found so abundantly in all parts of the conference as those of Preston Cooper. His preaching was popular, solemn, eloquent, and convincing, while it carried with it a vein of originality and independence which gave him a high position as a pulpit orator. And, withal, he was a man of the most meek and humble spirit; he carried with him to his grave the elements of true greatness.

COOPER, Dr. George P., Memphis, Tenn., one of the oldest citizens.

CORBIN, Dr. Charles F., Fort Ann, N. Y., July 29, æ. 69. The deceased has long been a worthy citizen of Washington Co., a man of stern integrity and unblemished reputation. He died lamented by a large circle of friends.

CORCORAN, Dennis, Esq., ——, June —, æ. —. A telegraphic despatch elsewhere mentions Dennis C. as among the killed by the explosion of the steamer Pennsylvania. This will be sorrowful intelligence to the thousands who have known the deceased for years, and appreciated his many fine personal and social qualities. Mr. C. was a native of Ireland, and came to New Orleans in the year 1834. Shortly afterwards, he commenced a brilliant career in the press, as journalist and reporter for the Picayune. He soon achieved for himself and that journal an eminent reputation for that genial humor and graphic felicity of style which distinguished him as a man and a writer. He then became one of the founders of the New Orleans Delta, and remained in it as a proprietor and editor, with slight interruptions, until 1857. A few months ago he established the Sunday Magazine in this city, which was suspended about two weeks since. At the November election of 1853, Mr. C. was elected on the democratic ticket a representative from New Orleans in the state legislature. Having served out his term, he was subsequently elected, and served for two sessions, as reporter of the debates of the Louisiana state Senate. When Mr. C. was chosen to this last position, his old and steadfast friend and early associate in journalism, David Martin, was acting as reporter of debates in the Louisiana House of Representatives. These two worked lovingly and ably together in the foundation of the present leading journals in New Orleans. More transitory than what they helped so largely to create, both have passed away.— *New Orleans Delta*, June 15.

CORNELL, George, Newport, R. I., May —. He was the last but two of the gallant survivors from R. I. of the battle of Lake Erie. He was one of the noble band of about three hundred, who accompanied Com. Perry from Newport to the lake in the war of 1812, and was with the commodore in the Lawrence at the battle of Lake Erie, and rendered brave and efficient service. He was an honest man, an excellent citizen, and a consistent Christian. We believe that Capt. Thomas Brownell, U. S. navy, of Newport, and Dr. Usher Parsons, of Providence, are the only survivors of the memorable battle in R. I. His remains were interred with military honors by the artillery company under Col. Carr, and respect for his services and memory was also shown by the attendance of the mayor and city council, officers of the army and navy resident here, and a long procession of his fellow-citizens. At a meeting of the board of aldermen on Thursday, appropriate resolutions were passed, and communicated to the family of the deceased.

CORNISH, Rev. Samuel E., Brooklyn, N. Y., Nov. 5, æ. 65. He came to New York prior to the year 1820, and immediately commenced organizing a church, for the convenience of colored persons of the Presbyterian faith, who were till then debarred from any accommodations for worship, except such as were offered by the "negro pews" in other churches. In this enterprise he was eminently successful, and in a few years the first colored Presbyterian church in this city was erected in Elm Street. In the year 1826, in connection with the late John B. Russworm, Esq., he established a weekly paper, called Freedom's Journal, which soon became famous as an opponent of the Colonization Society. For nearly forty years he has been connected, and his name identified, with every enterprise having for its object the elevation of his people and the maintenance of their rights. He was a philanthropist, a patriot, and a Christian.

COTTER, Col. Cyrus, Damariscotta, Me., June 5, æ. 52. For many years past he had been one of that active and energetic class of men, of which there are but few left, who, years since, commenced the hazardous business of ship building at D. with no other capital than probity and industry, and pursued it until success crowned their efforts, and built up around the Damariscotta Bridge a wealthy and populous village. As one of that class he was in the true sense a public man. In business transactions he was honest, and had the confidence of those with whom he dealt, at home and abroad. He was a public-spirited and honorable man, and at all times manifested a sincere interest in whatever concerned the public good. For several years he represented his native town, Nobleboro', in the state legislature, and acquitted himself with credit.

COTTON, Miss Mary, Attica, N. Y., Oct. 16, æ. 68. She was the daughter of Capt. Rowland Cotton, one of the fifth generation in a direct line from Rev. John Cotton, the first settled minister of Boston, Mass. She emigrated with her father, in 1806, from Cherry Valley to the "Plains," near Buffalo, where, in the scenes incident to a pioneer life, and to a border warfare, which for some years raged in Western New York, she developed those domestic virtues for which she has been so distinguished through life. She was an only daughter, and losing her mother early in life, the care of her father's family devolved upon her — duties that she faithfully discharged. In 1835 the family removed to Attica, where she has since lived, respected for her virtues and loved for her deeds of kindness and affection.

COVENHOVEN, Christian, New York, Feb. 21, æ. 80. Mr. C. was descended from our oldest Dutch families, and of Huguenot origin; his ancestors were among the first that arrived and settled on the Island of Manhattan, or New Amsterdam. The Van Couenhovens, or Van Schouvenhovens, were identified with the interests and prosperity of that city in many important positions from its first foundation. Mr. C.'s father and grandfather both served through the revolution with distinction and honor; he himself was conspicuous in furnishing means and influence to raise a company (of which he was lieutenant) that was attached to the 1st regiment of artillery during the war of 1812, and was stationed at Sandy Hook and adjacent places. He was also commander of the old North Fort and other important defences during the war.

COWLES, Solomon, Norfolk, Ct., April 7, æ. 79, and WILLIAM S. COWLES, a son, April 23, æ. 43. The father was born in N., and was one of the industrious, quiet, working farmers of Ct., whose energies were constantly taxed to make his lands more productive, more valuable, and more beautiful. He was a free and willing supporter of good institutions, and in all public matters and interests of the town, where he always had lived, he was ever ready to lend a helping hand. The son had spent many years in Macon, Ga., as a merchant, and had lately returned to N. to comfort his parents in their old age. His mother survives.

Cox, Mrs. Mary, Albany, N. Y., Sept. —, æ. 102. Mrs. C. was born in Ireland, and came to this country in 1849. She was then in her 94th year, but hale and hearty as she was when she was 60. She was grandmother to John Savage, at present a resident of Washington, who was forced to flee from Ireland during the rebellion in 1848, having taken side with Meagher, O'Brien, and others. Since Mrs. C came to America, she has resided with Dr. Cox, at Albany. She was a very extraordinary woman, has never been sick — seriously sick — in her life, her death being caused by old age. She was a woman of strong mind, and died in possession of all her faculties. Her sight and hearing were as good when she reached her 102d birthday as they were during her school days. She was a member of the Episcopal church, and lived and died an exemplary Christian.

CRAGIN, Francis W., M. D., Greenfield, N. H., July 26, æ. 55. Dr. C. was born in Greenfield, July 20, 1803. After a preliminary education, he commenced the study of medicine with John Ramsay, M. D., in the year 1827, and finished his medical education at the medical school at Hanover, under the special direction of Prof. Muzzey, in the year 1829. In the year 1830 he sailed for Surinam, and landed at Paramaribo, its capital; and there, in a foreign city, among strangers, without the aid of wealthy ancestors to buoy him up, he soon acquired the native dialect, and rose to distinction as a medical practitioner and surgeon. He possessed a taste for natural history, and amid the perplexities that are incident to his profession, he assiduously employed himself in collecting the various specimens in natural history which are so abundant in South America, and with scientific descriptions, sent them to the Boston Society of Natural History, of which society he was chosen an associate member, in the year 1837. For his numerous contributions he repeatedly received the thanks of the society, and after his death, the president, Prof. Jeffries Wyman, offered the following resolutions: —

"*Resolved*, that the members of the Boston Society of Natural History have learned with deep regret, the death of their late associate, Dr. Francis W. Cragin.

"*Resolved*, that in his death the society has lost one of its most generous friends and benefactors."

Nov. 10, 1834, Dr. C. was married to Miss Julia Ann, daughter of Hon. Jacob Richardson, of his native town, who went to Surinam; but the tropical climate proving detrimental to her delicate constitution, he returned with her to her paternal home, where she died of consumption. Subsequently, he married Miss Martha I., daughter of Rev. Bancroft Fowler, of Greenfield. She also went to Surinam, and there found her resting place, leaving one daughter. Dr. C. was appointed consul in 1847, and such was his fidelity, that he held the office until his health became so impaired, in 1857, that it was thought advisable by his friends, for him to leave the tropical climate of Surinam, and return to his paternal residence in Greenfield. With his health much improved, and with his usual enterprise, he commenced repairing it for a country mansion, and married Miss Mary A., daughter of Rev. John Le Bosquet, of Greenfield. In a few months his disease returned with increased severity, and he died much lamented.

CRANDALL, Benjamin, Montgomery, Ala., Oct. 25, æ. 99, the last surviving hero of the revolution in that section of the country. He was buried on the 26th with military honors.

CRANDALL, Rev. Joseph, Salisbury, ——, March 19, æ. 86.

CRANKSKA, William H., San Francisco, Cal., Oct. 24, æ. 40, late acting consul at Tahiti, a native of Providence, R. I.

CRANSTON, Mrs. Ruth, Harmony, O., Feb. 12, æ. 90, widow of the late James Cranston. She was born at Scituate, Providence Plantation, in what is now Rhode Island, in 1767. She was the daughter of Gideon and Prudence Austin, formerly Prudence Angel. She was married to James Cranston in February 1786; moved to Athens Co., O., in 1812, and since the death of her husband, which occurred in June, 1833, has resided with her daughter, Mrs. Pruden.

CRAWFORD, Hon. Joel, Early Co., Ga., April 5, æ. 75, a gentleman long and favorably known to the people of Georgia. He read law in the office of the Hon. Nicholas Hare, in the city of Augusta, and having taken the benefit of a course of law lectures in Litchfield, Ct., under the auspices of Judge Reeve, was admitted to plead and practise in the courts of Georgia, at the spring term of Wilkes Superior Court, in 1808. He commenced his career at the bar in Sparta, but in 1811 removed to Milledgeville, where he resided to the close of his professional labors. In the war of 1812 he enlisted as a volunteer in a corps of dragoons, commanded by Capt. Steele, and was shortly after breveted aide-de-camp to Gen. Floyd — a post which he retained to the end of the campaign. This brevet gave Mr. C. the rank of major, and imposed on him perils and responsibilities in our Indian wars of that day, of fearful import, but which were sustained by him throughout, with credit to himself and honor to the country. The theatre of his military achievements was in that part of Georgia which now constitutes part of the territory of Alabama. He bore himself gallantly in the battle of Autossee, which was fought on the left bank of the Tallapoosa River, about thirty miles above its confluence with the Coosa; and again at Cauleebce Swamp. In both these engagements he had his horse shot from under him. He encountered many other perils of less notoriety, and always enjoyed the fullest confidence of his commanding general, of his comrades in arms, and of his country. Major Crawford was elected for two terms, a representative in Congress from Georgia, under the general ticket system, 1817 to 1821, and declined a nomination for a third term, that he might recruit his private fortunes, which had been much reduced by the unthrifty vocations of public life. At the earliest practicable moment he abandoned his profession as a lawyer, and gave himself mainly to agricultural pursuits. He repeatedly represented his county in the state legislature, and discharged, at intervals in his long life, important ministerial agencies for the state. In 1826 he was commissioned by Governor Troup to the difficult and exposed service of adjusting the boundary line between the States of Alabama and Georgia. Everard Hamilton and Richard Blount were associated with him in this commission. In 1837 the legislature, by a joint ballot of both houses, elected Maj. C., Samuel Farris, and Charles Bolton, a board of commissioners for the survey, location, and construction of the Western and Atlantic Railroad. By his associates he was chosen president of the board — a post he continued to occupy until that great work was nearly completed, and until the board was dissolved. He was a kind father, a provident and indulgent master, a benevolent neighbor, a fast friend, and a chivalrous and devoted patriot.

CRAWFORD, John M., Esq., Washington Co., Miss., May 19, æ. 85, father of Dr. S. P. Crawford, of Greenville, and Rev. W. H. Crawford. He had lived to a good old age, and was truly a model man; was kind and affectionate, hardly ever known to speak an unkind word to any person, and took a great delight in the comfort and happiness of his family.

CRAWFORD, Thomas, Bossier Parish, La., Feb. 27, æ. 34, at the residence of Dr. Shippy. In 1841 he graduated from the Alabama University with high honors. He was a man of talents, and of a commanding personal appearance. In 1844 he married Miss M. E. Gilkey, of Pickens Co., daughter of Walter Gilkey. He was a lawyer of no common abilities. His practice was extensive, enjoying the confidence of all who knew him. Generous to a fault, a community now mourns his loss.

CRAWFORD, Rev. William, Louisa Co., Va., April 5, æ. 86. It would be unjust to a life such as his to attempt to portray it in an obituary notice. To an intellect of no ordinary cast he added a decision of character and integrity of purpose which placed him above the roll of common men. An elevated and comprehensive devotion to the sublime truths of Christianity adorned his life, and displayed itself in a wise benevolence and discriminating charity wherever objects worthy of either were found. In all the relations of social and domestic life his conduct was governed not only by the kindness of his heart, but by conscientious convictions of duty, which nothing could seduce from the path they commanded him to pursue.

CRAWFORD, William S., Danville,

Ind., Dec. 17, æ. 68. He was born in Ireland in 1790, and came to Philadelphia in 1807. On the breaking out of the war between the United States and Great Britain in 1812, he joined Capt. Langhorn's company of the first rifle regiment of Kentucky militia, and afterwards participated in the bloody and disastrous battle of River Raisin, where he was wounded by a shot through the arm, and taken prisoner by the Indians. Most of his brave companions in arms who were captured with him were subsequently slain by the tomahawk of the savages in his presence; but, through what almost seems a miraculous agency, he escaped with his life, and was conveyed by his savage captors to Malden, where he was ransomed for a trifle by a generous-hearted British officer, and set at liberty. He served out the term for which he enlisted in the army, was honorably discharged, and returned to Bourbon Co., Ky. Afterwards (but at what precise date we are not able to say) he settled in Henry or Shelby Co., Ky., where he married, and lived till the year 1828, when he came to Danville, and settled on the lot where he died. In 1831 he was appointed postmaster at Danville by President Jackson.

CRIPPEN, Mrs. Mary L., Moscow, Rush Co., Ind., March 30, æ. •18, wife of E. H. Crippen, M. D.

CROCKER, Calvin J., Washington, D. C., March 7, æ. 33, son of Hon. Ira Crocker, of Portland, Me. He was a member of the advance party of exploring engineers of the South Pass wagon-road expedition, and a man of most daring and resolute character.

CROCKER, Edward, Portsmouth, Va., Aug. —, æ. 68. He was on board the unfortunate Chesapeake when the collision with the Leopard took place. He was one of the crew of the old Ironsides, when she escaped from the British fleet out of Long Island Sound, and in the same vessel participated in the fight with the Java, in which she became a prize to the Americans.

CROMPSTON, Mrs. Eliza, Philadelphia, Pa., March 15, æ. 82, daughter of the late Rev. Samuel Magaw, D. D., of the Protestant Episcopal church.

CROOKER, Mrs. Hannah, Bath, Me., ——13, æ. 83. Mrs. C. was the relict of Mr. Jonathan H. Crooker, who died something over 50 years ago, and was the mother of Messrs. Charles and William D. Crooker, distinguished and enterprising merchants and ship builders of Bath. She was the eldest daughter of the celebrated Dr. Samuel Eaton Duncan, whose residence was near Harding's station on the Brunswick side of the New Meadows, some 60 and 70 years ago. Of this ancient and honorable family Mrs. C. was the last surviving member. The family consisted of three children — two daughters and a son. The famous Dr. Waldron, who practised in Bath, and is remembered by many of her older citizens, married the younger sister; and the son, Capt. Samuel E. Duncan, the father of George W., Capt. William H., and Charles E. Duncan, died in Bath, at a ripe age, about a year ago. Mrs. C., through a long life of varied fortune, has always maintained a high place in the affections of a large circle of relations and friends.

CROOKS, Washington, Chambersburg, Pa., May —, æ. —. The bar of Chambersburg bear testimony to his character as follows: —

"*Resolved*, that in the decease of Washington Crooks, Esq., society has lost a valuable member — one whose voice was ever heard in advocacy of those measures of reform advanced for the amelioration of the wronged and the promotion of the interests of the unfortunate and destitute; general education, a firm and ardent supporter and constant friend; Christianity, a humble follower and bold defender; his profession, an earnest student and eloquent advocate; and the family circle, a kind brother and tender husband.

"*Resolved*, that we cheerfully accord to him the best qualities that go to make up the true man. His intellect was of no ordinary character, and, under the adverse circumstances of poverty and ill health, boldly cut a way for itself to distinction among his fellows; his heart was large; his soul, sincere; and the pleadings of his eloquent tongue still echo through the hearts of his many friends."

CROOKS, Dr. Joseph, Fayetteville, Pa., Oct. 21, æ. 52, formerly of Lietersburg, Md. He was a kind father, an obliging neighbor, a good physician, an ornament to society; and his place will not easily be filled.

CROSS, Col. Hardy, Nansemond Co.,

Sept. —, æ. 83. Col. C. was one of the wealthiest and most useful citizens of the county. He leaves a widow and two daughters to lament their loss.

CROSWELL, Dr. Andrew, Mercer, Me., June 4, æ. 80. Dr. C. was born at Plymouth, Mass., April 9, 1778. He graduated at Harvard College in 1798, in the same class with the late Rev. William E. Channing, D.D., Rev. Joseph Tuckerman, D. D., and Hon. Joseph Story, LL. D. He studied medicine with Dr. Zaccheus Bartlett, of Plymouth. On completing his professional studies, he settled as physician in the town of Fayette, Me., and subsequently removed to Mercer, which was afterwards his permanent residence. He acquired an extensive practice; and by his skill and success he gained the entire confidence, not only of the people of the town in which he resided, but of all the neighboring towns, and was frequently called to long distances in consultation in difficult cases. He was a man of the kindest feelings; and to the indigent he was ever prompt to render his best services, without expectation of reward other than the consciousness of having relieved the sufferings of a fellow-being. He was justly entitled to the appellation the apostle bestowed upon St. Luke; namely, "the beloved physician." He married Susan Church, of Farmington, Me., by whom he had six children — four sons and two daughters. One of his daughters has deceased. All his other children, with his widow, survive him.

CROSWELL, Rev. Harry, D. D., New Haven, Ct., March 13, æ. 83. He had been rector of an Episcopal (Trinity) church there 43 years, to Jan. 1, 1856. He had officiated at 2553 baptisms, 873 marriages, 1842 burials. He was father of the late Rev. Dr. William Croswell, of Christ Church, Boston, and of Sherman, for many years editor of the Albany Argus, and of Frederick, for many years judge of the Probate Court of New Haven. A newspaper, the Balance, was edited by him from 1803 to 1808. This was rather a violent anti-Jefferson paper. For some of his remarks on Jefferson's conduct Mr. C. was prosecuted for libel. An account of his trial was published.

CROWE, Rev. Frederick, New York city, Nov. 7, æ. —. Mr. C. went from Great Britain, about 20 years ago, to Belize, and established himself as an independent missionary. After about 13 years' evangelical labor among the Spanish people, he became satisfied of the necessity of a wide circulation of the Scriptures. The only versions accessible were very defective; and he returned to Great Britain, and interested a number of Christians in Edinburgh and other places, who formed an association for procuring an improved edition of the Spanish Scriptures. He subsequently visited the United States, and secured the favor of the American Bible Union, under whose auspices an excellent translation was made, in conjunction with the friends of the cause in Great Britain. About two or three years ago he returned to the Central Spanish American States to resume his labors. He sustained himself in the field by teaching, and was supplied with copies of Scriptures by the American Bible Union. Every thing prospered with him till persecution hedged up his way. He was imprisoned, harassed, and at last driven by mob violence from the country. His life was in danger till he was safe on the steamer at Panama. His exposures and imprisonments brought on a fatal sickness. Since his arrival in New York, a few days before his death, he had been gradually sinking, and now lies in death, a martyr for the Word of God.

CULBERTSON, Joseph, Chambersburg, Pa., July 26, æ. 79. He was born Feb. 27, 1779, in that section of Franklin Co., Pa., known as Culbertson's Row, which had been settled by his forefathers prior to the revolutionary war. He was of Scotch descent, and possessed many of the striking qualities of that people. At an early age he embarked in mercantile business; at a later period of his life he was elected high sheriff of Franklin Co. He reared and educated a large family of children, some of whom have filled and now occupy prominent public positions. His second son, Alexander, was connected with the American Fur Company, where, by his energy, talent, and industry, he amassed a fortune, and conducted with great ability all the enterprises of that vast corporation. He is mentioned favorably by Irving in his Astoria. He contributed largely to the collections in the Smithsonian Institute, and has aided science in many of her various branches. One of his sons, the

Rev. Simpson Culbertson, after graduating at West Point as a cadet, abandoned the army and studied theology, and has for many years been zealously and efficiently laboring as a missionary in China. A younger son, the Rev. Thaddeus Culbertson, was just entering with much promise upon his career of usefulness when he was stricken down suddenly by death, Aug. 28, 1850. His daughter, Anna M., died in Christian triumph, April 8, 1858, just after her brother embarked on his return to his mission labors in China. Mr. C., for the last ten years of his life, was president of the Bank of Chambersburg; and perhaps much of the success of that institution might be traced to the character for honesty and truth that so characterized its head. He was a member of the Presbyterian church of Chambersburg, and gave full evidence of his genuine piety. For nearly half a century he had been associated with the interests of Chambersburg, and lived within its limits long enough to see a generation pass away. He had survived nearly all those with whom he had started in life; a few veterans like himself only remaining as specimens of a race of men now numbered with the dead. Full of years, surrounded by his family, loved and respected by the community in which he lived, and honored by all who knew him, he has gone down to a Christian's grave with all a Christian's hopes about him.

CUMING, Gov. T. B., Omaha, N. T., Mar. 23, æ. —. "Nothing," says a private letter, "could have occurred to cast a deeper gloom over this community. He was a universal favorite, and died without a personal enemy in the world." Gov. C. was, before his removal to Nebraska, the editor of a Democratic paper at Keokuk, Iowa, and exercised very considerable influence upon the politics of that state. He was a man of very considerable ability, and was successful in attaching friends to him wherever he went. On President Pierce's accession to the presidency, he selected Gov. C. for the office which he held at the time of his death. To native talents of the first order he added the advantages of classical learning and of wide experience. The whole territory has sustained an irreparable loss. The city of Omaha, for the benefit of which his best efforts had been exerted, and which is indebted to him in a greater degree than to any other man for the proud station she now occupies, deplores, as with one voice, his untimely decease. The loss of no man among us would have been as severely felt as that of Gov. C. The tolling of the bell which announced his death met with a mournful response from the hearts of all within the hearing of its sound.

CUMMINGS, James P. C., M. D., Fitchburg, Mass., Aug. 27, æ. 28, only child of Rev. Preston and Alona D. Cummings, of Leicester. He studied his profession with Dr. Trow, of Buckland, and Dr. Workman, of Worcester, and attended lectures at the Berkshire Medical Institution and Harvard University, where he received his degree on a special examination in 1850, and immediately commenced practice in Leicester, Mass. In May, 1855, he removed to Fitchburg, where he had a steadily increasing practice till Feb., 1858, when, by great exposure in the performance of his professional duty, he sickened and of consumption died. He was eminently successful and highly prized by his employers, and left behind him that which is rather to be chosen than great riches. He died lamented by all who knew him.

CURTIS, Judge ——, Lawrence, K. T., Feb. 15, æ. —. He was a member of the territorial legislature, formerly judge of probate, and for a period president of the convention which formed the Topeka Constitution.

CURTIS, Andrew J., Esq., (of Vicksburg, Miss.,) De Peyster, St. Lawrence Co., N. Y., July 5, æ. 30, at the residence of his father, Jonathan Curtis, Esq. Mr. C. was born in De Peyster, and there came to man's estate, when he emigrated south, and settled in Vicksburg, where he resided until Feb., 1858, when rapidly declining health compelled him to relinquish a lucrative business, in which he had amassed a respectable fortune during his eight years' sojourn in that city. He was descended from an ancestry of octogenarian age, and was himself of robust constitution until Sept., 1855, when a severe attack of yellow fever greatly impaired its vigor, and induced the fatal disease (consumption) in the prime of life and the very zenith of his usefulness. He had that about him which favorably impressed the beholder — in stature above the common height, perfect symmetry in form, manly features, cordial manners, fluent and impressive conversation. Sound judgment, quick perception, and indomitable energy were the characteristics of his mind; honesty, purity, and benevolence, the qualities of his heart. It was the fortune of Mr. C. to enjoy to a large extent the friendship and esteem of the community in which he lived, and to be honorably identified with its success and prosperity. He entered upon the stern realities of another world with satisfactory assurance and calm resignation.

CURTIS, David, Esq., Augusta, Oneida Co., N. Y., May 14, æ. 87. He migrated from his native place in Litchfield Co., Ct., in 1796, and was one of the earliest and most enterprising pioneers before whose vigor the wilderness of Central New York receded, to give place to the abodes of industry and civilization. He was a man of no less decided integrity than energy of character, and ever faithful to the public trusts committed to him, as well as to all the private relations of life.

CURTIS, Thomas M., Mobile, Ala., Oct. 9, æ. 38.

CURTIS, Joseph, Esq., Jamaica Plain, West Roxbury, Mass., Feb. 13, æ. 85 yrs. 4 mos. 20 days. His great-great-grandfather, William Curtis, with his wife, Sarah, and four children, came from England to America in the year 1632, and settled on a farm lying on Stony River, in Roxbury, where he had four more children born to him. His youngest child, Isaac, born in 1642, inherited the homestead, with the condition that he should take care of his parents in their old age. The emigrant, William, died Dec. 8, 1672, æ. 80. His wife, Sarah, died March 20, 1673, æ. 73. The old homestead is now in possession of the fifth Isaac Curtis, who has also a son of that name.

CURTISS, Rev. Amasa S., Holland Patent, Oneida Co., N. Y., Dec. 27, æ. 52. He was 30 years old when he left the farm for the duties of the ministry. After serving the Baptist church at Hastings a number of years, he preached successively at Rose Valley, Red Creek, Copenhagen, Westmoreland, South Butler, Holland Patent, and Steuben. He was eminently a man of faith and prayer, was mild and amiable in disposition, a good pastor, and spiritual and evangelical as a preacher. He was a man of an unblemished moral character, and in all the relations of life demeaned himself as a Christian, and won the respect and confidence of all.

CUTLER, Miss Lydia Belknap, Hanover, Mass., Dec. 18, æ. 64, at the residence of her brother, the Rev. Samuel Cutler, rector of St. Andrew's Church. Miss C. was the eldest child of Samuel and Lydia Prout Cutler, and was born in Newburyport, Mass., Nov. 2, 1794. She led a retired, but a most useful and devoted life, full of good works. She was Thought, to move others as hands. She was ever watchful, and knew when, where, and how a good deed should be performed. She was a patient Christian. It is well in this connection to record the melancholy catastrophe which terminated the lives of her parents. In their deaths they were not divided. June 28, 1832, being then on board the packet schooner Rob Roy, bound from Newburyport, Mass., to Portland, Me., by a sudden gust of wind the vessel was capsized, and they, with three others of their fellow-passengers, were drowned. The bodies were recovered, and on Sunday, July 1, were laid in the burial ground connected with the Episcopal church in Newburyport, of which, for many years, both had been communicants. They were most respectable and venerable people; and their sad end filled the town with intense anguish and deepest sorrow. The father was 79, and the mother 63.

CUTRIGHT, Mrs. Rebecca, Upshur Co., Va., Dec. 5, æ. 106. She was the first white woman who settled in the valley of the Buckhanon River, coming to Western Virginia when quite young, and living with her husband in a hollow tree at the mouth of Turkey Run, in what is now Upshur Co. The deceased retained all her faculties in vigor until the close of her long and eventful life, and on the morning of her decease caressed one of her great-grandchildren. Her descendants number over 400.

D.

DABNEY, Francis O., Beyrout, Syria, Dec. 26, æ. 28, of Boston. He was son of Charles William and Frances Alsop (Pomeroy) Dabney, and was born in Fayal, Azores, (where his father resides as American consul,) March 17, 1830. His mother was formerly of Brighton, Mass. He was fitted for college mostly under tutors in Fayal, and the last year under the instruction of Eben Smith Brooks, of Cincinnati, (H. U., 1835.) Immediately after graduating, he entered the counting room of Messrs. Dabney & Cunningham, of Boston, and was subsequently admitted as a partner. On the 15th of September last, he left New York for Liverpool, on business of the house. He was in perfect health until near the middle of December, when he was seized with an alarming illness, which in two weeks terminated fatally. Mr. Dabney had not gone far enough in life's journey to be known to many beyond the circle of his friends, but his energy and upright manliness struck all who came near him. Seldom is so much firmness and integrity and such a chivalrous sense of honor shown by one so young. For these noble qualities he might well be esteemed by all who knew him.

DALAND, Tucker, Esq., Salem, Mass., ———, æ. —. Mr. D. was born in Salem, in 1795, and was a grandson of the late Mr. Benjamin Daland, who was a prominent actor at the North Bridge, on that memorable day when Col. Leslie's regiment was defeated in the attempt to seize some cannon in North Salem, being the first demonstration of successful resistance of the "rebels" to the king's forces — an event imperishably connected with our revolutionary history. Mr. D. received his education at the classical school of the late Mr. William Biglow, at the period of a very high standard of intellectual and moral culture in Salem, for both male and female instruction. After leaving school, he entered the counting house of the late Joseph Peabody, Esq., and for a series of years Mr. D. was "the head and front" of the very extensive and successful business of that eminent merchant, whose confidence he enjoyed in the highest degree, continuing to fill important trusts with his usual skill and fidelity, after the death of his early patron and friend. Possessed of a vigorous constitution and a sound judgment, he was enabled to bring the full force of his experienced and comprehensive mind to bear upon his extensive business relations. As a merchant, he was eminently successful, of upright and honorable feelings, and of untiring industry. As a highly valuable and useful citizen, of sound morality and purity of mind, a great lover of his country, and a sincere friend and benefactor of the poor, Mr. D. had but few equals. As instances of his charities, which were dispensed not only without ostentation, but under the strictest promise of secrecy on the part of the almoners, it may not be improper now to mention that, within the last year or two, he has paid to one of the provision dealers, not less than three hundred dollars for meats furnished to the poor, and that during the last season he supplied the means for providing fifty loaves of bread per diem for a period of four months. On one occasion, casually ascertaining that a townsman, who was about to remove to the west, was arrested for debt as he was upon the point of starting in the cars, Mr. D. became responsible for the demand, which he fully discharged without a thought of recompense. These facts are enumerated only as illustrations of his method of benevolence, and of his kindly impulses. His home was the abode of domestic happiness and tranquillity, and of a generous hospitality. His memory will be long cherished, and the benefit of his example long felt.

DANA, A. W., Indianapolis, Ind., Nov. 27, æ. —, general superintendent of the Bellefontaine Railroad, formerly of Boston, Mass.

DANA, Mrs. Mehitable, Conway, N. H., Nov. 18, æ. 79, relict of the late Hon. Judah Dana, of Fryeburg, Me.

DANCE, William S., Esq., Powhattan C. H., Va., Feb. 11, æ. 69, clerk of the county.

DANE, Hon. Joseph, Kennebunk, Me., May 1, æ. 79. He was son of John and Jemima (Fellows) Dane, and was born in Beverly, Mass., Oct. 25, 1778. He was a descendant of John Dane, who emigrated from England, and settled in Ipswich, Mass., about the year 1648. Both his parents were natives of Ipswich. They died in Beverly, where they lived, the father, March 5, 1829, in his 80th year, and the mother, April, 1827, aged 76 years. Mr. D. was fitted for college at the Phillips Academy, Andover, and graduated at Harvard College, 1799, with the second honors of his class. After leaving college, he pursued his legal studies in the office and under the instructions of his uncle, Hon. Nathan Dane, of Beverly, (H. U., 1778,) and was admitted to the bar in Essex Co., in July, 1802. Besides the advantages to be derived from the large experience, exact and varied learning, and practical good sense of his immediate instructor, he could not fail to be benefited by the intimate association of the latter with Prescott, Jackson, Putnam, and Story, who were then beginning to be distinguished for professional excellence, and became the ornaments of the bar and the bench. After his admission to the bar, Mr. D. immediately began the practice of law in Kennebunk, at that time a part of the town of Wells, where he soon became distinguished as an able lawyer and an upright and safe counsellor. He continued in active practice in the profession until 1837, when he retired. As a practitioner he was courteous, faithful, and honest, and sought, by the influence of his own example, to elevate the character of the profession for integrity and moral excellence. "He concerned himself with the beginnings of controversies, not to inflame, but to extinguish them. He felt that he owed a duty to the community in which he lived, and whose peace he was bound to preserve. He was eminently a peacemaker, a composer of dissensions, and constantly aimed to prevent the mischiefs which follow in the train of litigation." To him may very justly be applied the language used in regard to another — that " he cast honor upon his honorable profession, and sought dignity, not from the ermine or the mace, but from a straight path and a spotless life." He was the last survivor of those who were members of the bar of York when he began practice ; among whom were the honored names of Mellen, King, Holmes, Hubbard, and Wallingford. In 1819 he was a member of the convention which framed the constitution of Maine, and took an active part in its proceedings and deliberations, and was one of the committee which draughted the constitution, Mr. Holmes being chairman. Associated with him in this important committee, among others, were Chief Justice Whitman, Generals Wingate and Chandler, Judges Bridge, Dana, and Parris. On the admission of Maine into the Union, in 1820, he was elected a member of the 16th Congress, from the first district, to complete the unexpired term made vacant by the election of Mr. Holmes to the Senate, and also a member of the 17th Congress. Subsequently he was in the state legislature, as a member of the House, in the years 1824, 1825, 1832, 1833, 1839, and 1840, and was a member of the Senate in 1829. In 1841 he was elected a member of the executive council of Maine, but declined to accept the office. He fulfilled the duties of the various and important public trusts confided to him, with acknowledged ability, great singleness of purpose, and with an earnest, patriotic desire to advance the public interest. After his retirement from the bar and from public duties, he always interested himself deeply in whatever was calculated to promote the welfare of the community. Few men have lived so long and enjoyed so largely and uniformly the confidence, respect, and esteem of their fellow-citizens. He married Oct., 1808, Miss Mary Clark, daughter of Hon. Jonas Clark, of Kennebunk, and granddaughter of the Rev. Jonas Clark, of Lexington, Mass., (H. U. 1752,) a lady of great excellence of character, who survives him. He had three children, two sons and a daughter. The sons survive him, and are prominent citizens of York Co. Hon. Nathan Dane, of Alfred, and Joseph Dane, Jr., of K. He was happy in his domestic and social relations, kind, affectionate and benevolent.

DANFORTH, Mrs. Naomi, Hillsboro', N. H., May 18, æ. 80. Her mother in her 100th year attended the funeral. Eighty years ago the present season, the mother, with the deceased in her arms, rode on horseback from Lempster through Washington and Hillsboro', most of the way by marked trees, crossed the Contoocook in a canoe, the horse swimming after, and visited the early settlers in Henniker.

DANIEL, Willie Augustus, Weldon, N. C., May 11, æ. 32, son of Hon. John

R. J. Daniel. Educated to business, he took upon himself the management of his father's plantation, — he being most of his time at Washington as a member of Congress — and evinced much judgment and energy, and remarkable promptness and sagacity in the adoption of means to the accomplishment of an end — a faculty indicative of a high order of intellect. In person the deceased was tall and well proportioned, with fine and well-developed features, and was exceedingly handsome and prepossessing in his appearance and demeanor. He possessed a strong mind, good understanding, a well-balanced judgment, and a tenacious memory. His heart was susceptible of deep and tender impressions, and he was magnanimous, generous, and benevolent, almost to a fault. He seemed to delight in doing good to others, rather than to himself.

DANIEL, Capt. W. J., Marion, Miss., Dec. 31, æ. —. Capt. D. had long been a citizen of Lauderdale Co., and has so demeaned himself that it is not unfair to say that no man in the country enjoyed more the confidence and esteem of his fellow-citizens. In the Mexican war Capt. D. raised a company of volunteers, of which he was chosen captain, and went to the tented field to serve his country. He discharged the duties of his office while engaged in the Mexican war, so as at once to gain the approbation of his superior officers, and the respect and love of his men. Capt. D., though laying no claims to brilliancy as a lawyer, was always regarded as possessing solid legal attainments. For years previous, and at the time of his death, he had a law partnership with the Hon. Sylvanus Evans, one of the first lawyers in East Mississippi.

DANIELS, Constans Freeman, New London, Ct., Oct. 20, æ. 69. He was editor of the Cheraw Spectator from 1825 to 1828, and of the Camden Journal from 1828 to 1833. Mr. D. was born in the town of Waterford, in the year 1789. He was educated for the profession of the law, studying first with the late Gen. Isham, then a leading member of the bar in this city, and afterwards with Judge Matthew Griswold, of Lyme. In 1821 he commenced to practise, locating in the town of Middle Haddam, in Middlesex Co., Ct. Four years later, in 1825, he removed to Cheraw, in South Carolina, where he commenced his editorial career as editor of the Cheraw Spectator. In 1828 he removed again to Camden, in the same state, where he published the Camden Journal, which in his hands was a stanch, unflinching Union paper, during the nullification excitement of those times. He continued in the charge of the Journal until the year 1833, when he returned to the north, and soon after became connected with the editorial department of the New York Courier and Enquirer. Four years later, in company with a Mr. Lang, he bought the New York Gazette, of which he was the editor until the year 1839. In that year he again became an associate editor with Gen. James Watson Webb, of the Courier and Enquirer, and remained connected with that journal until he finally removed in 1848, and took charge of the Chronicle. In the summer of 1857, after ten years of service as the editor of the Chronicle, he was attacked by severe illness, and compelled to retire from the active duties of his profession. His health and strength rapidly failed, and all measures adopted to effect his restoration to health were found to be unavailing. The Daily Star, in speaking of his death, says, "He was a man of more than ordinary ability — of extensive reading — high culture — high toned — independent — a generous friend and bitter enemy. For keen, pungent, biting paragraphs, he was hardly surpassed in the fraternity. He left a wide circle of friends to deplore his loss."

DARLING, Dr. George W., Constable, N. Y., June 15, æ. 61, formerly of Woodstock, Vt.

DAUBY, Martin Van Buren, Esq., San Francisco, Cal., March 16, æ. 27, son of Augustine G. Dauby of Utica, N. Y. He was a lawyer by profession, was gifted with fine mental endowments and good social qualities, which made him a favorite with his acquaintances in Utica.

DAVENPORT, Col. William, Philadelphia, Pa., April 12, æ. —. He distinguished himself at Chippewa and Bridgewater, in the war of 1812; also in the Black Hawk war, under Gen. Taylor.

DAVIDSON, Mrs. Ede Harris, Shelbyville, Tenn., March 15, æ. 37, wife of Hon. H. L. Davidson, and daughter of Robert P. and Eliza W. Harrison, of S. Mrs. D. was a native of S., and with the exception of a brief period, had spent the whole of her life there, and was well known to the whole community, and as truly beloved as she was generally known. It could not have been otherwise. Possessing an attractive person, easy and engaging manners, a heart full of kindness and overflowing with sympathy, she could only be known to be loved. To all those natural traits that adorn and beautify the character, were added the refining and sanctifying graces of Christianity. She knew no sloth in her Master's service, was ready for every good work, and equally prompt to partake of the happiness of the happy, and share the sorrows of the sorrowing. In all the varied relations of life, of daughter, wife, mother, sister, mistress, and friend — she was a model of warm and affectionate fidelity.

DAVIES, Edgar W., Esq., Williamsburg, N. Y., May 27, æ. 58. Many years ago Mr. D. published a paper, in New York, called The Old Countryman, and was also connected with other publications here and in Boston. Subsequently he adopted the profession of law reporter, and as such became widely known to our public men, judges, lawyers, and citizens generally; and from all who knew him he won respect and confidence by his gentle, unobtrusive manners, his integrity of character, and his love of truth. As law reporter, and in other capacities, he has been connected with The Sun for the last fourteen or fifteen years; and in discharging his responsible duties as a reporter, he was distinguished by his extreme caution, so scrupulously anxious was he to avoid committing an error, or doing an injury to any one unwittingly. In his private and domestic life he was of an amiable and affectionate disposition.

DAVIS, Dr. B. F., Post Oak Springs, Roane Co., Tenn., æ. about 35. He stood deservedly high as a successful physician, and an energetic farmer and citizen.

DAVIS, David, Brooklyn, N. Y., Nov. —, æ. 105. He was born near Morristown, N. J., in October, 1754. On the breaking out of the revolutionary war he resided in East Chester, Westchester Co., N. Y., and enlisted in the American army as a soldier, but being familiar with the management of horses, he was made a teamster, in which capacity he served in many of the battles of the revolution. At the close of the war he returned home, and remained on his farm until the troubles of 1812, when he was again called out, but did no active duty. He went to Brooklyn thirty years ago.

DAVIS, Gen. John, East Liberty, Pa., Nov. 29, æ. 87. He was born in Franklin Co. At an early age he desired military employment, and sought a position in the army of his country. He received commissions from Presidents Jefferson, Madison, and Monroe. As private and officer he served his country for fourteen years. In 1807 he, with a company for the south-west, descended the Ohio in keel boats. He served for seven years under command of Gen. Andrew Jackson. In the Indian wars in Florida he distinguished himself, and especially so at the battle of the Horseshoe. He was afterwards at the battle of New Orleans, as a captain in the army, and was one of Gen. Jackson's aids. Here he undertook a most dangerous duty, — that of obtaining a supply of ammunition for the American army, — which he successfully accomplished, with the loss of a number of men and the mules attached to the wagons. For his success in this hazardous undertaking he received the honorable appointment of brevet major. In 1815 he retired from the army, after the close of the war had rendered his active services no longer necessary to his country. During the administration of President Jackson he received the appointment of U. S. marshal for the western district of Pennsylvania.

DAVIS, Rev. S. -Hammer, Amelia Court House, Va., July —, æ. 28, pastor of the Presbyterian Church there. He was a native of Maryland, and a graduate of Hampden Sidney College.

DAVISON, Dr. Samuel, Greece, N. Y., Dec. 15, æ. 65. He was a much respected citizen and physician, and served as a justice of the peace.

DAY, Rev. David P., Webster City, Iowa, Oct. 16, æ. 55. He had been for many years a local preacher in the M. E. church, and none knew him but to love him. For the last two years he supplied the work on that frontier mission.

DEAN, Isaac, Adrian, Mich., March 3, æ. 86. He went to that place at a very early day. He assisted in the erection of the old flouring mill known as the "red mill," the first erected in the county. He also erected the first public house in that place, in 1828, then and now known as the "Exchange." During the early settlement of Southern Michigan Mr. D. was well known to all who in those trying times were seeking homes in that section, the then "far west," and he was always ready to lend a helping hand to those who needed aid. He had previously settled in New York, as early as 1791, in what was called Genesee Country, now town of Phelps, Ontario Co. His benevolence was confined to no sect or color; all who were in want found in him a friend ready to help, and in his upright life he was always respected.

DEANE, Dr. Ezra, Cambridge, Mass., Sept. 8, æ. 70, late of Biddeford, Me.

JAMES DEANE, M. D.,

Greenfield, Mass., June 8, æ. 57. He was born at Coleraine, Franklin Co., Mass., Feb. 24, 1801. Though called away in the full strength and vigor of manhood, he left behind him a name bright with every manly virtue, and which posterity will delight to honor. In his early days fortune favored him not; auspicious winds blew for him no favoring gale; but unbending integrity, firm purpose, and indomitable perseverance made him, in the brief half century in which he lived, what he was, and what he strove to be — the eminent physician and surgeon, the scientific discoverer, and the high-minded, noble man.

Born amid the rugged but picturesque hills of Western Massachusetts, his early years were spent in labor upon his father's farm, and his opportunities for obtaining an education were in no way superior to those enjoyed by others in like circumstances. He, however, early manifested an earnest desire for the acquisition of useful learning, and a strong disposition for study.

On arriving at the age of 21, he left his paternal home, and obtained a situation as clerk in the office of the judge of probate in Greenfield. Here he remained four or five years, at the end of which time he entered himself as a student of medicine, in the office of the late Dr. Brigham, of Utica, N. Y., then of G. He now found himself in a position better suited to his mind, and with a steadiness of purpose and zeal worthy of success, he bent the full strength of his talents to the study of the profession. He attended lectures at Columbia College, N. Y., and graduated there in 1831. Returning to Greenfield, he opened an office. Professional practice was slow in reaching him, and most men would have despaired of success; but not so with Dr. Deane. Though he must have felt much the need of encouragement, he did not yield to discouragements. His leisure was devoted to study, and he made himself no less the student now than while nominally so, and aimed to add to his storehouse of knowledge each day something that would better fit him for those arduous labors destined to devolve upon him in after years, when the high honors of brilliant professional success fell thickly around him.

For many years previous to his death he enjoyed an extensive and constantly increasing practice, and each year but added new honors to his fame. In his skill and judgment not only his patients, but his professional brethren, implicitly relied. As a counsellor he was often called many miles from his home, and as an operative surgeon he was eminently and widely distinguished.

It was in the early part of his practice that his attention was directed to the science of geology and its kindred branches. In 1835 he first pressed upon scientific notice his discovery of the fossil footprints in the red sandstone of the Connecticut valley. At the time of his death he was about publishing an elegantly illustrated work upon the subject, delineating and describing by his own hand the many different species of footprints he had discovered or caused to be discovered, the result of twenty-four years' investigation and labor. We trust it will yet be published, that the scientific world may reap its benefit. Considering the disadvantages under which he labored in early life, and the age at which he entered upon scientific and professional studies, the amount of labor he accomplished seems remarkable.

He was possessed of a versatile and active mind, and talents of no ordinary degree. He was emphatically self-taught and thoroughly versed, not only in the various branches of his profession, but upon subjects political and scientific in general. He was a frequent contributor to Silliman's Journal. In personal appearance he was singularly tall and symmetrical, and his bearing was dignified and majestic. Seen in the railroad car, or among his fellowmen any where, a stranger would have singled him out as one distinguished above the rest. His deportment was at all times unassuming; he never sought to make himself popular, and ever regarded such efforts with contempt. He was a man of few words, and never gave idle or hasty opinions. His conclusions were the result of consideration, and hence could be relied upon. No man could manifest greater coolness or deliberation than he, or firmness in cases requiring it; yet his delicacy and gentleness were remarkable. Eminently social and domestic, he was a most kind and devoted husband and father, and a true friend. Many were the anxious inquirers and expressions of solicitude made at his door, when it was announced that he lay upon the bed of sickness, and, alas, of death. All seemed anxious to do something for him who had beforetime ministered to their needs with so tender and skilful a hand. But all in vain were the efforts of family, physicians, and friends; he died after a brief illness of three weeks. Deep was the feeling manifested at the last sad rites of his burial. Hundreds, eager to show their tribute of respect and gratitude to his memory, crowded the church and its vestibule, and followed his remains to their last resting place upon the spot he himself had chosen. But not yet could he be suffered to rest unblessed by the community in which he had lived. Eight weeks after, citizens, friends, and mourners were gathered together to listen to the eulogy pronounced upon his life and character by Dr. Bowditch, of Boston.

At a meeting of the Boston Natural History Society, it was said by T. T. Bouvé,—

"Of his ability as a doctor of medicine others present are far more competent to speak than myself; but I quote the language of one well acquainted with him, in the statement that 'his success and skill were acknowledged in all the various branches of his profession, but were more especially conspicuous in operative surgery. In critical cases it is said that his coolness and presence of mind were unsurpassed.' 'No man,' says the same authority, 'ever took a more genuine pleasure in the relief of human suffering; and being called to most of the difficult cases within a large circuit of miles, the readiness with which he yielded to the frequent demands upon him only was equalled by the diligence and professional enthusiasm with which he prepared for his operations.'

"But it is in his character as a naturalist that we, members of the society, feel the most interest. None of us, I am sure, can be unmindful of his labors in working out and faithfully portraying the remarkable impressions of the rocks of the Connecticut valley, or of his yet more valuable and instructive observations upon these interesting monuments of past life. Whatever may be said of others who have honorably worked in the same field, this I think may be truly stated of Dr. D., that the first *scientific* observations on the footprints were made by him.

"Nearly a quarter of a century has gone by since he first called attention to these impressions; but yet, though absorbed much in the duties of his profession, he never lost his interest in them. To his mind, nurtured as it had become by their study, questions of important moment depended upon their full elucidation; and certainly he exhibited an untiring devotion in his labors towards the accomplishment of this end. We all know that he had for some time been engaged in the preparation of a work on the footprints of the Connecticut valley, now under publication by the Smithsonian Institute; and all are undoubtedly aware that, by a process of his own invention, he was able to lithograph and photograph them, so as to produce illustrations of singular fidelity, the color even of the stone in which they occur being exactly represented. How far he had progressed towards the completion of the text for this work is not yet known to us. The plates, I have the satisfaction of announcing, are all finished.

"Dr. D. always felt a strong interest

in our society, and he was anxious that our cabinet should possess a full suit of the impressions. To him your committee were much indebted for advice and assistance in procuring such as adorn your cabinet. It is a satisfaction now to know that he himself felt grateful to the society for the readiness with which it at all times, through your curator, loaned him such specimens as were needed for the illustration of his work. These were always unhesitatingly placed at his disposal.

"Dr. D. was quiet and unobtrusive in his manners, and always presented his observations with singular modesty. It is indeed painful to reflect that his manly form will never more come into our presence, nor his instructive speech greet our hearing.

"It is always a pleasure to know that those whom we have respected for scientific attainments were loved and honored in private life for their virtues. This pleasure we can fully enjoy in the case of our lamented associate. I cannot, perhaps, better close these remarks than by quoting the language of the friend in Greenfield who furnished me with some of the facts given concerning Dr. D. He says, ' To the community here his death is a loss not easily supplied. To many families it is only second to that of an immediate member. We mourn not only the loss of our physician, and of a useful fellow-citizen, but of one who, by the daily beauty of his life, and by numberless unremembered acts of kindness, made personal friends of all those who were in the habit of associating with him.'

"In conclusion I offer the following resolution:—

"*Resolved*, that the Boston Society of Natural History, highly appreciating the value and importance of the labors of the late Dr. James Deane, of Greenfield, in the investigation and elucidation of the fossil footprints of the Connecticut valley, recognize in his death a great loss, not only to themselves, with whom he was associated, but to all who feel interested in the progress of science."

HON. ALBERT G. DEAVITT,

Saratoga Springs, N. Y., Sept. 1, æ. 42, of South Bend, Ind. He was a brother of J. J. Deavitt, Esq., of St. Albans, Vt. The deceased was a native of Rensselaer Co., N. Y. In his boyhood he exhibited those fine qualities of head and heart which caused his friends to anticipate for him a distinguished and honorable future. And these pleasing anticipations were in a good degree realized. But in the meridian of his days, and at the moment when his earthly prospects seemed most flattering, the all-wise and inscrutable Ruler of human events saw fit to terminate his worldly career. After reading law at Plattsburg and Ogdensburg, Judge D. completed his legal studies, preparatory to his admission to the bar, in the office of the Hon. D. L. Seymour, of Troy, N. Y. And, after having practised at the bar of his native county a few years with ability and success, he removed to Indiana. He received military commissions from Govs. Bouck, of New York, and Whitcomb, of Indiana; and in March, 1857, he was appointed by Gov. Willard circuit judge of the 11th judicial circuit of Indiana, in the place of Hon. T. S. Stanfield, resigned.

Hon. Schuyler Colfax, in the St. Joseph Valley Register, published at South Bend, Ind., says, "We regret to announce the death of Judge A. G. Deavitt, of this town. He was one of our old citizens; and he has been regarded as a sound and able lawyer, an impartial judge, a good citizen, and a kind and affectionate husband and father. His death leaves a vacuum not easily filled."

Said another notice of him, " Many hearts will be saddened by this event, not only of those who admired the deceased for his talents and ability, who esteemed him for his honor, who were won to him in friendship by his kindness, but of many whose sympathies were with him and his family in his long and painful sickness. It was not permitted him to die in the bosom of his family, as he doubtless desired; but the affectionate hand of one whom he described, in the warm utterance of his heart, 'a good, noble brother,' was with him. It has not been permitted his friends and neighbors to follow his remains to their last resting place on earth; but in the cemetery of Saratoga, in a beautiful spot marked by a monument reared by fraternal love, and beneath the shade of a spreading pine, they will rest till the resurrection of the just.

"In the beginning of the long and painful sickness that came upon our brother, and from the midst of the dark and distressing providences that near two years ago carried a brother and a sister from beneath his roof to the grave, he turned his mind, with cheerful hope and assiduous care, to find the blessings in disguise of those deep glooms. He sought and found. The Bible, which he saw, and felt, and said would make heaven on earth, if men would live by it, became his rock; the Redeemer and his blood, his entire hope; and carefully and anxiously did he seek, in changed views, and feelings, and life, for the evidence that all was well. Whilst hope flattered him of recovery, and his friends entertained sanguine expectations of it, his chiefest desire of restoration was for his family's sake, and that he might teach his young children the fear of God."

The court and bar of St. Joseph Co., Ind., adopted the following resolutions:

"Whereas we have heard that the Hon. Albert G. Deavitt departed this life at Saratoga Springs, N. Y., on the 1st inst., therefore we, the members of the bar and officers of the court of South Bend, where the deceased has so long occupied the position of one of the most prominent members of the legal profession, —

"*Resolve*, 1. That in the death of the Hon. Albert G. Deavitt, the bar of South Bend has lost one of its most able and talented members. United with him by the ties of professional and social intercourse, we can but express our sorrow at this dispensation of Providence, and pay the tribute of affection due to the memory of our departed brother.

"2. We deeply sympathize with the bereaved family of the deceased, and hereby tender them our condolence in this afflicting dispensation."

DE COST, Capt. Nash, Skaneateles, N. Y., Jan. 27, æ. 75. He was well known in New York 30 years ago, as one of the most popular shipmasters of the "Swallow Tail" line of Liverpool packets. Those who had occasion to cross the Atlantic at that period will remember him as commander of the favorite packet ship York. Previous to his connection with that ship, he severally commanded the ships Euphrates, Cortez, and Averick, in all of which he not only gave entire satisfaction to owners, but also to those who took passage with him. The numerous gifts of silver plate which he possessed, and cherished in his advanced age, testified his popularity with his passenger friends. He was always a good friend of the sailor, and has often boasted that he never had occasion to flog a man who lived with him in the whole course of his life. He possessed a good heart; and it was always in the 'right place' when appealed to by those in distress. He was a sincere Christian, and died in the hope of a glorious immortality.

DEEN, Dr. O. L., Bolivar Co., Miss., Aug. 18, æ. 38. Dr. D., we believe, was born in Georgia. His father immigrated to Mississippi, and settled in Hinds Co., where he still lives, when the doctor was quite a boy, where he received a moral and honest training that characterized him through life. The doctor moved to Bolivar Co. some 10 or 12 years since, where he has practised his profession with success and untiring energy. He possessed some noble qualities in a high degree; was ever a friend to the poor, ever an energetic mover in matters that concerned the public good, and ever kind and genial in his nature. Appreciating and rewarding merit wherever found, and in all the relations and transactions in life, he was strictly honest and rigidly just; bold and fearless in asserting, and firm in sustaining, what he conceived to be right, but ever open to conviction. When told by his physician that he could live but a little while longer, he calmly said, "Well, I am satisfied with life, satisfied with my success; and, were it not for my wife and children, I would not be at all disconcerted."

DE FORREST, Dr. H. A., Rochester, N. Y., Nov. 24, æ. 44, at the house of Harvey Ely, Esq. He was a native of Watertown, Ct. He graduated at Yale, and pursued his medical studies there. At an early period of his practice he settled in Rochester, where he continued for about five years, with great success. He then offered his services to the American Board as a medical missionary, and was appointed to the Syrian mission. He was married, Aug. 6, 1840, to Miss E. S. Sargent, of Stockbridge, Ct., and in Sept., 1841, they sailed for

France, that the doctor might enjoy the advantages that Paris affords to the medical man. He reached Beirut in April, 1842, and continued in this foreign field about 12 years, when ill health compelled him to leave. As a physician, he was enabled to enter immediately upon his duties. He was, however, more than a mere physician. He pursued the study of the Arabic language; and, although he declined to assume the ministerial office, yet he cheerfully conducted religious meetings both in English and Arabic, with great acceptance. For many years also, as treasurer, he managed the finances of the Syrian mission with great ability, and in various ways relieved his clerical colleagues from the pressure of secular cares. He likewise assisted in conducting the Arabic press, both by translations and by editing books and tracts prepared by others. But it was to the cause of female education that he devoted most of his time and strength, and to this he consecrated his last affections. It became with him almost a passion. To leave it was his sorest trial; and to go back to Syria, and resume this chosen employment, was the one earthly hope cherished longest and abandoned last of all. And in that which he so loved he was eminently successful. Aided by his amiable and devoted wife, he originated and carried to great excellence the female seminary of the Syrian mission. The influence of this school upon the Arab community in favor of female education has been great, wide-spread, and permanent. Many happy families are rising up in Syria to bless his memory, whose self denying labors they themselves have been blessed with educated, refined, and pious mothers. So ardent was his zeal in this work that he could not be prevailed to relinquish it even temporarily until his robust constitution was so entirely broken down that it could never afterwards be restored. The editors of the Independent say of the deceased, "No Christian traveller from the United States could have visited Beirut within the past 15 years without perceiving that this modest and genial missionary physician was doing as great a work in elevating the women of Syria as was Mr. Calhoun in training young men for the ministry, and Dr. Smith in preparing the Bible for the people. Two of the editors of this journal have enjoyed the privilege at Beirut or at Abeth of worshipping with that Syrian household over which Dr. and Mrs. De Forrest presided with so much wisdom, and affection, and Christian grace; and gladly would we render a personal tribute to so good and useful a man."

DE GARAY, Jose, New York city, Sept. 21, æ. 57. He was a native of Mexico, and was born Sept. 21, 1801, and died upon the anniversary of his birthday. He was well known in the United States as the original projector of the Tehuantepec transit route across the continent, for which he obtained the grant from Santa Anna in 1841. The first grant having expired by limitation before its terms had been fulfilled, Senor De Garay succeeded in 1846 in having it renewed by Mariano Salas, then dictator. He leaves a son and daughter, and also several relatives living in France.

DE LONG, Hon. James A., Brownville, K. T., Nov. 25, æ. —. As a man, his aspirations were high and noble; as a citizen, kind-hearted and esteemed; as a neighbor, social and beloved; as a political adviser in the time of the struggles, ever mindful of the interests of the territory; as the representative of his county, he fulfilled his duties in the territorial legislature the most praiseworthy — ever true to his constituents and to the cause of freedom.

DELUOL, Rev. L. R., D. D., Baltimore, Md., ——, æ. —, formerly superior general of St. Mary's Seminary, and vicar general of this diocese. Dr. D. was a native of the south of France, was president of St. Mary's College of this city, and for many years superior of the Theological Seminary connected with that institution. During a long lifetime he devoted all his energies to the arduous duties of the priesthood, and in every respect was a model citizen and Christian.

DENIG, Edwin T., Esq., Pembina Settlement, British possessions, Sept. 6, æ. 47, second son of Dr. Geo. Denig, of Columbus, O. The deceased had been for many years a member, and actively engaged in the operations of the American Fur Company, having charge of one of the upper forts and trading posts situated at the mouth of the Yellow Stone River, where he spent twenty-five years of the best part of his life. His long residence among the Indians, his correct and Christian-like deportment in all his transactions, gave him unbounded influence among them, and rendered his services peculiarly valuable to the company. His acquaintance with the habits, manners, and language of the different tribes by which he was surrounded, has seldom been equalled, and resulted in his making several valuable communications on the ethnological and philological peculiarities of these different nations, which have been handsomely acknowledged by government, and printed in the archives of our national history. Becoming tired of such complete isolation, and wishing to confer upon his children the benefits of education, he severed his connection with the Fur Company in 1856, and removed to the Pembina Settlement, on the Red River of the north. At this point he found all the refining influences of civilization open to his access, with little or none of those social evils which mar the moral beauty of social existence in the more densely populated districts of our land. He purchased a large grazing farm, and established an interior trading post, and was actively engaged in both branches of business, when a short, but violent attack of fever terminated his existence. Brief as had been the period of his sojourn here, he had, nevertheless, secured the high regard and sincere attachment of quite a number of distinguished residents, some of whom have voluntarily evinced their esteem in communications addressed to his relatives in Columbus since his death.

DENISON, Rev. Henry Mandeville, Charleston, S. C., Sept. 28, æ. 35, rector of St. Peter's Church. He was a native of Pennsylvania, graduated at the Episcopal Theological Seminary in Fairfax Co., Va., and married a daughter of Ex-president Tyler. He formerly officiated in Brooklyn, N. Y., and Louisville, Ky.

DENISON, Mrs. Rachel, Royalton, Vt., Aug. 23, æ. 84, widow of Dr. Joseph A. Denison, and sister of the Rt. Rev. P. Chase, late of Illinois.

DENNETT, Hon. Mark, Portsmouth, N. H., Aug. 19, æ. 75.

DENNING, Col. R. W., St. Louis, Mo., Sept, 29, æ. —. Col. D. was formerly a well-known merchant in Chillicothe, O., where he had built up a reputation of spotless honor and strict integrity, which contributed to prosperity in business, and endeared him to a large circle of acquaintances in that city, who, doubtless, heard of his death with that sincere regret which can only attach to the loss of a valued friend. During his life his generous disposition, warm heart, and gentlemanly bearing attached him socially to every one with whom he came in contact, and such was the esteem which his presence inspired, that every companion at once became his friend.

DENNY, Major St. Clair, Pittsburg, Pa., paymaster of U. S. army, and formerly captain of the 5th regiment of infantry.

DEVENS, Dr. S., Lake Village, N. H., Aug. 30, æ. 49, formerly of Charlestown, Mass.

DEWEY, Dr. B. F., Cascade, Ia., April 18, æ. 41, son of Dr. Asa Dewey, of Boston. The deceased was an excellent physician, a very useful member of society, and highly respected by all who knew him.

DEWEY, David, M. D., Plainfield, Essex Co., N. J., April 28, æ. 73. Dr. D. was for more than forty years a practising physician. He was an active and influential citizen.

DEWOODY, Hon. John A., Des Arc, Ala. ——, æ. 30. He was a native of Limestone Co., Ala. He resided in Des Arc near five years. His business qualifications were of the first order, and since the organization of our municipal government, he has filled the office of mayor, having been elected four times in succession.

DICK, Thomas Morritt, M. D., near Sumpter, S. C., Aug. 30, æ. 54.

DICKEY, Ebenezer V., M. D., Oxford, Pa., July 31, æ. 36. He was the youngest son of the late Rev. Ebenezer Dickey, D. D., of the same place. He died in the house in which he was born, and in which his father died. He was a man of great force of character — able, dignified, and independent — and identified with all the public enterprises of the south-western part of the county. He was made president of the Baltimore Central Railroad Company, which position he resigned when elected, in the fall of 1856, to a seat in the legislature of the state; and at the organization of the Octoraro Bank, he was chosen, by universal consent, its president. He was in the prime of life, and his death has created a void it will be difficult to fill. The deceased stood highly in his profession as a medical man. In every position he was called upon to fill, he discharged his duty with ability.

DICKINSON, Mrs. Jane Louisa, Plainville, Ct., April 8, æ. 33, wife of Rev. J. L. Dickinson, and daughter of the Rev. Artemas Boies, who died in 1844, the honored and beloved pastor of the Second Church in New London. When 16 years of age, and a member of the seminary in South Hadley, which was her native place, she united with the church. Mrs. D. was admirably fitted for her station. Being the daughter of a clergyman, possessed of a cheerful and loving spirit, cultivated and refined by education and the grace of God, she was a helpmeet for her husband; and great indeed is the loss sustained by him and his bereaved family.

DICKINSON, Col. Alexander, Lewiston, N. Y., Oct. 31, æ. 68. Col. D. was born in New Jersey, July 4, 1790, and removed to our frontier in 1811. He was one of the oldest and most respected citizens of Niagara Co. He has held many offices of responsibility, and ever discharged the duties intrusted to him with credit to himself and honor to his constituents.

DICKINSON, Dr. R. Q., Albany, Ga., May 6, æ. 60, a man highly esteemed and well beloved, cut down, although past the meridian of his life, in the midst of his career of usefulness.

DICKSON, Hon. Samuel, M. D., Albany, N. Y., May 4, æ. —. He was the faithful representative of the Albany district in the last Congress. The Albany Co. Medical Society speak of him as an honored and useful member of the community, of the profession, and of the society; and that it is meet and proper that men who have been useful in their day and generation, both in public as well as in private life, should receive the plaudits of their fellow-men.

DIKE, Samuel, Weathersfield, Ct., Oct. 20, æ. 95, a revolutionary pensioner — a man of sterling integrity, and true Christian principle.

DILLON, Rev. Matthew, Peoria, Ill., Dec. 16, æ. —, pastor of Peoria, and late president of the University of St. Mary of the Lake, and pastor of the Church of the Holy Name, Chicago.

DIMOCK, Rev. Davis, Montrose, Pa., Sept. 27, æ. 82. He had been a Baptist preacher in the Wyoming region and Montrose for nearly sixty years, and was an associate judge of Susquehanna Co. for a quarter of a century. His father was an officer in the revolutionary army, and after the war removed with many others from Connecticut to the Wyoming Valley, and settled at Wilkesbarre. The subject of this sketch was then 14 years of age, just the age to have earlier impressions enforced, and childhood's bent strengthened, by the scenes of Indian massacre, and the personal narratives of a thousand thrilling incidents, which go to make up the history of Wyoming. He here labored on the farm and in the workshop; improved the scanty opportunities in his reach to gain knowledge by attending and teaching common schools; and was active in all of the political and other gatherings of the people. In June, 1797, he was united in marriage with Betsey Jenkins, of Tunkhannock, who became the mother of his twelve children, and the beloved and faithful partner of his toils and privations, as well as his hopes and enjoyments, during fifty-five years of his earthly pilgrimage. His labors, his manner of life and doctrines, have left their imprint, not only upon the journals and publications written by his own hands, but upon the records of the county, upon all the old church records and family altars in a wide area, from Great Bend to Wilkesbarre; and well might they be gathered into a volume for the perusal, edification, and profit of the living.

DIXON, Mrs. Eliza W., Westfield, N. Y., March 10, æ. 53, wife of Hon. Abram Dixon. The deceased was a daughter of Gen. Holt, one of the early settlers and prominent citizens of Buffalo, who emigrated from Cherry Valley, where Mrs. D. was born.

DOANE, Mrs. Mary H., Burlington, N. J., March 7, æ. 84, mother of Rt. Rev. Bishop Doane.

DODD, Rev. Dr. Thaddeus, Amwell Township, Pa., Jan. 16, æ. 82.

DODGE, Capt. David, West Cambridge, Mass., Nov. 5, æ. 75. Capt. D. was the youngest son of Barnabas Dodge of Dodge's Mills, Hamilton. His eldest brother, Oliver, graduated at Harvard University, and was settled in the ministry at Pomfret, Ct. Barnabas, the second son, who is well remembered by many of his contemporaries now living, died in

1802. Paul, the next younger, graduated at Brown University, was admitted to the bar, and opened an office at Burlington, Vt., where he died in 1807. Two sisters, Elizabeth, who was married to Asa Lamson, of Beverly, and, after his death, to Samuel Smith, of Ipswich,— and Eunice, who was married to Aaron Haskell, of Newburyport — have both since deceased at Ipswich; the former in 1816, and the latter, mother of George Haskell, Esq., of the present board of county commissioners, in 1851. Mr. D. was born at Hamilton in 1783, and though, from feeble health and other causes, he did not receive a collegiate education, he still had the benefit of much sound instruction from his father, who was distinguished for his proficiency in some branches of study, especially mathematics, numbering among his pupils the late Hon. Nathan Dane, a relative of the family. His early training and his native abilities secured for him some distinction while he was yet a young man. During the last war with England, he was appointed to the command of the Ipswich cavalry, and was called out to repel threatened invasion. In 1823 he was made Master of Unity Lodge of Free Masons at Ipswich. He also filled many town offices at different times, and represented his native town for several years in the legislature. In 1807 he married Huldah Dodge, of Hamilton, whom he survived only about eight months. His mills at Hamilton having been destroyed by fire in 1823, he went in 1828 to Salem, and here established works for the distillation of pyroligneous acid in Southfields, near the old lead factory. He afterwards removed to Lynn, and thence to West Cambridge. Mr. D. was a man of agreeable manners, of fine social qualities, and of extensive information, and obtained a large acquaintance with the intelligent men of his day. Like some others of his family, he possessed and cultivated a taste for music, and was ready and accurate with the pencil. He leaves three sons and two daughters living; three other children, all daughters, having died in his lifetime.

DODGE, W. W., Esq., Fort Wayne, Ind., Nov. 15, æ. 30, of Warsaw, Ind. He was born in the town of Athens, in the State of Ohio, January 3, 1829. He commenced the practice of law in the fall of 1854, in Paducah, Ky. In the year 1855 he removed to Fort Wayne, and pursued the practice of his profession there until the spring of 1858, when he removed to Warsaw, where he resided at the time of his death. He was a young man of fine talents, and for one of his experience possessed much legal ability.

DONALDSON, Mrs. Jemima, Danville, Pa., June 28, æ. 88, at the residence of her daughter, Mrs. Colt. She was mother of Judge William D., of Pottsville, and had lived a widow fifty years.

DOOLITTLE, Dr. R. B., Madison, N. Y., July 30, æ. 50.

DORR, Clifford, M. D., Somerville, Mass., Aug. 19, æ. 52. He was son of John Dorr, and was born in Boston, Nov. 2, 1805. He was fitted for college at the public Latin School in Boston. After graduating, he studied medicine under the instruction of Dr. George Hayward, of Boston, and received the degree of M. D. in 1829. He practised his profession in Braintree and Quincy, Mass., and for a short time in Matagorda, Texas. Sept. 6, 1840, he sailed from New York to Sydney, New South Wales, and returned by way of Calcutta and St. Helena, arriving at New York in January, 1842. In March, 1855, he was seized with a severe paralysis of the brain, from which he never recovered. He was never married.

DORR, Sullivan, Esq., Providence, R. I., March 3, æ. 79, father of the late Gov. Dorr. He was in early life engaged in the India trade, afterwards in manufacturing, but since 1838 has been president of the Washington Insurance Co. Few men have lived so long as Mr. D. who have commanded so great respect from his fellow-citizens. He went to Providence in the vigor of his manhood; there he was married, and resided more than fifty years, and educated a numerous family. He was a man of remarkable system, punctilious in all his engagements, industrious and prudent. He was a man of the highest integrity, and of scrupulous fidelity to all his obligations. Very few survive who were his contemporaries in early life. The venerable Dr. Crocker, who attended at the marriage festival, repeated the solemn burial service over the remains of his esteemed parishioner and friend. Those who knew him will derive instruction from his example, and the remembrance of his virtues will be pleasant.

DORRANCE, Dr. John, Peterboro', N. Y., Oct. 11, æ. 79, father of Hon. Daniel G. Dorrance, of Florence, N. Y.

DR. FREDERICK DORSEY,

Hagerstown, Md., Oct. 28, æ. 84. He was born in Anne Arundel Co., Md., in 1774. He was well educated, and in early life removed to Washington Co., where he spent the remainder of his days in the active pursuit of his profession, in the house in which he had lived since his marriage. He continued in active practice up to the hour of his last illness, a period of nearly seventy years, and, what is a most unprecedented circumstance, was associated in practice, at the time of his death, with his son and grandson.

Jefferson was his idol; Clay, Rochester, Pindal, the Fitzhughs, the Barnes, the Ringgolds, the Tilghmans, the Lawrences, the Spriggs, the Carrolls, the Buchanans, the Kershners, — all now gone, — were his early, intimate friends. He was a student, and continued through life a faithful disciple of Dr. Rush, perhaps the greatest physician that ever lived. No man was more ready to adopt any real improvement in the science of medicine than he was. He was one of the very first men in our country who adopted etherization in cases of surgical operations, and even before it had been generally used in the cities. Contrary to the general belief, he read, too, the current medical literature of the day; but the great source from whence he drew his knowledge was nature's fountain, experience, tested by his own sound judgment. Upon one subject he was, however, a true and unalterable Rushite: calomel and blood-letting were with him the alpha and omega of the profession.

No clouds of adversity or sorrow could long obscure the genial sunshine of his jovial heart. To the end of his days this inestimable blessing, cheerfulness, never forsook him. In all his business transactions he was strictly honest. He was for many years a member of the vestry of St. John's Parish, and had been also its warden, treasurer, and register.

DORSEY, H. A., M. D., Hopewell, Pa., May 25, æ. 27, son of I. H. Dorsey, M. D., of Huntingdon.

DOTON, Mrs. Harriet F. W., Pomfret, Vt., Nov. 18, æ. 29, wife of Hosea Doton, A. M., principal of the High School. Her maiden name was Ware, and she was born at Pomfret, Jan. 23, 1829; and though of a feeble constitution and delicate frame, she early acquired the rudiments of a good education, and formed habits of critical and serious thought, calm reflection, and rigid self-examination that afterwards became distinguishing traits in her character. Her mind was one of superior power. At the age of fifteen she began to teach with marked success, and in connection with her employment devoted herself to study, till almost every branch of science had been the subject of her investigation. She read and taught the elementary and higher mathematics with ease, and made an application of their principles to some of the more difficult problems in natural philosophy, to the calculations of all the ordinary astronomical phenomena, and to the development of the laws of planetary motions. In the summer of 1857 she received an invitation to take charge of Mrs. Gray's celebrated school for young ladies, in Tappahannock, Va., but she applied herself principally to astronomical calculations for publishers in Vermont and New Hampshire. On the 27th of May, 1858, she was married to Mr. Doton, a civil engineer, and in September of the same year, with her husband, yielding to the urgent solicitations of their friends, took charge of the Pomfret High School as principals. They had scarcely commenced their labor when she was attacked with the fatal disease of that climate, the typhoid fever, against which her slender and delicate frame struggled for nearly ten weeks, till her wasted form gave up its treasure, her pure spirit, to its Father and its God. As a teacher she was most happily and singularly successful. Wherever she was employed a high and elevating influence seemed to emanate from her soul, begetting a love of study, a thirst for the attainment of purer knowledge, and a higher and more glowing admiration for all that is truly great, good, and beautiful. But the crowning excellence of her character was her ardent devotedness to the Christian religion. She made it the one all-absorbing principle of life, the guiding star of all her acts.

DOTY, Mrs. Eleanor A., Amoy, China, Feb. 28, æ. 35, wife of Rev. Elihu Doty, missionary to China, and daughter of Hiram Smith, Esq., of Troy.

DOUGHERTY, Rev. Michael, Tuscaloosa, Ala., April 16, æ. —, pastor of the Catholic church.

DOUGLAS, Mrs. Lucy, New York, March 28, æ. 85, relict of the late Capt. Richard Douglas, of the Connecticut line of the revolutionary army. She has long drawn a pension from the government on account of the services of her husband in the revolution. He was an ensign at Bunker Hill, and a captain at Yorktown. A son, E. Douglas, Esq., resides in Bellefontaine, O.

DOUGLAS, William, Esq., Middletown, Conn., April 21, æ. 46. He was at the time of his death a member of the board of education, and also a member of the city council, being first alderman. His loss will be felt in every circle. He was a man universally admired for his sound moral principles and strict integrity; and his active participation and coöperation in any movement calculated to advance the interests of Middletown won the admiration of all progressive citizens. He was born in Northford, in the town of North Branford, Ct., Jan. 19, 1812. He was a son of William Douglas, one of the yeomanry of New Haven Co., who, when a boy of only 11 years of age, showed a spirit characteristic of the times that tried men's souls by taking a despatch from his uncle, Gen. Douglas, then in Plainfield, Ct., to Col. Ledyard, at Groton, the day before that awful massacre, swimming his horse across the River Thames, near New London. He was a grandson of Col. William Douglas, who was engaged in the old French war, and when a mere boy, only 16 years of age, held an office in the colonial army, which post he held in actual service until the close of the war, which ended in the surrender of Montcalm and the taking of Quebec by Gen. Wolfe in 1759, and subsequently, in our revolutionary struggle, distinguished himself as commander of a flotilla, on Lake Champlain, in the siege and taking of St. John, in 1775, and in taking a large number of prisoners from the enemy, together with a large amount of arms, ammunition, and stores. He was also colonel of a regiment from New Haven Co., which occupied a prominent post in the continental army at the battle of Long Island, where he was in principal command during the hottest of the fight. He also distinguished himself at the battles of New York, Harlem, White Plains, and skirmishes with the enemy about New York in 1776, in one of which battles he received his death stroke. In 1832 Mr. D. came to Middletown, where he commenced the machinist business in company with William H. Guild, under the firm of Guild & Douglas, with whom he continued in business until Aug. 19, 1839. At that period his brother, Benjamin Douglas, was associated with him in business under the firm of W. & B. Douglas, which name was continued up to the time of his death. He spent his business life of some 20 years in Middletown, and from a small commencement, in conjunction with his brother Benjamin, gradually increased the business which they established until they stood foremost in the ranks of inventors and manufacturers. William Douglas was possessed of a superior mind; and he bent its whole energies to the improvement of mechanism. As an inventor and machinist, he was acknowledged a superior by all; an honor to the science and trade, as well as an honor to the town. In his private life Mr. D. was uniformly kind and amiable; in religious sentiment, a Universalist. He leaves a wife and six children.

DOUGLASS, Rev. Richardson, D. D., Woodstock, Va., May 14, æ. —. He had been a minister of the gospel in the Baltimore conference for several years, and exemplified in his life the doctrines of religion, and expressed his willingness to "depart and be with Christ." As a theologian, he was sound and erudite; as a Christian gentleman, he was urbane and courteous; and, as a physician, he was scientific and skilful. The Methodist Episcopal church mourn their loss, as he was a local minister of high standing among them.

DOW, Rev. John G., Chelsea, Mass., May 18, æ. 78, of Newbury, Vt.

DOWNING, Capt. James, Waynesburg, O., Dec. 15, æ. 72. He was born in Brook Co., Va., in 1786. He emigrated to Stark Co. in 1805, and erected the first house in Sandy township. He hewed the logs himself, and went to Gaddenhutten and near Pekin to get white men to commence, and then procured Indians to assist in raising the logs. He also put out a crop of corn the same year. The year following his father and brothers removed from Virginia to Sandy township, where he has made his permanent home until about one year ago, when he took up his abode with his sister, Mrs. Thompson. In the war of 1812 Mr. D. entered the army as a volunteer, was elected captain, and served on the northern frontier until he was honorably discharged.

DRAKE, Dr. J. B., Greenville, Ill., Sept. 3, æ. 70. He was a native of Princeton, N. J., where early in life he graduated as A. B. in 1809; and subsequently he received a diploma from the Medical College of Ohio. In 1820, bent upon success in his profession, he came west, and commenced the practice of medicine in the counties of Bond and Montgomery, for a while making his residence at Hillsboro', but settled permanently in Greenville in 1827. From this period until the close of his life he made his profession his principal business. Both in practice and counsel the doctor had won for himself a high reputation. He was a fine scholar, and spent much of his pastime in reading the classics. So conversant was he with Virgil, Cæsar, and Homer, that he almost seemed to be one of the ancients. As a citizen, none were more universally esteemed, as possessing the unflinching and stern qualities of common honesty and sound integrity. In Dec., 1836, he was married to Mrs. Elizabeth Bird, sister of Rev. William Young, deceased, who, with their son Henry, an only child, now of mature age, are left to mourn the loss of an affectionate and worthy husband and father.

DRAKE, R. G., Esq., of the firm of Chapman & Drake, counsellors at law of Hartford, Ct. He died at the south in Feb., whither he had gone for the benefit of his health.

DRAPER, Hon. William, Pontiac, Mich., Aug. 8, æ. 78. He was son of James and Lois (Battle) Draper, and was born in that part of Dedham which is now within the limits of Dover, Mass., Feb. 12, 1780. He was fitted for college partly by Rev. Nathaniel Emmons, D. D., (Y. C., 1767,) of Franklin, Mass., and partly by Rev. Thomas Thacher, (H. U., 1775,) of Dedham. On leaving college, he went to Concord, Mass., and entered as a student at law in the office of John Leighton Tuttle, (H. U., 1796.) Having completed his legal studies and been admitted to the bar, he opened an office in Marlborough, Mass., where he acquired an extensive practice, and was quite successful as a lawyer. For ten years he was president of the Middlesex bar. In 1833 he went to Michigan, established himself in Pontiac, and was a citizen of that place during the remainder of his life. He occupied a prominent and distinguished position in the legal profession. At the time Congress passed the enabling act for the admission of Michigan into the Union, a convention was called under that act, that the people might determine whether they would accede to the proposition of Congress or not. Mr. D. was the president of the convention. He was president of the bar of Oakland Co., Michigan, for 20 years, and held the office at the time of his decease. While few of the high earthly honors were bestowed upon him, he had, what was far better, the deserved esteem and respect of every one who knew him. He was a Christian gentleman, upright, scrupulously so, and for 25 years was an exemplary member of the Congregational church in Pontiac. He retained his mental faculties to an extraordinary degree. About two years before his death there was a case pending in the Circuit Court of Michigan, in which he had a personal interest. He wrote out and read to the court an argument and brief of marked power and great research, and he was successful at last. Mr. D. was famed for his love of field sports, and it was his delight, in the last years of his life, to hunt and fish in and around the beautiful lakes of water that are so numerous in the vicinity of his late residence; and the principal reason of his visit to Mackinac, where he died, was his desire to gratify his taste in this respect. Mr. D. married, in 1810, Harriet Eliza Payne, a daughter of Major Phineas Payne, of Concord, Mass., of revolutionary memory. They had six children, four sons and two daughters, namely, William, Charles, Albert F., James, Eliza C., and Ann M., all now living except James, who was the youngest child. Charles graduated at Harvard College in 1833, and is a lawyer in Pontiac.

DRED, Charles, Esq., Duxbury, Mass., Feb. 4, æ. 88 years 10 months.

DRENNON, R. Henry, Pine Bluff, Ark., July 22, æ. 22. A graduate of Erskine College, at the early age of 19 Mr. D. commenced the study of law, a profession which in boyhood seems to have fascinated him, and in Dec., 1857, at Columbia, he was admitted to the practice. February following, he left his native state to pursue his profession in Pine Bluff, Ark. There, under the kind advice and encouragement of Gen. James, a distinguished lawyer of the place, he had every prospect of a noted and brilliant, as well as useful career.

DRUM, Hon. Augustus, Greensburg, Pa., Sept. 17, æ. 40. He was a son of the worthy Simon Drum, Esq., deceased, for so many years postmaster in Greensburg. Mr. D. was a man of splendid talents, and stood high in the legal profession. He had been a member of the State Senate, and of Congress, and had served his constituents faithfully and ably. The bar of Westmoreland Co.

Resolved, that his eminent ability as a lawyer, his short but brilliant professional career, inspire us with a most profound regard for his memory as a brother; and his high classic and literary attainments as a scholar, with his fine social qualities as a friend and citizen, rendered him a useful and agreeable member of society, justly entitled to the respect of all.

DUDLEY, C. E. I., Hamilton, N. Y., July 10, æ.—, by drowning in the Madison Reservoir. He was a member of the Sophomore class in the university, and teacher of Spanish in the Female Seminary. Mr. D. was from Delavan, Wis., and had been connected with the university three years, and had endeared himself to all by his kind and gentlemanly deportment and studious habits. Possessing fine talents, an ambition lofty and aspiring, a perseverance constant and unwavering, his friends had entertained high hopes of his usefulness, and predicted for him an honorable and brilliant future.

HON. JOHN DUER,

Chief Justice of the Superior Court of the city of New York, died at the residence of his son on Staten Island, Aug.

8, æ. 72. Hon. Judge Duer was born in 1784, in Orange Co., N. Y.; he was a grandson of William Alexander, the celebrated Lord Stirling — Col. William Duer, father of the judge, having married Catharine Alexander, a daughter of Lord Stirling, towards the close of the American revolution. William A. Duer, brother of the judge, president of Columbia College in this city, and previously circuit judge of the second circuit in this state, died only a few weeks before the chief justice.

Judge D. first practised law at Goshen, in Orange Co., with Beverly Johnson; and about forty years ago, in company with that gentleman, who was one of the most distinguished lawyers of his day, came to the city and commenced active practice. His chief fame as a lawyer was acquired by his conduct of several very prominent insurance cases, and he was universally regarded as the best insurance lawyer in the state. His work on insurances is considered as a standard authority.

In 1849, he was elected an associate justice of the Superior Court. After the death of Judge Oakley, he became chief justice, and held that position at the time of the accident, the results of which have prevented him from taking his seat upon the bench for several months. Judge D. was a prominent member of the Protestant Episcopal church, and sat, as a lay delegate, in the diocesan convention held in this city just before the memorable trial of Bishop Onderdonk.

Judge D. was selected as the orator on the occasion of the obsequies of Judge Kent, to give expression to the high esteem entertained by the bench and bar for that distinguished jurist. In this effort Judge D. made an admirable success. On other occasions he has also appeared before the public, concerned in various subjects, and unhesitatingly expressing his own views as he conceived to be right. In his personal relations Judge D. was a polished gentleman and an attached friend. His course while upon the bench added largely to the enviable fame he had already acquired as a member of the bar. The judge leaves a large family. His eldest son, William, formerly held a diplomatic station in South America.

Justice Bosworth, at a large meeting of the bar, addressed the meeting as follows: —

"My brethren of the bar and gentlemen: I feel wholly incompetent to say any thing on the present occasion. It is a sad one to all of us, and particularly so to myself and others occupying the same relation to the distinguished man whose death we mourn. At the same time, I deem it not inappropriate to the present occasion that I should state some things respecting the deceased which attached me to him, and made my affection for him personally as strong as the respect which I cherished for his learning, his great ability, and his unsullied integrity.

"It is in the light of the private personal acquaintance that I have had with him that I propose to speak on this occasion, trusting that others will take that more comprehensive and enlarged view which is required to present the man as he was and as he lived, and to do justice to his worth and services.

"I had no personal acquaintance with him prior to my election as a member of the court which, during some nine years, he has adorned with his learning, and the duties of which he has performed with untiring industry and fidelity.

"Conscious of his great genius, of his superior learning, and of his large experience, I was apprehensive, without knowing why, that he might be impatient on encountering views less mature than his own — that he possessed tenacity of impressions and opinions that might render consultations with those whom he could not but regard as his inferiors sometimes embarrassing, if not unpleasant.

"But it gives me sincere pleasure to say that I never met one who treated opinions adverse to his own with more courtesy, or discussed questions giving rise to conflicting views with more kindness, or who strove more to prevent final disagreement of opinion, when that was likely to occur, never causing even the slightest temporary dissatisfaction.

"Whether to the credit of the court or not, still it is true that the kindest personal relations have at all times existed between its members. So strong and unbroken has been this personal regard, that I do not think any member of it has ever failed to desire the reëlection of an incumbent whose term was about to expire, no matter what might be his politics, or who might be his competitor. I have no reason to doubt that this was as much the feeling at the time of my first election, and properly so, as at any time since then.

"Judge D. was at all times firm and resolute in his resistance to all outside efforts to remove a faithful and competent subordinate officer of the court, merely on the ground of his personal opinions, although it is the practice at present that each political party, in making nominations, should select those holding the same views that they cherish.

"Yet it was his view that no judge could add to the dignity of his office, or to his claims to personal confidence and regard, by exceeding any of his powers in proscribing competent and faithful subordinates merely on political grounds.

"No man was more industrious, or labored more faithfully, than he. He was so constituted that it was impossible for him to be inactive. He read much, and probably no judge in the state read more promptly, or with more care, every elementary treatise and every volume of reports, as from time to time they were issued from the press.

No judicial opinions excel his own in clearness, in fulness of illustration, in beauty of style, in the vigor of logic, or in the richness and variety of learning by which they were illustrated. However strong may have been his impressions upon the argument of a cause as it was presented, yet if it so happened that those impressions were formed in the absence from his mind of any fact justly entitled to affect the result, no one more readily than himself gave that fact its proper effect, or more readily yielded his impressions to the truth and justice of the case. He had another peculiar mental habit. He rarely, if ever, commenced to write an opinion until his examination of a case and the authorities bearing upon it had been completed.

"Hence writing was not to him an aid in the comparison of authorities, or in reaching legal conclusions; and hence his opinions, even when delivered at length, were generally unwritten, though delivered with as much precision of language as if they were written. His manuscript was mrely disfigured by alterations and interlineations, even in his largest and most labored opinions.

"It is gratifying to know that the last years of our distinguished brother were years of happiness to him and to his family, of usefulness to the community as well as to the profession, and of signal service to the court of which he was a member. "He took great pleasure in discharging the duties of his office. He was a truly great man, an eminent jurist, an upright judge — and I sincerely believe that no partiality or prejudice, fear or favor, or the apprehension of any consequences personal to himself, ever exercised the slightest influence over his deliberations, or for a single moment clouded his views or warped his judgment."

The Hon. Benjamin F. Butler read, with others, the following resolutions, prepared by the committee of arrangements, which were passed : —

"*Resolved*, that in the death of the Hon. John Duer, chief justice of the Superior Court of the city of New York, the legal profession, and the public at large, are called to mourn the loss of a judge whose genius and learning made him an ornament of the bench, upon which, with so much dignity, he presided, and whose uprightness, love of truth, and manly independence justly entitled him to the esteem and reverence of our whole community.

"*Resolved*, that while we thus express our sense of the high judicial abilities of our departed brother, and of the fidelity with which he discharged his duties on the bench, a just appreciation of his character and services prompts us to a special commemoration of the eloquence, learning, and brilliant talents which distinguished him as an advocate ; the scrupulous care with which, when at the bar, he sought to guard and promote the dignity and usefulness of his profession ; his efficient and honorable labors to improve the legislation and jurisprudence of our state, as one of the revisers of its statute laws ; his writings on an important branch of legal science, and other productions of his pen, particularly his beautiful tribute to the memory of the great commentator on American law ; his genial spirit and scholarly attainments ; his philanthropy and patriotism ; and above all, the unaffected Christian graces which illustrated and adorned his character and life."

DUER, Hon. William Alexander, New York, ——, æ. 78. He was brother of Chief Justice Duer, also a grandson of Lord Stirling, and claimed the title. He was for several years a distinguished member of the legislature of New York, representing Dutchess Co., and was a leader in the old federal party. In 1818 he removed to Albany, where he was again elected to represent that county in the same legislature. He joined the democratic party in 1818, and took ground against Governor Clinton. In 1823 he was appointed circuit judge for the circuit embracing Albany, Columbia, Rensselaer, and some other counties. After filling this office for several years, he removed to the city of New York, and was appointed president of Columbia College. He was the author of the Life of his ancestor, Lord Stirling, and of a work on constitutional jurisprudence.

DUNCAN, Greer B., New Orleans, La., at Cincinnati, O., on his way to Philadelphia, June 24, æ. 47. He had been for upwards of 25 years a prominent member of the Louisiana bar, and among his brethren none was more highly esteemed than Mr. D. He was an industrious and profound lawyer, a fluent and forcible speaker, an accomplished scholar, and a man beloved for many high and noble qualities. Though his death was not expected, his loss will be long deplored by many friends and the whole Louisiana bar.

DUNCAN, Mrs. Naomi, Antrim, N. H., Sept. 28, æ. 88, wife of Dea. Robert Duncan. She was of Scotch-Irish and Presbyterian descent. Her father, John Duncan, Esq., moved from Londonderry to Antrim in 1773, being the seventh settler in the town. He enjoyed the entire confidence of the people, and was by them repeatedly elected to important offices. He was an elder in the Presbyterian church 23 years, and died in 1823, æ. 89. At the time of her death Mrs. D. had been longer a resident of Antrim than any other living person, having come hither in her fourth year.

DUNHAM, George E., drowned in the Connecticut River at Springfield, Mass., July 17, æ. —. He was son of Austin C. Dunham, of Hartford, Ct., and a Junior in Yale College. Different club boats were practising for a "regatta," and young D.'s boat was capsized by a collision.

DUNHAM, Rev. H. R., Galena, Ill., May 3, æ. —, pastor of the Second Presbyterian Church. He was a native of Washington Co., N. Y., and was educated at Union College, then under the superintendence of the venerable Dr. Nott. The Galena papers speak very highly of the deceased as a Christian minister and a man.

DUNHAM, Dr. Thomas K., Jeffersonton, Ga., Dec. 8, æ. 40. He had lived many years at his late residence, and had, by social and professional intercourse, formed a large circle of acquaintance. His gentleness of manner and uniform courtesy won for him the highest admiration. By his kindness and ready sympathy, admiration was soon warmed into friendship; and friendship, by intimate association, always kindled into love. For it may be said of him, if ever of any man, that he was loved by his friends to a degree amounting to devotion. Whether in private or in public life, his warm congeniality, his generous heart, and pure motives never underwent a change. As a physician, he stood in the foremost rank; and in a wider field of labor he would have left as noble a monument to attest his intellect as now, in honor to his heart, is borne in the bosom of every friend.

DUNN, Col. Thomas H., Macon, Miss., July 13, æ. —. Col. D. had just been appointed consul to Havana. He was a politician, firm and uncompromising, but at the same time commanded a large share of the confidence and esteem of his political opponents. His social qualities were of a high order. He was in the meridian of life, full of high hopes and generous impulses. A wide circle of friends will mourn his untimely fate.

DURFEE, Rev. Simeon Borden, Tiverton, R. I., Feb. 23, æ. 30. He was son of the late Chief Justice Durfee, and graduated in 1851.

DURKEE, Gen. Chauncey, Canton, Mo., Dec. 2, æ. —. His history is identified with that of his country, and written upon the pathway of civilization. For nearly half a century he has been an active, busy, and enterprising citizen, ever ready to lend a helping hand to the needy. From St. Charles to the Iowa line he has left his footprints upon the highway of public duty. Ever ready to obey the call of his countrymen, whether in the tented field or in the civic walks of life, he alike distinguished himself as one of earth's noblemen. He was an officer in the Black Hawk war, commanded a company in the Mormon insurrection, and was a colonel in the service of the state in the settlement of the difficulty about the Iowa line. In every walk of life his urbane and gentlemanly demeanor won the esteem of all with whom he associated. His untiring energy and perseverance enabled him to surmount difficulties before which others would have quailed. Early in life he was left an orphan by the massacre of his father by the Indians, and at the same time he escaped the scalping knife and tomahawk by what was deemed by others miraculous. He concealed himself in a hollow log until an opportunity was afforded of eluding the vigilance of the savages, and then a four-mile race of life or death was before him. At one time, surrounded by the Indians, his sagacity enabled him to outwit them and reach the fort in safety, when a shout of joy went up to Heaven from a hundred happy hearts.

DURST, Maj. James H., Texas, near the Nueces, ———, æ. —. He participated in the storming of Bexar during the Texan revolution, at the age of 14, and was engaged in almost every battle up to the annexation of Texas. He was prominent in the Cherokee war, had served in the state Senate, and was deputy collector of the Brazos Santiago district at the time of his death.

DUVOL, Capt. Pres, Mattalang, Siam, April 27, æ. —. Capt. D. was formerly well known as a pilot and steamboat captain on the Ohio and Mississippi. He went to Siam some years ago, became a prominent officer of the Siamese navy, and performed a gallant feat in capturing a piratical fleet in the Gulf of Siam. He is said to have been engaged in mining in the mountains at the time of his death. He left a wife and child at Lancaster, O. He was a tall, noble-looking man, in the prime of life, when he left his native country.

DWIGHT, Miss Mary Ann, Morrisiana, N. Y., Nov. 4, æ. 52. Miss D. was born in Northampton, Mass., Sept. 17, 1806. Her father, Josiah Dwight, Esq., was a native of Springfield, Mass. Her mother was Rhoda Edwards, a granddaughter of President Edwards. She was one of a numerous family, and among them were three sisters at one birth. This occurred in the year of the great eclipse.

Mary Ann was the second born of the three. The eldest and youngest of the three, with their mother, still survive. She had only such advantages of education as were afforded in the ordinary day schools of a country village at that time. Her father had an excellent library, though not large, on which her taste was formed; and he had always that unparalleled means for training the young, the society of cultivated people at his house. Drawing and painting in water colors was almost the only accomplishment then acquired by young ladies, and the opportunity for gaining instruction in these was only infrequent and transient. Miss D. betrayed no more than ordinary talent, and did not look forward to teaching, or any great attainment in the art, though it was always to her a pleasant pursuit. At 20 she went to Amherst, Mass., and took lessons in drawing heads and shading in crayon of Mr. Cardella, an Italian, and a teacher in Mount Pleasant Institute. This instruction developed her talent, and awakened an interest which she had not felt before. It was now to her a study, and occupied all her time. She improved rapidly, and looked forward to painting miniatures. In 1833 she went to Boston, where she taught drawing, and was at the same time making progress herself, copied some fine engravings in crayon, and painted in water colors a miniature copy of the De Witt Family, by Rembrandt. This copy of hers is a beautiful work of art; and she would never part with it, though offered liberal sums of money. She now felt obliged to relinquish miniature painting from weakness of eyes; and soon after the sight of one eye, which had never been perfect, was wholly lost, though the defect was not apparent to the observer. To paint in oil was her next attempt; and she copied some fine pictures so successfully that she decided to relinquish teaching, and occupy herself only with painting, and in 1838 went to New York with this object in view. She was at first obliged, for want of means, to continue teaching, and was employed in Mrs. Lawrence's school. While there she published, for the use of the school, an elementary work on astronomy, making the illustrations herself, and also a compilation of "Poetry for the Young." After leaving this school, she taught drawing in classes, and at the same time devoted herself to copying pictures with gratifying success until she was interrupted by the great fire in 1845, which destroyed much unaccomplished work, and caused her much loss besides. She now returned to Northampton, and, having passed some months with her mother, she went to Saco, Me., and began her work on Grecian and Roman Mythology. This was published by Putnam in 1849, when she returned to New York. In 1850 she published Cowper's translation of Homer's Iliad, with notes and Flaxman's designs, and an abridgment of the Mythology for schools. From this time she devoted herself to giving instruction in drawing, and occasionally a course of lectures on art, and, though a sufferer from failing health, persevered in her habits of industry and application; and while employed in giving lessons in Miss Dutton's and Miss Peters's schools in New Haven and Miss Porter's in Farmington, going from one to another on alternate days, she prepared for the press an Introduction to the Study of Art, a work of nearly 300 duodecimo pages, published by Appleton in 1856. When this was done she did not rest, but began another work, — an abridgment of Lanzi's History of Painting, — and completed it, excepting the illustrations, which she had not health after to accomplish. She declined rapidly in the last year of her life, but allowed herself no invalid habit or indulgence, and taught her classes until the summer vacation. She was extremely well fitted by her patience, her gentleness, her sound knowledge, and her strong sense of duty, for a teacher. During all her life she was diligent and earnest in the duty of self-cultivation. Her range of reading was wide; but the particular department to which she was most attracted was that of art, with which she had made herself very well acquainted, both in theory and practice. She was patient in sickness, and endured suffering with uncomplaining fortitude. She seemed to have a spirit of the most perfect Christian faith, hope, love, charity, and patience, and a submission to the Father's will perfect and entire. She was buried in Northampton, her native place.

DYER, Dillis, Esq., Ramsay, Ky.,

Jan. 27, æ. 62. He was an esteemed citizen, several times a representative in the legislature of Kentucky, and subsequently a member of the state Senate, which position he filled with honor to himself and fidelity to his constituents.

DYER, Joseph, Enfield, N. H., April 5, æ. 85. He was born in Connecticut, but removed to New Hampshire when about 22 years old. He was a military officer several years. He became a member of the United Society (Shakers) in 1814, and has ever since that time been distinguished as a remarkably active supporter of the principles and interests of the society. He was a man of superior mental and physical vigor and activity, and retained them, in a great degree, until within a few of his last years. He was universally respected for his honesty, frankness, and sincerity of purpose, wherever he was known.

E.

EAGLE, Henry, Esq., Oswego, N. Y., Jan. 27, æ. 73. Mr. E. was a native of Prussia, and was born in Memel, on the borders of Russia. Soon after his minority he immigrated to this country; and, being a shipwright by trade, on arriving at New York he was engaged by Henry Eckford, the prominent shipbuilder. In 1809 Mr. Eagle came to Oswego, and superintended the construction of the U. S. brig Oneida the same year. During the war of 1812 he went to Sacketts Harbor to superintend, under Mr. Eckford, the building of the U. S. fleet to be employed on Lake Ontario. Subsequently he became interested in the coasting trade on the lakes, and was for several years master of one of his own vessels. Since that period he has been engaged in mercantile pursuits in this city until a recent date, when he retired from active business, having acquired a handsome competency. Mr. E. was ever regarded and esteemed as a man of honor, strict probity, kindly feeling, and sympathy, was of marked simplicity and unostentation, and enjoyed the cordial respect of the whole community. He has lived to see Oswego rise from a mere hamlet, having contributed much to its growth by his own efforts and enterprise. He has gone down to the grave full of years, like a "shock of corn fully ripened for the harvest," respected, beloved, and lamented by all.

EASILY, Col. John A., near Pickens Court House, S. C., Feb. 22, a distinguished citizen of South Carolina.

EASLEY, Mrs. Elizabeth A. P., Newport, Va., April 1, æ. 23, wife of Dr. W. D. Easley, and daughter of Dr. Isaac Pennington, of Chester Co., Pa. Her father was a skilful and eminent physician, a man of highly-cultivated mind and fine literary taste. He was a descendant of one of those English Quaker families who accompanied Penn to the new world. The family settled then where the largest part of them has always remained — in Chester Co., not far from Philadelphia. Her mother was the daughter of James Allen, Esq., of New Jersey, originally a Puritan family, who emigrated to New Jersey prior to the revolution, in which James, then a young man, took an active part when the foe invaded his native state.

EASTMAN, Rev. Samuel, Elkhorn, Wis., April 17, æ. 69. As a clergyman of the Baptist denomination he resided some years in Mississippi, Louisiana, and at Cincinnati. He then became a resident of New York city, where he planted the Stanton Street Baptist Church, which has since become one of the largest and most flourishing churches in that city, and from which has branched another large church. To this church he ministered many years. Partly on account of his failing health, he removed to his native town, Landaff, Grafton Co., N. H., fulfilling his vocation as minister, when his health would permit, at Landaff, Haverhill, and Meredith Village, N. H., and at Grafton and Rutland, Vt. In 1844 he moved to Wisconsin, where, in impaired health, he has lived a life of partial retirement from clerical duty, supplying occasionally destitute places.

EASTON, Dr. William, A. M., Smyrna, Pa., Nov. 7, æ. 27, son of Rev. William Easton. He was a graduate of Union College, Schenectady, N. Y., of the class of 1850, received his degree as M. D.

from Jefferson College in 1853, and followed his profession for some time afterwards in Cecil Co., Md. Modest and retiring in his habits, few but his intimate friends were aware of his ripe scholarship. To the close of his career he was a laborious student, and remarkable for classical and scientific acquirements in one so young. The Greek New Testament was his *vade-mecum*. He was an accomplished chemist, and willing, without regard to pecuniary compensation, to employ his skill and acquirements for the relief of the suffering.

EATON, Rev. Asa, Boston, March 24, æ. 79. He was born in Plaistow, N. H., July 25, 1778, was fitted for college by Rev. Giles Merrill, of Haverhill, Mass., (H. U. 1759,) and graduated at Harvard in 1803. After a brief preparatory course of theological studies, he was instituted rector of Christ Church in Boston, Oct. 23, 1805, where he labored diligently and faithfully until May, 1829, when he resigned his rectorship, and for eight years subsequently was employed as a city missionary, laboring among the destitute in Boston, and preaching to the poor in a hall where the seats were free. From 1837 to 1841 he was connected with a literary institution in New Jersey. For a short time previous to his death he was attached to the Church of the Advent in Boston. He was a distinguished member of the Masonic fraternity, and at one time held the office of deputy grand master of the Grand Lodge of Massachusetts. He was widely known throughout the country from his long connection with the Episcopal church, his blameless life, and his entire consecration to the work of the Christian ministry. His tall and commanding figure, with locks of snowy whiteness, attracted attention wherever he went; and his memory is revered as a beloved and faithful expounder of divine truth. He married, Oct. 9, 1813, Susannah Storer, youngest daughter of Ebenezer Storer, of Boston, (H.U. 1747,) and had six children, — three sons and three daughters, — of whom two sons and one daughter survive him. His wife died Nov. 26, 1853, æ. 71.

EATON, Mrs. Esther, North Haven, Ct., Aug. 27, æ. 96, relict of Calvin Eaton. She lived to see that which few see — nine descendants of the fifth generation.

EATON, Daniel, Youngstown, O., May 17, æ. 84. He was among the pioneer settlers, having removed to Ohio from Pennsylvania in 1803 or 1804. Soon after settling he erected a blast furnace at the mouth of Yellow Creek, near Poland Village. This was the first attempt made to manufacture iron in that section of Ohio, and, we believe, in the state. A few years afterwards he disposed of this establishment, and, in company with his brother James, erected a furnace at the mouth of Mosquito Creek, (now Niles,) which remained in successful operation for a long period of years. He was elected to the Ohio Senate from Trumbull Co. in 1815. He was several times a member of the legislature from Trumbull Co.

EATON, Hon. George C., Dallas Co., Ark., June 2, æ. 47. He was the son of Maj. John R. Eaton, was born in Granville Co., N. C., March 5, 1811, removed with his family to Arkansas in 1848. In politics he was a democrat, was a member of the legislature of Arkansas, and also represented his native county several years in old North Carolina, in the General Assembly. He had many personal friends, was a man of ardent attachments, social in his feelings, and had an extended acquaintance.

EDDY, James, Esq., Burlington, Vt., Aug. 22, æ. 49, general superintendent of the American Telegraph Company. He was a native of Ithaca, N. Y., was a gentleman of much energy of character, and as a telegraph manager he had no superiors. In private life he was amiable and unassuming, a gentleman in his bearing, and a Christian in his daily walks. He was one of the pioneers in the introduction of the magnetic telegraph at the east, and built the first line east of Boston, and between that city and Calais, Me., and at the time of his death was manager of between 3000 and 4000 miles of wire, extending through the New England States, and as far south as Philadelphia. The news of his death created great sorrow; all the offices of the company were draped in mourning, and at St. Johns, N. F., the flags of the shipping were put at half mast.

EDDY, Justin, Esq., Cuyahoga Falls, O., March 5, æ. 72. He and his brother Alanson were among the first, if not the first, settlers of Edinburgh, and for more than half a century, the deceased has been one of its most prominent and useful citizens. Long will he be held in affectionate remembrance by those who had the pleasure of his acquaintance.

EDELMAN, Joseph, Esq., Palmer, Pa., March 17, æ. 55. He was a man of many amiable qualities, and much respected wherever known. Last fall he was elected county commissioner, and made an excellent officer. His death will be a great loss to the board.

EDGLEY, Mrs. Marcia, East Corinth, Me., Oct. 2, æ. 107. She was born in Brentwood, N. H., in 1751. She was married about 1776. She lived but a few years with her husband, and was left a widow with an only child, a daughter. Some time during the last century, she emigrated to this state, and settled in China. She subsequently removed to this place, where she resided until her death. She was a woman of great energy and fortitude, amiability and Christian devotedness. Her vision, which had become dimmed, and which for nearly a score of years required the aid of glasses, was restored a few years since, and until within a few months past she could easily read the large print of her Bible without glasses. She retained to a remarkable degree the possession of her mental powers, until she had crossed the boundary line of her century.

EDMUNDS, Rev. James, Absecon, N. J., March 23, æ. —.

EDWARDS, Charles G., Esq., at St. Nicholas Hotel, New York, June 17, æ. —, formerly an eminent lawyer of Cahaba, Ala.

EDWARDS, Mrs. Lucinda, Virgil, N. Y., æ. 84, widow of Jonathan Edwards, of V. She was born, and spent the early part of her life, in West Stockbridge, Mass. In 1798 she emigrated with her husband to Yates Co., N. Y., which was then a new country. In 1802 they settled in Virgil, where they remained till death. They were the early and firm supporters of the worship of God, and were ever ready to give a cordial welcome to the early missionary. She was an intelligent and earnest friend of education, which led her to collect a few children, who, with her own, constituted a small school, which she instructed; thus establishing the first school held in the place. The few Christians who held to the doctrines of the Congregational church were collected together on the 28th of Feb., 1805, and were constituted, by the late Rev. Dr. Williston, a church of Christ, consisting of eight members, of whom she was the last survivor. During the long time of her membership of this church, she was its firm friend and supporter.

ELIOTT, Rev. Arthur W., Paris, Ill., Jan. 18, æ. 73. He was born in Baltimore Co., Md., in 1789, and came to Ohio in 1804.

ELLIOTT, Rev. Joseph, Monmouth, Ill., Aug. 17, æ. 69. He was a laborious and useful minister of the New Testament for 50 years. He was born in Mason, N. H., in 1789, and at the age of 26 he was ordered to the great work, and became a pastor, which office he filled in various places in New England, New York, and Ohio for 45 years; often with great success and extensive revivals of religion. He was also a very successful teacher of youth and young men for the ministry for many years, in addition to his pastoral labors. Always ready to do good, he was ever to be found at the post of duty, and willing to engage in any labor to instruct and bless mankind.

ELLIOTT, Rev. William H., Bowie Co., Texas, March 22, æ. 69, of the Texas district Methodist Protestant church. He entered the ministry in the State of Virginia, emigrated to the State of Tennessee in 1823, and soon after, preferring the form of government of the Methodist Protestant church, he joined the Tennessee conference, and continued on the itinerant list to the day of his death. He emigrated to Texas in 1836. He was of a strong mind and commanding voice, and though dead, he will ever live in the memory of all who knew him.

ELLIS, Rev. Ferdinand, Exeter, N. H., Feb. 20, æ. 79. He was born in Medway, Mass., in June, 1778. He graduated at Brown University, in 1801. After being employed four years as a tutor there, he entered upon ministerial labor in the Baptist denomination, as colleague with Rev. Dr. Stillman, in Boston. From thence he went to Marblehead, where he preached to the Baptist church and taught school. In 1817 he removed to Exeter.

ELLSWORTH, Hon. Henry L., Fairhaven, Ct., Dec. 27, æ. 67. He was twin brother to the Hon. Wm. W. Ellsworth, formerly governor, and now judge of the Superior Court of Errors of Ct., and the two were the youngest children of the Hon. Oliver Ellsworth, of Windsor, Ct., second chief justice of the United States. After graduating at Yale College in 1810, and studying law with Judge Gould at Litchfield, he married the only daughter of the Hon. Elizur Goodrich, of New Haven, and settled at Windsor, on the estate of his father, in the practice of his profession and the pursuits of agriculture. At the end of a few years he removed to Hartford, where he continued about eight or ten years, when he was appointed by Gen. Jackson commissioner among the Indian tribes to the south and west of Arkansas. While employed in this service he made extensive circuits towards the Rocky Mountains. In one of these he was accompanied by Washington Irving, who thus obtained the materials of his remarkable work upon our western prairies. At the end of more than two years, Mr. E. was called to Washington, and placed at the head of the United States patent office. He brought to the duties of this station, talents, a sound practical judgment, a quick insight into the characters of men, uncommon case and dexterity in the transaction of business, great powers of physical endurance, and an interest, amounting almost to enthusiasm, in the advancement of the useful arts and the progress of our country in the development of its physical resources. His attachment to the pursuits of agriculture led him, in addition to the ordinary patent office report, to commence a series of reports to Congress on the agricultural condition of the country, embodying information obtained by a correspondence to every part of the Union, and containing suggestions often of great importance for the improvement of the science to which he was so much devoted. He led the way in obtaining valuable seeds from foreign countries, and circulating them, by means of the post office, in the various parts of the United States to which they were suited. By his labors and perseverance the patent office was raised from a depressed condition, and rendered one of the most useful and popular departments of the government. At the expiration of about ten years, Mr. E. resigned his connection with the patent office, and established himself at Lafayette, Ind., in the purchase and settlement of United States land. His zeal and energy in this new employment was felt throughout the whole of Northern Indiana, and contributed greatly to the settlement of that part of the state. He was foremost in promoting every design of public improvement. He was a firm friend to the cause of temperance at a period of great laxity on this subject. He was a generous and consistent supporter of religious institutions, under the peculiar embarrassments to which they are liable in our new settlements. Throughout the whole of Northern Indiana he will long be remembered as a public benefactor.

ELMS, Rosington, Madison, Ind., March 14, æ. 70. He was an eminent and successful teacher of the most useful branches of practical and classical education. He removed from Brockville, Canada West, to this place about 18 years ago, and has been teaching here ever since that time, for, although originally ordained for the ministry, teaching was his forte. Some of his early pupils are among the most prominent men of Canada at this time, and very many of the best business young men of Madison give evidence of the excellency of his instruction.

ELTON, Dr. Samuel, Watertown, Ct., Dec. 8, æ. 78. He was long known as one of the most distinguished physicians in Litchfield Co., and was probably the oldest physician, having practised 59 years in his native town. His funeral was attended on Sunday by some 25 physicians from the neighboring towns, among whom was the venerable Dr. Williams, of New Milford, now the senior in the profession. The Episcopal church was crowded, and the services, conducted by Rev. Dr. Holcomb, were impressive. Resolutions were passed by the professional brethren of the deceased, expressive of their respect, &c.

"Whereas, Almighty God, in his wise providence, has been pleased to take from the field of usefulness and the scene of his earthly labors the venerable Dr. Samuel Elton, of Watertown, being the last of an unbroken succession of that honored name, who have for nearly a century discharged with great ability and unusual success, the arduous duties and self-denying labors of our useful and time-honored profession in that town, and

"Whereas, for nearly 60 years of this long period of time, our deceased brother, "in season and out of season," by night as well as by day, regardless of exposure to the pestilence which walketh in darkness, irrespective of pecuniary remuneration, and in spite of the infirmities of age, has devoted himself unreservedly to the calls and service of suffering humanity, therefore,

"*Resolved*, that such particular devotion and persevering assiduity to the calls and labors of a benevolent and noble profession are worthy of the example and commendation of his surviving brethren, and with the other virtues of his character, deserve to be held in grateful and lasting remembrance.

"*Resolved*, that in the death of Dr. Elton the public have lost a benefactor, the poor an unfailing friend, the cause of education an efficient supporter, the medical profession an able practitioner and wise counsellor, and his family and relatives a kind husband, indulgent father, and faithful friend."

ELY, Dr., Bombay, Jan. 17, æ. —, U. S. consul at Bombay.

EMERY, Rev. Allen, Madison Co., Va., Oct. 4, æ. 58. He had been for many years a minister in the old school Baptist church, and was always faithful, earnest, and devoted to the cause of his divine Master, and beloved by the members of his congregations.

EMERSON, Henry, Esq., Cincinnati, O., Aug. 27, æ. 62, a distinguished merchant of that city. He was born in Haverhill, Mass., in 1796, and removed to Cincinnati in 1818.

EMERY, Joshua, Portland, Me., Dec. 27, æ. 84. He was born in Biddeford, Me., April 10, 1774. He was originally a hatter in P., and afterwards, until the embargo times, was an extensive and prosperous merchant, on what is now Commercial Wharf. He had a large family, and some of his children are among our most active, intelligent, and successful men of business.

EMMET, Thomas A., Jr., New York city, Nov. 25, æ. 30, son of Thomas Addis Emmet, of N. Y.

EMMONS, Henry, Boston, Mass., Sept. 22, æ. 88, one of the oldest, if not the senior printer in B. The deceased was known to the present generation as an agent for the sale of several annual publications. He was formerly quite active in religious matters, and is reported never to have tasted ardent spirits or used tobacco. For the last 40 years he has not used tea or coffee, but has been a consistent cold water man.

ENOS, Hon. Truman, Westmoreland, N. Y., April 14, æ. 82. He has, for many years, been a prominent and honored citizen of Oneida, and has ever merited and enjoyed the confidence and esteem of his fellow-citizens. In the earlier and more vigorous period of his life, he filled, with great credit to himself, several important offices, in all of which he showed that he was "honest, capable, and faithful." In 1821 he was appointed one of the judges of the County Court of the county, which office he resigned in 1826, on his election to the state Senate. He was the representative of his Senate district, under its former organization, for four years. In his own town he discharged, for about 30 years, in a highly satisfactory manner, the duties of an honest and upright magistrate, and of a faithful representative of his town in the board of supervisors. He was a public-spirited citizen, ever ready to aid the poor, and to defend and succor the oppressed. He was active in promoting the cause of education, and fostering the interests of religion.

ERWIN, Dr. J. S., Aug. 6, for many years representative of McDowell Co., in the North Carolina legislature.

ETIEN, Assawis, May 21, æ. about 80, chief sangman of the Penobscot tribe. Assawis was born in 1778, and was elected governor in 1818. His disease was pleurisy, which he contracted while hunting and fishing. The funeral took place at Oldtown. All the Indians except those hunting afar off, and consequently not aware of the death of their aged chieftain, assembled on the island to share in the performance of his obsequies. The corpse had been brought by a steamer on Saturday, and deposited in the church. A black flag marked with the cross floated from the liberty pole. The church was decorated in black, and the first pew, already assigned for the governor, was dressed in mourning. Monday morning, at half past nine, the solemn high mass of requiem was celebrated by the Rev. Eugene Vetromile, and sung by the Indians in their language and manner. After the reading of the gospel, an interesting and most impressive sermon was delivered by Father Vetromile, and the ceremonies of interment were then performed according to the custom of the tribe. According to the ancient custom of the tribe, the Indians will mourn their departed chieftain a full year; and when the frosts of another winter shall have melted away, and the time of springing flowers shall have come again, they will meet together in festive throngs to elect a new governor.

EUBANKS, Dr. Wm. G., Greenwood, Ala., Sept. 22.

EUSTIS, Hon. George, New Orleans, La., Dec. 23, æ. 62. He was the oldest son of Jacob and Elizabeth (Gray) Eustis, and was born in Boston, Oct. 20, 1796. He was fitted for college at the Boston Latin School, and graduated at Harvard University in 1815, where he attained a high and enviable reputation in every branch of the prescribed studies of the institution. Soon after his graduation, which was with distinguished honors, he went abroad in the capacity of private secretary to his uncle, Governor Eustis, then minister to the Hague, the secretary of the legation being the late Alex. H. Everett, so well known for his varied attainments, and with whom he formed a friendship that was lifelong. At the Hague Judge Eustis began his legal studies, and drew from the clear fountains of the civil law of Holland, France, and Germany, those elementary principles and stores of learning which, at a later period, he was destined to exhibit to such advantage in his career at the bar and on the bench. He settled at New Orleans about the year 1822, and was not long in reaching high social and professional distinction. The bar of New Orleans then embraced some of the ablest juridical minds in the country. The learned, laborious, and eloquent Livingston ; the vigorous, ponderous, and sarcastic Mazureau ; the fluent, graphic, and sensible Grymes ; the well-read, sagacious, and vigilant Hennen ; and a host of other younger attorneys, many of whom have since reached the highest places in the profession, — were the formidable rivals among whom young Eustis was thrown to struggle and contend for the prizes of professional distinction. He was frequently a member of the state legislature, and in succession secretary of state, attorney general, and associate justice of the Supreme Court of the state, which last position he resigned to enter on a somewhat lengthened tour in Europe. He was also a leading member, as a conservative democrat, of the convention for amending the state constitution in 1845, and became the chief justice of the Supreme Court as it was remodelled by that instrument. His judicial decisions were marked by a clearness of style and logic, and a thorough acquaintance with law, which made them compare favorably with the best to be found in the English or American reports. After the adoption, in 1852, of the present constitution of the state, which provides for popular election of the judiciary, Judge Eustis retired from public life to resume practice at the bar under flattering circumstances. To his great professional learning Judge Eustis united an extensive acquaintance with English, French, and Spanish literature, and was esteemed by his large circle of friends a most entertaining and instructive companion ; and if his conversation was now and then dashed with sarcasm, it was often replete with genuine humor and racy wit. He was naturally of a vigorous mental and physical constitution, maintained by habits of out-door exercise, and his death, at the comparatively early age of 63, will cast a gloom over an extensive circle of acquaintances, not only in the state of his adoption, but in many other portions of the Union. In 1849 the honorary degree of Doctor of Laws was conferred upon him by Harvard University. He married, in 1825, Clarissa Allain, of Louisiana, by whom he had six children — four sons and two daughters. He has left a widow and several children, one of whom, the Hon. Geo. Eustis, Jr., has, during the last and present Congress, been the representative from the first congressional district of Louisiana. The bar of New Orleans say of him that during the long period in which he was engaged in the practice of his profession, he was justly regarded as one of its leading members. Distinguished alike for great learning, unwearied industry, and stainless purity of conduct, he will long be regretted, not only as a lost ornament of the bar, but as one whom all regarded as competent and willing to lend his aid to his brethren, who looked up to him for counsel and support. In his judicial career he exhibited great powers of mind, and great attainments, and these always in a manner condensed and clear. As a judge, no personal feelings, no professional attachments, no taint of prejudice, marred the justice of his decisions or the confidence of litigants. In all the various relations of life — at the hearthstone — in the social circle — his amiability and generosity tempered the sterner virtues into the gentle husband and father, and the confiding and forgiving friend. The loss of such a man, and such a lawyer, it will be difficult to replace, and will be long felt and deeply mourned.

EUSTIS, Horatio Sprague, at his plantation in Issaquene Co., Mississippi, Sept. 4, æ. 46. He was the son of General Abraham (H. U., 1804) and Rebecca (Sprague) Eustis, and was born at Fort Adams, Newport, R. I., Dec. 25, 1811. He was fitted for college at the Round Hill School, Northampton, Mass., under the superintendence of Joseph Green Cogswell, (H. U., 1806,) and George Bancroft, (H. U., 1817,) and graduated at Harvard in 1830. He studied law, went to the west, and finally settled as a lawyer in Natchez, where he continued in the practice of his profession, with the exception of an interval of a year or two, until his death. He married, May 10, 1838, Catharine, daughter of Henry Chotard, a planter. He left a widow and ten children, seven sons and three daughters.

EVANS, Dr. Asbury, Covington, Ky., Sept. 12, late professor of the Medical College of Ohio, and formerly of Louisville.

EVANS, Eleanor Tounson, Waverley, Ohio, March, 5, æ. 71, wife of Daniel Evans, daughter of William Tounson, and niece of Gen. Nathan Tounson, of Baltimore Co., Maryland.

EVANS, Dr. Jos. T., Marine Town, Ill., July 8, æ. 42.

JOSIAH J. EVANS,

Washington, D. C., May 6, æ. 72, senator from South Carolina. Mr. E. was born in South Carolina, Nov. 27, 1786, and was one of the earliest graduates of her infant college. He was of the class of 1808 — a distinguished class of 30, three of whom survive. He was educated to the bar, where he soon rose to eminence. At an early age he was sent to the legislature, and shortly after was made solicitor of his circuit, which post he held until 1830, when he was elevated to the bench. He continued there until he was, in 1852, chosen by the State of South Carolina to represent her in the Senate. He has filled every station he has occupied with untiring industry, scrupulous fidelity, and distinguished ability, and to the entire satisfaction of his state.

He was descended of Welsh parents, who settled on the Peedee River in the early settlement of that part of the country. He had lived his full threescore years and ten, and few have lived them better or enjoyed them more; for with a fond family and ample fortune, he was, in all his private as well as public relations, without blemish or reproach, and in South Carolina had ever only to indicate the position he desired to occupy, whether in society, in his profession, or in affairs, to have it accorded to him at once. He was well read and learned in his profession. His mind and memory were strongly imbued with the great principles of the common law, and he was particularly familiar with all legislative enactments and the decisions of courts. He was endowed by nature with a clear head, a well-balanced mind, and an unerring judgment. He was always cool, calm, and dispassionate, and never at fault on the bench. He never took sides in any case, as a judge, but always weighed the testimony carefully, and submitted it most impartially to the jury. In his charges on the law, he was plain, positive, direct, and decided.

He had great patience — a great virtue in a judge, next to those of honesty and learning. He was always kind and courteous to the bar; and yet no judge ever had more dignity of manner, commanded more respect in court, or despatched more promptly the business of the court.

Whilst Judge Evans was a wise statesman and a pure patriot, he was no politician, and had no relish for politics. Once only he consented to serve in the legislature, and that was just as he was starting in life. He had been brought up in the states rights school of politics, under the lead of Governor Williams and Judge Smith, of South Carolina, and Wm. H. Crawford, of Georgia. This threw him in opposition to Mr. Calhoun and his school of national politics. When the nullification controversy sprang up in South Carolina, Judge Evans was on the bench.

As a companion, he was always social,

pleasant and agreeable. He possessed great good humor and cheerfulness of disposition. I do not remember ever to have seen him depressed, sad, or melancholy. He enjoyed an anecdote or witticism, and would laugh most heartily over a good joke. He always conversed well, and made himself interesting to his friends. His religious creed was of the Episcopal faith. He was a regular attendant of that church, and a large contributor to its annual support; whilst he always manifested the most liberal consideration and respect for other denominations.

"At a meeting of the bar of Columbus, Hon. W. F. De Saussure remarked that the opinion has long since been stamped indelibly upon the public mind, that he was an able judge, a learned judge, emphatically a safe judge — patient and laborious, as we all can testify; ready in the application of the law to cases which came before him on the circuit; and where his judgment was satisfied as to the law and the justice of the case, not slow to assume the responsibility of indicating that judgment to the jury. His summing up was clear and unambiguous. He was never misled by refinements and subtlety, nor did he indulge in them himself. This formed no part of his intellectual constitution. The benevolence of his character begat a natural courtesy, which was set off by the native dignity of his manners, and rendered his intercourse with the public, his friends, and especially the bar, graceful and easy. I have never known him to have an angry collision with the profession, and I have had a large experience in one portion at least of the state. The gentleness of his bearing both in and out of court might seem to imply a lack of energy — infirmity of purpose. Nothing could be farther from the truth. He had well-formed opinions upon all subjects, which he was firm in maintaining; but his quiet nature shrank from eager controversy. His motto seemed to be, '*Suaviter in modo, fortiter in re.*'

"To pronounce an elaborate panegyric upon the life of one so long associated with your honors in the highest judicial functions, might seem to be superfluous; yet it is a relief to the heart to recall the memory of his virtues; and it may profit the public to review the foundations upon which rests his claim to their gratitude and love. For upwards of 45 years this distinguished citizen was engaged in the public service; 40 of these as commissioner of the Court of Equity, as a representative in the state legislature, as solicitor of the eastern circuit, and finally as a judge in the highest tribunals of law known to our system. How faithfully he discharged his duties in three of these departments your honors are the witnesses and the judges."

EVANS, Mrs. Mary, Hillsboro', O., Dec. 10, æ. 84. She was born in New Jersey in 1774. When young, her parents emigrated to Fayette Co., Pa., where, when only in her 15th year, she was married to Richard Evans, with whom she lived an eventful and happy life for the unusually long period of 63 years. Soon after their marriage, in 1789 or 1790, they emigrated to Kentucky. This was before the days of our palace steamboats; it was no pleasure trip. Conveyance down the Monongahela and Ohio was the slow and tedious flat boat, which, by keeping in the centre of the stream, they narrowly escaped the murderous rifle of the savages from either bank, so destructive of the life of the emigrant of those days. After living a few years, first in Bourbon Co., and afterwards on Cabin Creek, they determined to seek a new home. In 1799 Hugh Evans and his sons and sons-in-law explored this part of Ohio, and made purchase of a large part of the lower valley of Clear Creek, where, that fall, in the unbroken forest, they erected their cabin for the reception of their wives and children. The next spring they removed their families to their forest homes. The difficulty of that move may be judged from the fact that they had to cut the way through the forest for their wagons from the Ohio River. In this day of luxury and improvement we can little tell the trials of the wife and mother in the cabin of the pioneer. Often, in late years, has Mrs. E. been heard to recount the trials of that first year on Clear Creek, when, to use her own language, " more than fifty Indians to one white man came to her cabin." These often indulged in their savage orgies and mock fights to frighten her, when they found her alone with her helpless children. But no danger, no difficulty, impeded the onward progress of that hardy, determined band of pioneers. The forest gave way to the highly-cultivated farm, the cabin to the mansion; and Mrs. E. lived to hear the shrill note of the locomotive instead of the war whoop of the savage. Of that band of the first settlers on Clear Creek she was the last; the mother of 15 children, 12 of whom she saw married and settled in life.

EVANS, Rev. S. G., Randolph Co., N. C., Feb. 17, æ. 54.

EVANS, Gen. Thomas C., La Grange, Ga., May 5, æ. —. Gen. E. had filled many responsible public stations, and was highly esteemed for his many personal virtues. He was interred with Masonic and military honors.

EVERETT, Hon. Melatiah, Wrentham, Mass., Dec. 26, æ. 81. Mr. E. was probably the oldest member of the bar in Bristol Co., having been admitted in 1805. He was born in a part of Wrentham now included within the bounds of Foxboro', in June, 1777, and was graduated at Brown University in 1802, in the class with Henry Wheaton, John Whipple, Samuel Bugbee, and Milton Maxcy. Having pursued his legal studies with the late Judge Wheaton, he commenced practice in Attleboro', but subsequently removed to Foxboro', and finally to Wrentham, where he has resided for the last 25 years. In 1831 he represented his native town in the General Court, and in 1841 and 1842 he was elected to the Senate. He has also filled various offices in the town and county, having been an acting magistrate for a period of 50 years. In these various positions his fidelity and integrity deserved and won the respect and confidence of the public. Having for the last ten years retired in a great measure from services of a public kind, he busied himself with his farm and flowers, in the care of which he found much enjoyment. But his interest in public affairs did not subside; and, although he did not actively participate in politics, yet no man better knew their history, or more earnestly watched their progress. Well informed in relation to the events of our national history from the adoption of the federal constitution, his conversation upon those topics was both entertaining and instructive. But he desired to know whatever of interest was passing in the nation, state, and neighborhood. No one was more eager to read the daily prints. His newspaper was in his hands almost to the last. In his politics he was decidedly anti-slavery. His last public appearance was at the meeting in Worcester at which the republican party was organized, of which he was one of the vice presidents. His twin brother preceded him to the tomb only a few months. They had lived near each other for fourscore years. The subject of this notice was the last of seven brothers. Hon. Horace Everett, of Windsor, Vt., who died Jan. 30, 1851, was also one of the seven; he was 14 years in Congress, and received the degree of LL. D. During his long and severe sickness our friend uttered no complaint; he bore all without a murmur; and, though few enjoyed life better, yet he willingly bowed to the stroke which he could not shun. In all the relations of life he was exemplary — as a husband, counsellor, church member, and citizen. He was a friend of freedom, temperance, and learning.

EVERETT, Mrs. Nancy W., Roxbury, Mass., Nov. 20, æ. 59, wife of the late Thomas Everett, and daughter of the late Obadiah Wright, Esq., of Boston, Mass. A person so kindly benevolent as Mrs. E. should not pass to the tomb without a line of obituary. She was most emphatically a *cheerful Christian.* In 1841, 1842, 1843, she took an active part in the great temperance enterprise of those days, and filled the office of secretary in the Ladies' Benevolent Society for the Suppression of Intemperance, and her reports in that capacity would confer credit upon the best writers of the day. Her place as a model Christian cannot be easily supplied.

EWALT, John, Howland, O., Jan. 3, æ. 82. He was one of the pioneers of the county. He came here about the year 1801, when the only road to his late residence was an Indian trail through the woods, and when Warren contained only three dwellings, and those were log cabins. He brought with him a large variety of choice fruits, from which original stock, much of the good fruit of this vicinity has descended, and by his efforts and example did as much, perhaps, as any one for the improvement of horticulture in Trumbull Co. He sat upon the first jury impanelled under the state government of Ohio, and was identified with all the early history of the Reserve. Of a most genial and social disposition, he delighted to recount interesting passages in the events of his pioneer times, and his vivid memory and happy faculty of narration made his reminiscences a rich treat to all who had the pleasure of hearing them.

EWING, Hon. John, Vincennes, Ind., April 5, æ. 69. He some years ago filled a prominent place among the public men of Indiana. He was one of our oldest citizens. In his earlier days he was an active, enterprising man. He was at one time a merchant, and established, some thirty years ago, a paper known as the Wabash Transcript. His connection with this newspaper led him into political life, and he represented his county in both branches of the legislature, and his district once or twice in Congress. He was a man of acknowledged ability, stern integrity, and irreproachable honesty of purpose. The following is Mr. E.'s epitaph, which he wrote a few days before he died: "Here lies a man who loved Vincennes, his God, his country, and his friends."

F.

FAIRBANKS, Mrs. Sarah Catharine, St. Augustine, Florida, March 22, æ. —, wife of Hon. Geo. R. Fairbanks. Mrs. F. was the second daughter of Hon. Benjamin Wright, for a long period surrogate of Jefferson Co., N. Y., and Sarah, his wife, sixth daughter of Charles Ward. Her grandmother, Mrs. Charles Ward, was Mary, the youngest daughter of Philip Pell, Esq., of Westchester Co., and Glarianna Fridwell, and a direct descendent of John Pell, Esq., of Norfolk Co., Eng., Master of the King's Cup, who died in the year 1607, and whose descendants settled in Westchester Co., N. Y., and were known as lords of the manor of Pelham, in that county. * Her grandfather, Charles Ward, was a descendant of Andrew Ward, of Watertown, Mass., who accompanied the first settlers to Connecticut, and was a magistrate in 1636. The family motto of the Wards, "*Non nobis solum,*" was exemplified in a remarkable degree by the subject of this notice, as well also as by her mother and grandmother, the latter of whom died at Adams, Jeff. Co., N. Y., a few years since, at an advanced age. Distant friends of Mrs. F. cannot appreciate the loss to her immediate circle of influence in the death of this lovely woman. At home, in the church, in the community, she leaves a blank hardly to be filled. A natural buoyancy and energy had borne her through physical trials and many difficulties; but a true *faith* and lively *hope* had sanctified these to the formation of an earnest Christian character; so that any thing was ventured where duty called or human sympathy claimed her efforts. Her daily life was marked by utter unselfishness. "To do good and to distribute" seemed to be the law of her social intercourse. A *living* member of the church, she gave herself to its interests; and not by word only, but in deed, she labored for its advancement. Among the last thoughts and acts of her life were "cares and toils for it." In all parish work the pastor found in her a ready will and open hand to render aid according to her ability; and as God had blessed her with those things which the world needs for happiness, she only used them to secure her friends in everlasting habitations.

FAIRFAX, Mrs. Margaret, Vancluse, Va., —— ——, æ. 75, widow of Lord Thomas Fairfax.

FAIRFIELD, Mrs. L. J., Hillsdale, Mich., July 3, wife of Hon. Edmund B. Fairfield, LL. D., president of Hillsdale College. Mrs. F. was probably one of the best educated women of the state, having thirteen years ago taken the collegiate A. B. upon completing the full college course, including Latin, Greek, and Hebrew, and having subsequently, in regular course, received the higher degree of A. M. She died in full hope of immortality through Christ. She was a daughter of Dr. Jenison, formerly of Eaton Co., and a sister of Rev. C. A. Jenison.

FALES, Mrs. Sarah K. P., Quincy, Ill., Nov. 26, æ. 76, extensively known and

* Bolton's History of Westchester Co.

esteemed as a teacher of young ladies. This venerable and excellent woman retained her mental powers to the last, and continued to be, as in former days, a centre of attraction to a large circle of friends.

FARMAN, Benj. H., Lowell, Mass., Sept. 25, æ. 84. He was formerly of Bath, N. H., and was the first child born in that town that arrived to the age of manhood.

FARMER, Dr. William, New Lisbon, O., March 8, æ. 57. He was a man of unexceptionable character, unassuming manners, amiable disposition; and such was his urbanity, that he made fast friends of all with whom he became acquainted. He had a strong, vigorous, and highly cultivated mind. For upwards of 33 years he had been a practising physician, and had a wide-spread reputation as a skilful doctor, to which he was fully entitled. For nearly a quarter of a century he resided in Salineville, Col. Co., O. Last fall he removed to New Lisbon, where his professional services were duly appreciated.

FARNHAM, Maj. Gen. A. H., Hinsdale, Pa., April 19, æ. —.

FARRAR, George, M. D., Derry, N. H., Sept. 15, æ. 80. Dr. F. graduated at Dartmouth College, in the year 1800, and took his medical degree in 1803. He immediately entered upon the practice of his profession in Derry, and continued in active service as a physician for more than half a century. He was emphatically "the beloved physician." His practice was very extensive, and he was unsurpassed in his attention to his patients, cheerfully bestowing his labors upon the poor as well as the rich — all confided in his skill and his kindness. "The blessing of him that was ready to perish came upon him, and he caused the widow's heart to sing for joy." Dr. F. was a Christian of deep and consistent piety.

FARRINGTON, Dr. Joseph Jewett, Haverhill, Mass., Aug. 6, æ. 29. Dr. F. was of Concord, N. H., and leaves a large circle of friends who are deeply pained to part with one whose career of usefulness has been so suddenly checked, and to whom they had been attached by his goodness and professional acquirements.

FARWELL, Rev. John E., Fitchburg, Mass., Dec. 24, æ. 48. He was born at Ashby, Mass., Dec. 9, 1809, and was the child of religious parents. In 1836 he graduated at Amherst, and in 1839 at Andover Theological Seminary. He devoted himself to the mission work, was accepted by the board, and ordained at Ashby. His health failed, however, and he accepted a call to preach at Rochester, N. H., where he labored successfully for 10 years. After leaving R., he labored in various places for short periods. "The first impression one would receive of Mr. F.," says Rev. G. T. McCollom, in the funeral discourse, was, that " he was a gentle, meek, affectionate man. Other prominent traits were decision, child-like simplicity, and frankness. He was a man of great industry and perseverance. As a preacher, he was scriptural, faithful, useful; as a Christian, devout, loving, and holy. He was a man of rare judgment and foresight, and used these qualities in God's service."

FASSITT, Thomas S. R., Esq., Philadelphia, Pa., Dec. 1, æ. —, late a well-known and esteemed merchant. Mr. F. was a native of Philadelphia, but for several years has passed about one half of the year at his residence in Newport, R. I. He was a gentleman of great personal worth, and his loss will be keenly felt by many friends and acquaintances there.

FAULKNER, Charles J., near Alexandria, D. C., May 4, æ. 54. He was born in Berkeley Co., Va., received a public education, and was admitted to the bar in 1829. He had been a member of the House of Delegates, also of the Senate of Va., and was appointed commissioner to report upon the boundary between Virginia and Maryland. In 1851 he was elected a representative to Congress, and continued a member till his death.

FAXON, John, Boston, Mass., Oct. 7, æ. 46. He was well known to the printers of Boston during the last 25 years. The deceased had been a partner in the Boston Stereotype Foundry Company for the last ten years, prior to which period he was for many years engaged upon the Boston Atlas.

FEARING, Isaiah, Jr., Elizabeth City, N. C., ——— —, æ. 67. He was a native of Mass., but came to this place while quite a young man, and has long been known as one of the principal merchants of the town. He was a consistent member of the Methodist Episcopal church in the town, and a member of the board of stewards.

FENNER, Dr. L. H., Cleveland, O., May 5, æ. —, of Norwalk, Ct. He had been in poor health about two months, and a short time previous to his death he took up his abode at the Cleveland water cure, hoping to be benefited by hydropathic treatment. Dr. F. came to Norwalk a little more than a year ago, and became associated with Dr. Tiffy in the practice of medicine. His correct and gentlemanly deportment, together with the strict attention which he paid to the practice of his profession, caused him to be highly esteemed by our citizens generally. In his death, we feel that our town has lost one of its best inhabitants.

FENTON, Mrs. Judah, Winchester, Va., Jan. 29, æ. 103. The writer of this tribute to her memory was her near neighbor for many years, and has often been edified by a narrative of many incidents of the revolutionary war, and the commanding personage of General Washington, which she would propound with so much force and clearness of mind. The deceased was a native of Pennsylvania, and came to the county of Frederick about the close of the revolution, with her relatives, and settled at Neffsville, near Winchester, where she resided upwards of 70 years.

FERGUSON, Rev. John, Whately, Mass., Nov. 15, æ. —, formerly pastor of the First Congregational Church in Whately, and subsequently an agent of the American Tract Society. He was a Scotchman by birth, and had all the qualities of character which made the heroic Covenanters the Puritans of Scotland. He was sound, devout, venerable, and beloved, and has gone like an ancient patriarch to his rest.

FERRIS, Mrs. Lydia, Clarkson Centre, N. Y., Sept. 30, æ. 87. Mrs. F. was a native of Old Chester, N. H. She, with her first husband, whose name was Toll, emigrated to this place in 1806, and settled in the vicinity of what is now East Clarkson, when this region was mostly an unbroken wilderness, there being only an Indian trail from Genesee to the Niagara Rivers, where the Ridge Road was subsequently surveyed. In coming to this place, she, with her husband and infant child, crossed the Genesee River where the city of Rochester now stands, on a string piece of the first bridge built at that place, which was then in the course of erection.

FILLMORE, Rev. Daniel, Providence, R. I., Aug. 13, æ. 70. He was a native of Franklin, Ct., a member of one of the oldest and most respectable Methodist families in New England, and a relative of Ex-President Fillmore, whose branch of the family was from the same vicinity. He joined the itinerancy in 1811, and was appointed to the Falmouth circuit in Maine. He early rose to an honorable position among his brethren, and has since filled some of the most important stations in New England, as Portland, Lynn, Boston, Providence, New Bedford, and other places. He was twice stationed at Nantucket, Mass., viz., in 1825-6 and 1841-2. He was one of the first generation of Methodist preachers in New England, a few of whom, as Asa Kent, Ebenezer Blake, Lewis Bates, David Kilburn, and Daniel Webb, still live. Of the eleven who joined the New England conference at its session in Barnard, Vt., in 1811, of whom he was one, but two now remain — Aaron Lummus, now resident in Lynn, his native place, and the venerable William Marsh, of the East Maine conference. He was for many years the secretary of the old New England conference, the duties of which office he discharged with distinguished fidelity, and with an ability which has never been surpassed. Never, probably, have its duties been better performed. He was an ardent and active friend of education in the church, and for several years performed the duties of financial agent of the Wesleyan University for the Providence conference, with eminent tact and faithfulness, and without fee or reward. Many are the souls in all parts of New England who have been called to repentance by his successful labors, and are now members of the visible church. He was a fast friend of the church. He most cheerfully shared in the labors, struggles, poverty, and reproach of her early years; and he lived to share in her successes and triumphs, and to see her a power in the land; and to but few men in New England is she more indebted for these triumphs and successes than to him. To her were devoted the activity of his youth, the strength of his manhood, the counsels of his old age, and the prayers of his whole pious life. In 1852 he was put upon the superannuated list. Ardent in his piety, pure and unsullied in his character, calm and quiet in his spirit, kind and affectionate in his manners, zealous and active in his labors, eminently conservative in his principles, sound and able as a preacher, and faithful above many as a pastor, he has gone to his reward and to his rest, leaving behind him a name "which is as ointment poured forth," an unsullied reputation, and an example of Christian faithfulness and of ministerial fidelity.

FINLEY, Col. A. C., Clarksville, Va., Dec. 25, æ. 49. Col. F. was born in Rockbridge Co., and in early life connected himself with the Presbyterian church in Lexington, Va. For more than 20 years he had resided in Clarksville, where he held the office of cashier in the Exchange Bank. June 4, 1842, he was ordained to the office of ruling elder in the Presbyterian church. As a man of business, a friend, a Christian, and an office-bearer in the house of God, he was extensively and favorably known. In his disposition he was kind, conciliating, and confiding. In his business habits he was prompt, indefatigable, and laborious. In the service of God he was decided, regular, benevolent, and exemplary. In all the relations of life he was amiable, kind, and affectionate.

FINLEY, John, D. D., Greenville, Miss., Aug. 28, æ. 74. Dr. F. was born in Ayr, Scotland, March 10, 1784; entered the ministry about the year 1806; was chaplain to the Senate of New York during the administration of Gov. De Witt Clinton; and with great acceptability and success sustained the relation of pastor to the First Baptist Church in Baltimore, at Jackson, Tenn., Louisville, and at Memphis.

FISH, Dr. Erasmus D., Belvidere, N. J., Feb. 8, æ. 50.

FISHBURN, Prof. Junius M., of Washington College, Va., April —, æ. —. Prof. F. was a son-in-law of Dr. Junkin, president of the college, and was the professor of Latin and modern languages in that institution.

FISHER, Mrs. Harriet B., Amherst, Mass., Aug. 18, æ. 39, wife of Rev. George E. Fisher, and daughter of Jacob Holt, of West Brookfield, Mass. She resided in Amherst after 1841 to her marriage in 1850, her husband being at that time pastor of the Congregational church in Rutland, Mass. In Sept., 1852, Mr. F. was installed over the North Church in Amherst. Every one who knew her always esteemed and loved her. Her amiability, and gentleness, and quietness of spirit; her unpretending yet perfect fidelity to every trust; her prudence, and wisdom, and soundness of judgment; her self-sacrificing spirit, and untiring devotion to the welfare of all, — won the affection and confidence of every acquaintance. As a pastor's wife, "none named her but to praise."

FLAGG, Dr. Chandler, Marblehead, Mass., Sept. 10, æ. 77, a distinguished physician and most worthy citizen. The doctor was born at Grafton, Mass., Jan. 1, 1782. He graduated at Brown University in 1803, with all the honors of his *alma mater*, and after a thorough course of the study of medicine, entered upon its practice in Marblehead, where he rapidly rose to great eminence in his profession, which he held during a period of nearly 50 years. He was often sought as counsel in cases of difficulty and danger, and here he exhibited, in a marked degree, the soundness of his wisdom and judgment. He was a gentleman of the old school, and was remarkable for his urbanity and suavity of manners. He needed only to be known to secure the respect and friendship of his fellow-men. Through life he maintained his habit of daily study, which was diversified and extensive, finding special delight in that of the French language; the Bible and Prayer Book in this dialect were to him a source of instruction and comfort. Some years since he retired from the active duties of his profession; yet he is still remembered with gratitude by those who once had occasion for his services.

FLEECE, Dr. James, Lebanon, Ky., June 19, æ. —. Eminently successful in his profession, and profoundly respected and loved by his patients, he had a large circle of friends, who will feel his death as a great bereavement. His life was long and useful, and his memory will ever be fresh in the hearts of all who knew him. Let his virtues be imitated by us all. At a meeting of the members of the Medical Association of Lebanon, it was

"*Resolved*, now that his professional history has closed, after an active service of 37 years, it is no extravagance to say, that upon the arena of professional life, for energy and self-denying labor, none have surpassed him, and in his own sphere, few have ever met with a higher degree of appreciation, and whose loss will be more sensibly felt.

"*Resolved*, that as a private citizen, by his labor of love and spirit of public enterprise, the public heart feels a common sense of bereavement, now that his evergenial presence has passed from their midst."

FLEMING, John S., Esq., Goochland, Va., Aug. 31, æ. 67. The death of this distinguished man has deprived the bar of Virginia of one of its brightest ornaments, and society of one of its most genial spirits. Mr. F. was a man of decided genius, and of such eloquence that the lamented John Hampden Pleasants applied to him the title of the "forest-born Demosthenes." He had a strong understanding, a clear intellect, and overflowing wit and humor. But for his striking modesty and singular absence of ambition, he might have achieved a fame coëxtensive with the limits of the nation. His nature was as noble as his intellect was splendid.

FLEMING, Capt. William, Philadelphia, Pa., ———, æ. 76. He was one of our oldest and ablest mariners, having sailed out of Philadelphia for no less than 43 years. He was a man of remarkable intelligence and great purity of character, and, at the time of his decease, held the office of marine surveyor to the insurance companies.

FLETCHER, Dea. Ezra W., May 24, æ. 62. Dea. F. was born in Northbridge, Mass., in that part of the town now known as Whitinsville, Jan. 28, 1796. He was the son of Col. James and Margaret Wood Fletcher, and was the youngest of a family of ten children. His parents were persons of devoted piety, firm in their attachment to Puritan institutions, and were especially careful in the training of their children. His father was a man of more than ordinary strength of mind, and, by his practical wisdom and sound judgment, was well fitted to advise and direct in public affairs. Dea. F.'s early advantages for education were only such as were afforded in the common school in his native place. But such were his habits of application to study that he very soon acquired a knowledge of the English branches then taught in our schools. At the age of 16 or 17 he obtained a situation as clerk in the store of David Wilkinson, Esq., of Pawtucket, where he remained some three or four years. For a few years after closing his service here, he resided in his native place, acting as clerk and agent for a small manufacturing company then just organized. He was married March 25, 1819, to Laurinda Chapin, daughter of the late Dea. Phineas Chapin, of Uxbridge. They had four children, neither of whom has survived the father.* In the autumn of 1823 he removed to Jewett City, Ct., having engaged in the service of Messrs. Samuel & John Slater, the former of whom was the pioneer in the cotton manufacturing business of this country. In 1836 he entered into the service of Samuel Slater & Sons, of Providence, and continued until near the time of his death. He now reunited with the Richmond Street Church, and was chosen its deacon. This office he filled with great acceptance for six years, when he withdrew, and united with others in forming the Fourth Congregational Church. He was immediately chosen to the same office in this church. He subsequently joined in organizing the Central Church, but declined the office of deacon on account of increasing ill health. He continued a member of this church through the remainder of his life. For some years previous to his death his health had been failing. By the advice of his physicians he relinquished business in the spring of 1856, and took up his residence in his native village. He was encouraged to hope that the change would be the means of prolonging his life, even if he could not regain his health. He had always been greatly attached to the place of his birth, and to his near friends residing there, and now, in the days of his feebleness, his feelings prompted him to seek once more a home among them. It was soon evident that his disease was of such a nature as to forbid all hope of recovery. It did not, however, until a

* A son, Dr. EZRA W. FLETCHER, JR., graduated at Brown University, with distinguished rank as a scholar, in the class of 1839; studied medicine with Dr. Usher Parsons, of Providence; attended medical lectures in Boston and Philadelphia, and received his medical degree at Cambridge, in 1843. He spent two years in Paris and Vienna, commenced practice in Providence, R. I., but died greatly lamented June 25, 1847, æ. 26.

few weeks previous to his death, interfere seriously with his enjoyment of the society of his friends, or prevent him from attending public worship on the Sabbath, and meetings of conference and prayer. As he drew near to death his faith in Christ as an all-sufficient Saviour became stronger and stronger, and his hope of eternal blessedness brighter. Death to him had no terrors. "I have been an unprofitable servant," said he to a friend, "but if I am not greatly mistaken, Christ is very precious to me. His grace surrounds me; his love enriches me." His religious character was formed by direct contact with the Word of God, accompanied by the teachings of the Spirit. He loved the sacred book, and from the time that he began to hope that he was savingly interested in its truths he made it his habitual and prayerful study. He was a man of true Christian benevolence. He gave such direction as to the disposition of his property that more than one third of the whole will be appropriated to benevolent purposes. The sum that will be thus appropriated will not fall short of thirty thousand dollars. The property that enabled him thus to give liberally, was not, like that of many wealthy men, the result of speculation or successful traffic, but, with the exception of a small amount received from his father's estate, was the result of the annual savings from a salary never large, and which many of our city clerks would consider inadequate to meet their personal expenses. It would be impossible to give a just view of Dea. Fletcher's religious character without speaking of him as a man of prayer. He took a firm hold upon the promises which God has made to encourage his people in this duty, and he felt that they had no reason to hope for the divine blessing any further than they were willing to meet this duty. Many years ago he heard the remark made by a minister of the gospel, that the Christian needed to spend as much time every day in seeking supplies of spiritual food by communion with God in secret prayer as he spent in taking food for his body, and from that time till the close of his life, it is believed that he made his own practice conform to this. Three times, every day, was it his custom to retire from the world and pour out his desires to Him that seeth in secret. And thus did he obtain food for the nourishment of the spiritual life within him, and for preparing him for that higher service upon which he has now entered. Surely he that thus learns to walk with Christ on earth shall dwell with him in eternal glory.

FLETCHER, Samuel, Esq., Concord, N. H., Sept. 30, æ. 72. He was a native of Plymouth, N. H., born July 31, 1785. He was graduated at Dartmouth College, in the class of 1810; studied law with the late Samuel Green, Esq., afterwards a judge upon the bench of the Superior Court; was some time preceptor of Gilmanton Academy, but entered upon the practice of his profession in Concord about 1815, and continued in its successful pursuit until 1842, when, having been chosen treasurer of the Theological Institution and Phillips Academy, at Andover, Mass., he removed thither, and remained until 1850, when he returned to Concord. He was many years a trustee of Dartmouth College, which position he held until his death. He had represented Concord in the legislature, and during that portion of his life passed there, before declining health incapacitated him for active labors, bore an important part with contemporary citizens in shaping the character of the place of which he was long an influential and valuable inhabitant.

FLINN, Mrs. Sarah, Pittsburg, ——, March 15, æ. 78, consort of William Flinn, Esq. It is a tribute which nature owes to the living to cherish the memory of the dead. Mrs. F. was the daughter of David Sample, of Westmoreland Co., Pa., attorney at law, in which profession he occupied a very eminent position in his day. Mr. Sample, owing to the dangers to which his family were exposed from the frequent incursion of the Indians, especially in his absence from home, attending to official duties, removed them, for a short time, to Cumberland Co. It was in this county, near Big Spring, that Mrs. Flinn was born. It was her privilege to be able to point back to a father who was an ornament to the legal profession, who was esteemed for his urbanity, and beloved for his generosity; but she had a higher honor in that she could refer to a parentage who feared and served the Lord. Her father was no less a Christian than a gentleman or a lawyer. Mrs. Flinn finally cherished the religious instruction which had been inculcated by her pious parents in the morning of her days. Frequently has the writer heard her speak, with thankfulness and gratitude to God, of her parents.

FLOWERS, W. P., La Grange, Ga., Nov. 29, æ. 27. Mr. Flowers was a young man of liberal education, fine social qualities, and an unblemished Christian character. Few could boast of such combinations of virtues, or a brighter prospect for future usefulness. In the prime of manhood and career of usefulness he has been taken away; but his memory remains with those who knew and loved him.

FLYNT, Col. John P., Forsyth Co., Ga., Sept. 21, æ. 63. The deceased lived an exemplary life, noble in all the qualities that constitute a neighbor, a friend, and a father of a family. He was a man of a liberal heart, and always ready to respond to the calls of benevolence. The loss of such men is not only painful, but an irreparable misfortune to any community. He leaves behind a wife and two daughters.

FOLGER, Mrs. Mary, Ravenna, O., June 28, æ. 80. Mrs. F., formerly Mary Joy, was born on the Island of Nantucket, Mass., Jan. 24, 1778, and was married to Mayhew Folger in 1798, who was also a native of N. He was at that time engaged in the merchant service upon the ocean, but in 1810 concluded to try his fortune on shore, and removed to Chester Co., Pa., and in 1813 to Ohio, at that time the frontier state. The war of 1812 was conducted on the lakes and on land with frightful cruelty, and the trials of pioneer life were severe. In August, 1812, Capt. F., with his family, arrived at Kendall, expecting immediately to see the settlements overrun by the British and Indians; but a kind Providence ordered otherwise. By the victory of Com. Perry over the British fleet on Lake Erie, the aspect of things was entirely changed. Of the early settlers of Kendall, but three are believed to be living in the neighborhood. In 1828, Capt. F. removed to Massillon, where, on the 1st of Sept. of that year, he died. Mrs. F. was emphatically one of the excellent of this earth, even and cheerful, benevolent in heart, shedding around her a genial and pleasing influence. Five children survive her.

FOLWELL, William W., Romulus, N. Y., Oct. 13, æ. 90. He was born in Southampton, Penn., Jan. 28, 1768. He was graduated at Brown University, in 1793, with high honors. While in college he experienced religion, and was baptized by Dr. Stephen Gano. Soon after leaving school he was called to, but declined, the rhetorical chair in that ancient institution. In 1796 he was married. He served one term in the legislature of his native state, and in 1807 he went to the State of New York, and made large purchases of land, and proceeded to gratify his strong and early-developed taste for the cultivation of the soil. He took a deep interest in the election of Dr. O. C. Comstock to Congress. He was no office-seeker, no lover of stormy debate, but chose, from his naturally retiring disposition, and his love of rural life, to look out upon the great movements of his age from the eminence of a refined, dignified, and quiet, though unpretending, home.

FONTANE, Hon. Philip J., Key West, Florida, Aug. 28, æ. 52. He was one of the earliest settlers of the Key, (in 1823,) and possessing ample business capacity, united to great energy and industry, contributed greatly to its improvement. No settlers, no conveniences were here when he first took up his residence. Commencing active life poor, by the force of his own character he raised himself from the humblest to the most important and influential positions in the community in which he lived, being at the time of his death a member of the state legislature, mayor of the city, U. S. naval storekeeper, and acting Spanish consul,— filling his public trusts with great ability and credit to himself.

FOOT, Hon. George, Hernando, Miss., July 17, probate judge of De Soto Co.

FOOTE, Emerson, Savannah, Ga., Sept. 30, æ. —. He was a native of Springfield, Mass. Previous to his going to Georgia, some twelve years since, he had the superintendence of several important roads at the north. About the year 1846 he took charge of the Macon and Western Railroad, then in a most prostrate condition, but which under his management soon became one of the most prosperous roads in the south. In Sept., 1857, he was appointed to the superintendence of the Central Railroad, which position he filled with credit to himself. He was an exemplary citizen.

FOOTE, Dr. Thomas M., Buffalo, N. Y., Feb. 20, æ. 49. He was known throughout the Union as the editor of the Buffalo Commercial; and the grace, vigor, tact, and industry he displayed in its columns gave him a very high rank in the editorial fraternity. From the 1st of February, 1836, with but inconsiderable intermissions, he contributed to the editorial columns of the Commercial, and at the time of his decease he was one of its proprietors and editors. In 1849 he was appointed by President Taylor *chargé d'affaires* to Bogota, and returning next year, was sent by Mr. Fillmore to fill the same office at the court of Vienna, where he remained for some time. In 1855 he again visited Europe with Messrs. Fillmore and Jewett. He was one of the leading editors who advocated the principles of the whig party when it was in its zenith, when it boasted of its Clays and Websters. He gained laurels in many a hard-fought contest with some of the ablest writers in the state. In his controversies with Thurlow Weed, editor of the Albany Evening Journal, though he met "a foeman worthy of his steel," he came out of them with increased reputation. Foote's articles were distinguished by gracefulness of diction, directness and life, and oftentimes fairly sparkled with wit. His selections, too, were of a character that tended to elevate journalism. As a citizen, he was universally respected and esteemed. He was born in Clinton, N. Y., and was a graduate of Hamilton College in the class with Hon. George W. Clinton, of B. He was three times married, and leaves behind him a widow and two children.

FORD, Dr. Henry A., Gaboon Mission, West Africa, Feb. 2, æ. —. He was a missionary of the American Board.

FORDHAM, Peletiah, Esq., Sag Harbor, N. Y., æ. 72. He held the office of postmaster of that place under Mr. Fillmore, as well as other official positions.

FORESTI, E. Felice, Genoa, Italy, U. S. consul, August —, æ. —. He was an Italian exile, well known in New York as the patriotic co-sufferer with Silvio Pellico in the dungeons of Austria, where he spent twenty years of his life, and in 1835 was exiled to the United States, and who a year ago received from the president an appointment acceptable to all parties — that of consul to Genoa. More than five thousand persons are said to have been present at his funeral, among whom were the officers and crew of the U. S. frigate Wabash. It is intended by his fellow-countrymen to open a subscription for the erection of a marble monument to him. Ferdinand, upon the death of his father, the emperor, in 1835, ascending the throne, immediately passed a decree liberating the Italian patriots, but condemning them to a perpetual exile in America. On the 1st of August, 1836, Foresti, with the other prisoners, was transported by night to Trieste, whence, on the 3d, they sailed for America in the very same brig (the Usello) from which Koszta in Smyrna was dragged. Immediately upon their arrival in New York, they were received with much consideration by prominent citizens, and a week later their fellow-countrymen gave them a banquet. An interesting biographical sketch, written by Prof. Foresti himself, was published a little more than two years ago in the Watchman and Crusader, entitled "Twenty Years in the Dungeons of Austria," giving the particulars of his eventful life.

FORREST, John Lawrence, Cincinnati, O., ———, æ. 43. He was a native of Cork, Ireland, and was a contributor to the Irish press during the stirring times of 1848. During the year 1857 many of his pieces appeared in the Pilot, over the signature of "One of Ireland's Ballad Poets." The Pilot calls him one of Ireland's sweetest poets.

FOSTER, A. T., M. D., Portsmouth, Va., Nov. 10, æ. 42. He was born in Williamsburg, Va., and was educated in the College of William and Mary. He pursued his medical course of study in Philadelphia. Thus has passed away from the church a noble Christian, from his profession an able and skilful physician, from society a truly kind and wise counsellor, and from his afflicted family an affectionate husband and kind parent.

FOSTER, Dr. George B., Chicago, Ill., Nov. 6, æ. 30. He came here from Boston about three years since, and immediately devoted himself with great energy and zeal to his professional pursuits. Although a total stranger, he soon won a large circle of friends, and worked out for himself a high career of professional usefulness and honor. He was a young man of rare promise in his profession, and exhibited an aptness and fondness for it, which, accompanied by a thorough medical education, must soon have placed him in the front of medical men. He also possessed, in an eminent degree, that amiableness and gentleness of manner which render the physician a welcome visitor at all times at the bedside. While his death will be the most heavily felt in the immediate circles of his family and friends, the community have lost a most worthy member, and his profession a bright ornament.

FOSTER, John, Havana, Cuba, July 12, æ. —, a native of Maine. Mr. F. went to Cuba in 1843, and has spent the winter there since that time, with one or two exceptions. He was an excellent mechanic, and a true man in every respect. A countryman being taken down with the yellow fever, Mr. F. nursed him for six weeks, and, when convalescent, placed him on board a vessel for Boston. Mr. F. was soon taken by the yellow fever, and died in four days.

FOSTER, Mrs. Sarah M., Berlin City, Wis., Aug. 8, æ. 26, wife of Dr. J. A. Foster, and daughter of Azell Meritt, of Georgetown, N. J. Mrs. F. was an active and devoted member of the Methodist Episcopal church. Her piety illumined every circle in which she moved. Her long and wasting illness was a brilliant succession of Christian victories; and her death was another glorious exhibition of the power of grace to disarm death of its sting.

FOSTER, Capt. Thomas, Swannanoa, N. C., Dec. 24, æ. 84. Capt. F. represented his district in the state Senate in 1809, 1812, 1813, and 1814, and represented Buncombe in the House of Commons in 1817, and again in 1819. Blessed with a clear, strong, and comprehensive mind, his views on public questions were always eagerly sought and greatly respected. As a neighbor, a citizen, a father, and friend, he was comparatively faultless.

FOUST, Dr. Jacob, Sheffield, O., April 4, æ. 32.

FOX, James, Esq., Harrisburg, Pa., Feb. 28, a prominent lawyer, and widely known as a whig, the strictest of the sect.

FOX, Jedediah, Hancock, N. H., Sept. 21, æ. 77. He was one of the fine old men of the generation that is fast passing away, very much respected in the community where he had so long resided.

FRANCIS, Rev. Apollos, Norton, Mass., Dec. 26, æ. 87, a local preacher in the Methodist Episcopal church. He was a devoted servant of the Lord for more than a half century. He preached with great zeal, faith, and success, on circuits and stations with the itinerants. His religion led him to deal justly, love mercy, and walk with great humility and circumspection with his God. He was one of the pioneers of Methodism in Norton, Mansfield, Easton, Cumberland, Mass., Bristol, R. I., and other places in New England. His house was one of the homes of "the fathers," such as Brodhead, Pickering, Coye, Merritt, Snelling, and Dane. He was a good man; his memory is blessed.

FRANCIS, Ebenezer, Esq., Boston, Mass., Sept. 21, æ. 83. He was the son of Col. Ebenezer Francis; was born in Beverly, Mass., Oct. 15, 1775. His father was an officer in the revolutionary army, and was killed in battle in 1777. Mr. F. came to Boston when he was quite young, and was apprenticed to Jonathan Harris, who kept a dry goods store at No. 24 Cornhill, now Washington Street, with whom he was subsequently connected in business. About the year 1802 he established himself in business at No. 45 Long Wharf; but a few years afterwards he removed to Batterymarch Street, and subsequently to Broad Street, India Street, India Wharf, Kilby Street, and State Street. Possessing great financial skill, he exercised it with remarkable success, and accumulated an immense fortune, so that at the time of his death he was undoubtedly the wealthiest man, not only in Boston, but in New England. He was a director in the Boston Bank from 1809 to 1817. When the Suffolk Bank was chartered, Feb. 10, 1818, he was elected its first president, which office he held until 1825, when he declined a reëlection, but continued to serve as a director in the same bank for the nine following years. While president he originated the system of redeeming the bills of banks in other places, known as "the Suffolk Bank system," which has proved to be of great benefit in establishing a sound paper currency. He was one of the most efficient agents in founding the Massachusetts General Hospital in Boston, and was for several years its president, and chairman of the trustees. He was for many years president of the Cocheco Manufacturing Company in Dover, N. H. In 1827 he was elected treasurer of Harvard College, and held the office three years, during which time he succeeded in bringing order out of chaos in the regulation of its financial affairs; and on his retirement an elegant piece of plate was presented to him as a token of the appreciation of his great financial skill, and as a testimony of the value of his services, which he had rendered gratuitously while he was in office. The college also, in 1843, conferred upon him the honorary degree of A. M. Mr. F. married, Nov. 3, 1799, Elizabeth Thorndike, daughter of the Hon. Israel Thorndike, and had seven children, of whom two daughters only survive. They are the wives of Nathaniel I. Bowditch and Robert M. Mason, Esqs., of Boston. His wife died June 24, 1853, in the 75th year of her age. In all his extensive mercantile and business transactions Mr. F. was distinguished for his strict integrity. In private life he was of exceedingly sociable and affable deportment, and gifted with fine conversational powers. His success in the accumulation of wealth was the most remarkable instance we have ever had to record.

FREEMAN, Rt. Rev. George Washington, Little Rock, Ark., April 29, æ. 68. He was elected missionary bishop of the south-west 12 years ago, and has had under his jurisdiction the church in Texas and Arkansas. Few men have been more devoted to duty, and few men have had more calls for toil and sacrifice. He has been for many years anxious to obtain a bishop for Texas, and has been every time disappointed. He hardly lived to hear of the election of Mr. Weston, which took place only three days before his death, 600 miles from the chamber where the venerable pioneer was just then " shuffling off this mortal coil." Bishop Freeman was a High Churchman, very much esteemed and respected by every body. He was born in Sandwich, Mass., in 1790.

FREEMAN, Jonathan, Esq., Hanover, N. H., July 29, æ. 82. He was the second son of Hon. Jonathan Freeman, a representative in Congress from N. H., from 1797 to 1801, who died in 1808, in his 64th year, leaving a widow who survived him 38 years, and eight children, all of adult age at their father's decease, Asa Freeman, of Dover, and Peyton R. Freeman, of Portsmouth, N. H., being two of them. The above noticed death is the first (except, as is probable, that of the third son, who went to sea in 1809, and has not since been heard from) which has occurred in that family since their father's decease — a period of 22 days less than 50 years; the sum of the ages of the seven, being more than 521, and the average over 74 years.

FRENCH, Henry R., Ashland, Ky., May 15, æ. 39, editor of the Ashland Kentuckian. Mr. F. started the first daily newspaper in Texas, at Galveston, some 18 years since, and was, for some 12 years previous to 1856, editor of the Georgetown (Ky.) Herald.

FRENCH, Judge Hugh L., Jackson, Miss., —, —, æ. 50. He was a native of Virginia, but emigrated when six years of age, with his father, Mr. Hugh French, to Adair Co., Ky. He was a nephew of Col. Andrew Lewis, of revolutionary memory, his mother being a sister of that officer. Having been educated for the bar, he entered upon the discharge of his professional duties with characteristic fidelity, and established a reputation as a lawyer. His fellow-citizens repeatedly evinced their estimate of his talents and integrity by electing him to places of honor and profit.

FRENCH, Ira D., Esq., Cincinnati, O., Dec. —, æ. 35, a lawyer of whom the bar say, —

Whereas, Ira D. French, Esq., a member of this bar, has been taken, at the early age of 35, from our number by death; and whereas he commenced the study and the practice of the law in our midst, here formed his character as a lawyer, and rapidly attained to a position of distinction and usefulness, and before us presented an example of strict integrity, spotless morals, and social worth; and also of the aspirations, tastes, and attainments of the general scholar, in connection with high acquirements and unremitting industry as a lawyer, unusual facility and correctness as a practitioner, and unyielding devotion to all the demands of professional duty.

"*Resolved*, that with profound respect for the memory of our departed brother, we deplore his death, as a great loss to the community and our body, and personally to all of us."

FRENCH, Otis, M. D., Gilmanton Iron Works, N. H., April 9, æ. 53, a native of Sandwich, N. H. He received his medical degree at Dartmouth College, 1827, was in practice in Gilmanton nearly thirty years, where he acquired a deservedly high reputation, as well as a man and citizen as a physician. He represented the town in the General Court in 1843-4, and held other offices of trust; all of which he discharged with honor to himself and advantage to the community.

FRENCH, Mrs. Phebe, Sandown, N. H., April 19, æ. 78, wife of Rev. William French.

FRINK, John, Chicago, Ill., May 23, æ. 64. Mr. F. was one of the most remarkable men of the west. With limited opportunities in early life for the acquirement of an education other than what is implied in ability to read and write, he proved himself, in later years, capable of successfully conducting an immense business, with great profit to himself and with untold advantages to the west. Coming here at an early day — in 1838, we believe — he engaged extensively in mail-carrying, as a contractor under government, and for almost a quarter of a century was the head of that great stage company which, under his executive management, performed the mail service for half a dozen Western States. What difficulties there were to encounter — what patience, courage, and endurance were necessary for its successful prosecution — every old settler knows; and though John Frink has probably been more heartily cursed by weary and impatient travellers than any other man between the Atlantic and Pacific, now, when we can look back upon his labors, his obstacles and triumphs, we feel assured that no other man could have carried through what he did. The States of Illinois, Wisconsin, Iowa, Missouri, and Indiana owe more to his unequalled administrative ability, for their early settlement and mail facilities, than to the labor of any living soul. He continued in the business to which he was bred until his coaches were superseded by railroad trains; and then, with the enterprise which was a part of his being, at once interested himself largely in the new method of travel, becoming, as he was when he died, a large stockholder in an important line.

FROST, Rev. Barzillai, Concord, Mass., Dec. 8, æ. 54. Mr. Frost was born in Effingham, N. H., June 18, 1804. He was fitted for college at Exeter Academy, under the charge of Benjamin Abbot, LL. D., and graduated at that institution with the highest honors in 1827. He then entered the Sophomore class at Harvard University, and graduated with distinction in 1830, being a classmate with Hon. Charles Sumner, and the late Hon. Thomas Hopkinson. On leaving college he was appointed preceptor of Framingham Academy, which situation he held two years. In 1832, he entered the Divinity School at Cambridge, where he completed his theological studies in 1835. During this period he was appointed instructor in mathematics to the senior class in the college in place of Professor Farrar, who visited Europe for the benefit of his health. This situation he filled two years, pursuing his theological studies at the same time. February 1, 1837, he was ordained as colleague with Rev. Ezra Ripley, D. D., over the Unitarian church and society in Concord. Dr. Ripley died Sept. 21, 1841, at the age of 90 years, and Mr. Frost continued in the uninterrupted active and successful discharge of his duties as pastor until the autumn of 1855, when, in consequence of a severe cold, his lungs became seriously affected, and he was obliged to relinquish the performance of his pastoral duties. In February, 1856, he sailed for St. Thomas, and after spending nearly three months on that island, and on the Islands of Jamaica, Cuba, and St. Croix, he returned to the United States. His health continuing feeble, he sailed,

Nov. 24, for St. Croix, where he passed about five months; and on his return he visited the Island of Bermuda, where he remained several weeks. He arrived home the latter part of June, 1857. His health being still in a very precarious state, he was obliged, Sept. 13, 1857, to ask a dismission, which was granted with great reluctance, his parishioners unanimously expressing, on the occasion, their great regret that the interesting relation which had so long existed between them and their beloved pastor should be terminated, and manifesting in various ways their strong and affectionate regard for him. His pastoral relation closed Oct. 3, 1857. A few weeks before the termination of his connection with the church and society, he suffered a severe affliction in the departure from this life of his distinguished and excellent parishioner, the Hon. Samuel Hoar. One of the last, and probably the very last sermon which he wrote was that he preached on the Sabbath next after the interment of his lamented and faithful friend. It was a simple and plain, but able and interesting discourse. Though written by Mr. Frost while in a feeble state of health, it was a full and just tribute to the memory of a great and good man. For a period of about 20 years, Mr. Frost performed all the duties of an active, zealous, and faithful minister. Every good cause found in him an earnest and efficient friend and advocate. His ministry was a very useful and successful one. A satisfactory evidence of this is, that during the whole course of his labors at Concord, he secured the entire respect and enjoyed the uninterrupted confidence and friendship of Samuel Hoar. November 12, 1857, Mr. Frost, accompanied by his faithful and excellent wife, and his youngest son, a very interesting boy of about ten years of age, sailed for Fayal, one of the Azores, in the hope that it might restore him to health. After remaining at the island about eight months he returned to his native shore. He arrived at Boston about the middle of August last. On the arrival of Mr. Frost at Boston, he was in a very prostrated condition, and was borne from the ship to the residence of a friend in the city, where he remained about a week. He was then carried to Concord, and was there received into the house of his kind and faithful friend and physician, Dr. Josiah Bartlett. Finding himself in so comfortable a mansion, among a host of his friends, consisting of his former parishioners and other esteemed acquaintances, his spirits revived, and his strength seemed to be considerably improved. He rode out a few times, and had the satisfaction of taking a parting look at the places endeared to him as having been the scenes of the cares and pleasures with which he was conversant during his Christian ministry. He took great comfort in being able to see and converse with his dear friends once more. At length he began to grow weaker, and about the first of November the symptoms of a speedy dissolution were manifested; but he still lingered until December 8, when, in the presence of his wife and son, his faithful physician, and other dear friends, his spirit took its flight to another and a better world. Mr. F. married, June 1, 1837, Elmira Stone, youngest daughter of Mr. Daniel and Mrs. Sally (Buckminster) Stone, of Framingham. They had four children, two of whom died in infancy. Another died in Fayal. The surviving son graduated at Harvard University at the last commencement, and is now a student at law in the office of the Hon. E. R. Hoar.

FRY, Dr, Thomas, Pittsburg, Pa., Sept. 13, æ. 78.

FULLER, Col. George R., Chittenango, N. Y., May 18. He removed to Chittenango from Schenectady, at an early day, and was for many years the confidential agent of the late Hon. John B. Yates. He was warmly interested in all enterprises which tended to improve the place of his adoption, and gave liberally from his abundant means to objects which met his approval. To the prosperity of the "Yates Polytechnic Institute" he devoted much time and money, and to his efforts, in a great measure, is due the success with which it has met. A polished gentleman in his manners, urbane and courteous, he added that noblest work of God, "an honest man."

FULLER, Gen. Isham, Hart township, Ind., ——, ——, æ. 60. Gen. F. was an old citizen of the county, had represented it several years in the legislature, and had filled several offices of honor and trust. ●

FULLER, Dr. Lemuel, Attleboro', Mass., Dec. 7, æ. 81.

FUQUAY, Rev. Thomas, Sevier Co., Ark., April 22. æ. 64. He was a native of Kentucky, the son of Joseph and Judith Fuquay. He emigrated to the State of Arkansas in the year 1823, and was married to Delia Browning in the year 1826, and professed faith in Christ in 1831, under the ministry of the Rev. James Black, at a camp-meeting held near Washington, in Hempstead Co., Ark. It is not known at what time he commenced to preach the gospel. He was a man of strong native intellect, studious in the acquisition of knowledge, clear in doctrine, forcible in his arguments, and persuasive in his style of address. One of his distinguishing characteristics was, decision of character, combined with fixedness of purpose; yet he was frank and urbane in his manners, dignified in his deportment, both at home and abroad.

G.

GEN. JAMES GADSDEN, Charleston, S. C., Dec. 26, æ. 70. General G. was born in Charleston, May 15, 1788. His father was Philip Gadsden, Esq., the youngest son of Gen. Christopher E. Gadsden, and was a gentleman of high moral instincts, and of modest and retiring habits. He married early in life, and was the parent of 16 children. He reared to man and womanhood eight sons and four daughters. Seven of the former still survive, of which Christopher Gadsden, the bishop of the Protestant Episcopal church, is the eldest. The late district attorney, John Gadsden, (on one occasion the intendent of the city of Charleston,) recollected by many for his high moral and intellectual qualifications, was the second, and the subject of this memorial the third.

Col. Gadsden received the rudiments of his education at the Associated Academy of Charleston, supervised by Williams, Dwyer, Smith, Hughes, and Hedley; all instructors in succession, and each of them of high reputation in their respective departments in science and the classics. He completed his education at Yale College in New Haven, Ct., under the presidency of the celebrated Dr. T. Dwight. He was at that institution with the lamented Calhoun, who was his senior. His two brothers, the Rt. Rev. C. E. Gadsden, and John Gadsden, with the Hon. John W. Felder, of Orangeburg, were classmates with Mr. Calhoun.

In 1803 the intercourse with New York was uncertain and irregular. To reach New Haven, young Gadsden had to take passage for Newport, the captain stipulating to forward him to the place of his destination. From Newport he was shipped on board of a sloop navigating the Sound (passing almost in sight of New Haven) for New York. On his arrival at the latter place, he was transferred to one of the daily packets, a small craft of about 60 tons, which left Peck Slip every evening, the passengers paying for the transportation of their persons only, taking tea beforehand in New York, and expecting to breakfast in New Haven. It was the practice of these packets to receive all passengers who offered, without regard to accommodations; and when the multitude assembled, (after leaving the dock,) they had to cast lots for the few berths the vessel afforded.

Without consultation with parents or friends, he followed the just impulses of his inclinations, and what he considered his obligations, and applied, through Mr. Cheves, the then representative of Charleston district, for a commission in the army. He was promptly gratified with a lieutenancy in the corps of engineers, and was the first individual that had been appointed to that scientific arm of the service, without the previous education and discipline at West Point — Mr. Cheves contending that his previous education and attainments having well fitted him to fill the office honorably to himself and the country.

He immediately sought active service, and was in consequence ordered to report to Gen. Wilkinson, at Sacketts Harbor, the then head-quarters of that portion of the army, where extensive military preparations were in progress for the invasion of Canada and a march on Montreal. In descending the St. Lawrence, he was a volunteer in Capt. Sumter's company, in a successful repulse of two British gun brigs in their attack on an advanced wing of the American army, encamped for the night at French Creek. He was subsequently in the engagement at Williamsburg, and in most of the skirmishes (which Gen. Wilkinson denominates "scratchings in the rear") with the British, in their efforts to retard the advance of the Americans on Montreal, until circumstances induced the commanding general to recross the St. Lawrence, and to retire into winter quarters at French Mills and Chautaque Four Corners. When Wilkinson subsequently decided to retrieve his fortunes by a winter operation against the British posts on the St. Johns, Lieut. Gadsden marched with the army from the Four Corners, on La Cole Mill, where another repulse and exceedingly severe weather forced the general to fall back on Plattsburg. The extensive military preparations of the British, the next season, inclined the secretary of war to the opinion that New York was to be the object of attack, and Lieut. Gadsden was ordered to report to Gen. Swift, to aid in the construction of lines of defence, in advance of Brooklyn, and on Harlem Heights. His labors, however, were unnecessary, as the British directed their operations where the Americans were seemingly less prepared, but where, on the plains of New Orleans, they met with a signal and unexpected defeat from Gen. Jackson.

To compensate Lieut. Gadsden for his sore disappointment in this respect, he was detailed as the engineer to report to Col. Walbach, of the artillery, at Portsmouth, N. H., and coöperate with Gov. King in the capture of Castine, then in possession of the British. The necessary artillery trains, snow sledges, and other arrangements for a winter operation were all consummated, when the news of peace arrested all hostile movements against the enemy.

At the close of the war, Lieut. Gadsden was selected to join Gen. Jackson as an engineer, to examine and report on the military defences of the Gulf of Mexico frontier. In a few hours after an introduction and interview, Gen. Jackson tendered him the situation near his person, as confidential aide-de-camp, and they immediately proceeded to the execution of the military reconnoissance imposed. The next season Lieut. Gadsden was the first American engineer selected to review these examinations in coöperation with Gen. Bernard, and to report a system of defence for the Gulf. Not concurring in some of the views of Gen. Bernard, and although but a junior officer of engineers, he had the independence to record his dissent in a separate report, (an act of much temerity, but typical of the real independence of the man,) and the gratification afterwards of having his position sustained by many older members of the engineer corps. The next year he accompanied Gen. Jackson on the Seminole campaign and was at the battle of Mickasukey, and at the capture of St. Marks, where he found and secured Arbuthnot; and when Ambrister was subsequently arrested at the Suwance towns, Lieut. Gadsden descended the river with a detachment of troops and captured a schooner in the service of the incendiaries, on board of which were found the correspondence and documents which led to their condemnation and execution. The captain having refused to navigate the vessel, considering himself a prisoner of war, Lieut. Gadsden, with characteristic promptness, assumed the command, and made sail for the port of St. Marks, where he safely arrived with his prize, and rejoined the army on its return from the Suwance. At Pensacola he planned the approaches, and established the batteries within 400 yards of the glacis of Fort Barancas, which forced Gov. Massot to surrender at discretion.

At the close of this Indian contest, Lieut. Gadsden was promoted to a captaincy, and had, by a rule of service limiting aides-de-camp to lieutenants, to retire from the military family of Gen. Jackson, when he was detailed to take charge of the works to be constructed for the defence of the Gulf frontier. He was in progress with the fortifications designed for Mobile Bay, and the passes into Lake Pontchartrain, when a vacancy in the inspector's department again reunited him to the military staff of Gen. Jackson, as inspector general of the southern division of the army, with the rank of colonel. He accompanied Gen. Jackson to Pensacola, when he took possession of Florida as governor, and was instrumental in harmonizing a difference of opinion, which grew out of the treaty with the Spanish governor, Calliva, and which might have led to serious results.

On the reduction of the army in 1822, Col. Gadsden was detailed as inspector general; but subsequently, on the recommendation of a board of general officers charged with the arrangement of the new military organization of the army, he was transferred to the office of adjutant general, and in this capacity he served for some six or eight months with Mr. Calhoun, who was then secretary of war, and while he was maturing his plans for the reorganization of that department.

Under a commission from Mr. Monroe, he accomplished a treaty for removing the Seminole Indians from Middle to Southern Florida, and undertook an exploration of the peninsula. He penetrated by land to Cape Florida, at great hazard from vagabond Indians, and of health; having buried several of his party in the wilderness during his expedition. He was the first white man who ventured to cross on a low parallel of latitude from the Atlantic to the Gulf shore through those jungles, glades, fastnesses, and swamps, which afterwards became the theatre of many disasters, and of General Taylor's early and successful achievements in the field.

The Indians removed, Col. Gadsden settled in one of their villages, "Warcissa," near Tallahassee, from which they had retired, and sought the independence and seclusion of a planter with moderate beginnings.

Col. Gadsden was allured from his retreat to take part in the railroad enterprises of his native state, which had been stimulated by the progress of the system in all parts of the country.

He was one of the first, and we believe the first, who drew public attention to the value of Sullivan's Island, as a sea coast summer retreat for the citizens of South Carolina, the neighboring and South-western States, instead of resorting to the less favored positions of Cape May, Rockaway, and Nahant.

The manufacturing and the mechanic interests he likewise fostered, and to the extent of his mite, contributed in aid of both, and particularly to test the applicability of slave labor to the manipulations in each. With the eye of a statesman, looking in advance, he recognized in this policy new sources of productive labor (should the present fail or prove inadequate) for the slave population of the south.

The last public position of importance held by Gen. Gadsden was that of minister to Mexico, appointed by President Pierce. While in that country he made the celebrated "Gadsden purchase," acquiring a large slice of Mexico, now known as Arizona, for which the United States paid $10,000,000. He brought his own treaty to Washington, and it was confirmed by the Senate. He was succeeded in the Mexican mission by Mr. John Forsyth, who has just returned home, having closed the legation in consequence of difficulties with the Zuloaga government.

GAINES, Maj. John P., Oregon, ——— —, æ. —. Maj..G. was formerly a citizen of Kentucky. He was in the Mexican war, and taken prisoner by the enemy. On his return at the close of the war, he entered Congress, having been elected during his captivity, and served two sessions. In 1850 he was appointed governor of Oregon, by President Fillmore.

GAITHER, Gen. William Lingan, Montgomery Co., Md., at Berkeley Springs, Aug. 2, æ. 45, the only son of Henry Chew and Eliza Gaither. His father was a respectable citizen of the same county, the son of William Gaither, of Frederick Co., and nephew of Col. Henry Gaither, a gallant soldier of the revolution. He was a prominent politician, frequently a representative in the legislature of the state. He was one of the little band who volunteered to defend the press in Baltimore, at the time of the excitement in 1812, and was with Gen. Lingan, when he fell at the hands of a merciless mob. His mother was the daughter of Major William Worthington, also a citizen of Montgomery Co., well known for his hospitality. Gen. Wm. L. G. was the only child of his parents, and was brought up with all the tenderness and fond solicitude of an only son. Never, perhaps, was parental care more fully requited; for his filial affection and devotedness to his parents, especially to his aged mother, through her declining years of sickness and infirmity, was one of the marked features in his character. Nurtured and trained under wise parental influences, he grew up free from the besetting vices of youth; and when he entered upon political life, which he did at a very early age, it was with a character already well formed and matured, and with moral principles and habits well established. From these he never deviated in all the conflicts and temptations of public life. With natural abilities of a high order, well cultivated by reading and study, with manners gentle and courteous, though somewhat reserved, and with high sense of true honor, manliness, and integrity, he did not fail, early in life, to command the respect and secure the confidence of his fellow-citizens. At the age of 22 he was elected to represent Montgomery Co. in the House of Delegates of Md., and continued, with slight intermissions, until his death, a member of one or other of the branches of the legislature. For many years he was president of the state Senate, and at the time of his death was a member of that body — acknowledged to be one of its most useful and influential members. When not engaged in public business, having an ample patrimony, he spent his time in travelling, or on his country estate, in reading, social intercourse or private business. But his chief attention and study were directed to state affairs, which developed and made eminently useful his fine natural abilities. Being intimately and personally acquainted with the history and objects of state policy, and very familiar with the principles as well as the details of legislation, his influence was always strongly *felt*, even when not exerted so as to draw attention. His wisdom, firmness, and long experience, exercised a very healthful influence over the public councils. The bent of his mind always led him to view measures in the light of cautious prudence. As a party man, firm, reliable, conservative, he was a prominent leader of the whig party in the legislature. Upon the disorganization of the whig party in 1854-6, he supported the democratic party — being honestly persuaded, that, under the circumstances, such was the duty he owed to the best interests of his country. Gen. G. was also actively engaged in the promotion of internal improvements, such as railroads, &c. He was a director on the part of the state in the Baltimore and Ohio Railroad Company. In 1851 he was appointed by the executive a member of the board of examiners for West Point. He was also elector for president and vice president on several occasions, and considered it the proudest act of his life, to have cast the vote of Maryland for Henry Clay, for president, in 1844. His course was marked by dignity of bearing, honesty of purpose, and independence of action. Though reserved in his manner, he was always accessible on proper occasions. In private intercourse his conversation was always instructive, pleasing, and elevating. His intellect and character were most appreciated by those who knew him best. He affords an instance of a perfect gentleman, passing through public life without a stain. Gen. G. was brought up in the Episcopal church, of which his parents were members. He was always an attendant upon its services, and for many years a vestryman of his native parish. During his last illness, his mind was deeply engaged in the subject of religion. He died at the early age of 45, without family, but remembered for his virtues and public services.

GALLAND, Dr. Isaac, Fort Madison, Iowa, Sept. 27, æ. 69. From a personal acquaintance of nearly half a century with Indian life and conduct, there is little in the manners, the history, or the traditions of the children of the forest that he was not familiar with, and at the time of his death he was engaged in writing a work on the Black Hawk war, and its causes and incidents, for a knowledge of which his residence on the Upper Mississippi, at the date of that war, gave him peculiar advantages. He has, during the last 30 years, published many scraps of personal adventure and history, which have always been received by the public with pleasure and eagerness; for, aside from the stirring incidents related, he wielded a pen noted for both its wit and vigor. He was a kind and affectionate husband and father; and as a neighbor and friend, the sorrow for his death which this community shows is his best panegyric.

GALLISON, Elder William F., Foxcroft, Me., March 9, æ. 59. Elder G. belonged to the denomination of Free Will Baptists, and has been in communion with that church for many years. Two years since he was nominated as a candidate for the office of register of probate, and was elected to that office by a large majority. He has ever sustained the character of a faithful preacher and a good man.

GALLUP, Robert, Greene, N. Y., May 20, æ. 97, a revolutionary hero, and said to be the last survivor of the Fort Griswold massacre. Mr. G. took up his residence in Plymouth, Chenango Co., in 1807, where he resided for some years. After a short residence in Norwich, he came to Greene, where he has continued to dwell until his death. In pursuance of a resolution of citizens at a public meeting, minute guns were fired, the flag displayed at half mast, and the bells tolled, upon the occasion of his corpse leaving Greene, on its way to Plymouth, for interment. The body was escorted by a large procession, accompanied with music, to the bounds of the corporation. Suitable honors were paid to the deceased as his remains passed through Oxford and Norwich. At Norwich the fine artillery corps of Capt. Tyrrell escorted the body through the town, amidst the booming of cannon. Capt. Tyrrell's artillery went to Plymouth, and assisted in burying the old hero with appropriate military honors. Thus has passed away the last of that gallant band of patriots who were residents of the county of Chenango. But few remain — scarcely a hundred — of those gallant souls who serve to remind the present generation of the trying times of the past; and as, one by one, they drop from our sight, we feel a mournful satisfaction in knowing that they have witnessed the joyful fruit of their labors, and that their last hours are soothed by the grateful efforts of a free and happy people anxious to pay tribute to their valued services. Lie quiet in your graves, ye heroic men. Millions yet unborn shall do homage to your worth, and speak your names with holy reverence.

GARDNER, Hon. Henry, M. D., Boston, Mass., June 19, æ. 78. He was the son of Henry and Hannah Gardner, and was born in the old Province House in Boston, Aug. 2, 1779. His father, Henry Gardner, was born in Stow, Mass., Nov. 14, 1731, and graduated at Harvard College in 1750. He was judge of the Court of Common Pleas for Middlesex; and afterwards, on his removal to Boston, he was elected a councillor and treasurer of Massachusetts. He was also a member of the American Academy of Arts and Sciences. While holding the office of treasurer he resided in the Province House, where were vaults for the safe keeping of the provincial revenues. He died Oct. 8, 1782, in the 51st year of his age. His grandfather, Rev. John Gardner, was born in Charlestown, Mass., July 22, 1695; graduated at Harvard College in 1715; was ordained pastor of the Congregational church in Stow, Nov. 26, 1718; and died Jan. 10, 1775, in the 80th year of his age and 57th of his ministry. Dr. G. was fitted for college at Andover, and graduated at Harvard in 1798, being a classmate with Rev. Dr. Channing, Rev. Dr. Tuckerman, Judge Story, and Judge Fay. He studied medicine with Dr. John Warren, of Boston; received the degree of M. B. in 1801, and that of M. D. in 1811, but did not practise his profession many years after receiving the latter degree. According to the laws of primogeniture then existing, he, being the oldest son, inherited a double portion of his father's estate, which was large; and, being thus placed above the necessity of engaging in any stated business, he watched the growth of his wealth, and was his own master in the employment of his time. He resided many years in Dorchester, where he was highly esteemed by the people of that ancient town, who elected him a representative to the legislature in 1822, 1823, and 1824. He was chosen a senator from Norfolk district in 1825, 1826, and 1827. He was also a member from Dorchester of the convention in 1820 for revising the constitution of the state. Of late years he has declined all public offices, preferring the quiet of private life, and devoting himself to agricultural pursuits and the superintendence of his large estate. He was a gentleman of strict integrity, and was highly respected in the community. He married, 1st, May 17, 1803, Joanna Bird Everett, daughter of Rev. Moses Everett, of Dorchester. She died Feb. 7, 1807, leaving one daughter, who is now the wife of Daniel Denny, Esq., of Boston. He married, 2d, March 20, 1810, Clarissa Holbrook, daughter of Dr. Amos Holbrook, of Milton, Mass., by whom he had three children, — two daughters and a son, — of whom only the son — Hon. Henry Joseph Gardner, late governor of Massachusetts — is living. His second wife survives him.

GARDNER, Robert, Esq., Roxbury, Mass., Dec. 30, æ. 62, a well-known merchant, who had held many offices of honor and trust in the city government.

GARMAN, Charles, Bedford Co., Tenn., April 19, æ. 102, a revolutionary soldier.

GARTHWAIT, William S., Carthage, Ill., Jan. 24, æ. —, associate editor of the Carthage Republican. Capt. G. was a volunteer soldier during the Mexican war, under Col. Baker, and participated in some of the great battles between Vera Cruz and the city of Mexico. He was a brave and fearless soldier, and won the universal respect of his companions in arms and of his superior officers.

GATLING, Dr. John, Sunsbury, Gates Co., N. C., Nov. 23. In the death of Dr. G., Gates has lost one of her most influential, intelligent, and worthy citizens. For years he stood at the head of his profession. For the last 15 years he has turned his attention to agriculture and domestic affairs, in which he was eminently successful.

GAULT, Samuel E., Pembroke, N. H., Dec. 14, æ. 36. Mr. G. was a member of the legislature in 1856 and 1857, and was in every respect an excellent and true man, whose loss will be deeply felt by his aged father, Mr. Samuel Gault, and by a large circle of friends by whom he was respected, and to whom he was endeared by his manly character and many generous deeds.

GAYLORD, Thomas G., New York, ——, æ. —. Mr. G. was a valuable citizen of Cincinnati. He was emphatically a self-made man. His fellow-citizens regarded him as a gentleman of marked probity. As a business man, he was prompt, never allowing his paper to be protested; and he possessed a sagacious mind. He was a native of Utica, N.Y.; married at 22, and removed to Pittsburg, where he engaged in the queensware business with a small capital which he had accumulated. Thence he removed to Maysville, Ky., and subsequently to Portsmouth, O., where he laid the foundations of a handsome fortune in the manufacture of iron. About 12 years ago he removed to Cincinnati, where he has since remained. He was always actively engaged in business, and, when he died, was in New York upon business connected with his firm, T. G. Gaylord & Son. He was a very successful business man, and accumulated property estimated to be now worth $200,000. He left a widow and several children to mourn their bereavement.

GEORGE, Mrs. Sophia, Barnstead Parade, N. H., Feb. 13, æ. 79, wife of Rev. Enos George, pastor of the Congregational church in B.

GEORGE, Rev. Z. Jeter, Richmond, Va., April 6, æ. 23, pastor of the Manchester Baptist church.

GERMOND, Smith P., Washington, Dutchess Co., N. Y., —— —, æ. 50. Mr. G. was one of the best men in Dutchess Co., and had represented his town in the board of supervisors. He was about 50 years of age, in good circumstances, and leaves a wife and family.

GIBBS, Hon. Leman, Livonia, N. Y., June —, æ. 70. Judge G. was a highly esteemed citizen, and had long been prominent in public affairs in this town and county. For many years he was a county judge, justice of the peace, and supervisor, and represented his district in the Assembly a few years ago. He must have been among the earliest settlers in his town.

GIBSON, David, Jr., Jefferson Co., Miss., Dec. 12, æ. 97. He was born in (the now) Marion District, S. C., and remembered well the firing of cannon and ringing of bells when the declaration of July, 1776, was promulgated in the district; also many incidents connected with the early struggle that followed, in his native state, in which his family, father, brothers, and uncles participated. After the fall of Charlestown, they removed to East Tennessee, and spent a year. His descendants and connections are very numerous from South Carolina to California, and are, and have been, among our most useful citizens, comprising men of all honorable callings, preachers, teachers, learned professions, legislators, planters, and merchants. He was remarkable for the urbanity and dignity of his manners; the perfect integrity and uprightness of his daily walk and conversation; for the preservation and active use of his physical strength and mental faculties to within a few days of his death; but more than all was he remarkable for being a living exemplification of that faith on which the hope of a happy immortality beyond the grave is founded.

GILBERT, Daniel C., Esq. Vidalia, Miss., Oct. 22, æ. 25, at the residence of Lewis Pipes, in Adams Co., near Natchez, a member of the Louisiana bar. Mr. G. was born at the family residence in Concordia Parish, April 2, 1833, and was consequently in his 26th year. Classically educated, he completed his law studies at the university of Louisiana, was admitted to the bar in Concordia, opened a law office at Vidalia, and had been just nominated to the office of recorder of the parish. He was a young gentleman of decided character, of great moral firmness and unswerving integrity; warm and genial in his associations and friendships; true as steel to his word and principles, and a firm and consistent democrat in political faith. But the crowning glory of his character was love and reverence to his widowed mother, and a more than paternal care and oversight extended to his younger brothers, now in a course of collegiate education. The oldest son, he assumed the duties of guardian and head of the family immediately after the death of his lamented father, who was an eminent Louisiana planter.

GILBERT, Herman C., Buffalo, N. Y., July 9, w. —, commercial editor of the Buffalo Commercial Advertiser. His industry and accuracy were proverbial, and his services invaluable.

HON. JOHN JAMES GILCHRIST, Washington, D. C., April 29, æ. 49. Judicial services make men less conspicuous than political; but they are not less important or less useful; and the faculties and accomplishments they demand are not less high or less rare. But from the limited sphere in which the life of a judge moves, it is the more imperative duty of those who know his value to set forth, distinctly and carefully, his claims to the gratitude and reverence of the community which he has served.

John James Gilchrist was born in Medford, Mass., Feb. 16, 1809. His father, James Gilchrist, was a master of a vessel, and is yet well remembered by many, as a man of powerful frame, vigorous understanding, and great energy of character. He early acquired a competence, and removed, while his son was yet a child of tender years, to the beautiful village of Charlestown, in New Hampshire, where he bought a farm, and occupied himself in rural pursuits for the remainder of his life, wh'ch was brought to a close in the prime of his manhood, from the effects of an accident. Here the boyhood of Judge Gilchrist was mainly passed; and here he pursued, under the guidance of the Rev. Dr. Crosby, a portion of the studies preparatory to a collegiate course. He entered Harvard College in the autumn of 1824, and graduated 1828.

After leaving college he commenced the study of the law at Charlestown, under the guidance of the late William Briggs, an eccentric but very well read lawyer, who possessed a much larger and better collection of law books than country practitioners usually accumulate. Of these books, in that quiet village, in which there was so little to disturb or distract the mind of the student, Judge Gilchrist made most excellent use, and by a wide range of elementary reading laid the foundations of his ample stores of legal learning. From the office of Mr. Briggs, he went to the law school in Cambridge, where he was known as a most diligent student, ranging over the whole domain of the common law, and letting none of his opportunities pass by unimproved. Upon his admission to the bar, he formed a connection in business with the late Governor Hubbard, whose daughter he afterwards married; thus finding himself at once in good employment, and escaping the discipline of that dreary period between the expecting of clients and the coming of them. The next few years were passed in the diligent and successful practice of the law, but in such way that he was every day adding something to his stock of practical and available legal learning. As was naturally to be expected of a rising young lawyer, he took some part in the politics of his state, and was for more than a year a member of the legislature; but he always made the politician subservient to the lawyer, and his aspirations were professional, and not political. When, therefore, in 1840, at the early age of 31, he was appointed one of the associate justices of the Supreme Court of New Hampshire, it was with the general and hearty approval of the bar and the public. He was a very young man for such a post; a year younger than Judge Story was when he was made a judge, and also a year younger than Mr. Justice Buller when he was elevated to the King's Bench, at an age which startled all the venerable proprieties of Westminster Hall.

When, in 1848, the place of chief justice was made vacant by the resignation of Judge Parker, Judge Gilchrist had proved himself to be a man of such high judicial excellence, and to be possessed of such a principle of intellectual growth and progress, that the eyes of all were at once turned towards him as to one in natural succession to the dignity; and his appointment gave general satisfaction and equal assurance. In this high place he remained until the Court of Claims was created by Congress, when he was placed at the head of this tribunal by President Pierce, who was his warm personal friend, who had often appeared before him at the bar, and thus knew at first hand, and of his own knowledge, how eminently qualified he was for the responsible and laborious duties which were to be devolved upon him.

Thus of the 27 years which elapsed between his admission to the bar and his lamented death, 18 were passed in the discharge of judicial duties. It is as a judge, then, that we are to consider him; and by the manner in which he bore himself in this high office are we to try his claims to be held in gratitude and honor by those who come after him. He put his whole mind — all that he had and all that he was — into his judicial life; before the public he stood in no other aspect, and was known by them in no other character. When he first went upon the bench, we have little doubt that he contemplated it as, in all human probability, a life-long service; and we know that he determined to devote himself to it with entire singleness of purpose, and to leave nothing undone which could help to make him as good a judge as his gifts and powers would permit him to be. To this determination he adhered, never yielding to the seductions of indolence, and never turned aside by the temptations of political ambition. He had the advantage of an excellent preparation, both in book knowledge and in practice; and he had the further advantage of having an admirable judicial understanding, and a perfect judicial temperament. Thus upon the bench he was ever a growing man; and at the time of his death he would have been pronounced a magistrate of the first class, tried by any standard known to the bar in England or America.

His learning was ample, various, and serviceable. In depth and extent of legal lore, many of his judicial contemporaries may have equalled him, and a few may have excelled him. He had no professional pedantry, no vanity of legal antiquarianism, no taste for the obsolete curiosities of black letter learning. But he had a sufficient knowledge of the history, principles, and spirit of the common law, to view every subject that arose from its proper point of view, and in its just relations to kindred and collateral branches; and his patience of labor enabled him to investigate every question that required research, thoroughly and completely. He had in a high degree that fine legal perception which distinguishes the living principle from the accidental, and temporary forms through which it has been manifested. Having early taken a wide survey of the whole field of legal learning, and made an outline map of the region, it was a matter of course that his after-acquired knowledge should naturally and easily have fallen into place, been duly classified and arranged, and kept within easy reach, and ready for use.

The digest of New Hampshire reports, published by him in 1846, well illustrates his power of thorough and scientific classification. On examination, it will be found no servile copy of preceding compilations, but a work of independent investigation and original construction. The only criticism which it ever called forth, was on the part of those who complained that it was a departure from the stereotyped forms in which digests are usually cast, and thus to them less convenient for immediate reference — an objection to which no one could have assented who had used the book enough to comprehend its luminous method.

In presiding over the full bench, he was quick, attentive, and courteous. He rarely interrupted counsel in their arguments, unless he had reason to apprehend that he had failed to take the point intended to be conveyed; and when the necessary explanation had been given, he applied himself anew to his task of patient hearing. He knew that nothing is gained, in point of time, by interrupting counsel for the sake of answering them, and that such a course often leads to unprofitable and unseemly discussions. His judgments were rendered with perfect clearness, and are written with scholarlike accuracy and taste. His statement of facts was often made with such lucid and consecutive method as to leave little to be done in the way of legal reasoning and the application of legal principles.

But his fine judicial qualities were even more signally displayed in his sittings at Nisi Prius. Here a judge is constantly exposed to emergencies which put his faculties and resources to the severest tests; for no foresight can predict, no preparation can anticipate, the unexpected turns of a trial, or the sudden questions which arise, and must be at once settled. All these claims were met by Judge Gilchrist with an ease and self-possession, — a dignity and courtesy, — which nothing but conscious strength could give. He ruled his court without effort, and without his rule being uncomfortably felt. His own sweetness of temper and serenity of temperament had a natural and benignant influence upon the bar: his own manner was so collected and courteous, that it acted with contagious power upon others. In all the jar and heat of forensic strife, he never for a moment lost his temper, and was always ready, when the occasion required it, with a seasonable word or two to soothe the ruffled feelings of contending counsel. A gentleman of nice observation, who had long been a practitioner before him, states that he had never seen him, in a single instance, give way to the slightest expression of impatience or irritability. His delicate sense of humor often enabled him, when the zeal of counsel was presuming a little too much upon the good nature of the bench, to check them by an admonition in a playful form, which recalled them to their duty, but left no sting behind.

To the trial of a cause he gave strict and undivided attention. Not a word escaped from him, — not a look could be detected, — from which an inference could be drawn as to his impressions of the case. He took careful and full notes of the testimony: every thing that occurred which was necessary to be remembered was recorded, the exact point of each exception written down, and in matters of nicety submitted at once to the counsel, — so that when the trial was over, every one was ready to admit the absolute truthfulness of the record.

In charging the jury he stated with clearness and precision, but without any technicalities, the points of the case, and the exact questions to be determined by them, and read from his notes every thing which the witnesses had said material to those points. He was rarely heard to say that this or that witness proved such and such facts; but he stated clearly what had been said, but without any comment which would have intimated his own opinion, or led the jury to think that he had done so.

As we have before intimated, the public life of Judge Gilchrist was exclusively judicial; and by his long and able service in this department, he has earned a title to the lasting gratitude and reverence of the community. But in the hearts of his friends he has left other records and built other monuments. And he was rich in friends; for his tastes and sympathies were not fastidious, though discriminating; and his qualities of mind and character were such as to exert a strong attraction over all who came within his sphere. His love of literature continued unabated to the last: in the reading of good books he found constant refreshment and relaxation in the arduous duties of his judicial life. With the Latin and French languages he was entirely familiar, and he read their books with discriminating relish; but his chief pleasure was in constant communion with the best specimens of the literature of England and of his own country. His taste was manly, catholic, and independent, but with a natural preference for the writers who were popular in his boyhood and youth.

No one had a better claim than he to the "grand old name of gentleman," whether we regard the essential or the formal elements which make up that character — the inward sentiment or the external manifestation. He was a finished man even in small things. He was careful, for instance, and scrupulously neat in his dress and personal appearance, and did not fall into the common practice — just the reverse of what should be the case — of growing slovenly and neglectful as he grew older. So, too, his handwriting was both legible and beautiful, and he took great pains to keep it so, and to resist the injuring influences of the constant taking down of testimony from the lips of witnesses. The comfort of good judicial handwriting to lawyers, reporters, and printers, is more obvious than common.

Judge Gilchrist married in 1836 Miss Sarah Hubbard, daughter of the late Governor Hubbard: his widow and two children, a son and daughter, survive him. In the several domestic relations of son, husband, father, and brother, he was one of the kindest, most amiable, and most indulgent of men. His home in the beautiful village of Charlestown — a finely-situated, unostentatious, and most comfortable country house — was the seat of a simple and generous hospitality; and those of his friends who have been welcomed by him under his roof will sadly and tenderly recall the happy hours there spent, and the atmosphere of easy kindness which they breathed from the moment its threshold was crossed.

GILLETT, Charles L., Hudson, Wis., ——, æ. 52. He was born May 23, 1806, at Oneida Castle, N. Y., where his father officiated as missionary among the Oneida Indians. He was early adopted by the tribe, and christened Ahnoel, or turtle. He has been a prominent man in Hudson, entering into its interests, and laboring earnestly for its upbuilding and progress in its political, social, mental, and moral relations. As superintendent of public schools, he acted for several years with fidelity and efficiency. He was scrupulous and exact in business transactions, and unflinching in the discharge of duty. As a citizen, neighbor, and Christian man, his worth is known, and his loss is felt, by the community, but nowhere so fully as in the bosom of his family. Eminently domestic in his habits, home was the centre of all his earthly joys. In its quiet retreat, life's pleasures, his books, his farm, his flocks, his fruit, his family, afforded him unbounded happiness. A firm believer in Christianity and its high mission, his highest earthly aim was to acknowledge God in all his ways.

GILLIAM, Col. Leslie, Oxford, N. C., May 20, æ. 78. Few men have enjoyed as did Col. G. throughout life that unqualified attachment and esteem of his fellow-beings which forms the peculiar distinction of his mortal career. It is seldom, indeed, that so much weight of character as he always derived from his sterling integrity, singularly good sense, and commanding address, is relieved by an openness of heart, a simplicity of manner, and a benignity of disposition so childlike and complete. For more than 13 years he was the sheriff of Granville, at a time when the duties and perquisites of the office were alike very considerable. During this period the attributes just mentioned were strongly attested by the well-known sentiments of the public. Col. G. had rare advantages of person, a vigorous constitution, a large, athletic frame, a powerful voice, and was favored with a keen enjoyment of life. He lived in Oxford nearly 50 years, witnessed in his children the blessings inherited with his own moral traits, and in his last illness received unexampled attention from many sympathizing neighbors and friends.

GILLILAND, Hon. Samuel N., Nov. 5, æ. ——, senator from Attala and Lake Cos., Miss. The Senate say, —
"*Resolved*, that by the death of Judge Gilliland the State of Mississippi has lost a faithful public servant, whose zeal in behalf of her welfare is evinced by near 20 years of efficient service in her legislative councils, whose devotion was equalled alone by the energy and ability with which he discharged every duty assigned him, and whose private worth, public spirit, and untarnished integrity and purity of character as a citizen, was exemplified by his daily deportment."

GILMAN, Capt. Nathaniel, Exeter, N. H., —— ——, æ. 65, one of the most enterprising and valuable citizens of Exeter.

GILMAN, Rev. Josiah, Lynn, Mass., Nov. 1, æ. 67. He was born in Gilmanton, N. H., Dec. 17, 1791. His early advantages were limited; and he was trained in the muscular calling of a blacksmith, and followed it till he was 25 or 26 years old. He then turned his attention to study, and became a Universalist minister. For some time he preached as he had calls in various places; among others, in Rumney, N. H. He removed to Washington, N. H., preaching there and in Lempster. He gave a plain and straightforward ministry of truth, and was held in good esteem as a man and a minister by the people.

REV. SAMUEL GILMAN, D. D.,

(of Charleston, S. C.,) Kingston, Mass., Feb. 9, æ. 66, at the residence of his son-in-law, Rev. Charles J. Bowen. He was son of Frederick and Abigail H. (Somes) Gilman, and was born in Gloucester, Mass., Feb. 16, 1791. His father had been a very successful merchant in

Gloucester, but died insolvent nearly 60 years ago, his insolvency having been caused by the capture of several of his vessels by the French in 1798. He left a youthful widow and four male children; and when Samuel was about seven years old, his mother took him to Atkinson, N. H., to be educated in the academy there, under the charge of Rev. Stephen Peabody, (H. U. 1769,) whose quaint, primitive ways are described with inimitable humor in a biographical sketch by Dr. G., published in the Christian Examiner in 1847. Not long subsequently, the family removed to Salem, Mass., and Samuel was for some time employed as a clerk in the old Essex Bank. He graduated at Harvard College (1811) with high honors in a class remarkable for eminent talent. A poem, which he delivered on his graduation, on the Pleasures and Pains of the Student, was replete with humor, and elicited rapturous applause from a crowded audience. This poem he repeated on the evening of commencement day in 1852, at the residence of Hon. Edward Everett, in Boston, whither the class had been invited to celebrate the 41st anniversary of their graduation, and added a sequel, in which he gave a retrospect of the time from their graduation to that period, paying a brief and beautiful tribute to the memory of those of the class who had deceased. It concluded with the following fine compliment to their host, the Hon. Mr. Everett: —

"Stay yet, dear friends; the minstrel bids you toast,
In pure, bright water, our accomplished host.
Who gives, one need not say, our class its name,
Tinged with the lustre of his well-earned fame.
Health for his labors, for his cares relief,
To him, our first and last unenvied chief!"

These two poems were printed immediately afterwards, for distribution to the surviving members of the class.

Among the various pursuits which offered themselves to Dr. G.'s choice was that to which, by character and endowments, he was best adapted; and it was the profession which was the choice of his heart. He soon began the study of theology under the supervision of Drs. Ware and Kirkland, who then constituted the theological faculty. Fortunately for him, he was not hurried, like most young Americans, immediately and prematurely into professional life. He lingered long under the roof of his *alma mater*, maturing his mind, extending his knowledge, and laying up those intellectual and literary treasures which his future isolation rendered so important. In 1817 he was appointed tutor in mathematics at Harvard College, which office he held two years. Early in 1819 he went to Charleston, S. C., where he received a pastoral call as successor to the Rev. Anthony M. Foster; and, after a few months of probationary service, he was ordained, Dec. 1, 1819, as pastor of the Unitarian or Second Independent Church in that city. The ordination sermon was preached by Rev. Joseph Tuckerman, D. D., of Chelsea, Mass., (H. U. 1798.) Here he labored faithfully and acceptably until his last sickness. He was universally respected by the people of the city of his residence; and his influence extended far beyond the limits of the religious denomination with which he was connected. He was the life and soul of the New England Society of South Carolina, and was always hospitable to all visitors from the north. During his residence in Cambridge he was a frequent contributor to the North American Review, in which periodical his papers are marked by their polished elegance of diction, the grace and felicity of their illustrations, and their racy humor. Among his contributions were a series of able papers on the Philosophical Lectures of Dr. Thomas Brown, and translations of several of the satires of Boileau. One of his most noted essays was on the Influence of One National Literature upon Another. He also wrote a fine paper on the Writings of Edward Everett, his classmate and warm personal friend. After his removal to Charleston he continued to write for different periodicals, his contributions embracing a wide range of subjects, from profound philosophical discussions to sparkling satirical essays. A selection of these was published in a volume a few years since, under the title of Contributions to American Literature, Descriptive, Critical, Humorous, Biographical, Philosophical, and Poetical. Among his productions the Recollections of a New England Village Choir has, perhaps, become the most generally popular. For apt local description, a keen sense of the ludicrous, and a happy intuition of characteristic peculiarities, it has seldom been matched in the humorous literature of this country. Dr. G. possessed the gift of poetry, which he cultivated with no inconsiderable success. He had a luxuriant fancy, an excellent command of natural imagery, and great fluency of expression. As a pulpit orator he was affectionate and persuasive, equally removed from languor and vehemence, never boisterous, but always in earnest, loving the sphere of universal ethics rather than the subtilties of sectarian doctrine, and commending the great lessons he taught by the shining and noble example of his private life.

Dr. G. married, Oct. 14, 1819, Miss Caroline Howard, daughter of Samuel Howard, a shipwright of Boston — a lady of remarkable talents and acquirements. She is the author of several excellent books; viz., Oracles from the Poets, Recollections of a New England Housekeeper, New England Bride and Southern Matron, Poetry of Travelling in the United States, Tales and Ballads, and others.

Dr. G. had four daughters who survive him; viz., — Abby Louisa, wife of Francis J. Porcher, merchant of Charleston; Caroline H. Glover, widow of William Glover, planter, of South Carolina; Eliza W. Dodge, wife of Pickering Dodge, Esq., of Salem; Anna, wife of Rev. Charles J. Bowen, of Kingston, Mass. He had also a son, who died young. His widow survives him.

GLADDEN, Mrs. Elizabeth, Winnsboro', S. C., June —, æ. 106, the grandmother of Col. A. H. Gladden. Mrs. G. was married about the time of the outbreak of the war of the revolution, and was quite familiar with many of the scenes which occurred in the state during that dark period which "tried men's souls." She retained all her faculties in a great degree, until within the last few years, when her eyesight and memory partially failed. She was, as far as our knowledge extends, the oldest resident in the district. One by one the links which bind us to the last century are giving way.

GODDARD, Mrs. Anna, Orange, Mass., Aug. 27, æ. 82, widow of Henry Goddard, of Royalston, and mother of Hon. Josiah G. and David G., of Orange, and Sanford Goddard, of Montague.

GODMAN, Mrs. Angelica, Louisville, Ky., at the residence of her son-in-law, Dr. William Goldsmith, Jan. 27, æ. —. She was the daughter of Rembrandt Peale, and widow of John D. Godman, M. D., late Professor of Anatomy.

GOLDTHWAIT, Timothy, Manchester, Mass., June 16, æ. 96. He was born in Stoughton, Mass., May 5, 1762. He was married, Jan. 24, 1788, to Mary Briggs, with whom he lived 62 years. He removed to Maine and settled in Augusta in 1801. He has left a number of children, one of whom is the Rev. T. Goldthwait, of Waterville.

GOOCH, A. G., Esq., Tuscaloosa, Ala., Jan. 3, æ. —. Mr. G. was a highly respectable and influential citizen of Tuscaloosa, and for a long time held the office of clerk of the Federal Court of the middle district of Alabama.

GOODALE, Dea. David, Marlboro', Mass., Oct. 17, æ. 67. He was the son of Dea. Abner Goodale, and the brother of Mrs. Thurston, missionary to the Sandwich Islands, and a near relative of Rev. William Goodale, missionary at Constantinople. He was educated in the district school, and repaid the debt by teaching twenty-nine winters in succession, commencing when only nineteen years of age. In 1816 he united with the First Congregational Church in M. He attributed his religious impressions to the faithful instruction of his parents to early habits of reading the Scriptures, and especially to the lessons which he regularly learned from the Assembly's Catechism. In May, 1818, he established, with the assistance of six others, the first Sabbath school in his native place, and was an active member of it, as superintendent or teacher, to the day of his death. In 1819 he was married to Miss Melliscent Warren, of Marlboro', sister of Rev. Edward Warren, missionary to Ceylon. They had six children, four of whom survive. In Oct., 1823, at the death of his father, he was chosen to succeed him in the office of deacon, and at the time of his death was senior deacon of the church. Perhaps no features of his character were more marked than his decision, energy, and sagacity. His mind was clear, vigorous, resolved, and possessed the main qualities which fit men to be leaders. And yet there was blended with these qualities so much of prudence and forecast — so many conservative elements — as to make him singularly well balanced and judicious. He died Oct. 19, æ. 67.

GOODALL, Hon. John L., near Carthage, Tenn., ———, æ. —. Judge G. was one of the most revered members of the judiciary of that state — a man whose sterling traits of character eminently fitted him for the judicial station, and which made him an ornament to the bench. He presided for many years, and commanded universal respect. His personal and social qualities were such as to endear him to all with whom he mingled, and, at his death, he left as many and as devoted friends as any one in the district. The bar will feel keenly the loss of an upright judge, and the community a most estimable, generous, and public-spirited citizen.

GOODE, Dr. Thomas, Hot Springs, Va., April 2, at an advanced age. Dr. Goode was born and reared in Mecklenburg Co., Va. Early in life he selected the profession of medicine. Yielding to the impulses of a noble and tender nature, he refrained from the duties of his profession until he had availed himself of the best advantages. To secure these he pursued his studies for a time in Edinburgh, Scotland, then returning to the United States, completed his studies at Philadelphia, having spent in this way five years in preparatory study. Ten years of his professional life were spent in his native county, ten in Roanoke, then in May, 1833, he came to Bath, where he has since resided up to the time of his death. Those who knew him as a husband and brother, father and master, felt his excellence as a man of "great natural kindness of heart."

GOODNOW, Miss Grace, Westmoreland, N. H., Nov. 19, æ. 116. She was the oldest person in the county, and probably the oldest in the state. At the age of 100 years she was more active than many modern misses of 16.

GOODRICH, Chauncey, Esq., Burlington, Vt., Sept. 11, æ. 60. He was born in Hinsdale, Mass., whither his father, E. H. Goodrich, had moved from Weathersfield, Ct. He lived upon his father's farm, sometimes teaching school in the winter, till he was 19 years old, when he left home to engage in trade, for which he had always exhibited a predilection. He was connected with the book-publishing house of Oliver D. Cooke, Hartford, Ct., nearly six years; being engaged a good part of the time as travelling agent of the firm. While residing here, he attended the preaching of the then Episcopal Bishop of Connecticut, and became sincerely convinced of the claims of that denomination. From Hartford Mr. G. went to Castleton, Vt., in 1823, and in 1827 he removed to Burlington. In 1828 he was married to Arabella Marsh, a daughter of Daniel Marsh, Esq., of Hartford, Vt., and sister of the late President Marsh, of the University of Vermont. His wife died in 1835, leaving two daughters, of whom the elder survived him but a few weeks, dying December 4, 1858. For many years after removing to Burlington, he was one of the most active and efficient members of the Episcopal church there, giving freely of both time and money to the organizing of a society, building of a church edifice, raising of the rector's salary, &c. His chief business was the publication of school, law, and miscellaneous books, printing and bookselling. Although he had indifferent success in business, he was not confined in the exercise of his peculiar generosity, for which very many have occasion to remember him with gratitude. Not a few who have graduated at Vermont University, and are now engaged at the bar or in the pulpit, and many others who fill honorable places as editors and business men, owe their present position and influence in greater or less degree to his counsel and generous help, in furnishing money, books, board, &c., and waiting on them indefinitely for his own remuneration, when he did not make them a present outright of whatever assistance he rendered. His farm and fruit garden divided his attention with his book-publishing. As an amateur horticulturist he was very widely and favorably known, and probably did as much as any other man to introduce and improve the culture of fruit in Vermont. He was very active in the formation of the Champlain Horticultural Society, and contributed his full share, both as its chief officer for a time, and as a member of its committees, to make it both prosperous and useful. He was an occasional contributor to the press, on horticultural and agricultural subjects. A little work of his, the Northern Fruit Culturist, was quite extensively circulated. In pomology he was very enthusiastic, and used to say that the practical Christianity of a place was to be tested by a literal application of this rule, " By their *fruits* ye shall know them."

GOODRICH, Rev. H. P., Carondelet, Mo., May 17, at an advanced age.

GOODWIN, Mrs. Catharine T., Middletown, Ct., Oct. 18, æ. —, wife of Rev. Frederick J. Goodwin, D. D., Rector of the Church of the Holy Trinity. The church has lost a true woman — modest, unassuming, prudent, yet ready alike for duty and for sacrifice in the spirit of Christian charity.

GOODWIN, Hon. Thomas, South Berwick, Me., June 9, æ. 59. He was formerly engaged in political affairs, having served as chairman of the selectmen of his native town 17 years. He has also represented his town and county in both branches of the legislature. In all his political career, he was faithful in the discharge of every duty devolving upon him; he was just and honest in all his dealings with man; kind and obliging to his neighbors. His house and heart were always open to the poor.

GORDON, Gen. William F., Albemarle, N. C., July 21, æ. —. In early life Gen. Gordon attained a high position in the state, and although he has not participated in the strife of politics for many years past, yet to the day of his death he was esteemed among the worthiest of the democratic leaders. He was a rigid disciple of the state rights school, and an inflexible champion of the rights of the south. A fervid oratory was his most characteristic talent — an incorruptible integrity his distinguishing virtue. In the relations of private life he commanded universal respect, and among his more intimate friends he was regarded with a warm and constant affection. He was long an influential member of the state legislature. He served only one term in Congress, but that sufficed to give him a historic name, for he had the honor of proposing the sub-treasury system. At his death he held the commission of major general in the militia of Virginia.

GORDON, Rev. Joseph, Canton township, Pa., Feb. 28, æ. 38.

GORDON, Dr. J. B., Olivet, Mich., July 14, æ. 32. Dr. G. was purely self-made in his attainments. He was an only son of a family of six children. His father died when he was but two years old. At the age of 20 he commenced reading medicine with Dr. A. B. Sampson, then practising medicine at Sullivan, in this county, with whom he staid about four years, except as much of his time as he attended medical lectures, the first course of which he attended at Cleveland. He graduated at the State Medical School at Ann Arbor, Mich. After practising medicine about one year, he located permanently at Olivet, Mich. He married Charlotte A., only daughter of Horace Blinn, of Sullivan. Through his untiring efforts and undivided attention to his profession, he won for himself a laudable reputation as a gentleman and practitioner.

GORDON, William, Esq., Newton, Ala., Sept. 9, æ. —. At a meeting of the citizens of Newton, it was said, " Death has again visited our community, and in its mission has struck down, in the strength of manhood and in the prime of life, our esteemed friend and respected citizen, William Gordon, Esq. In the death of our friend the bar of Newton has lost one of its brightest ornaments, and the town of Newton and the community at large one of their best and most enterprising citizens."

GORE, Rev. Samuel, Freedom District, Carroll Co., Ind., Sept. 4, æ. 74. He closed his earthly career calmly and peacefully, and has gone to dwell forever in that heaven which he sought to obtain with ardor and zeal for many years.

GORHAM, Charles, Bedford Co., Tenn., April 19, æ. 103, a revolutionary soldier.

GOULD, Anthony, Albany, N. Y., ——, æ. —. He had lived in Albany some 30 years, commencing his business career with his uncle, William Gould, law bookseller, and afterwards in the extensive partnership of Gould, Banks, & Co. He accumulated a large fortune in business, and had but a little while ago retired from it, in the hope to spend the evening of his days in the quiet of country life. As an instance of his liberality, he was one of the original contributors to the purchase of Dr. Palmer's church, and paid besides annually $1000, until the debt upon it was extinguished.

GOULD, John, New Ipswich, N. H., Sept. 22, æ. 95. With the exception of a few months while connected with the army, his whole long life was spent in his native town, and, what is more remarkable, he died on nearly the exact spot of ground that gave him birth. His wife, with whom he had lived 63 years, died 3 years since, at the advanced age of 91.

GRAFTON, Rev. B. C., Cambridge, Mass., Jan. —, æ. 72. Mr. G. was first settled at West Cambridge, where he remained six years. Afterwards he was settled in Plymouth, Seekonk, Taunton, Wickford, R. I., and Stonington, Conn., and finally over the Baptist church in Medford for about one year, whence he removed to Cambridge, ten years and a half since. He continued to preach for churches destitute of a pastor, being so employed nearly every Sabbath. During the absence of Rev. Dr. Parker in Europe he supplied his pulpit for six months. For a period of 30 years he preached every Sunday with the exception of two. With great shrewdness and knowledge of the world, Mr. G. possessed a charming simplicity and amiability, which endeared him to all with whom he came in contact. He was universally and deservedly esteemed, and was one of the class of ministers, "the fathers," of whom but few remain.

GRAHAM, Dr. D. C., Newbury District, S. C., Oct. 7, æ. 35.

GRAHAM, Hon. William, Vallonia, Jackson Co., Ind., Aug. 17, æ. 76. Mr. G. was a member of the first constitutional convention of Indiana, which met at Corydon in 1816, and in 1837 was elected to Congress from his district. He had also been repeatedly a member of both branches of the General Assembly, and during one session was speaker of the House. Although by no means a brilliant man, Mr. G. was a useful legislator, and, as a neighbor, was highly respected. He had taken no active part in politics for nearly 20 years.

GRANT, Mrs. Caroline, Milwaukie, Wis., Feb. 23, æ. —. She was a daughter of the Hon. Ward Woodbridge, of Hartford, Conn. Milwaukie had been her residence for the past 12 years; and her loss there will be quite irreparable. Her energy of character and goodness of heart identified her with every benevolent undertaking. So useful, indeed, did her talents make her in all the charitable projects of the day

that her associates always advanced her to most prominent positions. Her gentleness and kindness to her friends in sickness as well as health will long be remembered. To many she was an angel in the sick chamber, ever ready to watch while others slept, and to perform every gentle and kindly office. In this duty, the care of the sick, this true womanly duty, she was eminent. Ever a true woman in the relations of friend, sister, daughter, wife, and mother, may her example be of value to her sex.

GRANT, Prof. John, Tallahassee, Fla., Aug. 2, æ. 53. He was born in Bristol, England, April 13, 1805, and was the son of the Rev. Jeremiah Grant, of the Wesleyan Methodist connection in England, and moved to this country with his family in April, 1831, landing in New York, where he was soon afterwards employed as lecturer in a lyceum. Being compelled by the cholera soon to abandon that post, he moved to New Jersey, where he remained three years as principal in a high school. He then removed to Georgia, and passed his time as principal or professor in high schools and colleges in Fort Gaines and Columbus, Ga., and Cuthbert and Glenville, Ala., until, about two years since, he took charge of the Female Academy in Tallahassee. Mr. G. was a practically scientific scholar, and sacrificed his life to the good of his race. Religion and the Bible, so far from being excluded from his school, were ever prominently presented to his pupils, as constituting the sanctifying element in all true education. Hence he ruled them with love, and not with fear.

GRANT, William B., Esq., Gardiner, Me., Nov. 18, æ. 66. Mr. G. had been president of the Gardiner Bank since 1854, the duties of which office he performed with much ability and scrupulous fidelity. He was a man possessed of an uncommon share of good sense, and was remarkable for the kindness of his manners, for the courteousness of his deportment, and for his amiable disposition.

GRAY, Curtis G., Fort Valley, Houston Co., Ga., March 27, æ. 82. He was a native Carolinian, but for the last 36 years lived in Georgia. The greater portion of that time was spent in teaching school; and perhaps he was excelled by few in teaching the elementary principles of education. Many who have been benefited by his instructions will say, Peace to his ashes.

GRAY, Reuben, Brooksville, Me., Nov. —, æ. 97. He was the first white male child born on the peninsula of Castine. He voted for Gen. Washington and for every democratic candidate for president up to the present day.

GRAY, William M., Sunbury, Pa., Sept. 21, æ. 66, a nephew of the late Gen. Hugh Brady, and an officer in the war of 1812.

HON. ELIPHALET GREELY,

Portland, Me., Aug. 3, æ. 74. He was born in North Yarmouth, Me., May 1, 1784, and was a son of Eliphalet Greely and Sarah Prince; his grandfather, Philip Greely, was born in Salisbury, Mass., June 9, 1711, moved to North Yarmouth, and was killed there by the Indians, Aug. 9, 1746. Their ancestor was Andrew Greely, who was living at Haverhill, Mass., in 1669, at which time he had charge of the ferry across the Merrimac River. He died in Salisbury, 1697, leaving several children, among whom were Andrew, Philip, Joseph, Benjamin, Westwood, and Mary, born between 1640 and 1660. The subject of this memoir is the sixth in descent from Andrew, through Philip, Jonathan the son of Philip, Philip the son of Jonathan, Eliphalet the son of Philip, and Eliphalet his father. His mother, Sarah Prince, was a direct descendant of the Rev. John Prince, rector of East Shefford, in Berkshire, England, whose son, Elder John Prince, born in 1610, emigrated to this country in 1633, and settled in Hull, Mass., where he died Aug. 6, 1676. His son, Thomas Prince, born in 1638, married Ruth Turner, daughter of John Turner and Mary Brewster, a granddaughter of Elder Wm. Brewster, first pastor of the old Plymouth Church; she was born in 1663. Their son, Benjamin Prince, born 1693, married Abiel Nelson, and had Paul Prince, born May 14, 1720. He married Hannah Cushing, daughter of David Cushing, born May 8, 1722, and died in 1814, æ. 92; her father, David, was born in 1694, and was a lineal descendant of Peter Cushing, of Norfolk, England, whose son, Matthew, came to Massachusetts, and settled in Hingham, in 1638. Thus honorably descended, Mr. Greely sustained, without blemish, the character of his respected ancestors through a long and active life. At the age of 18, following the example of the enterprising young men of his native town, the Blanchards, Sturdivants, Lorings, Yorks, &c., and at a period the most successful in our commercial history, he entered upon a seafaring life. He began as an apprentice on board of one of his father's vessels, and rose rapidly, by his activity and intelligence, through the various grades of service, until, at the age of 22 years, he found himself in full command of a ship. In this capacity he continued with unusual success about 11 years, during which time no disasters occurred to any vessel he commanded, and no losses of property or life. He was calm, cautious, firm; and while he maintained perfect discipline among his crews, by his dignity and reserve, he was most considerate of the comfort and good order of all in his employment. Having, by this unvaried success, accumulated sufficient property to justify the measure, he left the quarter deck for the more ample verge of the counting room and warehouse, and successfully, for the remainder of his life, pursued commercial operations. As his voyages were principally to the West Indies, in which the mercantile interests of our state were principally and profitably engaged, so he continued to pursue the same kind of business after leaving the ocean. He conducted his concerns on shore in the same methodical, quiet, and honorable manner that had characterized the more arduous and active duties of his early life. He wrote a beautiful hand; he was exact and accurate in accounts; he was prompt and punctual in all his dealings. By his uniform course of integrity, industry, and intelligent action, it could not be otherwise than that he should accumulate an independent property, which he used with the same propriety with which he acquired it. Prudent and economical without meanness, liberal and hospitable without ostentation or display, he enjoyed his property with simplicity and dignity, dispensing freely and judiciously to all good objects which sought or claimed his attention. A person of such fine qualities could not be permitted to remain in retirement, and his services were early sought for public and responsible employments. In 1825, the second year after its entering upon business, the Casco Bank elected him its president; and he continued, by annual elections, to hold the office near 30 years, to the time of his death — a sufficient proof of his financial skill, integrity, and good judgment. He fulfilled the duties of that responsible office to the entire approbation of the stockholders and successive boards of directors, and the capital stock was increased under his administration, from $100,000 to $600,000. His financial ability received executive commendation, in the year 1826, in his appointment by the Governor as one of the bank commissioners of the state— his associates being Judge Bridge, of Hallowell, and Judge Ware, of Portland; and in 1830 he was again appointed. In 1834 he was chosen to represent the city of Portland in the legislature; and in 1843, he was elected mayor of the city. This office he held, by successive elections, six years, to the general acceptance of his fellow-citizens; and it may be said, without fear of contradiction, that the financial concerns of the government were never more carefully and judiciously managed than during his administration. He considered himself, in this station, to be but the steward of the community over which he presided, and that he had no right to squander the public money on extravagant or unnecessary projects. If men who are placed in such responsible stations had more of his scrupulous and conscientious watchfulness, we should not hear of so much recklessness, dishonesty, and waste of public funds as are now continually and harshly grating on our ears. For many years, Mr. Greely was connected with various charitable institutions, and works of public improvement, in the city and state. He was a corporator of the Atlantic and St. Lawrence Railroad Company, one of the greatest projects of public improvement which had been undertaken in Maine, and for several years an active director. He was long a manager in the first savings institution established in the city. His interest for seamen never abated, and he was never weary in his endeavors to promote their moral and temporal well-being, by the establishment of comfortable homes for them on shore, and for their religious instruction. He was for many years treasurer of the Seamen's Friend Society, and of the Mariner's Church Association, to which he largely contributed of his pecuniary means. He was also for a long time treasurer of the Portland Manufacturing Company. And ever mindful of the cause of education, to which he paid particular attention, while mayor of the city, in the improved construction of school houses, and the course of instruction, he made provision by will to perpetuate his usefulness in the same direction. He provided that, after the death of his widow, the principal part of his estate should be applied to the founding and endowing of a high school in his native town. September 9, 1812, he married Elizabeth Loring, a daughter of Solomon Loring, of North Yarmouth, and moved to Portland in the November following, to the house in which he ever after lived, and from which he was carried to his last dwelling place. The Lorings came from Hull, Mass. Three brothers settled in North Yarmouth, viz., Rev. Nicholas, pastor of the 1st parish, (Harvard University, 1732,) ordained November 17, 1736; John and Solomon, the descendants of Thomas Loring, of Hull. Her grandmother, the mother of her father, was Alice Cushing, daughter of David Cushing, who was also a maternal ancestor of her husband, so that they both had the blood of Brewster, Prince, and Cushing, old, and venerable, and worthy names in our New England annals. They had no children; and, thus drawn closer together in a happy and congenial alliance, their lives glided smoothly and kindly along through a period of 46 years, until the tie was abruptly sundered by the death of her affectionate partner. Three brothers, all older than himself, survive; Philip, of Portland, long connected with him in business, aged 84; Jonathan, of Cumberland, aged 80; and the Rev. Allen, of Turner, aged 78. Few towns have furnished to society better members and more valued citizens than ancient North Yarmouth. It was there William Royal, the ancestor of the distinguished family, afterwards settled in Medford, began his humble life more than 200 years ago; the principal river still bearing his name. It was there Peter C. Brooks, the exemplary Boston merchant was born, his father being minister of the place. The succession of her ministers adorns her annals — Cutter, Loring, Brooks, Gilman, Brown, the learned president of Dartmouth College, and Asa Cummings, long a leader in the churches. In other professions and business, the Russells, the Mitchells, Lewises, Princes, Lorings, Blanchards, Stockbridges, Greelys, Sturdivants, Drinkwaters, Chandlers, Seaburys, Buxtons, and others whom we need not stop to mention, have illustrated her history. For sound conservative principles she has brought down her fame to the present day. Mr. Greely, one of this conservative town and race, was a finely formed and handsome man, of courteous and dignified, although somewhat reserved and formal manners; his deportment was always gentlemanly and proper. He was remarkably neat in his person, always well dressed, and uniformly exhibited the manners of an old school gentleman. His manly presence will long be missed in the streets he frequented — his business talents in the departments of commerce, and the sweet issues of his benevolence in the various channels of philanthropy and charity. But the world beyond, whose joys he fondly anticipated, and for which his daily walk prepared him, will afford a more ample field for the development of all the faculties of his higher and purer nature; and while the mourners go about the streets, we believe he is reaping in a better existence the fruits of a well-spent life.

GREEN, Dr. Henry Prentice, Madison, N. J., Oct. 15, æ. 59.

GREEN, Mrs. Betsey, Pittsfield, Mass., May 24, æ. 84, widow of Rev. Rob. Green.

GREEN, Rev. Zachariah, Hempstead, L. I., June 21, æ. 99. Thus has another of our country's cherished ones passed from the earth. The remnant of the band of our revolutionary patriots has been further diminished. The venerable man whose death is here announced combined every attraction to make his life useful and his death triumphant. First, a soldier of this country in the hour of her peril, he was then, for more than 60 years, a soldier of Christ. Honorably dismissed from the army, in consequence of wounds received at the battle of Whitemarsh, he graduated at Dartmouth College in 1781, and after finishing his studies, was ordained a minister of the Presbyterian church.

The vigor and intrepidity which had characterized him in the army were transferred to his holy calling. He counted nothing hard, not even his life dear unto him, if he might but bring honor to Christ and advance his kingdom. Retaining his faculties to the last, he exhibited a beautiful and attractive picture of patient, gentle, cheerful, and devout old age. Amid all his connections with and anxiety for the religious institutions with which he was associated, he never ceased to feel the liveliest interest in the welfare of his beloved country, for which he had sacrificed every thing but life and honor, and to cherish as a hallowed thing the memory of his two great commanders, Washington and Greene. He was a chaplain in the army in the war of 1812. His remains were followed by nearly all the inhabitants of the village. The occasion was very solemn, and when the coffin was lowered in the grave, there was not a dry eye in the vast concourse of people, old and young, that gathered to take the last look at their venerated pastor.

GREENARD, Mrs. Mary, New York, Dec. 6, æ. 81, relict of the late Nevingson Greenard. It is said that a good man never dies, but shall be had in everlasting remembrance. The parents of the deceased in very early life were brought to the knowledge of Christ through the powerful preaching of the Rev. Mr. Whitefield, and were among the first to enroll their names under the banner of the cross in the old Brick Church on Beckman Street. There her feet were early led by her Puritan parents to tread the courts of the Lord's house. It was always her delight to mingle and worship with God's people in his temple.

GREENLEAF, Miss Sarah P., Chester, Pa., Nov. 12, æ. —, daughter of the late Stephen Greenleaf, of Brattleboro', Vt., and teacher in the Upland Normal School. Society could ill afford to lose a character like hers. A mind well disciplined — a heart adorned with every Christian grace — a life devoted to usefulness, with an energy of purpose uncommon in these frivolous times — these were hers; and these, least of all, could the world afford to spare.

GRENNELL, Michael, Clinton, Wayne Co., Penn., Feb. 13, æ. 105. He was born in Saybrook, Ct., April 1, (March

20, O. S.,) 1752. In 1777, at the age of 25, he was united in marriage with Miss Susanna Balcom, by whom he had six children, four of whom survive him. His wife died in 1825. He took a deep interest in the revolutionary struggle, and early entered the regular army. Having been some months in the regular service, he was taken sick, and by the advice of the commanding officer he retired from the army, and returned home to recruit his enfeebled health. He did not return to the regular service, but volunteered, when necessary, for the defence of towns and military posts on the Hudson River and Long Island Sound, and also in the vicinity of Boston. He was in the city of New York in 1776, and witnessed the enthusiasm of the army and people on receiving the news of the declaration of independence. He also saw the people pull down the statue of King George, and ride it through the streets on a wooden horse. He distinctly recollected those stirring events, and frequently related them with great interest and animation. He voted at every presidential election in the United States, always supporting the democratic nominee, except in the case of Washington and Fremont.

GRIFFIN, Dr. James, Great Bend, Pa., Jan. 18, æ. 65. Dr. G. was a native of New Town, Ct., and practised medicine for several years in Schoharie County, N. Y., and for the last 12 years in Great Bend, Susquehanna County, Pa. As a physician he stood at the head of his profession, and possessed, to an unusual degree, the confidence of his patients, to a very extensive and laborious practice. As a citizen and civil magistrate, he held a high place in the respect and esteem of the community in which he lived; while in the more tender and endearing relations of brother, father, and husband, he was greatly beloved for his many virtues and excellences of both his head and his heart. In his death the poor have lost a friend indeed.

GRIFFIN, Rev. Samuel, Kingston, Pa., Nov. 9, æ. 63. His first license to exhort is dated June 19, 1824, and his first license to preach, Nov. 10, 1827. He was ordained deacon at the session of the Oneida conference at Manlius, N. Y., in 1832, by Bishop Hedding, and received elder's orders by the same, at the session of the same conference, at Neversink, N. Y., in 1839. He travelled for several years under the directions of the presiding elder, and was very useful, but never entered the travelling connection. His labors will long be remembered on Canaan, Pittston, Plainville, Providence, Abington, Newton, Nicholson, and Tunkhannock charges. Upon this territory he labored as a regular supply under the presiding elder, and when not employed, exercised the functions of a local preacher, for the space of 30 years, with great acceptance and usefulness. For the last three years of his life he resided in the village of Kingston. He was a good man, and a man of more than common abilities. He was a stirring preacher, and rendered efficient aid to many revivals of religion.

GRIFFING, Rev. James, Clairborne Co., Miss., July 12, æ. 76. He was a plain, substantial, unpretending man, a zealous local preacher, and a professor of religion for more than 50 years; and his piety was of that pure and fervent kind that sustains the Christian amid the conflicts of life, and envelops his dying bed with the halo of immortality.

GRIMES, James J., Cambridge, O., Nov. 26, æ. —. At a meeting of the members of the bar and officers of court, it was resolved, —

"That we feel deeply sensible of the loss which the profession and society have sustained in the death of brother Grimes, that we will cherish the memory of the deceased as a member of the bar, as a man and citizen endowed with excellent qualities of mind and possessed of noble traits of character."

GRISHAM, Jeremiah, Ouachita Parish, La., Sept. 20, æ. 106.

GROE, Rev. Samuel, Freedom District, Carroll Co., Md., Aug. 4, æ. 74.

GROTON, Hon. Nathaniel, Bath, Me., Oct. 25, æ. 64. Judge G. was found drowned in a small stream near home, by accident.

GUILD, Benjamin, Esq., Boston, Mass., March 30, æ. 73. He was a gentleman endeared to a wide circle of acquaintances, among whom his urbanity of manners and intelligence were highly appreciated. He graduated at Harvard University in the year 1804.

GWIN, Mrs. Mary, Brunswick Place, Miss., June 22, æ. 80, mother of Hon. Wm. W. Gwin, senator from California.

H.

HALE, Mrs. Esther, Hollis, N. H., Oct. 10, æ. 87, wife of the late Dr. William Hale. She was one of the oldest and most respected residents of H., and the last on the pension list.

HALE, Foster, ———, —, Nov. 24, æ. —, inventor of raised letters for the use of the blind.

HALL, Rev. Nathan H., D. D., Columbia, Mo., June 22, æ. 97, son of Rev. Randall Hall, of Garrard Co., Ky.

HALL, Joshua, Westminster, Vt., May 10, æ. 59. In early life Mr. H. directed his attention to the gospel ministry, but was obliged, on account of declining health, to give up his studies in that direction. Being gifted, however, with an ardent passion for music, he devoted himself to the acquisition of this "divine art," in the theory and practice of which he soon made himself proficient. For many years he was engaged as a leader of a choir, and as a teacher of classes in sacred music in various towns and cities in New England. His judgment and taste in respect to sacred music, and its appropriate use in the sanctuary, were remarkably correct; and his efforts to advance the interests of this important part of Christian worship — making it turn, as it ever should, to the praise and honor of God — will be long felt in those communities where his labors were enjoyed. He was a firm believer in the truths of the gospel, and ever held its ministers in high esteem. His death was joyful in the hope of immortality.

HALL, Col. Timothy Hilliard, Westminster, Vt., Dec. 14, æ. 55. He was the youngest son of the late Hon. Lot Hall, who in 1776 was a lieutenant of marines in the revolutionary war, was captured by the British, taken a prisoner to Scotland, but released, after much suffering and hardship. He returned to Barnstable Co., Mass., where he read law with the Hon. Shearjashub Bourne, and about the year 1780 removed to Westminster, Vt., and became a successful practitioner. In 1786 he married Miss Polly Homer, of Boston. They had five children — Daniel, Benjamin Homer, Mary Parrot, and two Timothy Hilliards. Daniel and Mary P. are still living. Lot Hall was a man of some distinction in Vermont; frequently a representative in the Assembly from his town; and, after Vermont was admitted to the Union, he was in 1793 one of the presidential electors. The votes were for Washington for president; and he was the bearer of the votes to Philadelphia. He was several years a judge of the Supreme Court, and held other offices of responsibility. He died May 17, 1809. Timothy Hilliard was six years old at the death of his father, and always lived with his widowed mother on the paternal homestead, which he inherited, till she was called to her final rest, in Feb., 1843. Timothy H. was bred a practical and working farmer, and took great satisfaction in cultivating his farm in the beautiful valley of the Connecticut, and by the application of modern fertilizers endeavored to make two spears of grass grow where only one grew before. In his flock and herd he was choice in his selections, and believed in cultivating a small farm, but cultivating it well. His house, out-houses, barns, sheds, garden, yards, and enclosures were fitted up in good taste, and to the passing traveller bore the appearance of good husbandry. In rotation with his townsmen, he was called to discharge the municipal duties of town offices, and was sheriff of Windham Co. for many years, which duties he discharged with fidelity. He never married.

HAMILTON, Laurens, Richmond, Va., July 6, æ. 23, drowned during an excursion of the New York National Guard, of which he was a member. He was grandson of Alexander Hamilton, and graduated at Columbia College.

HAMILTON, Henry R., M. D., Colesville, N. Y., June 26, æ. 49, a worthy man and an honorable physician. In 1850 he received from the medical department of the University of the City of New York the honorary degree of doctor in medicine — a compliment to his industry and zeal in the cultivation of his profession.

HAMMOND, William Gardner, a citizen of Long Island, June 19, æ. 59, great-grandson of Joseph Hammond, who came to this country from England early in the last century, and settled in Narragansett, where he was the proprietor of large estates. His father resided at Wickford, and was a well-known merchant. He was born in January, 1802, and graduated at Brown University in 1821. An accomplished scholar, with a love of the classics which amounted to enthusiasm, and a clear and retentive memory, he found his greatest pleasure in his books. He preferred that class of literature which treats of the science of government, and the biography of great and commanding intellect.

HAMMOND, Hon. John C., Crown Point, Essex Co., N. Y., Jan. 1, æ. 52. He was well and extensively known as one of the best business men in New York. He was a member of the well-known firm of Hammond & Co., and for upwards of 30 years was largely and successfully engaged in the mercantile lumber and iron business. He possessed a manly exterior, and was remarkable for his fine personal appearance. But what commanded general respect and universal esteem, were his straightforward, upright course as a man of business for nearly a third of a century, in one of the largest concerns in Northern New York, his perfectly moral conduct, his private benevolence, and his liberality in sustaining the Christian and charitable institutions of the day.

HAMPTON, Col. Wade, at a plantation on the Mississppi, Feb. 10, æ. —. The Charleston Courier says, "Col. H. was well and widely known throughout the South and beyond, as a gentleman and citizen of untiring public spirit, gallant demeanor, and high-toned courtesy and hospitality; in all points a noble representative of the best old school and class of Carolina planters. At the memorable defence of New Orleans, in Dec., 1814, and Jan. 8, 1815, he acted as a confidential and well approved aide-de-camp for Gen. Jackson, and with our esteemed fellow-citizen, Col. A. P. Hayne, shared largely in the confidence and closest regards of that sagacious chieftain, whose intuitive judgment of men was one of his most remarkable traits.

HAMTRAMCK, Col. John, Shepardston, Va., April 21, æ. 61, a highly respected citizen of the town, (for several years its mayor,) and a justice of the peace for the county. Col. H. was son of Gen. Hamtramck of the revolutionary army, who was also prominent as a compatriot of Gen. Harmer, in his sanguinary contest with the Indians. The deceased was born at Fort Wayne, Ind., whilst a battle with the Indians was raging. He was in service with Gen. Zachary Taylor, then a captain, on the Indian frontier. He graduated with distinction at West Point, was an officer of the United States army, and for several years an Indian agent. Devoted all his life to military studies, his last service was as commander of the regiment of Virginia volunteers in Mexico. His death created a void in the community in which he resided, where he was always prominent and public spirited.

HANCOCK, Thomas, Bath, N. H., May 28, æ. 70. He was a farmer by occupation. He cultivated his own land, but did not neglect mental culture or the companionship of books. He was intimately acquainted with the history of the town and its early settlers, and for many years kept a diary, carefully noting the most important occurrences. He took great delight in history and geography. His deportment was polite and obliging, and his conversation cheerful and engaging. He respected the rights of others, and avoided giving offence to any. He has left a widow, four sons, and three daughters, two elder sons, Henry and John, being in California. Mr. H. has left the example and reputation of an *honest man,* that will be enduring as the solid marble.

HANNA, Gen. Robert, Indianapolis, Ind., Nov. 19, æ. 72. Gen. H. was born in the Laurens District of South Carolina, April 6, 1786. When he was a mere boy, probably about 14, his father removed to the eastern part of the state, and subsequently settled in Brookville. This, we believe, was about 1802. Here Mr. H. grew up, and became an active and leading citizen. At the age of 23 he was appointed by Gov. Harrison sheriff of the eastern district of the territory, and he retained the office, we believe, till near the organization of the state government. After the organization, he was elected sheriff of the Franklin Court at one time, and it was during his occupancy of that office that the amusing adventure with Mrs. Frazer, related in Smith's Reminiscences, occurred. He was previously elected a member of the first constitutional convention, and at his death was the only member surviving, except, we believe, Mr. Holman, of Wayne. Afterwards he was appointed register of the land office, at the time that Gov. Noble was receiver, and both came to Indianapolis nearly at the same time, and but a little while after the removal of the seat of government here, in 1825. Since then he has lived here all the time, filling some of the most important stations in the gift of the people. When Gov. Ray was a candidate for re-election, he was warmly suported by Gen. H., and opposed by Gov. Noble. Gen. H.'s influence was then great: probably no man since has exerted a wider and stronger power than he, and his aid elected Ray. In return, when James Noble, then U. S. senator, died, leaving one year of his term unfilled, Gov. Ray appointed Gen. Hanna to the vacancy. Mr. Tipton, of Logansport, was regularly elected to the succeeding term. This was in 1832 or 1833, we believe. Subsequently Gen. H. was elected to the state Senate by the whigs, of whom he was a firm and active adherent, and was nominated for a second term, but was beaten by Wm. Stewart. This, we think, terminated his political career. Since then he has lived the quiet, honored life that his services and character had earned. In this hasty sketch we have omitted, no doubt, some points of his life that we might recall if we had time; but we have no opportunity now to do full justice to him. We trust some of our readers will do so for us. — *Indianapolis Weekly Journal.*

HANSON, Benaiah, Medina, O., Nov. 1, æ. 76. He was born at Windham, Me., Oct. 18, 1781. He was the youngest of 11 children. His mother's maiden name was Abigail Hays. His father, in the Memoir and Journals of Rev. Paul Coffin, D. D., is thus mentioned: "August 18, 1800. Rode to Windham, and lodged with Ichabod Hanson, who has 11 children, and never gave one of them a blow, and 20 grandchildren, and never lost one." Mr. Ichabod Hanson's father was a member of the Society of Friends; his wife was a Congregationalist. They resided at Dover, N. H., where they reared their large family. Friend Hanson, or his immediate ancestors, emigrated from England. When 90 years of age he took a journey of 60 miles to visit his son Ichabod, at Windham, Ct., somewhere between the years 1786 and 1788. Dr. B. Hanson, the subject of this sketch, after spending one term at Fryeburg, Me., entered Exeter Academy, where he remained four years. He commenced the study of medicine under the tuition of his brother-in-law, Dr. John Converse, of Durham, and after the usual course of study, was admitted to practice. During the last war with England he received a commission in the army, as a lieutenant in the 33d regiment of infantry, under the command of Col. Isaac Lane, brother of Col. Daniel Lane, of Belfast, Me., and was ordered to Plattsburg, and engaged in active service. At a subsequent period he entered the College of Physicians and Surgeons, in the city of New York, and graduated in 1825. The faculty at that time comprised W. J. McNevin, Israel Post, John W. Francis, Samuel L. Mitchell, David Hosack, and Valentine Mott. During his attendance at the medical college, he was a student in the office of David Hosack, with whom he studied two years. After graduating he removed to Western New York, and subsequently to Maumee City, O. Through the whole course of his practice, he was remarkably successful, and in the treatment of western fevers especially he was particularly fortunate. He spent 40 years in practice. His last years were particularly devoted to the study of the Bible. In 1811 he married Abigail Woodman, daughter of Capt. Joseph Woodman, of Buxton, Me. Capt. Woodman was the fifth Joseph of that name, and was descended from Joshua Woodman, the first man child born in Newbury, Mass., and the second interred in that place. He has left a widow and three children.

HANSON, Samuel, Esq., Winchester, Ky., Feb. 6, æ. 71. He was born in Alexandria, Va., and removed to Kentucky at an early period of his life, where he has ever since continued to reside. He was an eminent lawyer, alike distinguished for soundness of judgment and strength and clearness of intellect. Profound, practical, and endowed with untiring energy, he attained a conspicuous position as a member of his profession. He was repeatedly elected to the state legislature, and as a statesman, was remarkable for his sagacity, his large and comprehensive views, and his liberal, but yet conservative opinions. He was speaker of the Senate during the session of 1839–40, and discharged the duties of that office with signal promptitude and ability. In private life he was social, kind, and generous; an ardent and unfaltering friend, whose aid could be securely relied upon in any and every emergency.

HARDIN, L. B., Esq., Washington, D. C., March —, æ. —. He was for many years a most faithful officer in the navy department, and a most estimable gentleman. The fact of his having held the same prominent public position of disbursing clerk of the navy department for 27 years is a high testimonial as to his sterling qualities.

HARDING, Daniel F., Union, Me., ——, æ. 75, one of the oldest members of the Lincoln bar.

DR. ROBERT HARE,

Philadelphia, Pa., May 15, æ. 77. In the death of Dr. Hare science has to mourn the loss of one of her favorite sons. Our grief at this announcement should be softened by the reflection that he had passed the time assigned by the Psalmist. Ever since the beginning of the present century he has been known, and during many years of this period celebrated, for the zealous and successful prosecution of chemistry, and especially of electro-galvanism. His first discovery, the Compound or Oxy-hydrogen Blowpipe, was made in 1801, when he had not attained the age of manhood. Fed by oxygen and hydrogen gases, this instrument produced such an intense degree of heat as to melt the alkalies and the most refractory minerals and gems. By its aid, lime, barytes, strontian, and magnesia were decomposed, and their metallic bases evolved. He succeeded, many years subsequently, in reducing, by this blowpipe, 25 ounces of platina to a fluid state — a fact which he communicated, during a visit to England, to the chemical section of the British Association for the Advancement of Science. Since then he received from the American Academy of Arts and Sciences the Rumford medal for this instrument. In after years he introduced a modification of the Compound Blowpipe, which was fed by alcohol. He invented a new galvanic instrument, known as Hare's Calorimotor, of which, together with a new theory of galvanism, he gave an account in Silliman's Journal in 1819. Two years later we find him contributing a memoir in the same journal on some new modifications of galvanic apparatus, together with the outlines of a new theory of galvanism. By this apparatus, which he called the Galvanic Deflagrator, charcoal was ignited, and produced a light equal to the brilliancy of the sun, and too vivid to be borne by eyes of common strength. The combustion of the metals produced by it was peculiarly brilliant. Platina a quarter of an inch in diameter was instantly fused. The Galvanic Deflagrator was declared by Prof. Silliman, of Yale College, to be "the finest present made to this department of knowledge since the discovery of the pile of Volta and of the trough of Cruickshanks." About this time Dr. H. gave a description of an improved gasometer, and of a new eudiometer, invented by him. Among his other inventions, also detailed in Silliman's Journal, we may mention the Litrameter, an instrument for ascertaining the specific gravities of fluids; also the Hydrostatic Blowpipe, a modification of impelling power beyond what could possibly be obtained by the breath. He described also an apparatus for freezing water by the aid of sulphuric acid. Among his latest inventions was the Improved Barometer Gauge Eudiometer. Numerous were the improvements and modifications in chemical apparatus introduced by him to facilitate the works of the laboratory. His Single Gold Leaf Electroscope, doubtless suggested by Bennet's instrument with two gold leaves, is represented by Sir W. Snow Harris to manifest an astonishing sensitiveness to the smallest electrical force. To the materia medica Dr. H. contributed by his process for denarcotizing laudanum, and to toxicology by his method of detecting minute quantities of opium in solution. Dr. H. contributed papers on various subjects to the Transactions of the American Philosophical Society. One was on the Tornado, or Water Spout, with a detailed description of the remarkable storm at New Brunswick, a few years ago. He considered the atmospherical disturbances in these cases to be owing to an electrified current of air. His views were at variance with those of Col. Redfield, of New York, with whom he more than once debated the subject. The eminence of Dr. H. in his favorite branch caused him to be elected in 1818 to the chair of chemistry in the medical department of the University of Pennsylvania, which had been vacated by the transfer of Dr. John Redman Coxe to the chair of materia medica. Dr. H. retained this post until his resignation of it in 1847, or during a period of nearly 30 years. There have been many more attractive and brilliant lecturers — no one more honestly intent on instructing his class; and certainly no one, on either side of the Atlantic, performed his experiments on such a large scale, and with what we might almost call such a grand apparatus, more especially when he wished to exhibit the wonders of electricity and galvanism. It must have seemed to his auditors that when he sometimes paused in the very midst of an explanation, it was from no want of clear conception of his subject, nor for words, but because at the moment a new thought would present itself, and he straightway allowed himself to imagine the new combinations and the results that must follow. Beyond the contributions to science in the vehicles already mentioned, Dr. H. wrote but little. He was not the author of any systematic work; for his Compendium of Chemistry was intended for his pupils, and as a text-book to his lectures. In his pages, so copiously illustrated by drawings of different chemical apparatus and instruments used in his lectures, it showed what he did, if the letter-press fell short of telling what he said. Dr. H. was fond of discussing questions of political economy; and he occasionally issued brochures on those which most interested him at the moment. He had warm political predilections, and was never backward in expressing them. In early life he was a federalist, and in later times a whig. His frankness on such occasions, as on others which came up in the course of conversation, might seem to a stranger to be rather *brusque*; but they who knew him could readily acquit him of all intention to wound the feelings or to give pain to any fellow-being. He was, indeed, a man without guile, and, withal, given to fits of abstraction, so as at times to seem to be wanting in the amenities of life, which in his heart he felt inclined to cherish in society, as he did uniformly in his own family. He was not only placable, but magnanimous; and if he was sometimes chafed with the attempts made to deprive him of the merit of certain discoveries, or to underrate his scientific attainments, he seemed to be influenced more by a sense of justice than by considerations of personal vanity. Here we would fain terminate our brief and imperfect sketch of the labors and character of departed genius; but we have yet to advert to what is every where known, and silence respecting which could only pass for an idle affectation of friendship. Our readers know that we allude to the delusion under which Dr. Hare labored during the last few years of his life by a belief in " spiritualism," as the thing is misnamed, and in his ability to hold intercourse with the other world through an invisible but present medium. Surprise has been very generally felt that so zealous and successful a votary of science should have allowed himself to be mystified in this manner. But, without entering into recondite psychological inquiries, which would be out of place on the present occasion, we think that an explanation may be found in the original constitution of his mind, in the long and intense strain of his intellectual faculties during the many years in which he was uninterruptedly engaged in the studies of the closet and the experiments of the laboratory, and, finally, in the very nature of his favorite pursuits. He had long been in the habit of dealing with those subtile, diffusive, and imponderable substances, or, as they might be called, essences, which give rise to the phenomena of electricity and magnetism, and which penetrate all matter and pervade all space, and which assume such an endless variety of disguises, now amusing us in philosophical toys, now convulsing nature in the storm and the tornado, or causing mountains to vomit forth volcanic fires, and make an entire continent to tremble in the throes of an earthquake. Sent through the human frame, the electric agency imparts new life, and, for a moment, gives movement and expression to the dead. Dr. H., in the vigor of his days, had been accustomed to investigate the causes and nature of these proteiform appearances, to unmask some of their disguises, and to exercise the office of a vigilant observer and careful experimenter, while admitting only the deductions thus obtained. But with advanced age came a wearied and a worn mind, which, yielding more and more to habits of abstraction and absence from the outer world, allowed itself to imagine some changes, some disguises, of an ethereal and even spiritual nature, not differing much from, but only going a little beyond, those light, diffusive, and imponderable agencies with which he might be said to have long held communion. We leave to others the duty of showing that the secrets of the other, the spiritual world, and the revelations of God to man, have not been discovered by either genius, or learning, or science. The knowledge of all this lies in another direction, and is taught by other means, now happily, under the Christian dispensation, accessible to all. Dr. H. has left behind him a widow and three children — Judge Hare and his brother, now living in Maryland, and Mrs. Prime, in New York.

HARGRAVES, Mrs. Virginia, Columbus, Ga., June —, æ. —, wife of George Hargraves, Esq., and daughter of the late Hon. John Forsyth. In the death of this most estimable lady society has lost one of its best and most beautiful ornaments; for not only was she esteemed and beloved by those who were her more intimate associates, but all classes, from the highest to the lowest, speak her praises. To such as knew her well, and were on terms of daily intercourse, she was ever a warm and true friend, ready, with wholesome advice given in the spirit of love, to guide and restrain them, winning them by firm adherence to principle, and yet an unremitted gentleness of manner, to see and love the beauties of religion. But her chief ornament lay in that kind benevolence of heart she ever manifested towards God's poor, without further distinction than their peculiar necessities. A noble woman has fallen in Israel, and the Episcopal church has lost one of her brightest and purest members.

HARKNESS, Anthony, Cincinnati, O., May 17, æ. 65. He was a native of Rhode Island, and the pioneer manufacturer of locomotives in Cincinnati. He commenced business with a very slender capital, and has left a large estate, valued at over half a million of dollars.

HARNEY, B. F., M. D., Baton Rouge, La., Aug, 29, æ. 80. The Baton Rouge Advocate says, Dr. H. was born in Delaware, from whence he removed to Mississippi, soon after the completion of his medical education. When the late war with Great Britain was declared, he became connected with the army as volunteer surgeon, in which capacity he joined a volunteer company raised in Mississippi in 1814 for the protection of the frontier. He was subsequently received into the military service of the United States as surgeon, and shared the hardships and glories of the campaign of 1815. He also served in the Black Hawk and Florida wars, was appointed to the important position of medical director of the U. S. army during the Mexican war, and accompanied General Scott's command during its victorious march to the city of Mexico. His services were equally as available on the field of battle as by the couch of the wounded. During a guerilla attack he was slightly wounded in the ankle. Since his return from Mexico, and when not engaged in active service, he has resided here as surgeon of the U. S. garrison at this place. The many noble traits which adorned the character of Dr. H., as a man and a citizen, secured him the esteem and admiration of his friends and fellow-citizens. Dr. H. was the oldest surgeon in the U. S. army, and was, by seniority, entitled to the rank of surgeon general, which, we understand, he twice declined accepting. Gen. Wm. S. Harney, of the U. S. army, is a brother of the deceased, and his junior by a number of years.

HARPER, George K., Chambersburg, Pa., Jan. 13, æ. 79, formerly editor of the Franklin Repository, was born in Oxford, Philadelphia Co., in 1778, and removed to Chambersburg in 1794. At the age of 16 years he was employed in the printing office of his brother, Robert Harper, who then edited the Franklin Repository, the only newspaper in the county of Franklin. In that office Mr. George K. Harper continued to assist his brother until 1800, when he succeeded that brother as the exclusive editor of the Franklin Repository. Though the deceased was an avowed federalist of the Washington school, he was not intolerant, or even personally hostile or abusive, to those who differed with him in political sentiments. He commenced his editorship of the Repository during the exciting times that characterized the political contest between the friends of Adams and Jefferson for the presidency. In the second year of his editorship, (1801,) when the democratic party had supplanted the federal party in the administration of the federal government, the deceased, in the Repository of that year, announced to its patrons that the Repository shall not pursue a course of indiscriminate and unjustifiable abuse of the men now in power and their measures; nor, on the other hand, will it sink into apathy and servility; but, keeping aloof from licentiousness and indecorum, admit of free investigation of public men and measures. Though he was opposed to the declaration of war by Congress, in 1812, against England, yet when it was declared and waged, he took the side of his country in the contest of arms. He was lieutenant in a volunteer company of infantry in Chambersburg, under the command of Capt. Jeremiah Snider, which immediately equipped itself and marched to meet the enemy on the Canada frontier, then an extended wilderness, where the Indians roamed in alliance with British forces. After the service required, in an arduous campaign, in a country remote from the settlements and supplies, Mr. Harper returned to his family at Chambersburg. The paper during his absence was under the direction of Mr. William D. Bell, an apprentice, who was aided gratuitously by the supervision of two of Mr. Harper's friends. After his return from the military campaign, he resumed the editorship of the Repository, and though he was, by the law, exempt from further military services, yet when intelligence reached him of the near approach of the British army to Baltimore, and its demonstrations of attack on that exposed city, he again put on his arms and marched with all expedition to resist the arrogant and powerful enemy. He remained there until the enemy was repelled, the city of Baltimore saved from assault and capture, and the volunteers, of whom Mr. H. was one, were by the government allowed to return to their homes. After this he gave to the Repository his undivided attention until 1840, when he was appointed, by President Harrison, postmaster of Chambersburg, and relinquished the Repository. Though a more upright and capable public officer was not to be found in the community, yet he was allowed to retain this official station but a short time. On the death of President Harrison and the succession of President Tyler, Mr. Harper's relation to the new administration was embarrassing. His independence was an offence, and whilst his integrity and capacity was unimpeached, this veteran editor, soldier, patriot, and honest man of long service, was removed to give place to a youthful partisan. Mr. Harper being now without occupation his health and intellectual vigor gradually declined. During the forty years the Franklin Repository was under his editorship, it was a model family newspaper — free from all licentiousness, indecency, or indelicacy, the uniform advocate of religion and good morals, ever conservative in its principles, and the defender of peace, law, and order. Mr. Harper sustained all the relations of life with great propriety. He was a kind and attentive husband and father, and exemplary as a citizen and neighbor. Upright in his dealings, he was without litigation and controversy; yet no man was oftener called on as a referee or arbitrator to settle or pass opinion upon the controversies of others. He was always circumspect in his life and morals, and ever ready to discharge all the duties of a good citizen. He some years since made a profession of his faith in a crucified Redeemer, and was received as a member of the church, of which he was a consistent professor. His life was prolonged until within a few months of fourscore, in a community where he had lived for upwards of seventy years without reproach. He has left a large and respectable family to reverence his memory, amongst whom are his two sons, Kenton Harper, Esq., of Staunton, Va., and William Harper, Esq., of Romney, in the same state.

HARRIMAN, H. C., M. D.. Jerseyville, Ill., March 13, æ. 35.

HARRIS, Prof. Josiah, Prattville, Ala., Oct. 5, æ. 63. He was a native of York district, S. C., a graduate of Hampden Sidney College, and of the Theological Seminary of Virginia.

HARRIS, Samuel, Baltimore, Md., June —, æ. 84, of the well-known banking house of Samuel Harris and Sons.

Mr. H. was among our most highly esteemed citizens during his long life, and although a member of the Society of Friends, took part in the war of 1812 in defence of the city, and was slightly wounded at Fort McHenry.

HON. WILLIAM R. HARRIS, Memphis, Tenn., June 18, æ. 56, from injuries received by the explosion of the steamer Pennsylvania. Although this event was somewhat expected for the past two days, the intelligence struck the community with the profound grief of a sharp and unanticipated sorrow. His professional brethren have borne testimony below to the learning and integrity of the deceased in the exalted position in which he died. His personal worth, his kindly heart, and inflexible honor were equally prominent in the circle of his acquaintances. To make up the record of the good example of his life, we append this brief notice, prepared by a committee of the Memphis bar: "William R. Harris was born in Montgomery Co., N. C., in 1802. While he was yet an infant his parents removed to what now is Bedford Co. in this state, and settled upon the waters of Duck River. The death-like stillness of the primeval forests of that region had scarce been disturbed by the sound of the woodman's axe. Not a half dozen chimneys sent up their columns of blue smoke within 20 miles of the humble cabin where our future supreme judge was learning lessons of hardihood, of boldness, of manliness, of courage from his very cradle. There were then no court houses there, no magistrates, no churches, no school houses, but society was reduced to its integral elements, and each head of a family and master of a cabin had to assume over his own household all the patriarchal functions of prophet, priest, and king. After living upon Duck River some 10 or 12 years, the father of the subject of our notice removed to what is now Franklin Co., where his son William, after ploughing hard all summer to help his father maintain the family, enjoyed the advantage of going to the common field school during the three winter months. Arrived at the age of 21, we find that the sheriff of Franklin Co. deemed William R. Harris to be a youth of such energy and trustworthiness that he appointed him one of his deputies. But while riding as deputy, William did not neglect his studies; applying himself at night, he was able to keep up with his class in the English grammar school, and to read all of the few books to be had among the bold pioneers, his father's neighbors. Finally deeming himself to have sufficiently improved to permit of his studying law, he betook himself to the town of Lawrenceburg, and placed himself under the instruction of Isaac Cook, a lawyer of some eminence, of that place. To maintain himself while studying law, young Harris wrote in the office of the clerk of the Circuit Court, and thereby rendered himself perfectly familiar with all the forms of legal proceedings. Having obtained his license to practise his profession, young Harris determined to locate at the new and thriving village of Paris, in Henry Co. Here he rose rapidly into eminence and distinction at the bar, so much so, indeed, that, after he had been practising only some eight years, he was deemed worthy by the governor of the state to be appointed to fill a vacancy which had occurred upon the Circuit Court bench; and this appointment of the governor was confirmed by the legislature, which met shortly thereafter. This responsible position he continued to fill for many years, until he retired from the bench, and removed to the growing city of Memphis to practise law. Upon the death of Judge William B. Turley, in 1851, who was then acting as commercial and criminal judge of Memphis, William R. Harris was by the bar and the legislature deemed worthy to succeed so illustrious a predecessor. This post Judge H. continued to hold until the change in the Tennessee state constitution, in 1854, vacated his office. He did not seek to be reëlected, but returned to the practice of his profession, until the next year a vacancy through the resignation of Judge Totten occuring upon the supreme bench, Judge H. was tendered the appointment, by his excellency, Gov. Johnson, which he accepted. The popular vote of the state in a few months ratified this selection of the governor. Thus elevated to the highest judicial position of honor and of trust in the state, he continued to discharge the functions of his office with great fidelity and zeal, until June last, when his life of usefulness and honor was brought to a sudden and awful termination by the explosion of the ill-fated steamer Pennsylvania. The committee have thus given a brief outline of the life of the distinguished man whose untimely death we all so much deplore. Judge H. possessed many of the very noblest traits of character which it is possible for man or magistrate to have. He was a sincere, conscientious, brave, truthful man. He was an honest, impartial, just, fearless, and able judge." — *Memphis Bulletin.*

"The terrible casualty which befell the Hon. William R. Harris, on the steamer Pennsylvania, in common with hundreds of other devoted fellow-creatures, terminated in his death yesterday morning at six o'clock. Thus has been stricken down, in the meridian of manhood and in the zenith of an honorable and distinguished career, one of the soundest intellects and truest hearts that adorn our state. William R. Harris was a man of no ordinary mould. His mind was clear, direct, and logical, never sacrificing the substance to mere ornament, and always endowed with a force and perspicuousness that challenged opposition. When added to this was a spotless integrity and the habit of thorough application and research, it may be fairly claimed that his was a legal mind of of the first order. We shall not essay in this brief notice to do justice to those sterling attributes of character which won for Judge Harris the unbounded confidence of his fellow-men, and which elevated him successively to the highest positions at the bar and on the bench. It is sufficient here to state that no man could have enjoyed a higher degree of confidence from his neighbors and friends, which gradually extended itself until the whole people of the state placed him on their supreme judicial tribunal. He was stern and unbending in his integrity, warm and undying in his friendship, ardent in his feelings, and in an expressive phrase, often used but forcible in its application, 'a true man.' He leaves behind him a devoted family and a wide circle of personal friends to mourn his sad and irreparable loss. He was the elder brother of the governor of Tennessee, who has been at his bedside from the moment of his arrival from the scene of the disaster that caused his death. The whole community participates in the sorrow of those whose bereavement is inconsolable." — *Memphis Daily Appeal.*

HARRIS, Hon. Thomas L., Petersburg, Ill., Nov. 24, æ. 41. He was a native of Connecticut, whence he emigrated to Illinois, and settled in Springfield in 1842, he being then 25 years of age. He changed his residence to Petersburg the following year, and at once entered upon a lucrative law practice. Three years afterwards he was elected to the state Senate, which office he did not accept, owing to the breaking out of the Mexican war, for which he enlisted as a private, and was at once elected major of the fourth regiment of Illinois volunteers, in which he served with distinguished ability, acting a considerable part of the time as colonel. It was a party under him that planted a battery on a hill opposite Cerro Gordo, the night before the battle, a work which the Mexicans supposed to be superhuman. On his return from the war he was nominated by the democrats for a seat in Congress, and was triumphantly elected, though the opposition numbered 1500 majority, and his competitor was a great favorite with his party, and reputed to be the ablest lawyer in the state. In that memorable canvass Major H. gave an earnest of his subsequent brilliant career in the councils of the nation. Since that period he has had a national reputation. Though comparatively a young man, he ranked among the ablest debaters. At Washington, last winter, he was conveyed to the Hall of Representatives on a litter, to give his vote on the great question of the session. In a recumbent position, he cast his vote for popular sovereignty, which he had previously advocated in numberless speeches during the session. He was the leader in that body on the question, and exposed his very life, and hastened its termination, by his patriotic devotion to its advocacy. At intervals during the session he had hemorrhages of the lungs, and was advised to abandon his official labors, and seek in retirement a restoration of his health; but he persistently refused, saying that the crisis demanded his services, and they should be rendered, even at the cost of his life. His congressional efforts were enough to exhaust the strongest constitution. They have entered into the history of the country; they are familiar to all, and will never be forgotten while popular sovereignty and true republicanism exist in this country. Mr. H. was a man of great talents, and most remarkable nerve and energy. In Congress he was a leading man, and no member of the last session commanded more general respect. He was chairman of the committee on elections — a position requiring an unusual amount of labor, and the exercise of much ability; but he discharged the onerous duties imposed upon him in a highly satisfactory manner. If he had a fault, it was that of being too plain spoken and too firm in the support of what he conceived to be a proper course of conduct. He never stopped to polish his sentences so that they would glide smoothly into the understanding of an opponent; but he said what he thought in plain words, and sometimes this plainness amounted to rudeness. But, with all this, he was as kind-hearted a man as ever lived. Mr. H. was small in stature, and slightly formed. For a long time he had suffered from a pulmonary disease, contracted, it is supposed, by exposure in Mexico. During last winter he suffered much from this complaint, and was at times confined to his room for weeks. But, although reduced to the lowest possible state by his insidious enemy, he was always cheerful and pleasant, and his voice rang out in the house as clear as a trumpet. Many who knew him last winter, thought that he would hardly survive the labors of the session, and the intelligence of his death will be no surprise to them, although it will bring sorrow to many hearts. Nor was Maj. H. known only as a soldier, lawyer, and statesman. His many private virtues were preëminent. As a son, a husband, a father, and friend, he was a model of fidelity and attachment. He was, in every relation of life, frank, courteous, and truthful.

HARRIS, Stephen, M. D., Providence, R. I., Oct. 10, æ. 72. Dr. H. was born in Johnston, R. I., in 1786; entered Brown University, then R. I. College, where he remained, but did not graduate on account of the death of his father. He studied medicine with Dr. Caleb Fiske, an eminent practitioner, completed his education at Dartmouth College, and commenced the practice of his profession. He soon relinquished it on account of feeble health, but subsequently entered the business of cotton manufacturer. In connection with the late James Greene, Resolved Waterman, and others, he formed the Greene Manufacturing Company at River Point; afterwards became sole proprietor. At his death he was one of the largest manufacturers in Rhode Island. He was one of the founders of the R. I. Medical Society; but only three of his associates, it is believed, survive him.

HARRISON, Rev. Fosdick, Bridgewater, Ct., Feb. 9, æ. 76, for many years pastor of the Congregational church in Bethlehem.

HARRISON, Nathaniel, Brunswick Co., Va., Dec. 14, æ. 72, one of the Petersburg volunteers to Canada in the war of 1812.

HARRISON, Col. Robert Monroe, Kingston, Jamaica, May 24, æ. 90, U. S. consul. Col. H. was born in Virginia in 1768, a descendant of the ancient and honorable family of that name in Berkeley Co., and cousin of the late President Harrison. Having early shown a desire to become a sailor, his mother reluctantly allowed him to go to London to be instructed in navigation by the then celebrated Hamilton Moore. While going up the British Channel, he was pressed on board a small king's cutter, and afterwards transferred to other vessels of war. He was accustomed in after life to say he was greatly indebted to the discipline of a British man-of-war for the firmness and decision of character he possessed. After he procured a discharge, he travelled extensively upon the continent, visiting places of interest as far as St. Petersburg at the north, and Madrid at the south. He returned to the United States about the time of St. Clair's defeat, and received a commission of second lieutenant in the army, and joined Gen. Harrison's regiment. His health failing, he sought the mild climate of the south of France. He was appointed to the navy by Washington; and the date of commission was the same as that of Com. Rodgers. He was the friend and associate of Truxton, and resigned his commission during Jefferson's administration. He then went to Russia, and witnessed some of the stirring scenes consequent upon the invasion of Napoleon, and participated in the battle of Borodino. In Sweden he married a ward of Count Fersien, Swedish minister of state, afterwards stoned to death by the populace of Stockholm; and when the war of 1812 broke out he immediately offered his services to his own government, and on his way home was carried a prisoner to Cowes, England. From thence he went to St. Thomas, and there found a commission as consul for that place waiting for him. Since then he has served in the same capacity in several important places, and has been United States consul for the Island of Jamaica for the last 27 years. Says a writer (Dr. Otis, surgeon in the U. S. mail steamer service) in Harper's Magazine, "I there met our captain, who kindly invited me to accompany him on a visit to the venerable Col. Harrison, United States consul at Jamaica. Accepting with pleasure, we soon reached the consular residence through a beautiful grove of fig trees, whose broad leaves overshadowed our path. Its purple fruit, bursting with ripeness, hung within reach, while wide-leaved banana trees and waving cocoa palms towered up in other parts of the garden. All this, the captain told me, had been laid out and cultured under the immediate supervision of the consul's estimable lady. As we stepped over the polished floors of the veranda we were met by the consul himself. Greeting the captain, with great cordiality he extended his slightly trembling hand to me, saying, 'My countrymen are always welcome.' His appearance was imposing — of a medium height, erect and dignified bearing, with hair and long flowing beard as white as snow. I have seldom seen a more noble and venerable-looking man; and his gracious lady, to whom we were presented, reminded me of pictures of the courtly dames of the 'Old Dominion' in Washington's time. During the conversation which followed the captain alluded to the days of the revolution, when the colonel was an officer in the American navy, having received his warrant from Washington himself. I shall never forget the pleasure with which I listened while the old man 'fought his battles o'er again.' Among the many entertaining reminiscences which the aged veteran recalled, I managed to gather a few data in his own personal history. His hair had been frosted by the winters of 90 years, more than 70 of which had been spent in the service of his country; for many years a midshipman and lieutenant in our navy, he resigned only to be sent on a secret-service mission to Europe, where his abilities and devoted patriotism made his services more valuable; and finally, for more than 40 years American consul general to the British West Indies, and resident consul at Jamaica. His intellect was still unclouded, although a trembling intonation of voice, and a slight unsteadiness of hand and gait, gave proof that time, dealing never so gently, had begun to unstring his vigorous frame. After more than an hour of pleasant and instructive converse, we reluctantly bade the aged patriarch farewell, and, receiving his paternal blessing, departed. And I now look back upon that interview with our venerable consul as one of the most pleasing incidents of my life." Col. H. leaves a son, a lieutenant in the U. S. navy. His wife died some two or three years before him.

HARRISON, Thomas A., M. D., Fawnsdale, Marengo Co., Ala., Sept. 5, æ. 43. Dr. H. was a native of Virginia. He received a polished literary education, and subsequently graduated at a medical institute. After devoting a few years to the practice of his profession, he married an accomplished lady of North Carolina, and about 16 years ago emigrated to his late home. During his residence here he pursued the occupation of cotton planting on an extended scale, and with more than usual energy and system. The retirement of this mode of life afforded the opportunity, so congenial to his taste, for general reading and reflection. He was intimately acquainted with the current literature of the day, and frequently entertained his friends with discussions of the various dogmas set forth. He still more earnestly studied the political aspect of the times.

HART, Judge Samuel H., Loveland, O., Dec. —, æ. —. He was well known, and was some time since quite prominent as a politician and as a lawyer. He was serving his second term as city solicitor. He was a public-spirited man, distinguished for his activity, vigor, and enterprise. He possessed many manly qualities; and there are many who will receive deeply sorrowful impressions at the unhappy termination of his career. He leaves a large and interesting family.

HARWOOD, Rev. John, Big Spring, Hardin Co., Ky., June 12, æ. 49. He was born in Louisa Co., Va., Oct. 7, 1808. He was brought to see and feel his condition as a sinner during a protracted meeting in Breckenridge Co., on the Christmas of 1833, and joined the Methodist Episcopal church a short time afterwards, and was soon licensed to preach.

HASKELL, Dea. Ezra, Dover, N. H., March 27, æ. 77. He was born in New Gloucester, in the then District of Maine, March 12, 1781. The years of his youth were spent in the ordinary occupations of farmer life. Having fitted himself for college, and earned money to defray his expenses, he entered Bowdoin College in 1809, one year in advance; then removing to New Haven, he entered the Junior class in Yale College in 1810, graduating in 1811. He joined the First Church in Hallowell, March 27, 1803, making the period of his connection with the Christian church 55 years. He spent most of his life as an instructor of youth, in which employment he never neglected the claims of religion. For many years he was resident in Boston, and a member of Park Street Church, and one of the examining committee. From this church, with a few others, he was dismissed to build up a new church in Essex Street, of which Dr. Adams is now pastor. He was also an efficient helper in the building of the Phillips Church, South Boston. A member of the Howard Benevolent Society, he was ever active in doing good, visiting the prison, and teaching the inmates on the Sabbath. Though a teacher, his great study has been spent on theology, in which his attainments were very great, surpassed by very few, always clear, and to the point. He lived to see three sons in the ministry, and have them acknowledge him their best theological instructor. He adhered firmly to the doctrines of the Westminster Catechism, which, in his family, he often expounded with exceeding pungency and power. The whole Bible was his study, and the maturity of his faith was evinced both by his life and his death.

HASSLER, John J. S., Norfolk, Va., June 23, æ. 59, born in Switzerland; an assistant in the U. S. Coast Survey, and son of the late F. R. Hassler, first superintendent of the U. S. coast survey, and standardizing of weights and measures.

HASSLER, Madame Marianne Guiliard, Miller's Place, Suffolk Co., L. I., Feb. 25, æ. 88, relict of the late Gen. Ferdinand Rudolph Hassler, former head of the United States coast survey. She was descended from an ancient noble Swiss family, the Guiliard. In education she was highly accomplished. United by marriage in early life to Mr. Hassler, emigrating with him to this country, she shared the vicissitudes of his varied and distinguished career. At one time the denizen of a frontier forest home, at another dwelling in cities — every where a lady in mind and heart. Her husband held, in the early half of this century, the office of scientific ambassador to London and Paris, with the outfit and salary of a foreign minister. She accompanied him, and enjoyed and improved, while she graced, the circles of refined society at those great centres of fashion and intelligence. She was resident at Paris when the first consul of France donned the purple and became Emperor. She was present at his coronation, and at his return from Elba. Her recollections of that extraordinary man, and of his scarcely less extraordinary consort, Josephine, were in the highest degree interesting. The last 20 or 30 years of this lady's life were clouded by afflictions in the death of her husband and children. One of the latter, Charles Hassler, a surgeon in the navy, perished in the wreck of the steamer Atlantic, on the Long Island coast, where, though his bravery and coolness contributed to the salvation of others, it failed to secure him from a watery grave.

HATCH, James Lewis, Charleston, S, C., Sept. 25, æ. 25. Mr. H. was born, we believe, in 1833, in the vicinity of Portland, Me. With the particulars of his life and career, short as it was, we are not fully acquainted. Graduating at an early age, and after severe struggles and sacrifices in favor of a liberal education, he left Bowdoin College with flattering testimonials and credentials. He began some connection with the press before or during his college course, and was a correspondent and contributor for New England journals; among others, we believe, for the Portland Transcript and the Boston Post. The advice of physicians and friends induced a removal to the south, as a resort needed by impaired health, and in the winter of 1854-5 he arrived in Charleston, and soon entered the employment of Messrs. L. W. Spratt & Co., then editors and proprietors of the Charleston Standard. He continued in this relation two years or more, and was actively concerned in the editorial conduct of that journal, and, at intervals, was the acting editor-in-chief.

HATHAWAY, Hon. Elnathan P., Freetown, Mass., Jan. 23, æ. 61, Mr. H. was born in Freetown, Bristol Co., near the close of the last century, one of the somewhat numerous family of the late Dr. Hathaway, then of that place, but subsequently, and for many years, a resident of Ohio. After the usual preparation in the required studies of the time, Elnathan entered Brown University, and graduated with the class of 1818. He was diligent, well read, and orderly, and left the institution alike respected by the members of his class and the officers of the corporation. Shortly after his graduation, he entered his name in the law office of Hercules Cushman, Esq., of Freetown, with whom he pursued his studies, till admitted to the Bristol bar, when he became a partner in business with his instructor. By close application and fidelity in the discharge of professional duty, he early acquired the confidence of the community, and obtained the reputation of a safe and sound legal adviser. His practice became, in a short time, extensive and lucrative, and his labors were continued till necessity no longer compelled him to answer professional calls beyond his own personal convenience. Such, in a few words, is the material aspect of the life of the late Mr. H. Behind all this, there were elements in his character, not as obvious, because only brought into play on occasions outside his professional life, but nevertheless elements which, when understood, made him even more than he seemed to be. His social qualities were admirable, and his conversational powers of a pleasing order. When freed from the cares and perplexities of business, few men entered more heartily into the current and less important affairs of life. Though the tendency of his mind was eminently logical, he delighted to pass from demonstration to trust, and was never happier than when engaged in the lighter interchanges of thought. He possessed a keen relish for the salient points in ancient history, read with appreciative interest the great English dramatist, and knew the good things in the fictions of Sir Walter Scott almost by heart. All these occupied in his mind the place of an "afterpiece" in the great drama of his busy life. It was in his hours of relaxation that he shone brightest; it was at his own hearthstone that he made his happiest conquests over the affections of others. Though not an orator, in the ordinary sense of that term, as used in the United States, he was a ready and effective speaker, always securing attention by the clearness with which he arranged his thoughts. His arguments at the bar were to the point, for, unlike not a few of his countrymen, he could not or would not talk unless he had something to say. That he was a man of no ordinary stamp in his profession, is evident from the high estimation in which he was held by his contemporaries. These were such as Lemuel Williams, T. G. Coffin, Charles H. Warren, and Hezekiah Battelle; and of the succeeding generation, H. G. O. Colby, John H. Clifford, Nathaniel Morton, Baylies Sanford, and many others, all eminent in their profession, and men of whom Massachusetts may well be proud. With these gentlemen Mr. H. was often associated in important cases, and it is safe to say, no client ever had reason to complain of neglect, or of misapprehension on his part, and as little certainty on the part of the gentlemen above named. Patient, laborious investigation was his predominant characteristic, and he pursued this often long after others were more than satisfied. In politics Mr. H. was a democrat of the old school, and throughout his whole life an active member of that party. Well informed upon all the great principles of constitutional government, slight perturbations in public sentiment had little or no effect on his own clearly prescribed course of action. His opinions were generally the results of mature reflection, and when once formed were carried out to their legitimate consequences, regardless of momentary ebullitions of popular feeling. In this course he may have been considered a party man; but he never sunk the party man in the partisan. Claiming for himself nothing he was not ready to concede to others, he met his opponents frankly, and urged his own views with imperturbable good nature. So well understood was this trait in his character, that wherever known he was a general favorite among his political opponents. Several times, in the course of his life, Mr. H. represented his town in the General Court, and once or twice he held a seat in the Senate from Bristol Co. In both situations he acquitted himself with marked ability. He was also a member of the convention for the revisal of our state constitution in 1853, and often took part in the debates, and otherwise rendered substantial service in furthering the objects of the convention.

HATHORN, Rev. Samuel, West Gardiner, Me., Dec. 13, æ. 64.

HAWES, Hon. J. H. H., Troy, N. Y., Jan. 27, æ. —, at one time a member of Congress from New York city.

HAWES, Col. William F., Winthrop, Mass., Oct. 3, æ. 53. In the death of Col. H., Winthrop lost one of its most useful and valued citizens. Extensively engaged in manufactures, he gave employment to a large number of operatives. In his business relations, his frank, manly, and upright course won for him the confidence and respect of all. In former years, Col. H. resided in New Bedford, where he was a member of the vestry of Grace Church, and took an active part in the organization of that parish, and in the erection of the church. He was a sincere believer in the Christian faith, and in the distinctive principles of the Protestant Episcopal church. He was a graduate of Brown University, and was among the most intelligent of our business men.

HAWKINS, Hon. Micajah, Warner Co., N. C., Dec. 22, æ. 72. Under the tuition of the celebrated Marcus George, and the professors at Chapel Hill, he received a liberal education; and by that indomitable energy which never forsook him, he soon after acquired an independent fortune. In 1817 he was elected to represent his native county in the legislature, in both branches of which, and as representative to Congress from his district, he served, with the exception of a few years, until 1850. He was an active and useful magistrate for a number of years, a councillor of state, and arose, by meritorious services, to the rank of major-general in his division of the militia of the state. In politics he was a thorough democrat, and uncompromising states-right man, and while in Congress he gave a cordial and efficient support to those great measures of public policy which distinguished the administrations of General Jackson and Mr. Van Buren. He was endowed with correct judgment, decision, and unwavering firmness to principle. His generosity, hospitality, and personal popularity are too well known for comment.

HAWKINS, John D., Franklin Co., Va., Dec. 5, æ. 73. He was the last surviving child of Col. Philemon Hawkins, of Warren Co. Of liberal education, and having practised law many years, he was fitted for usefulness in all the walks of life. On his retirement from the profession of the law, he carried with him a knowledge and a capacity for business, which soon became the common property of his neighbors and friends; and to them, in the transaction of business and in other matters, his advice and aid were cheerfully and readily afforded. He was for many years presiding justice of Franklin Co.; and in that capacity his usefulness was extensively felt, and his efficient and impartial administration of justice gratefully acknowledged by all. For many successive years he represented Franklin Co. in the Senate branch of the legislature, in which he was an active and useful member, and exerted a marked influence over its proceedings. Endued with a liberal public spirit, he was among the earliest and most devoted friends of the cause of internal improvements, and ever after gave to it an earnest and zealous support. His home was the seat of hospitality; and visitors, strangers or friends, were always received with that cordiality and welcome which springs only from the warmest feelings of the heart. None went away without a desire to visit the hospitable mansion, ever gladdened as it was by the smiles and greetings of its kind-hearted occupants. He was the devoted and affectionate husband, the kind and tender parent, the humane master, the warm friend, and the good neighbor.

HAWKINS, John H. W., Parkersburg, Pa., Aug. 26, æ. 61, the friend of the drunkard. Mr. Hawkins's life was an eventful one. He was born in Baltimore in 1797. At an early age he went to school to Rev. A. McCain, a rigid disciplinarian, whose extensive use of the rod had a vicious effect upon the boy. At the age of 15 he was put an apprentice to the hatting business, where he served faithfully until he was 21, never wilfully disobeying his master but once; and that was during the last war, when the British effected a landing, and commenced a march on the city of Baltimore. Young H., then 17, desired to join the volunteers in defending his native city against the enemy. His master refused; but he went to the armory, was furnished with arms, and, by a forced march of 14 miles, he overtook the volunteers in time to enter the ranks before the engagement. During the battle a ball of the enemy passed through his hat. After the fight was over, and the American arms were victorious, he returned to his work and his mother, who was in a state of great alarm for the safety of her son. At the age of 15 he was converted, and joined the Methodist Episcopal church; was a constant attendant at a class and band, and generally beloved by all who knew him. At the close of his apprenticeship he had saved by overwork $25; he spent the whole of it in purchasing Bibles and spelling books, and paying the rent of a room to keep a Sabbath school for boys; for at that time there was no Sunday school for boys in his city, and his pious soul yearned to be the instrument in reclaiming the children whom he saw breaking God's holy day. During his apprenticeship and early manhood he was surrounded by those who were in the daily use of alcoholic drinks. In the workshop the bottle was always filled, inviting young and old to partake. In the convivial party and social gathering he was proffered the cup of friendship by the hands of fair women and venerable sires. Day by day his love for wine and strong drinks was strengthening, and day by day the love for his Saviour was weakening, until his appetite led him into the mire of intoxication and all the horrors of drunkenness. From the grog shops he had been often helped home by his companions to his house late at night, and thrust in the front door, where he has lain in a helpless state of intoxication. His family would come to his assistance; his little daughter Hannah, unable to raise him up, would bring pillows and blankets to keep him warm, and lie down by her dear father to keep him from harm. Such acts of kindness pierced his soul, and he would promise himself he would never drink to excess again; but the tempter came, and he fell, and each succeeding fall was lower and more degrading than the former. His friends gave him up for lost, and he began to despair for himself; but June 1, 1840, after one of the worst debauches he had ever had, which came near sending him to a drunkard's grave, his little daughter Hannah was made the instrument of her father's salvation. Coming to his bedside early in the morning, and supposing him asleep, she pressed a kiss of tender affection upon his bloated cheek. Then, kneeling down by his side, she lifted up her eyes and heart to heaven, and prayed in a whisper that God heard, and went to the ears of the sinful man. After this she silently left the room; but when he heard her steps dying away from the stairs he sprang from his bed, and knelt on the very spot where the child prayed, and cried penitentially to his God to hear the voice of intercession; and there, in that holy place, he vowed, and called upon God to help him up in his weakness, to forgive and raise him to the dignity of a man and Christian. For three days, like Saul of Tarsus, he struggled against a raging thirst, an enfeebled body, a weak mind, and one of the strongest temptations that can befall a mortal; but God, who is rich in mercy, came to his assistance. The bottle, at the request of her father, was broken by Hannah. At the invitation of six other bottle companions, he went to a carpenter's shop in the evening, and signed the Washingtonian pledge; and there these men pledged themselves to watch over and help each other to live temperate lives. Mr. H. was enabled to keep the pledge; he was soon restored to the church and class; and such was the confidence of his brethren that they elected him to the office of a local preacher. If his fall was rapid and ignominious, his rise was glorious, and proved a blessing to thousands. At this time Mr. H. was in the prime of life, in person well formed. He had a dignified and commanding appearance, carriage erect, in manners affable, a rich, melodious voice, and a strong constitution. He had all the requisites of a reformer

— boldness, discretion, energy, fortitude, firmness, and perseverance, together with the Christian virtues of self-denial, humility, benevolence, honesty, simplicity, and sincerity; looking to God for success, and giving him all the glory. Such was John Hawkins in 1840, when, with six other reformed drunkards in the city of Baltimore, they began their labor to urge the fallen to sign the temperance pledge. They followed the drunkard to his house, and with tears urged him to come to their meeting, and join their increasing army. Their success in that city was great. It was preaching glad news to the spirits in prison. The poor drunken sot exclaimed, "Well, if such a man as John Hawkins can be saved, I can;" and he signed the pledge, and himself became a temperance lecturer. In Baltimore there were in less than a year 12,000 that joined them. The Macedonian cry from New York was, "Come over and help us." Mr. H., with several of his associates, did come. Churches and halls were crowded. There was joy in desolate hearts; mothers and daughters, sisters and wives, felt that there was a way at last found to save their families from disgrace, and their husbands from death. The wilderness and the solitary place was made glad for them; and in a few months 10,000 drunkards in the city of New York left their cups, and joined the Washingtonians, as they were called. Boston was soon visited by Mr. H.; and 5,000 more in that city were added to their number. He continued his labors throughout New England; and it was estimated that there were in less than a year 75,000 more redeemed from their cups. He now gave himself up to the work of saving the drunkard. He travelled extensively through every state in the Union, save California; and such was the wonderful success of his labors and his coadjutors', that, in less than one year from the time he signed the pledge, there was estimated to be over 2,000 that had joined this new temperance movement. In writing to his sister, the widow of an Episcopal clergyman, he says, "I have lectured 54 times in 40 days, written 60 letters, travelled over 1,000 miles; and the best of all is, I am in good health, I live in peace with all mankind, and with a bright hope, which grows brighter and brighter to the perfect day, when my labors on earth shall cease, and I shall go to my reward." He continued his labors until June 28, when his health utterly failed him, and he literally broke down with excessive toil. At Boston he was taken sick, and confined to his room for some time. He proceeded by easy journeys to his son, the Rev. W. G. Hawkins, in Pequin Valley, Lancaster Co., Pa., where he enjoyed for several weeks the society of a large number of his relatives — a feast he had not enjoyed for years.

HAWKINS, Capt. J. H., Springfield, Mass., May 17, æ. —, U. S. inspector of firearms.

HAYES, Rev. Alonzo, Alexandria Co., Va., July 15, æ. 47, formerly of Barrington, N. H. Mr. H. was ordained and installed pastor of the Congregational church, West Barnstable, May 24, 1843, and dismissed July 9, 1850. Subsequently he removed to Dublin, N. H., where he labored for some time, as it is supposed, very successfully, in the ministry. From thence he removed to Alexandria Co., Va., where he died. Before he was ordained at Barnstable the parish had been reduced by repeated divisions, until but few remained to worship in the ancient church. The funds of the church, which had been preserved many years, and carefully transmitted from generation to generation, were, in a few years previous to his coming, exhausted. There was just that state of things which every one will readily perceive must have existed. Discouragement, perplexity, and consequent disagreement, pressed heavily upon the church and society. He was a diligent student; and his sermons were well written and instructive. But his power for good was in his earnest piety. His humility, patience, and Christ-like simplicity made a deep impression.

HAYES, Oliver Bliss, Nashville, Tenn., Nov. 1, æ. 76. He was born in South Hadley, Mass., May 21, 1783, and was the son of the Rev. Joel Hayes, an eminent Congregational minister of that town. After receiving the highest literary culture in the best New England schools, and qualifying himself for the profession of the law, he went to Baltimore, where he remained a short time, and finally settled in Nashville, early in

1808. About this time and contemporary with him were many great names at the Nashville bar, Whiteside, Overton, Grundy, Dickinson, and others, who have long since departed, and he, their last survivor, is now gone. There were likewise great interests involved, and great questions to be settled by the courts, particularly those growing out of the conflicting land titles of the country. By his genius, his tact, his knowledge of men, accurate business habits, the ready resources of his intellect, his power of investigation, and graceful and vehement elocution, he made a strong impression upon the public mind, and his services were eagerly sought for by the suitors in the courts. His practice was extended through a considerable portion of Middle Tennessee, and in most of the important causes he was retained as counsel. During the whole period of his professional career, which was continued to about 1830, he ranked with the ablest of his contemporaries. His fine conversational talent, cultivated taste, ready wit, and various knowledge, have rarely been surpassed, and made him exceedingly attractive in the social circle. Having acquired a competent estate, about the period before alluded to, he retired from his profession with the view of devoting himself to the ministry, and was ordained as a minister in the Presbyterian church. But commencing his labors at so late a period, and having no pastoral relation, it is not to be supposed he could acquire the same high distinction as in the former field. Yet the fervor of his piety, the fidelity with which he discharged the various duties assigned him by his brethren, and the ability of his occasional efforts will be attested by them all. In his own house he dispensed a liberal hospitality, and in the exercise of all the domestic virtues as a husband and father, his character shone with peculiar beauty and loveliness.

HAYS, Hon. Mills, Newberry township, Pa., June 2, æ. —. He was one of the associate judges of the courts of York Co., Pa., for five years, having been elected to the office in 1851, immediately after the amendment to the constitution providing for the election of judges.

HAZARD, Rev. Charles S., West Greenwich, R. I., July 27, æ. 36, son of Robert Hazard. He experienced religion in February, 1842, and soon after united with the M. E. church at East Greenwich, R. I. From this time onward for several years he devoted himself chiefly to the work of teaching — a profession in which he was esteemed and useful. In the spring of 1850 he was admitted to probation in the Providence conference, and stationed at Westport, Mass., where he labored two years. His next appointment was Attleboro', Mass., where he preached only a few months, when he was laid aside by a severe illness, from which he never fully recovered. For six years Bro. H. was an invalid, preaching and laboring to the extent of his ability, and bearing up bravely under a burden of disease and suffering. His natural endowments were of the most substantial and valuable kind. Free from the eccentricities of genius, his mind was sound and symmetrical. He was a vigorous thinker, and had informed himself by a careful study of men, as well as of books. As a Christian he was modest, devoted, and consistent. On all the great moral issues of the day he took right positions, and held them with firmness and courage. As a preacher he was interesting and profitable, aiming not at display, but at such a division of the word of God as would give to each a portion in due season. In the pastoral work he was faithful and beloved; it was among an inner circle of friends who knew him intimately that his excellences shone with serenest beauty. In the social circle he was cheerful, courteous, and companionable; his presence was a perpetual benediction.

HEADLEY, James H., Buffalo, N. Y., Oct. 12, æ. —, author of Sacred Plains, and other interesting works.

HEATON, Robert, New Orleans, Aug. 26, æ. 23, professor of mathematics in Dolbear's Commercial College.

HEDGES, Josiah, Tiffin, O., July 15, æ. 80. He was born in Berkeley Co., Va., April 9, 1778. He left his father's home at an early age, with the determination to carve out his own fortune. His first enterprise on his own account was a trading excursion to New Orleans, with fruit, which he flat-boated from Wheeling, Va., to that point, when the time occupied in making the voyage was six weeks, and when but few adventurous spirits would make the experiment, which was then hazardous and dangerous. He finally, in 1801, one year before Ohio was admitted as a state of this Union, settled in Belmont Co., where he for a number of years was one of its most active and prominent citizens. He was the first sheriff of Belmont Co., and also for a term of years the clerk of the court. Being then of a speculative mind, and being convinced that North-western Ohio was one of the garden spots of· the world, and that it would settle up with remarkable rapidity, Mr. H. made a journey to this region. He immediately determined upon entering the land upon which Tiffin is mostly built. At that time foot paths were worn around it, by persons who had looked at the land. Mr. H. then proceeded to the land office, and in 1820, at the land sales at Delaware, Ohio, he bought the land which was an unbroken forest. By a prudent and systematic course in disposing of his town lots, Mr. H. had the pleasure of seeing his town increase in population. For a number of years there was much rivalry between Fort Ball (now the second ward) as to which should be the county seat. By the persevering efforts of Mr. H., and by purchasing much of the property on the Fort Ball side, he succeeded in securing the location on the east side. This was in 1828. He then went to work, determined to effect the removal of the United States land office, then located at Delaware, to Tiffin. In this he was successful, and from that time onward Tiffin has progressed rapidly in wealth and population. In 1831 Mr. H. was chosen to represent the county, or the district of which the county was a portion, in the Ohio legislature. He served one session, but preferred paying more attention to his own private affairs, and declined any further political preferment. He was generous and just in his dealings with his fellow-men, and scrupulously honest, benevolent to all Christian denominations, having, with one or two exceptions, donated the lots upon which their churches are erected; and he was liberal towards all public improvements. In all the relations of life, public or private, he was a just and sincere man. He was a good citizen, and a true and steadfast friend. As a husband he was kind and obliging; as a

14

father, affectionate, generous, and indulgent.

HELM, Major Benjamin, Elizabethtown, Ky., Feb. 24, æ. 90. He was the last survivor of the memorable band of daring soldiers who took possession, and held, Sovern's Valley, the first white settlement made on the waters of Green River. The history of his life and times would make a volume interesting to many persons desirous to know the privations, toil, and danger through which the early settlers of the present Great West had to pass. He entered the service as a citizen soldier, and continued in it until the close of the Indian war by Gen. Wayne. Every able-bodied man, however, was thus enrolled; but a smaller number, the young, active, and more daring, were relied on, and called minute men, or rangers. They were expected to be ever ready, armed, and equipped for the saddle. The individual character of any one of those men would be truly interesting at this day, and posterity will search in vain for truthful narrations of those days and times. Amongst the occasional associates in arms of Major Helm were the gallant Gen. Cleaver, some of whose descendants now live in Ralls Co., Mo.; Gen. Hardin, whose descendants have filled high places in Kentucky, and many other Western States; Gen. McArthur, afterwards governor of Ohio; also the Vanmeters, Haycrafts, Haynes, and Maj. Helm's brothers, and many others, whose names are not known to the writer. The rangers, who watched over and defended the settlement in Sovern's Valley, were ever on the lookout. The attacks of the Indians were very frequent, and their lives always in danger; but the increase of population, and the close of the Indian war, at last brought this state of things to an end. Sovern's Valley became the county seat of Hardin, and the seat of justice was located between these several forts, and called Elizabethtown, and Major Helm purchased the land between the court house and his father's farm for a homestead. He served a few years as the representative of the county in the state councils; was appointed clerk of the Circuit and County Court. He married the daughter of Benjamin Edwards, of Nelson Co., and the oldest sister of the late Gov. Edwards, of Ill.;

settled upon his land, built himself a splendid suburban residence; continued to act as clerk of the county, and also, at the same time, was a successful merchant and neat farmer for many years. He lived in the style of an old Kentucky gentleman, and his house was a home for, and generally filled with, preachers, friends, and relatives. He raised a respectable family of children, who married to please him, and did well afterwards, and his last days were peaceful and quiet. The religious and moral character of Major H. was most extraordinary. He professed religion when a boy, having been baptized when a child by a clergyman of the church of England; he was always satisfied with his baptism; he did not then join a church, but did commence to qualify himself for the ministry. The active scenes in which he was constantly called to act his part for so many years, so engrossed his whole time, that this was abandoned. He was a Methodist in feeling and principle, but did not attach himself to the church until a short time before his death. He was benevolent. Some thirty years ago or more, the Methodist society of Elizabethtown purchased a lot and raised a small subscription to build a cheap frame house of worship. He took the contract for building the house, and to their surprise and gratification, delivered to them a large and splendid brick chapel, that cost him many thousands of dollars beyond the contract price. His wife and most of his children were at the time or soon after became members of this church, and afterwards he himself died a member of it.

HENDERSON, Lawson F., M. D., Madison Co., Miss., March 17, œ. —.

HENDERSON, Hon. James P., Washington, D. C., June 4, œ. 50. He was born in Lincoln Co., N. C., March 31, 1808; received a liberal education, and chose the profession of the law, to which he was always attached, and in which he was eminently successful. His health becoming affected, he went to Cuba; returning, he selected a location in Mississippi, until the invasion of Texas by the Mexicans awakened his energy, and he did much towards arousing the chivalry of the south. On repairing to Texas, he was appointed brigadier general of the Texan army. When the army was disbanded, he retired to private life till called to be the attorney general of the state, which office he retained until a vacancy occurred in the state department by the decease of Gen. Austin, the illustrious father of Texas, when Gen. Rusk having declined, Gen. H. was appointed to the office, and remained in it until 1837, when he was sent as minister to England and France, to negotiate the recognition of Texan independance. He returned from Europe in 1840, and resumed his profession at San Augustin, in partnership with Gen. Rusk, until 1843, declining a position in the cabinet. He was next appointed as assistant minister to Washington, whence returning, he resumed the profession of the law until the annexation of Texas was consummated. He was next a member of the convention from Augustin Co., and afterwards elected first governor of Texas. After some time, a requisition was made on Texas for troops for the Mexican war, and Gen. H. took command. He acted a conspicuous part at Monterey, and was commissioner to negotiate the articles of capitulation of the garrison. He declined a reëlection as governor of Texas, and since then has been recognized as an eminent citizen. On the death of Gen. Rusk, he was unanimously elected to the Senate. He was no ordinary man. He made his mark in Texas, and the nation was not unacquainted with his merits and virtues.

HENDLEY, Jesse, Spalding Co., Ga., July 2, œ. —.

HERBERT, James W., St. Thomas, Dec. 27, œ. —, American consul.

HERBERT, Henry William, New York, at the Stevens House, May 17, œ. 51. The death of this unfortunate gentleman, by his own hand, is announced above, with a full detail of the circumstances attending the melancholy event, as presented to the coroner's jury. Mr. H., though not widely known in general society, occupied a prominent position before the public, on account of his writings, most of which were of a popular character, and which extended over a singularly diversified range of subjects, from classical, historical, and critical disquisitions, to essays on field sports, natural history, and rural economy. His pen was no less vigorous and brilliant than it was versatile. His productions, although numerous and sometimes rapidly thrown off, were the fruit of large previous studies and rare accumulations of knowledge. Mr. H. was a native of England, but had resided in this country for nearly 30 years. He was born in London, April 7, 1807, and at the time of his death had but recently completed his 51st year. His father was the Hon. and Rev. William Herbert, Dean of Manchester, a person of considerable distinction as a poet, a man of science, and a politician, and a descendant of the noble house of Pembroke and Percy. Until the age of 12, Henry William H. was educated at home, under a private tutor, when he was sent to a private classical school for a short time, and then entered Eton College, April, 1820. In due time he was transferred to Cambridge, where he graduated in 1829. Soon after taking 'his first degree, he met with a sudden reverse of fortune, which reduced him from a state of comparative affluence; and thus cast upon his own resources, he determined to make the experiment of living in the United States. He came to this country towards the close of the year 1830, and at once found employment as the principal Greek teacher in the classical school of the Rev. Mr. Hudart, in this city — a position which he retained for about eight years. During this period, he turned his attention to authorship, and from 1833 to 1836 was editor of the American Monthly Magazine, a part of the time in connection with Mr. Charles F. Hoffman. His contributions to this periodical formed nearly half the contents of several numbers, and are said to have been marked by a fine spirit of scholarship. In 1834 he published his first historical novel, entitled The Brothers, a tale of the Fronde, which was followed in 1837 by Cromwell, in 1843 by Marmaduke Wyvil, and in 1848 by the Roman Traitor, a classical romance founded on the conspiracy of Catiline. He was also the author of Field Sports of the United States, and a variety of sporting sketches and essays, under the *nom de plume* of Frank Forrester, a metrical translation of the Agamemnon, and Prometheus of Æschylus, the Cavaliers of England, the Captains of the Old World, the Captains of the Roman Republic, and other historical works, besides a great variety of articles in different journals and magazines. His largest work, entitled The Horse and Horsemanship of America, was issued during the past year. Soon after his arrival in the United States, he married a lady in Maine, who died, leaving him a widower, with one child. He was married, for the second time, on the 16th of February last, to Miss Adela R. Budlong, of Providence, R. I.; but the happiness of the connection proved of short duration, and according to the statements in the letter of the deceased elsewhere published, the disappointment thus ensuing was the cause of the catastrophe which ended his life. Mr. H. was a man of an excitable and sensitive temperament, possessing uncommon powers of literary execution, and, when not under the influence of the erratic habits which were the bane of his life, and the sorrow of his friends, a model of professional industry and accomplishment. His residence, until quite recently, had been in a country place, near the city of Newark, called "The Cedars," which, it is understood, had been settled upon him by his relatives, without the power of alienation. In appearance, manner, and tone of mind, Mr. H. was always an Englishman, betraying a remarkable power of resistance to the characteristics of his adopted country.

HERDMAN, Capt. R., Pittsburg, Pa., June 4, æ. —.

HERRING, William, M. D., Harrisburg, Va., Sept. 14, æ. —. He was extensively known as a practitioner of medicine, and enjoyed a high degree of personal and professional popularity. During many years of extensive practice, he had endeared himself to the community by the kindness of his disposition.

HEWSTON, Mrs. Isabella, St. Clairsville, O., —— —, æ. 59, widow of Dr. Joseph Hewston.

HIBBARD, Col. John, Clay Co., Ky., March 14, æ. 83. He was a man of sterling integrity and unusual hospitality, of strong natural mind, and remarkable for his love of law and order. He lived in the county of Clay since 1804; he served in the legislature from that county in 1808, 1812, 1813; acted as sheriff and justice of the peace at different times for more than 40 years, and his promptness in the discharge of his duties made him a terror to evil doers. His social qualities will never be forgotten by the many friends as well as strangers who have chanced to visit him at his mountain home.

HICKEY, Thomas H., Boston, Mass., June 12, æ. 34. He was a native of

Portsmouth, N. H., but had resided in Boston since 1845. He enjoyed the respect and confidence of a wide circle of friends, who will testify to the purity of his life and the estimable qualities of his character. He was one of the earliest and most intelligent members of the Young Men's Christian Union, and took deep interest in its objects. Every worthy cause found in him a friend, and few men of his years have done more good, according to their abilities, than Mr. H.

HICKLIN, Jonathan H., near Pana, Christian Co., Ill., March 9, æ. 106 years 22 days. He was born in Virginia, Feb., 1752. At 22 he emigrated to Kentucky, and resided in the counties of Woodford and Fayette 36 years; was well known to the early settlers of Lexington. From Kentucky he removed to Busseron Prairie, Knox Co., Ind., where he lived 10 years, thence to Clark Co., Ill., on the hill, above the spring in the rock, near Livingston, 38 years. He was an extraordinary man, of pretty large stature, not fleshy, bony and muscular, particularly fond of the rifle, good marksman, killed many a buffalo and deer; was acquainted with Boone, with whom he had many a shot at the mark. His character assimilated strongly to that of Daniel Boone. — *Eastern Illinoisan.*

HICKMAN, Mrs. John, West Chester, Pa., Oct. 12, æ. —, wife of Hon. John Hickman. Mrs. H. was a lady of great talents and many endearing qualities. She resembled her glorious husband in many respects, and in nothing more than in the firmness of her friendship, the gentleness of her manners, and the kindness of her heart.

HICKMAN, Mrs. Sallie A., Shelbyville, Ky., May 24, æ. 27, wife of Dr. John F. Hickman.

HICKMAN, Elliott, M. D., Hickman's Bend, Ark., Dec. 10, æ. 77.

HICKS, Edward B., Brunswick, Ga., Nov. 28, æ. 70, a gentleman of high standing and unblemished character, and at an early day of his life a prominent member of the bar.

HIGBEE, D. C. M. D., Peoria, Ill., Feb. 21, æ. 48. He was a graduate of Transylvania University, and a practitioner of medicine for several years in Lexington, Ky.

HIGGINBOTHAM, Mrs., Greene Co., Ala., May, 7, æ. —, wife of Maj. G. G. Higginbotham.

HIGGINS, Rev. William, Richland Dist., S. C., July 4, æ. 79. He was born July 3, 1779, was baptized in Sept., 1805, ordained a deacon in 1825, and the same year was married to the eldest daughter of that eminently useful minister of the gospel, Rev. George Scott, whose memory is fondly cherished by many. He was for many years a licensed preacher, and the founder of the Colonel's Creek Baptist Church.

HIGGINS, Hon. W. A., Brenham, Texas, May 20, for many years chief justice of Washington Co., Texas.

HIGGINS, Newell F., Esq., Newark, N. J., Nov. 23, æ. 45.

HILDRETH, Mrs. Dolly, Dracut, Mass., Feb. 27, æ. 65, wife of Dr. Israel Hildreth, and mother of Fisher Ames Hildreth, Esq., of Lowell. She also leaves six daughters, one of whom is the wife of Gen. Benjamin F. Butler, of Lowell.

HILL, John, Davidson Co., Tenn., Dec. 5, æ. 77. He was born in Rockingham Co., N. C. He moved to Tennessee in December, 1809, and in 1814 enlisted as a soldier under Gen. Jackson, and was in the battle at New Orleans, Jan. 8, 1815. When a soldier, his conduct was such as secured the confidence of his general, and the affections of his fellow-soldiers. He professed religion late in life, not until he was 61 years old. He was baptized into the fellowship of Mill Creek Church, by Elder Whitsitt, in 1843, and was a consistent and much beloved member of that church when he died.

HILL, Mrs. Sarah A., Middletown, Ill., Nov. 15, æ. —, wife of Dr. G. Hill.

HILL, Hon. Samuel, New Brunswick, N. J., April 8, æ. 65, a native of New Brunswick, but late of Flemington, where he resided for many years, highly esteemed as a good citizen and an upright judge.

HILL, Mrs. Susannah Coit, Hartford, Ct., May 21, æ. 55. Mrs. H. was born in New York, and was the daughter of of Elisha Coit, Esq. With great depth of feeling and true delicacy, she had an unusually clear and vigorous understanding. It is rare, even among persons of as wide a range of reading and observation, and of as thoughtful habits, to find such good sense and calm wisdom. Her judicious views and reliable common sense marked her conversation even more strongly than the freshness and vivacity with which she expressed her thoughts. But there was no approach to that hardness which often renders this strength of character repulsive. The tenderness was equal to the tenacity of her affections. Her appreciative sympathies and ready manifestations of interest made her as companionable to the young, as she was to those of her own age. She held by bonds which only death can hallow those to whom she was united by natural ties, and she drew towards her, in every position she filled, the hearts of many friends. And all was most nobly complemented by her Christian graces. The spring of all her life was the love of the Lord Jesus Christ. She seemed to have attained that elevated position in which religion did not appear the duty so much as the joy of life. She delighted to do the will of God. It was not, however, till after spiritual struggles, protracted through many years, that she first obtained joy in the Holy Ghost. In 1831 she joined the church in New York, then under the care of Dr. Joel Parker, whom she always regarded as chiefly instrumental in her conversion. From this period there was a development of spiritual graces and active labors, in various forms of Christian benevolence, such as few exhibit.

HILL, Capt. James, Stoughton, Mass., March 17, æ. —, a prominent manufacturer of S.

HILL, Selah, Jersey City, N. J., Nov. 22, æ. —. He was a gentleman of high standing in the county, and within a few years past, has served as a member of the common council, board of water commissioners in Jersey City, and also in the board of chosen freeholders. At the time of his death, he was one of the directors of the Mechanics and Traders Bank, of Jersey City.

HILL, Capt. A. Powell, Culppeper, Va., March —, æ. 80. He was a member of the legislature for 20 years or more, and a magistrate of C. for a much longer time. He was in the assembly when the sovereign people were in the habit of electing, from inclination and interest, a considerable proportion of "substantial old farmers" as their deputies. Of that class he was a worthy and faithful representative. The "old farmer" delegates, in his day, possessed an influence far beyond their votes. They were, in fact, the leading and controlling members of the legislature.

HILL, A. N., Esq., Dover, N. H., April 2, æ. 70. He was an active Christian for 49 years, and contributed liberally to the various benevolent enterprises of the day. He was a firm magistrate, and died lamented as he had lived respected.

HILLEARY, Henry, Upper Marlboro', Md., March 17, æ. 52. The rector and vestry of Trinity Church, in that place, met, and

"*Resolved,* that in the death of Mr. H., the vestry have lost one of its most active members, the church one of its most zealous and consistent followers, and the community a kind and generous friend."

HILLER, Captain, Poughkeepsie, N. Y., June 1, æ. —.

HILLS, George, Boston, Mass., Sept. —, æ. —. A wealthy man. He left the following legacies to public objects: — Fifth Universalist Society, (Rev. T. B. Thayer's, in Warren Street,) $4000 ; the Association for the Relief of Aged Indigent Females, $1000 ; the Perkins Institution and Massachusetts Asylum for the Blind, $1000 ; the Massachusetts General Hospital, $1000.

HINDS, Ephraim, West Boylston, Mass., June 18, æ. 77. He was son of Benjamin and Tabitha (Holland) Hinds, and was born in that part of Shrewsbury which is now within the limits of West Boylston, Nov. 7, 1780. His father was a farmer, and one of the earliest settlers of the town. His mother was a native of Boylston. He was fitted for college partly at Leicester Academy, and partly by Rev. William Nash, of West Boylston, (Y. C. 1791.) After leaving college, he taught school in Boston, Watertown, Sterling, Lancaster, Mass., and several places in Vermont. After some years spent in teaching, he entered upon the study of law, under the instruction of Eleazar James, of Barre, Mass., (H. U. 1778.) On his admission to the bar, he began the practice of his profession in Barre, where he resided a short time, when he removed to Athol. From this town he went to Harvard, where he remained about 13 years ; thence to Marlboro', where he lived from 1833 to 1841 ; in South Brookfield, from May, 1841, to May, 1845 ; in South Orange from May to Nov., 1845 ; in Deerfield from Nov., 1845, to May, 1847 ; and in West Boylston from May, 1847, until his death. He married, April 28, 1823, Maria, daughter of Hutchins

Hapgood, of Petersham. He was greatly respected at the bar as a man of strict veracity, of unbending integrity, sound judgment, and practical wisdom. He had been unable to walk for more than a year before his death, in consequence of a severe rheumatic affection, but was uniformly cheerful and entirely submissive to the divine will. He was remarkable for his habits of punctuality, systematic arrangement of secular affairs, and rigid economy.

HINKLE, Samuel, Esq., Morgan Co., Ind., Sept. —, æ. 67. Mr. H. was a native of Pennsylvania, and went to Louisville at a very early period. He lived in Oldham Co. nearly 40 years, and removed to Indiana about five years ago. Few men were better known in Kentucky than he, and none more respected and beloved. He discharged faithfully and well all the manifold duties of life. He was a prominent and exemplary member of the Methodist church; and his house was the home of Methodist preachers and clergymen of all other denominations. It was the abode of hearty and generous hospitality. There is no pure and sterling quality of heart or mind that Mr. H. did not possess. He was a man of wealth, and, as such, he necessarily had many business transactions; yet he never in his life either sued or was sued; and this single fact is a most forcible illustration of his humanity and honesty.

HINMAN, Mrs. Martha A., Newbury, Vt., —— —, æ. —, widow of the late Dr. Clark T. Hinman, first president of the North-western University, near Chicago, and eldest daughter of the Hon. Timothy Morse, of Newbury.

HINMAN, Mrs. Phebe, Derby, Vt., July 14, æ. 88, widow of the late Hon. Timothy Hinman. Over 60 years ago, in company with the honored partner of her life, she removed from Connecticut, her native state, into the then wilderness portion of Northern Vermont; and close by the shore of a beautiful pond which now bears their name, with no white inhabitant or settlement nearer than Greensboro', a distance of 30 miles, they erected a rude cabin, and in the deep solitude of the trackless forests founded the beautiful and flourishing village of Derby. She had lived to see her children and her children's children to the third and fourth generations, to the number of 76, 66 of whom were living at her death, among whom was one grandchild 45 years of age; and 28 of the 66 were great-grandchildren.

HINTON, Gerard J. M. D., Gainesville, Fla., —— —, æ. —. He was a native of North Carolina, and was born near Raleigh, Nov. 10, 1831. He enjoyed all the advantages of a liberal education, and graduated at Wake Forest College in 1852. Turning his attention to the study of medicine, he graduated at the University of Pennsylvania in 1855.

HIRONS, Rev. William, Wilmington, Del., July 28, æ. 60. Mr. H. had been a prominent local preacher, and a warm advocate of the temperance and other philanthropic causes.

HITCHCOCK, Charles, New York, Dec. 10, æ. —, son of the late Judge Hitchcock, of New Haven.

HITT, John D., M. D., Warrenton, Fauquier Co., Va., Dec. 5, æ. 56. He was born in South Carolina, near the Georgia line, in the Edgefield District. About the year 1835 he came to Fauquier Co., and married in one of the oldest and most respectable families near Rectortown. Some ten years since, he lost his wife, since which time he has resided in Warrenton. Dr. H. was a man of decided mechanical genius and great inventive talent. His devotion to ingenious mechanical inventions had impoverished his fortunes, and reduced him to absolute want. He, however, possessed a fund of general information, that gave him place in social life rarely awarded to great eccentricities and fallen fortunes. He was a man of rare charity and kindness of heart. Sympathy for the suffering sick with him rose to heroic hazard and self-sacrifice. When the pestilence raged in Norfolk, and its loathsome breath forced the abandonment of the poor victims by their nearest in blood and affection, Mr. H. courted the perils of that awful occasion, and through the whole season ministered in kindness and love to the hapless sufferers.

HOBART, Hon. Aaron, East Bridgewater, Mass., Sept. 19, æ. 71. He was a son of Aaron Hobart and grandson of Aaron Hobart, and was born at Abington, June 26, 1787. His mother was Susan Adams, daughter of Elihu Adams, of Randolph, a younger brother of the elder President Adams. He entered

Brown University in 1801, and graduated in 1805. He studied law with Judge Mitchell, of East Bridgewater, and was admitted to practice in 1809. A few months after his admission to the bar he commenced practice at Abington; but, owing to ill health and by advice of his physician, he went to England in the autumn of 1810, and spent the ensuing winter there. He returned home in 1811, and opened an office at Hanover Four Corners, where he remained until his removal to East Bridgewater in 1824. In 1814 he was elected representative from Hanover, and in 1819 he was elected to the Senate. In 1820, Hon. *. Sampson having resigned his seat in Congress, Mr. H. was elected to fill the vacancy, and was also reëlected to the 17th, 18th, and 19th Congresses. He was a member of the executive council of Massachusetts in 1827, 1828, 1829, 1830, and 1831. In 1843 he was appointed judge of probate for Plymouth Co., which office he held until July 1, 1858, when his commission terminated by reorganization of the Courts of Probate and Insolvency. Judge H. was remarkable for his pleasant manners, the purity of his private life, and a conscientious and faithful discharge of every public duty.

HOBBS, Prentiss, Brighton, Mass., Aug. 28, æ. —. Mr. H. was a merchant in Boston upwards of 40 years, possessing great uprightness of character and unbending integrity. His transactions were numerous with all professions of men, and seemed to be marked with a degree of conscientious rectitude, as if he believed the record was made in heaven, to be spread before him in the future life which the departed entered. He was a rare specimen of mankind; and he has left a character which, for moral virtue and benevolence, is unsurpassed, if we rely upon the universal response from his numerous friends, who have been in daily intercourse with him for nearly a half-century. Possessing a sound judgment, he was a reliable and safe counsellor in all matters of trust. All who had the pleasure of his acquaintance will recognize the sweet expression of his countenance which greeted their approach, at once inviting their commands, whether for *his* profit or *their* emolument. His whole life is a type of eloquence, speaking in a language enduring and binding upon the morals of mankind. Such a life may be compared to pulpit eloquence, which we hold unsurpassed in guiding aright the masses of the world. In his dealings he sought no advantage to promote his interest at the loss of another. He firmly believed in reciprocity of trade. He was a native of Weston, Mass.

HODGDON, Elder Jacob, St. Louis, Mo., April 16, æ. 65. He was born in Hardin Co., Ky., as we are informed, Jan. 3, 1793; united with the Baptist church in Kentucky in 1812, and with the Christian church in Jacksonville, Ill., in 1833. He moved to Pike's Co. in 1833, and to Pittsfield in 1838. He was the exemplification of all that ennobles man — a laborer in example, in word, and in deed. He was not slothful in business; for, by his industry and prudence, he had acquired much of this world's goods.

HODGES, Jerry, M. D., Petersham, Mass., April 3, æ. 71, a native of Norton, Mass.

HOFFEDITZ, Theodore S., D. D., Nazareth, Pa., Aug. 2, æ. 75.

HOFFORD, Mrs. Hannah, Beverly, N. J., æ. 63, widow of the late John Hofford, Esq., of Plumstead, Bucks Co., Pa. Her father, M. Lourie, was an ardent patriot and soldier of the revolution, acting with marked bravery in several important battles during that trying period, and cherishing in after life in the minds of his children a warm attachment to their country, for whose liberties he fought. Mrs. Hofford was a woman of great kindness of heart, a sincere and useful Christian, and died in the full hope of a blessed immortality. She leaves four children surviving her. Her oldest son, Rev. M. L. Hofford, A. M., a graduate of Princeton College and Theological Seminary, is, at present, principal of a Classical Institute at Beverly, N. J.

HOGAN, Thomas, Chapel Hill, N. C., July 4, æ. 75. Mr. H. had been much identified with Chapel Hill from its foundation. He assisted in laying the walls of the east building about 65 years ago. Since that time his life had been spent in the immediate vicinity of the university, and through long years of patient industry he had risen from poverty to independence. He found a ready market for his surplus productions in the village, and especially among the members of the faculty, and from an early period down to the times of their respective deaths, enjoyed the friendship and confidence of President Caldwell and Dr. Mitchell. He bore upon his character traces of the rugged scenes through which poverty and early orphanage compelled him to pass. Until the last three or four years he had been emphatically a son of toil. He was a stern, shrewd man, sociable in his habits, honest in his dealings, and faithful to his friends. Although strict in pecuniary matters, and the master of what he had by slow accumulation, Mr. Hogan dispensed liberally to his children, as each became settled in life; and probably, at the time of his death, had distributed to each of them fully as much as he had retained.

HOISINGTON, Rev. H. R., Saybrook, Ct., May 16, æ. 56. Mr. H. was a native of Vergennes, Vt., but removed in early life to Buffalo, N. Y., where he was hopefully converted through the reading of the "Shepherd of Salisbury Plain," at the request of a pious mother. He graduated at Williams College and Auburn Seminary, was settled at Aurora, N. Y., in 1831, and embarked for Ceylon in 1833. He was compelled by ill health to return to his native land in 1842, but in 1844 he went again to Ceylon, where he labored six additional years. His connection with the American Board continued two years longer, during which time he visited many churches. He afterwards supplied the pulpit of the Congregational church in Williamstown two years and a half, and was installed at Centerbrook, in April, 1857, where he labored with devoted constancy till the day of his death.

HOLCOMB, Mrs. Hannah, Mason, Warren Co., Ohio, Dec. 30, æ. 86. She was born March 22, 1771, in Salisbury, Litchfield Co., Ct., where her parents, David and Lois Everest, had resided from their birth. Mrs. Holcomb, being one out of 13 sons and daughters, in that puritanic family, was married in September, 1786, to Dr. Jonathan Holcomb, of Sheffield, Berkshire Co., Mass. Dr. H. was born at Sheffield, Mass., June 19, 1762, and was a graduate of Yale College, Ct., in 1784-5, and after a thorough course in the study of medicine, removed early in life to New Jersey, practising his profession in that state and Pennsylvania for many years; emigrating with his family in the spring of 1814 to Warren Co., Ohio, where they resided until his decease, Oct. 1, 1847. Mrs. H. became a member of the Presbyterian church while yet under the care of her father and mother, and continued a practical Christian, under all the varied changes through which she was called to pass, for more than 70 years, until summoned to the enjoyment of a harvest of good works, far away, in that beautiful land of rest.

HOLLAND, Isaac, Washington, D. C., Nov. —, æ. 63. He was for a long time, the efficient and accomplished clerk of Messrs. Blair & Rives, publishers of the Daily Globe. Subsequently he was elected doorkeeper to the United States Senate, and held that office at the time of his decease. He was the father of Stewart Holland, the gallant youth, whose death on board the ill-fated steamer Arctic afforded an instance of such heroism and faithfulness to duty as to elicit the spontaneous plaudits of the country, while his loss was universally regretted.

HOLLIDAY, Louis P., Esq., Tallahassee, Fla., of Memphis, Tenn., Nov. 30, æ. —. Mr. H. resided in Kentucky, but was extensively known throughout the Union, he having been for several years president of the Cairo and New Orleans Railroad Company. All who knew him loved him for his many generous and noble traits of character.

HOLLINGWORTH, Rev. J. H., Syracuse, N. Y., June 2, agent of the Children's Aid Society.

HOLMES, Dea. Daniel, Wilson, Niagara Co., N. Y., May 26, æ. 69. Dea. H., the second son of Dea. John Holmes, was born July 3, 1789, in Charlton, Saratoga Co., N. Y. In his youth there were no Sabbath schools in the county, and children were not conversed with on the subject of personal religion, as they are at the present day. His parents required their children to observe the Sabbath strictly, and to repeat to them the Catechism on every Lord's day. He assisted his father in the pursuit of agriculture. He was an obedient son, and a kind brother, and, with the rest of the family, attended the preaching of Rev. Joseph Sweetman, pastor of the First Presbyterian Church in Charlton. He was married, Feb. 12, 1811, to the second daughter of Hon. Judge Taylor, of Charlton. In May, 1812, they moved to Carlisle, Schoharie Co. In Sept., 1813, Mr. H. and his wife united with the Presbyterian church in Carlisle. In June, 1817, there being no canal or railroad, he shouldered his pack, and travelled on foot over 700 miles, and purchased a lot of land, lying between the 12 and 18 mile creeks, in what is now the town of Wilson, Niagara Co., N. Y., on the shore of Lake Ontario, which he occupied till called to give an account of his stewardship. In Feb., 1818, Mr. H. removed his family from Carlisle to their new home in the wilderness, two and a half miles east of his lot, till a log house could be erected, into which they removed in April, although it was destitute of door or windows, upper floor, chimney or hearth, but where hearty thanks were offered to Almighty God for his watchful care, and his blessing sought for the future. Before leaving the shanty the opening spring had broken up the ice in the creek near by, and when Sabbath came, the few people who were scattered about in the woods, rushed to the creek and lake in pursuit of fish. The heart of Mr. H. was pained to see the Sabbath so desecrated, and he gave notice that there would be a religious meeting on the next Sabbath, in a little log school house, standing a little west of what is now the village of Olcott. The house was filled with hearers. Mr. H. conducted the meeting by reading the Scriptures, prayer, and singing, and reading a sermon from Rom. i. 16 : " For I am not ashamed of the gospel of Christ, for it is the power of God unto salvation to every one that believeth." At the close of the meeting there was a request that a similar meeting might be held the next Sabbath. When the weather became warm enough, the meetings were removed to a barn in the vicinity, that more people might be accommodated. These were the first meetings of the kind ever held in the vicinity. After the first summer they were held four miles south-west of his residence, and one and a half miles south of what is now the village of Wilson. His practice was to go every Sabbath morning, during the summer, five miles west, on the lake shore road, and have a Sabbath school, and conduct a religious service by praying, singing, and reading a sermon, and then go to the place above mentioned, and conduct a similar meeting and Sabbath school, and this last mentioned meeting was kept up regularly till a house of worship was built, and a stated supply for the pulpit procured. The travel necessary to sustain these and the weekly prayer meetings, and funerals which he was often called to attend, was invariably performed on foot for the first five years. He was in the habit of distributing religious tracts on Sabbath desecration and other sins, as opportunity offered In January, 1819, through the instrumentality of Mr. H., a Presbyterian church was organized, by the Rev. David M. Smith, of Lewiston, consisting of his father and mother, his sister and her husband, himself and wife, six in number. At the formation of the church Daniel Holmes and John Holmes, his father, (who had removed here also,) were set apart and ordained ruling elders; which office he faithfully discharged to the day of his death. Although for the first fifteen years the church was nearly all the time destitute of the labors of a minister, — not being able to support one, — yet in 1835, in the annual report made to the presbytery, they numbered 117. Since 1835, the church have enjoyed the stated ministrations of the word. As the deceased was ever ready and willing to spend his time to promote the interests of religion, so he was ready, even beyond his ability, to give of his means for the building up of Christ's kingdom. He made no small sacrifice to secure the erection of a house of worship, which was completed and dedicated February 12, 1835. All the benevolent enterprises of the day received his hearty coöperation. He was truly a Christian philanthropist. He was instrumental in the formation of the first temperance society ever formed in Wilson, and was an efficient member of all the different temperance organizations, in that town, to the time of his death. He was a warm friend of human rights. Truly did he remember those in bonds as bound with them ; and warmly did he defend the right of free discussion in the days of mobocracy, which prevailed to such an alarming extent in 1836-7. He was a hearty supporter of our common school system, and aided in erecting the first school house built in Wilson. Truly may it be said of him, that he was ever ready for every good word and work. He said to the minister present, "Forty years ago last month I read the first sermon to this people, from these words: 'I am not ashamed of the gospel of Christ, for it is the power of God unto salvation to every one that believeth,'" and requested that his funeral sermon might be preached from the same text.

HOLMES, J. P., M. D., Evansville, Ind., April 15, æ. —. The Evansville (Ind.) Journal, under the head of "A Homeless Stranger," has the following interesting notice of the death of an eminent stranger: "A week ago, on Saturday, the steamer Union brought from Green River an apparently poor and afflicted man, past the age of 80. One eye had been destroyed by a cancer, and the other, by sympathy, was so swollen and affected as to be sightless. One leg was paralyzed, and the poor sufferer seemed utterly helpless, destitute, and friendless. No one knew whence he came, nor whither he was bound, except from the desire he expressed to be taken to Memphis. As the steamer was going no farther down the river, he was placed on Messrs. O'Riley & Co.'s wharf-boat, on the deck of which he lay unattended and uncared for from Saturday evening until Sunday afternoon, when his condition became known to Dr. A. C. Hallock, our good Samaritan, who visited him and found him in a most afflicted condition,—helpless, blind, suffering with pain, and a mind wandering in delirium. The doctor, by intercession with "Old Aunt Hannah," the black nurse, induced her to give up her only bed, and take him in and attend upon him. He was bathed, clean clothes were procured for him, and his cancer dressed. He refused medicine, appeared to have a perfect knowledge of the nature of his disease and condition, said that there was no medicine that could help him, and that he only wanted care and quiet. He remained with his faithful nurse, who was unremitting in her attentions to him, by day and night, and he was visited daily by Drs. Hallock and Casselberry, who ministered to his necessities. The progress of his disease was rapid, and he sank fast under its effects, and on Thursday night he expired, alone, in the house of the good negro woman who had given him shelter, with no friend or clergy to soothe his spirit in its last mortal agony. On examining his effects after his death, papers were found which proved him to have been Dr. John Pocock Holmes, a member of the College of Surgeons of London. Among them was an original certificate of Sir Astley Cooper, testifying to his qualifications as a surgeon, with numerous testimonials from other eminent surgeons of his ability and faithfulness as a member of their profession. It appeared from other original papers, that he had been, previous to 1827, 16 years a surgeon in the employ of the Hudson Bay Company, at their various posts on this continent. In 1827 he was a practising surgeon in London, holding intercourse with the most eminent men. Among the papers he appears to have preserved with care, is a card of invitation from the lord mayor and mayoress of London to dine at the Mansion House on the 12th of May, the year not mentioned. But the papers which he seems to have deemed the most precious, are a package of letters from Capt. Parry, the great Arctic explorer, with whom he seems to have enjoyed a free and cordial intimacy. It appears that the deceased had rendered some important service as a chemist, and from knowledge he had gained in the Hudson Bay Company's service, in the manufacture of pemmican for the exploring expedition, for which Capt. Parry gives him much praise, and the Admiralty voted him an acknowledgment of £150. Capt. Parry invites him, in free and familiar terms, to call at his house in London, and at another time, to visit him on board the Hecla, at the Nore, before sailing. The notes and letters of the celebrated explorer are interesting and valuable as autographs. Among his effects, found since his death, were two large and beautiful gold medals, awarded to 'Dr. John Pollock Holmes, by medical societies, for his valuable invention of obstetrical and surgical instruments.' There is also a large number of letters from eminent and professional men—from the nobility, and medical and scientific societies, acknowledging the receipt of 'Dr. John P. Holmes's very valuable and able treatise on consumption and asthma.' There are two cards of invitation to Dr. J. P. Holmes and lady, to dine at Guildhall, on the occasion when Queen Victoria honored the mayor and common council with her presence."

A gentleman residing near Nashville, Tenn., gives the following additional facts: "I have been personally acquainted with Dr. Holmes since his arrival in this country in 1841. I was at that time living in Williamsburg, opposite New York. He became a constant visitor at my house. He was known in New York and Williamsburg as a man of science in his profession. I was then contemplating coming west, and the doctor expressed a wish to come with me, and said, as he was getting old, he would like to live and end his days with me. His friends settling in Tennessee, the doctor remained with them four years. At the end of that time he made the acquaintance of a person from Mississippi, who induced him to go with him into that state, where he became inveigled into some scheme of speculation, by which he lost, I suppose, nearly all his money. When he left me, he had between $15,000 and $20,000 in money and securities. After his misfortunes in Mississippi, he wandered, mortified and broken-hearted, to the settlement of Shakers at West Union, where he buried himself from the knowledge and intercourse of his friends."

HOLT, George M., Mobile, Ala., May 29, æ. —. He was, we believe, a native of Georgia, but early removed to Alabama, where he ever afterwards resided. In the earlier days of Mobile he was one of her most prominent and public-spirited citizens, dispensing a generous and elegant hospitality to strangers, and first in "every good word and work" calculated to advance the interests of Mobile. In later years he led a more quiet and retired life, but never lost the respect and confidence of his fellow-citizens. He was a man of strong will and decided opinions, but was governed by what he believed to be the right. He had for some time been in infirm health, and his decease was not altogether unexpected. At the time of his death he held the office of clerk in the United States Circuit Court for his district, and was a faithful and efficient officer.

HOLT, Mrs. Ann R., Wight Co., Va., Dec. 3, æ. 46, wife of Dr. John Q. Holt.

HOLT, Michael W., M. D., Alamanace Co., N. C., May 23, æ. 48. Dr. Holt was highly esteemed as a citizen and as a physician, and his kind and conciliatory manners secured the favor of all who knew him. He represented the county of Orange in the House of Commons in 1840, while associated with Alamanace, and was a member of the Senate in the last legislature for the district of Randolph and Alamanace.

HOLT, Thomas M., M. D., Esopus, N. Y., May 23, æ. 66.

HOLT, Mrs. Virginia P., Montgomery, Ala., Aug. 20, æ. —, wife of Dr. J. W. Holt.

HOOKER, James, Esq., Poughkeepsie, N. Y., Sept. 11, æ. 60. He was one of the wealthiest and most respected citizens of P.

HOOPER, John H., Esq., Greensburg, Pa., Oct. 21, æ. —, for a time one of the editors of the Greensburg Herald. He was a young man of industry and good natural qualifications. He secured a fair education, and was admitted to the bar as a practising attorney. In the last campaign he was the candidate of the opposition for clerk of the courts.

HOPKINS, Captain John, Georgetown, D. C., Nov. 25, æ. —.

HOPKINS, Howell, Esq., Philadelphia, Pa., June 4, æ. —. He entered at the bar in 1814, and became a distinguished lawyer.

HOPKINS, Walter, New Orleans, La., Sept. 10, æ. 32. Mr. H. was born in Aug., 1826, in London. He came to the United States about five years ago, and first made his home in New Orleans. He was in many respects a remarkable man — in all respects a gentleman. He had been an editor of the Charleston Courier, and of the Delta, of the Times, and of the Courier, in New Orleans. He universally commanded respect in all situations, and though he died a stranger in a strange land, he was surrounded to the last by sympathizing friends.

HOPPER, Mrs. Mary, Sag Harbor, L. I., Dec. 12, æ. 78, mother of Rev. Edward Hopper. The maiden name of this venerable lady and truly pious disciple of Christ was See, and she came of an old Huguenot family that settled in the early colonial times in Westchester Co., where she was born, near Tarrytown. She resided many years in the city of New York, and attended the old Collegiate Church in Fulton Street, since better known as the North Dutch, having been a professor of religion for half a century, and sitting under the ministries of

Rev. Drs. Kuypers, Brownlee, Dewitt, and Knox. Manifold and most excellent were the virtues that adorned her character and made her life blessed. It was mainly through her toils and prayers that her son was led, under God, to enter upon the ministration of his truth; and for the past 15 years she had been a communicant in the churches of his charge.

HOPPER, Hon. Judge P. B., Centerville, Md., March 27, æ. —. He was an eminent member of the bar, and filled many positions of responsibility in Maryland with great credit. At the first election under the new constitution, he was chosen to preside as judge over the fourth judicial district. In this position he discharged his duties with strict fidelity. In his own neighborhood, and wherever known, no one was more highly esteemed for his unblemished character than the deceased. He was a member of the Methodist Protestant church from its formation until the time of his death, having been a member of the convention of 1828 which formed that magnificent instrument, embodying the principle of mutual rights of ministry and laymen; and his love for the principles of the church continued unabated, he advocating and defending them zealously, and sustaining them liberally by his means and labors until the end of his life.

HORN, Rev. Rodderick, Pawnee Co., Nebraska, Jan. 8, æ.—

HORNER, Mrs. Maria L., Hamilton village, West Philadelphia, Pa., May 24, æ.—.

HORROCKS, William, Philadelphia, Pa., June 13, æ. 38. Mr. H. was extensively known as an active and enterprising business man, and was universally esteemed for his uprightness and stern integrity. Closely identified with the interests of Frankford, both as a borough and afterwards as a part of the consolidated city, he enjoyed in a rare degree the confidence and esteem of his fellow-citizens, and had served them with marked approval, first in their own local government, and subsequently in the councils of the city. As a legislator he was liberal, public-spirited and sagacious, seeking always to make right his guide, and prompt in the discharge of every duty. He had been for many years largely engaged in business, and while amassing wealth had sought so to employ his means as to contribute to the general prosperity, and promote the happiness of his fellow-men.

HORTON, Benjamin, Avon, Oakland Co., Mich., Nov. 6, æ. 75. He was born Nov. 10, 1783, in Northumberland Co., Pa. In 1809 he emigrated to Upper Canada, and was married the next year to Jane, daughter of Christian Zavits, of Wainfleet, (now Port Colburn, Lincoln Co., Niagara Dist.) In 1820 he removed to Yarmouth, Elgin Co., and in Feb., 1825, to Michigan, where he has since resided. He was elected to offices of trust in his township, and always served his neighbors faithfully and well. During the last nine years of the territorial organization he served as justice of the peace by appointment from Gov. Lewis Cass.

HORTON, John A., Newark, N. J., December —, æ. —, distinguished as a scientific farmer.

HOSMER, Mrs. Elizabeth B., Leominster, Mass., Dec. 3, æ. 72. She was a consistent member of the Baptist church in L., and will be lamented by a large circle of friends. For fourteen years she served as a faithful matron in the Theological Seminary at Newton. Her attention and fidelity to the students endeared her to many a heart.

HOTCHKISS, Elisha, near Aurora, Ind., June 10, æ. 80. Mr. H. was a native of New Haven, Conn., where he spent several years of his early life. He was a lawyer by profession, and liberally educated, having graduated at Dartmouth College, in the same class with Daniel Webster; and the writer of this brief notice has often heard that great statesman speak of his old friend and classmate with regard and affection.

Mr. H. commenced the practice of the law in Vermont, where for several years he held the office of county judge. He emigrated to Cincinnati in 1818, and he soon attached to himself many friends, who saw his real worth, and learned by a longer acquaintance how to value it. He served as mayor of the city of Cincinnati for many years, with the approbation of his fellow-citizens, and high honor to himself. His unobtrusive manners, sound judgment, large experience, and stern integrity, marked him as a man to be loved as well as trusted; and he vindicated, to the last, the reputation he had borne through every change of fortune.

HOTCHKISS, Dea. Elijah, Waterbury, Ct., May 5, æ. 92.

HOTCHKISS, Abraham V., E. Lewiston, N. Y., May 9, æ. 50. Mr. Hotchkiss came to Lewiston about 20 years ago, from Oneida Co. He was first engaged in the dry goods business, and afterwards appointed postmaster at Lewiston, which office he held about 8 years. In 1853 he was appointed collector of customs for the District of Niagara, by President Pierce, which office he held with honor to himself and credit to the government. He was respected as a citizen both at home and abroad, and those who knew him best will regret his sudden and unexpected departure. As a politician, he was an active, working democrat, ever ready with open hand and purse for the good cause he advocated. He was a faithful friend to the press in his county, having on two occasions aided in the establishment of democratic papers.

HOUGH, Wm. Mosely, Madison, Dane Co., Wis., Dec. 18, æ. —. Mr. H. held at the time of his death, and had held during four years, the office of county surveyor; to which for two years past has been added that of city engineer. Previous to his removal to Madison, in the spring of 1853, he had been for many years engaged in teaching, as principal in various high schools and academies in Pennsylvania and New Jersey. As a man of intelligence and literary taste, of accurate and energetic business habits, of thorough uprightness and firm religious principles, he had become widely known and highly esteemed by the people of Dane Co.

HOUGHTON, Mrs. Juliana, Philadelphia, Pa., Aug. 22, æ. 38, wife of D. C. Houghton, D. D.

HOW, Mrs. Mira, Haverhill, Mass., Dec. 23, æ. 68, wife of Col. Jacob How.

HOWARD, Capt. Harrison, Conneaut, O., May 9, æ. 46. From early boyhood he had followed the lake, and for many years been prominently identified with the lake commerce. No one was more highly prized for his business connections, his general intelligence, and his social qualities, sharing the respect, and esteem, and the confidence of all. He was a man of remarkably even temperament, retiring in his habits, and even under the most trying pecuniary difficulties in past years his spirits never flagged.

HOWARD, Henry M., Sullivan's Island, Sept. 10, æ. 40. He was at his death, and had been for many years, naval officer in the Charleston custom house. The duties of his office were discharged with uniform exactness and fidelity. He was not less diligent and earnest in reference to the obligations and duties of social life. None performed them better. His quiet, unobtrusive manners covered an excellent heart, steadfast and affectionate to his friends, courteous to his acquaintances and strangers, ready to do kind offices at all times, and warmly grateful always in receiving them.

HOWARD, Mrs. Jane W., Bradford, Vt., Aug. 9, æ. 31, wife of Dr. W. H. M. Howard.

HOWARD, Mrs. Laura B., Bangor, Me., March 27, æ. 28, wife of Rev. Roger S. Howard, principal of Girls' High School.

HOWARD, Mrs. Lydia Eaton, Weathersfield, Vt., May 10, æ. 37, wife of Mr. John Howard, and daughter of Jeremiah and the late Hannah H. Bemis. She followed her mother's example in consecrating her heart and life to God when a child. Thus early she confessed Christ publicly by receiving baptism and uniting with the Methodist Episcopal church, of which she continued a worthy member until her Saviour called her home. In her correspondence religion was the absorbing topic — how the Christian should live, and how he might expect to die. How often has she thus urged upon the writer of this notice fidelity to the cause of Christ in the great work of winning souls! and as often has he been stimulated to greater devotion to the work whereunto God hath called him. Consumption slowly but surely prosecuted its work of desolation with Mrs. H.; and she long knew that she must shake hands with Death. The prospect beyond the grave was unclouded; but how could she leave her loved companion and her dear children? Ah! that struggle was long and severe, but the victory was obtained. Christianity is sufficient for any emergency — be it recorded to the glory of God — for the living, for the dying.

HOWE, Hon. Chester, Elmira, N. Y., March —, æ. 50.

HOWE, Mrs. Mary Ann, Waukegan, Ill., June 12, æ. 60, wife of Rev. Elbridge Howe. She was a native of Providence, R. I.

HOWELL, Rev. Seth, Oxford, Butler Co., O., Feb. 18, æ. —. He was a native of Wales, but for some years had been settled in the ministry at Mount Sterling, in the Columbus presbytery, and more recently at Stony Hill.

HOYT, Mrs. Emeline C., Natick, Mass., Sept. 14, æ. 39, wife of Dr. John Hoyt.

HOYT, Mrs. Margaret, Hunter's Bottom, Ky., Sept. 14, æ. 91. She was a native of New York, and landed at Maysville, Ky., 70 years ago. She was the first white woman in Cincinnati.

HOYT, Mrs. Sarah, Norwalk, O., Aug. 20, æ. 87, the last survivor of the Wyoming massacre.

HOYT, Dea. Stephen, New Road, N. Y., March 27, æ. 84.

HUBBARD, Rev. Ebenezer, near Nashville, Tenn., Sept. 2, æ. 74. He was son of Rev. Ebenezer (H. U. 1777) and Abigail (Glover) Hubbard, and was born in Marblehead, Mass., Nov. 12, 1783. His father was born in Concord, Mass., May 22, 1758; was ordained at Marblehead, Jan. 1, 1783; and died Dec. 15, 1800, æ. 42. His mother was daughter of Col. Jonathan Glover, of Marblehead. Mr. H. was fitted for college at the public classical school or academy in Marblehead. After leaving college, he studied divinity with Rev. Timothy Flint, of Lunenburg, Mass., (H. U. 1800,) who married his sister Abigail. He was ordained pastor of the Second Church in Newbury, Mass., May 11, 1809. This pastoral relation was dissolved Oct. 16, 1810; and he was installed over the church in Middleton, Mass., Nov. 27, 1816; resigned his charge April 29, 1828; was installed at Lunenburg, Dec. 10, 1828. He was always a Trinitarian, as he declared, and, as he called himself, a moderate Calvinist, but was very liberal in his feelings towards Unitarians, and would not unfrequently exchange with clergymen of that denomination. Mr. H. continued pastor of the church in Lunenburg until Nov. 20, 1833, when his connection with the society was dissolved. He studied medicine, but never practised regularly, except, perhaps, in Boxford, or rather in Lunenburg, while he was a pastor there. In June, 1838, he removed to the west, and taught school a while in Trenton, Tenn., and afterwards in Paris, Tenn. In 1843 or 1844 he removed to Fulton Co., Ky., and settled on a farm in Hickman, which a son, dying, left him, and which he called Clergyman's Retreat. For some years he pursued the farming business, overseeing it and attending to his garden, while in his leisure hours he read books and wrote sermons, preaching sometimes, but having no charge. He liked the investigation of literary and scientific subjects.

HUBBARD, Mrs. Elizabeth, Albany, N. Y., Oct. 19, æ. 82, wife of the late Hon. Timothy Pitkin, and daughter of the late Rev. Dr. Hubbard, of New Haven, Conn.

HUDSON, Prof. T. B., Olmstead, O., April 2, æ. 39. Prof. H. was born in Chester, Geauga Co., O., in 1819. His father was a physician. At 18 he entered the Western Reserve College, where he studied and nearly accomplished the course, but left before graduating, and returned home. His father's circumstances did not admit of much aid for him, so that he was indebted chiefly to his own self-sustaining energy. His thirst for knowledge and perseverance carried him through difficulties which would have disheartened a less resolute mind. When the Oberlin Institution was opened he formed in the principles of the school his own views of learning; and in 1837 or 1838 he was called to teach mathematics. For 20 years he had been connected with Oberlin College as a professor of mathematics and the languages. The intelligence of Prof. H.'s death will carry sincere and poignant grief wherever this good man has visited, pleading for the enslaved. There will the tidings of his painful death occasion great grief, that such a powerful champion of liberty has fallen in times of trial and peril.

HUDSON, Barzillai, Torrington, Conn., March 19, æ. 78.

HUFFARD, Mrs. Mary, Jacksonville, Ala., Sept. 14, æ. 46, wife of Rev. William Huffard.

HUGER, Daniel, Charleston, S. C., Nov. 13, æ. 80. Surrounded by a devoted family, his habits were those of retirement, but not of seclusion. He was always ready to make his contributions of sentiment and of cheerfulness to the social circle. This was the field of his choice. He never sought nor desired public distinction. His mind was cultivated, but neither biased nor prejudiced. His feelings were gentle and kind, but always manly and candid. His ambition was to be right, and his only fear was to do wrong. His manner was the unostentatious bearing of a refined and conscious gentleman; and his urbanity had its source in the humility of the Christian. He professed what he believed; and his unwavering purpose was to act what he professed. His piety was not of impulse or of influence, but that of an honest thinker, whose own labor, with his Master's help, had wrought out his own conclusion. His research had commenced in youth; its fruits were the pleasure and the solace of his maturer years, and the rich but modest ornament of his old age. A Churchman himself, he yet considered other men as the children of God. Stanch and uncompromising in his own opinions, he yet deemed the privilege of thinking an inheritance from Heaven. He held no scrutiny over the tenets of others. Charitable and generous, he measured alms with none, but gave cheerfully as God had given him ability, though with a secret hand; and, when denial was necessary, he began invariably with himself. Truth was his cardinal principle, and justice his natural attribute.

HUGHES, Hon. Voley, Mendon, N. Y., Dec. 21, æ. 52, late mayor of Kenosha, Wis., and brother of John M., Arthur, and Hazen Hughes, of Cleveland.

HUGHES, David G., M. D., Hot Springs Co., Ark., June 7.

HUGHES, Mrs. Elizabeth C., Montezuma, O., æ. 54. She was born in Hartford, Conn., in 1804; emigrated west upwards of 20 years ago, and had been a resident of Ohio most of this time; in her 15th year experienced religion, and united with the church. Her piety was uniform and growing until she was taken to her final rest. In 1851 Mrs. H. removed to the village of Montezuma. The village had no Presbyterian church at this time. In a short time after her removal here a Presbyterian church was organized, consisting of five members; but there was but one male member in the organization. They had no house of worship of their own. All the members were poor in the things of this world, except Mrs. H. Soon after the organization of the church a plan was entered upon to erect a Presbyterian church. On March 5, 1854, she had the privilege to witness the erection of a comfortable and a neat house consecrated to the service of the triune God. Mrs. H., in connection with her self-denying pastor, John Hawks, contributed largely of their substance towards this noble enterprise, which is an honor to the place.

HULL, John C., Louisville, Ky., Aug. 26, æ. —. Recognized by the business community as a man of remarkable enterprise, energy, and usefulness, Mr. H. was equally known and endeared to his friends by the most attractive personal qualities. Chivalric, generous, humane, courteous, benevolent, charitable in the largest and noblest sense, every enterprise intended to advance the prosperity of the city of his choice received his cordial and active support; and every effort in behalf of suffering indigence was equally sure of his sympathy and aid. In his nearer and dearer domestic relations, Mr. H. was a rare example of unselfish affection. Left at an early age the protector of orphaned sisters and other bereft relatives, the better part of his life was entirely devoted to their welfare. Endowed with qualities such as these, Mr. H. received but his due in the warm affections of all who knew him.

HULL, P. P., Marysville, Cal., ——, æ. 34, formerly a lawyer of Mansfield, O., but at the time of his death one of the proprietors and editors of the San Francisco Town Talk. He was a printer, and had been connected with the newspaper business in San Francisco almost all the time since his arrival in the state, in 1850. He served his time in Mansfield, O., where his widowed mother still resides, and afterwards read law with his uncle, James Purdy, of Mansfield. He was born in that city in 1824. In his native state he was respected and loved by a large circle of friends; and in California, especially among his typographical and editorial brethren, he was eminently popular.

HUMPHREY, H. W., M. D., Iowa City, Iowa, —— ——, æ. 50.

HUMPHREY, Rev. Aaron, Beloit, Wis., Oct. 10, æ. 88. Mr. H. commenced his ministerial labors in the Methodist connection. Upon entering the Episcopal church, he officiated for some years in the diocese of Connecticut; was rector of St. Luke's, Lanesboro', from 1820 to 1830, when he removed into the diocese of New York. After serving, for some time, the parishes of Waddington and Ogdensburg, he organized a parish at Beloit, Wis., and continued to labor there until the infirmities of age obliged him to seek rest. For more than half a century, he faithfully discharged the duties of the ministry, and is remembered with respect by those who, at different periods, constituted his charge.

HUMPHRIES, J. R., Boonsboro', Md., May 23, æ. 41, a native of Wilmington, Del., and long a member of the Methodist Episcopal church. At the time of his death he filled the office of justice of the peace, the duties of which he discharged, so far as we are aware, with general acceptability, and in this respect his place cannot easily be filled. He was also school commissioner for the district for several years past, and in this respect, too, he acted to the satisfaction of the public.

HUNT, Freeman, Brooklyn, N. Y., Aug. 3, æ. 54. Mr. H. was preëminently a self-made man. He originated and executed the plans which have given him a reputation as a writer upon commercial affairs, and which redounded to his success in material prosperity. He was born in Quincy, Mass., in March, 1804, and was, consequently, 54 years of age at the time of his death. His father, Nathan Hunt, a shipmaster, died when Freeman was but three years of age. His ancestors, on both sides, were among the early inhabitants of the colony. His educational advantages in youth were limited to a few years' instruction in the country school, and at the age of 12 he left his home for Boston, and entered the office of the Boston Evening Gazette, in a position of general usefulness; among his duties was that of serving subscribers with the paper. Soon after, he apprenticed himself to the printing business. Subsequently, he went to Springfield, Mass., where he continued his labors as a compositor; but, desiring a larger field to satisfy his ambition, he returned to Boston, and became connected with the Boston Traveller. While here as a compositor, he sent several articles to the editor, which were published; and, inquiry being made as to their authorship, he confessed their source. Thereafter he rose in the establishment until he attained a respectable position. He first became a publisher soon after his apprenticeship expired, by establishing the Ladies' Magazine, of which Mrs. Sarah J. Hale, who had just brought out her first novel, was the editress. The magazine succeeded, and the success determined him to enlarge the scope of his labors. He accordingly sold out, and commenced the republication of the Penny Magazine, which reached a sale of 5000 copies within a year after its commencement. This work he soon abandoned, and became connected with the Bewick Company, an association of authors, artists, printers, and bookbinders, as the managing director. Being without capital, it required first-rate financiering ability to enable the association to carry out their object; but Mr. Hunt was equal to the task, and it was during this time that he projected the American Magazine of Useful and Entertaining Knowledge, the editorial department of which he conducted until he ceased his connection with the company. He also published, in Boston, in connection with a Mr. Putnam, the Juvenile Miscellany, which went through several volumes before it passed into other hands. He collated, also, two volumes of American Association, which met with a large sale. In 1831 he removed to New York, and soon after established a weekly paper called the Traveller. During this time he projected A Comprehensive Atlas, which he brought out in 1834. Subsequently, a series of letters, written to the Boston press, were published in a small volume entitled Letters About the Hudson. The volume met with a ready sale, and passed through three editions. In 1837 he conceived the project of the Merchants' Magazine, the details of which he fully elaborated during subsequent months, when he commenced canvassing for its support. In July, 1839, the first number was printed; his means being exhausted, the Hon. James M. Stevenson, of Troy, loaned him $300 to pay the expense of its publication. On the delivery of the first number he collected the subscription; since which event Mr. Hunt continued to increase in prosperity until his death. The Merchants' Magazine has now passed through 19 volumes, with a steady increasing subscription. It is taken by commercial men in all parts of the world. Mr. Hunt was thrice married. His first wife lived but a few months after marriage. Three children were born of the second marriage, two of whom are deceased — the eldest, John Fredericks Hunt, about a year since. A daughter of 15 years is the only one of the three living. His third wife, who survives him, is the daughter of the Hon. William Parmenter, of East Cambridge, Mass. A young son is the only issue of his third marriage.

HUNT, Rev. Aaron, Armenia, N. Y., April 25, æ. 90. He was a member of the New York Methodist Conference during the long period of 67 years. He was the father of Rev. A. Hunt, Jr., now of Whitlockville, Westchester Co., N. Y.

HUNT, Rev. John B., North Easton, Mass., Oct. 10, æ. 39, at one time pastor of the Methodist Episcopal church, at Hingham, Mass.

HUNT, Rev. Holloway W., Hunterdon Co., N. Y., Jan. 11, æ. 89. For seven years in his early ministry he was pastor of the churches of Newton and Sparta. His first wife was Susan, daughter of Judge Jonathan Willis, of Newton, to whom he was united in marriage in 1795. The average ages of this venerable man, his parents, grandparents, and seven brothers and sisters, would overreach 85 years. For 40 years he was pastor of the churches of Bethlehem, Kingwood, and Alexandria, — a field now occupied by five Presbyterian ministers, besides several other denominations.

HUNT, Hon. Alvah, New York city, Oct. 28, æ. 60. He was engaged through a long period in mercantile pursuits, in which he became successful. He was at various times honored by offices of trust and prominence in the state. He was twice sent to the state Senate from his district, and twice consecutively was he elected as treasurer of the state. Possessed, as he was, of decided executive ability, with a ready and extended knowledge of men and of the means of political advancement, he exerted, at times, a large influence in the political organization with which he acted. During the few later years of his life, he withdrew from the arena of politics, and resided in the city of New York, and until the time of his death, was connected with the Des Moines Navigation and Improvement Company, as treasurer. He was a self-made man, having risen to the position he occupied, from a condition of poverty, by native force of talent and character.

HUNTER, John C., Savannah, Ga., May 22, late purser in the U. S. navy.

HUNTER, Robert W., Junior, Prince George's Co., Md., Sept. 22. He was a native, and long a resident, of Alexandria, and one of the most skilful and successful ship-builders in the country.

HUNTINGTON, George, M. D., Poughkeepsie, N. Y., Nov. 6, æ. 37, formerly of Pittsfield, Mass.

HUNTINGTON, Abel, M. D., East Hampton, L. I., May 18, æ. 81. Dr. H. was originally from Connecticut, but settled in early life in East Hampton, as a practising physician. He became very skilful and very popular in his profession, and enjoyed in a very eminent degree the affection, the confidence, and respect of the people among whom he practised. Dr. H. held several public offices during his life. He was twice elected to Congress during the administration of Gen. Jackson's second term. He was a member of the convention to revise the state constitution in 1846, and during President Polk's administration he held the office of collector of the customs in Sag Harbor. He was an active politician of the Jackson, Silas Wright, and Van Buren school, and took a very prominent part in all the public meetings and conventions during the earlier and more active part of his life.

HUNTINGTON, Daniel, New London, Ct., May 21, æ. 70. Mr. Huntington was born in Norwich, Ct., Oct. 17, 1788. He was the second son of Gen. Jedediah Huntington, who was born in the town of Norwich, Ct., Aug. 15, 1743. Gen. H., at the commencement of the American revolution, joined the army, commanded a regiment in 1775, and held the rank of brigadier general towards the close of the war. He uniformly enjoyed the esteem and intimate confidence of Gen. Washington. He filled many offices of trust in his own state, and was collector at the port of New London under four presidents. The son bore an impressive resemblance to his father in person, mind, manner, and character. He was educated at Yale College, in the class of 1807. His first settlement in the ministry at North Bridgewater, Mass., continued twenty years, and his labors from time to time were abundantly blessed. From this harvest field disease compelled him to retire, and for seven years he was a resident of New London, recruiting his health, but actively engaged in educating young ladies in the higher branches of study, for which his fine literary taste eminently qualified him. His health restored, he accepted a second call from a portion of his church in Bridgewater who had formed a new society. Here he labored again thirteen years, winning souls to Christ, but the providence of God ordered that he should again leave this field, and return to the home of his youth, and pass the evening of his days amid the scenes of his earliest aspirations. From that day for about six years, till near the time of his departure, he continued to preach the gospel " in season and out of season," as " the open door was set before him." At the time when the Master called him he was " diligent in business, fervent in spirit, serving the Lord," preaching his last sermon at Mohican, just four weeks before the messenger of death met him. The physical sufferings of his last days were very great, but no complaining or murmuring words fell from his lips. With him patience had her perfect work. He died as he had lived, with a firm, unwavering trust in God. The day before his death his faith expressed itself, as it had often done in days of health and joyousness, in the voice of song :—

" There shall I bathe my weary soul
In seas of heavenly rest,
And not a wave of trouble roll
Across my peaceful breast."

So has passed away to his rest one eminently devoted to the happiness of his family and friends, the honor of the Redeemer, and the salvation of men. Far more delightful than easy would it be to portray the refined sensibilities, the generous sympathies, the self-forgetting spirit of sacrifices, and the heartfelt devotion to the world's welfare, that marked the life and formed the elements of character in this departed servant of God; and but for his unfeigned humility and the extreme modesty that imposed a constant restraint on the forth-puttings of his native genius, and this exclusive "respect to the recompense of reward," he had shone with far superior brilliancy in the starry firmament of earth's ambition, though less splendidly in that nobler firmament where stars never set and the sun no more goes down.

HUNTSMAN, Rev. John, Prospect Grove, Scotland Co., Mo., Sept. 13. He was born in Franklin Co., Pa., July 29, 1803, was converted in the 17th year of his age, and joined the Methodist Episcopal church. He joined the Ohio conference, Methodist Protestant church, in 1833; was for several years a laborious minister in the Pittsburg conference. In 1846 he removed to Missouri; and here he found himself without a membership, or an association in the ministry; but notwithstanding all this, he found a few noble men and women who loved the principles of the Methodist Protestant church, scattered about within 40 to 60 miles, and he formed them into societies, which, under a kind Providence, has resulted in what is now Des Moines Mission.

HURD, Mrs. Mary Ann Twichell, Amesbury, Mass., Oct. 11, æ. 29, wife of Y. G. Hurd, M. D., a native of Acworth, N. H.

HURD, Rev. George E., Dover, N. H., Oct. 16, æ. 28, minister of the Protestant Episcopal church of the diocese of N. H., and son of Hon. Ezekiel Hurd.

HURST, Thomas P., Chillicothe, O., May —, æ. —, an eminent lawyer.

HURXTHALL, F. D., Massillon, O., Dec. 1, æ. 80. He emigrated from Prussia in 1805, and became a merchant in Baltimore — was one of the defenders of Baltimore in the war of 1812. After that he removed to Clearfield Co., Pa., and from thence he became a citizen of Massillon in 1832.

HUTCHINSON, Mrs. Mary A., Charlotte, N. C., July 1, æ. 23, wife of Dr. E. Nye Hutchinson.

HUTCHINSON, Haley, Montgomery Co., Ala., December 2, æ. 65, a very wealthy planter.

I.

IMLAY, William H., Hartford, Ct., ——, æ. 79. He was born in Hartford, Jan. 25, 1780, and commenced business for himself at the age of 18. One of his first acts was to assume and pay off his father's debts. Men whose means of information are ample have boldly asserted that he did more business in his lifetime than was ever done by any other man who ever lived in Connecticut. His operations reached from Georgia to Michigan, and the locality, even to the day of his death, seemed to him unimportant, provided there was a good prospect of profit. He was largely interested in the Atlantic Dock speculations, in timber lands in the North-west, in country stores in Alabama, and in paper-mills in Windsor. He was an early and energetic friend of the New Haven, Hartford, and Springfield Railroads, and subsequently of the Providence and Fishkill Railroad. In matters of public utility, he did not stop to consult his private interests before giving them his support. He recently informed a friend that his estate would have been fully $100,000 better off if he had left to others the construction of the latter road. Twenty-five years ago he might have retired from business with an annual income of over $20,000 ; and the accumulation of that income, added to his then existing capital, would have made him the wealthiest man in the state at the time of his death. But he determined not to rust out, and died, a striking example of a man fairly worn out by hard work.

IRONS, Dexter, Mystic Bridge, Ct., May 25, æ. 51, well known to the public for the many fine ships which he has constructed.

IRVINE, Alexander, Esq., Bedford Co., Va., Nov. 30, one of the most respected and honorable citizens of the commonwealth.

IRWIN, Col. M. W., St. Paul, Min., Nov. 23, æ. 38, son of Calander Irwin. He was a native of Uniontown, Pa., and was the editor of a democratic journal in that county. He afterwards removed to St. Louis, and became the principal editor of the St. Louis Union. In 1853 President Pierce appointed Col. Irwin marshal for the territory of Minnesota, and in the summer of that year he removed to St. Paul, where he resided up to his death.

ISAACS, Edward M., New Ipswich, N. H., Sept. 5, æ. —. He was for many years prominent, both in business and in politics, and, though he had not reached the prime of life, had acquired a marked position and influence in society. In 1853 he was supported by the whigs for the office of secretary of state. In 1857 he was selected as an aide-de-camp by Gov. Haile, and at the time of his death was a member of the legislature from New Ipswich. By his death the people of New Ipswich have lost a public-spirited citizen and a generous-hearted friend.

J.

JACKSON, Albion, Onondaga Valley, N. Y., Dec. 22, æ. 57. Mr. J. was the first white child born in Syracuse.

JACKSON, Mrs. Elizabeth Willing, Philadelphia, Penn., Aug. 5, æ. 91. She was one of those relics of the classic era of our country, whose departure deserves especial note. She belonged to the well-known Willing family, with which so many of the early memories of this city are connected, having been the sister of Richard Willing. It is through her husband, however, that she is best known in Philadelphia. Maj. Wm. Jackson was an aid to Gen. Washington, and his private secretary. Subsequently to the revolutionary war, Maj. Jackson became a public man of considerable influence. He was chosen to deliver the funeral oration in Philadelphia for his old friend, Washington, and the address is said to have been a very fine one. For a number of years he was the publisher of a popular Philadelphia daily evening paper called the Commercial Register.

JACKSON, Timothy, Boston, Mass., Oct. 31. æ. —. He was accidentally run over and killed on one of the city railroads. He was distinguished as an inventor. The celebrated hotel annunciator, the heavy ordnance by which the walls of the Malakoff and Redan were battered down and a breach made for the French and English troops at the storming of Sebastopol; the novelty sewing machine, and many other new and useful inventions were his. He is said to have been a man of great amiability and excellence of character, but, like too many other inventors, he reaped little pecuniary benefit from his inventions. He left a wife and five children in destitute circumstances.

JACKSON, William H., Westmoreland, Oneida Co., N. Y., æ. 27. He was, for a time, student, and afterwards teacher, in Rome Academy. He graduated with honor at Hamilton College, and afterward devoted himself, successfully, to teaching and the study of law. He was soon to have entered upon his profession in New York city.

JACOBS, Gen. S. D., Natchez, May —. æ. —, at the mansion of his father-in-law, Capt. John B. Nevitt. Born in the Carolinas, Gen. Jacobs commenced a brilliant professional career in Tennessee, from which he was taken into the service of the federal government at Washington, for many years as assistant postmaster general. A better official never pressed that honored tripod of office. Gen. J. became a planter of Texas.

JAMISON, Rev. Francis B., St. Vincent College, Cape Girardeau, Mo., Nov. —, æ. 58. He was a descendant of the early Catholic settlers of Maryland, and was born near Frederic City. In his early youth he entered the Mount St. Mary's College, Emmetsburg, where he distinguished himself by his talents, and the facility with which he advanced in the paths of literature and science.

REV. JACOB J. JANEWAY, D. D.,

New Brunswick, N. J., June 27, æ. 84. Dr. J. was born in New York city, in 1776; he graduated at Columbia College, and pursued his theological studies with the venerable Dr. Livingston, of the Reformed Dutch church. In 1799 he assumed the pastoral charge of the Second Presbyterian Church, Philadelphia, as colleague with Dr. Green, and sustained for 30 years that relation, either as colleague or sole pastor. He removed to Pittsburg in 1828, when he was chosen by the general assembly of his church first professor of theology in the newly-erected Western Theological Seminary. During the last 30 years of his life, he resided chiefly in New Brunswick, sustaining, for part of the time, the relation of pastor of the Reformed Dutch Church, and vice president of Rutgers College. The adult life of Dr. J. was passed in the period marked by the rise and advance of our country, and the development of the great religious charities of the day. Before the war of independence, he was carried, when a child, from New York, then occupied by the enemy, and, with his father's family obliged frequently to remove from before the invaders, he lived to see the rise and growth of the greatest empire of the age. Entering the church of his adoption, the Presbyterian, when 266 ministers was the entire number, he left it when, in both branches, over 4000 rejoiced in her service. Dr. J. was identified with the growth and success of the religious charities of the day. One of the founders of the oldest Bible Society in our country, the Philadelphia Bible Society, he watched the expansion, and rejoiced to contribute to a cause he held so dear. Notwithstanding the labors of his parochial charge, then, and up to the time of his leaving it, the largest and most influential of the denomination in Philadelphia, he conducted, as chairman of the committee, the entire concerns of the Home Missions of the Presbyterian church. For their success he labored and prayed, and after its enlargement in 1829, by the general assembly, he continued a member, and for many years was its presiding officer. Active in the promotion of theological education, he took a prominent part in founding the Theological Seminary at Princeton, contributed to its funds, and was active in securing its endowment — a director for nearly 40 years, an intimate and cherished friend of its professors, the two eldest of whom he followed to their graves. He succeeded the first president of the board of directors, Dr. Green, and continued their presiding officer to the end of his life. Living as he did in New Brunswick, yet for years, with distinguished punctuality, he attended the weekly meetings of the executive committee of foreign missions, in their rooms at New York, till increasing infirmities and advancing age warned him to retire. Dr. J. has published a good deal on theological subjects. His easy and perspicuous style made his writings acceptable to the religious public. Remarkable for great exactness in all his habits, possessing a singular equanimity and self-possession, easy in his manners, he was greatly beloved. Firm and decided in his theological opinions, he advanced them with dignity; he so conducted controversy, that his opponents were soothed by his suavity, and thus were saved the usual fate of controversialists. Inheriting an ample estate, he used it with great liberality, and in contributing to religious and other charities, is believed to have given away per year one fifth of his income. A man of no ordinary intellect, he was always a diligent student, and maintained the habit till the end of life; for much study is believed by his friends to have shortened a life, which, though protracted, might, through great constitutional vigor, have been still more prolonged. Few men have passed through so long a life, and mingled so much with society, who have maintained so much consistency, and escaped all taint and blemish. The piety of Dr. J. was his crowning glory. Converted at the early age of 19, he walked with God, and is believed, for the greater part of his life, to have had an unshaken assurance of his acceptance in Christ. Modest, he instinctively shrank from the free expression of his religious feelings, except to his most intimate friends. His holy life proved his fellowship with God. Venerated for years, and surviving the mass of his contemporaries, his younger brethren regarded him with filial esteem. His last sickness was protracted, though painless, the extraordinary vigor of his frame giving way by slow degrees to the power of disease.

JARVIS, Mrs. Mary Coggswell, Baltimore, Md., Aug. 16, æ. 79, relict of the late Leonard Jarvis, Esq. By her death about $50,000 becomes awarded to Har- vard University and a charitable institution in the city of Baltimore, divided equally between them.

JAUNCEY, Joseph, M. D., Westport, Conn., April 7, æ. —, eldest son of the late Dr. Joseph Jauncey, of New York.

HON. WILLIAM JAY,

Bedford, Westchester Co., N. Y., Nov. 4, æ. 69. Mr. Jay was born at New York, June 16, 1789. He was fitted for college at New Haven by Mr. Henry Davis, afterwards president of Hamilton College, N. Y. He entered Yale in 1804, and took his degree in 1807. Returning to Albany, he entered the office of John B. Hewry, Esq. His health interfering with the practice of his profession, he rejoined his father's family, and assisted him in the management of his estate at Bedford, which William inherited on the death of his father in 1829. In 1812 he married Augusta McVickar, of New York. She died in April, 1857, soon after the death of Mr. Jay's sisters, Mrs. Banyer and Miss Ann Jay. Subsequently to his marriage Mr. Jay was appointed first judge of Westchester Co.; and he was continued upon the bench by successive governors, of opposite politics, through the varied changes of party, until 1843. Excepting the judgeship, we believe Mr. Jay held no public office. Gen. Jackson, while president, appointed him to an important Indian commissionership; but the office, which had been unsought, was declined.

Judge Jay, with a competent fortune, a cultivated and active mind, a fondness for intellectual labor, during a life of elegant leisure, consecrated his superior powers, unostentatiously and unremittingly, to the cause of humanity and religion, being willing, in imitation of his divine Lord, when incurring opposition or reproach, to make himself of no reputation, if need be, in the pursuit of what he deemed a righteous course. Born to affluence, he held his property as a steward of the great Proprietor; not necessitated to professional labor, he made the suffering and the oppressed his client; whether on the judicial bench or in the circle of intellectual or scientific friends, he aimed to be just and useful, and was willing to labor with the friends of God and man, in season and out of season, whether the cause was popular or unpopular, disregarding human praise or censure, so that he could stand approved to his own conscience, and especially to Him for whom he looked habitually as his present all-seeing, as well as his final Judge. Mr. Jay was thorough in his researches, scrupulous in the use of language, truthful in his statements, dignified in controversy, faultless in rebuking iniquity, firm as a rock in the maintenance of his honest and well-wrought opinions, liberal in the use of his wealth for the promotion of human happiness and the protection and defence of the wronged. He had the singular good fortune to write with just severity against the delinquencies of time-serving men and associations held in popular estimation, and yet retain the respect and confidence of the community. But it was not merely good fortune; it was also the result of his carefulness as to facts, his gentlemanly yet independent style, his uniform fairness, his disinterestedness, his unswerving integrity, and his entire freedom from gross personalities. He instinctively shrank from sinking the gentleman in the controversialist, imputing bad motives to all whom he felt bound to oppose, or seeking, by trick or artifice, to win a victory over an opponent. He might appropriately have borne upon his escutcheon the motto, "Be just and fear not." He was just; he was fearless; he was upright before God and man.

In religion he was a Low-Church Episcopalian, and a devoted and conscientious Churchman; yet he was free from bigotry and intolerance, and liberal in his estimation of the tenets and usages of Christians of other denominations. Wherever he recognized in another the image of Christ he cordially took him by the hand as a Christian brother, and yielded him his confidence. He was, from an early age, a frequent delegate to the Episcopal convention of the diocese of New York, and was consistent in opposing all attempts to change the doctrines, constitution, or liturgy of the church.

Mr. Jay was a friend to the Bible, tract, peace, temperance, Sunday school, Sabbath, missionary, education, and anti-slavery causes. He was a patriot as well as a philanthropist and Christian, and entered with prudent zeal into the political agitations of the times. He was president of the Westchester Bible Society, and a vice president of the American Bible Society, president of the American Peace Society, foreign corresponding secretary of the American Anti-Slavery Society, and afterwards vice president of the American and Foreign Anti-Slavery Society. He contributed to the funds of all the above-named societies, and advocated their claims by his pen and tongue so long as their acts met his approbation, and no longer.

During the last 25 years Mr. Jay has been an outspoken abolitionist in principle and action. He was no more ashamed of the name of abolitionist than he was of the name of Christian. He had a hereditary kindness for the people of color, whom he recognized as citizens of the country which gave them birth. He deemed the slave a brother by creation and redemption, and in his will has bequeathed, perhaps, the first legacy ever given for the relief of fugitives from slavery.

In politics he was, like his honored father, Chief Justice Jay, a federalist of the old school, then a whig, then a free-soiler, then a republican.

The different societies to which he belonged passed resolutions of respect and condolence. The bar of Westchester Co. say,—

"Whereas, since the last term of the court of this county, the hand of death has removed from among us the Hon. William Jay, for a quarter of a century the presiding officer of the Court of Common Pleas, whose official career was marked by extensive learning, punctilious attention to his duties, strict and fearless uprightness, as well as by uniform courtesy towards the bar and all others with whom he was brought into contact, and whose life was noted for a conscientious observance of justice towards all, for eminent usefulness, and every virtue ennobling to human character, thus securing for him the veneration and regard of all classes of his fellow-citizens, therefore

"*Resolved,* that Judge Jay, by the purity and simplicity of his life, by his liberality towards every measure deemed by him to be conducive to the benefit of his fellow-men, by his strict justice, by his hatred of oppression and wrong by or upon whomsoever inflicted, by his love for those cherished truths which regulated his conduct and sustained and cheered him at the termination of his career, has left behind him an example worthy of our studious imitation, and that the reverence with which the name and character of our departed friend were mentioned every where, illustrates the truth of the inspired declaration that 'the memory of the just is blessed.'"

Judge Robinson at the meeting remarked "that he felt himself obligated to join in this tribute to the memory of Judge Jay from the peculiar relations that had existed between them. He had been born within sight of his mansion, and enjoyed his friendship from his youth upwards. He gave me his confidence and his approbation. The success attending me was ever to him a source of pleasure, as, indeed, was the prosperity of every young man of his acquaintance.

"From 1818 till 1843 he was judge of this court. His judicial career was worthy of his noble sire, John Jay, the statesman of the revolution, the author of the glorious state constitution of 1777, and the first head of the United States Supreme Court. He was a model officer, a just judge. He dispensed justice from the bench with learning and wisdom, with stern integrity, and the strictest impartiality. His neighbors, his friends, strangers, the rich and the poor, were punished alike for violation of law.

"During the 25 years that he was judge of this county, no trial, civil or criminal, occupied more than one day. It may appear strange to the younger members of the bar that so great rapidity, so great saving of time, could be exercised in the dispensing of justice, and the rights of all be regarded. But Judge Jay was a jurist of the highest attainments. Whenever a point was raised he was familiar with it, and the law applicable to it, and usually decided it without argument. If either party sought to introduce irrelevant or improper testimony, he would reject it immediately, before the other party had time to raise an objection. It will thus be perceived by all familiar with trials, and who are aware how much time is occupied in arguing motions, and in the introduction of irrelevant testimony, how it was that Judge Jay, by divesting the proceedings of all this useless rubbish, and confining them to the main issues, was enabled to dispose of cases so summarily, and at the same time so justly. He was just to the prosecution; he was just to the prisoner; and he regarded the interests of the people.

"He was an exemplary citizen. Those with whom he differed in sentiment always conceded to him sincerity, purity, and integrity. He was religious without intolerance, upright without bigotry, merciful and generous without weakness. As a man in private, public, and Christian life, he was a rare model. By his death, the community in which he lived has lost one of its most useful members, humanity one of its brightest ornaments, Christianity one of its noblest exemplars."

Mr. Jay's writings are numerous. His contributions to the public press were very frequent. He was fond of thus employing his gifted pen; and editors seldom refused his neat, logical, apposite, and convincing contributions. He often wrote anonymously, but never hesitated to write under his own signature, either in addressing public bodies, the people, or individuals, when he deemed it necessary. He wrote many pamphlets, anonymous or bearing his own name, on various subjects. In 1826 he received a prize for an essay on the Sabbath as a Civil Institution, and in 1827 another for an essay on the Sabbath as a Divine Institution. In 1830 he was honored with a medal from the Anti-Duelling Society of Georgia for the best essay on Duelling. In 1833 he published two octavo volumes of the Life and Writings of John Jay; and since that date he has published various volumes on African Colonization, Peace, and Slavery, which have been widely circulated at home, and some of them have been reprinted in England. He has left, we understand, a commentary on the Old and New Testament, and probably other writings, which may yet be laid before the public. Mr. Jay's writings on the anti-slavery question have been more numerous than on any other subject; and yet, as is seen, he was not a man of "one idea." His political, his humane, and his religious feelings, in connection with his hereditary and characteristic love of liberty, led him early to espouse the cause of the free people of color and the slave.

Judge Jay twice visited Europe in the pursuit of health — first in 1843, when he travelled also in Egypt, and again in 1856, when he paid a short visit to England. His correspondence for many years was very extensive, especially with the leaders of the anti-slavery movement in the United States. He was the last of the children of Chief Justice Jay, his brother, Peter Augustus, having died in 1844, and his two sisters in 1856. He leaves behind him a son and three daughters, his two eldest daughters having died before him.

Chief Justice Jay, father of William, was the great-grandson of Pierre Jay, a Protestant merchant of Rochelle, France, who, on the revocation of the edict of Nantes, fled to England. Augustus Jay, the son of Pierre, emigrated to New York, where in 1697 he married Anne Maria, daughter of Belthasar Bayard. At the age of 85 he died, leaving one son, Peter, who married Mary, daughter of Jacobus Van Cortlandt, of New York. Peter died at Poughkeepsie, N. Y., in 1782, leaving John, who was born in New York, Dec. 12, 1745. John was educated at King's College, read law, and married Sarah Livingston, daughter of William Livingston, afterwards governor of New Jersey. He died May 17, 1829, æ. 84.

Peter Augustus Jay, brother of William, died Feb. 20, 1843. He was president of the New York Historical Society, and vice president of the American Bible Society, and had been recorder of New York. Miss Ann Jay and Mrs. Banyer, sisters, died in 1856, having bequeathed more than $31,000 to various charitable societies.

JEFFRIES, Richard, Georgetown, D. C., July 20, æ. 69.

JENKS, Joseph R., Philadelphia, Pa., June 26, æ. 91, a well-known citizen of Philadelphia, and an esteemed member of the Society of Friends, was for many years a successful merchant; was benevolent, upright, and honorable, and from time to time occupied various offices of trust, the duties of which he discharged with scrupulous fidelity. He was, in all the relations of life, a pure-hearted, high-minded, and honorable man.

JESSEE, Philip, New Garden, Russell Co., Va., Dec. 1, æ. 120. It is stated that a short time before his death he was able to attend to his own household affairs, and that while in his 100th year he cut and split 100 rails. He was a man respected by all who knew him.

JETER, Col. S. B., Nottoway Co., Va., April 2, æ. 76, a prominent citizen of Nottoway Co. He had served his county in the various capacities of justice, sheriff, commissioner of the revenue, &c., and was generally respected in the community.

JEWETT, Hon. Freeborn G., Skaneateles, N. Y., Jan 27, æ. 68. Judge J. came to reside in our county at an early day — as early as 1815 or 1816. He studied law in the office of Col. Samuel Young, and on taking up his residence in Skaneateles, entered into partnership with James Porter, formerly a representative in Congress from that district. Young J. had not been long in his new home before he was chosen to the office of justice of the peace, the duties of which were satisfactorily discharged. While holding that office, he was appointed surrogate — a position he held several years. In 1827 he was a member of the Assembly. In 1830 he was elected to Congress, against his wishes. Serving in that body for one term, he declined a renomination. In 1846 Gov. Wright appointed him a justice of the Supreme Court, and in the year subsequent he was elected to the office of judge of the Court of Appeals. In 1853 he was reëlected; but his health failing somewhat, he resigned the office at the end of two years. After his retirement from the bench, his health improved, and he has since been actively engaged in the management of his private affairs. The death of Judge J. will be widely and sincerely mourned. In all the relations of life he bore a stainless character. He was a self-made man. The career of such a man affords a forcible illustration of what may be accomplished by a steady adherence to the duties and responsibilities of life. As a judge he gave entire satisfaction to the bar of the state, and secured in an eminent degree their confidence and respect, showing himself an accomplished lawyer and a dignified, impartial, and painstaking judge. Very many of his judicial opinions have been reported, and many of them contain well-considered and thorough discussions of questions of magnitude and interest, and will always be cited with respect. He possessed a clear

and well-balanced mind, great good sense, and sterling integrity.
JEWETT, James M., Aurora, Portage Co., O., Dec. 9, æ. 70. He was the fifth generation from the original settlers of the name, consisting of two brothers and a nephew, who emigrated to this country in 1638, (from England,) and settled in Rowley, Mass. From this family all of the name in this country, acquainted with their origin, can trace their descent. A singular circumstance in connection with this family is the fact that the original homestead yet remains in the family, and has been occupied by those who have filled the office of deacon in the Congregational church for over 200 years. A clock brought from England 18 years after the landing of the Pilgrims at Plymouth Rock, still does duty in the old family mansion.

JOHNSON, Dr. A. H., Lynnville, Ill., Dec. 4, æ. 35.

JOHNSON, Leonard, Triangle, N. Y., æ. 59, a graduate of Amherst College.

JOHNSON, Mrs. Mary, Baltimore, Md., Sept. 13, æ. 55, relict of the late Chancellor John Johnson.

JOHNSON, Mrs. Mary E., Nashville, Tenn., May 22, æ. —, wife of Col. B. R. Johnson, professor in the Nashville Military University, and daughter of Daniel G. Hatch, Esq., of Covington, Ky., formerly of Exeter, N. H.

JOHNSON, Peter, Esq., West Troy, N. Y., April —, æ. 60, an old resident of West Troy, and a lawyer of the old school — a straightforward, frank, honest man.

JOHNSON, Dr. William M., Alamance Co., N. C., Oct. 15, æ. —. Dr. J. had for a number of years been connected with the Spirit of the Age as associate editor ; he was a pleasant writer, and a very zealous and efficient friend of temperance.

JOHNSON, Willis, M. D., Mason, N. H., Oct. 2. æ. 72. He was born in Sturbridge, Mass., Dec. 21, 1786, and commenced the practice of medicine in Jaffrey, N. H., in Aug. 1807, before he was 21 years of age. He removed to Mason in July, 1814, where he lived 44 years useful and respected. He filled the office of town clerk 22 years, and was chairman of a board of selectmen five years, and held other offices in the town and county. As a physician his services were highly appreciated, and he was unusually successful, so that he was under the necessity of prescribing for many of the sick after he was unable to visit them, by learning their state from their friends, or by their going to his room to receive advice and prescriptions.

JOHNSTON, E. H., Esq., of Galena, N. Y., at Dubuque, Iowa, Aug. 19, æ. 39, for three years past the principal of the Galena Classical Institute ; a most valuable citizen and an estimable man. He went to Galena in October, 1855, and assumed the charge of the Institute, which he conducted successfully up to the present time. Possessed of considerable experience as a teacher, of great energy of character, and devoted to his calling, under his auspices the Institute became at once flourishing. It was owing entirely to his persistent exertions that the new Institute building on Seminary Hill was commenced, and carried forward to completion. Mr. J. was a native of Sidney, Delaware Co., N. Y. After obtaining his education, he was engaged for four years as a teacher in Albany, and left there for Galena. He leaves a wife and two children.

JOHNSTON, Rev. James, York Co., Pa., March —, æ. —, for 30 or 40 years the pastor of an Associate Reformed church in Mansfield, Ohio.

JOHNSTON, Mrs. Mary Charlotte, S. C., June 9, æ. 58, relict of Rev. Cyrus Johnston, D. D., formerly pastor of the Presbyterian church in that town. For upwards of 30 years she was a consistent member of the Presbyterian church, and for a quarter of a century the devoted wife of one of its most laborious and zealous ministers. In every relation of life she sustained her part nobly and well.

JOLLY, Rev. Hugh, Coeymans, N. Y., April 20, æ. 89, an earnest and consistent minister of the gospel, and a Methodist preacher for more than 60 years.

JONES, Dr. Anson, Houston, Texas, Jan. 8, æ. —. Dr. Jones has been prominently connected with public affairs in Texas for many years. He was a native of Louisiana, but emigrated to Texas in 1833, and at once took part in the struggles of the republic for independence. He joined the army, raised a company of volunteers, was at the battle of San Jacinto, received the appointment of judge advocate general, and held various military positions during the years 1836 and 1837. In 1837 he was

16

elected to the second Congress of Texas, from Brazoria Co. In the following year he was appointed minister of Texas to the United States; was recalled in 1839, and elected state senator in the place of Hon. William H. Wharton, deceased. In 1840 he was chosen president of the Senate, and, in the absence of Gen. Lamar, became ex-officio vice president of the republic. In 1841 he was elected secretary of state — an office he filled with marked ability for three years. He was the last president of the republic, having been elected to that station in 1845. In February, 1846, the republic was annexed to the United States, and Dr. J. relinquished his authority; two years of his presidential term being yet unexpired. Dr. J. was regarded with great affection by the people of Texas, who were unanimous in ascribing to him measures which resulted in the independence of the young republic.

JONES, Archibald, Esq., Frankfort, Me., Feb. 8, æ. 81, a native of Worcester, Mass., whence he removed to Frankfort in 1802, and was consequently one of the earliest settlers of the town. He was a lawyer by profession, and the first who commenced practice in Frankfort. At the time of his death we believe he was the oldest member of the Waldo bar. His whole life was without spot or blemish. He was a Christian, not only by profession, but also in practice. In him the poor and afflicted always found a friend and comforter.

JONES, Benjamin, Oakland, O., April 9, æ. 52. He was the son of Catlit and Sarah Jones, who emigrated from Virginia to Columbiana Co., O., about the first of the present century. Catlit Jones accompanied Daniel Boone in his first adventure in Kentucky. On the occasion of the capture of Col. Boone's daughter and another distinguished lady by the Indians, Mr. Jones was one of the "twelve brave men" who volunteered and perilled their lives to rescue these young ladies from their savage captors. While with Col. Boone in guarding the "corn patch" against the Indians, he received a severe wound in the arm. He was also an officer in the revolutionary war. Afterwards he joined the Society of Friends, and resolved "to beat his sword into a ploughshare and his spear into a pruning hook," and was an acceptable minister in that society. Benjamin was also a member of the Society of Friends. He leaves two brothers, a bereaved wife, and eight children, to mourn his death. He was a general reader, and was familiar with the solid literature of the age; was remarkable for the precision and extent of his knowledge of all subjects upon which he conversed. He took a lively interest in agricultural improvements, and by the judicious application of fertilizers and subsoiling had greatly increased the productiveness of his farm. He was the friend to popular education. He took a deep interest in the antislavery movement, and was a zealous advocate of the rights of man, and of the interests of free labor against the aggressions of American slavery.

JONES, Charles A., Rochester, N. Y., Jan. 25, æ. —. His more intimate friends were aware that his health had been impaired ever since his visit to Washington at the time of President Buchanan's inauguration. Within a fortnight he returned from a business visit to Washington, and was then quite debilitated, but resolutely refused to succumb to the insidious disease lurking in his system. His large contracts for erecting government buildings in Chicago and Milwaukie occupied his mind, and furnished excitement for his enterprise, so that he "had not time to be sick." The death of his son-in-law, Mr. Bruff, a week before, was undoubtedly a severe stroke; for upon him he placed great confidence and dependence in carrying on his extensive contracts. Mr. J. had resided in Rochester upwards of 20 years.

JONES, Edmund Loftin, Chapel Hill, N. C., Nov. 24, æ. 19. He was a member of the Junior class in the university, of high standing in scholarship and deportment, and distinguished for good natural abilities, perseverance, and diligence. To these may be added truthfulness, amiability of temper, and warmth of affection. His fine face and person, and his winning, kind manners, caused him to be much admired by all; but by his family and personal friends he was most dearly loved.

JONES, Mrs. Elizabeth, Hart Co., Ga., Oct. 9, æ. 86. Her parents, Joseph and Mary Henderson, moved from Virginia when she was about 11 years of age, and settled on Cold Water Creek, Elbert Co., Ga. In 1795 she was married to James Jones, with whom she lived a devoted and happy life for 63 years, raising a large and respected family. We are rarely called upon to record the death of one who has spent so large a life of usefulness and devotion to the church of Christ. She was 70 years or more a member of the Methodist church. The Henderson family were among the pioneers of Methodism in this section of Georgia.

JONES, Dr. Henry J., Louisville, Ky., May 13, æ. 45, formerly of St. Louis, but for many years a practising physician in Louisville.

JONES, Dr. Isaac, Washington, Ark., Feb. 11, æ. —. He was originally from Orange Co., N. C., where he stood at the head of his profession; emigrated to Hempstead Co., Ark., many years ago; took the lead in his profession; was distinguished for his enterprising disposition; was kind and liberal in his views, as well as benevolent to the poor and needy. Dr. J. was emphatically a gentleman and a scholar, and was one of the most extensive cotton planters in the state. He leaves a widow and several children to mourn his loss.

JONES, Judge Lewis, Urbana, Ill., Dec. 25, æ. —.

JONES, Gen. James J., Basle, Switzerland, Sept. 4, æ. —. For many years in his earlier life he took an active and efficient interest in the military establishment of New York, in which he held the rank of major general of the third division of infantry; and he was distinguished not only as a good disciplinarian, but for his pure and honorable character and popular qualities. His services in the financial and charitable institutions of the city have been constant and important. As a trustee of the savings bank, of the New York Life Insurance and Trust Company, of the New York Hospital, as a vestryman of Trinity Church, and in administering many private trusts of great responsibility, he has been eminently faithful and wise. In private life Gen. J. was honored and beloved. His ample fortune was, alike from principle and impulse, applied in doing good.

JONES, John A., Texas, Aug. 12, æ. —, formerly a member of the Maryland legislature from St. Mary's Co.

JONES, John P., Sullivan Co., N. Y., æ. 80. He was one of the founders of Monticello, has been State senator, and in 1856 was a Fremont elector.

JONES, Miss Lucy Y., St. Leon, Va., Oct. 31, æ. —, eldest daughter of Mrs. Helen Jones, of Mecklenburg Co., Va. She was a daughter of James Y. Jones, Esq., formerly of Jefferson Co., and granddaughter of Joseph H. Jones, Esq., who died at Smithfield in 1822.

JONES, Mrs. Maria B., Geneva, N. Y., Dec. 23, æ. 67, widow of the Hon. Samuel W. Jones, and daughter of the late James C. Duane, of Schenectady.

JONES, Mrs. Minerva A., Medfield, Mass., Jan. 31, æ. 29, wife of D. W. Jones, M. D. In the life and character of Mrs. J. there was a rare combination of Christian virtues and personal charms. With a gracefulness of manner and a sweetness of disposition peculiarly her own, were united an intellectual culture and a consistent piety, which not only rendered her an agreeable companion, but secured for her at once a prominent place in the affections and confidence of all who knew her.

JONES, Samuel B., Esq., late of Carrollton, Miss., July 29, æ. —, at the residence of his friend James Minter, on Tallahatchie River, and formerly a member of the Carrollton bar. He was a man of many excellent traits of character; especially was he remarkable for the generosity of his disposition, and the benevolence of his heart. Raised in the counsels of an educated and a polite circle of relations, his early associations matured into an urbanity of manners which marked his course in riper years. Reared for the legal profession by an uncle who was a distinguished member of that profession, he attained membership with the Mississippi bar. Honorable by nature and by cultivation, he was conspicuous alike for his high sense of honor and his integrity of purpose. His native affability and his cultivated courtesy won the approval and insured the respect of enlightened associates; and his agreeable companionship in his social intercourse told of the noble qualities of his heart, and the valued qualifications of his mind.

JONES, Dr. Sterling Henry, late of Green Co., Ala., March 2, æ. 28. He was lost by the burning of the Eliza Battle. He was the eldest son of the late B. B. Jones and Elizabeth D. Jones, now of

Sumter Co., Ala. After receiving his education, he studied medicine in the office of Dr. Pearson, of Pickens Co. He then attended his first course of lectures in Philadelphia, and afterwards graduated at the Medical College in New Orleans, La., and commenced the practice of medicine in Sumter Co. Shortly after he was married to Miss Mary Owens, of Pickens Co. His fortune being ample, he turned his attention more directly to agriculture, and settled near Gainsville, where he lived several years. Becoming dissatisfied with his location, he sold out, and purchased a plantation in Greene Co. last year — made a crop, and was on his way to Mobile to receive the proceeds and to lay in his family supplies. He bade fair to make a very successful planter. Dr. J. was born in Tuscaloosa Co., Ala., and from youth to manhood combined every quality to endear his relatives and acquaintances.

JONES, Com. Thomas Ap Catesby, Georgetown, D. C., May 31, æ. 69. He was a native of Virginia, and was born in the year 1789. He entered the navy as a midshipman in the year 1805, and received his commission as a captain in 1829. He was first brought prominently into public notice in the year 1814, at the time when the British naval expedition against New Orleans entered Lake Borgne. Com. J., then a lieutenant, had command of a division of five gun-boats, carrying 23 guns and 183 men. The British force that he was appointed to intercept, consisted of 40 or 50 barges or boats built for this special duty, carrying 42 guns, and 600 or 800 men. After a gallant resistance the little American flotilla was compelled to surrender, Lieutenant Jones having been early disabled by a shot. His conduct in the affair was universally commended. That the victory was dearly bought by the British is proved by the fact that their loss, as officially reported, was 95 — more than half the number of Americans engaged, and, by American witnesses of the affair, the loss is even said to have been 300 or 400. In 1842, when he had command of the Pacific squadron, while lying at Callao, he received unofficial information which led him to believe that a war between the United States and Mexico was inevitable. He was led to believe that through intrigues at Mexico, a cession of Mexican territory to Great Britain was contemplated. He suddenly set sail with a squadron of four vessels in order to forestall the supposed designs of the British admiral. On arriving before Monterey, some circumstances confirmed his suspicions; he summoned the governor to surrender the place, which was done, and Oct. 20, 1842, the American flag rose over the old fort, and a proclamation was issued explaining to the people the strange movement. For this indiscreet but well-meant seizure of Monterey, in a time of peace, Com. J. was suspended from service for a time, and in 1855 was placed upon the reserved list by the naval board.

JONES, Worster, Claremont, N. H., Dec. 20, æ. 75. He was a native of Claremont, belonged to a large and respectable family, and was one of the most useful and worthy citizens.

JORDAN, Reuben, Sr., Monticello, Jasper Co., Ga., May 23, æ. 69. Mr. J. was a native of North Carolina. His father emigrated to Georgia when he was a child, and settled in Oglethorpe Co., where Mr. J. resided for more than thirty years. He then removed to Jasper Co., where he resided till his death. He represented both the counties of Oglethorpe and Jasper several times in the legislature of the state. He possessed a mind naturally vigorous and acute, which had been enlarged and disciplined by reading and reflection, which, added to fine conversational powers and genial feelings, rendered him both an instructive and agreeable companion. Firm in his principles, frank and bold in his maintenance of them, sternly upright in all his dealings, he enjoyed the confidence of his fellow-citizens while living, and died calm, self-possessed, and fearless.

JOSEPH, Joseph L., New York, June 4, æ. 61. The New York Herald gives the following correct history of the once noted, but for many years almost forgotten name that heads this article. It says, "Previous to the panic of 1837, the banking house of Joseph Brothers was reported to be the wealthiest in this country. Certain it is that their operations were on a most extensive scale, and their liabilities when they failed were counted by millions. The Josephs were the agents of the Rothschilds in this country; and so unbounded was their credit, that when the crash came their failure did more to precipitate the great panic of 1837 than any other one event of the time. In fact, their failure was very similar to, and produced pretty much the same effect as did that of the Ohio Life and Trust Company, in 1857. The house occupied by the Josephs stood on the same lot as the house now occupied by Brown Brothers & Co.; and what was a little singular, the house, which was new, fell a few days before the firm did commercially. The fall took place at midnight and no one was injured. On Saturday, it was announced that Joseph L. Joseph, who was the head of this once great banking firm, was dead. Since the failure the brothers have pursued various occupations, but have never been heard of as bankers.

JOURDAN, Thomas, Williamson Co., Ill., April 12, æ. 56. His history is connected with that of Illinois. His father, Thomas Jourdan, emigrated from Tennessee while he was yet young, in 1787. In the war of 1812, they built a fort which was known as Jourdan's Fort, in the present county of Williamson, eight miles south-east of Frankfort. In the course of the war the Indians made several attacks upon the garrison, when they chanced to go out of the fort; but owing to the skill and bravery of the soldiers, who were principally of the Jourdans and Whitesides, they succeeded in saving the women and children from Indian massacre. The subject of this sketch was then but a youth; nevertheless he was one of the most daring, and was always foremost in any enterprise, however perilous. His courage and bravery were unsurpassed. He afterwards married and settled within half a mile of the old fort, and lived on the same farm until his death.

JOYNES, Thomas R., Sr., Accomac, Va., Sept. 12, æ. 69. He was an able lawyer, who rose to success and fortune by his own exertions, and was distinguished in the state convention of 1829–30 by his great powers as a debater and statist. He was remarkable for his quickness, clearness, and accuracy. He was the compeer of the brilliant Upshur, and was to him what Fox was to Pitt in Parliament. He has been for many years the Nestor of the eastern shore, where his loss will be felt most, and where his memory will long be cherished as an able and good man in all the relations of life. He leaves a widow, and a large family of children, of whom, two of his sons, already known for their worth, are William T. Joynes, Esq., of Petersburg, and Dr. L. S. Joynes, one of the professors of the Medical College of Richmond.

REV. BETHEL JUDD, D. D.,

Wilmington, Del., April 8, æ. 82. He was a clergyman of the diocese of Western New York, but for some years past spent much of his time at the residence of his son in Wilmington. He was born in Watertown, Ct., in 1776, and graduated at Yale College in 1797, under the presidency of Dr. Dwight. He immediately entered upon preparation for the ministry, pursuing his studies under the direction of the Rev. Dr. Bowden, of Cheshire, Ct. He was ordained deacon by Bishop Benjamin Moore, of N. Y., in 1798. For the space of 60 years he made full proof of his ministry, being favored with almost unbroken health, and in labors more abundant. He was, at different periods, actively engaged in the dioceses of Ct., N. Y., Western N. Y., Md., N. C., and Fla. He was officiating in Hudson, N. Y., at the same time that the late Bishop Chase was laboring in that diocese. He was one of the early presidents of St. John's College, Annapolis, and also rector of the church in that city. He was one of the pioneers of the church in North Carolina, where he organized several parishes and draughted a constitution for the diocese, when the number of its clergy should entitle it to be admitted as such. Among the missionary stations which he held was St. Augustine, Fla. For about 15 years he was rector of St. James's Church, New London, Ct., the parish of which Bishop Seabury was once incumbent. This charge he resigned on being appointed president of the Episcopal Academy in Cheshire, Ct. Dr. Judd retained, in a remarkable degree, his physical and mental vigor, and his energy was very little impaired by the burden of years. Witin a month of his death he occupied the pulpit, proclaiming the unsearchable riches of Christ with a fervor and animation surpassed by few younger men, and his pen has been busy during the past winter in producing articles for one of the religious journals. He was a ripe scholar, an earnest, evangelical, and effective preacher, a courteous gentleman, and a godly man. His end was eminently peaceful and blessed. He was enabled in his dying hour to take up, with humble confidence, the utterance of the great apostle, "I am now ready to be offered, and the time of my departure is at hand. I have fought a good fight, I have finished my course, I have kept the faith. Henceforth there is laid up for me a crown of righteousness, which the Lord, the righteous Judge, shall give on that day to all who love his appearing." And with much emphasis he added, "We do love his appearing." Thus closed in calm serenity a life that dates from the period of our colonial dependence, and a ministry that commenced in the last century. "Your fathers, where are they? And do the prophets live forever?" The funeral service was solemnized in St. Andrew's Church, Wilmington, on Saturday, April 10, nearly all the neighboring clergy of the diocese of Delaware being present, and the Rev. Messrs. Breck, Ridgely, Parker, and Newbold acting as pall-bearers. The bishop of the diocese officiated in the service, assisted in the lesson by the Rev. S. C. Brinckle. With many tears and affectionate regrets, the remains of this venerable servant of Christ were committed to the tomb.

JUDSON, David L., Birmingham, Ct., March 8, æ. 27. He was a graduate of Yale College, class of 1851, and son of the late Donald Judson, Esq.

JULIAN, Hon. George H., Forsyth Co., Ga., Oct. 23, æ. 45. In all the relations of life, of son, brother, husband, father, citizen, neighbor, and friend, he was a model man — a bright, shining ensample to all persons who would fulfil their appointed and appropriate destiny on earth. It may be said, with perfect truthfulness, that, in this instance, a good man has fallen in the prime of his life, and in the midst of his usefulness to family, church, and country. Blessed with a handsome competency of this world's goods, made and accumulated by his own persevering industry, painstaking, and economy, — possessed of a charitable, benevolent, and large heart, — it is impossible to estimate the heavy loss the county of Forsyth has sustained in the death of this prudent, orderly, and most estimable gentleman. To his stricken widow and little son (an only child) the bereavement is heart-rending and irreparable; and outside of his own immediate circle, at home, none will feel the severity of this inscrutable stroke of Providence more sensibly than those families and persons in his neighborhood, who were the recipients of his overflowing kindness and liberal, unselfish generosity. The widow and the orphan, the poor and afflicted, never sought his aid or appealed to his bounty in vain. No deserving person did he ever turn empty away. Often has he been known to provide the destitute and suffering poor with money, from his purse, to purchase provisions and the necessaries of life, when he himself had not in his barns and smoke-houses wherewith to supply their wants. His charity embraced all within its compass, and every body loved him. He died, as he had lived, lamented and beloved by all who came in contact with him, and, as is believed, without an enemy in the world. In 1855, the people of Forsyth county, appreciating the character and worth of Mr. J., honored themselves by elevating him, by a large majority, to a seat in the legislature of Georgia; and in 1857 he was again reëlected to the same responsible position by his fellow-citizens.

JUNEAU, Paul, Juneau, Dodge Co., Wis., Aug. 13, æ. 35. He was the second son of the late Solomon Juneau, the founder of Milwaukie, and the first-born of that revered pioneer after his permanent settlement at the flourishing commercial emporium of Wisconsin, now more than 40 years since, where Paul was born, April 28, 1823. He was consequently in the 35th year of his age at the time he was unexpectedly taken away by a most sad casualty. During the last years of his life his residence has been in Dodge Co. In 1849 he was elected member of the Assembly from the Theresa district. In 1852 he was chosen register of deeds, which office he held for four years, discharging its duties to the satisfaction of the people who had placed him there. Faithful, courteous, and prompt, he won the confidence and esteem of all who knew him, and at length surrendered his responsible office with the full consciousness of having impartially discharged every public obligation that devolved upon him. At the time of his sudden and shocking death, he was a member of the present Assembly from his district, and also clerk of the Circuit Court of Dodge Co. He was a prudent and considerate legislator, zealously guarding the interests of his constituents, and solicitous to promote the welfare of the whole state — an esteemed and upright citizen — a man of integrity and honor, who had troops of friends — true to his party, above reproach, and without an enemy. Among all the multitude of mourners, there was not one, beyond the circle of the departed's nearest and dearest relatives, who exhibited a deeper or sincerer sorrow than an aged and silver-haired Indian, who in sadness and grief followed his lost friend to his final place of repose, weeping like a child, and showing that though he belongs to a race the poets have described as

"Stoics of the wood — men without a tear,"

he was not destitute of the sympathies which belong to humanity in every age and every clime. There was something touching and affecting in seeing an old Indian — a lonely and neglected stranger amidst the intruding crowds who have driven his people from the beautiful land of his ancestors — coming from his distant forest home to witness the burial of one in whose veins flowed the blood of his tribe, and whose family had ever been the guardian and vindicator of his injured nation. But such are the contrasts and such the vicissitudes of life.

JUSTICE, Capt. John, Millcreek, Pa., July 6, æ. 71. Capt. J. came to Erie during the late war with Great Britain, for the purpose of aiding in the construction of Perry's fleet. Marrying some time afterwards, he settled in the place permanently, residing for the last 25 years just outside the city limits. By indefatigable industry he secured a competency, and was ever held in high esteem for his integrity and personal worth.

K.

HON. JOHN KENT KANE, Philadelphia, Feb. 21, æ. 63, judge of the United States District Court for the eastern district of Pennsylvania. He was a son of John Kane, whose father emigrated from Ireland in 1756. Judge Kane's mother was a Miss Van Rensselaer, of New York. He was educated at Yale College, and then studied law in Philadelphia, in the office of the late Judge Hopkinson. He was admitted to the bar April 8, 1817, and soon took rank among its members as one of the most promising of their number. He was originally a federalist in politics, but in the Jackson times he gave in his adhesion to the democratic party, and was elected by them several times to the state legislature. He was also at one time their candidate for mayor, and held, for a time, the office of city solicitor. In 1845 he was appointed by Gov. Shunk attorney general of the state. This office he resigned in June, 1846, when, on the decease of Judge Randall, of the United States District Court, President Polk appointed him to fill the vacancy. This office he continued to hold up to the time of his death. His judicial decisions have generally been regarded as entitling him to the confidence of the public and his own profession. He was an able rather than a brilliant lawyer, his mind being well stored with precedents, and guided by strong practical sense. He exposed himself to a good deal of obloquy by his decision in the Passmore Williamson case; and at the time of his death a suit was pending against him for false imprisonment, at the suit of that person. There is no doubt, however, that in that, as in all other decisions, Judge K. was animated by a strict sense of duty, and only acted in accordance with the dictates of his conscience. Since the death of his distinguished son the tributes of condolence and respect which he received from all parts of the world must have consoled him for any feelings of hostility that might have been excited against him by his course on that question. There is no doubt, however, that his son's premature end preyed greatly on his spirits, and hastened the termination of his own days. Thus death has, in a brief period, claimed as its victims two of the most distinguished members of a family which, through its different branches, had for more than a century rendered important services to the country. Mrs. Kane, who survives him, was Miss Jane Leiper, a descendant of Thomas Leiper, of the revolution, and intimate personal friend of Jefferson. A daughter and three sons also survive. The latter are Col. Thomas L. Kane, who is now in California, R. Patterson Kane, Esq., a member of the bar and of the common council of Philadelphia, and Dr. John K. Kane, who accompanied the searching expedition sent out in quest of the second arctic expedition of the late Dr. E. K. Kane, and who is now in Paris.

Judge K. was a gentleman of fine abilities, a good lawyer, and a learned judge. He was also an accomplished belles-lettres scholar, and an adept in the graceful accomplishments of society. Few men of our acquaintance were more courtly in manner, or better calculated to impress upon the observer the idea of a perfect gentleman. Whether at the bar, on the bench, in political life, or in society, he never, for an instant, lost his self-possession, or was betrayed into a rude word or a display of temper. He was a member of various artistic and scientific societies, such as the Musical Fund Society, the Academy of the Fine Arts, and the American Philosophical Society, and exercised high influence in all of them. However men may have differed from him on political questions, there are none that will deny him the possession of most winning social qualities, and of great firmness and tenacity of purpose in every thing that he undertook.

KAVANAUGH, Dandridge W., Lawrenceburg. Ky., April 24, æ. 32. He was a young and very promising lawyer; and as a husband, father, son, a friend, and good citizen, his loss will be deeply felt. He had been for many years an exemplary and consistent member of the Christian church, and met death with Christian fortitude and resignation.

KEARSLEY, Mrs. ——, Detroit, Mich., Jan. 7, æ. ——, wife of the venerable Maj. Kearsley. She had lived in D. during the memory of the present generation, having been one of those who were pioneers of the prosperity of Detroit.

KELLER, Rev. J. B., Carlisle, Pa., Nov. 30, æ. 33.

KELLOGG, Edward, Brooklyn, N. Y., April 29, æ. 68. He was known to the public as the author of a work on political economy, entitled Labor and Other Capital. His loss, though at a ripe age, and by no means unexpected, will occasion deep regret to numerous relatives and acquaintances.

KELLY, Rev. Alexander, Mount Pleasant Mission, Kentucky conference, July 7, æ. 27. His deep piety, his ardent zeal for Christ, and his evident gift for usefulness, procured for him the recommendation of his class to the quarterly conference, when, without a dissenting voice, he was licensed to preach. He maintained his good standing as a preacher, was useful, and very much esteemed by all who knew him.

KELLY, Col. John W., Callaway Co., Mo., Oct. ——, æ. ——. For many years Col. K. represented Holt Co.; and two years ago he ran on the ticket with Col. Benton for lieutenant governor, since which time he has lived in retirement upon his farm in Callaway Co.

KEMPTON, Paul, New Bedford, Mass., Sept. 11, æ. 84. He built the house in which he resided, and occupied it for a period of 49 years. Mr. K. was in the early part of his life, for a series of years, collector of taxes and a constable, and has also held several other important offices, all of which he discharged with acceptance. At the time he held the collectorship he was in the habit of notifying delinquents by chalking the amount due upon the doors of their houses and places of occupation, considering it preferable to the modern process of issuing a twenty-cents summons. The distinguishing traits of Mr. K.'s character were firmness and strict integrity.

KENDALL, Rev. William C., West Falls, Erie Co., N. Y., March 1, æ. ——. Mr. K. was, at the time of his death, in the midst of one of the most extensive revivals with which this part of the state was ever visited. His end was triumphant.

KENDALL, Capt. Robert R., Freeport, Me., May 23, æ. 85. He was an officer in the war of 1812-15, and was engaged in the battle of Plattsburg.

KENNEDY, Andrew, Esq., Charlestown, Va., Feb. 27, æ. 61. As a member of the bar in early life, and latterly as an intelligent and efficient magistrate of the county, and at the same time presiding over the banking institution of this place, there is but one voice going up from the whole community, proclaiming in terms of peculiar emphasis, truly, and faithfully, "He acted well his part."

KENT, George L., California, March —, æ. —, formerly of New Hampshire, a young man of excellent culture and fine character. He was the only son of George Kent, Esq., now of Bangor, Me., and was known as a gentleman of rare amiability, purity, and talents. He had been in California nine years.

KETCHAM, Israel, Brooklyn, N. Y., July 22, æ. 85. He was a resident of New York and Brooklyn for the last 57 years, but born near Poughkeepsie, Dutchess Co., from whence he removed at the age of 21. In the early part of his life he enjoyed the friendship and confidence of Dewitt Clinton, Judge Spencer, and other leading men. He was born Feb. 22, 1782. Few men are possessed of more energy of character than was developed by him.

KETCHUM, George H., Cincinnati, Ohio, May 17, æ. —, of the legal firm of Ketchum & Headington, of that city. He was formerly a citizen of Versailles, Ky., and was an intelligent, agreeable gentleman — one of the most prominent lawyers of the Cincinnati bar, and a man of spotless integrity.

KILBOURN, Myron, Baltimore, Henry Co., Iowa, March 7, æ. 56, a graduate of Hamilton College. He was a pioneer of Henry Co., of which he was one of the earliest magistrates.

KILGORE, John, Esq., Cincinnati, Ohio, April —, æ. 61. He was president of the Little Miami Railroad, and is said to have been worth a million of dollars, the earnings of his own industry. He was a native of England, but had lived in Cincinnati since 1818, actively engaged in mercantile and subsequently in banking business.

KILINGLING, John, Lebanon, Warren Co., Ohio, Dec. —, æ. 50. He was penurious in habit, and although it was generally known that he was wealthy, there were but few who even guessed at a tithe of his riches. Upon opening the will, it was found that he had died leaving $750,000 worth of property in this country and in Germany. His direction for the disposition of this sum is equally novel and unsophisticated. By his will, it is provided that the money shall be deposited in a bank, the principal never to be touched, but the interest to be devoted to the education of the Protestant Germans in this state. His acquaintances were few, and like most of those who exist only for the hoarding of wealth, he formed no friendships.

KILLUM, Mrs. Rebecca, Hillsborough, N. H., ——, æ. 102. She was a native of Billerica, Mass., where she was married 81 years ago. Her husband was drafted for the army soon after. While encamped near Boston, under Gen. Washington, Mrs. K. walked from Billerica to the camp, carrying his supply of clothing. She retained her faculties till a few weeks before her death.

KIMBALL, Mrs. Abigail, Bath, N. H., July 17, æ. 63, wife of Capt. James Kimball. She was mother of 15 children. Six of her sons live in Waukesha, Wis., one in Newton, Ia., and one son and three daughters in Bath, N. H. Her husband is a farmer. They began with but little property besides their own earnings, but by a course of industry and economy' acquired, ultimately, an abundance. For many years she spun, wove, colored, cut, and made, the clothes of her family. She was ever willing and ready to lend a helping hand to the poor, and to discharge all the duties of her responsible situation. She was twice married, her first husband having been killed in the war of 1812. Her departure is mourned by a numerous circle of relatives and friends. "Her children arise up and call her blessed; her husband also, and he praiseth her."

KIMBALL, John Hazen, Barton, Vt., Feb. 21, æ. 62, eldest son of the late Judge Kimball, of that place.

KIMBALL, Samuel A., Esq., Concord, N. H., Oct. 14, æ. 77, was son of the late Dea. John Kimball. He graduated at Dartmouth College in 1806. He was once preceptor of Gilmanton Academy. He had represented Concord in the legislature, and had held the office of clerk of the Senate.

KIMBALL, Mrs. Susannah, Goffstown, N. H., —— 16, æ. 73. She was daughter of Dea. Oliver Everett, of Sharon, and sister of Hon. Otis Everett, of Boston. She left her home in 1813, and became the wife of Capt. Nathaniel Kimball, and a foster-mother of four children. Possessed of good intellectual and educational attainments, and having received from pious parents the best domestic and religious training, she was prepared to enter on the duties of these relations with hopes of great usefulness. These hopes were fully realized. For the space of 45 years, in the family, in social life, and in the church of God, it will be said of her, "She did what she could." She exhibited an eminent example of discretion, industry, benevolence, and piety. Capt. Nathaniel Kimball was born in Bradford, Mass. His parents were Lieut. Daniel, and Mrs. Elizabeth Kimball, of honorable and precious memory. His three brothers, Rev. Daniel Kimball, of Needham, Rev. David T. Kimball, of Ipswich, and Samuel Kimball, Esq., of Goffstown, have lived more than 50 years with their respective wives. The ages of the four brothers and of their sister, Mrs. Jane Gage, of Londonderry, average 77 years; all of whom are enjoying a healthful old age.

KING, Gen. Benjamin, Abington, Mass., May 27, æ. 64. In the death of this worthy citizen the whole community feel a loss. As a man of business he was extensively known, and his influence widely felt. The poor found in him a friend and helper; the sick and sorrowing, a heart to sympathize with them in their afflictions; the cheerful and happy, one to participate in their joys; the Christian and philanthropist, encouragement from his heart and hand. For many years he had been an active and influential member of the First Congregational Church, and for a succession of years was president of the Palestine Missionary Society. He was for 24 years president of the Weymouth Bank.

KING, Charles G., Esq., Boston, Mass., Feb. 26, æ. —, a man whose uniform amiability of character and kindly disposition rendered him universally popular. He was the son of the late Gedney King, and succeeded him in business; and for many years the store in Broad Street was the resort of all those who had use for mathematical instruments. He was formerly a trustee of the Massachusetts Charitable Mechanic Association, and in every position in life he fulfilled his duty, and has died respected and beloved by all who know how warm and generous a heart has ceased to beat.

KING, Col. Henry, McKinley, Marengo Co., Ala., July 13, æ. 64. He was a native of N. C., but early removed to Madison Co., Ala. Upon the breaking out of the war of 1812, he enlisted as a private in the ranks of Gen. Jackson's army, and was with the old hero at the celebrated battle of New Orleans. He returned to his home, not long, however, to enjoy retirement, for his fellow-citizens soon selected him as one of the members of the electoral ticket for the state at large during Jackson's first presidential campaign. With a well-balanced mind and a vigorous intellect, he inflicted stalwart blows upon the opposition, and did much to secure for old Hickory a glorious victory. He was nine consecutive sessions a member of the state legislature from Madison Co., and was ranked as one of its most efficient members.

KINNEY, Col. William C., Belleville, Ill., Oct. 24, æ. 43. He was a son of Ex-Lieutenant Governor Kinney. He was a native of Illinois, and served his county and state with credit in various public capacities. In his death the community in which he resided has lost a valuable citizen, and society a member whose many brilliant qualities greatly adorned it. Col. K. was a brother-in-law of Gov. Bissell.

KINNICUT, Hon. Thomas, Worcester, Mass., Jan. 22, æ. 57. He was born in Warren, R. I., Nov. 30, 1800, graduated at Brown University in 1822, studied law, and was admitted to the Worcester bar in Sept., 1825. He was frequently a representative from Worcester in the state legislature, and in 1842 was speaker of the House, and was again chosen in 1844; but his failing health compelled him to resign the chair. He was senator from Worcester Co. in 1838 and 1839. He was a trustee of the State Lunatic Hospital, treasurer of the board of education, and held many honorable trusts in his county. In 1848 he was appointed judge of probate for Worcester Co., and he held this office at the time of his death. He was a scholar of refined taste and varied acquirements, a well-read and judicious lawyer, a high-minded politician, and an upright and honorable man. He enjoyed in a high degree the confidence and esteem of his fellow-citizens.

KINSMAN, Hon. Newell, Montpelier, Vt., Dec. —, æ. 63. He was born in Springfield, N. H., June 21, 1795. He removed to Vt. about 1815, and during his life occupied many honorable public positions. He was twice elected representative in the General Assembly from the town of Barre, served two years in the state Senate from Washington Co., and was two years states's attorney for the county, fulfilling all his duties with honor to himself and to the acceptance of his constituents.

KNAPP, Daniel, Esq., Gainesville, Wyoming Co., N. Y., Sept. 13, æ. 80. He had been a resident of the county (formerly Genesee, now Wyoming) for more than half a century, served his country in the war of 1812–15, was in the celebrated sortie of Fort Erie, as adjutant under Gen. Brown, was universally known in his county, and as universally respected by all.

KNICKERBACKER, John Hale, Troy, N. Y., June 17, æ. 29, son of Abm. Knickerbacker, and Mary Ann Hale, his wife, of Schaghticoke, N. Y. The cultivation of the fine arts was to him a pleasant recreation. But he was delighted in studying the records of the past, as well in general history as in the more difficult search into family genealogies. Of these he had collected records very far back of all the families from whom he sprang — Knickerbacker, Hale, Nazro, and Coffin. His earliest ancestor in this country upon his father's side was John, Lord Berghen, who served as a captain in the Netherland navy under Count Wm. Frederic of Nassau, at the attack upon Antwerp in 1650. After the death of William second Prince of Orange, he took the name of Knickerbacker, and came to this country in 1674. He was the descendant of the celebrated Anthony van Berghen, who was created Marquis of Berghen and K. G. F. by the Emperor Charles V., and being sent an envoy to Spain by Wm. of Orange, was there cruelly sacrificed by Philip II. for his adherence to the principles of the revolution in the Netherlands. John Berghen Knickerbacker, grandson of the first emigrant to America, was born at Albany, N. Y. He purchased lands in Albany, now Rensselaer Co., in 1709, comprising the beautiful valley between the Hudson and Hoosac Rivers, called by the Algonquin Indians, who inhabited it, Schaghticoke, or Min-gling-waters, from the union of three rivers within its limits. He named it the "Valley of Peace." John Hale Knickerbacker was of the fifth descent who had lived upon the same spot. He cherished a warm regard for his ancestral home, and now lies in its family burial-place, surrounded by those he loved and venerated in life. He graduated at Union College, Schenectady, N. Y., and attended the Rensselaer Polytechnic School, where he studied natural science, preparatory to the study of medicine. He acquired a knowledge of several modern languages, but most particularly the Low Dutch, in which he corresponded with gentlemen in Holland upon the subject of his researches. He was writing, at the time of his death, an epitome of the grammar of the Dutch Language, which he had mastered under great difficulties. He was a member of the Protestant Episcopal church, and died, as he had lived, a humble Christian.

KNIGHT, Hon. Jonathan, West Pike Run township, Pa., Nov. 22, æ. —. He was elected to Congress from the 20th district in 1854, and was one of the most popular members of that body. He was never a violent partisan, and had more reputation as a civil engineer, in which profession he was quite eminent, than as a politician. He was, we believe, the chief engineer of the Baltimore and Ohio Railroad in the infancy of that enterprise, and enjoyed a wide reputation as a safe, prudent, and reliable man in all matters connected with his profession. Chosen repeatedly to positions of public trust and responsibility, he never abused the confidence of his fellow-citizens, but invariably acquitted himself with the scrupulous fidelity which marked his whole career. In his younger days he was chosen county commissioner — a compliment rarely bestowed upon one of his years. He was afterwards elected a member of the Senate of Pennsylvania — a position which he filled with eminent credit to himself, and to the entire satisfaction of his constituents. His loss will be felt in all ranks of society. His benevolence and humanity were unsurpassed in any community. Want and poverty never went from his door unrelieved. He was truly a friend to the destitute and needy. He has lived a model life; and his firmness and devotion to conscientious principle were felt and appreciated alike in the halls of legislation and in the private social circle.

KNIGHT, Sylvester, Easthampton, Mass., Nov. 22, æ. 85, father of Hon. H. G. Knight.

KNOWLTON, Thos., Willington, Conn., April 14, æ. 92. He was the son of Col. Thos. Knowlton, a distinguished officer and patriot of the revolution. Like the father, the son was a devoted friend of his country, and, though young, served in the army in the same war for a period of some 18 months.

KNOX, Rev. Dr. John, New York city, —— 8, æ. —. Dr. K. was a steadfast, gentle, moderate man; very earnest in his work; of a solemnity of manner that made his words by their very sound like the messages of another world; a pastor who mingled for so many years with his people at their homes as well as in the public worship; who appreciated and was companion of their happiness and their sorrows; and who in all these years, while he was compelled often to be in the knot of the intricacies of the web of family affairs, knew how to walk the narrow golden line of the Christian friend that never forgot to be wise while he was sympathizing. The fathers of the church were his familiar friends. He knew Livingston and Linn, and learned from their exalted school the dignity and prudence which made his 'fraternity with those by whose side he stood on the very last Sabbath of his life one of uninterrupted brotherhood. De Witt, Vermilye, Chambers, felt in their inmost heart that they possessed in their senior a counsellor who had learned of the pious dead the lesson of love to the living. There are memories connected with Dr. K.'s care and solicitude for these many years over the orphans of John G. Leake's blessed endowment, that need no human annals. Theirs is the language that is graven so that the inscription shall remain on the "new earth." It is thrilling to the heart to possess the name of a great man, while our ear has life to delight at the sound; but it is better joy to be known as a good man. This righteous and venerable man deserved this latter and this better word; and the church declares it his well-earned name.

KOWNSLAR, Franklin A., Esq., Lexington, Mo., May 11, æ. —. At a meeting of the members of the bar, and the officers of the different courts in the city of Lexington, the following resolutions were unanimously adopted :—

"Whereas our friend and brother, Franklin A. Kownslar, Esq., a member of the Lexington bar, has, in the inscrutable dispensation of an all-wise Providence, been suddenly called from the courts of earth to the bar of the supreme Judge of the universe, and whereas we, his brethren in the profession, and officers of our courts, who are left, deplore his loss, and are again led to contemplate with mournful feelings the uncertainty of life and the certainty of death, yet, amidst all of our sadness at this unlooked-for and sorrowful event, realizing, as we do, a full consciousness and recollection of the high moral character, strict integrity, exalted sense of honor, great intelligence, and legal learning of the deceased, we feel impelled, by the high respect and esteem we entertained for him in life, now in his death to give expression to the deep emotions we feel on this solemn occasion. Therefore

"*Resolved*, that in the death of Franklin A. Kownslar, Esq., the community has lost a valuable citizen, the church a consistent and useful member, society a true and virtuous man, the bar a bright ornament, and ourselves a courteous, dignified, and honorable companion and compeer."

KUYKENDAL, B. J., Benton, Mo., March 13, æ. 33. Mr. K. was a native of South Carolina, and partook of that noble and chivalrous spirit which characterizes her sons. He did his country valuable service during the war with Mexico, in the ranks of the Palmetto regiment. His health was seriously impaired by exposure in Mexico, and he never regained it. He became a citizen of Missouri about four years ago. His noble bearing and generous disposition won for him the love and respect of all who knew him.

L.

LABAGH, Rev. Peter, D. D., ——, ——, Nov. —, æ. 84. Dr. L. was born in New York city, being descended from an ancient family of that name early connected with the colonial affairs of the Dutch government. He was licensed to preach the gospel in 1796 by the Classis of Hackensack, at the same time with the late James Spencer Cannon, D. D.

LABAR, Leonard, Stroud, Pa., æ. 82. He was one of our oldest and most respected citizens, and his death is universally regretted.

LACKET, Clarence D., New York city, March —, æ. 59.

LACKET, Grenville A., New York city, March —, æ. 53.

Clarence D. Lacket, Esq., a member of the New York bar, died suddenly on Monday afternoon of congestion of the lungs. His unexpected decease so affected his brother, Grenville A. Lacket, that he was yesterday morning attacked with apoplexy and died in a few hours. The Post says, "They were most estimable men; their relations through life had been singularly close; they lived together, worked together, and died together."

LACKEY, Hon. William, Jeffersonville, Ind., April 13, mayor of the city, was an honorable man and a sincere Christian.

LA FARGE, John, Glen Cove, L. I., —— —, æ. 72. He was a native of France, and has resided in this country for upwards of 40 years. He was at St. Domingo during the massacres, and was one of the very few whites who escaped. He leaves a large estate, principally in real property, of which the hotel bearing his name forms a part. He was a heavy real estate owner in Jefferson and Lewis Cos., having purchased, a few years since, all the lands owned by Joseph Bonaparte in those counties. The ground on which the Free Academy now stands, and several lots in Lexington Avenue, were also his property. He married late in life, and leaves a widow and a large family of children. He was a man of kindly nature and agreeable manners, and will be much missed by a large circle of friends.

LAKE, Daniel, Castleton, Vt., Oct. 4, æ. 90. He was born at Woodbury, Ct., Nov. 5, 1768. His father, Gershom Lake, was one of the bold adventurers who came into the wilderness of Vermont, then called the New State, and its settlers Green Mountain Boys. Gershom Lake came to Castleton, with his wife, in 1772, leaving their son Daniel with a relative in his native town, where he remained until he was 17 years of age. He then came to Castleton to live with his parents, to comfort and support them in their pilgrimage. This duty he faithfully performed, remembering the commandment with promise. His mother lived to 97 years of age, and was kindly cherished to the last. His father died much younger. Daniel Lake married Zipporah Tracy, of Richmond, Mass. Their children were four sons and three daughters. His wife and one daughter have deceased; three sons have gone to the Western States; the other children remain in Castleton. Mr. L. was industrious and peaceful in his habits, unassuming in his manners, sedate and contemplative in company with his Christian friends. He read the Bible much for instruction, and meditated upon it to imbibe its spirit and hold communion with his Saviour, by prayer and praise, night and day. His brother, Chester Lake, died at High Forest, Min., Nov. 3, æ. 57, formerly of Castleton. His daughter, Mrs. Betsey Dwyer, died at Montgomery, Vt., May 8, 1851, æ. 48.

LAMAR, Thomas B., M. D., Macon, Ga., April 14, æ. 58, an eminent physician and urbane Christian gentleman.

LAMB, Reuben A., Jamaica Plain, Mass., Nov. 22, æ. 57. He was a native of Vermont, but removed to this vicinity about 25 years ago. He was well known in business circles as a merchant, and noted for integrity and honorable dealing. Twenty years since he became the subject of the renewing grace of God, and made a public profession of his faith; and although naturally modest and self-distrustful, his confidence in Christ never wavered. His piety was deep, mellow, and scriptural: he enjoyed religion. When the Mather Church was organized at Jamaica Plain, five

17

years ago, his was the first name on the list, and the almost hopeless enterprise leaned mainly on him; it was dear to his heart, and no man rejoiced more at its growing prosperity. Universally esteemed in society, a pillar in the church, devoted in the family, his loss will be deeply felt.

LANCASTER, Ann Terrell, Jackson, Tenn., Oct. 21, æ. 57, wife of Samuel Lancaster, Esq. She was a daughter of the venerable Capt. John Lynch, formerly of Lynchburg, Va., who died in 1842, and was descended from a long line of honorable and patriotic ancestors.

LANDRUM, George T., Lexington, Ga., Aug. 10, æ. 29, son of William and Jane Landrum, was born in Oglethorpe Co., June 14, 1829, and was the youngest brother of Rev. S. Landrum, of Macon, Ga. He graduated at the State University, at Athens, Ga., in 1851, with the second honors of his class. During his college course, he endeared himself to both students and faculty by an exhibition of qualities of head and heart which do honor to human nature. In the fall of 1851 he was admitted to the bar. It was said that so complete was his mastery of Blackstone's Commentaries, that he could easily give a correct analysis of any chapter designated. His industry and energy were great; and he was rapidly rising in wealth, position, and honor, at his death. As a lawyer, he was intelligent, successful, and enjoyed a large practice. As a man, he was generous, noble, and commanded esteem and admiration. As a friend, he was sincere, faithful, and devoted. In all the domestic relations, he was kind, genial, and self-denying.

LANDRUM, F. A., M. D., Washington, Ill., July 8, æ. 48. He was born in Louisa Co., Va., in 1809. In 1830 he commenced the practice of medicine, associated with Dr. Daniel Roberts, at Winchester, Scott Co., then quite a small village; and in 1839 came to Pike Co. and settled there, when at that time but few inroads had been made upon the domains of the free inhabitants of forest and prairie. Few men have filled a more active or useful post in society. Serving 12 years as justice of the peace, filling many other useful and honorable stations, when at that early day it required some leading character to forward the interests of the infant settlement, he seems to have been the man suited to the times — was not only a peacemaker when a difficulty arose among the settlers, but was the medical as well as the financial adviser of the community in which he lived. As a physician and a useful citizen, he was much esteemed; as a friend, he was frank and true; as a husband, kind and affectionate; and as a father, wise and indulgent; and by that untiring energy, economy, and perseverance, which characterized his whole life, had collected enough of the good things of life to leave his family a liberal competency.

LANE, Gilbert Cooke, Cornwall, Ct., Nov. 10, a graduate and afterwards tutor of Middlebury College.

LANE, Martin, Cambridgeport, Mass., Oct. 16, æ. 73, for nearly 30 years cashier of the Cambridge Bank. He was a native of Northampton, a brother of Hon. Ebenezer Lane, the former chief justice of Ohio, and was much respected for his integrity and simplicity of character. One son, Prof. Lane, of Harvard College, survives him.

LANGDON, Capt. George, Martinez, Cal., Feb. 8, æ. 56, formerly of Portsmouth, N. H. In life, he was useful and respected; in his death, happy and resigned. He was to his enemies fearless, to his friends a brother. It will be long before the native Californians forget the services he has rendered them.

LANSING, Judge Jacob, Albany, N. Y., May 20, æ. 65. He was once, and for a term of years, judge of Albany Co. His profession was that of a lawyer, and in years gone by, Judge L. was in the possession of an extended and lucrative practice.

LANSING, Louisa, Washington, D. C., Feb. 27, æ. 34. She was author of the Little Commodore, and a sister of Commodore Brese.

LARKIN, Rev. John, New York city, Dec. 18, æ. —, one of the ministers of the Roman Catholic Church of St. Francis Xavier, in New York.

LARKIN, Thomas O., San Francisco, Cal., Oct. 27, æ. 56. Mr. L. was born in Charlestown, Mass., Sept. 16, 1802. He went to California in April, 1832. He was married in 1833, on board of an American vessel, at Monterey, and his children were the first of American parentage, paternal and maternal, born upon California soil. He was appointed United States consul in 1844, to reside at Monterey, and was the first and last that ever held that appointment in this country. It is enough to say that in every respect he performed the duties of the office with advantage to his country and imperishable honor to himself. Throughout the war, which resulted in giving California to the United States, Mr. Larkin pursued a line of patriotic purpose that has crowned his name and his memory with undying honor. In the broadest sense of the expression, he was a great-hearted patriot, who loved his country and his countrymen, as was evidenced by his untiring zeal and his great-hearted generosity in the times when the test was made by which this title was earned. Such services deserved and received, through the secretary of state of the United States, the " thanks of the president for his attention, for so many years, to the cause of his country."

LARNED, George, Thompson, Ct., June 9, æ. 82, father of Prof. Larned, of Yale College.

LASCELLES, Henry A., Panama, New Grenada, Nov. 30, æ. 31, a telegraph operator to Panama Railroad Company.

LATHROP, Leopold, Madison, Wis., April 26, æ. 24, a son of Chancellor Lathrop, of the university. He was very generally known as a young man gifted with intellectual powers far above the ordinary range. He was born in Clinton, N. Y., in August, 1835. He entered the Wisconsin State University, and subsequently continued his studies at the Michigan State University, and was admitted as an attorney at 18. After practising a few months, he removed to Nebraska, and was engaged in the practice of the law there, and also edited a weekly newspaper at Florence.

LAWRENCE, Richard M., Hamburg, N. Y., May 7, æ. 76. He was a surveyor, and was an assistant to the late Martin Ryerson, who was selected by Gov. Morris, the elder, then one of the commissioners for laying out and regulating the Island of New York, in avenues and streets. Mr. L., afterwards, (also at the instance of Mr. Morris, who was then a large proprietor in St. Lawrence Co., N. Y.,) went into the Black River country as a surveyor, and at the day of his death still held a commission as deputy surveyor of the State of New Jersey. He was a firm believer in holy writ, and died as becomes a Christian.

LAYTON, John, Petersburg, Pa., Dec. 17, æ. 36. Mr. L. was prominently connected with the press of Pittsburg for many years, having commenced as clerk of the Morning Post, of which he subsequently became part owner. He was elected to the common council in 1856, and again in 1857, and labored faithfully for the interests of his constituents.

LEACOCK, James H., New Orleans, La., Aug. 22, æ. 22. He was the son of Rev. Mr. Leacock, well known and much admired and beloved in Kentucky as a clergyman and a man, and now officiating in the ministry in New Orleans. Young Mr. L. graduated at the Kentucky Military Institute, June 15, and, against the earnest solicitations of all his friends, went to New Orleans.

LEAR, Sarah Ann, Camden, Ark., Nov. 23, æ. 49. Her paternal relations were heroes of the revolution — her father, William Wright Winn, being a son of Gen. Winn, of Winnsboro', Fairfield District, S. C. While young, she emigrated to Alabama, where she was married, and where she became a member of the Presbyterian church.

LEARNED, Ebenezer, New London, Ct., Sept. 10, æ. 78. Mr. L. was a native of New London, and of course one of its oldest inhabitants. He entered Yale College when 17 years of age. Upon leaving college he commenced teaching school, pursuing, at the same time, the study of the law, the practice of which he commenced at Groton ; but he returned soon to New London, where his professional career was one of uninterrupted success, enjoying, in the mean time, the confidence and friendship of all classes of citizens. His residence and office, for half a century, were in the mansion from which his remains were taken. He retired, several years ago, from the active duties of his profession, with an ample fortune, to enjoy the society of his family and friends.

LEAVITT, Rev. Nehemiah, East Rumford, Me., —— —, æ. 85, a native of Deerfield, formerly of Raymond, N. H.

LEE, Abraham, Bath, Md., April 29, æ. 79, of wounds received by his being thrown from a horse. He was among the earliest settlers of Franklin Co., having emigrated from Kentucky in the fall of 1807, while the war whoop of the savage was yet heard in the White Water Valley, and afterwards rendered important service to the government as surveyor of the public lands.

LEE, Mrs. ——, Washington, D. C., ——, w. 90. Mrs. Lee was the widow of one of Washington's aide-de-camps, and retained a vivid recollection of revolutionary scenes. Washington "gave her away" at her marriage, and honored her with a wedding dinner at Mount Vernon.

LEE, Robert P., D. D., Montgomery, N. Y., ——, w. —. The consistory of the church say, —

"Whereas it has pleased the great Head of the church to remove from us by death our highly-esteemed pastor, the Rev. Robert P. Lee, D. D., we desire to express our high appreciation of his worth as a man, and of his services in the relation which he has sustained to us as our pastor. Therefore

"Resolved, that, with sentiments of unfeigned gratitude to God, we cherish a sense of his great goodness in allowing us for nearly 30 years to enjoy the inestimable blessing of the wise counsels, the consistent Christian example, and faithful labors of his servant whose loss we are now called to mourn. By his dignified and exemplary deportment he secured the respect, not merely of the members of his own flock, but of all who knew him, and did honor to the sacred office with which he was invested. With great fidelity and diligence he preached the doctrines of the gospel, and urged the performance of the duties which it enjoins, thereby making it manifest to the consciences of his hearers that his governing aim was to preach 'Jesus Christ, and him crucified,' as the only ground of hope to fallen men, and the principal means of promoting the sanctification of his followers. With him the religious training of the children and youth of his charge was an object of deep and abiding interest. In labors to impart to them biblical and catechetical instruction he was diligent and untiring. With mournful satisfaction we cherish the remembrance of his kind, sympathizing visits to our families in seasons of affliction, his words of counsel and consolation, his fervent prayers to God for us, and his services of pastoral fidelity and love, when we were called to follow endeared friends and kindred to the grave. Under the sorrows produced by the thought that we are to see his face and hear his voice no more, we are comforted by the firm belief that his spirit is now among the glorified in heaven, enjoying the blessed recompense secured by divine promise to the faithful servant of the Lord Jesus."

LEECH, David, Leechburg, Pa., Nov. 3, w. 69. Mr. L. was well known in the community. It may be said that he was the pioneer of internal improvements in Pennsylvania. He was one of the contractors for making the canal; and before the main line of communication between Philadelphia and Pittsburg was completed he commenced the work of transportation, and, in the face of many and great difficulties, succeeded in establishing freight lines over the entire route, thus giving to our citizens the earliest possible benefit of our great system of improvements. On the completion of the main line he perfected his arrangements, affording the advantage of complete lines both for passengers and freight, which were of essential advantage to our travelling and business community, and gave no slight impetus to the trade of Philadelphia with the west. He has been actively engaged, at different stages of his career, in different works of public improvement in Pennsylvania, apart from his connection with the main line, and exhibited the same energy and activity in all his operations.

LEHMAN, Rev. Jacob, Hellam, York Co., Pa., May 14, w. 54. He held the office of bishop in the Mennonist persuasion, and was highly esteemed, not only among those of his own denomination, but by all who had the pleasure of his acquaintance.

LEHMANOWSKI, Col. ——, Hamburg, Clark Co., Ind., —— —, w. 88, the illustrious Pole who served under Napoleon during the times of the republic and the empire. He was among the first to rally to the standard of the Little Corporal, and never betrayed his trust or his master, from the siege of Toulon to the final overthrow and exile. For his devotedness he suffered imprisonment in the loathsome dungeons of Paris, and at last exile. He was buried with Masonic honors, and while he lived could boast of being one of the officers that initiated the great Napoleon into the mysteries of that ancient and honorable order. Col. L. is widely known in the United States by his lectures on Napoleon, which he delivered four or five years ago in different parts of the country. He was an old campaigner, and, besides his vast store of information and reminiscence, was an interesting man personally. The theory of Napoleon, who "made his soldiers fight with their legs instead of their muskets," — those long forced marches by which he won such marvellous triumphs, and taught gray-haired generals the value of minutes in war, — all this was forcibly illustrated in the frame of the veteran. Those long marches had given to the sinews of his legs a prodigious power. He has frequently been known to stand upright without support, raise the calf of one leg to a right angle with the other, and in that position support a full-grown and large-sized man standing erect on the outstretched heel. He will be remembered by all who saw him as a wonderful man, physically and mentally.

LEHRE, Col. Thomas, Summerville, S. C., Dec. 28, æ. 64. He passed his life in different offices, with fidelity and devotion to duty. At the time of his decease he was president of the Charleston Savings Institution, and also a director in the Bank of the State of South Carolina. For a number of years, beginning in 1834, he was judge of the Court of Ordinary for Charleston district. He resigned this office in 1847, on account of declining health. He had represented St. Thomas and St. Dennis in both branches of the legislature, and for a period represented the city parishes in the House of Representatives.

LELAND, A. L., M. D., Detroit, Mich., ———, æ. 40. Dr. L. had been a resident of Detroit about 14 years, and had won the esteem of all who knew him by his urbane manners, his integrity of character, and his humane disposition. He was a native of Massachusetts, and graduated at Cambridge in 1838 with distinguished credit. He occupied a prominent and very enviable position in the profession to which he belonged, and would have achieved distinction and fortune had his life been spared.

LELAND, Joseph W., Esq., Saco, Me., Sept. 7, æ. 53, county attorney for many years.

LEONARD, Horatio, Esq., Raynham, Mass., ———, æ. 78. He was born in 1780, and was appointed sheriff of Bristol Co. at the age of 21 years. He held the office until 1811, when he was removed by Gov. Gerry, and Noah Claflin, Esq., of Attleboro', appointed, who held the office but one year. On the reëlection of Gov. Strong Mr. L. was reappointed sheriff, which office he continued to hold under all administrations until 1844, a period of 42 years in all, when he resigned, and Mr. Danforth received the appointment. Col. Zephaniah Leonard (father of Horatio) held the office almost half a century before his son received the appointment. They were influential and highly-respected citizens, and enjoyed the confidence and esteem of their fellow-citizens.

LESLIE, Jonathan, South Mills, N. C., Feb. 28, æ. —, a native of Scotland, but for a long time a resident of the city of Richmond. Mr. L. was a contractor on the Albemarle and Chesapeake Canal; and wherever he was known he was highly esteemed and respected for his moral worth and amiability.

LEWIS, Elijah, Roxbury, Mass., Dec. 15, æ. 83. Mr. L. was a wealthy and much respected citizen of Roxbury. He held the offices of selectman, representative, alderman, and various other official positions. He was accustomed to take very active exercise for the benefit of his health, even to the last of his life.

LEWIS, John, Frankfort, Ky., ———, æ. 75. Mr. L. was a veteran teacher. He was the author of a novel of considerable interest, entitled "A Tale of the Great Kanawha."

LEWIS, Rev. Lester, Middletown, Ct., Feb. 7, æ. 40, pastor of First Baptist Church in that place.

LEWIS, Rev. Lincoln, Upper Gilmanton, N. H., æ. —.

LEWIS, Morgan G., M. D., Buffalo, N. Y., Feb. 8.

LEWIS, Timothy, Belvidere, Ill., June 2, æ. 94. He might almost be said to be like Logan, "last of his race," as we apprehend but few men who took any part in the stirring scenes of the revolution are yet among us. He was born in Ashfield, Mass., May 24, 1764. He was brought up in Vermont, and lived there for a good portion of his life. At the age of 15 he entered the army, and was in it at the time when Arnold undertook to sell out the American army at West Point. His father furnished supplies to the army, and was drafted. The subject of our sketch, at that time a large, stout youth, was accepted in his father's stead, he having volunteered to go; so he shouldered his musket and started with the rest. He had an iron constitution, and never kept his bed from sickness a whole day until his last sickness. He was one of the iron men whom that age gave birth to, and when he died, dropped gently away, like one going to sleep.

LIBBY, Abraham, Belfast, Me., Nov. 16, æ. 83. He was one of the early settlers of Belfast, having resided there more than half a century. He was born in Rye, N. H., and learned the trade of a joiner, at Candia, in that state. At the age of 22 he removed to Montville, Me., whence he removed to Belfast in 1801. He was a man of a remarkably athletic and vigorous constitution, possessing that energy, firmness, and independence of character so characteristic of the pioneers of Maine. He took a lively interest in public affairs, and was noted for his fervent and abiding patriotism. Nurtured in the revolution, he was inflexibly devoted to the principles of Jefferson, Madison, and Jackson, and voted for every democratic president from Jefferson to Buchanan. He died, as he had lived, an honest man, a good citizen, a faithful friend, and an affectionate father.

LINCOLN, Deborah T., Boston, Mass., March 25, æ. 87, relict of the late Charles Lincoln, Esq., formerly of Hingham, Mass. She was highly respected in life, — in death affectionately remembered.

LINCOLN, Henry S., New York city, Dec. 2, æ. 33. Mr. L. was a graduate of Union College, Schenectady, where his studious habits, refined scholastic taste, integrity of character, and gentlemanly bearing, secured for him that universal respect and esteem which followed him into after life. He chose the law for his vocation, the study of which he commenced at Saratoga Springs. But, notwithstanding his strong predilection for the legal profession, his ardent love for medical science enabled him, by industry, perseverance, and economy, to graduate as a member of the medical profession. Determining at this point, in accordance with his original intention, to devote himself entirely to the practice of law, he removed to the city of New York, where, in the midst of the most encouraging success, and brilliant prospects, he was suddenly arrested by disease, and called to part with all that was dear to him on earth.

LINCOLN, Capt. Jacob, Eastport, Me., March 14, æ. 91. He was born in Hingham, Mass., March 19, 1767. His wife died in 1840, at the age of 70, and he was again married to a lady who survives him, as does one brother, upwards of 80, at Hingham, and a sister, aged 94, at Cohasset, Mass. He also leaves the legacy of his good name to a numerous body of descendants and connections. He was clerk of the first town meeting in Eastport, held May 11, 1798.

LINDSEY, Keziah, Norridgewock, Me., Feb. 16, æ. 96. She was one of the first settlers of the town, having lived on the same farm 75 years, and been a member of the Congregational church 60 years.

LINDSEY, Mrs. Lucy, Lynn, Mass., June 19, æ. 68, widow of the late Rev. John Lindsey.

LINSLEY, Mrs. P. H., Greenwich, Ct., Jan. 20, æ. 75, wife of Rev. Dr. Linsley, formerly pastor of the South Church, Hartford, Ct., and also of Park Street Church, Boston, Mass. The following extract is from the sermon preached at her funeral by Rev. Dr. Hawes: "I am not accustomed to eulogize the dead, and were I disposed to do so, I should feel restrained, on the present occasion, by the known wishes of the deceased. But it is due to the grace of God, which made her what she was, and has now, I doubt not, taken her to her home in heaven, to pay a passing tribute to her memory — to speak of her piety and usefulness as a Christian; of her cheerful trust in the Saviour; of her tender, untiring interest in the welfare of others; of her patience in suffering, and her peace and hope in death. In these particulars she deserves to be held up as an example of rare excellence, and worthy of the imitation of all who knew her. Mrs. L. was born in Bennington, Vt., in 1784, and was the youngest of seven children, all of whom are now deceased. It tells well for the Christian training which these children received from their devotedly pious parents, and for the faithfulness of God to his covenant promises, that of their children, numbering 20 or more, and now in the midst of life, all, or nearly all, are hopefully Christians, and of the highest respectability. Six of them are in professional life, and four are ministers of the gospel. At the age of four, Mrs. L. lost her mother, and at 16, her father. Left thus an orphan, she was placed under the guardianship of Gov. Tichenor, who, at her own request, sent her to the then distinguished school for young ladies, under the care of Miss Pierce, in Litchfield. She there received a thorough education, which, with other favorable influences operating to develop and establish her character, fitted her to fill, with dignity and usefulness, the different stations she was subsequently called to occupy. Naturally gay, buoyant in her spirits, and fond of the attentions and ways of the world, it required the discipline of severe trials and afflictions to teach her the true end of life, to bow her will to God, and bring her to choose Christ in faith and love, as her Saviour and her all. This discipline, with the attending influences of God's Spirit, was effectual. She gave herself to her Redeemer, and in 1812 made a public profession of religion, which she continued to adorn by a living piety and a growing meetness for heaven, till the end of her course on earth. She possessed a mind naturally active and vigorous, well balanced and well cultivated; her temper was uncommonly frank, affectionate, and cheerful; her heart alive to every social feeling and every benevolent impulse; her sense of duty clear and discriminating, and eminently tender and active; ever affectionately regardful of the welfare of others, she never seemed happier than when making them happy; all crowned with a warm, devoted spirit of piety — these were the prominent traits of her character, and combined as they were, in her case, in just proportion and harmony, they formed her to be esteemed and loved by all who knew her, and to exert a decided and useful influence in every station in which she was called to act. She had a strongly marked character — a character that was felt, and felt for good, by all with whom she had much intercourse. Her religion was heartfelt and devoted, a living principle of feeling and action, of light and peace and salvation; and like a comely garment, it sat easily and gracefully about her. She loved her Bible, and she loved prayer; and I have seldom known a person who had a better acquaintance with the truth and spirit of the Scriptures, or was more careful to apply them to the practical concerns of life. When good was to be done, she always had a heart and a hand ready to bear a part in doing it; and many, very many, in different parts of the land where she has resided, when they hear of her death, will be reminded of impulses to good which they received from her conversation, her example, and her prayers, and they will all gratefully cherish her memory now that she is gone. When, some months ago, the sad accident occurred, if so we may call it, which confined her to her room to go out no more, she regarded it as a monition that the time of her departure was near. It gave her no uneasiness, no alarm; she looked to the end with calmness and unwavering Christian hope. "I dread dying," she said, "but am not afraid to be dead."

LINTON, Nathan, Wilmington, O., Feb. 11, æ. 81. He was born on the banks of the Delaware River, Bucks Co., Penn., Jan. 17, 1778, and with his father's family emigrated thence to Ohio, in 1802. The family stopped first at Waynesville, Warren Co., then a place of considerable note. In 1804, he raised his first crop in the limits of what is now Clinton Co., and has, from that time to this, steadily cultivated the same lands. In 1805, his father's family moved into the hewed log house, which is still standing in a dilapidated condition on the home farm. He commenced his career as a surveyor, in Ohio, in 1803. He married Rachel Smith, who then resided on Walnut Creek, in Highland Co., Jan. 31, 1806, and in 1807, moved his young bride into a log cabin, which stood upon the same ground since occupied by his residence. During the summer of that year, while absent on a surveying excursion, a fearful tornado passed over his residence, unroofing, and blowing large forest trees upon the cabin, his wife, all alone, taking shelter under the puncheon floor, and under the bed, seemingly the only place of safety she could have found. When the county was organized, in 1810, he was appointed surveyor, which office he held for a period of about 20 years, when he declined a reappointment. From that time to the day of his death, he held various positions of trust and confidence.

LIPPITT, Rev. Edward, Dudley, Mass., June 23, æ. 64. He was born in Cranston, R. I., and was converted in the autumn of 1821, while residing at Killingly, Ct. At a quarterly conference of the New London District, held in Hebron, June, 1823, he was licensed as a local preacher; this relation he sustained till the time of his death. At a session of the New England conference held in Springfield, May, 1831, he was ordained as a deacon by Bishop Hedding. He was a man of strong mind and firm purpose, untiring in his efforts to promote the cause of Christ and the interests of the church. As a husband and father, kind and affectionate; as a citizen, active and useful. Though suddenly prostrated with fever, he was fully prepared for the great change which awaited him. His last hours were marked with the greatest triumph.

LISON, James S., M. D., New York city, Dec. 24, æ. 51. Few men have exhibited in life a more devoted example of true Christian character; none have been in death more deeply lamented. Fully relying on the atoning merits of his Saviour, he quietly breathed his last in the happy expectation of a glorious immortality beyond the grave.

LITCHFIELD, John H., Porto Cabello, Feb. —, æ. —, American consul at Porto Cabello, after three days' illness of paralysis.

LITTELL, Samuel, West township, Columbiana Co., Ohio, Feb. 7, æ. 79. He was a native of Fayette Co., Penn., where he lived until 1838, when he removed to Wayne Co., Ohio, and resided there until about a year before his decease, when the infirmity of age induced him to sell his property, and remove to a point where he could enjoy the society, and almost daily intercourse, of eight of his ten children. Mr. L. was a man of strong mind, a great reader, a deep thinker, a close and profound reasoner, with a mind fully stored, and a memory tenacious enough to render available and pleasing the knowledge gained through so many years. He wrote and spoke with clearness and perspicuity, and in this exercise he delighted. He published much — taking an active part in all the exciting subjects of his day, and especially in favor of the temperance reformation. He was a firm believer in the Christian religion, an Old Side Baptist by profession; and this profession he honored and adorned by a long life, so devoted to morality and religion, that nearly all his descendants, who have arrived at adult age, are children of the covenant.

LIVESAY, Rev. Joshua, Suffolk, Va., Aug. —, æ. —.

LIVINGSTON, Hon. Robert, Lisbon, N. Y., Nov. 26, æ. 90. He came to the town of Lisbon in 1803, located himself on a farm, about a mile below Galloupville, and resided on it until his death. He was appointed one of the judges of the Court of Common Pleas of St. Lawrence Co., in 1810, and held the office until 1826. He was a justice of the peace in that town about 20 years, and was several times elected supervisor of it. He discharged the duties of those offices with unquestioned integrity, eminent good sense, and always to the satisfaction of the public.

LLOYD, Aaron, Waterford, Pa., July 6, æ. 84. He was born in Essex Co., N. J., and emigrated to Erie Co., Pa., in July, 1815, where he resided until his death. He was a lover of his country and her institutions, and in the last war with England, served his country's cause in the army 18 months, and was in the battles of Chippewa and Lundy's Lane.

LOGAN, Judge William, Succasunna, Morris Co., N. Y., Nov. 27, æ. —, a member of the House of Assembly for three terms.

LONGSTREET, Jas. C., Calhoun, Ga., July 11, æ. —. Col. L. was a young man of splendid natural talents, and an elegantly cultivated mind. He had attained an eminence in his profession which rendered him an ornament to the bar and an honor to his country. In the discharge of his official duties, he displayed that ability and fidelity which proved him admirably suited to the task assigned him. Those with whom he was cast socially esteemed him most highly on account of his amiability, intelligence, and gentlemanly bearing.

*

LOOMIS, Earl, M. D., Oneida, Madison Co., N. Y., June —, æ. 63. He was a partner in the practice of medicine with Dr. J. W. Hamer, late of Skippackville, Montgomery Co.

LOOMIS, Mrs. Sarah G., Bennington, Vt., Oct. 21, æ. 67. In a community where Mrs. L. has been so widely known and loved, an extended notice of her character is not necessary. The style in which she was the priceless ornament of a meek and quiet spirit, so comely upon her, and which she seemed never to put off, will not soon be forgotten; and it is believed that the fragrant remembrance of her intelligent fidelity in her domestic and social relations, her unassuming but practical benevolence, her humble confidence in Christ, and her steadfast interest in his blessed cause, will long refresh the hearts of surviving friends.

LOOMIS, Gustavus H., M. D., Montpelier, Vt., May 22, æ. 41, at the residence of Hon. John Spalding. He was eldest son of the late Hon. Jeduthun Loomis, of Montpelier.

LORAS, Rt. Rev. Matthias, Dubuque, Iowa, Feb. 19, æ. 66. The bishop was born in Lyons, France, in May, 1791. He was in the sacred ministry 43 years, 15 as the president of a college in France, and 28 in this country, eight of which were in the service of the church at Mobile, and 20 in Dubuque as the bishop of the diocese. Few men have been more loved and respected by the community at large than he. His life was not only a useful, but an eventful one, and closely allied with the early history of Dubuque.

LORD, Jeremiah, Kennebunk, Me., Nov. 28, æ. 75. In 1805, Mr. L., while a seaman on board a Kennebunk ship called the Olive Branch, bound from Nantes to Cadiz, was impressed on board an English frigate of 32 guns, belonging to the fleet under Lord Nelson, then stationed off Cadiz, waiting for the French and Spanish fleets to put to sea. Oct. 21, 1805, was fought the renowned naval battle of Trafalgar. As no ship of less than 64 guns was admitted in the line of battle, the duty of this frigate at the time was to assist disabled ships. After the action was over, this vessel, being uninjured and a rapid sailer, was detailed from the fleet to convey to England news of the victory and death of Lord Nelson. A few days after the frigate arrived at Plymouth, the American consul there released Mr. Lord from his imprisonment of nine weeks and two days, and he was returned to the ship from which he was originally taken. Consequently Mr. L. was a spectator and participator in this great naval engagement, although not actually in a station of much danger. The noise of the battle and the horrid sights which he witnessed on board some of the disabled ships, often haunted his memory. As a husband, father, and neighbor, he was kind and obliging; as a citizen, he was esteemed, having been one of the selectmen of Kennebunk for seven successive years, and in 1833 was a member of the state legislature.

LORD, Rev. John, Portland, Me., Aug. 2, æ. 67.

LORING, Ellis G., Boston, Mass., May 24, æ. 52. Many just and graceful tributes to the memory of the late Ellis Gray Loring have been elicited from various quarters. but none more felicitous than that by Wm. Lloyd Garrison, in remarks before the anti-slavery convention. Long intimate with Mr. L. and identified in the same great cause, no one can more thoroughly appreciate his excellence of character than Mr. Garrison. After describing Mr. L.'s early and constant association with the friends of the slave, Mr. Garrison concludes as follows: "Our friend risked, it will be remembered, his professional success in thus early espousing the anti-slavery cause; he risked his social standing, which was one of great importance to himself; but he was willing to risk every thing — fortune, professional fame, success, reputation, life itself. He was eminently conscientious, and that made him morally courageous and independent; and wherever he felt that duty required him to stand, he had it in his nature to plant his feet, let the consequences be what they might. Mr. L. set a noble example, as a lawyer, in opposition to the proscriptive and hateful spirit of colorphobia, which still prevails so extensively in our land. I believe he was the first lawyer who ever took a colored boy into his office, in order to train him up to the profession of the law. He did so, and with a resolute purpose, though there were many to laugh and sneer; and we have now, among the lawyers of Boston, that same colored boy, grown to full manhood, occupying a respectable position, and pursuing daily his professional avocation in the courts, in the person of Robert Morris, Esq. Mr. L. also distinguished himself by his legal ability in the celebrated case of the slave girl Med, which came up in the Supreme Court of this state many years ago, before Judge Shaw, whereby we obtained the decision that a slave, having been brought into Massachusetts by his or her pretended owner, hereby became free. Mr. President, we are all mortal — all steadily on the march to the spirit-world. Our days are numbered, and short at the longest. 'The line is forming on the other side.' How much work remains to be done! Let us who are left behind endeavor to be all the more zealous, active, determined, in prosecuting the noblest cause that can challenge human sympathy and effort, and thus be instrumental, under God, in putting an end to the most dreadful system of oppression the world has ever known. I stand here to bless the memory of Ellis Gray Loring — to acknowledge my deep indebtedness to him for his early kindness, efficient coöperation, and lasting friendship. I stand here, also, to express my heartfelt sympathy for his beloved wife and almost idolized daughter, whose sorrow I would share and alleviate. Let me say, in justice to Mrs. L., and as an act of grateful remembrance, that she was at least as early in the field in behalf of the oppressed as her lamented husband. In this cause, from the start, twain were one — with but one heart, one pulsation, ever seeing eye to eye, and working steadily together. Let no one infer, from the fact that for a few years past he has been comparatively out of sight, that Mr. L. had lost his interest in the anti-slavery cause; for that he never lost. But, after the cheering extension of the cause, and its friends had become multitudinous, he followed his natural bent, which was always for retirement, and not for publicity. Enough that when there were few to plead for those in bondage, — in spite of his taste and temperament, his social position and professional respectability, — in the darkest and stormiest period of our terrible struggle, he was ready for public exposure and popular contumely, for self-denying labor and heroic enterprise, gracefully withdrawing himself from observation only as others advanced, yet keeping the flame of his philanthropy as pure and bright as in the beginning."

LOUNSBERRY, John S., M. D., Philadelphia, Pa., Dec. 2, æ. 37.

LOVELACE, Rev. Thomas, Pleasant Gap, Pittsylvania Co., Va., Nov. 27, æ. 64. He was a member of the primitive Baptist church from early life to the time of his death, and was an active and laborious preacher of the gospel for more than thirty years, occupying a prominent and influential position in the denomination. The whole course of his life was marked by a stern integrity, a high sense of duty, and inflexible purpose; indeed, he combined those traits of character which make a man an upright and useful citizen, confining his labors chiefly to the church of which he was a member.

LOVELL, Rev. Stephen, Boston, Mass., Aug. 4, æ. 59, assistant editor of the Boston Olive Branch. He became converted when 18 years old, and subsequently entered the ministry of the Methodist denomination, in which he labored zealously for 30 years. His devotion to whatever can make men better; his integrity, industry, and piety; his fine qualities as a man, citizen, and neighbor; his virtues as a husband, father, and friend; his heroic endurance of physical pain; his willingness and desire to die, made him a rare man — a rare Christian.

LOVET, Bartholomew, Jefferson, Mo., June 14, æ. 93. He was born in Thomaston, in 1765, about 11 years before the declaration of independence of the United States. At the age of 27, he was baptized, with his wife, then 22 years of age, by Elder Andrew Fuller, of Warren. Two brothers and two sisters of the deceased survive, who are very aged.

LOWE, Judge Wm., Frederick, Md., Aug. 7, æ. 69. He was an estimable man and citizen, and had been a judge of the Orphans' Court for upwards of six years, in which position he did his duty as one of the guardians and protectors of the widow and the orphan. He was a resident of Frederick twenty odd years, during which time he served in various capacities, and by his kindness of heart and upright conduct made many friends.

LUCAS, Col. Edward, Harper's Ferry, Va., March 4, æ. —, paymaster of the Harper's Ferry armory. He was an officer of the war of 1812, and had been a member of the Virginia legislature and Congress.

LUDLOW, Capt. Charles S., Dec. 28, æ. 50. He died suddenly at sea, during a gale, on board Vanderbilt steamer Ariel. "It was now blowing furiously; and the immense waves, as they leaped upwards, broke like waterspouts around the ship, or, combing, fell like immense breakers upon the ocean beach. The forward part of the wheel houses on each side were broken in, and the round houses were both washed away. At 11 A. M. the ship settled deeply in the trough of the swell, and a tremendous sea broke upon the forward deck. Capt. Ludlow,. at the instant, was cautioned by the second mate, who was standing near him, to 'look out;' but he had scarcely spoken the words when all were submerged apparently ten feet under water. Both the first and second mates were badly injured; and for the instant it was thought that the steamer had foundered. The main hatch was broken in by the sea, and many tons of water went below. Capt. L. was knocked down, and the heavy drag, composed of plank and timbers, struck him in the side. He was found lying upon his back, with his cap washed off, his eyes closed, and apparently insensible. In this condition he was conveyed to his room. He revived sufficiently to speak a few words, the last of which were, 'Tell the commodore I died at the post of duty.' He then sunk back, and expired. The injury was apparently on the left side, two or three of the ribs being broken, and the fragments penetrating the heart."

LUDWIG, Col. Jacob, Waldoboro', Mo., Nov. 3, æ. 82. Col. L. was of German descent. His father, Capt. Jacob Ludwig, was one of the German emigrants who settled at Waldoboro' in 1748, was an orderly sergeant in the French and Indian wars, commanded a company in the war of the revolution, and was the first representative from Waldoboro' to the General Court of Massachusetts. Col. L. had few early advantages of education, but, possessing a strong and active mind, he improved every opportunity to acquire knowledge. He frequently represented Waldoboro' both in the legislature of Massachusetts and of Maine. He was one of the selectmen of the town for more than a quarter of a century, and a deputy sheriff more than thirty years.

LUSK, James, Jefferson, Mo., March 5, æ. 37. He was long connected with the press of Missouri, and a prominent actor in the political scenes of the state. He was public printer for a number of years. In his private relations he was a courteous, dignified gentleman, and highly esteemed by a large circle of acquaintances and friends.

LUTTERLOH, Gen. Charles, Chatham Co., N. C., Aug. 27, æ. 74. He volunteered in the war of 1812 as a private, but was very soon promoted to the rank of first lieutenant, which rank he held and continued in the service until peace was declared, since which time he devoted his attention to agricultural pursuits.

LUTTON, Rev. Robert, Philadelphia, Pa., Dec. 5, æ. 67.

LYMAN, Mrs. Rhoda Huntington, Arcade, Wyoming Co., N. Y., June 22, æ. 91, relict of the late Rev. William Lyman, D. D. Mrs. L. was born at Lebanon, Ct., in 1767, where she resided during the revolutionary war, with the stirring incidents of which she was familiar, Lebanon being for some time head-quarters for Lafayette and others. For over 30 years her husband was pastor of the Congregational church in Millington Society, East Haddam, Ct., she sharing his labors. In 1825-6 they removed to Western New York, and in 1827 to Arcade, where Dr. L. died, June 5, 1833, æ. 69, and where Mrs. L. has since resided, some of her children being settled there. She was sister of Rev. Dan Huntington, of Hadley, Mass., and aunt of Rev. Prof. F. D. Huntington, of Harvard University. For her superior social and intellectual endowments, her cultivated mind and manners, and for her many Christian precepts and examples, she will long be remembered. The temperance, anti-slavery, anti-sectarian, and moral reforms found in her a warm friend. In her last days, as always, but with increased earnestness, she exhorted all around her to "live for Christ," while she longed to depart and be with him. The close of life with her was intelligently peaceful; and her remains lie beside her husband's in a beautiful grove in the Arcade Rural Cemetery. Dr. L. was a native of Lebanon, Ct., a graduate of Yale College, class of 1787, and soon after became pastor of the Congregational church in Millington Society, East Haddam, Ct., where he labored for over 30 years, when he removed to Western New York, and in 1827 to Arcade. He was a man of more than ordinary mental force and originality. His conversational and discursive powers are seldom surpassed; and hence, on marriage, ordination, funeral, and like occasions, he was a general favorite. Although he died soon after the opening of the temperance and anti-slavery discussions of this century, yet he had already become fully enlisted in these reforms. His sympathies were at once with the right; and long will his memory be cherished by his numerous family and other friends.

LYON, Robert, New York, March 10, æ. 49. Mr. L. was the second son of a respectable London tradesman, named Wolfe Lyon, and was born in that city, Jan. 15, 1810. He came to America in 1844, and established an umbrella manufactory, which did not succeed; and a beloved brother lost his life, which he sacrificed rather than lose property intrusted to his care at the fire in San Francisco in 1851. He subsequently turned his attention to journalism, and established the Asmonean, as a Jewish organ, Oct. 26, 1849. It is still in existence as a weekly paper. He also edited the New York Mercantile Journal. Of his public career and private life the Asmonean says, "As a public man, Robert Lyon was known to and honored with the confidence of Henry Clay, Gen. Cass, and Daniel Webster. His high standing among the leaders of the press enabled him on many occasions to render useful service to the community, while at all times he was ready to write, speak, and act in the cause of charity, of freedom, of mental and moral progress. In private life, exemplary as a husband and father, abstemious in his habits, simple in his tastes, firm in his friendships, he was justly endeared to an extensive circle of friends.

M.

MABRY, Lucine, M. D., Anderson District, S. C., June 3, æ. 23. Dr. M. graduated at the Jefferson Medical College, Philadelphia, and commenced the arduous duties of his profession in the village of Mount Carmel.

MACAULAY, John P., M. D., San Francisco, Cal., —— —, æ. —. The medical profession of San Francisco, at a public meeting, say of him, —

"*Resolved*, that in his death we recognize a loss, to the members of our local profession, of a zealous and devoted brother; to his patients, of a kind and conscientious friend and physician; and to those connected with him by ties of consanguinity, of a relative, whose intellectual, moral, and social character entitled him to their warmest affections, and of whose professional career they might well be proud."

MACKAY, Francis L., Calcutta, Hindostan, July 8, æ. 21. He was the second son of Robert C. Mackay, Esq., one of the most respected and influential merchants of Boston. He early evinced a taste for business. Though but 21 years of age, his integrity had endeared him, not only to his many friends at home, but to his countrymen and associates at Calcutta.

MACKAY, Andrew J., Council Bluffs, Iowa, Aug. —, æ. —. He was a young man of fine attainments, a ready and graceful writer, a fluent speaker, and a sound thinker. He left Council Bluffs in Dec., 1855, after which time he was employed upon the Madison (Wis.) Argus and Democrat, as local editor.

MACKEY, Rev. E. D., Princess Anne, Md., Sept. 6, æ. —. He was a remarkable man. The accomplishments of the gentleman so blended with the graces of a Christian that humanity was ennobled in his person, and religion seemed to have a natural home in his heart. Mr. M. was an intelligent Christian. His intellectual ability, and his proficiency in many branches of education, are shown in the history of his life while a youthful scholar in a high school, a student in the College of New Jersey, and a theological student in the seminary at Princeton. He graduated at the college in Princeton with the highest honor in one of the largest classes that ever went out from the walls of that venerable institution. But his soul was devoted to God, and his mental energies were directed towards the advancement of Christ's kingdom. Perhaps no one ever left the seminary who was more beloved and respected by the professors, or had a higher reputation among his classmates for deep, sincere, humble piety, or proficiency in theological science, than Mr. M.

MACKIE, Peter, M. D., Wareham, Mass., March 23, æ. 72.

MACPHERSON, John B., Gettysburg, Ga., ——— ——, æ. 69, for 40 years the cashier of the Bank of Gettysburg.

MADDUX, Edward, ———, Ky., May 21, æ. 48, a native of Farquhar Co., Va. He was a lieutenant in the Missouri volunteers in the Florida war, and was in the battle of Okechobee. He was also a soldier in the Mexican war. He was a man of fine intellect and generous impulses.

MAGILL, James, Stone Valley, Huntingdon Co., Pa., Oct. 17, æ. 71, father of the Rev. Wm. C. Magill, deceased.

MAGOON, Stephen S., New Hampton, N. H., Aug. 14, æ. 76. Long in business, he lived and died an honest man, and highly respected by the entire community.

MAGRUDER, John T., near the camp of the 6th column Utah forces, on the Big Blue River, June 28, æ. 22, son of A. Magruder, Esq., of Washington city, formerly of Charlottesville, Va. Scarcely a year ago Lieut. M. left the Military Academy as a graduate to enter the cavalry arm of the service. During the short time he was connected with the army he proved himself inferior to no young officer in the zeal and ability with which he discharged his duties, and full worthy of the confidence reposed in him by his superiors in rank.

MAGUIRE, Edward C., D. D., Fredericksburg, Va., Oct. 8, for nearly half a century pastor of St. George's Church, of that city. A clergyman who has been a member of the diocese of Virginia all his life speaks of the deceased as "a man freer from faults than any one he ever knew."

MAHARREY, William H., Philadelphia, Pa., Aug. 29, was a native of Augusta, Ga., and highly esteemed for his manly character, his business capacity, his devoted friendship, and his generous and charitable deeds. He was for many years a worthy and efficient member of the city council; at one time sheriff of Richmond Co.; and in all his public and private relations a worthy and a true man.

MAIDLOW, Edmund, Scott township, Ill., Oct. 23, æ. 50. He filled several posts of public trust and honor, with credit to himself and to the entire satisfaction of the public. He was several years county commissioner, superintended the building of the court house, and was president of the Agricultural and Horticultural Society.

MAKEPEACE, Dea. Lysander, Norton, Mass., Jan. 24, æ. 87 yrs. 5 mos. He was born in Norton, Aug. 22, 1771. His paternal ancestor in the fourth remove, Thomas Makepeace, came from England to Dorchester in 1635, and died there in 1667. He was the ancestor of all the Makepeaces in America. The subject of this notice was chosen deacon of the Congregational church in Norton, April 1, 1803. At one time he was largely engaged in the manufacture of cotton fabrics, and for many years was one of the most prominent and useful citizens of his native town, having filled many responsible places with credit.

MALLERY, Rev. S. S., Willington, Conn., March 12, æ. 58. Mr. M. was at Willington attending revival meetings, and laid down his work with his harness on.

MALTBIE, Rev. E. D., ———, ———, ———, æ. ——. The presbytery with which he was connected express the feeling "that in the death of their brother they sustain a great loss — the loss of one who was valiant for the truth and for the purity and order of the church of Christ; at the same time one of deep, intelligent, and productive piety; one who had greatly endeared himself to his brethren as a judicious counsellor, a kind associate, and a steadfast friend; one, too, who was greatly respected, and exerted the happiest influence in the several places where he was successively located, and whose loss will be especially felt in the community where his last years were spent, and where his efforts were unwearied in devising and furthering so many works of charity and piety.'

MANDEVILLE, Henry, D. D., Mobile, Ala., Oct. 2, æ. 53. Dr. M. was born in the village of Kinderhook, N. Y., in 1804, and became a member of Christ's church at the age of 16. He graduated at Union College in 1826, and immediately after entered the Theological Seminary at New Brunswick, N. J. He was first called to a country church near Newburg, N. Y. God blessed his labors, and the church was built up, established, and refreshed by an extensive revival. He went to Geneva, and there organized and built the Dutch Reformed church. His labors were appreciated by the people and blessed of God. After three years' residence and labor in Geneva, his reputation as a scholar and preacher began to extend. The church of Dr. Bethune, at Utica, having become vacant, without ever having heard him preach, he was invited by its members to supply the vacancy. The confidence of the church and congregation in his ability, learning, eloquence, and piety was not disappointed or misplaced. The literary acquirements of Dr. M., the purity of his style, the impressiveness of his delivery, and his reputation as a pulpit orator, were now known, appreciated, and recognized. He was called to fill the chair of professor of elocution in Hamilton College, New York. He discharged the duties of this responsible office faithfully, profitably, and acceptably for eight years. Having written a work on Elocution, and prepared for our colleges and academies other books that have been extensively used and approved, he went temporarily to Albany to superintend their publication. While there he was invited to take charge of a Presbyterian church, his connection heretofore having been with the Dutch Reformed church. His anxiety to preach the unsearchable riches of Christ, to sound the gospel trumpet, and call sinners to repentance, induced him to resign the professor's chair, and assume again the pastor's duties and responsibilities. His labors in Albany were owned of God, and the church was blessed with a revival. At this time he became identified with the great temperance reform movement that then agitated New York. He was conservative in his sentiments, and contributed by his productions to the great moral revolution that has blessed both church and state by the change it has wrought in the habits and feelings of the people. In the fall of 1852 the health of Mrs. M. induced him to seek a more genial clime; and he was invited to fill the pulpit of this church, that was then temporarily vacant. He remained with us during that winter and spring, and so completely won the confidence and affection of the members and congregation that when the pulpit was subsequently vacated he was invited with singular unanimity to return and become their pastor. He accepted the invitation; and since Nov., 1854, and up to the time of his death, he labored with us faithfully and efficiently. As a preacher, he had few superiors. He was instructive, impressive, and faithful. He invested every theme he discussed with new and striking charms. His sermons were always suggestive. He addressed the understanding of his hearers rather than their fears. He seldom presented the terrors of the law. He left Sinai in its awful grandeur for Calvary with its bleeding Victim.

MANNY, John H., West Rockford, Ill., —— ——, æ. —, inventor of the famous reaping machine. A local paper says, "The name and fame of John H. Manny is written and re-written with each revolving season upon the whole broad surface of our prairie country."

MANSFIELD, Joseph, Lynnfield, Mass., ——, æ. —. Mr. M. descended from a family remarkable for their longevity. His father, Mr. Andrew Mansfield, died at the age of 92 years, who was the eldest brother of a family of three brothers and six sisters, making a family of nine, whose ages at the time of their deaths were as follows: Sarah, 72 years; Mary, 83; Andrew, (mentioned above), 92; Joseph, 77; Hannah, 81; Elizabeth, 79; Rebecca, 74; Rachel, 64; Timothy, 89. They were all married and had 51 children, viz., 29 sons, and 22 daughters.

MANSFIELD, Rev. Z. H., Norwich, Ct., April 16, æ. 47.

MARCH, Lieut. J. Howard, Dec. 21, æ. —, on board storeship Relief, during the passage from Aspinwall to New York.

MARDEN, Jonathan, M. D., Quincy, Mass., March 3, æ. 54. His superior intelligence, his clear perceptions of truth and duty, and his steady, fearless, and manful performance of duty at all costs and hazards, his love of sound doctrine, and of the order and purity of the gospel, were traits of commanding prominence in his character and life, which made him endeared and useful while he lived, and render it forever true of him, that "though dead he yet speaketh."

MARIM, Charles, Esq., Leipsic, Kent Co., Delaware, March 26, æ. 54, for many years he occupied a high standing as a public man. In early life he was several times successively returned to the legislature, and always occupied a leading position in that body. As one of the founders of the Delaware free school system, his memory merited the gratitude as well as the high regard of all the friends of popular education. He occupied the honorable office of secretary of state during the term of Gov. Comegys, and was also the secretary of the convention, which met at Dover in 1852, to frame a new constitution for the state. These important offices he filled with ability. He was a law student of Hon. J. M. Clayton, but being possessed of an ample patrimony, soon after his admission to the bar, he retired from the field, where his talents might have placed him in the first rank of his profession, and for many years occupied the beautiful farm, "Chipping Norton," which descended to him from his ancestors. Much of his time was devoted to literature, and few men of his opportunities have acquired greater facility in writing, or could clothe their thoughts in more beautiful language, than he. His character was eminently social; fond of his friends, — they idolized him, — in his palmy days he loved to have them about him, and many an hour has been happily spent in listening to his lively and agreeable conversation, abounding always in humorous sallies. Though a humorist, he had his times of serious meditation. A true believer in the Christian faith, his profession of love to the Saviour of mankind was pure, and without the semblance of hypocrisy he acknowledged his sinfulness.

MARKHAM, James B., M. D., Somerville, Dallas Co., Ala., Dec. 12, w. 48.

MARKHAM, Rev. Robert A., Somerville, Dallas Co., Ala., Dec. 19, w. 28; both brothers to John G. Markham, editor of the Paulding (Miss.) Clarion.

MARKS, Gen. William, Beaver, Pa., April 10, w. 78. He was one of the oldest inhabitants in Western Pennsylvania. His father emigrated to this country about 1785. Gen. M. settled on the south side of the Monongahela River, then almost a wilderness and for some years afterwards subjected severely to the bloody incursions of the Pawnee and other hostile tribes of Indians. Notwithstanding the limited advantages he enjoyed for education, he early made himself conspicuous as one of the most able and successful politicians in Pennsylvania. He entered the House, a representative, about 1810, and continued until 1820, when he was elected to the Senate, of which body he was elected speaker in 1821, and over which he continued to preside until 1827, when he was elected to the United States Senate, in which he served until 1833, thus making an unbroken period of political service of 23 years. During this time he was the contemporary and friend of Samuel Sitgreaves, John Sergeant, Walter Forward, Abner Lacock, Richard Coulter, William Wilkins, and many other statesmen of power in the commonwealth. Of his contemporaries and compeers, the great and venerable Senator from Alleghany alone survives him, and may his honored life be yet long spared. In the Senate of the United States he served with Calhoun, Webster, Benton, Berrien, Hayne, Van Buren, and others whose names are honored in the land. During his term he was the chairman of the committees on agriculture, and upon engrossed bills, and a member of the committee on military affairs. He was distinguished as a hard-working member, and when he participated in debate, which was seldom, he was always calm, courteous, and brief, and neither in debate nor as presiding officer, did he ever offend, or receive offence, from any fellow member. He entered political life during the administration of Thomas Jefferson. He was a democrat of the old school, and in 1812 was selected by the democratic caucus to move, in the Pennsylvania legislature, the resolutions supporting the administration of Mr. Madison in the war with Great Britain. He supported the administration of John Quincy Adams, and always regarded it as the wisest and purest since the days of Washington. For five years he was associated with Col. Benton in the Senate committee* on military affairs. Here there was some conflict of political sentiment, but to the end of their days they were warm and attached friends, always keeping up the courtesies of friendship. They were about the same age, died on the same day, and within a few hours of each other. Gen. M. was a sincere and consistent Christian, and for the last 20 years was an elder in the Presbyterian church.

MARLOW, Alfred Pryor, New Town, Ala., May 5, æ. 62. He was one of the first settlers of New Town, having moved there in 1819. In the war of 1812, at the age of 17, he enlisted as a volunteer in Maj. Edmundson's company of Tennessee Mounted Riflemen, and served in the battle of New Orleans. He was a man of strong prejudices, but withal kind and generous.

MARQUIS, S. F., M. D., Folsom's Bar, Cal., Nov. 4, æ. 40, formerly of New Cumberland, Hancock Co., Va. He was a man of more than ordinary ability, intelligence, and enterprise, and had attained to considerable eminence in his profession. He left home for California in 1852, and returning after an absence of about two years, left again for California, April 12, 1854.

MARSH, James M., Dubuque, Iowa, ———, æ. ——. For 23 years he was engaged in surveying the lands of the United States in Michigan, Wisconsin, Iowa, and Minnesota. "He commenced the struggle of life a penniless and friendless boy, and closed it surrounded by magnificence, honored by all who had dealt with him and known him, enjoying an enviable reputation as a man of science, and possessing an unblemished moral character."

MARSH, Sarah, Heath, Mass., May 9, æ. 100 years, eight months, seven days. Through her long life she never was sick over three weeks' time in the aggregate, and enjoyed good health until within a few days of her death, when she was prostrated by a fit. During her last sickness she was entirely free from pain, and died evidently from old age. She left a numerous posterity, extending to the fifth generation, numbering about 200 lineal descendants. One hundred and seventy survived her. She had been a professor of religion 82 years, and died in the Christian faith.

BENJAMIN MARSHALL,

Troy, N. Y., Dec. 2, æ. 76. He was born in Huddersfield, England, in 1782. His ancestors were the founders of the place, having built the second house there. The deceased was the youngest of six brothers. When very young, he was engaged in the cotton manufacture, and at the early age of twenty came to this country with his brother Joseph, bringing an invoice of goods. They landed at New York, in August, 1803. That city had then hardly begun to grow, and its limited extent may be inferred from the fact that in consequence of the prevalence of cholera in the town, he accepted an invitation of two friends to take refuge with them in the country at the old Stuyvesant mansion, which stood on what is now Thirteenth Street. One of these friends, Francis Thompson, had a store on Beekman Street, and was largely engaged in the importation of woollen goods. With him Mr. M. became connected in business, importing cotton manufactures and making remittances in cotton. This business led him to become interested in shipping. It also resulted in his passing his winters in Georgia, where he studied the growth of cotton. The embargo of 1808 interrupted the business, which was terminated by the war of 1812. In 1814 Mr. M., with Jeremiah Thompson, resumed the ordinary shipping and importing business in Pearl Street. In 1818, he conceived the idea of establishing a periodical packet line between New York and Liverpool. The inexperienced men of the time scouted such a suggestion. The idea of having ships sail on regular days, in despite of wind and weather, seemed to them preposterous. But the line was established by Mr. Marshall, the Thompson Brothers, and Francis Wright and Son. The first ship, the James Monroe, sailed in January, 1819, in a north-easterly snow storm. The venture was a success, and in four years a dozen other lines had been established upon the same principles. The line of which Mr. Marshall was founder, from its well-known signal of a tar-barrel hoisted at the mast-head, was called the Black Ball line — a designation which it bears to this day.

In 1825, satisfied, from the increased growth of cotton, and the existing tariff on imported goods, that the manufacture of cotton must become one of the most important and profitable interests of the country, he concluded to withdraw from commerce, and devote all his energies and capital to it. This was an occupation most congenial with his humane and charitable disposition. It gave him an opportunity to put his ample means in such a shape that the greatest possible good would result from them. It enabled him to place employment within the reach of the needy, to clothe the naked, and to see shapening themselves on every hand the indubitable evidences of his genius and enterprise.

In 1826 Mr. Benjamin Marshall and his brother Joseph established at Hudson the Print Works, and in Troy, what was known as the Ida Cotton Mill, at the outset an establishment of limited extent. These works were carried on together until 1834, when the connection was dissolved, Benjamin taking the factory in Troy.

One of the great enterprises of Mr. Marshall's life was the establishment of the New York Mills, in Oneida Co., in N. Y., until fifteen years ago the most extensive establishment of the kind in the Union. The goods manufactured at these mills always commanded considerable more in the market than those of other works. One peculiar feature in this connection deserves especial notice, because it is suggestive of a noble peculiarity in the character of Mr. M., and teaches a lesson we would that every capitalist, whose abundant means enable him to pursue the same course, should learn. In connection with his partner in the works, Mr. B. S. Walcott, he manifested a most lively interest in the welfare of his employees — physical, intellectual, and spiritual alike. He was continually devising new schemes for their benefit. One of the finest tracts of land in that vicinity was purchased and apportioned off as a play-ground for the operatives, and provided with every needed apparatus for recreation and its attending development of physical power. Evening schools were established, with the most competent tutors, where all who liked were furnished tuition free of charge. Thus body and mind were strengthened together. Beyond the regular course of instruction, lectures were secured every year on physiology, phrenology, anatomy, geography, natural philosophy, chemistry, and astronomy. The religious wants of the operatives were also carefully attended to without any sectarian basis. Two large churches were erected, one Presbyterian, the other Methodist; and connected with each was an admirably arranged Sabbath school. Money was given with equal liberality to each. Hundreds of young men now engaged in various honorable pursuits can look back with thankful hearts to the New York Mills, as the ports from which they started on the voyage of life, freighted with good resolutions, and with those treasures of knowledge that are the most valuable possessions of honest ambition.

The great idea of Mr. M.'s life, we have seen, was to so use his capital as to give employment and consequent support to the greatest possible number of human beings, and to be instrumental in bringing out such products as would add great value to the possessions of the community. He never in his life was interested in the manufacture of a worthless article, or the fate of a fancy stock. His energies were always employed for a purpose. He always paid his employees well, and by every means in his power stimulated them to laudable effort, because he realized that in this way their value, too, would be enhanced, as producing agents in the community. This was the predominant and beautiful trait in the life of this truly useful man.

The practical benevolence of Mr. M., though continuously and unostentatiously employed in the channels we have named, was not confined to them. The mammoth business establishments he has erected will be no more enduring monuments of the true greatness and worth of his character, than the charitable institutions he founded. His benevolence was not posthumous. The "Marshall Infirmary," the most complete and well-ordered establishment of the kind in this section of the country, had its foundation originally in the generous impulses of his heart. His first donation to this institution was $25,000, and every year since its establishment he has expended $2000 in its maintenance. His personal and unremitting attention has been given to it, and hundreds of sufferers have had occasion to thank him for the comforts so freely bestowed upon them when they were languishing from disease. The hospital for patients suffering from infectious diseases was founded upon his suggestion and with his generous aid. The Lunatic Asylum is another child of his sympathy, and within the last year he has given his personal attention to its erection, and shown the most lively interest in it.

The Troy "Marshall Factories" may be considered the results exclusively of Benjamin's enterprise, sagacity, and genius. He resided in Troy; he built them under his constant and direct supervision. They rose and grew under his eyes, and he looked upon their success, and upon their auxiliary benefits, as upon success achieved and benefits conferred by "pet offspring." The commencement of these works were the wooden mills, at the foot of the hill, on the bank of the stream. Afterwards, or about 1840, he conceived and constructed the tunnel through the rocky margin of the Poestenkill, from above the falls, giving a power of more than 150 feet fall, and one of the best in the world. Mill after mill — all fine and extensive brick structures — rose year after year, until every available position between the mouth of the tunnel and the bed of the stream far below was occupied. Some of these mills employ hundreds of operatives. Some he ran himself, and others he leased on the most liberal terms to other manufacturers, whose success promised to contribute to the benefit of industry and the prosperity of the city. He was ready to aid in every way in his power the introduction here of new branches of manufacture; also to introduce every improvement known in his particular branch of manufacturing. Besides, he was of an inventive turn of mind, and there are many improvements in manufacturing machinery the results of his genius. These works on the bank and slope of the Poestenkill are estimated to have cost him half a million of dollars. They alone are a splendid monument to his enterprise and genius. And it is a living, breathing monument, for it has made that portion of the city what it is, and will contribute to its growth, during a long period of time to come.

It has been well said, that Mr. M., in his career of 55 years upon our shores, had driven his commercial bark in triumph among innumerable breakers, over the shoals and sands of fluctuating credit, through the forced calms of non-intercourse and embargo, and survived unharmed the storms of war. Then from the infancy to the maturity of his manufacturing enterprises, he had seen hundreds of his collaborators sink under the ruins of establishments prostrated by changes in national policy, and by violent financial convulsions; and was yet enabled to carry his own, various as they were, through all the changes of tariffs, the demolition of the national and the successive extinction of hundreds of state banks, and through all the effects upon credit produced by state repudiations and almost universal bankruptcy, as well as through periods of expansions not less dangerous, and of unreal as well as real prosperity. This triumph was not accidental; it was the natural result of his forecast and skill.

He was not only a noble, he was in many respects a peculiar man. He was the possessor of great wealth, yet there was not the slightest tinge of the aristocrat in or about him. He would meet his poorest employee on terms of equality as between man and man. He was courteous and affable to all without a show or feeling of condescension, a devout Christian without making any pretensions to piety, a truly honest man, " the noblest work of God," without assuming, by word or act, to be better than other men. Without disparagement to others who have gone before him to the grave, it may be said without fear of contradiction, that he had done more for his fellow-men, and more to benefit the city, than any other citizen that Troy has lost. It will be long, we fear, before we look upon his like again.

He outlived the space of threescore years and ten allotted to man; he did not fear death, nor sigh at his approach on his own account; he would have deferred the stroke only that he might do further good to others. How many have heard him discuss magnificent schemes of enterprise and benevolence, and then express his regret that his age would prevent him aiding in their consummation and witnessing their success. He seemed, really, too good a man to grow old and die. Perennial vigor and undecaying manhood for him would have been a blessing to mankind.

In his domestic relations he was in some respects fortunate, and in others unfortunate. As we learn from a statement furnished by him, in 1853, to the publishers of a biographical magazine, (and from which we have derived many of the facts of his early history,) he was married in New York, in the year 1813, to Niobe Stanton, the daughter of a Captain John Stanton, a gentleman of some influence in the locality of his residence. She died in 1823, before his removal to Troy. With this lady he lived in uninterrupted harmony until her death, and did not marry a second time. She was a devout and benevolent woman, and acquitted herself well in the appropriate field of usefulness. He had one son by this marriage, who, it is said, was a promising youth, but became the victim of an incurable malady, while on a European tour some fifteen or twenty years ago. He died about two years since, leaving his surviving parent childless. His family has been chiefly composed, since the death of his wife, of relations who had come from England. He was a member of a Christian church 34 years. As a church attendant he was a model; he was rarely absent from his place in the church; indeed he was never absent unless kept away by a providential interposition. In his will he directs the Ida Mills property (value of some $500,000,) to be run during certain lives of his friends, one half the income to be given to the American Bible Society, American Home Missionary Society, and American Tract Society, and the other half to the Marshall Infirmary, but ultimately to be sold and divided in the same proportions to the same societies.

MARSHALL, Francis, Tuscaloosa, Ala., March 5, æ. 68. He was a native of Virginia, was born in Powhatan, reared in New Kent, and was married to Miss Ann E. Howle, of the latter county. While a citizen of Virginia he held important offices of honor and trust, was an officer in the war of 1812, and exhibited a patriotic spirit in defence of his country's cause. Obliging and benevolent, urbane and companionable, he had the sincere respect of his intimate friends.

MARSHALL, Jonas, Fitchburg, Mass., Dec. 31, æ. 90. He left ten shares of Fitchburg Railroad stock, the income thereof to be distributed among poor widows and those who have not called upon the town for assistance.

MARSHALL, Nicholas T., Cincinnati, O., ———, æ. —, a well-known physician and able professor in the Medical College of Ohio.

MARTIN, Hannibal, M. D., Olney, near Moundsville, Va., Aug. 3, æ. 31. He graduated with honor at the college commencement, which took place last March; and, having ever applied himself diligently to his studies, he returned shattered in health, and consumption found him an easy prey.

MARTIN, Col. Moses, Rahway, N. J., Jan. 5, æ. 73. The colonel was a prominent actor in the last war with Great Britain; and, as a civilian, few men have had more warm-hearted or more devoted friends. For 40 years, with one or two exceptions, he filled the office of overseer of the poor of his township, with credit to himself and to the entire satisfaction of his constituents. He held this office until the day of his death; and this fact speaks volumes in favor of the high esteem in which he was held.

MARTIN, Tillerton H., Corinth, Vt., Dec. 18, æ. 99, one of the revolutionary soldiers, who fought desperately for his country. His last words were, " Long may the liberty flag wave; for I am going home to die no more."

MASON, Rev. C. C., Centre, Wis., Sept. 26, æ. 58. Mr. M. was born in Yorkshire, England, Dec. 21, 1800; experienced the saving grace of God at the age of 17; at once entered upon the work of an itinerant in the ranks of the Wesleyan Methodists, and was extensively known as the "boy preacher." In July, 1830, he came over to this country, and remained about a year, during which time he continued to preach the gospel, mostly in Saratoga Co., N. Y., and became extensively known in that region of country as an eloquent, faithful, and successful preacher. In 1831 he returned to the place of his nativity, where he remained about five years, when he again started for this country, leaving his family behind; commenced preaching as a local preacher under the presiding elder of Williamsburg, Mass. He then joined the New England conference, and was appointed to Coleraine, Mass., and various other places in New England.

MASON, Elisha, Litchfield, Conn., June 1, æ. 100. He was born in Litchfield, Conn., April 5, 1759, and at the time of his decease was the last of the revolutionary pensioners in his native town. Not long since he stated to a friend that on being discharged from the public service, at or near the Highlands on the Hudson, he was paid off in continental money, and started home on foot. Reaching Danbury at evening, he remained there over night, and in the morning tendered his money in payment for his bill, which was refused. He finally offered the landlord $40 for his keeping, which was rejected; and he, as a last resort, pawned his rifle. In this way were thousands of revolutionary soldiers rewarded for their services. Mr. M. married Lucretia Webster, a descendant of Gov. Webster, Jan. 5, 1785, with whom he lived 68 years. Twelve children were born to him. One of the sons, Stephen, graduated at Williams College, and was for several years pastor of the Congregational church at Washington, Ct.; is now a resident of Michigan. The late Ebenezer Porter Mason, a very distinguished astronomer and mathematician, whose memoirs were published by Prof. Olmsted, of Yale College, was grandson of the subject of this sketch. Mr. M. was a highly-esteemed citizen, a member of the First Church in Litchfield, and held important offices in the town.

MASON, Mrs. Elizabeth A., Dahlonega, Ga., Feb. 9, æ. 65, relict of the late Rev. David H. Mason, at the residence of her son, Dr. Zelotes H. Mason. She was born May 4, 1793, in Philadelphia, Pa., and in 1814 married to David H. Mason, of Ashford, Conn., who died Aug. 29, 1848, in his 65th year. He was eminent as a mechanician, and for several years was connected in business with M. W. Baldwin, of Philadelphia, Pa. In 1837 he was appointed coiner in the United States branch mint, Dahlonega, Ga., which office he held until his death. Late in life he was ordained as a minister of the Presbyterian church. His Christian character endeared him to all his acquaintances. Mrs. M. was an earnest, active Christian, seeking by every means in her power to advance the cause of the Redeemer. During a short residence in Lowell, Mass., in 1825 and 1826, she was the means, in the noted revival in that place, of stirring up Christians, and, by personal conversation, of leading many persons to Christ. She knew by experience the value of religion, and sought to impress upon others the necessity of a change of heart, and, when she realized that she had been the means of doing good, gave all the glory to God, that he had used such a feeble instrument to advance his cause. She mourned over her shortcomings, and sought for the grace of God to help her infirmities.

MASON, Rev. Francis, Adams Creek, N. C., Oct. 14, æ. 63 yrs. 2 mos. He had been a member of the Methodist Episcopal church for 45 years, 35 a class leader, and the last 8 years of his life he had been engaged as a local preacher in proclaiming the gospel of Christ.

MASON, Mrs. Mary, Boston, Mass., April 10, æ. 80, relict of the Hon. Jeremiah Mason. She was a native of Amherst, N. H. Her father was from Ireland. Maternally she was descended from the clan of the McGregors of Scotland. One of her sisters was the wife of Dr. Appleton, president of Bowdoin College, and mother of Mrs. John Aiken and Mrs. Gen. Pierce. A sister still living is Mrs. Amos Lawrence, of Boston.

MASON, Miss Virginia Wallace, Hagerstown, Md., Oct. 6, æ. 38. She was born at Montpelier, (the estate of her father,) Washington Co., Md., in April, 1820. She belonged to the Virginia family of Masons, so distinguished in the annals of the state, and was the granddaughter of Thomson Mason, and grand-niece of the great George Mason, both of whom were so prominent in our revolutionary history. Her father was the late John Thomson Mason, one of the most eminent lawyers of his day; and she was a sister of Judge Mason, (of the same name,) now collector of the port of Baltimore. Her father removed from Virginia to Maryland, where he passed the remainder of his life. Miss M. was highly esteemed for the noble qualities of her head and heart, resembling her father very much in the character of her mind and disposition. She enjoyed the confidence of many warm and devoted friends; and few persons died more regretted. Indeed, such was the esteem in which she was held in the community in which she lived, and so awfully sudden was her death, that its announcement almost led to an involuntary suspension of business, in the general manifestation of sympathy and sorrow. She never married, and left a considerable estate, a part of which were slaves, whom she proposed in her will to manumit.

MASSEE, Rev. William, Dunnville, Dunn Co., Wis., Feb. 16, æ. 76. He was born in England, where he was converted in his 19th year. At the age of 24 he was licensed to preach as a local preacher in the Wesleyan Methodist connection. In the early part of his life he was favored with the ministrations of Dr. Adam Clarke, Richard Watson, Robert Newton, and others of precious memory. About 1819 he came to America, and settled in Oneida Co., N. Y. He continued to labor as a local preacher until disabled by disease about 15 years ago. When his strength was no longer sufficient to preach, he served the church as class leader for a time; but even this power soon failed. In 1856 he came with part of his family to Wisconsin.

MASTEN, William, M. D., Albany, N. Y., March 10, æ. 54.

MATHIS, Henry, Barton Co., Mo., July 19, æ. 76, an old soldier, who had served in the last war with Great Britain, and in the defence of the north-western frontier against the Indians.

MATLOCK, Rev. Samuel M., Warren Co., Ky., Jan. 8, æ. 57. He was born in North Carolina, but early removed to Kentucky, and settled in Warren Co., where he lived until his death. He was licensed to preach the gospel Oct. 8, 1836, at Mount Olivet, in Warren Co., and was ordained Oct. 8, 1842, at Pleasant Grove, Simpson Co. He spent more than 20 years in preaching the gospel. His life was a living commentary on the Christian religion, an example that will live in the memory of those who knew his devotion to the cause of Christianity.

MATTHEWS, Capt. Jonathan, Monson, Me., Feb. 8, æ. 75. He was one of the first county commissioners of Piscataquis Co.

MATTINGLY, Sallie R., Bardstown, Ky., Dec. 22, daughter of the late Judge Roane, of Virginia, and granddaughter of Patrick Henry.

MAXEY, Mrs. Mary B., Prince William Parish, S. C., Dec. 31, æ. 81, widow of Milton M. Maxey, Esq., lawyer at Beaufort, S. C.

MAXWELL, Hon. Sylvester, Charlemont, Mass., Dec. 21, æ. 83, the youngest son of Col. Hugh Maxwell, of the continental army, through the revolutionary war, from Bunker Hill to the evacuation of New York.

MAXWELL, Thomas, Saugerties, Ulster Co., N. Y., ——, æ. 72. He was an officer under Wellington, and followed through his campaign upon the continent. He was actively engaged in all the battles of that memorable campaign which closed with the sanguinary struggle on the plains of Waterloo. In 1826, accompanied by his family, he set sail for the new world, and settled in Greene Co., N. Y., from whence he removed to Saugerties, where he purchased a farm and resided thereon to the time of his death, prosperous in worldly matters, and respected and esteemed by all who knew him.

MAY, Rev. Edward H., Philadelphia, Pa., Aug. 28, æ. 74, late secretary of the Seaman's Friend Society, in Philadelphia, and formerly pastor of the Reformed Dutch Church, in 21st Street, New York.

MAYER, Rev. J. C., New Orleans, La., Aug. 24, æ. —.

MAYER, Rev. Philip F., Philadelphia, Pa., April 16, æ. 77. He was over 50 years in the ministry. He was for many years president of the Pennsylvania Institution for the Deaf and Dumb, president of the Philadelphia Dispensary, and a trustee of the University of Pennsylvania. He was much beloved by his congregation, and highly esteemed for his piety, his learning, and his many other admirable qualities, by people of all denominations.

McARTHUR, Hon. Duncan, Chillicothe, O., April —, æ. —. The Chillicothe Gazette announces the death of Allen C. McArthur, the last immediate descendant of Gov. McArthur. It is stated that he was appointed a colonel in the regular service, and "afterwards, upon the resignation of Gen. Harrison, became commander-in-chief of the army of the North-west."

McCALLISTER, William, Beaver, Beaver Co., Pa., Sept. 21, æ. —, formerly clerk of the courts, and more recently register and recorder of Beaver Co.

McCARTHY, John F., ——, ——, Oct. 8, æ. —, formerly assistant foreman in the New Orleans Delta office, and foreman of the Times of that city. He was a native of Washington city, graduated at Georgetown College, D. C., after which he graduated at the Law School of Harvard University. Subsequently Mr. McC. was professor of mathematics and ancient languages in the Washington Seminary, and a practitioner of law in Washington and St. Louis.

McCLARY, Mary, Williamsburg District, S. C., Aug. 27, æ. 84. She was one of the few who lingered here as a relic of a past generation. She was born Feb. 14, 1774, amid the threatening events which led to the war of the revolution, and had a distinct recollection of many of the fearful and bloody scenes enacted during the invasions of Tarleton and Wemyss. The house-burnings, plunderings, murders, and other calamities inflicted on the friends of liberty in that part of the country, could never be effaced from the memory of childhood, even down to her death. She became the second wife of David McClary. Jan. 9, 1798, he having first married Mary Witherspoon in 1791.

McCLELLAN, Hon. John, ——, ——, æ. —. He was the son of Gen. Samuel McClellan, of the revolutionary army, and was born at Woodstock, Ct., Jan. 4, 1767, and graduated in 1785. He studied law with the late Gov. Samuel Huntington, of Norwich, and began its practice in his native town, in 1787, and faithfully attended to the business of his office for 65 years, and was at his death the oldest counsellor at law in Connecticut. The records of the town and of the state will show that he had his full share in the confidence of his fellow-citizens, as he was elected more than 30 times to the state legislature, and was a member of the convention which formed the present constitution of Connecticut. The last time that he received the suffrages of his fellow-citizens was in 1847, when he was chosen an elector of president and vice-president of the United States, and voted for Taylor and Fillmore. Mr. McClellan was extremely happy in all his domestic relations, and was sure to create pleasant feelings in every circle in which he moved. Like others of his generation, he was full of interesting anecdotes and reminiscences. He married the only daughter of William Williams, a signer of the Declaration of Independence. He left two sons and three daughters.

McCLELLAND, Adaline Evertson, New Brunswick, N. J., Aug. 25, æ. 18, youngest daughter of the Rev. Alexander McClelland, D. D.

McCLUNG, Susan, Maysville, O., Nov. 2, æ. —, relict of Hon. William McClung, and mother of Rev. John A. McClung and the celebrated Col. McClung, of Mississppi. She was the daughter of Col. Thomas Marshall, of revolutionary memory, and a sister of the distinguished John Marshall, chief justice of the United States.

McCLURE, Andrew, Botetourt Co., Va., Nov. 9, æ. —, a minister of the Dunkard sect.

McCONN, P. H., Brunswick, Ga., Oct. 13, æ. 34. At the time of his death he was a member of the city council of Brunswick, and clerk of the Glynn Superior Court.

McCONNELL, E. E., M. D., Clarksville, Johnson Co., Ark., July 25, æ. 59. He was, at the time of his death, a citizen of Johnson Co., and had resided there since the year 1837, and was universally respected and beloved. Sterling honesty — a disposition to take a lively interest in the misfortunes of others, and kindness of heart, were the dominant characteristics of his nature, and which made his departure from among us mourned by all. He was the father of a large family, whom he loved with a parental fondness that knew no bounds. In short, he was the best of parents, the best of husbands, a true friend, and a lover of his fellow-men.

McCORKLE, Capt. Henry, Colliers-town, Va., Oct. 25, æ. 67. He was born Feb. 14, 1791, and was the son of William McCorkle, who served with usefulness at Yorktown, and the grandson of another revolutionary soldier, who was killed at the battle of the Cowpens. Capt. McCorkle himself was at Norfolk in the last war, having volunteered in the place of his brother-in-law, Mr. William Hamilton, well known afterwards as an elder in the Lexington church, and who had been drafted in the company of Capt. Robert White, also an elder in the same Presbyterian connection. The history of Capt. McCorkle's life, for the last 30 years, was one of faithful attention to the duties of a citizen and a father, in both of which relations he was remarkable for the purity of his moral character and the integrity of his business acts.

McCOSKRY, Mrs. Alison Nisbet, New York city, May 30, æ. 85, widow of the late Dr. McCoskry, of Carlisle, Pa.

McCOY, Ada, Jacksonville, Ill., Feb. 5, æ. —, wife of Rev. Asa S. McCoy, president of the Illinois Female College.

McCREEDY, James, Plattsburg, N. Y., Aug. 7, æ. 76, a resident of Plattsburg for 73 years, and a member of the first five families that settled in that town, of whom only two now survive.

McCULLOCH, George P., Morristown, N. J., June 1, æ. 83. He was the projector of the Morris Canal, and by his writings and energy succeeded in accomplishing that valuable public improvement. The Newark Advertiser says that he was born in Scotland, but at an early period established himself as a teacher in this country, in which position he gave direction to the minds of some of the ablest men of the present time. He was the father-in-law of Hon. J. W. Miller, late U. S. Senator from New Jersey.

McCULLOCH, Col. Thomas, Abingdon, Ia., Jan. 18, æ. 62. Judge McCulloch was a native of Washington Co., Va., and is well remembered by most of the old and prominent citizens of that county. He emigrated to Iowa in the fall of 1847, previous to which time he had been for upwards of 20 years a prominent citizen of Washington Co. He was sheriff for a term of years, and for three years was a member of the Virginia legislature. He had also been a member of the Iowa legislature. For upwards of two years previous to his death, he held the office of judge of the County Court of Jefferson Co., in Iowa, and was re-elected and entered into his second term in the summer of 1857. He was a man of sound judgment, excellent common sense, sterling integrity, and great moral worth, and possessed the happy faculty of gaining hosts of friends wherever he was known.

McCURDY, Lavinia S., Logan Co., Ky., Feb. 3, æ. 78. Her father, Thomas Sharp, a revolutionary soldier, who fought at King's Mountain and elsewhere in that contest, removed to Kentucky about the year 1796.

McDANIEL, Samuel, Butler Co., O., Oct. 9, æ. 61. He was a native of New Jersey, but went to Ohio more than 40 years ago. He made the journey, as many others of the earlier settlers of the country, on foot, carrying all his effects on his person. By a life of industry and economy, he attained to a competency. He was a good husband and father, a kind neighbor and friend, conscientiously living the faith he professed.

McDIVIT, Hon. James, Emmetsburg, Pa., Nov. 13, at an advanced age, for a number of years associate judge of the county. He was a worthy man and an excellent citizen.

McDONALD, Rev. Alexander, Shelby Co., Ala., March 18, æ. 76. He was born in Virginia, Christmas day, 1781. He moved to Tennessee, and settled in Giles Co., then almost a wilderness, in 1808. So soon as he had cleared away the brush and cane, and built a rude cabin for the protection of his family, to use his own language, he cast about him to see what arrangement could be made for the worship of the true and living God; for at that time he was a preacher of the gospel. Within 15 miles of him he found six members of his own church, the Methodist. These were collected together, a class formed, and a church site selected, which was called Mount Pisgah. Here Mr. McDonald lived a great many years, a part of which time he was in the itinerancy. From Tennessee he removed to Mississippi, where he remained until about three years ago. He was a strong man, and a good and useful man. He retained his zeal to the last, preaching almost every Sunday.

McDOUGALD, James, Paulding, Miss., Sept. 30, æ. —. The Paulding bar regard the deceased as "a warm friend, a learned attorney, a generous opponent, and a faithful and vigilant ally and associate in the practice."

McEWEN, Timothy, Evans, N. Y., May 27, æ. 71. Mr. McEwen removed from Utica to Evans previous to the last war with Great Britain, and lost considerable property when the British forces sacked the village of Buffalo. He was actively engaged in manufacturing pursuits for many years. He was prominent in the early history of Buffalo, and labored earnestly in its welfare.

HON. JOHN A. McEWEN,

Nashville, Tenn., Dec. 3, æ. 34. He was born in Lincoln Co., Nov. 28, 1824, and at the time of his death had just passed his 34th anniversary. His parents removed to Nashville at an early day, and he was brought up and educated there. Taking a broad and thorough primary course in the schools of the city, he went thence to the University of Nashville, where he graduated with distinguished credit at the age of 18 years.

He immediately became a tutor in the university, and secured alike the love and admiration of the students in this new sphere, as he had done while a school companion and classmate. A year or two afterwards, he entered upon the study of the law in this city, and in due course was prepared and admitted to the bar. He rapidly rose to eminence, and for several years past has occupied a front position at a bar distinguished for its juridical ability, dignity, and general learning. But during all his arduous study as a theoretical and practical lawyer, he never forgot his earlier attachment to the classics, ancient and modern, and at his decease was one of the most thorough and finished scholars of his age in the country. Neither did he neglect the current literature of the day, nor the progress of the sciences, but kept up with the advances in both. As if to make his accomplishments universal, he devoted a proportion of his time to the study of politics; as a science, however, rather than as a means of foisting himself into public station. Of course talents so splendid, and attainments so varied, could not rust for want of use. He was always in action. In 1851-2 he edited, with great success and ability, the Daily Gazette, of Nashville. His brilliant oratory brought him importunities from various colleges and committees for speeches and orations, with many of which he complied. When the new buildings for the University of Nashville were about to be erected, the trustees selected him as the orator on the occasion.

On the establishment of the Southern Commercial College, he was selected to give a course of lectures to the students of that institution, on mercantile and general commercial law, which he did with eminent ability and success. He was next elected mayor of Nashville, which office he filled with all the energy his now failing constitution allowed. He was forced, before the expiration of his term, to measurably vacate the office, in travelling for his health.

In the multiplicity of all his labors, he never forgot the claims of religion, and having early connected himself with the First Presbyterian Church of the city, he was punctual in his attendance and devout in his services at the altar of Christianity, and for many years labored in that fruitful vineyard of the church and the Sabbath school. His manner was ever polite, genial, and amiable, and invariably won the respect and warm esteem of all his acquaintance.

At a public meeting of the citizens of Nashville, Hon. Andrew Ewing said in substance —

"It becomes my painful duty to announce to you the death of John A. McEwen. He departed this life yesterday evening, about 7 o'clock, in the 35th year of his age. Fifteen months have elapsed since his friends were first startled by a painful rumor that his health was endangered. He struggled bravely for life, but the die was cast. He sank slowly and surely — the angel of death waited for him until yesterday. But now, all is over — the bow is broken, the music is hushed, and his strife for life done. I cannot, if I would, trust myself to speak of the crushed hopes and wounded hearts of his family. Those only can estimate the grief who have lost such a son, husband, and father.

"He was eminently a child of the people, and a missionary in the cause of their advancement and progress. From his first entrance into manhood until his close as mayor of our city, all his powers were devoted to the building up and cherishing public schools, sustaining other charitable institutions, lecturing, speaking, and thinking for the masses. He had no element of a demagogue, flattering, cozening, and betraying those who trusted him; on the contrary, he was remarkably candid, upright, and truthful to a fault. The last great speech of his life was devoted to portraying the difference between a demagogue and a philanthropist. He understood the distinction, and well did his life exemplify the position he had chosen.

"He believed in the continued progress of mankind, and ardently struck his blows for the cause. He died with his mind fixed on the opinion of a millennium on earth, and his glazed eyes intently gazing on the glorious future.

"It is difficult to magnify the influence of Mr. McEwen on his immediate contemporaries and the rising generation. At the bar, on the hustings, in the lecture room, and in social life, his high bearing, his untainted morality, his buoyancy of spirits, and his candid nature diffused happiness and gladness wherever he went; his pathway amongst men, like a vessel on the ocean at night, left a train of light behind. We, members of the bar, can well remember how his wit and joyousness often soothed the asperities of our contests and smouldered all the embers of heart-burnings and jealousy. We can never forget the kindliness of his disposition or the trumpet tones of his eloquence, as they rung out again and again in the walls of our old court room.

"He is gone, struck down in the meridian of life, and in all the aspects which I have presented it: it is a sad and mournful dispensation. But not so, probably, to him; he never lived to prove the hollowness of friendship, the sounding brass of patriotism, the utter neglect by the masses of those who spend their lives in their service. He passed away with warm faith in the purity of the majority of the people, with full belief that his efforts would be understood and appreciated by those for whom he labored. His battle is fought, and his contest done; he has been taken from the evil to come."

Portions only of the eloquent speech of Mr. Ewing are taken. When he had finished, he presented the following preamble to resolutions which were passed:

"The people of Nashville were shocked, yesterday morning, with the information that their brilliant and accomplished fellow-citizen, John A. McEwen, was in the agony of death. Although many of us were aware that his health was feeble, and his chances for recovery very doubtful, no person was prepared for his sudden death. It seemed almost impossible that one so gifted, so active, and so full of life as he was but a short time since, could thus droop and perish in so short a period; but he is gone, and all that we can do is to offer our tribute of esteem for his memory, and endeavor to imitate his virtues. Mr. McEwen was eminently a child of the people, and throughout life a missionary for their interest and improvement; his kind heart revelled in philanthropy, and his brilliant intellect was constantly employed in obeying its dictates. He commenced his manhood with a tutorship in the University of Nashville, and when he passed to the bar, and thence to the mayorship of the city, his attention was still directed to the public schools and other eleemosynary institutions of our city; his high spirits, his chivalric feelings, his warm enthusiasm lent a strength and power to his efforts that will be long remembered by those who were familiar with him. It is impossible, in the brief space allotted to us now, to give even a passing review of his services to this community, or to examine the peculiar qualities of his mind; he was too strongly endowed with the qualities that charm and adorn social existence; and his departure is too afflicting for us to form a fair estimate of what he was. When time has softened and lightened our grief, we then can weigh his merits, and more correctly estimate our loss. As Mr. McEwen belonged to no particular class of society, and his life was exhausted in a struggle for the progress and advancement of mankind, it is eminently proper that he should be buried and lamented by the whole people. Therefore

"*Resolved*, that we deeply deplore the death of John A. McEwen, and that we warmly sympathize with the sorrow of his afflicted family and relations.

"*Resolved*, that the public authorities of the city be requested to tender his family a public funeral for the deceased, and that we all join in this demonstration."

McGIFFIN, George Wallace, Washington, Pa., Dec. 28, æ. 35. He was a son of the late Thomas McGiffin, Esq., an eminent member of the Washington Co. bar. After his graduation at Washington College, in 1841, at the early age of 19, he prosecuted, for some time, the study of medicine under the instruction of James Stevens, M. D., of Washington, but was led to abandon the pursuit of this profession on account of the want of sufficient physical strength for his toils. He then turned his attention to the law, and, after a three years' course of study in the office of the late Hon. T. M. T. McKennan, was admitted to the bar in 1846.

McGINNIS, Hugh B., Galena, Jo Daviess Co., Ill., Oct. 17, æ. 32. The members of the Galena bar, at a public meeting, passed the following resolution: —

"*Resolved*, that we cherish the highest respect for the professional zeal, learning, and ability of the deceased, for his energy of character, and the integrity of his professional life, for the social qualities and estimable virtues which he displayed as a man, a citizen, and a friend."

McGREGOR, Lewis, Red Bluff, Cal., Aug. 17, æ. 38. He was a native of Kintail, in Ross-shire, West Highlands of Scotland, where his father, William McGregor, still resides. They are descended from the celebrated McGregor clan that flourished in the days of Rob Roy, to whose time their family records and traditions still run back. The deceased was for 12 years a soldier in the British army in India, and afterwards travelled nearly all over the three continents. He was one of the pioneer teamsters of the Sacramento Valley, and at the time of his death was the owner of several large teams, and was extensively engaged in transporting goods to Shasta and other northern towns.

McGREGOR, Lieut. William Gray, Belise, La., Aug. 16, æ. 26. Lieut. McG. was a native of Newport, R. I. He was an officer of much promise. By his energetic spirit, his generous and noble character, his intelligence, and most exemplary conduct while in the discharge of his official duty, he secured the unqualified esteem of his superiors, and bade fair, at no distant day, to rank high in the service to which he was attached.

McGUIRE, Rev. E. C., D. D., Fredericksburg, Va., Oct. 8, æ. 65. He was born in the ancient borough of Winchester, in 1793, and commenced his long and honored ministry in Fredericksburg, in Oct., 1813, when he was barely 20 years of age. From that day, with a singleness of purpose and a laborious diligence never surpassed, he pursued the even tenor of his way. Noiselessly and without pretence, he, as the instrument of Heaven, accomplished a great work. Under his faithful culture, his congregation greatly multiplied in numbers, and flourished in all its higher spiritual interests. In the lapse of 45 long years he kept himself free from the slightest reproach, even from them that are without; and, in the affectionate estimation of all his fellow-Christians, he adorned the doctrine of his Lord and Saviour in all the beauty of holiness. He discharged his high offices as an ambassador from God through those long years in three different church edifices, and to as many successive generations of Christian worshippers. The whole of the present generation in his own communion he baptized, the whole of the past generation he buried, until, at last, he left a world growing stranger in the ceaseless flow of change, to find himself far more at home in that heaven where the friends and parishioners of his early life had gathered before him.

McINTYRE, Hon. Archibald, Albany, N. Y., May 5, æ. 85. He was a Scotchman, but came to this country while a child, and has occupied prominent positions for many years. He was Assemblyman from Montgomery Co. from 1798 to 1802, and again in 1804; occupied the office of state comptroller from 1806 to 1821; was elected United States senator in 1822, and filled that place for six years; and afterwards contracted with the state, in connection with John B. Yates, to manage its lotteries, until those enterprises were prohibited by the new constitution.

McKEE, William K., Esq., Punxsutawney, Pa., Feb. 8, æ. —, prosecuting attorney.

McKEEN, Miss Catharine, Mount Leon, Ohio Co., Va., July 20, æ. 33. She was a daughter of the Rev. Silas McKeen, of Bradford, Vt.; a young lady of fine talents and superior attainments in learning, decidedly pious, and highly esteemed as a teacher. Her last years of active service were spent at Mount Holyoke — an institution which she greatly loved, and in whose prosperity, even to the last, she felt deeply interested.

McKEEN, Col. Thomas, Easton, Me., Nov. 25, æ. 96. He was a native of Ireland, and emigrated to the United States in 1783, before the conclusion of peace with Great Britain. For 37 years he was either president or cashier of the Easton Bank, and also held in the course of his life several other important posts of civil trust. He left an estate valued at about a quarter of a million dollars. It is said that Col. McKeen, when a boy, heard the first gun fired by the celebrated Paul Jones in his great fight with the Serapis and Countess of Scarborough.

McKENNA, Rev. Patrick, Brooklyn,

N. Y., —— —, æ. 39. He was a native of Tydavnet, Monaghan Co., Ireland, was educated at St. John's College, Fordham, and was ordained by the Most Rev. Archbishop Hughes.

McKENNEY, Col. Thos. L., New York city, Feb. 20, æ. 74. He was formerly an Indian agent, and wrote, some years ago, an interesting work on the Indians.

McLANE, Mrs. Sarah, Indianapolis, Ind., Dec. 24, æ. —, widow of Gen. Jeremiah McLane, a soldier of the revolutionary war, and one of the early pioneers of Ohio. Gen. McLane settled at Chillicothe in 1790. He was secretary of state of Ohio for a period of 12 years. In 1816 Gen. McLane and family removed from Chillicothe to Columbus. He repeatedly represented the Franklin district in Congress. He was a democrat, and the district was largely whig; but his fellow-citizens held the veteran and patriot in such estimation that for their suffrages no man could beat him. He "died in harness," having departed this life while a member of Congress. Mrs. McLane continued to reside in Columbus until 1854. Since then she lived with her son at Indianapolis. This venerable gentlewoman was of an age at the time of the revolution to have had the great events then acting vividly impressed upon her memory. She could doubtless remember what seem to us, by their very grandeur and tremendous import, to have been the acts of some remoter heroic age. Having reached womanhood in 1790, when she came with her husband to Ohio, she witnessed for nearly three quarters of a century afterwards the marvellous and uninterrupted progress of the west. Mrs. McLane's virtues equalled her longevity. She was the happy mother of a numerous and prosperous offspring.

McLEAN, Hon. John, Salem, Washington Co., N. Y., Dec. 5, æ. 65. He was a native, and always a resident, of Warren Co. His father was one of the most distinguished citizens of the county, holding among other offices the office of judge for a long time, and was one of her representatives in the state legislature. The deceased was not only one of the most distinguished citizens of the county, but the peer of any in the state. After graduating at Union College, he studied law, in part with Hon. Gideon Hawley, of Albany, and part of the time in Salem, at which time Justices Nelson and Willard were his fellow-students. In 1818 he was admitted to the bar, and entered into business in partnership with the Hon. John Crary, of Salem; and shortly after he was appointed examiner in chancery, which place he filled for a time, and then was appointed master in chancery, which places he held under Chancellors Kent and Walworth, and performed the duties thereof with such ability as to elicit the encomium from them of being the best officer in the state. During the years 1829 to and including 1832 he represented Washington Co. in the Senate of New York, and in 1837 he was again elected to the same office, to fill the vacancy of I. W. Bishop, who resigned. After holding the office of one of the county judges for a while, he was appointed in 1835, by Gov. Marcy, first judge of Washington Co., which office he held until 1847, performing its duties with such ability, and credit to himself, and honor to the bench, as to attract much business to that court from the Circuit Court. In 1835 he was also appointed a regent of the university, which office he held up to the time of his decease. In political life he was an associate of the best men of the democratic party in its best days, a friend of Silas Wright and Gov. Marcy. Gov. Wright appointed him one of the commissioners to establish ferries between New York and Long Island. His colleagues in that service were George P. Barker, of Erie, and Samuel Cheever, of Saratoga. It may be truly said of him, that, instead of office honoring him, he honored the office. His well-balanced and discriminating mind, his instinctive sense of justice and equity, his due appreciation of the principles on which they are founded, his stern independence and decision of character, his high sense of honor, and his inflexible uprightness of heart, connected with a dignity of mind and manner softened by a grace peculiarly his own, probably qualified and designated him most preëminently to adorn and elevate the bench, although at the same time fitting him for any civil station, however high and honorable, to which man is invited. In private life his many virtues were remarkably preëminent. He was honest in all his relations with his fellow-man, a pattern of punctuality in his engagements and appointments, always courteous and always dignified in his intercourse with others, ever manifesting a deep interest in the character and welfare of young men around him, and eager to encourage and stimulate merit wherever it was exhibited.

McLELLAN, Hon. John, Woodstock, Conn., Aug. 1, æ. 90 yrs. 6 mos., among the fruits of the revival of 1858 in the church at Woodstock. He was for many years a man of prominence in Windham Co. Among his surviving children is the wife of Prof. Silliman, Sen., of New Haven.

McLEMORE, Col. Chas., ——, Ark., Oct. 27, æ. 51. He died away from home on a western tour. He was born in Hancock Co., Ga., March 9, 1808. As an evidence of the high appreciation of his commanding abilities, he was repeatedly sent to the legislature of Alabama by the old whig party, in its days of ascendency. He filled the position of senator from Chambers Co. for a long series of years in succession. While in the legislature, he offered determined resistance to all schemes which contemplated the depletion of the state treasury, or which foreboded the least detriment to the interests of his constituents. He was several times elected president of the Senate, for which position his dignified bearing, combined with his affable manners, peculiarly fitted him. For a few years previous to his death, he led a secluded life, preferring the enjoyments of home to the busy turmoil of political life. In the private circles of life, he combined all those elements of character which tend to create friendly relations of the most intimate and lasting kind.

McLENDON, Mrs. C. A., Le Grange, Kilgore, on Bayou Macon, Madison Parish, La., Oct. 19, æ. 24.

McMYNN, Mrs. Ella W., Racine, Wis., June 18, æ. 32. She was a native of Vermont, and her maiden name was Wiley. She went to Wisconsin in 1849, and engaged in teaching in the village of Waukesha. After nearly two years she was invited to Kenosha to continue her vocation of teaching. There she was united in marriage to Mr. McMynn, her surviving companion. As a teacher of youth, she had few superiors. Gifted with a high order of intellect, and having acquired a thorough education, her mind exercised, almost voluntarily, a masterly control over the minds of her pupils. They always acknowledged her influence, and yielded without controversy to its sway. Her labors in the schoolroom were quiet and unobtrusive, yet always effectual.

McNEIL, Bernard, M. D., Philadelphia, Pa., Nov. 9, æ. 73.

McPHERSON, John B., Gettysburg, Pa., Jan. 4, æ. 68. He was born Nov. 15, 1789, near Gettysburg, Pa., on the farm upon which his ancestors settled when they emigrated to this country, about 1730. He received a fair education in the academies in Gettysburg and York. He spent several years of his early manhood in Frederick, Md., with an uncle, for one year was clerk in the Branch Bank located in that place. He was married April 25, 1810, in Frederick, to Miss Catharine Lenhart, of York, Pa., a sister of William Lenhart, the distinguished mathematician. In 1814 he removed to Gettysburg. He was elected cashier of the bank in Gettysburg, which post he filled until his death. Much of this time, he performed all the duties, never wearying in their discharge. He was a most faithful, patient, competent, accurate, and popular officer. He was punctual, painstaking, and prompt. His manners were mild and unobtrusive, but he possessed great decision and firmness of character happily blended with gentleness. He was large-hearted, and took an active interest in every movement which promised to promote the moral or material welfare of the community. He was intelligent and well read, and was an early patron and efficient friend of Pennsylvania College, located at Gettysburg, of whose board of trustees he was president at the time of his decease. He was among the oldest bank officers in the country. He died leaving a whole community to mourn his loss. His name was a household word in the county, and a synonyme of purity. He left several children, the youngest of whom, Edward, is a member elect to the thirty-sixth Congress. His widow survived him about one year.

MEAD, Capt. Joshua R., Northampton, Mass., Aug. 16, æ. 62. To an active, vigorous, and inquiring mind and superior judgment were added industry, energy, and perseverance rarely equalled, a hopefulness of disposition that cheered him onward amidst the gloomiest and most discouraging circumstances. He was a prominent and useful citizen, a kind, generous, and hospitable friend and neighbor, a most considerate and affectionate husband, a truly doting parent.

MEADE, Mrs. Mary M., Dinwiddie, Va., March —, æ. 80, mother of the Hon. Richard Kidder Meade, U. S. minister to Brazil.

MEAKER, Valorus, M. D., Waterville, Me., Oct. 31, æ. 49.

MEARS, Dea. Elijah, Boston, Mass., March 2, æ. 80. He was born in Tewksbury, Mass., and in early life came to Boston, where, in 1800, he commenced business as a partner in the well-known firm of Kilham & Mears. In 1806 he was baptized by the Rev. Thomas Baldwin, D. D., and became a member of the Second, now the Baldwin Place Baptist Church. In 1828 he removed his relation to the Federal Street, now Rowe Street Church, of which, in 1837, he was elected a deacon. Though naturally modest and retiring, few men were better known in the community than Dea. M., and all who knew him are certain that he has left behind him no better man. His religious convictions were deep, and his life, to an uncommon degree, was conformed to his belief. His morality, founded on the Christian basis, was a structure of great symmetry and beauty. So true was he in all the relations of life, that he could stand erect and look any human being in the face, apprehensive of no charge of malversation. He had a strong love of right, and no one suspected him of the slightest deviation. He was conscientiously just, and yet as conscientiously benevolent. Seldom are righteousness and goodness so happily blended in the same character. Rigorously exact in all his dealings with others, he was remarkably tender and charitable towards wrong doers, and ready to put the best possible construction upon every man's motives and intentions. His whole life, after he became a Christian, was a lovely illustration of the purifying, regulating, elevating power of deep-seated religious principle.

MEARS, Richard, Peacham, Vt., Sept. 2, æ. 92. Mr. M. went to Peacham at the age of 22 years, more than 70 years ago, and was truly one of the pioneers of the town. It is said of him that he was one of the most hardy and industrious men that ever lived; that it was a usual thing for him to fell an acre of trees in a day.

MEAUX, Thomas, M. D., Coverty, Amelia Co., Va., Dec. 3, æ. 66, a Virginia gentleman of the old school, kind and courteous in manners, exemplary in all the relations of life, as father, husband, friend, and neighbor.

MEGGISON, Hon. Joseph C., Columbus, Ala., March 29, æ. —, at the residence of Col. Robert Robson. He was formerly judge of the district of which Galveston composed a part. He was a Virginian by birth, but removed to Mobile, and from that city to Galveston in 1839. He was a man of good abilities, and of a most gentle and kindly disposition.

MELLEN, Joshua, Wayland, Mass., Feb. 22, æ. 94, father of Chief Justice Mellen.

MERCER, Hon. Charles Fenton, ——, —, — —, æ. —, entered Congress from Virginia in 1817, and served continuously till 1840 — a period of 24 years. He was a firm and ardent supporter of the administrations of Monroe and John Quincy Adams, and a decided though moderate opponent of those of Jackson and Van Buren. He was an advocate of protection to home industry, along with Thomas Newton, Philip Doddridge, and the most enlightened though not the most numerous portion of the representatives of Virginia in those days. He was also an early and steadfast advocate of national improvement by roads and canals. The cause of African colonization had no steadier friend; and we believe he was for some years president of the American Colonization Society. Though his district (that directly against Washington) was often opposed to him in politics, he was seldom opposed, and, we think, never beaten. After his retirement from Congress at a ripe age he withdrew from all active participation in politics. Though not a great, he was a wise and good man, who left behind him a record of usefulness and a spotless name.

MERCER, W. V. I., Waterloo, N. Y., Dec. 15, æ. —, cashier of the Seneca Bank.

MERCER, George Weedon, Washington, D. C., Sept. 9, æ. 41, son of the late Col. Hugh Mercer, of Fredericksburg, Va., and grandson of Gen. Mercer, of the revolution. The deceased was a quiet and retiring, but a noble-hearted and most estimable man. He was guileless, confiding, affectionate, and eminently faithful in all the duties intrusted to him. Few have led a life more free from those frailties and blemishes which so often mar the symmetry of human character.

MERRIAM, Ebenezer, West Brookfield, Mass., Oct. 1, æ. 80, a veteran printer and publisher. He was born at Leicester, Mass., Dec. 15, 1777, and commenced as an apprentice to Isaiah Thomas at Worcester in 1790, when only about 13 years of age; and, after remaining there till 1796, he went to Boston for a few months. Then, under the patronage of Mr. Thomas, he established himself at Brookfield, (now West Brookfield,) at that time an important centre, and commenced in 1797 the publication of the Massachusetts Repository and Farmer's Journal, the Spy being the only other paper printed in the county. The Repository was continued for three years, being printed on the press formerly used by Benjamin Franklin; but, for want of sufficient patronage, Mr. M. gave up its further publication, and in 1800 supplied his office with the necessary material for doing book and job work. In this business he was now assisted by a brother — the father of the Messrs. George and Charles Merriam, of Springfield, Mass.; and for 51 years the office was continued without change, and with almost uninterrupted prosperity. Mr. M.'s business was for many years the publication of such books as Danford's and Eustis's Reports, Chitty's Pleadings, Chitty's Criminal Law, &c., of each of which there were several editions. He also printed many of the New York Reports for the New York booksellers, Connecticut Reports for the publishers, Saunders's Reports, with various other law books. His law-book printing amounted to some 60,000 volumes. In 1814 and 1815, before stereotyping came into vogue, he printed 12,000 octavo Bibles, putting 1800 reams of paper into the edition. Various editions of Watts's Psalms and Hymns, Perry's Dictionary, Fiske's and Webster's Spelling Books, and other books, were also printed by him. The average number of boys in his office was about eight; and the whole number who went through a regular apprenticeship was some 62. Only about half of these are now living; and they are widely scattered throughout the country. In a letter to a friend, written in 1856, Mr. M. says he scarcely ever lost a week in the whole time he continued in business, from sickness or any other cause. He says, "I began without pecuniary means, and shall probably leave the world the same. Owing to my manner of doing business, my losses have been heavy, from $1000 to $5000 at a time, besides other smaller debts in abundance. I have dealt with knaves, rogues, and fools, and many honest men. I have no reflections to cast upon myself, that I have not been industrious and frugal." He was elected a member of the legislature, and filled many public trusts. He died in Christian faith and hope.

MERRILL, Dea. Enos, Milton, Vt., Aug. 9, æ. 90. He was a native of West Hartford, Ct., but at the age of 17 removed to Castleton, Vt., where he lived until Oct., 1856. His residence in Castleton commenced immediately after the revolution, when all was new and as yet unformed. He was present at the installation of the first pastor, and took an active part in laying the foundations of society and religious institutions. In 1790 he became a member of the church, and in 1809 was chosen deacon, in which office he served constantly until his removal in 1856 — a period of 66 years.

MERRILL, Jonathan H., M. D., Salem, N. H., Sept. 1, æ. 57, a highly-esteemed practising physician.

MERRY, Mrs. Phila B., Pawtucket, Mass., Sept. 9, æ. 71. Mrs. M. was of the Andover family of Tyler, in the fifth generation. 1. Job Tyler, of Andover, afterwards of Mendon. 2. Samuel Tyler, of Mendon. 3. Ebenezer Tyler, of Attleboro'. 4. William Tyler, of Providence. 5. Phila Benson, the youngest of 15 children, was born in Providence, Dec. 31, 1787, and married Barney Merry, Esq., Oct. 12, 1807.

METCALF, Hon. Ralph, Claremont, N. H., Aug. 26, æ. 62. Gov. M. was a native of North Charlestown, N. H. He entered Dartmouth College in 1819, and graduated in the class of 1823. In 1825 he began the practice of law at Newport, and five years after was elected secretary of state — an office which he held for several years. He also had a clerkship at Washington for a short time. In 1852 he was chairman of the committee for compiling the laws of the state, and in 1852 and 1853 was a member of the House from Newport. He was elected governor in March, 1855, and was reëlected the next year.

MEYERS, Mrs. Salome, Palmer township, Pa., Feb. 25, æ. 88. She and her deceased husband were both natives of Bucks Co., whence they removed to Northampton Co. 57 years ago. Peter Meyers was a soldier in the American revolution when he was 18 years of age, and subsequently one of the earliest pioneers of Kentucky. He died 38 years ago.

MICHLER, Mrs. Fannie K., New York, N. Y., Oct. 4, wife of Lieut. N. Michler, of the Topographical Corps of Engineers, U. S. A., and daughter of the late Judge Kirtland, of New York.

MIDDLEKAUFF, Rev. D. S., Christian Co., Ill., July 31, æ. —, son of the late Leonard Middlekauff, Sen.

MILBURN, Gen. William, St. Louis, Mo., April 12, æ. —. Gen. M. was born in England, but came to this country at a very early age, and was educated in Virginia. He emigrated to Missouri in 1817, and became deputy surveyor under Gen. Rector, and in that capacity surveyed a large portion of the lands in Missouri. Afterwards he was appointed chief clerk in the surveyor general's office, which office he held until he received the appointment of surveyor general of Illinois and Missouri from President Van Buren. On the change of administration he was removed, solely on political grounds. In 1842 he was elected sheriff of St. Louis Co., which office he held for two consecutive terms. Since that time he lived a retired life, cultivating his farm, and enjoying that repose rendered necessary by long and arduous public services. In all the offices which he held he discharged his duty faithfully, honestly, and satisfactorily, and was generally regarded as a man of great kindness of heart, and honorable in all his transactions.

MILLER, Abraham, Philadelphia, Pa., June 30, æ. 78. The death of this gentleman forcibly recalls to mind events no longer within the recollection of any not of mature years. For years an active and intelligent member of the councils of his native city, he was transferred to represent the same constituents in the Assembly, at Harrisburg, where his distinguished services, as the head of the committee on inland navigation and internal improvement were widely acknowledged. He was then transferred to the state Senate, where his clearness of intellect, purity of principles, and force of character gave him extensive influence. He was the first man in Pennsylvania to propose the revision and abolition of the usury laws,—a measure which, startling the prejudices of those who had not looked into it, is only now, after 20 years' discussion, about to be carried into execution. His mind was of a decided literary turn; in early life a constant poetical correspondent of the then popular journals of the city; and, in later years, his Memorials of the Past, printed for private circulation only, still gives pleasure to those who possess it. But perhaps his strongest characteristic was his unobtrusive benevolence. For many years his anonymous contributions, under various signatures and initials, have been very large indeed; and it was only when no longer able to take charge of business that they became known to his most intimate friends. We subjoin a list of his bequests —

Penn. Inst. for Deaf and Dumb,	$6,000
Orphan's Society of Philadelphia,	2,000
Bible Society of Philadelphia,	2,000
Board of Domestic Missions of Philadelphia,	2,000
Pennsylvania Hospital,	2,000
Union Benevolent Asso. of Phila.,	1,500
The Franklin Institute,	1,000
Widows' and Single Women's Society,	1,000
Walnut Street Charity School,	1,000
Philadelphia Dispensary,	1,000
Penn. Inst. for the Instruction of the Blind,	1,000
Wills's Hosp'l for Lame and Blind,	1,000
Penn. Colonization Society,	1,000
Northern Home for Friendless Children,	1,000
Union Temporary Home for do.,	1,000
Prison Society,	500
Apprentices' Library Company,	500
Academy of Fine Arts,	500
Northern and Southern Dispensaries, each,	500

After numerous legacies of a private nature, Mr. Miller gave the residue of his estate to the Pennsylvania Hospital.

MILLER, F. W., M. D., Portage, Wis., —— 12, æ. 40. Dr. M. was one of the early settlers of Portage, widely known and sincerely respected; as a physician, he was devoted to his profession, and well qualified to practise it successfully; he was prompt, skilful, and attentive; ready for any emergency, and generally judicious in an extremity; the children of poverty never sought his services in vain, or received his *grudging* attention. He had many eminent and remarkable qualities; his impulses were generous, his motives honorable, and his instincts true to humanity; he was always at the post of danger — courageous, self-sacrificing, and self-reliant.

MILLER, Capt. John, Cumberland Co., Va., March 25, æ. 73. Capt. Miller was a prominent man of his county. He received a liberal education at Princeton College, at that day one of the best literary institutions of the country, soon after his return from which he entered on the study of the law, which, however, he did not long continue to practise. Possessed of an ample fortune, he devoted himself to agricultural pursuits, and to the acquisition of such knowledge as might fit him for enlarged usefulness. Soon after his entrance on the duties of active life, the war of 1812 demanded his patriotic services, which he promptly and cheerfully rendered, as captain of the celebrated troop of Cumberland. His fellow-citizens had a high appreciation of his qualifications for usefulness, and called him, for several years, to represent them in the state legislature. In all the varied relations of life he was most exemplary, and worthy of imitation. As a citizen, a friend, a neighbor, a husband, a father, a master, he left a reputation pure and unsullied. There was nothing contracted, nothing little or low about him. He was a Virginia gentleman, in a lofty sense of that term. But his crowning excellence was his sincere Christian piety. His religious character was strongly built on Christian principle. It was the result of intelligent views of God's revealed truth, and the cordial reception of that truth in an honest and humble heart. The result was, a lovely Christian life.

MILLER, Washington, M. D., Sunderland, Mass., May 17, æ. 61.

MILLER, Hon. William, Portage, Wis., June 5, æ. —. At a special meeting of the common council of Portage, the following resolution was passed unanimously: —

"*Resolved*, that in the decease of William Miller, Esq., the Board has lost a prompt and careful guardian of the interests of the city; the community one of their oldest, most active and industrious citizens; and his friends a faithful counsellor and steadfast supporter."

MINER, John D. L., M. D., Chardon, O., May 19, æ. 32.

MINOR, Lucian, Williamsburg, Va., July 6, æ. —. He was, for some time previous to his death, in declining health, so much so as not to have been able to discharge the duties of his chair in William and Mary College, in which institution he was professor of law. Mr. Minor was conspicuous for his ardent advocacy of the temperance cause, and next to Gen. John H. Cocke, of Fluvanna, was perhaps the most zealous adherent of total abstinence in Virginia. It was through his agency that John B. Gough, the eloquent cold-water missionary, first visited Virginia several years ago, before he became famous in England. Mr. Minor served the interests of the temperance reform as an orator himself on very many occasions; nor was he less active with the pen than with the tongue, having written with equal ability and earnestness in behalf of total abstinence in newspapers, periodicals, and pamphlets. As a literary man, he might have acquired an enviable fame, had he directed his energies undividedly to letters. His style was pure, his scholarship profound and extensive, and his taste remarkably correct. The pages of the Southern Literary Messenger bear abundant evidence of his facility in composition, both didactic and imaginative, upon gay or grave subjects. He wrote sometimes for the North American Review, and his articles therein were noted for their good sense and nervous English. The longest literary effort of his that we can now call to mind was his biography of Professor John A. G. Davis, of the University of Virginia, whose violent death in 1840 caused so painful a thrill throughout the length and breadth of the land. As a lawyer, Mr.

Minor was known rather for the extent and accuracy of his learning, than for any commanding success in the courts. For many years he resided in the county of Louisa, where he was especially esteemed, and where he filled the office of prosecuting attorney. Disdaining every thing like artifice, he sought in the practice of his profession only the elucidation of truth and the enforcement of justice, and he has been known frequently to decline the conduct of causes which he thought unsustained by right. As professor of law at William and Mary College, he maintained the high standard of legal proficiency which has always marked that venerable school, and, until his strength began to fail him, labored with unflagging perseverance to bring back to the halls of the old seminary the numbers that in other days flocked thither for instruction.

MINOT, GEORGE, Reading, Mass., April 16, æ. 41. He was son of Hon. Stephen (H. U. 1801) and Rebecca (Trask) Minot, and was born in Haverhill, Mass., Jan. 5, 1817. His father is a son of Capt. Jonas Minot, of Concord, Mass., (where he was born, Sept. 28, 1776,) and has been a lawyer in Haverhill. He was appointed a judge of the Circuit Court of Common Pleas, and held the office until 1820, when the law which created that court was repealed. In 1824 he was appointed county attorney for Essex, which office he resigned in 1830. He still resides in Haverhill. Mr. Minot's mother was a daughter of Samuel Trask, of Bradford, Mass., and deceased several years since. He began to fit for college at Haverhill Academy, and concluded his preparatory studies at Phillips Academy, in Exeter, N. H. Immediately after graduating, (H. U. 1836,) he entered the law school in Cambridge, where he remained two years, when he left, and completed his legal studies in the office of the Hon. Rufus Choate, (D. C. 1819.) He was admitted to the Suffolk bar in April, 1839, and immediately opened an office in Boston. He rose rapidly to distinction, and soon attained to an eminent rank in his profession. Possessing a mind remarkably clear and logical, his counsel was sought in important and intricate cases, which required great acumen, keen discernment, and a nice discrimination. But he was more widely known by his editorial labors. He was the careful and accurate editor of the United States Statutes at Large during ten years. He also rendered valuable assistance to the late Mr. Peters in the preparation of the first eight volumes of the Statutes, published in 1848; the full and complete general index of which was the exclusive result of his labors. His name is also familiar to the legal profession as associate reporter of the decisions of the late Judge Levi Woodbury in the first Circuit Court, and his edition of the nine volumes of English Admiralty Reports, republished by Little, Brown, & Co., in 1854, bears evidence of his industry and learning in this branch of his profession. In 1844 he edited the work which has made his name familiar to every Massachusetts lawyer — the Digest of the Decisions of the Supreme Court of the state, to which he added a supplement in 1852, and, until compelled by the state of his health to lay aside his labors, he was intending to recast the entire work, and, including the later reports, to make it more completely useful to the profession, more just to his own reputation, and that of the court, whose learning and ability it would illustrate. Mr. Minot was for many years solicitor of the Boston and Maine Railroad Corporation. As such he was called on to advise in many very delicate and difficult controversies and deliberations; and in all he was remarkable at once for honesty of purpose, firmness, and discretion. Beyond his profession he read and speculated more variously and more independently than most men of any profession. Elegant literature, music, — of which, in its science and practice he was a lover and master, — politics, theology, in its relations to a religion revealed in the Bible, and to that philosophy which performs its main achievement in conciliating faith with reason, were its recreations. To sacred music and poetry he devoted himself with fervor. He married, first, in 1844, Mrs. Emily P. Ogle, widow of Dr. Richard Ogle, of Demarara, an Englishman by birth. She was the daughter of Dr. Gallup, formerly of Woodstock, Vt., but who resided many years at the Hague, Netherlands, where he married Susan Maria Eversdyk, a Dutch lady, and where this daughter was born. She died in Boston, Nov. 21, 1853, and Mr.

Minot married, second, Dec. 12, 1854, Miss Elizabeth Dawes, daughter of Thomas Dawes, (H. U. 1801,) a lawyer in Boston, and granddaughter of Hon. Thomas Dawes, (H. U. 1777,) who is well remembered by the elder portion of the community as the learned judge successively of Probate, the Municipal, and the Supreme Courts. He left two children, a son by his first wife and a daughter by his second wife. As a citizen, many will bear testimony to his private virtues and his excellence in all the social relations. As a son, he was all that could be desired, attentive, respectful, and affectionate. He was a loving and considerate husband, and the fondest father. He had important trusts reposed in him by friends and relations, who knew their confidence in his ability and integrity could never be shaken, or their hope in him disappointed except by death. Fidelity to the dictates of conscience was his ruling principle of action. His faith in religion was firm, and attended him through life, and shone forth in the perfect resignation with which he bowed to the appointments of Heaven, although he had all that man could desire to render life attractive.

MINOT, Mrs. William, Boston, Mass., ———, æ. —. Mrs. M.'s intellect was of a very high order, and of rare comprehensive power, while her candid temper preserved the balance of her mind, and rendered her judgment just and impartial. She possessed a keen power of analysis and patient investigation, a quickness of perception combined with deliberation in her decisions; she could take in a large circle in her range of thought, and yet detect a minute flaw in any process of reasoning, so that her opinions were of rare value. These powers she chiefly applied to the philosophy of social and domestic life, where her feelings fully entered, giving warmth and brilliancy to all the fibres of those innumerable hearts which looked up to her for advice, instruction, and sympathy. Her days were all marked by an even, flowing beneficence, not confined exclusively to the poor, but spontaneously enriching every social circle, from the world of art and fashion down to the humblest walks of life. Her systematic arrangement of time enabled her to do so much more than usual that the results of her exertions seemed to most persons the effect of miraculous powers, rather than the simple process of giving to every hour its appropriate work. As president of the Bethesda Society she showed her zeal and executive powers no less than her humanity. Hers was not a weak compassion expended in tears, but she aided the unfortunate inmates of that institution by encouraging assurances that they had yet powers which, in spite of past misuse, might enable them to improve themselves and assist others. Mrs. M.'s talents and taste in painting continued to be exercised up to her last illness. Her love of nature, and her delight in preserving, by the sketches of her pencil, every scene of beauty and interest, will recall her to her friends in many a beautiful familiar spot with which her spirit is identified. Perhaps much of the serenity by which she was so distinguished may have been connected with her sympathy for nature in all its beautiful forms. Faithful as a wife, a mother, a sister, and a friend, judging others as she would be judged, her life was marked by obedience to Christian laws; and the hope and trust which her heavenly Father gives to those who try to do his will have been her reward and the consolation of her friends.

MINTURN, Edward, M. D., Philadelphia, Pa., Sept. 6, æ. 27.

MITCHELL, Rev. Charles, Holston conference, Va., June 6, æ. 44. He was born in Smythe Co., Va., Feb. 28, 1814; was married to Miss Sarah Barret, Dec. 2, 1835. He joined the Methodist Episcopal church, and professed religion while in his youth; was licensed to preach in 1847 by Rev. William Hicks, presiding elder on the Wytheville district. He was employed by the presiding elders to travel in 1849, 1850, and 1851, and received elder's orders at the hands of Bishop Early in Knoxville, Tenn., Oct. 28, 1856.

MITCHELL, Edward S., Brunswick, Me., Oct. 27, æ. 29, principal of Brunswick High School.

MITCHELL, J. K., M. D., Philadelphia, Pa., April 4, grand master of the Grand Lodge of Freemasons of Pennsylvania. Dr. M. was born in Sheppardstown, Va., May 12, 1798. His father was a native of Scotland, where the son was sent in 1807 to be educated after his father's decease. In 1816 he returned, and took up his residence in Philadelphia, and entered upon the study of medicine under the tuition of the celebrated Dr. Chapman. His health becoming impaired, he made a voyage to China, where he ultimately accepted the situation of surgeon in one of the ships connected with the China trade. During his residence in China he wrote a number of literary articles of a high order for the magazines and periodicals. Feb. 5, 1833, he was united in marriage with Miss Sarah Matilda Henry, daughter of Alexander Henry, Esq., of Philadelphia. During the same year he was elected physician to the Almshouse Infirmary at Blockley. In 1828 he was elected to the same situation in the Pennsylvania Hospital, and was one of the regular lecturers at the Franklin Institute from 1833 to 1838. In April, 1841, he was unanimously elected professor of the practice of medicine in the Philadelphia Jefferson Medical College, which place he filled with the highest credit to himself until his decease. His scientific, literary, poetical, and miscellaneous productions are of a high order of excellence. As a physician, he stood among the most eminent of the profession; as a writer, he was brilliant and profound; as a citizen, he was justly honored and admired.

MITCHELL, Samuel, Frankfort, Md., Oct. 18, æ. 76, one of the early settlers of Clinton Co., and one of the first associate judges.

MITCHELL, Rev. William B., Hyde Park, Oct. 27, æ. —.

MIXER, Warren N., drowned on the way from Amoor River, Eastern Siberia, to San Francisco, Nov. 10, æ. 30. He was a native of Buffalo, brother of Dr. S. F. Mixer, of Buffalo. He had been superintending the construction at the Amoor of two steamers for the Russian government, and was a talented and energetic man, and one whose sterling integrity and amiability endeared him to his friends. His enterprise and skill in his profession gave great promise of future usefulness.

MOBBY, Rev. Zalmon, Canaan, Ct., Sept. 17, æ. 66. In early life he was pastor of the Baptist church in Bristol, and afterwards pastor of the Fourth Baptist Church in Pawtuxet. He graduated at Brown in the class of 1817.

MONELL, Mrs. Mary E., Newburg, N. Y., Oct. 22, æ. about 38, wife of John J. Monell, and daughter of Hon. N. B. Smith, of Woodbury, Ct. She was the rightful inheritor by birth of rare mental gifts. The daughter of parents themselves richly endowed by nature and liberalized by culture, she grew up into womanhood the object of mingled admiration and affection on the part not only of the circle to which she belonged, but of all who knew her. To a temperament constitutionally cheerful and happy, and to a mind and character well poised, she added the refinements of an exquisite taste, a cultivated intellect, a heart warm with all womanly affections, and ennobled by a sincere Christian faith. From her many natural gifts and her admirable use of them, her death has left a very unusual void in the community where she resided. In her beautiful home on the Hudson, she was a rare model of lovely tenderness and goodness. But she is a loss scarcely less to society at large than to her own circle and family. With her high mental endowments and her most winning personal loveliness, she had a breadth of human charity and Christian liberality of which the whole community felt the influence. From this inborn and undeniable superiority, this instinctive nobleness and truthfulness, she became the leader in all the good works of the neighborhood, in the furtherance of liberal public objects as well as in the refinements of home and the hospitalities of the drawing room. To all classes her death is a loss that will be thought truly irreparable; while, for the relatives and more intimate friends whom she has left, it will be long before she can be mentioned without a tear at the heart.

MONTGOMERY, R., M. D., Xenia, O., Aug. 15, æ. 60. He was a man of fine literary attainments, and was at one time a regular contributor to Blackwood and other magazines.

MONTGOMERY, Robert, Little Fishing Creek, near Danville, Pa., Jan. 31, æ. 84. He was an early settler of Trumbull Co., having located in Poland township in 1806, where, with others, he established the first iron works in that part of Ohio. In 1816 he removed to Coltsville. He was distinguished as a theoretical and practical agriculturist, was possessed of a peculiarly investigating mind, and a man of varied and extensive information. He retained his intellectual faculties in full perfection until near the close of life, and died in the faith of the Christian religion.

MONTGOMERY, William, M. D., Shippenburg, Pa., Sept. 22, æ. 23.

MOODEY, Rev. Pliny, Kirtland, O., April 4, æ. 33.

MOODY, Hon. Stephen, æ. 75.

MOODY, Mrs. Frances, æ. 85.

Entombed March 24, 1858, Stephen Moody, Esq., who died at Gilmanton, N. H., April 21, 1842, and Mrs. Frances Moody, his widow, who died at Hanover, N. H., March 22, 1858, at the residence of her son-in-law, Prof. Crosby. The remains were deposited in the tomb of the late Joseph Cutler, Esq., in St. Paul's Churchyard, in Newburyport, according to an arrangement of some years' standing. These facts furnish but another expression of the strong attachment of the former natives of New England to the place of their birth or early associations, and of their desire to have their last resting place amidst the scenes of their youth. Mr. M., we are informed, was born upon the old Moody farm, opposite the old Newbury (Newtown) meeting house, now occupied by Mr. M. Ridgeway, a descendant of the family. This farm has been in the Caleb Moody family, through four successive men of that name, to his father. Mrs. M. was the daughter of William Coffin, one of the eminent business men of Newburyport, whose farm and house were upon the rising swell of land beyond Pipe-stave hill, and whose ancient house is still standing. After the death of Mr. Coffin, his widow removed to Newburyport, and lived for many years on High Street, in the house removed by the building of the railroad. Mrs. M. was the sister of the late Tristram Coffin, one of the eminent merchants of this place at the opening of this century, and of the old firm of Coffin & Otis. She was also sister of Mrs. Marquand, wife of Joseph Marquand, once a princely merchant here, and for many years collector of customs. Mr. M. graduated at Cambridge in the distinguished class of which the Hon. Josiah Quincy was a member. He read law with the late Hon. Levi Lincoln, of Worcester, and settled in Gilmanton, where he spent his life, eminent in his profession, widely known and greatly useful in all the relations of life. These two individuals, whose memory is tenderly cherished and reverenced by the survivors, were eminently people of the old school, as their abundant and uniform hospitality, their dignified and courteous manners, their sacred keeping of the Sabbath, and the strict moral and religious training of their household fully show. Both experimentally embraced the gospel of Jesus, and "died in faith." They were joined in marriage by the late Rev. John Andrews, D. D., and their children were baptized by Rt. Rev. Edward Bass, D. D., and Rev. James Morss, D. D., late rectors of St. Paul's Church. They had only three children, daughters, who married, and are wives of Hon. N. Crosby, of Lowell, Mass., Rev. Prof. Rood, of Vt., and Prof. Crosby, of the Dartmouth Medical College. — *Newburyport* (Mass.) *Herald.*

MOONEY, Mrs. Sarah, Meredith, N. H., Dec. 14, æ. 89. Mrs. M. was the daughter of Judge Smith, who was one of the first settlers of the town of Meredith. Possessing a mind of no common order, she was able accurately to relate the various incidents of her life up to the hour of her death. She lived to see fall about her very many of her kindred; but however tender the tie that was sundered, she ever submitted with that pious resignation which characterizes the sincere Christian. Judges Mooney and Smith were rich specimens of the New England men who laid the foundations of society in our country towns. Rising generations will long bless the memories of such men.

MOORES, Rev. Josiah, Columbia Co., Ark., Aug. 19, æ. 82. He was born in North Carolina, Feb., 1776, and joined the M. E. church in 1799; emigrated at an early day to Kentucky, and thence to Tennessee, where he raised a large family; for the last ten years he had been in Arkansas; was ordained deacon by Bishop Roberts, in Shelbyville, Tenn. Nov., 1825. He was a faithful, consistent Christian, and a great lover of the peculiar doctrines and usages of the M. E. church. He was a Methodist of the old stamp, and knew all the old Methodist preachers of Middle Tennessee and North Alabama. He attended, in the days of his strength, camp meetings far and near, and was never known to miss circuit-preaching when he was able to go, whether in the week or on the Sabbath.

MOORHEAD, Maj. James, Kittanning, Armstrong Co., Pa., Oct. 18, æ. 66. He was at one time one of the most prominent citizens of the community in Armstrong Co. He ably represented it in the legislature, and was highly esteemed for his public and private virtues.

MOORHEAD, Hon. John, Fairfield Township, Westmoreland Co., Pa., Dec. 8, æ. 66. He was born in Derry Township, April 23, 1793, and soon after his arrival, at the age of 21 years, removed to his late residence, where he continued to live until the time of his decease. He held several highly responsible and important offices, the duties of which were discharged in a fair and impartial manner, and with due regard to the public interest. In 1835 he was commissioned a justice of the peace of Fairfield Township, by Gov. Wolf, and in 1841 he was commissioned by Gov. Porter, an associate judge of the several courts of Westmoreland Co., under the amended constitution of 1837 and 1838, for five years, and at the expiration of that period was again commissioned, by the lamented Gov. Shunk, for another term. During the time of his being on the bench, by the uprightness of his conduct, discriminating judgment and candid manner in the discharge of his judicial functions, he commanded the respect and esteem of his colleagues on the bench, the bar, and his fellow-citizens.

MORFIT, John C., M. D., Chicago, Ill., Jan. 8, æ. —.

MORGAN, Mrs. Rebecca, Jeffersonville, Ind., Dec. —, æ. 80. She was a native of Virginia, and settled at Springville, Clark Co., at a very early day. She was a resident of Jeffersonville 56 years, and entertained the first trustees of the town, and the first court of Clark Co. She was twice married, and the mother of the first white child born in Clark Co.

MORGAN, Mrs. Jane Gilman, Washington, O., ——— 13, æ. 49, wife of D. T. Morgan, Esq., and daughter of the late Dudley Woodbridge, Esq., of Marietta, O. The character of this estimable lady deserves a far more extended tribute than the columns of a newspaper will allow. She was descended, in a direct line, from the well-known Congregational clergyman, the Rev. John Woodbridge, whose grandfather was driven out of England, in the reign of Elizabeth, for Puritanism, and who himself immigrated to this country in 1634, settled as the first minister in Newbury, Mass., married a daughter of the Hon. Thomas Dudley, governor of the colony, and was first of a line of clergymen, (all named John, and all eldest sons,) extending through six or seven generations. Mrs. M. herself was a child of the grace of God, thus signalized in the generations of her pious ancestry.

MORRILL, Hon. Samuel, Concord, N. H., Sept. 7, æ. 79. Dr. M. was a native of Epping; was admitted in early life to the practice of medicine, which he commenced in Salisbury. In 1800 he removed to Epsom, where he held important local offices, and in 1819 became a resident of Concord. He was appointed in 1821 a justice of the Court of Sessions, represented the town of Concord in the legislature of 1822, was the first register of deeds of Merrimack Co., was judge of probate of said county from 1823 to 1828, when he was chosen treasurer of the state. Upon the organization of the N. H. Savings Bank in Concord in 1830, he was chosen treasurer, and continued to discharge his duties as such, as he had those of all his other trusts, with signal fidelity, till his resignation in 1856.

MORRILL, Jeremiah, Boscawen, N. H., June 4, æ. 83.

MORRILL, Joseph, Boscawen, N. H., March 31, æ. 93.

MORRIS, Edward A., Springfield, Mass., Sept. 2, æ. 57, at the residence of his brother, Judge Oliver B. Morris. He was born in Wilbraham, Mass., March 14, 1801, but early in life removed to Springfield, and entered the service of Moses Bliss, merchant, on State Street. Samuel Reynolds was at the same time a clerk for Daniel Bontecou, on Main Street; and the two young men, after attaining majority, united in business under the name of Reynolds & Morris, and for 25 years were among the leading merchants of the town, occupying the stand now held by Mr. A. M. Lincoln. Industry and integrity, in a high degree, marked their business conduct, and achieved their due reward. Some ten years since, they gave up trade, and Mr. Reynolds became president of the Chicopee Bank, and while in that position died. Mr. Morris, several years later, followed him in a bank presidency, succeeding Mr. Benjamin Day in the Springfield Bank, and now, at a similar remove, has followed his old friend and partner to the grave. Both were often alike called to service in our municipal affairs, and Mr. Morris was the leading member of the board of assessors for some years. Intelligent and sensible in all business and public affairs; conscientious in the discharge of every duty; just to friends and generous to all; kind and genial in temperament; pure and pious in all his life, — few men were more widely known or better beloved in the community than Mr. Morris. His death is a public loss. He was never married, but through the families of his brothers had a wide range of relatives, by all of whom he was held in esteem and love. The following resolutions by the directors of the Springfield Bank are but the voice of the business community upon his life and death : —

"*Resolved*, that while he has by a long and useful life won high respect as a valuable citizen and a Christian gentleman, and while his death is therefore an affliction in which all our citizens must have part, it calls upon us, who have been associated with him in the discharge of common duties, for a special expression of our share in the general sorrow.

"*Resolved*, that by a long and honorable performance of many and various business trusts, he was entitled to the respect awarded for unquestioned integrity and fidelity in such duties; that by faithful attention to his duties while a director, and by special devotion to the interests of the bank since he was elected president, he has won our highest confidence, and is entitled to a grateful remembrance."

MORRIS, William Gardner, M. D., Delhi, N. Y., June 13, æ. 31.

MORRIS, Jacob, Long Branch, Pa., Aug. —, æ. 80, a veteran of the war of 1812. He first enlisted at Shrewsbury, and the next day joined a detachment of the army at Trenton, and soon marched for the scene of action. He served two and a half years, and was in the battle of Lundy's Lane, where he received a severe wound in the leg from a cannon ball. He was principally employed in Canada and on the frontier.

MORSE, Eliakim, M. D., Watertown, Mass., Jan. 9, æ. 98. He was, in early life, an active business man, doing a considerable importing trade, particularly in the article of drugs, and, it is said, was one of the first, if not the first, to despatch a vessel from this country to Europe upon the close of the revolutionary war. For a long period, however, he lived in retiracy, upon a beautiful estate in Watertown, occasionally riding about on horseback or in his carriage, the form of the latter, pertaining, as it did, to the days of Washington, exciting general attention. He was a firm adherent of the late whig party, and was unshaken in his political faith until the day of his death. His last appearance at a political meeting was as vice president of an assemblage of that party at Faneuil Hall, in connection with the position of Daniel Webster.

MORSE, Benjamin F., M. D., Fremont, O., April 26, æ. 45. The larger part of his active life as a physician was spent in Peru, Huron Co., O., where his skill and fidelity in his profession, and his character as a man and a Christian, gave him an honorable standing among an extensive circle of friends and acquaintances.

MOSELY, Major Thomas, Sarcoxie, Jasper Co., Mo., July 16, æ. 66. He was born in Woodford Co., Ky., July 12, 1792. He emigrated to Missouri in 1819, and upon the organization of the state government, was appointed clerk of the Circuit Court of Madison Co.

MOTT, Mrs. Emma D., Winterset, Ill., Sept. 23, æ. 26. She was born in Grafton, Windham Co., Vt., in 1832. She was the daughter of Dea. P. W. Dean, a man of eminence as a citizen and a Christian. From pious parents she received early religious instruction, and also a liberal education, graduating from the Ludlow Academy, Vt., and the Meredith Academy, N. H. For three years she was preceptress of the Baptist Seminary at Derby, Vt., and in Nov., 1856, she was married to Frederick Mott, an attorney at law of Derby Line, Vt. In the spring of 1857 she and her husband both received appointments as teachers in the Iowa Central University, and went to that state for the purpose of entering said institution, but the financial revulsion had been so great, the proposed endowment of the college was incomplete, and they were led to turn their attention elsewhere.

MULBETT, Hon. James, Fredonia, N. Y., Sept. 10, æ. 78. A local paper says, "He was born at Guilford, Vt., where his father, a not affluent farmer, taught him the toil of a farmer's life, until he was old enough to learn a trade. He then worked for some years at the business of a cabinet maker. Quitting this as an occupation uncongenial to his mind and wishes, he next tried a mercantile life. This he also abandoned after a brief period, and commenced the study of the law in 1813 or 1814, under the direction and in the office of Hon. Jacob Houghton. He went to reside in Fredonia, Chautauque Co., in 1810, soon after the organization of the county, and has continued to reside in that village ever since, except a very brief period before his elevation to the bench. He represented Chautauque Co. as a member of the legislature in 1823 and 1824, was for several years district attorney of the county, and was elected one of the justices of the Supreme Court, at the first judicial election under the new constitution in 1847, and was reëlected in 1851. Borne down by ill health, he resigned his office in 1856, and has now terminated a long, eventful, useful, and finally a Christian life. In all the relations of life, whether as citizen, lawyer, or judge, his genial disposition, his quick perceptions, and his uncompromising love of justice, commended him to the esteem and regard of all who were so fortunate as to know him, and he always enjoyed a large share in the affections of his associates and the community in which he lived; and his death leaves. a void which will always remain unfilled.

MULLIKEN, Samuel, Newburyport, Mass., Nov. 29, æ. 89. He was known for many years as cashier, successively, of the old Newburyport Bank, and of the present Merchants Bank, of that city. He served in these two institutions more than 40 years, having resigned his office in 1851, at the age of 82. He was probably the oldest bank officer, in regular, active service, in the country at that time. His recollections went back to the early history of the revolution. The battles of Lexington and Bunker Hill, the "Ipswich Alarm," the encampment and embarkation at this place of Arnold's expedition, and all the principal events and prominent actors of that period and of our whole revolutionary history, were fresh in his memory. The Daltons, the Tracys, the Jacksons, the Greenleafs, the Johnsons, Parsons, Bradburys, &c., of Newburyport, were within his personal knowledge, and were many of them his contemporaries and associates. When a pilgrim pursues a long journey without stumbling, he becomes from that very circumstance worthy of double respect. We look on his age as we do on the autumnal flowers, which continue to blow when the frost has withered all around them. Life is but a variety of temptations; and the man that has been sober in youth, and cheerful in age, and honest in all his connections, leaves us a beautiful example. Such was our aged and respected fellow-citizen whose death we record. His integrity, his temperance, his uniformity, his wonderful art of making life calmly pleasant, are worthy of careful imitation and constant remembrance. It is not enough to speak of his integrity; there was a peculiar security which every one felt in every trust committed to his hand. For him to depart from integrity was as little to be expected as a deviation in one of the great laws of nature. His principles were founded on religion, and therefore they were immovable. He had cultivated his mind; he had guarded his heart; he had bowed to the authority of his God. In the parlor, at the desk, in the walk, he was the agreeable companion. He was a close observer of events and men, and hence his conversation had all the charms of a colloquial history. Nowhere did he shine more than at his own fireside, surrounded by the smiles of his affectionate household.

MULVEY, B. C., M. D., Saco, Me., July —, æ. —. He graduated at Brunswick in 1831, and immediately entered upon the duties of his profession. For many years he was extensively known and highly appreciated, both as a skilful surgeon and a good physician. He was an accomplished scholar and a true gentleman, and possessed uncommon powers of application. He had acquired a great amount of knowledge upon all subjects relating to his profession, and his judgment was remarkable. His great tact in the most difficult cases could not but render him a popular doctor, and make a demand for his services far and near. He would exhaust the powers of his own nature for the comfort of his patients, and was kind and sympathetic almost to a fault, never distressing any one upon whom he had a demand.

MUNCE, Capt. Thomas S., Natchez, Miss., Aug. 14, æ. 44, a native of N. He was educated at Washington College, Penn., commenced the study of law in the office of Hon. R. J. Walker in N., but left for an office in the Mississippi Railroad Bank, was long a member and ultimately captain of that noted volunteer company, the Natchez Fencibles, went to the Mexican war in the second regiment of Mississippi rifles as first lieutenant in Capt., afterwards Col., now Gen. Charles Clarke's company, served there, and returned as adjutant of his regiment.

MUNROE, Mrs. Lucelia T., Bradford, Mass., Sep'. 20, æ. 46, wife of Rev. Nathan Munroe, one of the editors of the Boston Recorder. Mrs. M. was a native of South Reading, where she spent her earlier years. In the course of her education she was connected with Bradford Academy, and afterwards with the school of Rev. Mr. Brace, in Hartford, Ct. At this latter institution she was graduated. In 1836 she was a teacher for a short time in Bradford Academy, under the care of Miss Abigail C. Hasseltine. She here became acquainted with Rev. Nathan Munroe, the pastor of the church in Bradford, to whom she was married in 1842. In the discharge of the varied duties of the Christian woman, wife, and mother, with great fidelity and affection, she passed the remainder of her years, until early on Monday morning, Sept. 20, and at such an hour as she thought not, she was called to her final rest. Some would say she was suddenly arrested in the midst of unfinished plans of usefulness. Why not say she was permitted to pass from hope to fruition sooner than she had dared to expect? Among her Christian excellences was a conscientiousness that covered every moral act. It was not reserved for great occasions, but was kept strong, and healthy, and active by daily use. She had excellent practical judgment; in other words, a broad and sound common sense. She had a comprehensive mind, well-balanced and well-furnished, and which, therefore, could not but work well upon all questions submitted to it. She had a large measure of Christian charity; the love that believeth all things good, and thinketh no evil, putting a charitable construction upon the conduct of those who were not present to defend themselves. Her character seems an eminently practical and useful one for this world; best fitted to help us through this rugged scene smoothly, while at the same time imparting the largest amount of happiness to others. It was not a combination of angelic graces, but of human virtues energized and sweetened by a living Christian spirit, and all employed in doing good for the Master's sake.

MUNSELL, Hezekiah, Hoosic Falls, Rensselaer Co., N. Y., April 15, æ. 86. He was a lawyer, and in earlier days held a prominent position among the profession in Rensselaer Co. He was an educated man, and was highly esteemed and respected by the citizens of Hoosic. He had held various town offices of trust and responsibility, and was the author of Munsell's English Grammar, a work extensively used in the schools at one time. He was also, some years ago, an active democratic politician.

MURDOCK, Oscar, Esq., Charlestown, Mass., June 26, æ. 30, son of Col. Judson and Judith M. Murdock of C. He was born in Hubbardstown, but his father, having lived many years in Boston prior to 1850, when he moved to Charlestown, trained his son by clerkship to assume the responsibilities of business. He entered, therefore, early upon a career of business and public life, and was widely known and appreciated. He was elected a member of the common council in 1855 and 1856, and last year as a member of the board of aldermen. As a city official he was always prompt and attentive to the duties imposed, and being possessed of pleasing and cordial manners, was highly esteemed by his associates. At his death he had widely extended his business and responsibilities as a merchant in Boston, and seemed really to have but just entered upon the great sphere of his opening influence. The board of aldermen say, "We cheerfully bear witness to his worth, and to the public loss which his death has occasioned, that, while we remember the faithful officer, we should not forget the generous and noble-hearted friend, or the social virtues which he possessed, and which make his death so great a bereavement to relatives and friends."

MYERS, Col. Michael, Madison, Wis., May 22, æ. 65. He was formerly a colonel in the U. S. army, and had been sheriff of Kenosha Co.

N.

NAPIER, Mrs. Elizabeth B., Marion, S. C., Aug. 15, æ. 40, wife of Rev. Robert Napier, for 24 years an exemplary Christian, and down to the last year of her useful life a member of the Sabbath school, studying the word of God with her children. In death her faith was strong and triumphant.

HON. FREDERICK NASH, Hillsboro', N. C., Dec. 4, æ. 76, the venerable and beloved chief justice of N. C. He was the son of Abner Nash, Gov. of N. C. in 1799, and a nephew of Gen. Francis Nash, who fell mortally wounded while fighting for his country at the battle of Brandywine. Judge N. was born in Newburn, in 1781. He represented that borough in the House of Commons in 1804 and 1805. In 1818 he was elected a judge of the Superior Court, which he resigned in 1819. In 1827 and 1828, he represented Hillsboro' in the House of Commons. In 1836 he was again elected a judge of the Superior Court, from which, in 1844, he was transferred to the Supreme Court bench, which dignified position he occupied until his death, with credit to himself and to the state.

NEALE, Dr. Thomas, Romney, Va., May 6, æ. —. late of Jackson City, Mo. He was one of five sons of the late Thomas Neale, a wealthy and admired citizen of Va., and after completing his education, he made the tour of Europe. Soon after his return he commenced the study of medicine, and removed to the "far west," where he spent his long and useful life. He was a remarkably kind and affectionate husband and father, ever just, talented, and learned; and no man ever stood higher for uprightness in all his business transactions with his fellow-men. He has left a widow and two children. He was buried with the honors and ceremonies of Freemasonry.

NEELY, Hon. B. H., Batesville, Ark., Aug. 28, æ. —. He had been judge of the Circuit Court, and was held in high esteem by all who knew him.

NELSON, A. F., Bath, Me., Dec. 19, æ. 65. He was a native of England, and one of the crew of the Boxer, at the time of her sanguinary engagement with the Enterprise, in the war of 1812.

HON. ALBERT HOBART NELSON, at the McLean Hospital, Somerville, June 27, æ. 46, of Woburn, Mass. He was born in Milford, Mass., March, 1812, where his father, John Nelson, was a practising physician. He entered Harvard College in the class of 1832, and was graduated that year with honors. In the same class was his associate on the Superior Court bench, Judge Abbott. Mr. N. studied law under the direction and in the office of the late Hon. Samuel Hoar, of Concord, for a long time one of the leading members of the Middlesex bar. In 1839 he entered upon the practice of his profession, at Concord, and in 1842 removed to Woburn, where he has since resided. About the year 1846 he was appointed district attorney for the Middlesex district, and filled the station in a most satisfactory manner, until ill health compelled him to resign. The Senate chamber was his post for two successive sessions; and while there, his practical common sense and facility of expression made him a useful and valued senator. He was appointed a councillor under the American regime in 1854, and continued in that position until transferred to the chief justiceship of the Superior Court of Suffolk Co., in the fall of 1855. He sat on the bench until last spring, when he was obliged to resign in consequence of continued ill health; severe shocks of paralysis completely mastering him, and bearing him to the grave.

Mr. N. was a warm-hearted, generous man, a valuable, public-spirited citizen, an able and accomplished lawyer. In his intercourse with his fellow-men he was popular. The adaptation of his mind to all classes of people was most ready and perfect. Intuitive perceptive faculties were improved upon by the requisitions of the profession which he had chosen. His excellent taste and cultivated intellect made him an acquisition every where. His ease and gracefulness of manner placed any one with whom he came in contact upon a friendly and familiar footing, and he had a genial manner, which recommended itself and shed a delightful charm around him. As a citizen, Woburn had reason to be proud of him, for he was always ready, willing, and eager to improve and adorn the town by valuable suggestions, practical opinions, and material aid. Schools and public institutions were benefited by his large experience and generous views, and his valuable services will long be remembered and appreciated. His courteousness and urbanity of manner were peculiarly appreciated by his brother members of his profession. His kindness and consideration for younger and less experienced gentlemen of the profession were marked, and in these respects he set a noble example, worthy of emulation. The Suffolk bar were pleased at his appointment, and he confirmed their kind opinion of him by his patient consideration of causes, by his ready despatch of business, by his quickness of perception of legal points, and, above all, by his gentlemanly and kind bearing to all.

At a session of the Superior Court in Boston, of which he had been chief justice, the four judges being present, C. W. Cooley, Esq., district attorney of the committee, upon offering resolutions of respect and condolence of the Suffolk bar, among other things said, referring to his appointment to the office of chief justice of the new court, that his remaining associates on that bench would bear witness that he appreciated the responsibility of his position; that he entered upon his duties with a generous ambition and purpose that none of them should be left unperformed, and that the court should be a useful and successful one. All will agree that he was energetic, prompt, and faithful, and that he did his duty invariably well. "It was my fortune," said the district attorney, "to be connected with the court during the whole period of his service. He had a comprehensive mind, embracing at a glance all the facts relating to a case. He was ready in his recollection of the law, and he accurately and forcibly applied it. His learning was such that he always acquitted himself with great credit, and he had that large basis of common sense which led him to appreciate what the law ought to be; and he hardly ever failed to conform to the law as it had been before announced.

Judge N. was a gentleman, on the bench, of urbane manners and the kindest disposition. He won the affection of all who were connected with him. It is no injustice to others to say that in almost all particulars he was regarded as a model judge."

Mr. Cooley, in behalf of the bar, requested the following resolutions to be entered upon the records of the court; to which Chief Justice Allen briefly responded.

"*Resolved*, that the late Chief Justice, thus cut off in the full strength of his manhood, is entitled to the respectful recollection of all who can appreciate that rare combination of talent and learning, with personal and official integrity, kindness of heart, sweetness of temper, and an unfailing courtesy of demeanor, at the bar and on the bench, of which he furnished so signal an example.

"*Resolved*, that we deplore his death, because of his usefulness and lofty promise as a jurist and a judge, because of his attractiveness and beauty of personal character, and because we sympathize with his bereaved family and surviving friends."

In the Court of Common Pleas, Judge Bishop said, "His intellectual attainments and capacity made him an eminent lawyer, and his courteousness in the practice of his profession was worthy of all praise. His integrity and faithfulness as a public officer were in accordance with strict fidelity to duty. As a member of the bar he exhibited what all of us love, and what has great power—strict honesty and great integrity. He was a man of great intellectual scope."

NELSON, Morgan, Esq., Wheeling, Va., Dec. 25, æ. —. Mr. N. went to Wheeling from New England about 40 years ago, and has been engaged in the practice of law during that period, and although of serious and reserved manner, was always urbane and respectful in his deportment towards his brethren at the bar, and charitable in his construction of the motives of others. His loss will be long and deservedly felt in the domestic circle in which he moved. He also occupied a high position in the Masonic body, and has filled the highest offices therein during a long term of years. The resolutions of the city council, and of the members of the bar, speak of him in honorable terms. The council, having been informed of the death of Morgan Nelson, Esq., doth, on motion, "*Resolved*, that in the death of Morgan Nelson, so long a citizen of the place, and so favorably known to us all, our city and our community have sustained a deep and heartfelt loss.

"*Resolved*, that though not recently one of our body, yet we cannot but be mindful of his long and valuable services as a member of this body, and also as mayor of this city — a position always pleasant to the council, from the unaffected and courteous manner which ever distinguished his official relations; and that this council takes this melancholy occasion to testify alike to his official integrity and his private virtues."

NESMITH, Mrs. Margaret, Windham, N. H., Dec. 4, æ. 71, wife of Col. Jacob M. Nesmith.

NETTLES, Dr. Joseph A., Philadelphia, Pa., July 7, æ. —, suddenly, at the Girard House, a resident of the parish of East Baton Rouge, and a man of wealth. The Alumni Association of Centenary College of La., where he graduated in 1849, say of him, that "in the loss of our brother, this association has been deprived of a faithful and valued member, society of a useful and respected citizen, and his family and friends of one whose kind heart and gentle nature endeared him to all.

NEVINS, John J., Washington, D. C., April 15, æ. —. He graduated at Georgetown College, and always resided in the District. He was among the most efficient clerks employed in the census office under Mr. Kennedy, where his knowledge of foreign languages and his talents as a statistician rendered his services of great value. From the census office he was transferred to the department of state, where he was highly esteemed for his varied talents and excellent characteristics.

NEW, Dr. Walter Wyatt, Hinds Co., Miss., Feb. 28, æ. 67, surgeon in the United States army during the war of 1812. He was a son of Col. Anthony New, of Virginia, and subsequently of Kentucky. He served fourteen years in the navy, and was promoted on account of his eminent merit from the post of assistant surgeon to that of fleet surgeon. He was in active service during the war of 1812, and was in several of the battles with Commodore Bainbridge, Porter, and Perry, and at the close of the war was presented by Congress with a medal in acknowledgment of his services.

NEWBERRY, Hon. Amasa Stoughton, Sangerfield, N. Y., March 15, æ. 56. He was one of the most prominent citizens of his town and county; and his name and influence were widely known as those of an upright, reliable, and honorable man. Throughout his life he was a warm supporter of the institutions of religion; and in his end he embraced its consolations, and trusted in its promises.

NEWBOLD, George, ———, ———, ———, æ. about 76, the venerable and highly-respected president of the Bank of America, in New York city. He left New York in his usual health, intending to visit his brother-in-law, Dr. Fox, at Andalusia, Pa.; but whether he died there or at his brother's, in Georgetown, N. J., does not appear. He was for many years prominently identified with the financial and banking history of New York. Having been previously cashier and director of the Bank of America, he became, May 15, 1832, president, and held that office until his death. He was familiar with Gallatin, Worth, and Wilkes, and other eminent contemporaries.

NEWELL, Charles, West Newbury, June 23, æ. 22, son of the late Hon. Moses Newell.

NEWELL, John, Woodstock, Ill., June 29, æ. 90. "Father Newell" was born at Salem, Mass., Jan. 31, 1768. He was married Sept. 1, 1791, and moved to New Hampshire, where he resided nearly 60 years. Some eight years since he came to Woodstock to spend the remainder of his days with his children, three of whom reside there. He had lived more than 60 years a consistent Christian life, always cheerful and contented, and ready to speak a word in behalf of that cause which lay so near his heart. He leaves a wife, with whom he had lived for nearly 70 years, and a large number of children, grandchildren, and friends to mourn his absence.

NEWELL, Hon. Moses, West Newbury, Mass., March 12, æ. 65. "This has been a mournful day in West Newbury. A melancholy has settled upon all our population at the funeral of Hon. Moses Newell — respected, honored, and beloved for his many manly and noble qualities of character, and for his many benevolent and useful acts in life. Col. N. has left many good men and respected citizens behind him; but we know not one in whom the community in which he was born, and for 65 years had lived, had more implicit confidence. Faithfully and honestly, with few words and many acts, he performed his duties as a man, and a citizen, and a Christian, and has left a reputation honorable to head and heart. Col. N. was the son of Joseph Newell, Esq., one of the most prominent and active citizens of 'Ould Newbury,' who deceased more than 30 years ago; and the son inherited those qualities that had endeared the father to all his acquaintances, as he also succeeded him in the cultivation of the ancestral acres, being especially devoted to farming life. There practically and scientifically he was at home; his instincts, thoughts, desires, and sympathies fitted him for a New England farmer. He was the largest landholder in West Newbury. His homestead, upon which he had erected convenient and elegant buildings, embraced a fine tract — even as a prairie, and as rich as the virgin soil of the west, yielding abundant harvests. His out-lands were extensive in this and neighboring towns; and in his extensive pastures, which enclosed the highest hill in this vicinity, fed his flocks, and herds of new and improved stock, which he had introduced to improve the milking qualities of the cows of his native town; and to this end he had done more than any other person, expending time, money, and labor. As a farmer his reputation was not confined within narrow limits. He was one of the trustees of the Essex Agricultural Society as early as 1823, and so continued until 1852, when he was chosen president. For four years he presided over the society with marked ability; and the farmers of Essex will not soon forget the urbanity with which he conducted their annual meeting, nor the enthusiasm that he so largely infused into all their transactions. In 1856 he resigned his position, but not the labors or duties of an active member of the society. He was also a member of the state Board of Agriculture, and one of the trustees having the charge and supervision of the state farm at Westboro', and was 'one of the most efficient members of the United States Agricultural Society. It was only in January last that he attended the annual meeting of the national society at Washington. His interest in the promotion of this great industrial pursuit of the country was second to no other man's. He declined no duty, grudged no time or expense, for its advancement. He was always at his post when any thing was to be done. His advice was freely sought in all matters pertaining to the interests of agriculture, and was always as freely given. Here none were wiser in counsel, none more efficient in action, than he. The farmers of the county have in him lost one of their noblest representatives and most devoted friends.'" — *Newburyport Herald*. That Mr. N. was also held in high estimation by the citizens generally of the county is evidenced by the fact that for six years, from 1835 to 1841, he filled the office of county commissioner by their suffrages, and soon after this period was by them elected to the Senate of the commonwealth, entering this branch of the legislature in 1850. He also filled numerous other important public trusts with marked intelligence, promptness, and fidelity. His life has been one of great activity and usefulness in the service of the public, more from a sense of duty and a desire of benefiting others than from any regard to his own fame or aggrandizement. He was eminently disinterested in his motives of action.

NEWELL, Zebina, Esq., Keene, N. H., March —, æ. —, president of the Cheshire Co. Bank.

NEWHALL, Hon. Francis S., Lynn, Mass., Feb. —, æ. —. He was well known as a leader of the boot and shoe trade, and as president of the Laighton Bank. He had been a member of both branches of the legislature.

NEWHALL, Isaac, Lynn, Mass., July 6, æ. 75. He was no ordinary man. He was for several years, and during the second war, a merchant at Salem, where he had accumulated a small fortune, but which was lost by the fall of merchandise on the restoration of peace. After that time he removed to Macon, Ga., where he resided for several years, and then removed to Lynn, where he has since lived. He was a man of studious habits and extensive reading, fond of literature, and remarkably well-informed upon the subjects of British letters and politics. He was the writer of a series of papers upon the authorship of "Junius," which attracted no little attention among men of learning, while they exhibited the rare ability and learning of their author.

NEWTON, Dr. George M., ———, ———, ———, æ. 48. Dr. N. was born in ———, in the year 1810. After completing his collegiate career at the University of Georgia, he engaged in the study of medicine; and, graduating with honor at the University of Pennsylvania, he spent several years in the schools and hospitals of Paris. Soon after his return to his native city, he was elected to the chair of physiology in the Medical College of Georgia, but was subsequently transferred to the chair of anatomy, which he filled for about 20 years, with distinguished ability. It may be said with truth that he had in this position no superiors, and but few equals. About two years ago he retired from the duties of his profession, carrying with him, in his retirement, the profound respect of his colleagues, and of hundreds of physicians scattered over the land, who had had the good fortune to be his pupils. He never engaged in the active duties of his profession. An ample fortune enabled him to devote his time to the cultivation of literature and science. His mind was clear, acute, and vigorous. His judgment was rarely at fault. His will was resolute, and he never faltered in carrying out his plans and purposes. Had necessity compelled him to exert his faculties, he would have reached the highest rank in his profession. But his merit was excelled by his modesty; and he shrunk from the public gaze, and revealed his character in all its excellences only to his friends. His integrity was unimpeachable, while his benevolence was large, but unostentatious. In his death our city has lost one of its most valued citizens.

NEWTON, Isaac, New York city, ———, æ. 61. He was a son of a soldier of the revolution, and was born in the town of Schodack, Rensselaer Co., N. Y., Jan. 10, 1794. He went early to New York, and was clerk to William Chapman, who long kept a store on the corner of Broadway and Division Street. He was the first man who established a line of tow boats on the Hudson River, in 1829. He continued in the tow boat business till 1845. He also was the first to introduce the sharp bow and stern of steamboats. About the year 1835 he built the steamer Balloon. Shortly after this he built the North America, then the South America. In 1836, the celebrated "People's Line," from New York to Albany, was established, and in 1840 was placed under the superintendence of Mr. Newton. The Hendrick Hudson was put on this line by him, as was also the New World, which in 1852 left New York at 7 o'clock, A. M., and reached Albany at 2:15 o'clock, P. M., having accomplished the trip in six hours and fifty minutes. The Isaac Newton was also built and placed on the line under his supervision. For the last 30 years he resided in New York, having a fine summer residence, however, at Fort Lee.

NEWTON, John, M. D., Vermilion Co., Ind., June 16, æ. 36. During his protracted illness his heart was comforted by the consolations of the gospel of Christ, and he died in the full hope of a glorious immortality.

NICHOLS, Mrs. Elizabeth, Poughkeepsie, N. Y., Oct. 22, æ. 79, relict of Gideon Nichols, formerly of Hempstead, L. I., and the mother of the Rev. Edwin A. Nichols. She was the oldest and last surviving child of John Ferdinand Smyth Stuart, a prominent loyalist of the last century, and captain of the Queen's Rangers in the war of the revolution. She was a consistent Christian and faithful churchwoman, and highly esteemed by all who knew her.

NICHOLS, H. Brayton, Esq., on board the ill-fated steamer Pennsylvania, æ. ———, of Gonzales, Texas. The brilliant and highly cultivated intellect shall yield no more fruit on earth, but a tender memory will be enshrined henceforth and forever in the hearts of those who knew and loved him. It is hardly necessary to say that Mr. Nichols came to Gonzales about four years ago, and took charge of the Gonzales College as principal, all the arduous duties of which he discharged with faithfulness and ability. He afterwards entered the practice of law in connection with H. S. Parker, Esq., of Gonzales. A short time since the firm was dissolved, and Mr. Nichols left us with the intention of visiting his parents in Western New York, and returning about the first of August; but alas for all human hopes, he never reached the home circle. Truly, "in the midst of life we are in death."—*Gonzales (Texas) Inquirer.*

NICHOLS, Rev. James, Whately, Mass., Dec. 14, æ. 64. He was born in Northampton, April 13, 1794, converted in Cummington, May 1, 1828, and licensed to preach in 1832. He preached under the presiding elder on Granville circuit two years, and then joined the New England conference on trial, and was returned to Granville circuit another year. He labored two years at Somers, Ct., one year on Chatham and Lyme circuit, two years at Ludlow, two years at Three Rivers, one year at Jenksville, one year at Savoy, and two years at Leeds, in Northampton. At the conference of 1847 he took a certificate of location, but continued to labor as follows: two years longer at Leeds, Northampton, nearly a year at Greenfield, to supply the place of Bro. Jones, who left on account of ill health, nearly two years at Duckville, Palmer. From that time until July, 1853, he preached occasionally, as time and health permitted, when increasing infirmities compelled him to desist. During the 20 years of Bro. Nichols's ministerial life he was quite successful in his labors, and was much beloved by those who knew him.

NICOLLS, Gen. Joseph, Jefferson Co., Miss., Aug. 12, æ. 67. He was a native of Dochetshire, Md., from which place he emigrated, in 1810, to the then small town of Port Gibson. He married in Port Gibson, and resided there, and its immediate vicinity, for 34 years. In 1844 he removed to Madison Parish, La., where he continued a highly esteemed and useful citizen up to the time of his death. He was in active service for 12 months in the Florida war, in 1813 and 1814, being lieutenant and adjutant general. He arrived at high distinction as a Free and Accepted Mason, and died honored and cherished by all who knew him.

NICHOLSON, Mrs. Sarah, Palmyra, N. Y., Dec. 1, æ. 78, widow of the late John Nicholson, Esq., formerly of Albany, N. Y. She was a native of Albany; her husband, many years since, was a representative in Congress from Herkimer Co., and was afterwards, for many years, a magistrate in that city. Mrs. N. was well known to the older inhabitants of Albany, by whom she was highly respected. She had, for several years past, resided in New York city.

NICOL, Andrew, St. Petersburg, Va., Jan. 5, æ. 55. He was by birth a Scotchman. He was educated in an agricultural school; and after coming to Virginia he was intrusted with the management of some of the finest farms on James River. After the establishment of the model and experimental farm of the Union Society, he was unanimously elected to the office of superintendent; but declining health compelled him to retire after the expiration of two years. Being well known to the farming community, and enjoying the public confidence, he then opened an agricultural warehouse in St. Petersburg, and received a large share of patronage. It was as associate editor of the St. Petersburg (Va.) Farmer, for about two years, that the writer of this notice became intimately acquainted with him. His range of agricultural information was very extensive; he wrote with facility as well as force; and the columns of the Farmer were enriched by many valuable contributions from his pen. He was eminently a useful man; his personal qualities were of the highest order; in his business transactions he was scrupulously just and honorable. In short, he illustrated in his life the character of a Christian gentleman, and died lamented by all who knew him.

NIEBELL, Edward Sterling, Wilkesbarre, Pa., March 14, æ. 25. He was born in Wilkesbarre, but at an early age his family removed to Wayne Co. His father was a German, and held a commission in the armies of Napoleon — fought at Austerlitz, Leipsic, Waterloo, and other great conflicts of that wonderful man. After the downfall of the emperor he came to this country, and, we believe, first settled in Pike Co., establishing himself in business with some little capital. Ill luck attended him there, and he subsequently removed to Wilkesbarre, and then after a few years removed to Wayne Co., where he still resides at a good old age. When about 17 young N. entered the office of the Wayne County Herald as an apprentice at printing. His generous friend, Mr.

Beardslee, the editor of that paper, gave him much kind encouragement, and when he completed his time of service he was not only a good workman, but possessed a large share of solid information upon most literary, scientific, and political subjects. In 1835, with an old press and scanty type, — with slender means and no friends of wealth and influence to aid him, in fact with every discouragement, apparently, staring him in the face, — he boldly set out upon the wide and doubtful sea of journalism. Working 14 hours a day at the case, and spending a large share of the night in reading and writing, he issued but a few numbers of his little Herald before it attracted the favorable attention of leading politicians, and offers were made him to remove to Wilkesbarre and take charge of the Union, which he soon did. By nature he was retiring, and for that reason few, comparatively, fully understood and appreciated him. To those with whom he mingled freely he was frank, confiding, and generous to a fault.

NOBLE, Mrs. Sophia, Chelsea, Vt., July 10, æ. 66, widow of the late Rev. Calvin Noble, of Chelsea. She was born in Sharon, Vt., Aug. 24, 1791. Eight years after this, her father, Rev. Lathrop Thompson, was installed the first pastor of the Congregational church in Chelsea; and from that time this was her home, till called by the Master, as we trust, to a higher "mansion." In Dec., 1807, she was united in marriage with Rev. Calvin Noble, who a few months previous had succeeded her father in the pastorate of the church. It was some ten years later than this, that she made a public profession of her faith in Christ. Since the death of her husband in 1834, other pastors have filled his place; and others younger have occupied the place of pastor's wife; but such have invariably found her the wise counsellor and the firm friend.

NOLAND, Charles Fenton Mercer, Little Rock, Ark., June 23, æ. 46. He had acquired reputation as a pleasant and humorous writer, under the *nom de plume* of "Pete Whetstone." He was personally well known through the Mississippi Valley.

NORTH, Dr. Erasmus D., Westfield, Mass., June 17, æ. 51. He was born in New London, graduated at the University of N. C., in 1828, came to New Haven, and was made instructor of elocution in Yale College in 1831, which he resigned in 1834. Since that time he has devoted himself to scientific and literary studies, residing chiefly at Westfield, and for some time past had been preparing for the press an edition of the poems of his friend, Dr. Percival, accompanied by a biographical sketch.

NORTON, Mrs. Abigail, Buffalo, N. Y., Jan. 24, æ. 87, relict of Hon. Ebenezer F. Norton, and mother of Mrs. Albert H. Tracy, of Buffalo. She has resided here since 1815, at which time the late Mr. Norton was the attorney of the Niagara Bank, the first banking institution that was chartered in New York west of Canandaigua.

NORTON, Rev. Jacob, Billerica, Mass., Jan. 17, æ. 94. Mr. N. was the son of Sam'l Norton, and was born in Abington, Mass., Feb. 12, 1764, and consequently had attained to the great age of 93 years, 11 months, and 5 days. He was prepared for college partly at Hingham Academy, and partly with the Rev. James Briggs, of Cummington. He graduated with distinction at Harvard in 1786, and at the time of his death he was the oldest surviving graduate of the college. He studied divinity with the Rev. Perez Fobes, of Raynham, and was ordained over the Congregational church in Weymouth, Oct. 10, 1787, where he continued his pastoral labors for 37 years, until 1824, when he resigned his charge, and in a few years afterwards removed to Billerica, where he resided during the remainder of his long life. In 1789, he married Elizabeth Cranch, the eldest daughter of Hon. Richard Cranch, of Braintree, (now Quincy,) sister of the late Judge William Cranch, of Washington, D. C., and niece of the wife of President John Adams. His wife died Jan. 28, 1811, æ. 46. In 1813 he married Mary Bowers, of Billerica, daughter of Josiah Bowers. She died March 26, 1842, æ. 76. He leaves two daughters, eleven grandchildren, and eleven great-grandchildren. He outlived five sons and one daughter. Two of his sons, Richard Cranch Norton and William Smith Norton, graduated at Harvard College in 1808 and 1812 respectively. Mr. Norton retained his mental and physical powers to a remarkable degree until past the age of 90. For the last year or two he spent most of his time during the day reading, and without glasses, which he never used, with the exception of a short time, and then laid them aside as useless.

NORTON, John, Lexington, Ky., Feb. 9, æ, 75. He was a native of Lancaster Co., Pa., and was married in 1807 to the estimable lady whom he followed to the grave only about 12 months ago. He was a citizen of Lexington nearly 50 years, and in that time had been engaged extensively and successfully in commercial pursuits, and had been intimately identified with the growth and prosperity of the city. He was connected financially with all, and officially with some, of the public internal improvements which were designed to contribute to the improvement of Lexington and its vicinity; and some of the improvements were successfully prosecuted under his faithful and vigilant superintendence. He was educated at a time and under circumstances favorable to the cultivation of a manly and dignified character, and if his virtues were not attractive, they were inflexible almost to severity and sternness. Such were the men of that generation — characterized by simplicity, firmness, and integrity; men, "whose words were bonds — whose promises oaths."

NORTON, Hon. Luman, Bennington, Vt., April 27, æ. 73. He was born in Williamstown, Mass., in 1785, but in his early infancy his father removed into Bennington with his family, where the deceased spent his days. His youth was passed in laborious industry, and notwithstanding the few advantages which were presented to obtain an education at that early day, his love of learning, united with great perseverance, enabled him to acquire an education, by his almost unassisted efforts, much in advance of the youth of his time. He was literally a self-taught man, and became well versed in the history of his own and foreign countries. Noted for his urbanity and kindness, in all his intercourse with others he exhibited the distinguishing marks of the true gentleman. His naturally thoughtful and inquiring mind led him thoroughly to consider a subject before he acted. He was universally respected, and his life may well be said to have presented an example worthy of imitation by the youth of the present day, both in general courtesy and in what may be accomplished as a scholar, by well-directed personal industry and toil. Few men read more to the purpose than the deceased. He was often called to fill offices of honor and trust by his fellow-citizens, and no one could say that he was not faithful to the trusts confided to him. For several years he occupied a seat on the bench as one of the assistant judges of the county, and a few years since was elected a representative of Bennington in the state legislature, and in these positions he won many friends. During the last years of his life he made a public profession of Christ, and was confirmed in the Episcopal church, and continued a consistent and faithful member of the same to his death.

NORWOOD, Samuel, Esq., Roxbury, Mass., Sept. 30, æ. 80, formerly well known as a respected citizen of Boston. He occupied the same house in Spring Street for 40 years, and was one of the oldest members of the Brattle Square church.

NOWLIN, Rev. Robert W., Berryville, Clarke Co., Va., April —, æ. 33, of the Protestant Episcopal church, formerly of Amherst Co., Va. He died as a Christian should die, having on "the whole armor of God."

NUDD, David, Hampton, N. H., Nov. 2, æ. 69. He was born at Hampton, April, 1789, and died Nov. 2, 1858. His ancestors were among the original settlers of the town in 1838, and his pedigree can be traced on the town and church records of the place, without interruption, from that early period. He had limited means of early education, but improved them well, and was amply qualified for transacting every branch of the extensive business in which he became engaged. His natural endowments were of an extraordinary character, and no man who knew much of him could fail of being impressed with his remarkable powers of mind. Soon after arriving at manhood, and long before general attention had been much attracted to the lucrative business of our coast fisheries, Mr. Nudd turned his attention to that business, and invested in it all the means he had, and all the energies he possessed. For a long time, few men north of Boston had as much property invested in that business as he had, and between Newburyport and Portsmouth there was no man, except Mr. Nudd, who comprehended the field of enterprise, in which he labored with signal success. He built a large number of vessels at Hampton, for his own use, and for sale, and thus opened a new business and contributed essentially to the prosperity of the people. When the coast fisheries became a regular business, all along the seaboard, Mr. Nudd had made an ample fortune, and was yet a comparatively young man. When, in conducting the fishing business, he found large outlays in foreign salt necessary, with characteristic decision and enterprise he resolved to manufacture his own salt, and at once built extensive salt works at the Landing, so called, in Hampton, which works he kept in successful operation from their construction, about 1825, till about 1835, when, having pretty much given up the fisheries, he abandoned the manufacture of salt. The Hampton River was too crooked to enable him to bring his vessels to the high land above the marshes, where they could be reached by his teams, and as early as 1820 he excavated a canal of half a mile in length, of ample width and depth, at a large expense, by which the river was much shortened, and new and important facilities gained; and at the end of the canal built a valuable wharf and warehouse, since of great use to himself and the people of the town. He inaugurated the business of transporting potatoes, by water, from Hampton and the adjoining towns, to Boston, using his vessels in the fall of the year for this purpose, more or less, from 1820 to the period of his death. In early manhood there was no public highway, not encumbered by gates, from the thickly-settled portion of Hampton, to Hampton Beach. He formed a company, who built the Boar's Head Hotel about 30 years ago, and he himself built another house there soon after, and some years later still another, the Granite House, so called. He early became sole proprietor of the property, which he retained to the period of his death. The gates were long ago removed from the road, and the path to the Beach became as well known as the road to mill. By this imperfect allusion to the items of business in which

Mr. Nudd was engaged, it will be seen that, for a quiet town like Hampton, he must have done his full share to make a 'smart' town. The truth is, he was in his day so far before other men in enterprise between Portsmouth and Newburyport, that he had no rivals; and it is doubted whether, in the history of those intermediate towns, any other man has ever exhibited equal enterprise and talent, or made so important an impression upon the interest of the locality in which he spent his days. He was a firm believer in the truths of revelation, and on all occasions spoke of Jesus Christ as the undoubted Saviour of the world.

NUTE, Capt. Andrew, Madbury, N. H., Dec. 29, æ. 99. Capt. Nute was born in Dover, April 29, 1759. In 1775, when a few weeks over the age of 16, he marched from Dover to join the continental army at Cambridge, as a waiter for his uncle, Lieut. Paul Nute, in the company of volunteers, commanded by Capt. Andrew Drew, arriving at headquarters on the morning after the battle of Bunker Hill. Soon after the close of the war, Capt. Nute married and settled in the wilderness of New Durham, where he cleared himself a farm, and in 1793 he removed with his family to the town of Madbury, where he lived distinguished for his industry, morality, patriotism, and love of liberty. In 1810, such was his passion for arms, that he took command of the Madbury militia, and in the war of 1812 marched his company to Portsmouth, being then about 55 years of age. In the year 1843, at the age of 83, he experienced and professed the religion of Christ. His recollection of all the important events and distinguished men of the revolution was, until within a short time, as fresh in his memory as when they actually transpired, and he would frequently entertain his neighbors and friends with thrilling anecdotes of Washington and his illustrious compeers.

NYE, Miss Adeline, Walpole, Mass., Sept. 14, æ. 32. Miss Nye was known in this vicinity as a successful school teacher. She had taught for about 12 years in Walpole, Dedham, Abington, and in Virginia. Her instructions were thorough, her manners gentle, her conscientiousness all-pervading. The children loved her, and felt that her influence was that of a kind and judicious friend.

NYE, A. R., Esq., New Bedford, Mass., Aug. 8, æ. 50, of the firm of T. & A. R. Nye. During his active career he filled the offices of representative in the General Court, and member of the city council, and as a merchant was ever distinguished for his energy and enterprise.

NYE, Shadrack E., Yazoo city, Miss., Oct. 17, æ. —, long known as a leading member of the Yazoo bar. He was remarkable for his simplicity of disposition, his kind, good temper, and generous nature; noted for his public spirit and private charities. The poor and desponding, never turned from him without assistance and a cheering word. The loss of this good man is a misfortune to the whole community.

O.

OAKFORD, Dr. Paita, Peru, S. A., March 19, æ. —, U. S. consul at Tumbez.

OAKLEY, Hon. Zophar B., Huntington, L. I., Feb. 5, æ. 64. Mr. O. was born in Huntington, Suffolk Co., N. Y., Oct. 6, 1793. His ancestors, on either side, were among the earliest English settlers of Long Island, tracing back nearly 200 years. They were sturdy yeomen of the Puritan stamp, son following father in humble, honest pursuits, and bequeathing, in turn, to posterity the priceless legacy of a good name. The boyhood of Mr. O. was passed on a farm, privileged only with the limited means of education common to the rural population of that period. With more than ordinary mental activity and taste, no opportunities within his reach were unimproved. Those who knew him as a boy remember the facility with which he could apply himself equally to books or ingenious handiwork, and that his eye was quick to detect the beautiful in nature or art. His whole subsequent life amply justified the prophecy of his boyhood. After no little hesitation in the choice of a pursuit, he resolved to become a merchant; and barely on the verge of manhood, with little capital beyond a clear head and willing hand, opened a store in the principal village of his native town, where for forty years he pursued a steadily increasing, and for many years the most extensive, trade in that section of L. I., a trade which, while prosperous to himself, was so conducted that it might safely challenge a single record of wrong dealing to rise against it. During all this long business career, his life was governed by well considered and unvarying rules. His manners were gentle and courteous at all times, and his temper calm and even. Prompt to do what needed to be done, he was never impatient of necessary delays. Free from covetousness and penuriousness, he looked as carefully to the littles as to the greats; one of his maxims being, that "fractions make wholes." He had "a place for every thing and every thing in its place." No man knew the power of money better, and none ever used money with less abuse of its power. In connection with his business he never gave but one note, feeling that it was better to rise slowly, on his actual resources, than rapidly, with the perpetual risk of falling, on credit, and never opened a bank account, but for nearly half a century transacted his extensive money affairs through the well-known New York house of Willets — a memorable evidence of mercantile probity on both sides. In politics, without pretension or desire for prominence, he was among the opponents of the so-called democratic party; but it was through his activity and zeal in the temperance cause that he attained, or rather consented to, political distinction. Frequently filling the highest offices of his native town, he was induced by the temperance interest to stand for the legislature in 1851, being the first representative the opposition was enabled to elect. In the legislature he was distinguished for working rather than talking, but public life was too distasteful for him to desire its continuance. Delicate health in his later years also warned him to keep to the quiet of his beautiful rural home. Scrupulously observant of the Sabbath, a firm believer in the gospel, a man of daily family prayer and Bible reading, he was from early manhood a church member of the Universalist denomination, and the principal founder of the Universalist church in his native town, to the support of which he bequeathed $5000. Of his faith, as illustrated by its fruit in his life, it need only be said, that many who were most bitterly opposed to it, preferred him for their arbiter or executor to any of their own religious brethren. He was a warm friend of education, and gave $1000 towards founding the fine public school recently established in his native town. Mr. O. was twice married; first, to Abigail Chichester, (sister of Abner Chichester, a well-known retired merchant and capitalist of N. Y.,) by whom he had five children: Polly B., (married to Elbert Carll, treasurer of Suffolk Co., N. Y.,) deceased; Margaret C., deceased; Juliet M., married to Henry S. Smith, (a distinguished merchant and well-beloved citizen of L. I.,) both deceased; Catharine C., married to Carlos D. Stuart, (known as a poet, and for several years editorially connected with the N. Y. Daily Press,) and Ianthe, deceased; — second, to Charlotte Brown, by whom he had one child, Mary, deceased. His only surviving of six daughters is the above-mentioned Catharine C. But after all, what was most memorable in Mr. O.'s life and character was the even tenor with which he pursued his way, striving with every day to do some useful thing, and to let no day's duty go by to the morrow. His steps were all in the paths of service and benefaction; his ledger of life was as carefully posted as his business ledger; so that, when the hour came, "of which no man knoweth" in advance, he was ready to pass, fearless, through "the valley and shadow of death." And passing, he has left a memory of peaceful, upright example, that will not perish with his generation. Many a wayside tree planted by his hand to beautify the landscape, and many a flower cultivated by him to shed its fragrance for every passer-by, will long plead for kindly thought of him, in whom the gentle and kindly elements so mixed, that it would be scarcely exaggerating to say, in the language of the poet,

"From nature's mould ne'er came a better man."

OBDYCKE, Stacy B., Esq., Springfield, Ill., July 3, æ. —, one of the oldest citizens of the state. He emigrated from one of the Eastern States to Illinois in 1816, and settled in Kaskaskia, whence he removed many years ago to Springfield. He was an honorable, high-minded man, and his social qualities drew around him many friends.

O'BRYAN, Jordan, Cooper Co., Mo., March 14, æ. 64. He was a native of North Carolina, born Sept. 17, 1794, emigrated to Kentucky in 1807, and to Missouri in 1818. He served as a representative in the the first Missouri legislature, and afterwards in the state Senate. He was one of the riflemen who did work in the trenches at the battle of New Orleans, and we have heard him repeatedly state, that it was a popular error that General Jackson's riflemen were protected by cotton bales; the idea was a fallacy. He said there was a quantity of cotton bales as a protection to the artillery, but nothing of the kind where the riflemen did such fatal execution. We have frequently heard him describe the terrible effect of grape shot, as he witnessed it in that battle upon advancing bodies of men. He was one of the oldest citizens of Cooper Co., always much esteemed in his public as well as his private character.

O'CONNELL, Patrick, Columbia, S. C., —— 21, æ. 75. He died full of years and merits, cheered by the presence of his two sons, the Rev. Messrs. O'Connell, of Columbia.

ODELL, Mrs. Sarah Bartlett, Greenland, N. H., Aug. 15, æ. 65. In infancy she was dedicated to God by her parents, Philip and Elizabeth Towle. The former was grandson of Philip Towle, born in 1698, and descendant of one of the band of the Mayflower; and the latter a most estimable woman, and mother of ten children, of whom the subject of this memorial was the eldest. Mrs. Towle died Nov., 1857, æ. 88. Her childhood was spent in those "stirring times" when the alarm of war carried a terror with it unknown to these days of peace. It was within her remembrance that a messenger came from the sea shore in hot haste with the news that the "British were landing," which caused many of the people of Hampton to flee to the swamps and woods for safety, having first secured their silver and pewter utensils by throwing them into their wells. Mrs. O. spent a few years of the early part of her life in Portsmouth, where it was often her privilege to sit under the ministry of the learned and faithful Dr. Buckminster, and where, doubtless, she received religious impressions, which exerted a strong influence on her subsequent life. She was married Oct. 18, 1818, and became the mother of eight children, five of whom are now living. At the early age of sixteen she experienced a change of heart, and made public profession of her faith in Christ. Her Christian life ever after evinced the purity and sincerity of that profession, her closet and the family altar daily bearing witness that her treasure was in heaven, and that her "adorning was in that which is not corruptible, even the ornament of a meek and quiet spirit." Her originality of character and tender regard for the welfare of others, united with much gentleness and sweetness of manner, made her the valued friend, the affectionate mother and wife. "The heart of her husband did safely trust in her, and her children rise up and call her blessed."

ODIORNE, Samuel, Kittery, Me., March 29, æ. 56. He had been attached to the U. S. navy yard at Portsmouth, N. H., for about 35 years.

O'DONNELL, Cornelius, Fort' Vancouver, W. T., Oct. 3, æ. —, late first sergeant of Company H., 4th infantry U. S. army. He went to Oregon with the first detatchment of troops, arriving in May, 1849, under command of Major Hathaway, and had seen much service in the everglades of Florida and on the fields of Mexico. He fought in the battles of Palo Alto, Resaca de la Palma, Monterey, Vera Cruz, Cerra Gorda, Contreras, Churubusco, Molino del Rey, and at the taking of Chepultepec, and capture of the city of Mexico, serving in the last-named engagement with Drum's battery.

OGBURN, E. W., Greensboro', —, ——, æ. —. A prudent man in business, a judicious legislator, and a faithful administrator of justice. His was the lead in every movement whose object was benevolence or the promotion of the good of community; and especially in the cause of education was he a faithful laborer. For the last ten years he has filled the office of chairman of the board of superintendents of common schools for Guilford Co., and the entire state is much indebted to him for the increasing prosperity and perfecting of the system of common schools. The prosperity of Greensboro' Female College is also greatly indebted to the efficiency of his labors as trustee, which position, we believe, he has held from its commencement.

OKEMOS, chief, Lansing, ——, Dec. 5, supposed to have been over 100 years old. He was familiar with the events connected with the wars of 1792, and fought both for and against St. Clair and Wayne. He was a noted war chief 66 years ago, and carried with him credentials of his valor in long scars from his shoulders downwards, and transversely upon the sternum, from sabre cuts, received from one of Mad Anthony's troopers. He had also a cut in the head which left an indentation in which a person could place three fingers.

OLIVE, James, Lexington, Miss., May 2, æ. 74, at the residence of his son-in-law, John M. West, Esq. He was at an early period admitted to the bar in Georgia, and removed to Mississippi in 1835, where he resumed the practice and continued it for some years, and distinguished himself as a sound jurist and able advocate; courteous and affable, he won the respect and esteem which were due to his talent and worth; his ear was quick to catch the cry of distress, and his hand to relieve the want of the needy; patriotic in his feelings, he warmly defended those measures which he considered conducive to his country's interest, and firmly resisted those that he believed injurious; his arguments were clear, logical, bold, and fearless; his words were the true sentiments of his heart. He retired from his profession in 1844, and up to his last illness devoted his time to investigating and discussing the great questions of political interest which were before the people.

OLIVER, Francis J., Middletown, Ct., Aug. 21, æ. 81. He was the son of Ebenezer and Susannah (Johonnot) Oliver, and was born in Boston, Oct. 10, 1777. He pursued his preparatory studies at the Public Latin School in Boston; graduated at Harvard College in 1795, and was the last survivor but one of his class, Rev. Caleb Bradley, of Portland, Me., being, at the time of Mr. Oliver's death, the only one living. He was a merchant, and began business in Boston in 1805. In 1815 he entered into copartnership with the late Cornelius Coolidge, which was dissolved two years afterwards. June 13, 1818, the American Insurance Company in Boston was incorparated, and Mr. Oliver was elected its first president. This office he continued to hold until the autumn of 1835, when he resigned it, and was elected president of the City Bank, where he continued by successive re-elections until 1840, when he removed to Middletown, and there passed the remainder of his life. He was elected a representative to the legislature in 1822 and 1823, and was a member of the Boston common council in 1823, 1824, 1825, and 1828, and was its president in 1824 and 1825. In all these stations he discharged the various duties with the strictest fidelity and integrity. In his political principles he was an ardent federalist, and being a gentleman of fine personal appearance, great suavity of manner, and fluency of speech, he was often called upon to preside at public meetings. He married, first, Mary Caroline, daughter of Richard Alsop, of Middletown, who died Aug. 29, 1819, æ. 28; and he married, for his second wife, Mary Charlotte, daughter of Ebenezer Jackson, of Middletown. Mr. Oliver was a gentleman of unblemished moral character, and was for many years a warden of the King's Chapel, Boston.

BISHOP HENRY U. ONDERDONK.

The life of Bishop Henry U. Onderdonk is interwoven with no unimportant part of the history of the church; and the place he occupied, both as a bishop and a writer, will demand a full and impartial biography from some able hand. He was son of Dr. John Onderdonk, and was born in New York city, in 1789. After leaving college he chose the medical profession, and in order to secure the best advantages for this noble study, he proceeded first to London, and then to Edinburgh, and at the university of this last place obtained his degree of M. D. He returned to his native country, and after practising for a short time the profession for which he had so well qualified himself, the real bent of his mind and heart directed him to the work of the ministry. He entered upon his new studies with characteristic zeal and industry, and in the Convention Journal of 1816, Bishop Hobart reports him as ordained deacon and priest within the preceding year. Bishop Brownell was ordained deacon at the same time with him, and Bishops Brownell, Onderdonk, and Henshaw were ordained priests together. Only one of the three is now left. Jan. 14, 1816, soon after his ordination, Mr. Onderdonk went as a missionary to Canandaigua, then one of the outposts of the church in the diocese. The zeal with which he engaged in his work is shown by the fact that a church was built and consecrated within the year, and the missionary station soon grew into a flourishing parish, of which the missionary became rector in 1818. Nor did he confine his labors to one spot. All the towns and villages around, some of them distant, shared the benefit of his unceasing labors, and not a few of the now important parishes of that region can claim him as their founder. One of his early missionary reports has the following interesting notice: "March 1st, I held the first service in Rochesterville, (now Rochester;) July 19, organized a congregation there under the name of St. Luke's, Genesee Falls."

In 1820 he became rector of St. Ann's Church, Brooklyn, then the only Episcopal church in what is now called "the city of churches." In proof of the estimation in which he was already held in the diocese, he was made a member of the standing committee that same year. The general character for ability and devotion in his work, which he won as rector of St. Ann's, was proved by his election to the high office of bishop, to which, if any thing could add elevation, higher honor was imparted by sharing this office with Bishop White. Bishop Onderdonk was consecrated in Philadelphia, Oct. 25, 1827. Of this event Bishop Hobart thus speaks, in one of those admirable addresses which contained so much in so few words. To the New York Convention of 1828 he says, "I assisted on Thursday, Oct. 25, in the consecration of Henry U. Onderdonk into the office of bishop, to act as assistant bishop of Pennsylvania, and to succeed the present bishop in case of survivorship. In the removal of Bishop Onderdonk, this diocese, where he had distinguished himself by talents and by zeal in the discharge of his pastoral duties, sustained a great loss. The prospects, ardently cherished, of his great usefulness in the more extended sphere to which the good providence of God has called him, are fully realized." So soon did the quick eye of Bishop Hobart discover the true character of the new bishop. And we have heard those more conversant with the history of that time speak of the strong impression made upon the church at large by "the wonderful activity" of Bishop Onderdonk.

His popularity as a preacher, in every part of the diocese, was steadfast and abiding, for it rested upon a deep and solid foundation. Every discourse exhibited the power of a mighty intellect, thoroughly disciplined, always fully awake, and with not a single faculty slumbering on its post. He was a true watchman, with all the powers and faculties of his mind ever on the alert, guarding vigilantly every point against the assaults of error. He never left his subject half finished, but every sermon was a complete and masterly discussion of its proper theme. And he had that power, not always the gift of intellectual preachers, which gave interest to all his discourses. He placed his reasons not only in a strong, but in a clear and plain light. The intellectual hearer felt his strength; the plain and unlettered man rejoiced to hear hard things made so easy to be understood. But his two volumes of sermons, his rich legacy to the church, will tell all this better than many volumes written about it. And the congregations of learned and unlearned, which were always attracted to the churches when he preached, from his earliest to his latest ministry in Pennsylvania, more fully attested the truth of all we have said.

In his administration of all business matters he always commanded the respect of a class of men whom the clergy sometimes offend by looseness and negligence in such matters. He did not think strength of mind thrown away upon small matters. Prompt and punctual to the moment of every appointment, scrupulous in the fulfilment of the minutest duties, accurate in every letter and document, he was most careful never to cause any trouble to others by his own negligence. The distinguished layman, who acted for so many years as secretary of the convention of Pennsylvania, has often said that he never received a letter or document from Bishop Onderdonk which was not ready to be filed. In the administration of the public services of the church, or in presiding over the convention, at the meeting of a board or committee, or in the examination of candidates, or in any of the multifarious duties of his office, he brought the whole force of his mind to bear upon the matter in hand. The consequence was, that whatever he undertook to do was sure to be well done.

As a controversial writer — and the American church has produced few, if any, greater — he always commanded the respect, and often the esteem, of his opponent. This was especially manifested in his controversy with Dr. Barnes, out of which grew his great tract, Episcopacy tested by Scripture. We speak from certain knowledge, from what we have heard Dr. Barnes himself say within a few years, when we declare that he entertained the highest personal respect and esteem for Bishop Onderdonk, and expressed the deepest concern that the bishop should be restored to his ministry. He moreover said that this was the general feeling among his friends and brethren.

It was in the year 1845 that Bishop Onderdonk resigned his office as diocesan of Pennsylvania. Happily, most happily, all harsh or unkind feelings, begotten in that hour, have died, and found their grave in silence before the heart now quiet had ceased to beat. Many are now the voices to thank God that the action of the last meeting of the house of bishops was no longer delayed. Many will bless God that their ears were permitted to hear the familiar voice of their old and beloved bishop in the earthly sanctuary, before it sank into the silence of the grave. It must now, indeed, be a grateful thought to the churchmen of Philadelphia, that in almost every parish in that city, without exception, the bishop had been invited to officiate since his restoration. This undoubted evidence of the universal satisfaction felt in the resumption of his office must have been most grateful to the bishop's heart, and we rejoice that this happy memory rests upon his grave.

In all his season of trial there was a calm and uncomplaining submission. Not a breath or murmur, not a harsh word, not an unkind thought was ever expressed. An undiminished interest in all that affected the weal or woe of the church, an ever-vigilant watchfulness over all her concerns, proved how deep and strong a regard for her interest was in his heart. He showed that truest power of greatness which manifests its strength in submission. It was the presence of this mighty power of divine grace, not, as some thought, the absence of strong and acute feeling, which brought such a calm over the troubled waters. It is the strength, the power, which gives the Christian his victory over the world.—*N. Y. Churchman.*

ONDERDONK, Miss Susanna, Orange, N. J., Feb. 27, æ. 65, eldest daughter of the late Dr. John Onderdonk, of New York, and sister of the Rt. Rev. Bishops Henry U. and Benjamin T. Onderdonk.

OSBORN, Rev. Ethan, Fairfield Co., N. J., May 1, æ. 100, having been born in Litchfield, Conn., Aug. 21, 1758. At the age of 17, Mr. O. volunteered as a private soldier in the revolutionary army, was in the campaign of 1776, and in the retreat through N. J. The greater part of his regiment were taken prisoners at Fort Washington, but he escaped through the happy accident, or, as he called it, a " merciful Providence," of being absent on sick leave for a few days at the time the fort surrendered. His fellow-soldiers who were taken, died or suffered terribly in the " Old Sugar House " or the prison ship. On the expiration of his term of service, he returned to his father's home in Conn., and afterwards went through the regular course of studies at Dartmouth College. He was one of four graduates of that institution, all lately living, whose combined ages exceeded 400 years. At the age of 27 he was licensed as a minister in the Presbyterian church, and his first and only charge was the Old Stone church, at Fairfield, N. J., where he resided altogether 70 years. He was ordained in the year 1789, and resigned his charge, as active pastor, in 1844, making a period of 54 years of uninterrupted labors over one flock. During his ministry in this small country church he baptized about 1000 persons, performed about the same number of marriages, and buried about 1500 persons in the same churchyard where he has himself at length been laid at rest.

OSBORN, Mrs. Lydia B., Kennebunk, Me., Dec. 24, æ. 72, widow of Hon. James Osborn. In the discharge of life's duties, she was faithful, and died peacefully, trusting in her Saviour. She was born in Kennebunkport, and was a daughter of Dea. Seth Burnham, who was born in Kennebunkport, (then Arundel,) March 9, 1760, and died Nov. 17, 1846. He was much employed in public and private trusts, and was extensively known as an upright, intelligent man and good citizen. For many years he was occupied in surveying lands in the western part of the state. In 1812 and 1813 he represented the town in the Mass. legislature, and was for 45 years actively engaged in town affairs, and was for a period deputy collector of customs.

OSBORNE, Lewis, Esq., Easthampton, L. I., Aug. 14, æ. 76, brother of the late Thomas Osborne, of Fredonia. The most important portion of his life was spent upon the ocean wave. Prior to the last war with England, he was impressed in Liverpool, and by frequent changes from ship to ship eluded the most diligent search of the American consul and his friends. At length he was sent to the Mediterranean, and was in the blockading fleet off Toulon, under the Earl of Exmouth. It was here that he accidentally learned many months after it had taken place, that war existed between his country and England, and he at once refused to do further duty. After enduring the severest punishments, he was at length, on his peremptory demand, taken before the earl himself, who, upon his relating his story, ordered him to be treated as a prisoner of war, and he was transferred to a prison ship, and from thence to Dartmoor, where he was at the time of the Shortland massacre, and narrowly escaped with his life, one of his companions being shot dead by his side. He returned home in a cartel with the exchanged prisoners, in 1815, and took up his residence in Easthampton, his native place, where he resided until his death.

OSHKOSH, Keshena, Shawano Co., Aug. 29, æ. 70. His father was the head chief of the Menomonees, but dying young, the succession was disputed. In 1827, however, at the treaty of Butte Des Morts, Gen. Cass, the U. S. commissioner, after hearing the claims of the different contestants, formally recognized Oshkosh as the head chief, and his authority as such was henceforth undisputed. He was a native of Wisconsin, and a fine specimen of his race. He was one of the " landmarks " of Northern Wisconsin, a good friend to the whites, and an honored chief to the Menomonees.

OTIS, Alfred II., Esq., Boston, May

18, æ. 43. Mr. O. was for many years engaged in business in Dover, N. H., as a merchant, where he endeared himself to a host of friends by his honesty, probity, and fair dealing. Ever industrious and economical, he accumulated a fortune in Dover, and some few years ago removed to Boston in order to go into a more extensive business. Mr. Otis married a daughter of the late Samuel Dunn, Esq., of Dover, and in 1844 represented that city in the legislature.

OTIS, Mrs. Judith, Beloit, Wis., Feb. 20, æ. 85, widow of the late Rev. Nathaniel Otis. He died Aug. 5, 1851, at Beloit, æ. 72, having been devoted to the ministry more than 40 years, mostly in various places in the State of New York, the early part of his life having been spent as a mechanic. During his ministry his records show that he immersed more than 1400 persons, and married about 300 couples. He was distinguished for his success in healing divisions among brethren, and building up feeble churches, and gathering the "scattered" in the fold. Mrs. O. was peculiarly qualified to aid him in his labors by devoting herself to the temporal concerns of the family, that he might the better devote himself to the spiritual demands of souls committed from time to time to his charge. They "fought the good fight," and entered into rest in the fulness of the triumphs of faith.

WILLIAM FOSTER OTIS, ESQ., of Boston, Mass., at Versailles, France, May 29, æ. 56. He was son of the late Hon. Harrison Gray Otis, who was son of Samuel Alleyne Otis, of Boston, who was son of Judge James Otis, of West Barnstable, Mass., and brother of James Otis, the distinguished revolutionary patriot and statesman. The father of James was Col. John Otis, who lived in Hingham in 1636, and was son of John Otis, of Barnstable, England. Col. John O. was councillor for 21 years, judge of probate, and chief justice of the Court of Common Pleas. James Otis, his son, was also a colonel, judge of probate, and chief justice of the Court of Common Pleas, but above all deserves honor and remembrance as the father of the distinguished James, whose life has been so eloquently drawn by Mr. Tudor.

SAMUEL ALLEYNE OTIS, grandfather of William Foster Otis, was an eminently useful and important man inhis day. The New England Palladium said of him:—

"This much lamented fellow-citizen was son of the late Hon. James Otis, of Barnstable, whose life was devoted to the service of his country, and brother of the celebrated scholar, statesman, and patriot of the same name, who led the way to the American revolution. Imbued with a strong attachment to the principles of his father and elder brother, and liberally educated under their influence, Mr. Otis was himself an early and decided friend to the liberties of his country. In 1776 he was chosen a representative for Boston, and afterwards to the convention which framed the constitution of Massachusetts; he was also appointed a member of the board of war; a commissioner with General Lincoln and President Phillips to receive the submission and promised indemnity to the insurgents, and a delegate to the old Congress, in which capacity he served until the adoption of the federal constitution. He then became the first elected secretary of the Senate of the United States, and continued to discharge the duties of that office, from the first day of the organization of that body to the close of the last session, without the absence or intermission of a single day. No higher eulogium can be expressed upon his fidelity, industry, and accuracy in this responsible station, than his continuance in it, amid the struggles and collisions of parties, without a sacrifice or concealment of his political opinions, which differed from those of the majority of that body, whose good will and respect he conciliated by his exemplary attention to his duty, and by the amenity of his manners.

"His private character was adorned by all the moral and domestic virtues and accomplishments, and modelled upon the principles of our holy religion, which, from his youth, were openly professed and conscientiously adopted as the rule of his conduct in all his public and private relations. He died at Washington, D. C., April 22, 1814, æ. 73. Of his eight children only one is now living. Mr. Samuel Alleyne Otis, one of the sons, died at Newburyport, Oct. 27, 1814, æ. 44. It was also said of him that he was 'a man tenderly beloved by his family and friends, highly esteemed by a large circle of acquaintance, possessed of a high sense of honor, and distinguished for integrity. By his agreeable manners, gentlemanly deportment, and general intelligence, he maintained an elevated position in society, and sustained the high reputation of the honorable family to which he belonged. As a sound and active politician, his death will be deeply lamented.' His son, Rev. George Otis, graduated at Harvard, in 1815, and became rector of Christ's Church in Cambridge, and died in Cambridge, Feb. 25, 1828, æ. 31, — a young man of rare scholarship and charming piety. He had been a tutor and professor, and very successful as a clergyman."

HON. HARRISON GRAY OTIS, died in Boston, Oct. 28, 1848, æ. 83, having filled a large place in public influence and social relations. He graduated at Harvard in 1783, and early became a successful practitioner at the bar. He was the companion and rival of such men as Parsons, Ames, Lowell, Cabot, Gore. He was an eminent lawyer, a leader in the whig school of politics, and a most graceful and eloquent orator. He was many years in the legislature, filling the speaker's chair, and for six years the seat of president of the senate. He followed Fisher Ames in Congress, and after was five years United States senator, a judge of the Boston Court of Common Pleas, and third mayor of the city.

"During the most animated contests between the federal and democratic parties, he took an active part; and no man in the commonwealth enjoyed a greater popularity, or in a higher degree the confidence, of his political friends, or was able to move by his eloquence a popular assembly more powerfully. He had few equals in the amenity of his manners, or the grace, vivacity, and interest of his conversation on almost all subjects. He retained his vigor of intellect in a remarkable degree to the end of his long term of life, which closed in the full maturity of advanced age, as full of honors as of years."

The following notice from a correspondent pays a just tribute to the memory of this good man: —

"William Foster Otis was born in Boston, Dec. 1, 1801. He was the son of Harrison Gray Otis, a statesman and orator of the highest distinction, whose public life, early graced by an appointment under Washington's administration, continued through various offices, federal, state, and municipal, for more than 40 years. The honors and services of the father were not without effect upon the son, who, after graduating at Harvard College in 1821, and being admitted to the Boston bar, took a leading part in the volunteer corps of Boston, became a member of the Massachusetts House of Representatives, (1830-'32,) delivered a fourth of July oration, which excited a great sensation, before the young men of Boston, (1831,) was for several years the president of a Young Men's Temperance Society, and thus began a career in public with every promise of brilliant success. In 1831 he married Emily Marshall, of Boston, whose exceeding beauty was the least of the charms by which she won his affection, and retained it unshared. She died in 1836, leaving three children, one of whom, the only son, died at the age of 12. A natural disinclination for the pursuits of the public man, enhanced first by the joys, then by the sorrows, of his domestic life, together with the early decline of his health, resulted in the retirement of Mr. Otis from scenes and exertions in which most men, situated as he was, would have been absorbed. He became a member of the Protestant Episcopal church, and to the interests and duties connected with his new relations he gave the best years of his life and the best powers of his nature; as a parishioner of the Church of the Advent in Boston, supporting its teachings and its charities, constant in his attendance upon its services, and losing no opportunity to promote its best influences, yet always charitable towards those who were not of his own fold, and always rejoicing in all good works by whomsoever done. Mr. Otis lived a life of comparative seclusion, but of extended beneficence. His character, beautiful while he was on earth, becomes more beautiful to those who gaze after him; child-like, humble, full of humor, overflowing with tender sympathies and affections, universally considerate, as courteous to the lowly as to the eminent, perfectly honest and true, he was the invariable gentleman, and as far as is possible to humanity, the invariable Christian, a loyal subject of the kingdom not of this world. He was travelling through Europe when death overtook him, without warning, yet not unprepared, on the 29th of May, 1858. On the 17th of June, he was buried by the side of his kindred at Mount Auburn."

OTHOUT, John, New York city, Jan. 28, æ. 69. He was president of the Bank of New York, and a highly valued citizen.

OTTO, Dr. John B., Reading, Pa., Aug. 2, æ. 72. Dr. Otto was the oldest physician of Reading. He studied medicine under his father, a celebrated physician of the old school, and after graduating at the University of Pennsylvania, commenced the practice of his profession in his native place, where he enjoyed an extensive practice during his long and active life, and relinquished it only some six months ago, when the inroads of disease, and the infirmities of age, confined him to his house. He was universally respected and beloved, and his death, even though he had passed the ripe old age of threescore and ten, will be deeply mourned; and to many a household, where his presence in its seasons of sickness was so eagerly sought and welcomed, his departure has created a void that years may not fill. To the poor, especially, will his death be a bereavement, for they never appealed to his benevolent sympathies in vain. His purse and his advice and attendance were equally at their service at all times.

ROBERT OWEN,

——, ——, ——, ——, æ. 87. The following sketch from the N. Y. Post will be found interesting as well as accurate:—

"Our despatches by the Europa announce the death of Robert Owen, at one time, perhaps, the most famous man of his day. He was in the 88th year of his age, having been born in Wales in the year 1771. He distinguished himself quite early at school, but before he was eighteen he engaged in the cotton manufacturing business, into which he was instrumental in introducing the machinery of Arkwright, then a great improvement. His factories, called the Chorlton Mills, were situated near Manchester, and became very lucrative.

"But he was induced, after a few years, to remove to New Lanark, between Edinburgh and Glasgow, in Scotland, where Arkwright had founded a number of factories, in connection with David Dale, an enterprising and benevolent man. Mr. O. married the daughter of Dale, and was taken into partnership. His sympathies in behalf of the working classes concurring with those of Dale, they commenced together a practical reform in regard to their dwelling-houses, their hours of labor, and the education of their children, which was conducted for some time under such flattering promises of success, that it attracted the attention of philanthropists and statesmen in all parts of the world. As there were more than a thousand persons employed in the mills, about half of them under eighteen years of age, a fine field was presented for the display of their benevolent activity.

"Mr. O. succeeded, we believe, in shortening the duration of the children's labors, and in enabling them to attend his school, where the intellectual system, as it was called, or the system of teaching by objects, was first put in practice. In the evening, and on Sundays the adults were instructed by lectures, objects, diagrams, and books, so that the place soon put on a scholastic air, quite unusual in the manufacturing towns of Scotland or England. As he instituted, at the same time, a police which, though it was carried on without punishments, was rigid, his community was regarded as a model community. He himself considered it so, and he began to commend it as an example for all the earth. The late Duke of Kent, father of the present Queen of Great Britain, became very much interested in Mr. O.'s experiments, and through his influence the aristocracy and clergy of England lent him their countenance. But unfortunately, he connected his scheme for the practical improvement of the working classes with certain religious and social doctrines, which soon deprived him of the support of those eminent orders. Adopting a grossly materialistic theory of life, he held that men were entirely the creatures of circumstances, and that all that was necessary for the thorough regeneration of society, was a change in its external conditions. Improve the circumstances by which the child is surrounded, he said, and you improve the child. All the difference which subsists between the most polished and kind-hearted man of a civilized, and the most rude and cruel man of a barbarous country, is a difference in their circumstances. The civilized man, placed in New Zealand, would have been a savage, and the New Zealand savage, placed amid the means and appliances of an educated family of London or Paris, would have been a civilized man.

"There was enough of truth, and of the most important truth, in his theory to commend it to the attention of the world, and particularly of the classes for whose benefit it was specially intended. He was considered an oracle by them, and, indeed, the fame which he acquired and the reputed success of his practical scheme attracted towards him the regards of sovereigns. The King of Prussia, we think it was, sent for him, and consulted him in respect to the establishment and management of model villages in Prussia. He lived also on terms of familiarity with the King of France, and he made several voyages to Mexico, at the request of the government, to introduce his reforms into that country. On one of these visits (in 1828) he requested from the Mexican ministry the control of the states of Coahuila and Texas, for the purpose of testing his system of social organization on the largest scale. But as those provinces were not within the gift of the ministry, they offered him, as an alternative, a district of some hundred and fifty miles in breadth on the Pacific coast, north of the Gulf of California. Mr. O., for some reason or other, did not accept it; and it is curious to remark that, if he had, the gold mines of California would probably have been discovered twenty years before they were, and he become the richest man in all the world.

"The riches, however, would not have tempted him from the prosecution of his scheme, in which he was indefatigable, making in behalf of it many voyages across the Atlantic, visiting the crowned heads and great ministers of Europe, and the presidents of the North and South American republics, writing in the newspapers and periodicals, and lecturing before associations and meetings. He was enabled to do all this, because his manufacturing experiment had brought him a fortune of half a million of dollars and more, all of which, we presume, he expended in his various benevolent projects.

"In 1825 he purchased New Harmony, in Indiana, which was owned by the Harmonists, a band of German socialists under Rapp, (since the founder of Economy, near Pittsburg,) and he made a trial of his system there with the assistance of his son, Robert Dale Owen, now our minister at Naples. For a while it flourished, even beyond the market of western towns generally; but so far as it was a new experiment of social life, it failed.

"He was the author of several books on social science, the principal of which were the New Moral World, wherein he discussed his doctrines at length, in a simple and unpretending style, but with considerable clearness and vigor. He was, in fact, a monomaniac on the subject of socialism; he talked of nothing else, wrote of nothing else, lived for nothing else; and, in almost any other cause, might have compelled success. Even in that he would have succeeded to a much larger extent, if he had not connected the practical provisions of it with an erroneous philosophy and an avowed disbelief in Christianity. The latter, however, towards the close of his life, he yielded, through the influence, it is said, of the 'spiritual' communications.

"His last work was an autobiography, which abounds in the most interesting details of his career.

"He was a man of kindliest nature, sincere and truthful, and of the most unreserving generosity both in his judgments of men and in his conduct towards them. Nothing ever ruffled his temper, nothing could abate his energy; and, though he failed in the chief object of his long and busy life, it must still be said, to his credit, that he did more than any other man towards directing the attention of society in England to the melioration of the condition of the working classes."

OWEN, Maj. Solomon, Lisle, Broome Co., N. Y., April 7, æ. 88. A native of Stockbridge, Berkshire Co., Mass., he came to L. and became a settled resident more than 60 years ago. Some 30 years since he became a member of the Congregational church in L.; and in that relation, whatever duties devolved upon him he was ever prompt to discharge with characteristic fidelity and decision. As a citizen, a neighbor, and a man, he was respected and beloved; and as a professed disciple and follower of Christ, he sustained the honor of that profession as an intelligent and exemplary Christian. He manfully did his part in clearing away the ancient wilderness, and in grappling with the difficulties and the hardships incident to a new and thinly-settled region. Providence blessed him in his active, persevering diligence, and gave him a competence; blessed him with a numerous household, who were trained to become, in turn, a comfort and a blessing to their parents.

OWEN, Dr. W. J., Midway, Barbour Co., Ala., Nov. —, æ. 54. As a neighbor, he was kind; as a friend, he was warm and unchanging; as a father, he commanded the respect and love of his children, and the proverbial peace and quiet of his happy home fully indicated his long years of devotedness as a husband; as a Christian, he was ever looked upon as an example worthy the imitation of all.

OWSLEY, Mrs. Elizabeth, Richmond, Ky., April 17, æ. 70, consort of the Hon. Wm. Owsley, late Gov. of Ky. This venerable lady was one of the very few still lingering among us, the memorials of a former century. Her birth was almost synchronous with the origin of the federal constitution, and her life, extending from 1788 to 1858, covers the whole period of that vast experiment, commenced and carried on beneath its auspices. During one of the most momentous periods of its history, she was identified, in the person of her honored husband, with one of the most memorable struggles which have marked its progress, and lived to enjoy, along with him, the reward of his integrity and firmness in the highest office which the voice of an approving people can bestow. After the toils and honors of public life were passed, they sought together a peaceful retirement in the immediate vicinity of Danville; and there, in the quiet cemetery of that beautiful village her mortal remains have found their last repose.

P.

PAGE, Elder Richard, Walker Co., Texas, Nov. 28, æ. 80. He was born in South Carolina, where he lived till he arrived at the age of manhood, when he moved to Lincoln Co., Ga. He served his country in 1812. He was a laborious and devoted minister of the gospel, up to the time of his death. He left six children, all of whom are members of the Baptist church.

PACKARD, Rev. Heman, New Orleans, La., Feb. 11, æ. —.

PAGE, Capt. Benjamin, New York, N. Y., Apr. 16, æ. 47, U. S. navy. Capt. Page at the time of his death was on the retired list. He was born in England, entered the United States service Dec. 17, 1810, and attained the rank of captain in 1841. He had seen eighteen years' active service, and was last at sea in 1850.

PAGE, Robert F., M. D., Campbell C. H., Va., Nov. 10, æ. 38.

PAGE, Mrs. Anna, Washington, D. C., Aug. 31, æ. 84, youngest child of the late Henry Lee, of Virginia, and sister to the officer of that name of revolutionary memory, and of Charles Lee, attorney general under Washington. In early life she was united in marriage to William Byrd Page, of Va.

PAINE, Geo. Burgess, Leghorn, Italy, Dec. 9, æ. 24. On leaving college he pursued the study of theology for a year with his uncle, Rt. Rev. George Burgess, of Maine, and afterwards at the General Seminary of the Episcopal church in N. Y. He had completed the studies prescribed for ordination in the Episcopal church, and in the summer of 1858 had gone abroad for the purpose of spending some time in study and travel in Europe and in the East. He died after a brief illness of fever at Leghorn.

*PALMER, Andrew Y., Belfast, Me., June 25, æ. 46. In the characteristics of his mind Mr. P. was acute and critical. He was never satisfied with a half-examination of any thing, whether in law, literature, or the more exact sciences. Aside from his character as a citizen and a lawyer, the deceased was an ardent lover of nature. He delighted in the green woods and the fresh lakes, the night bivouac, and the sports of the angle and the gun, that have been dignified by many good and noted men. These relaxations he regarded with reason as beneficial to men of sedentary professions. He was the architect of his own reputation. He was not born to wealth or education. His earlier acquirements of law and of books were made in hours snatched from the duties of mechanical apprenticeship.

PARISH, Levi H., Washington, D. C., Feb. 14, æ. 64. Mr. P. was a clerk in the general post office department, which position he held some 20 years. During the first few years of his residence at the national capital, he was the Washington correspondent of the Rochester Advertiser. He was a soldier in the war of 1812, and was wounded at the battle of Queenstown.

PARKER, Col. Charles, Snow Hill, Md., Jan. 31, æ. 70. Col. P. was one of the oldest and most reputable citizens of Worcester. He served in various positions, always with credit to himself and advantage to his fellow-citizens. He was several times returned to the House of Delegates of the state, filled the offices of sheriff, county commissioner, county surveyor, &c., and at his death was collector of the port of Snow Hill. He was a man of generous impulses; benevolent to the poor and distressed, a kind and obliging neighbor, a true friend, and an honest man.

PARKER, Elizabeth, Durham, Me., June 22d, æ. nearly 115. She was the oldest person in the state of Maine at the time of her death. She was born in 1743, 33 years before the declaration of independence. Till she was about 110 she possessed bodily vigor sufficient to enable her to work in the garden, an employment she took great delight in.

PARKER, Rev. Armistead, St. Louis, Mo., June 28, æ. 50.

PARKER, Elijah, Keene, N. H., Aug. 26, æ. 82. He was for many years a practising lawyer in K., and a worthy citizen of the town. Among his children are Rev. Mr. Parker, of Concord, and H. G. Parker, Esq., of Boston.

PARKER, Isaac, Boston, Mass., May 28, æ. 70. He was the senior member of the house of Parker, Wilder, & Co., the president of the Traders Bank, and occupied several other places of trust. He leaves a name and character worthy of grateful remembrance.

PARKER, Hon. Jacob, Mansfield, O., Jan. —, æ. —, formerly president judge of Common Pleas in the Richland District, of which Knox Co. formed a part. He was a man of more than ordinary talent, and had the reputation of being an upright judge and a good citizen. He died at an advanced age.

PARKER, Mrs. Jerusha, Reading, Ms., Oct. 30, æ. 94. She never buried a child, and five followed her remains to the grave: one has been a missionary to the Sandwich Islands 26 years.

PARKER, David Sneed, M. D., Davie Co., N. C., May 3, æ. 35. Dr. Parker graduated at the Medical University of New York in 1850, and practised his profession with success for several years in his native county. He was a dutiful son, an affectionate brother, and a fearless, frank, and independent man.

PARKER, Rev. J. H., Salisbury, N. C., Sept. 16, æ. 45, rector of St. Luke's Church. He was born Jan. 21, 1813, in Tawboro', and graduated at Chapel Hill, in 1832, with the first distinction. He was a delegate to the Gen. P. E. Convention, from Alabama, in 1844. In 1846 he was ordained deacon, and the next year presbyter. After preaching a short time in the churches in the neighboring country, he succeeded the Rev. T. F. Davis (now Bishop of South Carolina) as rector of St. Luke's Church. At the mature age of 33, in the possession of a competent estate, and thus with the prospect of having temporal enjoyment in his power, he devoted himself to the self-sacrificing duties of a minister of the gospel. This parish was his first and only settled charge. He loved his work, and he loved his flock; and their affection and sympathy was the present reward and delight, without which he felt he could not live.

PARKER, Elizabeth, Groton, Mass., Dec. 3, æ. 92. She was the mother of 13 children, besides whom her descendants numbered 42 grandchildren and 22 great-grandchildren.

PARKER, Mary R., Kenosha, Wis., July 17, æ. 63. "Thus has passed away one who, for 43 years, had exhibited the graces of the Christian character, by patience, meekness, forbearance, purity, resignation; and by the activity of her benevolence she adorned and recommended the doctrine of God her Saviour."

PARKMAN, Catharine Scollay, West

Roxbury, Mass., Sept. 4, æ. 34, wife of Francis Parkman, Esq., and daughter of Dr. Jacob Bigelow.

PARSHALL, Dea. Isaac, Hartland, Livingston Co., Mich., Feb. 21, æ. 65. At the close of his days he expressed his continued attachment to the domestic mission and educational interests of the denomination, by legacies of $500 to the former and nearly $2000 to the latter.

PATTEN, John, Hancock, Mass., Aug. 16, æ. 98, the last revolutionary pensioner of Pittsfield.

PATTEN, Robert, Esq., Amesbury, Mass., Feb. 27, æ. 81, president of the Powow River Bank.

PATTERSON, John, Esq., Freehold, N. J., March 7, æ. —. Mr. Patterson was a lawyer by profession, though for the last few years his health has not been such as to warrant him in applying himself very closely to it. In political affairs he always took an active part, and held at the time of his death the clerkship of Monmouth Co., to which office he was elected in 1855.

PATTERSON, Mrs. Jane C., Pittsburg, Pa., March 15, æ. 80, widow of Rev. Robert Patterson, who died Sept. 5, 1854, æ. 81. Mrs. Patterson was the third child of Col. John Canon, the founder and proprietor of Canonsburg, Pa., where she was born Dec. 20, 1778. She was the last survivor of her father's numerous family. In her childhood and youth she shared in the hardships and trials of the early settlers of the west, of which she retained, to old age, a vivid recollection. Her memory went back to the times when the Indians were no unwonted visitors in the settlements of the whites; and the hospitality of no one did they enjoy more frequently than that of Col. Canon. She well remembered the building, by her father, of the old mill in Canonsburg, one of the first in all the west, and to which the farmers from a great distance around brought their grain. She also remembered the building of the stone academy in Canonsburg, in 1791, when, though but a child, she assisted in preparing the meals for the workmen engaged in its erection. Indeed, the entire history of that academy passed under her eye, from its commencement in 1791 until its charter as a college in 1802. With all its teachers during that period, and with many of its students, she was personally acquainted; and of the character and standing of almost all she had some knowledge. Many of the actors in the whiskey insurrection, in 1794, were well known to Mrs. Patterson, who could recall a variety of incidents that showed the intense excitement under which the western country was at that time laboring. With all the first ministers west of the mountains, the fathers of the Presbyterian church in valley of the Mississippi, she was well acquainted, and had frequently heard them preach. Of the stirring scenes of the great revival of 1802 she was fond of speaking, for her own heart had been deeply moved by the pervading and solemn influences of the time. Her conversation in later life was enriched, as may well be supposed, with many reminiscences of a period which, with its simple manners, modes of thought, and ways of life, as well as with its peculiar hardships, has so entirely passed away, and of which, during her last years, the deceased was one of the few remaining relics. Would that the unaffected piety and self-denying spirit of our fathers and mothers might revive in the hearts and shine in the lives of their children.

PATTERSON, Mary D., Huntington, Luzerne Co., Pa., June 10, æ. 79. This venerable lady was a member of the Methodist Episcopal church for more than 60 years. She was the second daughter of the late Col. Nathan Denison, who bravely commanded the left wing of our little army in the battle of Wyoming.

PATTISON, John P., M. D., Easton, Ct., Dec. 30, æ. 66.

JOHN MERCER PATTON,

Richmond, Va., Oct. 29, æ. 62. The following notice is extracted from a eulogy, delivered by the Hon. John S. Pendleton, at the court house at the November term of the Circuit Court:—

"This meeting has been called in order that the Circuit Court for the county of Culpepper, the members of the bar, the officers of the court, and other citizens present, may unite, in expressing in suitable and permanent form, their sentiments of affection and respect for the character and memory of John Mercer Patton, of whose recent decease they have heard with sensations of profound sorrow.

"It is of peculiar propriety that such a proceeding should be had here; for he was for years an eminent advocate at this bar — it was this district he represented with so much distinction in the Congress of the United States — and it was in this immediate vicinity that, for many years past, he had his occasional residence. Such tributes, when cordially rendered, are proper everywhere, uniting the graces of spontaneous justice to the illustrious dead, with the chances of profitable suggestions to those who survive.

"John Mercer Patton was not educated, in the first place, for the profession of the law, but for that of medicine. The latter he never practised at all — indeed, he determined never to practice, some time before he finished his course. He was thoroughly educated, passing with credit through his academic and collegiate course, (at Princeton,) and graduating also in the Medical College of Philadelphia. He then commenced the study of the law, and in a short time came to the bar.

"He commenced the great struggle of life, it is true, with all the accomplishments appropriate to his age, and with the prestige of an honored name and a distinguished lineage; but of any of the adventitious aids of fortune, or of special patronage, he had literally none.

"He took a high aim in the beginning, and commenced his career in the Chancery Court of Fredericksburg, Va. You, sir, know better than I do what the bar and the business of that court were at that time; for you yourself were a practitioner in it. I know enough of it to remember that it had jurisdiction of the business of an extensive and opulent district — was regularly attended by scores of lawyers, the élite of their respective counties, which, in considerable number, formed the district — a local bar numerous and able; and occasionally the great lights of the profession from other sections — all of whom divided amongst them, in various proportions, the honors and the profits of its extensive business.

"It is not for me to make, or seem to make, invidious distinctions among the members of the bar at Fredericksburg at that time. To name all, even of equal, and of high merit, would be impossible for me, speaking from my memory alone; to name a portion, however unimportant it might be to those omitted, would nevertheless be to do an act of injustice very repugnant to my own feelings. I may yet, without the slightest impropriety, refer to three or four by name, who, not being strictly of the district, form a class to themselves.

"Robert Stanard, of Richmond, of whom I never heard, in those days, but as the first, or second, or third lawyer of Virginia, practised in that court at the time I speak of. Walter Jones, of Washington city, that man of prodigious mind, whose wonderful intellect, strong in all the resources of varied learning, and refulgent with the brightest gifts of genius, eloquence, and wit, had made him for years the pride and ornament of the highest judicial forum of the republic, was an occasional practitioner in the Chancery Court of Fredericksburg. John Scott, of Fauquier, who, distinguished in early life for great abilities, had a mind that seemed to grow on to the close — whose sturdy talents were equal to any call, and carried him from every field with increased reputation. Philip P. Barbour — "*nomen venerabile que clarum*" — who, though the last I shall name, yet not the least; a man who is remembered, and always will be remembered by the whole country, with respect and veneration, whether as a lawyer, a statesman, or a judge.

"These were the men, with others of scarce inferior fame, in competition with whom Mr. Patton's professional noviciate was passed and tested. With what directness, expedition, and éclat, he marched firmly and unwaveringly to the front rank of the bar, you, sir, remember as well as I, until we saw him, at an age when young men in this country but rarely begin to gain a footing, — in England never, — ranking with the most successful counsellors, and enjoying and enlarging the largest, and, I presume, the most profitable practice in the court.

"When John M. Patton had passed his thirtieth year of age, a little, a vacancy occurred in the representation in Congress, of the district in which he resided, by reason of the appointment of Philip P. Barbour to a seat on the bench of the Federal Court.

"Upon an active canvass of the district, Mr. Patton was elected, and was there afterwards three times reëlected, without even a nominal opposition, on any occasion — a compliment paid to no other man of my acquaintance in Virginia at any time.

"To use a word reappearing in vogue, the fifth *decade* of the constitution was distinguished, above all others, for the great number of able and eloquent men who met in the one or the other House of Congress. Virginia, always well represented, was particularly strong for the greater part of that time. In the Senate she had Tazewell, Tyler, Rives, and Leigh; in the House, our present Senators Hunter and Mason, our present Governor Wise, the present minister to France, John Robertson, Fenton Mercer, Philip Doddridge, George C. Dromgoole, and others, whom I cannot at the present moment recall. All the states had great men. South Carolina, Kentucky, and Massachusetts — three opposition states in Jackson's administration — had of themselves intellectual capital enough to set up any ordinary Congress; Clay, Webster, Calhoun, William C. Preston, Crittenden, Choate, John Quincy Adams, Hayne, Everett, Legare, Hamilton, McDuffie, Menefee, Warren Davis, Waddy Thompson. To take only one out of many from several of the other states, there was Mangum, Forsyth, Porter, Prentiss, King, Bell, Benton, Corwin, Cass, Buchanan, Horace Binney, Silas Wright. It seemed, by common consent, to have been the object of the whole country to depute to that high arena the intellectual giants of the republic, that they might there meet, and measure arms. It was in that period of time, that most of the great measures of national policy were discussed, and many of them settled.

"It was in such a Congress that Mr. Patton made his first appearance. Into the wrangles, and squabbles, and personalities, which, to greater or less extent occur, and will always occur, he never entered. He was far above any possible participation in those exhibitions, whether in their comic or tragic scenes. But in the grave and important discussions he took always a prominent and distinguished part. I speak what I know to be true, (for after a brief interval, I followed him in that position,) when I say, that with all men whose opinions were worth considering, he left behind him, when he retired from Congress, a reputation and character, as a statesman and gentleman, than which no man in America, on a similar term of service, ever left a higher.

"As upon his own motion he first went into Congress, so, of his own accord, he retired — resigning his seat for the purpose of resuming the practice of his profession. He had been six or seven years in Congress, and was, of course, rusting, to some extent, in his profession. But he again took a high aim.

"He settled at once at Richmond, with the intention to confine himself chiefly, if not entirely, to the Supreme Court of Appeals.

"Lawyers in every part of the United States know that, beginning with the close of the revolution, with John Marshall, Edmund Pendleton, and George Wythe, down to the present hour, the bench and the bar of Richmond have been preëminently distinguished, as well for the learning and ability of their numerous members, as for their vigilant and scrupulous maintenance of the dignity and honor of their profession.

"I believe there was scarcely ever a time when that bar commanded a more general veneration, that at the particular time to which I refer.

"I will make no discriminations among the living: of the dead I may speak. Benjamin W. Leigh, Chapman Johnson, Robert Stanard, John R. Cooke, and Samuel Taylor were then the leaders of the Richmond bar, and were in the zenith of their extensive and well-merited fame.

"My impression is, that Mr. Patton, at the time he came to Richmond, had few or no cases in the Court of Appeals — none, I think, in that or in any other court of Richmond. I am not positively certain as to this fact, though I lived with him, in his own house, during his first winter in Richmond, being then myself a member of the legislature.

"How soon he got a footing in that court we all know — with how quick and firm a step he marched right onward and upward, until we saw him serenely perched on the very highest pinnacle of professional eminence, enjoying without vanity or ostentation, as he had acquired without envy or ill will, the high position of the undisputed and indisputable championship of the bar of Virginia, all Virginia knows. As to the manner in which he bore himself in that "high calling" let the Richmond bar be heard. Its resolutions on the occasion of his death I have embodied in those I propose to submit.

"But, sir, he is gone. Never again shall we feel his cordial grasp, or meet his genial smile, when in his annual visits he came amongst us, laying off his ponderous armor, and coming, for a season, to recover his wasted strength, and refresh his fatigued faculties in the balmy breezes of his mountain home.

"When death strikes down the foremost of a noble profession, whose dignity and influence he had long signally contributed to uphold and advance, the public, as well as personal, sympathy is oppressed by the afflicting calamity. Such is the melancholy, distressing occasion of this mournful and mourning assemblage. The sad privilege alone remains to us, as a body, to record the sorrow wherewith we are penetrated, as individuals, at the departure of the Hon. John Mercer Patton, our late noble and revered brother.

"The occasion does not permit even an outline of his high endowments and accomplishments. Of these there was the sure and unerring attestation, proceeding from the general anxiety to retain and appropriate his personal services. Each revolving year, to the close of his distinguished life, teemed with such tributes to his superiority, and so earnest, zealous, untiring, devoted, was he, that not even the admonition of his inexorable labors, in their wasting effect upon his health, could abate his diligence and ardor. He had chosen, as the mark of a worthy and generous ambition, the fame of an advocate and counsellor, and nobly won his way to their loftiest heights. At a bar proud in its memories of master spirits, of a Leigh, a Johnson, a Stanard, of a Marshall, a Wirt, a Wickham, at an earlier period — our deceased brother was honored for the brilliant success with which he sustained and renewed its glories. Providence was munificent in her gifts, and he was faithful in obediently devoting them to the allotment of human exertion in which they qualified him to shine.

"It need not be said he was disciplined, learned, accomplished in all the arts of an advocate; for this, and much more, is implied in the foremost position he so long and nobly occupied at the bar. The courts were indebted to him for his severe and lucid exposition of principles, and their application; his brethren for the bright example of his forensic and social life; his clients for his illustrious ability and devotion in representing them; and the country not less for his magnanimity, urbanity, generosity, and invincible propriety."

PATTON, William, Warm Springs, Buncombe Co., N. C., June 27, æ. 63. Mr. Patton was born in Wilks Co., in the mountain region of North Carolina, and educated at the old Menton Academy in Buncombe. Removing at an early period, he embarked in mercantile pursuits, and, during a long life, was recognized as a useful, enterprising, and public-spirited citizen. After his retirement from business, some years since, Mr. Patton resided during the summer months in the vicinity of Asheville, N. C. The local journals, noticing the sad event, represent him as having probably done more than any other person to bring out the resources of that region, and deplore his death as a man of benevolence and usefulness, whose loss would be felt by all, and especially by the poor of his county, to whom he was, in an eminent degree, a friend. His sound judgment, his unostentatious charity, his urbanity, his kindly spirit, and manliness of character, won many friends, who deplore his loss, and will preserve his memory green.

PAUL, John H., M. D., Dover, N. H., Nov. 12, æ. 40. Dr. Paul was a regularly educated physician, having graduated at Jefferson Medical College, Philadelphia, in 1846. He was a good physician, but for many years past devoted himself mainly to practical dental surgery. He was a worthy citizen and an estimable man in all the relations of life.

PAYNE, Americus V., Goochland Co., Va., June 29, æ. 60. In early life Dr. Payne received a liberal academic education, preparatory to the study of medicine, and was placed under the pupilage of one of the most distinguished physicians and surgeons in the city of Richmond, viz., the late Dr. McCaw. He subsequently attended the lectures in the University of Pennsylvania, and became the private pupil of Drs. Chapman and Gibson, two of the most distinguished professors connected with that institution. Having received the highest honors which could there be conferred on him, he returned to Virginia, and in his native county (if not at the very place of his birth) commenced the establishment of a professional reputation which, increasing with his years, was almost unrivalled, and can never be forgotten by those who best knew him, until they shall, like him, pass away. Ardently devoted to his profession, all the energies of his body and mind were directed in that channel. Medicine was his constant theme and study. With a well-stored mind his preception was keen, and he delighted to combat the most intricate and direful diseases.

PEARSON, Capt. Thomas, Nashua, N. H., Dec. 14, æ. 74. Capt. P. witnessed the entire growth of what now constitutes Nashua proper, and was always closely identified with it. He was a most worthy and excellent man in every connection of life, whether as friend, neighbor, or townsman.

PEARSON, Rev. Ora, Peacham, Vt., July 5, æ. 60. He was born in Chittenden, Vt., Oct. 6, 1797, fitted for college at Rutland with Saml. Walker, Esq., graduated at Middlebury College in 1820, and at Andover Theological Seminary in 1824. The following year he preached in Gaines, Cambria, and Ridgeway, N. Y. In March, 1826, he became pastor of the Congregational church in Kingston, N. H. June 15 of the same year, he was married to Mary Kimball, of Barton, Vt., daughter of the late Hon. John Kimball, one of the early settlers of that town, who died, after a highly useful life, May 9, 1844, æ. 74, and granddaughter of Dea. John Kimball, one of the early settlers of Concord, N. H. Mr. P. and wife became the parents of six children, all of whom survive him except the eldest, a young man of much promise, who died at Indianapolis, Ind., Nov. 10, 1856, æ. 28. Mr. P. continued his ministerial labors at Kingston nearly eight years, when he removed to Barton, where he preached two years, and went from thence to Compton, Canada East, where he labored as missionary of the N. H. Missionary Society, three and a half years. In 1839 he was installed over the Congregtional churches in Barton and Glover, Vt., where he preached the succeeding six years. From 1845 until 1851 he was volume agent of the American Tract Society in Northern Vt. From Aug., 1851, till his death, his residence was in Peacham. Though compelled in the latter part of his life, from loss of his eyesight, to relinquish the responsibilities of a pastor, yet he loved to preach the gospel, and as far as he was able did preach, and God owned and blessed his labors. He came home about the 1st of April, from revival labors in Orleans Co., and not long after laid himself on the bed of sickness, whereon he died in a calm and joyful hope of a happy, endless rest. As a minister he was Christ-like, conscientious, tender, earnest, preaching the word in season and out of season, sowing beside all waters, living out what he preached so well as to manifest heartiness and sincerity in his work.

PECK, Rev. John M., Rock Spring, Ill., March 15, æ. 69. We find the following interesting notice of Dr. Peck in a St. Louis paper. "So goes out the light of one of the most useful men that the Mississippi Valley has ever known. It is looking back a good while to say that Mr. P. was a resident of St. Louis and a Baptist minister as early as 1818, that he, and Rev. J. E. Welch, who yet survives him, organized the first Baptist church in St. Louis. Dr. P. was not only an extraordinary man in the pulpit, but he was an accurate observer of men and things, the seasons and the changes connected with them, and treasured up in his daily journal all that seemed to him remarkable in the material world. The amount of labor performed by him was extraordinary. He was never idle. He was always writing, or doing something for the good of his fellow-man. He was a tolerant man, asserting his own opinions firmly, yet modestly, and conceding to others the full enjoyment of their own peculiar views on all questions. Possibly, no man in the Valley of the Mississippi was so familiar with its local history as he; and although he may have done much to preserve this history by his writings, it may be cause of regret that a few years more were not allotted to him, in which to chronicle and write down things which, it is feared, may have died with him, from the imperfect manner in which his notes were kept."

PECK, Hon. Henry E., New Haven, Ct., May 6, æ. 53. He was the youngest son of Nathan Peck, Esq., who for many years was a prominent and much respected citizen of New Haven. He entered Yale College at the age of 14, and graduated with honor in the class of 1823. He immediately entered the law school at New Haven, and was admitted to the practice of his profession, which, however, becoming distasteful to him, he soon abandoned, and turned his attention to other pursuits. In 1829 he purchased, in connection with the late L. K. Dow, Esq., and united and edited, the New Haven Journal and Chronicle. In the same year, also, he established the New Haven Advertiser, the first attempt at publishing a semi-weekly paper in the city of New Haven. In 1833, in connection with A. Newton, Esq., he originated and commenced the republication of Blackwood and other foreign quarterlies — a work of great difficulty at the time, in consequence of the irregularity and uncertainty in receiving the original by sailing packets. In 1839 he engaged in commercial pursuits in connection with his brothers, and spent a large portion of each succeeding year from 1840 to 1845 in the West Indies. He represented his native town in the legislature of Conn. in 1847, 1848, and 1850. In 1851 he was elected to the Senate of Conn., and was chosen president of that body. In both branches of the legislature of the state he was a leading member, and was distinguished for his courtesy, ability, and fidelity. The following tribute appeared in the daily papers of New Haven, the day after his decease: "The death of the Hon. Henry E. Peck, of this city, will be universally regretted. He had long held a high position in this community as a public-spirited citizen, and as a gentleman of estimable character and honorable instincts. If Mr. P. was remarkable for any one estimable quality more than another, it was for his keen moral and intellectual perceptions. He was instinctively honest, prompt to note distinctions between right and wrong, as he was to detect fallacies in reasoning, intrepid in exposing and denouncing error, and in vindicating the truth. He acted in all things from a conscientious sense of his responsibilities, never permitting considerations of expediency or policy to interfere with what he felt to be his duty, nor stopping short in the pursuit of his object, until convinced by persevering and unavailing effort that its achievement was impracticable. He read much, and thought more. Hence his opinions on all subjects to which he gave his attention, and these embraced a wide range, were matured opinions, sincerely entertained and frankly and earnestly expressed, and if resolutely and tenaciously maintained at times, yet always with deference to the views and opinions of others. His aims were elevated, his impulses generous, his tastes cultivated and refined, and his social qualities attractive and estimable. These characteristics gave Mr. P. position and deserved influence wherever he was called upon to act. They exhibited themselves during his academical and collegiate course, in the law school, and throughout his connection with the public press and the excitement of the political arena. They were fully developed in his maturer years by an intelligent and successful application of his energies to mercantile pursuits, in his active and leading participation in all public enterprises having in view the prosperity and beauty of the city of his birth and residence, or the education and moral culture of the masses, and by his faithfulness and ability as a representative in both branches of the state legislature. They were also finely illustrated in his 'daily walk and conversation,' which were truly those of a polished Christian gentleman, with whom it was both an honor and a pleasure to be associated in public and in private life. Mr. P. was, at the time of his death, as during the previous year, one of the vestrymen of Trinity Church, and one of its most active and efficient members, and died in the complete realization of the hopes and faith of the Christian. Having fulfilled an important mission on earth, he leaves a lustrous example of unobtrusive but sterling worth, and of extended and permanent usefulness.

PEIRCE, Waldo T., Esq., Bangor, Me., May 1, æ. 53. Although still in the prime of life, Mr. P. was one of the oldest of the Bangor merchants, having commenced business there more than thirty years ago. In company with his brother, the late Hayward Peirce, he, during all that time, transacted an extensive and profitable business, which grew with the growth of the city, from the days when her merchants were few, and her population but a tithe of its present number. As a business man, he was an honor to his profession, and as a citizen, highly respected.

PELTZ, Philip, M. D., Philadelphia, Pa., July 22, æ. 55.

PENDLETON, Capt. Joseph, Isleboro', Md., Sept. 21, æ. 89. He was a native of Stonington, Ct., and served in the revolutionary war as a "powder boy," where he received wounds, the scars of which he carried to his grave.

PENFIELD, Eldridge II., M. D., Topeka, K. T., Dec. 12, æ. 38. He was born in the town of Rocky Hill, Conn., in 1821. At an early age he removed to Hartford, and afterwards to Middletown. The winter of 1855-6 he spent in Philadelphia, and the following spring went to Kansas with the Connecticut colony, the principal part of which located at Waubonsa.

PERKINS, Rev. John W., Boston, Mass., Feb. —, æ. 43. He was born in Chelsea, Vt., and joined the Vermont conference, in 1842, where he preached about seven years with much success, and then transferred his connection to the New England conference, of which he was ever a most useful and valued member. Under the direction of this conference, he was stationed for two years as pastor of the First Church at Salem, and then transferred to the Liberty Street Church, Newburyport, where his labors were crowned with success. After this he was transferred to Medford, where he remained one year, and then took charge of the church at Melrose. During his two years of service at the latter place, through his instrumentality a church was built, and the society attained a good degree of vitality and usefulness. One year ago last April he was assigned to the Church Street Church in Boston, of which he was the pastor at the time of his death.

PERKINS, William H., (of Rochester, Monroe Co., N. Y.,) Utica, May 12, æ. 39, from injuries received by the railroad disaster at Sauquoit Bridge on the New York Central Railroad. Mr. P. was born in Litchfield, Ct., July 11, 1819, and moved with his father's family to Genesee, N. Y., in 1824. He came to Rochester in 1835. In 1839 he entered the house of E. F. Smith & Co. as a clerk, and became a partner in 1842. After several successive changes of partners, Mr. P., in 1856, retired from the house of which he had been a prominent member, and to whose great success his high business character and sterling integrity had largely contributed. In 1851 he was elected treasurer of Monroe Co., holding the office for three years. He was twice married — in 1842 to Miss Montague, of Troy, N. Y., who died in 1844; in 1848, to a daughter of Rev. Chester Dewey, D. D., professor in the University of Rochester. He was for many years a member, trustee, and treasurer of the First Presbyterian Church. He left a wife and two children. The funeral services were performed in Rochester, May 15; and on the following day, (Sunday,) a sermon appropriate to the occasion was preached by his pastor, the Rev. J. H. McIlvaine, D. D. By the sad event of Mr. P.'s death the whole city was moved, and gloom settled upon the hearts of thousands who knew him only to respect and love. Dr. McIlvaine, in his sermon, says, "He was my best friend, of whom it will be difficult for me to speak. But you will bear with me. He was the first of the residents of this city with whom I ever exchanged a word; and, without the circle of his own family and connections, there is none to whom his sorrowful death is so great an affliction as it is to me. He was yet a young man, of strong frame and robust health. His face, to me at least, was a model of manly beauty. He was a man of a high and pure sense of honor, of great energy, combined with what is often wanting to such traits — a wise prudence and a liberal caution. His business reputation was unblemished. Eminently judicious, he was one upon whom not only his own family and connections, but also many others, leaned much for advice and counsel in times of difficulty and embarrassment. Withal he was ambitious, but in that sense of the word which excludes jealousy, and which seeks to rise by fair and honorable means alone. God prospered him, and thus enabled him to support a liberality for the welfare of others that was never known and will never be known to the public. There was no pecuniary sacrifice that he would not make for his friends. I believe that in this respect his was one of the most enlarged and liberal hearts that God has made. With these traits he combined elegant tastes and accomplishments, and the first of genial natures. Strongly discriminative in his preferences and friendships, he was yet without enemies. Hence this general grief, this testimony of universal respect. He had all that peculiar and lovely simplicity, and wholeheartedness and constancy in friendship, which could see no faults in his friends. This perhaps was the most striking trait of his character, as manifested to those who enjoyed his intimacy. Where he loved, it was with his whole heart. To the church, in which he first made profession of his faith in Christ; to this congregation, for whose interests and welfare his cares and toils were unsparingly given; to the choir, in which he had served with untiring faithfulness for many years, — his loss is indeed irreparable. Thus, in a wide circle of friends, in the respect of all men, in his business connections and success, in his fulness of health and strength, in the affection of parents, brothers, and sisters, in the love of his wife and of his two infant children, he had every thing to make life happy, and to promise a long enjoyment of its blessings. Last Sabbath he was there in his place in the choir, where his seat now stands vacant and crowned with wreaths of funereal flowers. On Monday he bade farewell to his family, to meet the calls of business in a distant city. On the route he was waited for by the angel of death. The darkness of night, with the uncertainties and dangers of night travelling, had passed, whilst he had been whirled in safety on his journey. The spires of a neighboring city were in sight, when there occurred one of those fearful railway disasters, which, from more than heathenish recklessness of human life, have now become a constant element in our calculations of life and death in this (with respect to all such matters) horribly misgoverned country. Two trains meet, both at full speed, upon different tracks, in passing a rotten bridge. The bridge gives way, as often it had been predicted that it would. The passenger cars of one of the trains are precipitated into the gulf, against the stone abutments, and driven up one into the other, like the slides of a telescope. I cannot describe what followed; it is too horrible. But many were killed; many others were crippled for life. The wonder is that any escaped. There my friend was crushed; and many hearts that were not there were crushed with his mangled body. Without a moment's warning, in the pride of health, in the midst of all his plans and schemes for the future, in the buoyancy of hope, in the fulness of his mind's energy, in the abundance of his joys, there his great heart was crushed."

PERLEY, John, Ipswich. West Parish, Mass., Aug. 20, æ. 90. Mr. P. listened to the booming cannon on Bunker Hill in 1775, with trembling anxiety for the vanquishing of the British, and was afterwards active to overcome that rebellious people led on by Shays. He devoted his after life to agriculture, and was ever opposed to every form of oppression.

PERRY, Com. Matthew C., New York, March 4, æ. 63. Com. P. was born in South Kingston, on Narragansett Bay, R. I. His mother was Sarah Alexander. His father was Christopher Raymond Perry, who became an officer of the infant marine of the United States in 1798. His elder brother was Oliver H. Perry, the hero of the battle of Lake Erie. The first of the Perry family in this country emigrated to Massachusetts from Devonshire, England, about the middle of the seventeenth century. Matthew C. Perry entered the United States navy as a midshipman Jan. 16, 1809, when he immediately joined the schooner Revenge, from which he was soon after transferred to the frigate President. In Nov., 1813, he was ordered to the frigate United States, and in April, 1814, was sent back to the President. Towards the end of 1814 he was ordered to the brig Chippewa, from which vessel he was transferred to the navy yard at Brooklyn with the rank of lieutenant. He thus learned the duties of his profession amid the stirring events of the war of 1812 with Great Britain, when every officer of our little navy was more or less in active service. In Aug., 1819, he was ordered to the ship Cyane, which was sent to the coast of Africa, to aid the efforts of the Colonization Society in its attempt to found a settlement of free blacks upon the Island of Sherbro, near Sierra Leone. The mortality at Sherbro was so great that it became evident no colony could be planted there; and Lieut. P. selected Mesurado Cape as a more suitable locality for a town. He therefore fixed the locality of the first settlement of Liberia. In May, 1831, Lieut. P. was put in command of the schooner Shark, in which vessel he twice visited the colony of Mesurado. In the same vessel he also cruised the waters of the West Indies, and captured several pirates. On his return, he was again attached to the Brooklyn navy yard, where he remained until 1824, when he was ordered to the North Carolina, of 96 guns, under the command of Com. John Rodgers. In this ship he served as first lieutenant, and captain of the fleet, during her whole cruise. He was then promoted to the rank of commander, and took charge of the recruiting service at Boston, in which employment he continued until 1830, when he took command of the corvette Concord, in which he conveyed John Randolph, as United States minister, to St. Petersburg, and afterwards cruised three years in the Mediterranean. When home again, he was once more actively employed at the Brooklyn navy yard as superintendent of a school of gun practice, and in the organization of a steam naval service. He was at this time promoted to the rank of captain, and was offered the command of the exploring expedition afterwards given to Com. Wilkes, but for various reasons declined it. In 1838 Capt. P. was sent to Europe to visit the dock yards and lighthouses, and collect from personal inspection such facts as might be useful in improving those departments of the United States service. Early in 1839 he submitted his report to the government, and resumed his duties as superintendent of gun practice, and in preparing plans for the construction and equipment of the Missouri and the Mississippi, the first two ocean steamers in our navy. While thus employed he was appointed to the chief command of the Brooklyn navy yard, in which position he remained two years, when, at his own request, he was appointed to the command of the African squadron, sent out under the provisions of the Ashburton treaty. He succeeded so well in carrying out the provisions of the treaty that he received the commendation of both the British and American governments. In 1846 he sailed as second in command to Com. Connor, to the Gulf of Mexico, and on the retirement of that officer in March assumed the chief command in time to direct the naval bombardment of Vera Cruz. Com. P.'s "able coöperation" in the siege of Vera Cruz was cordially acknowledged by Gen. Scott in his official despatches. But the most distinguished service in his long career was the expedition to Japan, which sailed from the U. S. Nov. 24, 1852, and in command of which Com. P. negotiated the treaty with Japan, signed on the last day of March, 1854. The important events connected with this expedition are still fresh in the public mind, and we need not now do more than refer to them. The disease which caused Com. P.'s death was gout in the stomach. He had complained of feeling poorly for several days past, but was not considered in danger until the hour of his death, about two o'clock in the morning. We believe he leaves a widow and six children, three sons and three daughters. One of the sons is now consul at Hong Kong. Of the daughters, two are married (Mrs. John Hone and Mrs. Auguste Belmont,) and one remains single. The wife of the Rev. Dr. Vinton, of Trinity Church, N. Y., is a niece of Com. Matthew C. Perry and a daughter of Com. Oliver H. Perry. The deceased had served at sea for a period of 25 years, and on the shore more than 17 years, and had only been unemployed about six years during the whole time since his entrance into the navy.

PERRY, Hon. Robert C., Lexington, Holmes Co., Miss. Jan. 14, æ. 45. He was born in North Carolina, and at an early age emigrated with his father to Tennessee, and in or near Pulaski he studied law under Judge Bramlett. He emigrated to Mississippi in 1836, and settled in Carthage, Leake Co., practising his profession, until some time in 1842, when he married in Holmes Co., and remained a citizen of Holmes until the time of his death. In his life he held the offices of district attorney and circuit judge. How these offices, in a strict performance of the several duties of the same, were performed by him, the records of the county show. How his duties as husband, father, master, and friend were performed, the memory of those who knew him best will best attest.

PERRY, Hon. George, Saxton's River, Vt., Aug. 22, æ. 51. In 1857 he was a faithful member of the state Senate, but had declined a reëlection on account of his health. He was a member of a large manufacturing firm at Saxton's River, where his loss will be keenly felt. As a neighbor and citizen he was most highly esteemed and beloved, and the whole community feel that a heavy stroke has come upon them.

HON. JOHN S. PETERS,

Hebron, Ct., March 30, æ. 85. Mr. P. was born in Hebron, Conn., Sept. 21, 1772. His father, Bemslie Peters, was a native of Hebron, as was also his mother, whose maiden name was Annis Shipman. They had seven children, of whom the subject of this sketch was the fifth. Their parental ancestors were English, and their traditionary history, as handed down from father to son, is as follows: Lord Peters, of ———, England, had three sons, Thomas, Hugh, and William, all of whom were liberally educated men, and all dissenters from the established religion. They formed a part of that little band, who, to escape persecution, fled to Holland, and from thence, in 1620, came to Plymouth, Mass. Thomas, the eldest brother, was a clergyman, and settled at Saybrook, where he died, leaving no children. He was one of the founders of Yale College, first located at Saybrook, and removed to New Haven in 1700; and his library, which he bequeathed to the college, formed the nucleus of the present extensive one of that institution.

Hugh, the second brother, was also a clergyman, and settled at Salem, Mass., where he resided until the rebellion against Charles I. had made some progress, when he returned to England, and took an active part in the support of Cromwell. On the restoration of Charles II., he died on the scaffold, a traitor or martyr, according to the opinion or fashion of the day. He had one child, a daughter, who married a highly respectable citizen of Boston, whose name is not known.

William was a merchant, and settled at Mendon, Mass. He left a large family, and from him, it is believed, all of the name now living in New England descended. John Peters, one of the descendants of William, removed from Mendon to Hebron in 1718, and was one of the first settlers of the town. He left a large family, among whom were Rev. Samuel Peters, D. D., and Bemslie Peters, the father of John S. Peters. In the year 1774, Bemslie Peters removed with his family to Mooretown, Vt., to act as the land agent of his brother Samuel, and Gov. Moore, of New York, who had jointly purchased the township; but in consequence of their failure to procure a title to the land they had purchased, and entertaining fears of a murderous descent of Canadian Indians, a war between Great Britain and the colonies being in embryo, he returned with his family to Hebron the year following.

On the breaking out of the revolutionary war, Bemslie Peters, with most of the other descendants of John Peters then living in Hebron, took the side of the king, and were determined royalists. He continued to reside in Hebron with his family until 1777, when he went to N. Y. city, then in the possession of the royal forces, and soon after sailed for England, and joined his brother Samuel in London. For his royalty he obtained a captain's commission, and resided in England until 1794, when he drew a large tract of land near Little York, in Upper Canada, to which place he removed, and died in the year 1799.

The family of Bemslie Peters were left by him in moderate pecuniary circumstances, and wholly dependent upon the mother, who discharged her duty to them faithfully. At the age of 18 John S. became a teacher, and continued to teach the dsitrict school for the four succeeding winters. At the age of 20, having made choice of the medical profession, he commenced its study with Dr. Benjamin Peters, of Marbletown, Ulster Co., N. Y., and with Dr. Abner Moseley of Glastenbury. In Nov., 1776, he went to Philadelphia to complete his professional studies, and there attended the anatomical lectures of Drs. Shipen and Wistar, the medical lectures of Dr. Woodhouse, and the Medical Institute of Dr. Rush. He returned to Hebron in March, 1797, and established himself as a physician.

Dr. Peters was considered a very skilful physician, and had an extensive practice in his own and the adjoining towns. He was a man of studious habits, and his active mind was well stored and enriched with the best and most valuable medical literature of the day. In addition to this, he possessed a mass of invaluable practical knowledge, obtained in his arduous every-day practice. He was esteemed and honored by his professional brethren, having filled various offices in the county and state medical societies, at one time president of the state society. He likewise so possessed the good will of the voters of Connecticut that they raised him to some very prominent political stations. In 1827 he was elected lieutenant governor, and continued in this office through 1830. In 1831 he was elected governor, and again in 1832.

Dr. P. possessed a good physical constitution, and up to within two years of his death enjoyed perfect health. When in the 84th year of his age, he made the following memorandum in his note-book: "I am now in my 84th year; I enjoy good health, and have a competency of this world's goods, and am waiting patiently for that change which I know must soon come. I have had my full share of the labors of a country physician, and more of political offices and labors than ordinarily fall to the share of one citizen."

In his religion he was a sincere Christian and a humble worshipper. His parents, and the Peters family generally, were Episcopalians. He was ardently attached to the church, and contributed liberally of his means to its support. To the parish of St. Peter's Church, in Hebron, he was a munificent benefactor. He was for many years a member of the corporation of Trinity College, which institution conferred upon him the degree of LL. D. Both as a physician and a man, he had a strong hold upon the affection of his townsmen. Dr. P. lived and died a bachelor.

PETERS, John R., New York city, Apr. 24, æ. 75. He was the eldest son of Gen. Absalom Peters, of Hebron, Conn., and was born at Wentworth, N. H., in 1783. He commenced his business education in Groton, Mass., in the same establishment with the late Amos and William Lawrence, of Boston, went from there to Troy, N. Y., where he carried on a successful business for several years, and removed to New York in 1814, where he has resided ever since. As a leading merchant of the latter city, he did much by his enterprise in developing the cotton trade of the south, where he had extensive business connections for many years, and sent, in 1816, the first vessel cleared from N. Y. for Mobile.

PHELPS, Hon. Charles B., suddenly, at Roxbury, Ct., Dec. 21, æ. 71, of Woodbury, Ct. He was a member of the bar 51 years, and a member of both branches of the state legislature, speaker of the House, and judge of the Litchfield County Courts. At a public meeting of the citizens of Woodbury, the following resolution was passed: —

"*Resolved*, that we are not willing to let this occasion pass without expressing our sense of the qualities of the man, the large legal knowledge to which he had attained, the reputation he had achieved, the unusual justness of his judgments as a judge, — never, in the long period of 26 years, having had one of the judgments of his Probate Court set aside, — the breadth of his reading, the keenness of his wit, the force of his eloquence, and the general excellence of his qualities as a man of force and success, either with assemblies or at the bar. The large and generous nature, also, that belonged to him; the nobleness and warmth of his heart; the depth and tenderness of his feelings, and the readiness and promptness of his sympathies for all the poor and the distressed; his generous appreciation, also, of the institutions of religion to the stability and purity of society, the worth of schools and colleges, and the necessity of sound books; for all of which, though not till very lately a professionally religious man, he always gave a liberal proportion of his means. His value, also, among us, as one of the men of the past; his taste for letters; his antiquarian disposition, and the love by that disposition accumulated; his form and countenance ever suggestive of good old times and good old feelings, telling us with a force words fail to do, that kindness of heart, pity for the poor, and good feeling to the various classes of men, are not necessarily a part of any man's creed, any sect, or any profession. And finally, that we shall long remember him as a magnanimous friend and father, the sincerity of whose attachments and the wisdom of whose counsels we could not doubt; and his memory will be dear to us, and his grave green in our recollections, 'till life shall pass.'"

PHELPS, Anson G., Esq., New York city, May 18, æ. 39. Mr. Phelps was one of the most distinguished of the young merchants of New York for philanthropy, public spirit, and wealth with which to carry out the benevolence of his heart. He was only son of the late Anson G. Phelps, Esq., whose munificence, both during his life and in his bequests by will, is universally known. Both father and son were members of the firm of "Phelps, Dodge, & Co." It is not too much to say, that no man of his age could be more missed from mercantile, religious, and philanthropic circles of our city than Mr. Phelps.

PHILBRICK, Edward, Concord, N. H., Aug. 20, æ. 90. He was for about 20 years one of the doorkeepers of the House of Representatives.

PHILLEO, Calvin W., Esq., Suffield, Ct., June 30, æ. 30. He was born in Vernon, N. Y., June 14, 1822, and was the only son of the Rev. Calvin Philleo, a preacher of considerable repute in the Baptist denomination, who removed to Suffield, Ct., where he was settled for several years. After receiving a good academical education, he studied law with the late Hon. George S. Catlin, of Windham, Ct., and was admitted to the bar of Hartford Co. in 1845. In 1847 he opened an office in Suffield, and, in 1849, married Miss Elizabeth Pense Norton, daughter of Daniel W. Norton. He obtained considerable professional practice, and a very respectable position at the Hartford County bar. His mind was eminently logical, and his briefs in the Supreme Court, which were generally expanded into full arguments, were fine specimens of logical reasoning. His attention was, however, during the last few years of his life, in some measure diverted to another and more attractive field of labor. He became a pleasing and graceful writer of fiction in Graham's Magazine, in Putnam's Magazine, in Harper's Magazine, and the Atlantic Monthly. Mr. Philleo had reached that happy point in human life, where a period of early struggles left behind makes brighter, by the contrast, a future of seemingly sure reward. This future of his imagination he surrendered, keenly disappointed, yet with a placid mind, to the greater future of reality. The memory of his warm, genial nature, his uprightness, and his many excellences, will be cherished by a broad circle of hearty and intimate friends.

PHILLIPS, Hariet C., Newburyport, Mass., Oct. 2, æ. —, wife of Samuel Phillips, Esq., and daughter of Zebedee Cook, Esq., of N.

PICKARD, Rev. John H., Caswell Co., N. C., Sept. 11, æ. 75. Mr. Pickard went to Caswell Co. in the year 1816, and commenced preaching at Bethesda Church as a licentiate. In Nov., 1817, he was ordained to the full work of the gospel ministry, by the presbytery of Orange. He continued his labors at Bethesda for upwards of 30 years. He was an earnest preacher of the gospel, and a man noted for his piety.

PICKETT, Col. Albert J., New Montgomery, Ala., Oct. 19, æ. —. Col. Pickett had long been well known in Alabama as an amiable and accomplished gentleman; and beyond the bounds of the states his name was made familiar to the general ear by his History of Alabama. He was one of those men, of whom so few are found among us, who, born to a life of ease, leisure, and abundance, choose to devote their time to intellectual pursuits. He was a member of the bar, but, we believe, never sought distinction there; but his mind was never idle, and his pen but seldom. His writings are scattered anonymously through the papers and periodicals of the country, and could they be collected, would form no insignificant "mental pyramid;" but he is little known as a writer except by his History of Alabama.

PIERCE, S. B., Esq., Augusta, Perry Co., Miss., April 17, æ. —, killed by the accidental discharge of his gun. Mr. Pierce was a native of Jackson, Miss., had represented Hancock Co. in the legislature, had been mayor of the city of Shieldsboro', and was a rising member of the bar.

PIERCE, Mrs. Lucy, Brookline, Mass., —— 12, æ. 80, widow of the late Rev. John Pierce, D. D., and a descendant of Mary, sister of Benjamin Franklin.

PIERCE, Asahel, Calais, Vt., Aug. 19, æ. 87. Mr. Pierce went into Vermont in the summer of 1795, purchasing a lot of land in the wilderness at the easterly part of the town of Calais, and commenced cutting down the forest preparatory to making a farm. In March, 1798, he moved his wife from the town of Rehoboth, Mass., into a log house, constructed on his premises.

PIERPONT, Robert R., Nappa Co., Cal., Nov. 5, æ. 34, a native of Rutland, Vt. He was one of the early settlers of Nappa, and went to California in 1849. In the practice of his profession he secured the confidence of all classes, and was universally esteemed for his probity and manliness of character.

PIERSON, Rev. Daniel, Bowdoinham, Me., April 24, æ. 79.

PILCHER, Gen. William A., Louisville, Ky., Aug. 14, æ. —. He was for some months mayor of Louisville, and for many years distinguished as a leading politician and lawyer all over the state. Gen. P. was at one time the democratic candidate for lieutenant governor of Ky., and canvassed and spoke in every county in the state. On the organization of the American party, he attached himself to it, and remained a fast and zealous friend of its principles up to his death. He was a man of talents, and highly esteemed in the society where he moved.

PILLSBURY, Hon. T., Danville, Texas, Dec. 23, æ. 68. He was a member of the Maine legislature, and some 20 years ago or more a candidate for Congress in the Eastport district. Failing of his election, he removed to Texas, and became judge of the Probate Court of Brazoria Co., and representative from the same county, in the Texas Congress. He was an ardent advocate of the annexation of Texas. He was the first representative from the western district in the Congress of the United States. He served but one term, not having been of the order of men to make a decided impression in that body. He was a man who could rarely go wrong, because he *felt* right. Such men always exert an abiding moral influence.

PINCKNEY, Mrs. Amelia, Annapolis, Md., Nov. 4, æ. 79. An Annapolis paper says, "Her industry was wonderful. The records of the state department bear evidence of a skill in penmanship, and a capacity for business, rarely met with in a woman. After her seventieth year she wrote 1500 closely written pages, full of the stores of her rich mind and cultivated taste, solely for the perusal and gratification of those who cheered the last years of her bodily suffering. In all this tribute of affection there is no sacrifice of the truth she loved so well — no exaggeration of the reality. As an evidence of the powers of her mind, and the rapidity of her mental conception, we may mention, that, when past her seventieth year, she wrote in six weeks 500 verses of excellent poetry, on the subject of the Queens of England, without the erasure of a line or change of a word.

PITCHER, Major M. S., Astor House, New York city, Sept. 17, of Sandy Hill, N. Y., æ. —. Major P. was appointed a captain in the 10th regiment of U. S. infantry during the Mexican war, and served with his regiment on the Rio Grande. Near the close of the war he was raised to the rank of major. He left the service when the 10 regiments raised for the war were disbanded. A few years ago, when four new regiments were added to the army, Maj. P. was appointed to a captaincy in the 9th regiment.

PITKIN, Rev. S. Dwight, Woodbridge, N. J., Sept. 30, æ. 36, at the residence of Walter Brewster. Mr. Pitkin was born in Ellerton, Ct., June 20, 1822 — graduated at Amherst College — studied theology three years in New York, and one year at New Haven, Ct. — spent one year preaching in Wisconsin, and went to Battle Creek in Oct., 1848, where he remained nine years. As a speaker, there are few who did not admire the elegance of his language and the perspicuity of his thought. In the fact that for eight years he drew around him the largest and most intelligent congregation in the place, and through the whole time made such progress that the interest and admiration of his audience increased as the time flowed on, and knew no ebb up to the day of his departure, is ample testimony of his efficiency in this respect. He was an industrious student, and gave his congregation the first fruits of that industry.

PLATT, John Freligh, Plattsburg, N. Y., Feb. 25, æ. 20, son of Moses Kent Platt, Esq. Mr. Platt was fitted for college at the early age of 12 or 13 years. At the age of 15 he entered the Sophomore class at Williams College. Owing to the failure of health he remained in college, at this time, but a single term. After regaining his health, he reëntered the Sophomore class in Sept., 1855. More careful of his health, and wiser in his purposes of a college education, he no longer devoted his attention exclusively to text books; he read much, and thought and wrote still more; and, as a natural consequence, with one of such brilliant talents, he won and maintained the reputation of being a close, accurate, far-reaching thinker. Less than a year since, his appearance was quite remarkable for health and strength. The last of April, 1857, he took cold, which, through neglect, settled into consumption; and he was obliged to return home in the early part of May. During his sickness, his ability to call up all his theoretical knowledge, and make it speak to his views, was noticeable, even in the shortest conversation. For the last few weeks of his life the burden of his talk, was the wonderful love of Christ, how every thing in the universe speaks it, and how every motive, which can influence a rational being, calls upon us to exercise it towards God and man; with what earnestness, with what impressiveness, with what melting tenderness, he besought his friends not to neglect it, no one who heard can ever forget. The paternal wisdom which secured for him the rarest educational advantages, and the fidelity of his early instructors, were richly rewarded by the commanding position, which, as a scholar and man, he maintained among his fellows. The habits of mind which he thus early formed, strengthened with his years, had already awakened high anticipations for his success and usefulness in the intellectual world.

PLATT, Rev. Isaac W., West Farms, Westchester Co., N. Y., Feb. 9, æ. 69.

PLATT, Joseph, Canfield, O., Jan. 15, æ. 87. The deceased was one of the old pioneers of that section, having removed from Massachusetts to Canfield Township in 1818.

PLATT, Mrs. Martha A., Columbus O., Sept. 10, æ. —. She was a decided Christian — meek, unobtrusive, yet earnest and self-denying. She ever evinced her hope in the humble endeavor, by the careful culture of her heart, to be more Christ-like. Solicitous for the welfare of Zion, she did what she could; and cheerfully suffered what was appointed to her in the kingdom and patience of Jesus Christ.

PLATT, Hon. Robert, Plattsburg, N. Y., May 16, æ. 79.

PLUMMER, Edwin, Portland, Me., May 29, æ. 33. He was a man quite above the ordinary rank, and in a literary point of view had reached a very respectable eminence. Acquiring, in his nonage, the printer's art, he soon stepped from the "case" to the higher walks of publisher and editor. He edited the Norway Advertiser, and afterwards started in Portland, several years since, a literary paper, the Northern Pioneer, and more recently the Eclectic, both of which won much credit for Mr. P., and a large circulation. He was a poet of no mean power. Some of his effusions were most beautifully conceived and expressed. As a prose writer, his lectures before societies, in this and other sections of the country, as well as his newspaper essays, placed him in a high rank. Above all, he was an honest man.

POMEROY, Rev. Thaddeus De Witt, Onondaga Co., N. Y., April 14, æ. 76, formerly of Gorham, Me.

POPE, Rev. Augustus Russell, Somerville, Mass., May 24, æ. 39. He was son of Lemuel and Sally Belknap (Russell) Pope, and was born in Boston, Jan. 25, 1819. His father was for many years president of the Boston Insurance Company, and died in Roxbury in 1851. Mr. P., soon after graduating at Harvard, 1839, entered the Divinity School in Cambridge, where he pursued his theological studies. He was ordained pastor of the Unitarian church in Kingston, Mass., April 19, 1843, where he faithfully discharged his ministerial duties until June, 1849, when he resigned his pastoral charge, and was afterwards installed over the Unitarian church in Somerville. He continued to labor with great acceptance to the people of his charge until his death, with the exception of a few months, about two years since, during which period he acted as state agent and lecturer for the Massachusetts Board of Education. He was a man of great energy and industry. He possessed talents well adapted to the profession he had chosen, and personal characteristics imbued with Christian virtues, which made him eminently useful as a minister, and beloved and respected as a man by a large circle of acquaintances.

PORTER, William T., New York city, ——, æ. 52. Mr. Porter was a native of Vermont, and his first occupation was that of a printer. He emigrated to New York about 25 years ago, and for some time practised his vocation in a book-printing establishment. He afterwards established a weekly journal called the Constellation, which was merged into the Spirit of the Times which was established by Mr. John Richards, and of which Mr. Porter was sole editor. As a journalist he was always generous and fair; as a writer, elegant, spirited, and graceful; as a gentleman, he won the esteem of all who met him. His last work was the obituary notice of the late John C. Stevens. Mr. Porter was connected with the family of the Hon. Rufus Choate, and other distinguished persons in New England. He was the last of four brothers, three of whom were journalists, and died in the harness.

PORTER, William M., Esq., Pittsburg, Pa., Nov. —, æ. 33. The deceased was a gentleman of rare endowments, and a versatile and ready writer. Having received a liberal education at the Western University, he afterwards studied law under Andrew Burke, Esq. Inheriting an ample fortune, with a mind disinclined to the labors and strife of the legal profession, he never entered on the practice of the law. Many of his essays had extensive circulation, and were read with marked approval. He had a large family connection in this county, and innumerable personal friends, who will long cherish his memory, and regret his early death.

PORTER, Charles, Haverhill, Mass., Oct. 24, æ. 71. Mr. P. was for many years a prominent citizen of Haverhill, and did much towards the present business prosperity. He was formerly a successful and respected merchant in New York; and, after he settled down in Haverhill, he erected a large number of substantial blocks of stores, and in many other ways contributed largely towards moving the wheels of trade. By the business men of this vicinity, with whom his intercourse was frequent and pleasant, Mr. P. will be much regretted. During an active business life, extending over so many years, he amassed a large property, and, like a wise man, used it as the Lord's.

PORTER, Rev. Calvin, East Paw-Paw, De Kalb Co., Ill., Nov. 22, æ. 64.

POST, Rev. Reuben, D. D., Charleston, S. C., Sept. 24, æ. 66. He was a native of Vermont, a graduate of Middlebury College, and in 1813, of Princeton Seminary. After a brief term of missionary service in Virginia, he was in 1819 ordained as pastor of the First Presbyterian church in Washington, D. C., where he remained until his removal to Charleston, as pastor of the Circular Church in Feb., 1836. During the period of his residence in Washington, under President Jackson's administration, he was for two successive terms chosen chaplain of the House of Representatives. His long pastorate in Charleston had rendered him one of the landmarks of the community, where, though naturally of a timid and unobtrusive nature, he was ever ready to take his part, when called upon, in matters of public interest. In the sphere of his ordinary labors, few men have been more punctual and faithful in the discharge of their stated duties. All in contact with him must have admitted the zeal, almost amounting to pertinacity, with which, under an increasing weight of years and infirmity, he fulfilled his pastoral duties. The most characteristic feature of his piety was reverence, a pervading sense of the presence and scrutiny of God, and the solemnities of eternity; and this perhaps imparted to his preaching its prevailing monitory and searching tone, its gravity and solemnity. His intercourse with other evangelical denominations was characterized by the widest liberality, though he was decided in his denominational preference and doctrinal convictions. He was third upon the roll of the Charleston presbytery in ecclesiastical seniority; and no one of its old members rejoiced more cordially in the reunion by which an unfortunate division had been healed. The board of supervisors of the High School at Charleston, of which Dr. P. was the president, at a special meeting passed the following among other resolutions:—

Resolved, that in the death of the Rev. Dr. Reuben Post we have lost an excellent president of this board, a Christian gentleman, who was devoted to his duties, and performed them with unfailing punctuality, urbanity, and wisdom; we shall ever remember with gratitude his valuable services to our school; we shall strive to imitate his example; we will respect and cherish his memory."

POTTER, Paraclete, Esq., Milwaukie, Wis., Feb. 3, æ. 78. Mr. P. was a native of Dutchess Co., and one of its most prominent citizens for many years. Being by trade a printer, he commenced the business of printing and bookselling as early as 1806, at which time he also took charge of the Poughkeepsie Journal newspaper, which he purchased of Nicholas Power, its founder. He continued in the same business until 1834, being all that time sole editor of the Journal — a period of 28 years. An active politician, he was until 1816 a zealous member of the federal party, then a supporter of Dewitt Clinton, and subsequently of Gen. Jackson. After he left his editorial labors he became very active in promoting the improvements which for a time marked the progress of Poughkeepsie. In 1841 he removed to Milwaukie, where he remained until death closed his career. With a character above the reach of reproach, he was a man of marked talent, and in general knowledge had few superiors in the country.

POTTER, Rev. Ray, Pawtucket, R. I., March 1, æ. 62.

POTTINGER, Hon. John, Jefferson, Berks Co., Pa., April 25, æ. —, was one of the representatives of Berks Co. in the state legislature during the years 1832, 1833, and 1834, and again in 1842, and was state senator for the term which included the years 1847, 1848, and 1849. He was at all times faithful to the interests of his constituents, and in public and private life maintained an unblemished character.

POTTS, Rev. R., Waynesburg, Pa., Nov. 21, æ. —.

POWELL, Robert M., Esq., Forks of Capon, Hampshire Co., Va., Oct. 17, æ. 58. He had been twice elected to represent his county in the legislature of Virginia, and was, at the time of his decease, a member of that body. He also served for some years as school commissioner and justice of the peace. He was kind and courteous in his intercourse with his fellow-men, and was ever thoughtful of the rights and feelings of all with whom he had to do. He was upright and honorable in his business transactions, and firm and undeviating in his friendships.

POWER, William, M. D., New York city, Sept. 14, æ. 60. He was a native of Ireland, and received his professional education in the great school of Dublin, and, to comply with the then laws of this state, received the diploma of M. D. in New York. For over 30 years he has been a medical practitioner among us. occupying a distinguished position, serving, without distinction, the rich and poor. Indeed, few physicians have ever done more for his poor countrymen than he. His frank and noble character commanded for him the respect and esteem not only of his own countrymen, but of all who knew him. The arduous toil of professional life gradually developed in him organic disease of the heart, from the effects of which he lingered for the last two years.

POWER, John Henry, M. D., Aberdeen, O., Sept. 4, æ. 33. Dr. P. was born and raised in Aberdeen. He completed his medical education in one of the medical colleges in Cincinnati, in the winter of 1854–55, and emigrated to Canton, Lewis Co., Mo., on the Upper Mississippi, where for one year he was earnestly and successfully engaged in his profession.

POWERS, William L., Bloomington, Ill., Aug. 28, æ. 53.

POWERS, Mrs. Azubah C., Phillipston, Mass., Aug. 31, æ. 76, wife of Oliver Powers, Esq., and mother of Rev. Philander O. Powers, missionary of the A. B. C. F. M. to the Armenians of Asiatic Turkey.

PRATT, W. H., M. D., Buffalo, N. Y., Nov. 28, æ. —

PRATT, Elder Cyprian S., Harmony, Me., July 8, æ. 51. He was born in Hebron, Me.; experienced religion about 1831, on Fox Island; subsequently united with the Free-will Baptists. He was licensed to preach by the Exeter quarterly meeting, June 18, 1833. In the June following he was ordained by a council appointed by the quarterly meeting, in the town of Brighton. For several years he devoted most of his time to travelling and preaching among the destitute churches, holding protracted meetings, &c. The Lord blessed his labors in the conversion of many sinners, and to the edification of the church. After the organization of the Wellington quarterly meeting his labors were, for many years, principally confined within its limits. The last of his labors were bestowed upon the town of Richmond, when failing health admonished him that his work in the gospel field was nearly over.

PREBLE, Maj. Henry, Woolwich, Me., March 6, æ. 45. He was a lieutenant of infantry in the Aroostook war in 1839, in the controversy about the northern boundary, and for several years a member of one of the large shipbuilding firms in Bath. He spent most of his life, however, upon a large and valuable farm which he received from an uncle. He married an accomplished lady in Bath in 1837, and left five children.

PRESCOTT, Miss Sarah, Boston, Mass., June 18, æ. 86, daughter of the late Hon. James Prescott, Sen., of Groton, and niece of Col. William Prescott, the hero of Bunker Hill.

PRESCOTT, William, Esq., Sanbornton, N. H., July 13, æ. 80. He was one of those noble veterans who took his pack on his shoulder and started for the far-famed township, and laid the foundation for many privileges to be enjoyed by coming generations.

PRESSEY, John, Esq., Sutton, N. H., Aug. 17, æ. 81. Mr. P. was one of the most aged and respectable citizens of the town of Sutton. Having lived a long time in the town, his circle of acquaintances was somewhat extensive; and by his uprightness of character and urbanity of manners he gained the confidence and respect of all who knew him. He had repeatedly been elected to the various offices within the gift of the people of the town, all of which he filled with marked ability and the strictest fidelity.

PRETLOW, P. R., M. D., Pineville, Monroe Co., Ala., May 26, æ. 53. Successful as a physician, accomplished as a gentleman, a man of inflexible integrity, and of unsullied honor.

PRICE, Mrs. Ruth, Bridgewater, Mass., Aug. 5, æ. 83, the last revolutionary pensioner in the town.

PRICE, Edwin, M. D., Brunswick, Mo., Jan. 24, æ. 62. He was born in Prince Edward Co., Va., Sept. 10, 1795. He received his academical education at Hampden Sidney College, Va., and graduated at the Medical College in New York in 1819. He first entered on the duties of his profession in 1821, in Charlotte Co., Va., in the vicinity of "John Randolph of Roanoke," in whose family, among others, the youthful doctor was the chosen physician. In 1838 he removed with his family to Howard Co., Mo., and one year later settled himself permanently in the then infant town of Brunswick. Dr. P. was gifted with a strong and vigorous intellect, a quick and accurate perception. Outside of his profession, he was a high-minded, large-hearted, kind, and polite gentleman. Sociable, lively, and humorous, his presence was welcome and agreeable in every company. Independent of the thorough education of his own children, he was the zealous advocate and generous patron of schools and colleges. Religion, too, claimed him as her friend. Her churches were uniformly reared with his aid; her ministers had a home at his house, and many of them a warm place in his heart.

PRINGLE, Rev. William, Ryegate, Vt., Dec. 14, æ. 66. He was born in Perth, Scotland, in 1791, came to this country in 1828, and preached near Albany, N. Y., until the succeeding year, when he was settled as pastor of the Associate Church of Ryegate, in which congregation he labored until seven years since, when he resigned his charge. He was very punctual in his habits. It was his motto to begin the day with God, and so to end it. He was ever most conscientious in his private duties.

PRIOR, A. G., M. D., Burns Depot, N. Y., March 12, æ. 42, a useful and worthy citizen, a physician of ability, and very successful in the practice of medicine.

PROAL, William H., M. D., Wappurgen Falls, Poughkeepsie, N. Y., July 16, æ. 37.

PUGH, Col. William E., Kosciusko, Miss., March 8, a citizen of Yazoo City, Miss. The members of the Attala Co. bar, in attendance upon the Circuit Court at Kosciusko, —

"*Resolved*, that in the death of Col. Pugh the profession of which he was a member has lost a worthy, honorable, and prominent member, and the community a useful, good, and dignified citizen."

PURDY, Jotham, M. D., Elmira, N. Y., ——, æ. —.

PURVIANCE, Robert, Sen., Baltimore, Md., ——, æ. —, one of the oldest citizens of Baltimore city, a descendant of a distinguished patriot of the revolution, and of one of the founders of said city. Mr. P.'s family originally were French Protestant Huguenots, who, in the reign of Louis XIV., were compelled, by the bitter persecution of the Catholics, to leave their native country. They sought an asylum in the north of Ireland, whence Mr. P.'s father, Robert, and Samuel, his uncle, emigrated in 1754, and in 1763 established a commercial house in Baltimore. True always to the principles of civil and religious liberty, they warmly espoused the cause of the grievances of the colonies against the mother country, and as early as 1768 were in correspondence with the celebrated John Hancock and others on the subject. Messrs. Samuel and Robert Purviance subsequently became intimate and corresponded with John Hancock, Richard Henry Lee, Henry Laurens, Robert Morris, Lafayette, and other leaders of the revolution, particularly during the memorable and disastrous winter of 1777-78, when Congress, driven out from Philadelphia by the British, held its sessions in Baltimore, on the corner of Liberty Street and Baltimore, old Congress Hall; and they shortly afterwards became the financial agents of the government; and to the good cause of independence their ample means were most liberally contributed. To the clothing of Lafayette's soldiers, before their advance to Yorktown, they were also the largest Baltimore contributors. Several of Lafayette's officers, Count Rochambeau and others, made their homes at the hospitable residences of Messrs. S. and R. Purviance. Mr. Samuel Purviance, who did most useful service during the revolution as chairman of the celebrated Whig Club and Committee of Safety of Baltimore town, was unfortunately, after the close of the war, and in 1788, captured by the Indians, on the Ohio River, near the present site of Cincinnati, and was never afterwards heard of. His brother Robert, after the adoption of the federal constitution, was appointed by Gen. Washington United States collector for the district of Baltimore, and enjoyed the honor, under the successive administrations of Adams and Jefferson. Mr. Robert Purviance, his son, was honored during his life by a few public trusts, and did good service at the battle of North Point. He was the youngest brother of the late Judge Purviance, so advantageously known, if not to the present generation, at least to their fathers and grandfathers, by his successful and honorable career of 35 years' practice at the Baltimore bar, and of nearly 20 years on the bench, who died in Baltimore in 1854, æ. 81. Mr. Robert Purviance throughout life was a most constant attendant at the First Presbyterian Church in the city of Baltimore, of which church his ancestors were among the principal founders, nearly 100 years since.

PUTNAM, Schuyler, Elyria, O., ———, æ. 69. Mr. P. was a grandson of Gen. Putnam, of revolutionary memory, who immortalized himself in early times by killing the wolf, and afterwards on the battle field. He was for many years a faithful magistrate in this place, and at the time of his death was a member of the Lorain bar.

Q.

GEN. JOHN ANTHONY QUITMAN, Natchez, Miss., July 17, æ. 60. Gen. Q. was born in Rhinebeck, in Dutchess Co., N. Y., on the banks of the Hudson, Sept. 1, 1799. His father, who was a native of Prussia, was a Lutheran clergyman and a man of fine cultivation. His grandfather was a distinguished Prussian general. He received his education at Mount Airy, above Germantown, in Philadelphia Co., and at the age of only 20 was elected to a professorship in the Mount Airy College, near Philadelphia. Preferring the law, he soon resigned his professorship, and commenced the practice of law in Chillicothe, O. Here he remained about one year, and in 1822 came to Natchez, where he settled permanently and spent the rest of his life. His talents and business habits soon enabled him to form a law partnership with the late W. B. Griffith, Esq., a distinguished member of the bar, which at once brought him into notice, and opened his way to fortune and fame. In 1827 he made his entry into politics, by accepting a seat in the legislature, where he was placed at the head of the judiciary committee, and won for himself marked distinction by the manner in which he discharged the duties of that responsible position. In the following year he was appointed by Gov. Brandon chancellor of the state, to fill a vacancy, and was at the next session of the legislature unanimously continued in the office. He remained chancellor until 1831, when he was chosen a member of the convention to revise the state constitution, and in that body, as formerly in the legislature, he was placed at the head of the judiciary committee. When the new constitution made all offices subject to the popular vote, he was replaced on the chancellor's bench without any opposition. It is worthy of especial remark in this connection, as showing the penetrating and sagacious turn of his mind, that in the constitutional convention he submitted a resolution to prohibit the legislature from borrowing money for banking purposes. It is useless to say how fully subsequent events vindicated the correctness of his views. In 1834 he retired from the chancellorship, and in the following year was chosen to the state Senate from Adams Co. Immediately after the elections took place, the Senate was convened in extra session, by proclamation of the secretary of state, to elect a president, who would become acting governor of the state by the expiration of Gov. Runnel's term of service. The Senate met, and Gen. Q. was elected, and entered upon the discharge of the duties of governor. His message to the two houses at the regular session of 1836, is still recollected as a remarkably able document, in which he promulged the views respecting state rights, and the institution of African slavery, to which he adhered with such consistency and advocated with such ability to the end of his life.

He retired from political life in 1836, but the struggle between Texas and Mexico soon brought him prominently before the public, as the ardent advocate and unflinching friend of the cause of liberty and independence in the republic of Texas. Together with Gen. Felix Houston, now no more, he did much to aid the gallant band of patriots in wresting from the grasp of Mexican tyranny and insolence "the Lone Star," which, having surrendered the attributes of a republic, put on the robes of a state, and entered into the Union.

When Texas achieved her independence he returned to private life, but continued to evince an interest for the prosperity of the state, and the construction of the lines of railroads, then just in their germ.

He was at one time grand master of the Masons, member of the Scientific Lyceum, and received the honorary degree of A. M. from Princeton College, and the still more acceptable one of LL. D. from Lagrange College, Ky. From 1839 to 1845 he lived comparatively a retired life, but was always fond of military societies and affairs, and the splendid companies at Natchez stand as monuments of his skill and enterprise in imparting ease and elegance in tactics to those under his control and management.

When war was declared with Mexico, a wider field was opened for the display of heroism and military talents than had yet been presented to his view. The soul of the gallant Quitman was prompted not alone by a desire to defend the honor and glory of his country, but within his bosom he felt as if it were one of "the big wars which make ambition virtue," and he yearned to marshal a chosen band of soldiers under the folds of his country's flag, and lead them on to victory or death. He was appointed brigadier general in the U. S. army in 1845, and in 1847 major general in the regular service.

History records his disinterested patriotism, his valor, unconquerable bravery, and all the attributes of a successful chieftain. His name is immortally linked with that of Chepultepec, Monterey, Contreras, Puebla, and other battle fields rendered memorable in the Mexican war. He never emerged from a battle save with his banners flying and victory perched upon his standard. To his memory belongs the honor of raising the first American flag that ever floated above the capital of Mexico. To him belongs the imperishable glory of having been the first civil and military governor of Mexico; the first and the last of Americans who have ruled in the ancient halls of the Montezumas.

The war now being over, he soon after returned to the United States, and received from his admiring countrymen his full share of the honors and applause showered upon the gallant chiefs who had led our armies to victory on a foreign soil.

At the Baltimore democratic convention of 1848 he received a very complimentary vote for the position of vice president, and in the same year was nominated by the democratic state convention of Mississippi for presidential elector. In 1849 he was nominated for the office of governor, and elected by more than ten thousand majority. He was one of the leading spirits of the south in the memorable years of 1849, '50, and '51. During his term of service the memorable struggle growing out of what are termed the compromise measures, convulsed Congress and the country, and in 1851, while the canvass was in progress, a convention clothed with the sovereignty of the people decided in favor of submission, and he, promptly bowing to the mandate, retired from the field.

In 1854 he was elected to Congress by a large majority. In 1856 he was re-elected by an increased majority, and occupied always an influential and honorable position in the House. In politics Gen. Q. was a state rights democrat, far more conservative and less ultra in his views than was usually believed. He was a Union man on principle, from conviction, and thorough patriotism; but he was opposed to consolidation, and may have looked calmly and philosophically to the disruption of the Union, not with a desire of its consummation, but in certain events as a remedy for less endurable evils. On the passage of the English Lecompton bill, he voted against it, with the republicans and Americans. This was in opposition to nearly all the rest of the south; but he gave good and sufficient reasons for it, which satisfied his constituency.

Gen. Q. was the brother-in-law of the late lamented Philip F. Mayer, the venerable Lutheran clergyman who died recently in Natchez, after fifty years' service in that ancient religious denomination. He had many friends in Philadelphia, and many admirers. His visit there in 1847, '48, after the war, was an ovation. In private life he was an accomplished, courteous gentleman, a warmhearted friend, and a genial companion. He was respected by men of all parties in Congress for his personal qualities. He was rather slightly made, and his face, though not eminently handsome, was marked with decision, self-reliance, and that repose which generally characterizes the faces of men who command men with success.

Gen. Q. was possessed of large fortune, and so far has left his family well off. Several plantations in Mississippi and Louisiana made up the bulk of Gen. Q.'s private fortune; but these were of great value, and his sugar crop alone is said to have been worth $50,000 per annum. He leaves a widow and several children. One of his daughters was married June 20, 1858, to Lieut. Lovell, of the navy, an officer who has served efficiently as commander of the Water Witch, and also in the arctic explorations.

At a meeting of the Natchez bar, Josiah Winchester, Esq., in the chair, the following report was presented: —

"As members of the Natchez Bar, we have met together to give voice to our sorrow at the decease of our late friend and brother, John Anthony Quitman. The virtue that was lovely in life should not be forgotten in death, and the sweet odor of a good man's example and memory should not be sepulchred in his tomb. All that was merely earthly of our departed friend will this day be consigned to earth; but the priceless gem that lay enshrined in the casket, reset by the master workman, will shine on in its wonted, yet increasing purity and lustre. The surroundings of the day and the occasion, attest that the deceased was no ordinary man, and that this is no ordinary mourning. The sullen booming of the cannon — the national colors at half-flag — the drapery of woe that shrouds our doors — the marts of business closed — the gathering of the people, silent and decorous — all bespeak that a mighty one has fallen. And nature herself, as if in sympathy with the hearts of her children, has temporarily veiled her sunshine in obscurity and gloom.

"But our grief is not confined to the limits of professional brotherhood. The area of the deceased was circumscribed by no such narrow boundaries. 'Twas his good fortune to be many-minded, and to belong exclusively to no sect or class. And while, as a jurist, he occupied a position second to few, in other departments, also, he stood foremost among his peers. Scarcely an office he did not fill, and none, which filling, he did not adorn. And it was his curious felicity, whatever his hand found to do, to do it not only well, but to permeate it with something of his own marked and peculiar individuality. As one of our own fraternity, he possessed many and high distinctive traits. To rich stores of juridical learning were added the graces of more general literature; and around a mind innate, strong, almost rugged, were entwined many of the lighter and airier charms of forensic eloquence. As a counsellor, his judgment was cautious and clear, reaching its conclusions not quickly, but by the slow and laborious process of logic. As an advocate, his utterance partook of his reasoning temperament, and was usually grave and measured. But not unfrequently his thoughts flowed even more copiously than his speech, and then the pent-up powers struggled for an outlet. Always self-poised, he was seldom taken by surprise, and never thrown from his balance; and though more at home in the heavier drill and training of the profession, he was not inapt with the lighter weapons, and cut-and-thrust practice of the bar. In all his intercourse with his brethren, he was a very Bayard in courtesy; nor was his courtly demeanor wanting in the more genial features of a winning personal kindness. To his younger brethren, particularly, he combined all the endearing softness of the gentler sex with the nobler and manlier nature of his own. And few, or none, are now present here, who, at some period of his professional career, have not received from his good word, or counsel, or smile of encouragement and approval, — or may be by way of more substantial helping hand, — an impetus to their onward and upward course.

"But it was in his great office of chancellor, that he conjoined and illustrated all the solid and sterling qualities of his nature and judicial education. As the great English advocate said of the great English judge, he sat upon the bench a very embodiment of the pure and awful form of justice. The judicial ermine caught a new whiteness from the stainless purity of its wearer. Thoroughly embued with the principles of that department of jurisprudence; himself mainly the author of the provision in our organic law which appointed that mode for its administration; painstaking and scrupulous almost to a fault; diligent in research and laborious in examination; holding the scales of the balance with the most delicate touch, and without variableness or shadow of bias; guided by enlarged and liberal views of his duties, and yet assiduous to decide not by the crooked cord of distinction, but according to "the golden metewand of justice," he so laid the foundation and built up the structure of that division of our law, as to leave to its successors only the easier duty of moulding it into symmetry and form.

"And what shall we declare of him in other walks and relations of life?

"No less a soldier than a civilian, he carried the eagles of his country into the very halls of the Aztecs, and in binding his own brow with laurels, he added an equally unfading chaplet to the military glories of the Union.

"No less a statesman than a soldier, he illustrated the annals of the nation with a copiousness of political wisdom, with a grasp and tenacity of purpose, with a lofty honor and uncompromising integrity, that made him the idol of his own party, and the admiration of his opponents.

"But after all, it was in the more familiar and every-day walks of life, in the near and kindly relations of citizen, neighbor, head of a family, and a friend, that our departed brother linked to him his fellow-men with hooks of strongest steel. His manners so simple and genial; his presence so dignified, and yet so attractive; his conversation chaste and instructive; an ear ever open to the tale of distress, or appeal of charity; generous to lavishness; of ample means, and even careless in the dispensation of his bounty; loyal to all the engagements of business, and ever ready to foster the enterprises of the day; of knightly fealty to the circle of his own fireside, and the most indulgent of parents, — all these, and other lineaments, made up the mere human portraiture of his character. Be it therefore

"*Resolved*, that in the departure from among us of such a one, in the very midst of his usefulness and in the zenith of his fame, we unite with our fellow-citizens and the people at large in deploring (while we bow to it) the inscrutable providence that has wrought such a work."

R.

RALSTON, Robert, Philadelphia, Pa., March 20, æ. —. He was a prominent and useful citizen of Philadelphia.

RANDALL, Mrs. Mary, Waukesha, Wis., Sept. 15, æ. 37, wife of Gov. Randall. She was a woman of exalted virtues, and her loss will be severely felt by all whose good fortune it was to know her as a friend and neighbor. A few years since Mrs. R. buried her only child — a sorrow from which she has never sought relief, save in the hope of union with the object of a fond mother's affection beyond the grave.

RANDEL, Dr. John M., Philadelphia, Pa., July 13, æ. 27.

RANDOLPH, Miss Mary, Plainfield, N. J., Sept. 2, æ. 60, daughter of Dr. Robert F. Randolph, deceased, formerly of Plainfield, and sister of Judge Joseph F. Randolph, ex-member of Congress.

RANDOLPH, Robert Lee, Eastern View, Fauquier Co., Va., Jan. 26, æ. 67, son of the late Col. Robert Randolph, of revolutionary service, from whom he inherited a good name and an ample fortune. To native refinement and strong good sense he superadded the graces of a liberal and finished education.

RANTOUL, Hon. Robert, Beverly, Mass., —— —, æ. —. His son, Hon. Robert Rantoul, Jr., died some years since in Washington, where his commanding talents had given him a high reputation. The decease of the father will attract less wide notice than that of the son. His was a local reputation. He was not known out of New England, but where known was recognized as a representative man. He had all the New England peculiarities in their best forms. Of unbending integrity, his justice in all his dealings was of that nature which prevents pauperism. Never was a contract of his disputed or delayed. Never was right sacrificed to expediency. He never hesitated to follow his convictions, from any fear of comment or criticism. He settled many estates, filled constantly offices of trust, was the first man thought of in private life as an arbiter; and in his political relations was often the choice of his opponents to conduct investigations and serve on committees where integrity and impartiality were required. It was well understood that no personal or party motive could make Robert Rantoul swerve from the trust reposed in him. In a word, he was what is truly called a good citizen, ever reliable in all his relations, never admitting that a lower code of morals can be recognized in public and political than in private matters. He died full of years and honors, and will be remembered by local historians as one of the stanch federalists of the days when the federalists had an organization. He was one of the last to relinquish his old party ties, and when he did so found a home, like many others of his school, in the ranks of the democracy; but at last, he gave his voice, his vote, and his influence in favor of the principles of the republican party.

RAWLE, William, Esq., Philadelphia, Pa., Aug. 9, æ. 71, an old and esteemed member of the Philadelphia bar. Mr. R. was the son of the late distinguished William Rawle, Esq., who resided on Third Street, near Spruce. He was married to a daughter of the late Edward Tilghman, Esq. He had entered his 71st year when he died. Mr. Rawle is best known to the legal profession as a reporter of the decisions of the Supreme Court of Pennsylvania, and in the performance of his duties in that office he labored carefully and industriously. There are 17 volumes of Sergeant and Rawle, 5 volumes of Rawle, and 1 volume of Rawle, Penrose, and Watts. He was also the author of an excellent work, published in 1829, called a View of the Constitution of the United States.

RAWLE, Samuel B., Macao, China, Sept. 2, æ. —, United States consul at that port.

RECORD, Rev. John, Winchester, Ill., Feb. 9, æ. 56.

REED, Dr. George H., Danbury, Ct., Dec. 17, æ. 22. Few young men of our acquaintance have entered upon the preparatory studies for a profession under more favorable circumstances than did the deceased. Having successfully mastered the preliminaries, he entered the

New York College of Physicians and Surgeons, at which he recently graduated. Dr. Reed was a "friend of pleasant memory." Unobtrusive in manners, correct, and at the same time generous in his estimate of character, with no relish for the unreal and mere show of life, a firm, unyielding advocate of Christianity by example as well as profession, — the influence of the deceased recommended his character to all, and especially the young, who would rationally enjoy this life, and enter in a full state of preparation upon the life in the future.

REED, Henry R., Lancaster, Pa., ——, æ. —, late cashier of the Farmers Bank of Lancaster. He was one of our most worthy and highly-esteemed citizens, enjoying the confidence, both as a business man and citizen, of all who had the pleasure of his acquaintance; and few men had a more extensive acquaintance than Mr. R.

REED, Rev. Isaac, Olney, Ill., Jan. 13, æ. 70, one of the pioneers of Illinois.

REED, William D., Louisville, Ky., May 30, a member of the bar of that city, and formerly of Frankfort, Ky. During the last 10 or 15 years he had figured not a little in Kentucky politics. He was at one time secretary of state in Kentucky.

REEVES, Rev. James, Carroll Co., Ga., April 6, æ. 74.

REIFF, Benjamin, Lower Salford, Montgomery Co., Pa., July 17, æ. 70. He held the office of justice of the peace for 42 years, and served four years as a member of the House of Representatives, and four years as a member of the state Senate. In all the varied relations of life he enjoyed the confidence and esteem of his fellow-citizens.

REYNOLDS, Hon. James, St. Catharine Springs, Canada, Aug. 25, æ. —, ex-member of the U. S. Senate from New York. Mr. R. was an active politician of the Henry Clay school, and a devoted personal friend of Mr. Clay. Since the organization of the American party he acted with them faithfully and consistently, and at the time of his death was president of the general committee of New York city.

REYNOLDS, John, Natchez, La., Sept. 8, æ. 58, at the mansion of his brother, Charles Reynolds, Esq. He was born in the city of Philadelphia in 1799. From the early age of about 21 years he had made New Orleans and Louisiana his home, with the exception of some three years spent in the city of his nativity devoted to that noble pursuit in which all his faculties were engaged — the study of architecture. To this he devoted his whole soul, and drank into its spirit, not so much as a means of subsistence and gain as a joy and an absorbing passion. Louisiana and its metropolitan city abound with edifices erected from his designs; and long will they stand, unharmed by the battling elements, as the monuments of his taste, skill, and energy. Probably one of the last labors of his pencil was an unfinished sketch of the Judah Touro Orphan Asylum, soon to be inaugurated among the crowning charities of New Orleans. He has one monument to the utility and durability of his designs in the Carradine buildings in Natchez.

REYNOLDS, Dr. R. T., Philadelphia, Pa., Aug. 21, æ. 47.

REYNOLDS, Dr. Samuel M., Marion District, S. C., Nov. 10, æ. 36. Dr. R. was a native of Camden, but for several years a practising physician in the Marion District. He graduated at the South Carolina College, and was highly esteemed by his associates and friends.

RHODES, Dr. D. C., Alexandria, La., Aug. 30, æ. 28. The doctor was a gentleman of noble impulses; and, though enjoying an ample estate, and careering to a princely fortune, he was ever kind and unostentatious. Urbane in his manners, and sympathetic in his feelings, he was every where welcomed to the social hearth.

RICE, Rev. J. H., Wattsburg, Penn., June 21, æ. 58. He had long been a minister of the Presbyterian denomination.

RICE, Rev. Jacob, Truxville, Pa., Dec. 25, æ. 75, a local preacher of the Methodist church.

RICE, Sir Walter, St. Charles, Mo., March 31, æ. 59.

RICHARDS, Dr. James A., New Haven, Conn., July 3, æ. 30. Dr. R. was engaged in the service of Beloit College for a portion of 1856; and, but for his precarious health, would have received a permanent appointment as professor of natural science. After leaving here he passed a year on the eastern continent. A voyage of some months on the

Nile seemed to be of benefit; but, on his return to this country, his difficulties returned, and it was soon evident that consumption had fixed its fatal grasp upon him. He met the disappointment of his hopes and plans of life with Christian resignation.

RICHARDSON, Hon. James, Dedham, Mass., June 7, æ. 77. Mr. R. was a well-known lawyer of Norfolk Co., having practised at its bar for half a century. He was a native of Medfield, and graduated at Harvard University in the class of 1797, in which were Rev. Dr. Jenks and Judge White, of Salem, now living, and the late Dr. Warren, of Boston, and Chief Justice Richardson, of New Hampshire, deceased. He pursued his professional studies in the office of the Hon. Fisher Ames, was admitted to the bar in the fall of 1800, and began the practice of the law in Dedham, where he continued it till within a few years of his decease. He was for some time a law partner with Mr. Ames — a connection which was dissolved by the death of the latter in 1808. He held several honorable offices in the commonwealth. He was a member of the Senate in 1813, a member of the constitutional convention of 1820, and a member of the Council in 1834 and in 1835. He also was a master in chancery and a trial justice in connection with his professional practice. He was much interested in measures designed for public improvement, such as the construction of turnpikes and the establishment of manufactures. He was at one time a considerable owner in manufactories, though he never abandoned the practice of his profession. He was one of the projectors of the Dedham Bank, and was president of the Norfolk Mutual Fire Insurance Company from 1833 until April, 1857. He delivered a poem before the Phi Beta Kappa Society at Cambridge, and addresses on several public occasions, among which were a Fourth of July oration at Dedham in 1808, being on the day of the death of Fisher Ames, to which event the oration contains an allusion, and an address delivered before the Norfolk bar, at their request, in 1837, upon the profession and practice of the law. The poem and the addresses were printed. His politics in early life were of the federal school, of which Mr. Ames was an eminent supporter; and he retained those views through life, though he acted with new parties as new times demanded. He was a man of decided political opinions, and he maintained them with ardor and firmness on all occasions. As a lawyer, if he did not excel as an advocate, or possess in a great degree qualities which attract popular favor, he had what is of more value than either in his profession — a clear and discriminating judgment, and an ample knowledge of legal principles derived from the very fountains of jurisprudence. He was emphatically a lawyer of the old school, and regarded with much jealousy the many modifications in the common law, which modern legislation has effected. In the prime of his professional career he had a successful practice, and was known in the county as a safe and learned counsellor. He was president of the Norfolk bar, and held that position at his death. He was a man of fine sensibilities, fond of letters, especially of the classics and of early English poetry, of elevated views of life and character, especially as applicable to his own profession. He retained his physical vigor to a remarkable degree till about a year before his death, when he experienced a fall, after which he was confined to his house till death.

RICHARDSON, Mrs. Harriet, Stratford, Conn., Oct. 5, æ. —, widow of the late James E. Richardson, of Philadelphia, and daughter of the Rev. Dr. Archibald Maclay, of New York.

RICHARDSON, Gen. Samuel M., Pelham, N. H., March 11, æ. 82, brother of the late Chief Justice Richardson, of Chester, N. H. He was several years in the legislature, and was once supported by the whig party as their candidate for Congress. He was in service during the war of 1812, and proceeded to Portsmouth at the time it was supposed that an attack would be made by the British upon this town.

RICHEY, Samuel E., Spring Township, Pa., Aug. 21, æ. 29. Mr. R. read law in the office of Benjamin F. Junkin, Esq., and, after his admission to the bar, removed to Mifflintown, and commenced the practice of the law with excellent prospects of success. He was an honest and upright citizen.

RICHMOND, Rollin M., St. Louis, Mo., Aug. 13, æ. —, of Quindaro, Kansas, formerly of Barnard, Vt. He was a graduate of the University of Vermont, of the class of 1857.

RICHMOND, Rev. William, New York, Sept. 19, æ. 60. Thus has closed, for this world, a ministry full of labors. Mr. R. was born in Dighton, Mass., Dec. 11, 1797. Receiving his early education among the Congregationalists, he entered upon a course of study preparatory for the bar. While yet a youth, at Union College, his attention being drawn to the claims of the Protestant Episcopal church, he was baptized in St. George's, Schenectady, and studied for the holy ministry under the direction of Bishop Hobart, and received as his guides in the study of the Holy Scripture the standard theologians of the English church. The first 18 months of his ministry were given to missionary work in the vicinity of Philadelphia, of Pittsburg, and in Ohio. In the spring of 1820 he was called to the rectorship of St. Michael's Church, Bloomingdale, and St. James's, Hamilton Square, (vacant by the resignation of Dr. Jarvis,) and entered upon his duties in the summer of the same year. He continued, with a short intermission, rector of St. Michael's Church until called to his rest. It was as rector of these churches that Mr. R., for many years, was moved to labors requiring more than common strength and faith, and in which he was sustained by the divine presence, and by the liberal hands and faithful hearts of those who were about him. Taught by his Master to be ever ready with sympathy and aid for suffering men, his daily work was to carry comfort to the sick and sorrowing, and, so far as was in his power, the needed aid to every stricken brother. There are many who remember that hand which never withheld, which, in the whole upper part of the island, was ready with its gift at every door of poverty, prompted by the belief that that gift carried a double blessing which was bestowed for love of Christ. It was the often expressed opinion of the deceased, that, both for those who have and those who want, the best charitable provision which can be made is to establish a church at every point at which there is a remote hope that the worship of God can be supported, because every church becomes at once a centre of good works.

Accordingly, his policy was, in each little village, to gather and organize a congregation, and, if possible, establish a regular weekly service. For 20 years, in pursuance of this policy, he performed each Sunday four or more full services, besides his week-day lectures. Long before his work was done he beheld the fruit of such labor, in the firm establishment, at almost every point thus early chosen by him, of a congregation, with its consecrated house of prayer, ministered to by its own pastor. Throughout his whole ministry he was an interested and active member of the General Board of Missions. The records of the diocesan committee preserve the memory of his zeal for the missionary work of the state, in their acknowledgment of his effectual help in the day of need. At a meeting of the clergy of the Protestant Episcopal church in the city of New York, held in St. Michael's Church, Bloomingdale, on the occasion of his funeral, the Rev. S. H. Turner, D. D., in the chair, —

"*Resolved*, that we are thankful for the privilege of bearing a full and cordial testimony to the determination and unreservedness with which, by God's grace, our brother beloved gave himself to his office, and devoted his abilities, talents, and means, during a ministry of 39 years, to the inculcating and spreading of gospel truth, the repelling from the church of erroneous and strange doctrines, and the rendering of a faithful service, both by word and good example, to the glory of the Saviour's name, and the edification of the divine household."

RICKEY, William W., M. D., Avon, Livingston Co., N. Y., Dec. 13, æ. 46. He was a native of the town of Sparta, Livingston Co. He pursued his professional studies at a medical institution in a western state, where he graduated; subsequently the honorary degree of M. D. was conferred upon him by the New York Medical College. For some years Dr. Rickey resided in Ohio — at Cleveland, Toledo, Newark, and Dresden. Under the administration of Mr. Polk, he was appointed postmaster of the latter place; and he was also private secretary to Gov. Wood during that gentleman's occupancy of the gubernatorial chair of Ohio. His career was considerably prolific of adventure, and on several occasions he narrowly escaped a violent death. He was on board the river steamboat Oronoco, near Louisville, in 1836, when the boat blew up, and a large number of persons were killed. Twenty years later he was a passenger on the Ospray, from Carthagena, (whither he had been for the benefit of his health,) for New York, when the steamer took fire in the harbor of Kingston, Jamaica, and sank. Having been appointed, through the influence of Gen. Cass, to the post of surgeon in the ocean steamer Pacific, Dr. Rickey served in that capacity between two and three years; but his health failing him, he accepted the invitation of John C. Nash, Esq., of this city, whose brother-in-law he was, to remain in Rochester during one trip, and the Pacific sailed without him. She never was heard from again.

RICKS, Richard H., La Grange, Franklin Co., Ala., Feb. 20, æ. —, formerly a representative and senator in the legislature from Hampton Co., Ala.

RIDDLE, Mrs. Elizabeth B., Jersey City, N. J., Dec. 3, æ. —, wife of the Rev. David H. Riddle, D. D., and daughter of the late Rev. Matthew Brown, D. D. To the many friends who knew this lady personally, no remark is necessary to assure them of her true piety, and her many excellent qualities. It may be interesting to them, however, to be informed of the peacefulness of her closing days.

RIDDLE, Robert M., Pittsburg, Pa., Dec. 18, æ. 46, one of the oldest and most experienced editors of Pittsburg. He was a son of Judge James Riddle, and brother to the late Mrs. Dr. Gazzam, and the present Mrs. Judge Shaler. All the members of Judge Riddle's large family were persons of ability and marked character, and most of them have been cut off, one by one, during the last few years. In 1837 he became proprietor and editor of the old Pennsylvania Advocate, then, we believe, what was called national republican in politics. During the brief administration of Gen. Harrison, he relinquished the editorship of that journal, to become postmaster, to which position he was appointed by the general. About the close of Mr. Tyler's term of office, he purchased of Mr. J. Heron Foster the Spirit of the Age, and soon afterwards merged it into the press now known as the Commercial Journal. To this paper he was constantly attached, as proprietor and active manager, down to the 22d of last March, when, owing to failing health, his connection with it was dissolved. In 1853 he was elected by the whig party as mayor of the city of Pittsburg, which post he filled, with credit to himself and with benefit to the city, one term; at the same time fulfilling his onerous duties as conductor of the aforesaid paper. As an editor he was highly accomplished, and successful. Although not ranking as a very profound reasoner, he was a most brilliant and instructive writer, and the emanations from his pen have been generally admired. In person he was tall, slender, and of dignified presence, and in manner affable, courteous, and sociable — interesting in conversation, and a pleasant companion. He leaves a wife and five children to mourn their bereavement.

RIDDLE, Rev. Walter, Boontown, N. J., Jan. 31, æ. 36. He was born in the north of Ireland, May 18, 1822, and emigrated to this country with his parents previous to his recollection, and settled in Bloomfield, N. J. At the age of fourteen he was converted to God, and joined the Methodist Episcopal church. In a short time he was licensed to exercise his talents, which were of no ordinary character, in the local ministry. He was an able minister of Christ, and when able to labor for his Master was always more than acceptable.

RIDGELY, Absalom, Annapolis, Ind., March 12, æ. 30, junior editor and proprietor of the Annapolis Republican. At the time of his death he was secretary and treasurer of the Annapolis and Elkridge Railroad Company, and treasurer of the corporation of Annapolis. He was for several years a resident of this city. Remarkable for his quiet and amiable deportment, he gained, as he deserved, the respect and esteem of all who knew him.

RIGGS, Elias, Elkhart Prairie, Ind., Jan. 1, æ. 84. The deceased was a highly respectable citizen of the county, of which he has been a resident since 1827, he being the earliest settler upon Elkhart Prairie.

RIGGS, Hon. Jeremiah, Fentonville, Mich., June 22, æ. 80.

RING, Hon. Chas., Lubec, Me., June 7, æ. 47, a member of the present Senate of Maine. He was born at North Yarmouth, (now Yarmouth,) Sept. 8, 1811, so that he died in the 47th year of his age. He was the youngest son of Dr.

Andrew Ring, of North Yarmouth. In early life he removed to Lubec, where he engaged successfully in trade, and secured the confidence and good will of the community. He filled various local offices, and was also a member of the House of Representatives in 1841. He was chosen senator in 1856, and reëlected in 1857, running above his ticket. He was distinguished for his entire fairness and excellent common sense. He was a man of most liberal views on all questions, and ready to take his share of responsibility on any measure that came up for action. He was an ardent friend of public improvements, and took an active interest in passing the policy of opening of the public lands of Maine, by the Aroostook Railway, at the late session of the legislature. He married a Miss Ruggles, of Calais, in 1845, by whom he had four children, all of whom survive him. Few men will be more missed in the region of his home.

RINGGOLD, Mrs. Susan B., Fredericksburg, Va., Dec. 10, æ., —, relict of the late Thomas Lee Ringgold, U. S. N., and only child of Hon. A. P. Upshur, who, at the time of his sudden death on board the Princeton, in 1844, was filling the office of secretary of state.

RIPLEY, Rev. Lincoln, Waterford, Me., ———, æ. 96. He was a native of Barre in the Commonwealth of Massachusetts, and a graduate of Dartmouth College, and at the time of his death believed to be the oldest graduate of that institution, with the exception of the Rev. Mr. Sawyer, of Bangor. He was one of a family of nineteen children from the same parents. The late Rev. Dr. Ripley, of Concord, Mass., was his brother. He was settled in Waterford early in life, and continued pastor of the church until he was dismissed at his own request, and was succeeded by Rev. John A. Douglass. While in active ministry he was, among the people of his charge, devoted to every good word and work. No acts of piety, no works of benevolence and charity, no systems of moral reform were neglected by him.

RISING, Abraham, Southwick, Mass., June 25, æ. 99. He was at the taking of Gen. Burgoyne's army at Saratoga, and was 17 years old when he entered the army as a substitute for the man that was drafted.

ROBB, Rev. W. C., De Soto Co., Miss.,
March 11, æ. —, at the residence of Col. Miller. When told by his physician that he must die, he closed his eyes a few moments, and said, " I am ready ;" then realizing more fully than ever before the fulness of the gospel of our Lord Jesus Christ, and the glory that awaited the self-sacrificing itinerant minister of that gospel. His end was not only peaceful, but triumphant. Mr. R. filled the most important appointments in his conference. This was his fourth year on the Memphis district. He has been more zealous and useful each succeeding year. Never did he preach with more power than he did during his last visits to his charges. He had many warm friends, who cherish his memory.

ROBE, Campbell, Esq., West Union, O., Nov. 14, æ. 27. At the time of his death he was occupying the position of clerk of the Court of Common Pleas, treasurer of the Agricultural Society, and superintendent of the union school. Community is thus bereft of one of its noblest sons, and society of one of its dearest and most highly esteemed members. Kindness, generosity, and cheerfulness were traits in his character which commanded the admiration of all.

ROBERTON, Dr. John, Philadelphia, Pa., Jan. 29, æ. 74. The deceased was well known in Philadelphia, and elsewhere. He was a native of Scotland, but came to this country many years ago. He was for some time engaged as a teacher at Charleston, S. C., and while there he was the preceptor of Col. John C. Fremont. For the past 20 years he has been a private teacher of the higher branches of learning in Philadelphia. He was respected and esteemed by all who knew him.

ROBERTS, Rev. Palmer, Seneca Falls, N. Y., April 19, æ. 78. He was a superannuated member of the East Genesee conference. His conversion was in Hunterdon Co., N. J., Sept., 1804, and he joined the conference on probation in 1811, and has ever since maintained his Christian integrity by the purity and innocence of his life.

ROBERTS, Dr. Alonzo, Lancaster, Ill., Feb. 26, æ. 42.

ROBINSON, Hon. Enoch Brown, Carrollton, La., Jan. 15, æ. 41. He was a native of Deerfield, N. H., but for 20 years has been a resident of Carrollton.

ROBINSON, Henry Edward, (of Washington, D. C.,) —— —., —— 9, æ. 34. Some 20 years ago, he was for a time employed as a clerk in a store. During the past twelve years, and up to within a few months, he had filled a responsible position in the pension department at Washington. He was a man of excellent business talents, of noble impulses, irreproachable character, and Christian virtue.

ROBINSON, Elder Joseph, Hallowell, Me., —— —, æ. 84. He was for many years a minister in the Free Will Baptist connection.

ROBINSON, Dr. L. G., Detroit, Mich., May —, æ. —. He was a graduate of Oberlin College, we believe, and received his diploma at the Albany Medical University. He has been a resident of Detroit for some years, and was gradually rising to a prominent position in the ranks of the profession to which he was devoted, heart and mind. Some three years since he originated the Medical Independent, a monthly professional journal, which he conducted with ability and success, and which has recently been consolidated with the other medical journal published in Detroit. He was a man of quiet but earnest character, and had gathered to himself many warm personal friends, who mourn his loss.

ROBINSON, Hon. Thomas, Ellsworth, Me., July 2, æ. 57. He was born in Litchfield, in 1801. He entered Waterville College in 1823, and graduated with honor in the class of 1827. After his graduation he came to Ellsworth, and entered the law office of the late John G. Deane, Esq. After completing his professional duties, he established himself in Jefferson, Lincoln Co., where he remained about one year, and then returned to Ellsworth, where he continued to reside until his death. He was a good lawyer and a successful advocate, possessed of excellent judgment and practical good sense. In his intercourse with his professional brethren he was uniformly courteous, and high-minded and honorable in his practice. He was social and companionable, and few men possessed or deserve to have more personal friends; and his sudden and premature death cast a gloom over the whole community. No one ever questioned the strict integrity of his character in all the relations of life, and few ever enjoyed more fully the entire confidence of the community in which he lived. He received frequent tokens of

24 *

the public confidence, and was extensively known throughout the state. He had been a member of both branches of the state legislature, and was several times the candidate of his political friends for a seat in Congress from that district, and in 1840, we think, he was one of the presidential electors. At a meeting of the Hancock bar, —

"*Resolved*, that the intelligence of the death of Hon. Thomas Robinson, late president of the Hancock bar, was received by its members with emotions of pain and deep sensibility, and that while we deplore the loss of a most valuable and able member of our profession, the public have also sustained an irreparable loss in the death of a most estimable citizen, whose kindness, liberality, and strict integrity of character secured him the attachment and confidence of the whole community."

ROBINSON, Zaccheus, Southboro', Mass., Jan. 17, æ. 93. His aged partner still survives, being 85 years old.

ROCKWOOD, Rev. Elisha, D. D., Swanzey, N. H., June 19, æ. 80, pastor of the Congregational church. He was the son of Elisha Rockwood, of Chesterfield, N. H., and was born May 9, 1778. We trace his descent from Elisha, of Groton, Nathaniel, of Medfield, Nathaniel R., of Wrentham, and Richard, of Dorchester, Mass., all of whom were men of sturdy principle and moral worth; and some of them were highly respected officers in church and state. The subject of our present narrative grew up highly respected till the age of 20 years, when he became a member of Dartmouth College, and soon after was hopefully converted. He was graduated with high honors at the commencement of 1802, amidst some of the Rev. Brown Emerson, D. D., and Dr. Amos Twitchell. After his graduation he became a preceptor of Plymouth Academy for two years; and he was then appointed a tutor in Dartmouth College, which office he retained two years, highly esteemed by the students and the faculty. It was during his tutorship that he pursued the study of theology, and became well indoctrinated in the faith once delivered to the saints. One of his compeers, the Rev. Roswell Shurtleff, D. D., who survives him, has borne ample testimony to the integrity, urbanity, and worth of Mr. R., in the early years of his history. He was always and every where the Christian gentleman of the old school, and of an enviable character. Oct. 26, 1808, he was ordained pastor of the Congregational church in Westboro', Mass., where he had labored for a considerable time, till all were prepared to welcome him in the name of the Lord. He was favored with a quiet and prosperous ministry for 26¼ years, during which time he enjoyed several interesting seasons of revival; and 354 were added to the church, 452 were baptized, and 210 couples were joined in marriage. Westboro' was his first love, and the home of his heart; and he might have continued there honored and beloved, had not an unhappy difficulty arisen concerning the erection of a meeting house. This resulted in his dismission in 1835. Many were the regrets of his friends; and many would have given much could he have been restored to that pastorate. During the period which succeeded his dismission, and before his installation at Swanzey, he met with the appalling affliction of the sudden death of his wife by apoplexy. What added to his distress in these circumstances was the fact that he was more than one hundred miles from his home. This wife of his youth, and the mother of his children, was an estimable woman — the daughter of the Hon. Breck Parkman, of Westboro', and granddaughter of the Rev. Ebenezer Parkman, the first minister of Westboro', whose praise is in the churches. Soon after the sad bereavement above-mentioned he went to Swanzey as a candidate for settlement; and, after two or three months, he was installed with great unanimity in Nov., 1836 — almost 22 years since. He afterwards married for his second companion the widow of Rev. Osgood Herrick, the much-beloved pastor of Millbury, Mass., whose record is on high. In 1855 the board of Dartmouth College showed their respect for his talents, character, and attainments, by conferring upon him the degree of doctor of divinity. That he possessed a *well-balanced* and *cultivated mind*, all acknowledge. His doctrines were of the Puritan stamp, as set forth in the admirable compend of the Westminster Assembly. His manner of discussing doctrines was clear and direct. The trumpet never gave an uncertain sound.

He never shrank from a bold and manly defence of the gospel.

RODDAN, Rev. John T., Boston, Mass., Dec. 3, æ. 40, pastor of the Catholic church in Purchase Street, at the residence of Bishop Fitzpatrick, in South Street. He was a graduate of the College of the Propaganda, at Rome, and was a man of uncommon ability. He was for several years a missionary priest in Quincy and Randolph; but for the past two years he had been stationed in Boston. He was for some time, we believe, the leading editor of the Boston Pilot, and was also well known as a lecturer before various Catholic societies through the country. He was a priest in all for about ten years, and was universally beloved. He gave his whole heart to his calling, and his place will be hard to fill.

MRS. ANNA MARIA RODGERS,

New London, Conn., Dec. 7, æ. 60. Mrs. R. was a most remarkable woman — remarkable for the intrinsic excellence of her own character, and also as the connecting link between two families of great personal bravery and brilliant exploits in our naval history. Her father, Capt. Christopher Raymond Perry, U. S. N., although very young at the time of the revolution, served in our infant navy with great distinction. He was in the action of the Watt and the Trumbull, the hardest-fought naval battle during that war, and was confined for some months in the dreadful Jersey prison ship; but immediately upon his release he again sailed in a privateer to harass the enemy's own coast. Capt. Perry received his post captain's commission in 1798. Early in the 19th century the navy was nearly disbanded, and Com. Perry was appointed collector of Newport, then a large commercial port. His five sons were all officers of the American navy; and all distinguished themselves during the war of 1812-14. Among them were Commodores Oliver Hazard and Matthew Calbraith Perry. One of them, Alexander I. Perry, at 10 years of age, was a midshipman, and acted as aid to his brother during the action on Lake Erie, and received a ball through his chapeau. At that early age Congress voted him a sword. He was drowned in the Mediterranean, æ. 20. Anna Maria married, at the age of 16, Capt. George W. Rodgers, a distinguished officer, also belonging to a highly patriotic family. His father was a colonel in one of the Maryland regiments during the war; and his elder brother, Com. John Rodgers, was one of the most gallant officers of the last war with England, and was for many years president of the board of navy commissioners. He died at Philadelphia, Aug. 1, 1838, æ. 73, the senior commander of the navy. A sister was the wife of the celebrated William Pinkney, of Maryland. Com. Geo. W. Rodgers entered the service in April, 1804, and received his post captain's commission in March, 1825. In 1832 he hoisted his broad pennant in command of the squadron on the coast of Brazil, having also a diplomatic mission to that government. A few months after he assumed the command he died at Buenos Ayres, March 21, 1832, æ. 45, after a short illness, universally beloved and respected. The utmost honors were paid to his memory by the government and citizens of Buenos Ayres, where he was buried. In 1850 the United States government ordered that his remains should be brought to his native country in the United States ship Lexington; and they were reinterred in Cedar Grove Cemetery, New London, where those of his wife now lie by his side. Their three eldest sons fought bravely throughout the Mexican war, two of them lieutenants in the navy, and one in the army. The latter, Lieut. Alexander Perry Rodgers, of the 4th infantry, U. S. A., after serving with distinguished gallantry through the war, and being honorably mentioned in despatches, fell, mortally wounded, while leading the "forlorn hope" of his regiment to the attack on Chapultepec. An extract of a letter published at the time says, "We entered the capital with less than 4000 men; 3000 brave spirits were killed or wounded. Among the former was the brave, gifted, beautiful, good, and generous Lieut. Alexander P. Rodgers. He was beloved and respected by all the army who knew him, and gave promise of being a brilliant, as he was already a most gallant soldier. Poor Rodgers! Barely 22 years old, he fell at the head of his company in the storming party at Chapultepec, pierced by a bullet through the forehead, and yielded up his brave spirit to the God of battles with a smile on his handsome face, as the shouts of his comrades in victory rang a sweet requiem to his soul. His life had been pure and unsullied, and his death was without pain, calm, and glorious." His remains were also brought home, and lie beside those of his parents. Lieut. R. H. Smith, 3d artillery, U. S. A., a son-in-law of Mrs. R., also served gallantly through the Mexican war, and was wounded at Monterey. He was lost in the steamer San Francisco, while on her passage with United States troops to California, Dec. 24, 1853. It will be seen by the foregoing how indissolubly Mrs. R. was connected with the history of the country, in whose service the blood of those near and dear to her had been so freely shed. She instilled into the minds of her children, who regarded her with the reverential affection such a character could not fail to inspire, her own sentiments of ardent patriotism, and the fire, the courage, and national consecration of both families, the most rigid regard for honor and integrity, and true, unfeigned Christianity. Added to these lofty qualities, in all the relations of daughter, wife, mother, friend, and woman, her life was a model to her sex; and to all who came within the reach of her influence her death was a heavy loss.

She was a lady highly esteemed and beloved for her native qualities of heart and mind. Her life was marked by those vicissitudes which test characters severely. At the age of 32 she was deprived of her noble husband, and left with the care of a large family of children. Well, however, did she improve the heavy responsibility thus imposed, ordering her household admirably with affection and the force of inborn character.

She was distinguished for great personal beauty, together with a noble and courteous bearing; indeed, she was one of those rare specimens of high-toned American aristocracy so seldom found at the present day.

Her hospitality, for which she was also remarkable, was never an affectation, but always genuine and sincere. Her home was a centre of attraction; and all who came within its genial influence loved to frequent it, never failing to be impressed alike by the gentleness and dignity of its maternal head.

To her unusual natural graces were added those of Christian character. Her love for the church was deep and abiding; and largely in the eyes of "Him who seeth in secret" has it been the beneficiary of her kindness and liberality. In her last moments and protracted illness she gave the most gratifying assurances of the presence of that peace which is the Christian's peculiar heritage in death. Long will her memory be cherished as a guiding influence by many to whom, "though dead," she "yet speaketh."

ROGERS, John W., New York, Sept. 16, æ. 39, eldest son of the late Dr. Samuel Rogers, of Plymouth, N. H.

ROGERS, Rev. Joshua M., Easton, Pa., March 1, æ. 75, first rector of Trinity Church, Watertown, N. Y.

ROGERS, Nathaniel Leverett, Salem, Mass., July 31, æ. 73. Although, some years past, retired from active life, Mr. R. was formerly one of our most influential citizens. The early death of his father, by whom he was fitted, prevented his acquiring a collegiate education; but he received a year's instruction at the famous Phillips Exeter Academy, previous to entering as clerk, about 1800, the widely-celebrated mercantile house of Messrs. George Crowninshield & Son, of Salem. Remaining there three years, he sailed as clerk on board their new ship America. Continuing to follow the seas, as master and supercargo, for many years, he became a distinguished merchant, second to none of our enterprising New England men in opening and prosecuting new voyages to foreign lands, and was especially the pioneer and founder, from the United States, of the Zanzibar and New Holland trades, and, as head of the house of N. L. Rogers & Brothers, was known in almost all quarters where American commerce unfurled her flag. Though averse to and invariably declining office, he held many responsible positions upwards of 30 years ago, as cashier of the Commercial, first president of the Mercantile Bank, and president of the East India Marine Society, and willingly, for a long time, discharged the more humble duties of a committee man in our schools, being always deeply interested in the cause of public education, was a member of the legislature and of the town selectmen, and at times chairman of the board. Generous by nature, the prosperity of others, whether friends or strangers, afforded him delight. His sociability, conciliatory manners, with excellent conversational powers, and a peculiar pleasantness and modesty of disposition, devoid of pride or ostentation, won regard from most classes of men. It may be interesting to add that he was born at Ipswich, Mass., in 1785, and removed with his parents to Salem soon after. His mother was Abigail, daughter of Col. Abraham Dodge, of Ipswich, a revolutionary patriot and soldier. She is yet well recollected, by our elderly people, as teacher for many years of the first school hereabouts of those days, for the instruction of young ladies. His father was also a teacher of a private as well as of the public Latin school in Salem, and died young in 1799. He was the youngest child and only son of the Rev. Nathaniel Rogers, of Ipswich, who died in 1775, the last of four ministers, who successively from father to son were pastors of the First Church there, one of whom was also a physician and president of Harvard College in 1684. His father, Rev. Nathaniel Rogers, who fled the persecution of the hierarchy, and settled there in 1636, was son of Rev. John Rogers, of Dedham, "the most noted Puritan of England," a grandson of John Rogers, prebendary of St. Paul's, and the first martyr of Queen Mary's reign.

ROGERS, Richard P., St. Charles, Mo., Aug. 25, æ. 26, counsellor at law. He was a man of sterling worth and integrity, a high-toned gentleman, and a sincere and fast friend. He was a ripe scholar, and in literary attainments was excelled by few. He was studious, temperate, strictly moral, and at heart a Christian. He was young in the practice of law, but gave unmistakable evidence that he would soon rank with the most prominent in his profession.

ROGERS, Dr. Samuel, Plymouth, N. H., Aug. 29, æ. 72. Dr. R. commenced the practice of medicine in Plymouth at the age of 21 years, where he continued till disabled by infirmity, with occasional interruptions by reason of illness, with more than an average share of success. Through unwearied attention and an active sympathy he won and retained the confidence and esteem of his patients, and secured an extensive practice. His was an ardent nature; and, though less demonstrative than many, yet his family and friends could never doubt his affection, which was reciprocated to the last, with a fond and unfaltering devotion. His father, John Rogers, was a successful physician at Plymouth, a graduate of Harvard College, 1777, who was son of Rev. John Rogers, of Leominster, Mass. Dr. Samuel was brother of N. P. Rogers, who died Oct. 16, 1846, known as an accomplished scholar, but ultra advocate of freedom.

ROLSTON, John, Natchez, Miss., ——1, æ. 42, at the residence of his brother-in-law, Giles M. Hillyer. He was a lawyer, and attained a respectable standing at the bar of Mobile. He also succeeded his father as notary of the Bank of Mobile, which office he held until his health failed him. He discharged all his public trusts faithfully and honestly.

ROOSEVELT, Elbert, Pelham, Westchester Co., N. Y., Nov. 2, æ. 91, a descendant of the ancient family of Roosevelt, of New York city.

ROOT, Mrs. Harriet Allen, Pittsfield, Mass., Oct. 19, æ. 58, wife of Dr. Oliver S. Root, and daughter of Hon. Phinehas Allen, senior editor of the Pittsfield Sun.

RORBACH, Samuel, Esq., Newton, Sussex Co., N. J., Feb. 19, æ. 76, for 15 years judge of the Court of Common Pleas of that county.

Ross, Prof. D. Barton, Haddensfield, N. J., March —, æ. 38, widely known south as the author of the "Southern Eclectic Reader."

ROULILAC, John G., Marianna, Fla., July 16, æ. 62. He was a native of Martin Co., N. C., but had resided in Florida for the last 14 years. The Marianna Patriot thus speaks of him: "He was possessor of a clear head and well-balanced judgment. He had learning, industry, patience, and remarkable equanimity, and to these qualities added a spotless integrity, set off by the graces of urbanity and high-toned courtesy.

ROUNSEVILLE, Miss Polly, Freetown, Mass., Aug. 20, æ. 78, daughter of Thomas and Philena Rounseville. She was great-granddaughter to the first Rounseville, who settled in Freetown about the year 1700.

ROWE, Cyrus, Esq., Nevada, Cal.,

Dec. 12, æ. —. Mr. Rowe, in company with Robert White, Esq., established the Republican Journal, in 1829, and was connected with the paper for the ensuing 20 years, as one of its publishers and proprietors, and as a contributor to its columns. From his active habits and practical turn of mind, however, Mr. Rowe was able more efficiently to contribute to the prosperity of the enterprise by devoting his time to the business details of the office, and by his exertions in this department the prosperity of the establishment was much increased.

ROWE, William Henry, Boston, Mass., July 22, æ. 27. He was a son of Samuel and Lydia Ann (Fletcher) Rowe, and was born in Boston, Oct. 6, 1830, and fitted for college at the Boston Latin School, where a Franklin medal was awarded to him for his superior scholarship. He was a diligent student, his conduct was unexceptionable, and he graduated with high honors at Harvard in 1853. He was induced, by the flattering prospects held out for young lawyers, to go to Davenport, Iowa, where he entered the office of Hon. John P. Cook, who was at that time a representative in Congress from Iowa. Here he finished his legal studies, and in March, 1856, he was admitted to the bar in Davenport. He immediately began practice, still continuing in the office of Mr. Cook. His success was very great, and he was soon in full practice with a brilliant prospect before him. He was a man of great energy, and a too constant attention to business probably affected his health.

RUNNELS, Harvey H., Fort Madison, Iowa, Sept. 21, æ. 26. Mr. R. was a native of New Hampshire, where the early portion of his life was passed, previous to 1856. He had selected the law as his profession, and finished his legal studies at the Cincinnati Law School during the winter term of 1856–57, and after his admission at Burlington, he returned to Fort Madison and commenced practice. Although a young man, he succeeded in acquiring a good practice, and was rapidly rising in the profession. A few weeks previous to his decease he had formed a partnership with Gen. T. S. Espy, of Fort Madison, and his future prospects were as bright as any young member of the bar.

RUSSELL, Rev. Daniel Livermore, Hannibal, Mo., —— —, æ. 58.

RUSSELL, Capt. Henry, Brooklyn, N. Y., æ. 72. Capt. Russell was one of the oldest and most respected shipmasters in the United States — born in Boston, Mass., a son of the late Major Benjamin Russell, editor and proprietor for many years of that well-known paper, the Columbian Centinel.

RYLAND, Maj. E. M., St. Louis, Mo., Oct. —, æ. —. The Chamber of Commerce of St. Louis, having heard of the sudden demise of Maj. Ryland, president of the board, and impressed with the profoundest sorrow at the event, a dispensation which deprives our commercial circle of one of its most honorable and energetic members, the community of a valuable citizen, the Chamber of its highest officer, capable in every particular for the discharge of the important duties of the position, and desirous to testify in proper manner, as a body, their sense of the many virtues of the deceased, and the high estimation in which he was held by the members individually and collectively, therefore

"*Resolved*, that in the death of Maj. Ryland, the commercial circles of St. Louis have lost one of their most intelligent, honorable, and energetic members; that this Chamber has sustained a bereavement of no ordinary character, in his decease, as a member and an officer, in both of which positions he had the entire confidence and esteem of the board."

S.

SACKETT, C. D., New York city, March 8, æ. 59, and

SACKETT, G. A., New York city, March 9, æ. 53, — brothers; they were most esteemed men — their relations through life had been singularly close — they lived together, worked together, died together. The bar of New York will not readily supply their places.— *N. Y. Eve. Post.*

SAFFARRANS, Col. Daniel, Memphis, Tenn., —— —, æ. 59. A Memphis paper says, "Col. Saffarrans was born Feb. 22, 1799, in the State of Virginia. Early in life he removed to Gallatin, in Tennessee, where, by energy, industry, and attention to business, he acquired wealth and position. He was a man of uncommon enterprise, energy, and decision. His public spirit always placed him in the front rank of the communities in which he lived. Some ten years ago he enjoyed the distinction of being regarded as one of the leading spirits in promoting that high degree of prosperity which we now enjoy as a community. He was always respected for his public spirit and the high tone he assumed, and his death will be sincerely lamented by a large circle of friends and by an attached family."

SAFFORD, William, M. D., West Gardiner, Me., Dec. 14, æ. 59.

SAGE, Mrs. Ruth P., Ware, Mass., Dec. 10, æ. 69. She was born in Blandford, Mass., Sept. 23, 1789, and was the daughter of Capt. Abner Pease, a native of Somers, Ct., and a soldier in the revolutionary war. Her mother, Chloe Viets, a native of Becket, Mass., was a woman of rare excellence in her mental endowments and her Christian character. The advantages of education enjoyed by Mrs. Sage were far beyond what were common in those days. She was married to Orrin Sage May 4, 1817, and continued to reside in Blandford until 1848, when he removed to Ware, Mass., and became president of the bank in that place. While unable to be active and efficient in the more public duties of the Christian, her heart was alive to all the interests of religion, and her works of benevolence and charity were felt by those who saw or knew but little of her person. Mrs. Sage leaves two daughters, one the wife of William Hyde, Esq., of Ware.

SALMOND, Edward A., M. D., Camden, S. C., April 22, æ. 28. Dr. Salmond possessed many noble attributes, a mind highly gifted, and a generous spirit. He had served for several terms as a member of the town council, and was twice elected intendant.

SALTONSTALL, Mrs. Mary E., Salem, Mass., —— —, æ. 70, widow of Hon. Leverett Saltonstall. The Salem Gazette says, "Mrs. Saltonstall was one of the few surviving representatives of the palmy days of Salem. United in marriage to a man who made still more eminent an honored name, she was early called to fill a prominent position in social life, which she adorned by her varied and sterling qualities. Of a kindly heart, an elastic and energetic mind, and a transparent spirit, added to the grace of a refined and courtly manner, she drew to herself a numerous circle of friends, who knew how to value both her character and her society. Her house was the scene of a hospitable welcome to every order of merit. The intelligent stranger, no less than the familiar guest, was made to feel the attractions of an inviting home.

SAMPLE, Samuel, M. D., Holmes, Miss., July 6, æ. 48. He was a native of the Abbeville District, South Carolina, and was reared and educated in that state. At an early age he graduated with distinction at the College of Medicine, in Charleston, S. C. Two years after he removed to Mississippi, and commenced the practice of his profession, in which he continued through the long space of 25 years. As a physician, he ranked as one of the first in his section of the country, and was an honor to the profession; as a citizen, correct in his deportment and gentlemanly in his bearing, fair and honest in his dealings with his fellow-men; as a husband, father, and master, he was kind, lenient, forgiving, and forbearing in his disposition.

SAMPSON, Zephaniah, Esq., Boston, Mass., Oct. 2, æ. 81. He was born in November, 1777, in the town of Braintree, went to Boston when 12 years of age, and served his apprenticeship as a bricklayer with Dea. William Bell. He was associated in the business of building, for many years, with the Hon. Charles Wells, one of the past mayors of Boston. Subsequently he was for several years superintendent of streets. In every situation in life he was upright, industrious, and worthy of all confidence. With a heart full of sympathy for the distressed, he did all within his power to diminish the sufferings of others.

SANBORN, Mrs. Huldah, Sanbornton, N. H., April 1, æ. 96. She was a daughter of Dea. Christopher Smith, of Northampton. She married Dr. S., and went to Sanbornton in the early settlement of the town. She was a woman of unusual energy and decision of character. Kind to the poor, sympathizing with the afflicted, always ready to minister to the sick, she was held in high esteem by all who knew her. Perhaps the best expression of her excellent character can be given in the words of one who was her pastor for nearly 50 years, uttered at her funeral: "A kind neighbor, a faithful wife, an affectionate mother, and an exemplary Christian." For more than 75 years she was a member of the Congregational church in Sanbornton, uniting with it, in company with her husband, March 23, 1783.

SANBORN, Nathan, M. D., Henniker, N. H., Dec. 15, æ. 67. Dr. Sanborn commenced the practice of medicine, in Henniker, in the year 1816, since which time he has been actively engaged in the duties of his profession, until within the past year. He joined the New Hampshire Medical Society in 1821, and was a very constant attendant upon all its meetings. He attended a course of medical lectures, and received a diploma from Dartmouth College, in 1833. He made a public profession of religion and joined the church in 1834. As a physician, by his discretion and skill he acquired the confidence of the community, and by his suavity of manners, together with his superior mental endowments, he won the respect and esteem of all with whom he was brought in contact.

SANDERS, Maj. John, Fort Delaware, Pea Patch Island, entrance of Delaware River, July 29, æ. 50. Maj. Sanders was a native of Kentucky. He was one of a remarkable family. An ornament to the United States army, of which he was an officer, he was distinguished for genius and scholarship of the highest order. In the corps of topographical engineers he was conspicuous. He was chief engineer under General Worth, and planned the attack of the Texan Rangers upon the Bishop's Palace at Monterey; he also distinguished himself at the siege of Vera Cruz. He, for a number of years, superintended the improvements attempted by the general government on the Ohio River. His plans were never carried so far as to enable the public to test their full value. Fort Delaware is a monument of his experience and care. To him, more than to any other man, is Philadelphia indebted for the successful manner in which its insecure foundations have been repaired and fortified, and the work itself pushed to its present forward state. Maj. Sanders was a gentleman of high character, warm heart, and great good sense. At the time of his decease he was looking forward to a brilliant career, and, until within a few days before his death, was in excellent health. He was the grandson of the late celebrated George Nichols, of Kentucky, son of Lewis Sanders, Esq., of that state, a politician of great influence, son-in-law of Hon. William Wilkins, of Pennsylvania, (secretary of war under Mr. Tyler,) and brother of the well-known George N. Sanders, Esq., of New York.

SANFORD, Jonathan R., Reading, Ct., Aug. 21, æ. 76. Through a long life, the deceased enjoyed, in an eminent degree, the confidence and respect of his fellow-citizens. In 1808 he was appointed to fill the office of town clerk and treasurer of his native town, and held those offices by consecutive annual appointments from that time to his death, a period of half a century. Besides filling, for several years, the office of judge of probate for the district of Reading, representing at different periods his native town in the state legislature, he discharged the duties of various trusts, both of a public and private nature, exhibiting in all his acts a sternness of integrity and purity of purpose seldom equalled. The consolations of that religion which cheered and comforted him through life were his solace and support in death.

SANFORD, Cyrenus, Buffalo, Ill., May 28, æ. 83. Mr. Sanford was born in Connecticut in 1775, and at an early age settled in a place called Hubbell Hill, in Delaware Co., N. Y. For 40 years he tilled the rocky soil of "Old Delaware," when, in 1833, he became satisfied of the superior farming facilities of Illinois, as a place where he could settle his large family of children, with a prospect of their future prosperity. In this year he made a tedious journey thither, with a design to view the different portions of Illinois, and to determine the locality which offered the most favorable inducements for a settlement. After having examined different portions of the state, he was finally attracted by the beauty and fertility of the region of Buffalo Grove, and determined to make it his future abode. In 1834 he moved to the town of Buffalo, and carried with him nearly all of his children, many of whom at that time had families. They purchased large tracts of prairie and timber land, and erected a sawmill on Buffalo Creek, at an angle of "Two-Mile Grove," in the town of Jordan, Whiteside Co., and commenced in earnest the work of improvement and progression. The condition of the town, at its primitive settlement, has a story which is frequently told, but never without interest to the rising generations. At the time Mr. Sanford's family settled, there were barely five families within the territory, bounded by Freeport, Oregon, Dixon, Sterling, and Mt. Carroll. The heads of those families were Mr. Elisha Doty, Oliver Kellogg, Samuel Reed, and —— Bush, in the region of Buffalo, and Mr. John Ankany, in the vicinity of Elkhorn Grove. The present flourishing town of Dixon, at that time, consisted exclusively of the humble log cabin of the venerable John Dixon, who is still living. Mr. Sanford's posterity is numerous, and consists at present of eight children, about ninety grandchildren, and about forty great-grandchildren, making in all about one hundred and thirty-eight souls, most of whom form at this time a worthy portion of the large population of the town of Buffalo. The children of Mr. Sanford, coming hither at a favorable period to select and purchase lands, have in consequence, by judicious management, become men of material wealth, and of unexceptionable integrity.

SANFORD, Capt. Thomas B., Brooklyn, N. Y., March 4, æ. —, at the residence of Capt. Charles B. Sanford. He was the well-known master of the steamers of the "Sanford Line."

SARGEANT, Dea. Sewell, Stockbridge, Mass., Aug. 3, æ. 69, a descendant of the "Missionary Sargeant."

SARGEANT, Edward E., Grand Rapids, Mich., April 15, æ. 37, brother to B. C. Sargeant, of Lowell, Mass., and a former resident of Lowell. Mr. Sargeant was a native of Hillsboro', N. H. By the bounty of an elder sister, he fitted for college at Newbury (Vt.) Seminary, and graduated at Dartmouth College with honor in 1843. He went to Georgia, and spent two years in charge of the Edenton Female Seminary, at the same time studying law with Judge Merriwether. He was admitted to the bar in 1845, in Macon, and returned to New Hampshire, where he pursued his studies in the office of Judge Wilcox, in Orford. In the fall of 1846, he went to Grand Rapids. After about a year, Mr. Sargeant was employed in the office of Bell & Martin, which eventuated in his becoming a partner in the firm. He afterwards never lacked business, and won for himself an enviable distinction in his profession. In consequence of failing health, he spent some seven months in Europe in 1854, and on his return, edited for a time the Grand Rapids Enquirer, and resumed the practice of law. His principal characteristics were, a clear and well-disciplined mind, a gentle, modest, and unassuming deportment, and an undeviating adherence to moral principle. He was greatly esteemed as a lawyer, and suitable testimonials of regard and esteem were adopted by the Grand Rapids bar.

SARGEANT, Alfred Dexter, Lowell, Mass., Sept. 15, æ. 26. Mr. Sargeant was born at New Bedford, Mass., Nov. 14, 1832. In 1849, when in his 17th year, he became a student in Newbury (Vt.) Seminary, where he remained ten terms, during which time he fitted for college. When he left the Seminary, he entered the M. E. Book Room, at New York, and remained, increasing in favor with those who knew him, till he became sole proprietor of a printing establishment at Milford, Mass., at the same time entering upon the work of editing the Milford Journal. He succeeded beyond his own expectation, or that of his friends. But his health failed under his laborious efforts, which were too much for his constitution. Mr. Sargeant was a young man of more than ordinary talent, and possessed great and uncommon amiability of temper and self-possession. Wherever known, he was respected and loved.

SARGENT, Henry, M. D., Worcester, Mass., ———, æ. —. At the annual meeting of the Worcester District Medical Society, Dr. Henry Clark, of Worcester, delivered an oration, in which he paid the following tribute to the memory of Dr. Sargent: "Since writing the address that I am about to read to you, he whom you elected to fill the place that I now occupy has been removed by death. It would be more in accordance with my own feelings were I to make his character the only theme of my remarks at this time, and could I portray it in fitting terms the hour would be profitably spent. It would be wise in us to contemplate a life so blameless as was his, as it could but exert a holy influence upon our own. In the death of Dr. Sargent we have lost one of our most active, scientific, and beloved members; one who ever exerted an elevating influence, and one, who, in his intercourse with his patients and professional brethren, was a model physician. Endowed by nature with a liberal mind and a generous heart, and educated in the best medical institutions of this and foreign countries, he had placed his standard of professional excellence very high. The exercise of his profession was to him something more than a mere matter of business. He had a genuine love for the study of medicine, and practised it with a spirit of true benevolence. The satisfaction of feeling that he had alleviated human suffering, or prolonged human life, was to him a greater reward than any pecuniary compensation. No one despised more than he those who have no *other than a mercenary interest in their profession, who regard it as a mere craft, and who, in the practice of it, cater to the prejudices and wishes of their patients without regard to their highest good. No feelings of jealousy or envy ever instilled their poison into his soul, and no one ever doubted for a moment the honesty of his purpose or the purity of his motives. He never disparaged the reputation of his medical brethren, or sought to advance himself at the expense of others. The performance of offices of love and kindness was to him a genuine and never-failing source of happiness. In 'seeking others' good' he found his own. But few have ever lived more in accordance with the golden rule of Christianity. This spirit of kindness and disinterestedness was one of his most striking characteristics, and it endeared him to his patients and to all who knew him in a remarkable degree. How truly may we say of him, 'None knew him but to love him, nor named him but to praise'! While we mourn the loss of such a one from our number, let the memory of his life stimulate us to a faithful discharge of all our duties, that we, like him, may be useful in life and honored in death."

SAUNDERSON, William P., Hollis, N. H., Nov. 12, æ. 51. Few men could be more missed in the community than Mr. S. As a citizen he was universally esteemed and beloved. No one took a deeper interest in the social and religious prosperity of the town than he. In his business transactions he exhibited good judgment and unwavering integrity. He was a successful farmer, and did much to keep up that high tone of agricultural interest for which his town is noted; and not a little to sustain that interest throughout the county. For many years he was a warm and active member of the religious society with which he was connected, and gave to it most cheerfully, so far as was needed, his time, money, and influence.

SAVAGE, James Sullivan, Southboro', Mass., Nov. 8, æ. 54. He was born at Redfield, Me. He came to Boston in 1825, possessed of nothing but his art as a stone-mason, and a clear head, resolute will, and an honest heart. He was soon at work, and after three or four years of subordinate service rose to be a master builder, and as such reared, in a few years, many substantial edifices in the city. His reputation grew with his works, and, in 1833, having been previously employed on the Bunker Hill Monument, he became a contractor with the federal government for extensive repairs and structures at Forts Warren and Independence, which occupied him about six years. He next contracted to complete the monument from the height of 80 feet, at which it had stood for some eight or ten years for want of means. This work of 80 feet he had superintended, but not in the capacity of contractor. This completion of the monument was effected in about three years, and showed Mr. Savage's capacity for structural achievement. In the course of it he invented the well-known and immensely useful lifting and locating derrick, patented in his name, and worked it with steam power. The great saving of time and money thus secured to the work made his contract a fortunate one. To its profits he, for a stipulated time after its completion, added those derived from visitors to the summit, ascending and descending by a steam car in the well made by the circular stairs within the walls of the monument. The monument completed his success as a man of business, and its last stone placed, at six o'clock on the morning of July 23, 1843, under the excitement of roaring cannon and a shouting multitude, satisfied him in his art. He practised it only occasionally after this. In 1845 he served the city as alderman, under Mr. Davis as mayor, and then retired to the pleasant farm he had purchased at Southboro', as the reward and solace of a life, though somewhat care-worn, yet still young and vigorous. Here he could indulge his taste for reading and reflecting. Here life was no longer a servitude. Here he was spared 13 years of peaceful enjoyment, qualified only towards its close by a chronic difficulty, making the study of health a necessary care. Mr. Savage was one of those strong, self-made, pure-minded men, who pursue their pathway in life without show, because they are without selfishness, and without noise; because they have true courage, tempered with self-respect, and moved by high claims of duty. He began the world as a mechanic operative, like the famed Stephenson, and ended it a contractor and builder, and a high representative of that valued and respected class. He was successful, not by chance, but by energy, endurance, and honesty. He was trusted, not merely because he could do well, but because he always would do well. With him there was no evasion in pretence or execution. Fidelity was a necessity of his nature — fidelity in thinking as well as acting. He never came to results by stumbling upon them or guessing at them, but he produced them by clear thinking and energetic action. Mr. Savage was for some 20 years a Boston man, and these qualities, though veiled by a modesty that knew no boasting, early brought him to the knowledge and confidence of our trading men, to whose care great interests were intrusted; and thus while yet a young man he was employed as a constructor of several of our most enduring public works.

SAVAGE, Rev. Amos, New Haven, Ct., —— ——, æ. 60, state agent of Tract Society for Connecticut.

SAVARY, Joseph, Groveland, Mass.,

Nov. 3, æ. 61, a gentleman whose high standard of moral integrity, and pleasing social deportment secured the esteem of a large circle of friends.

SAWTELLE, Mrs. Elizabeth, Augusta, Me., March 28, æ. 85.

SAWYER, Rev. John, better known as "Father Sawyer," Bangor, Me., Oct. 14, æ. 103. He was born in Hebron, Ct., Oct. 9, 1755. In his 12th year his parents removed to the town of Orford, N. H. Orford was then a new place; the first white settler having arrived there only three years before. Of course the Sawyer family were subject to all the privations and hardships of a new settlement. Of these, the young man of whom we speak (for he was then young) encountered his full share for the next 12 years. During this period a church was established in Orford and a minister settled, and Mr. Sawyer became a hopeful subject of renewing grace. It was during this period, also, that the war of the revolution commenced; and in the year 1777, when only 22 years of age, Mr. Sawyer volunteered, under Capt. Chandler, of Piermont, N. H., to repel the advances of Gen. Burgoyne. He was at Saratoga, at the surrender of Burgoyne, and shared in all the rejoicings of that eventful day. Having had but few advantages of school education, on his return from the army he entered Dartmouth College, and graduated in 1786. On leaving college, Mr. Sawyer had no hesitancy as to his future course of life. He studied theology for a time with President Wheelock, and for a longer time with the late Dr. Spring, of Newburyport; and commenced preaching within a year after leaving college. He preached his first sermon in Orford, and was earnestly invited to settle there; but not feeling fully competent to take upon himself the responsibilities of a pastor, he deferred for a time acceding to the request. Having preached in different places for nearly two years, he returned to Orford, and was ordained pastor of that church, in October, 1787. He made it a condition of his ordination, that the church should relinquish a practice which had been continued from its first organization, viz., that of baptizing children on what was termed the half-way covenant. He continued in the ministry about nine years, when he accepted a call to become pastor of a church in Boothbay, Me. He continued at Boothbay about 10 years, when, at his own request, he was dismissed, and removed to New Castle. From this period his labors as a home missionary commenced, in the prosecution of which he travelled, in all directions, through the forests, and among the wilder portions of Maine. About 50 years ago he went to Bangor as teacher and preacher at a salary of $200. He was a man of high aims, large and comprehensive views, and very laborious and precise in the performance of his duties. He was devoted to his ministry. He preached because he loved the work. He was eminently a man of prayer, and his success was in no small part due to his power in prayer. He was one of the founders of the Bangor Theological Seminary. Nearly up to the time of his death he continued to labor, teaching and preaching in Bangor and vicinity as when a young man, and we may almost say of him, as of Enoch, "He was not, for the Lord took him."

SAWYER, Hon. Jos., Piermont, N. H., July 4, æ. 72. For many years he occupied a prominent position in the political party to which he belonged, and was honored by his party with nominations to several high offices, showing that he enjoyed the confidence and respect of his political friends, as he did that of the whole community, for the uprightness and integrity with which he discharged the every-day duties of life. He was none the less revered in his private and social relations. Every one seemed to confide in him, and like a father or guardian he moved among his fellow-townsmen, who confided in him for counsel, and trusted his judgment in any difficulty. He was a faithful guardian of the educational interests of the town, not for the good of his own family alone, but in all parts of the town, he often, by his presence, cheered the school room, encouraging and animating the pupils in their intellectual labors. His earnest and affectionate appeals, awaking in them high aspirations and inciting to noble purposes, will long, very long be remembered as tributes to his memory. In the temperance cause, and indeed in all moral and social reforms, he was ever at his post, and the position usually assigned him was among the foremost and most responsible. He was, indeed, the useful, the true, the good man. He was in a remarkable degree careful of the education, happiness, and advancement of his children, and he leaves them the rich legacy of a power to meet life in any of its forms with credit and success.

SAWYER, Hosea, Esq., Dover, N. H., May 17, æ. 75.

SAXTON, Jehiel, Newburg, O., March 16, æ. 76. He was one of the pioneers of Cuyahoga Co., having moved into Newburg, in September, 1819, from Bristol, Addison Co., Vt. He was a soldier in the war of 1812, and was at the battle of Plattsburg. In all the social and domestic relations of life he sustained an irreproachable character for integrity and kindness. He ever seemed more anxious to do justice to others than exact it from them. Though a firm adherent to whatever he believed correct principles, he was always courteous to those who differed from him in matters of opinion.

SCAMMAN, Hon. John F., Biddeford, Me., June 23, æ. 71. He was a member of the first legislature of Maine after it was set off from Massachusetts. He was at another time collector of the customs at Saco, and at a period when the commercial interests were much larger than at present. He was elected subsequently to the legislature of the state, and again under Polk's administration to the halls of Congress. And faithfully he served the public amid all the strife of opinion and all the sophistries of demagogues. Unseduced by the phantom of ambition or by the sordid thirst for gold, he went to the place of power an honest man, and, what is better, returned an honest man. The simple law of right was always his chosen law, and the approval of his conscience his best reward. For him the race of ambition, which in these degenerate days so dazzles the multitude, had no charm. As a God-fearing man he always thought first and highest of his accountability to him, and therefore no honor with him was equal to the honor of the righteous, and no wealth so valuable as the wealth of a good name. But his character, apart from his public life, is likewise very much to be revered. As a religious man he was a steadfast attendant upon the worship of the sanctuary. Few men can point to so many Sabbaths spent in the house of God during a long and eventful life. He was a member of the Episcopal church, having received the rite of confirmation by Bishop Burgess, the present bishop of the state. Piety with him, however, was not a form of godliness, but a living principle within, regulating and governing his life.

SCARBOROUGH, Ira, M. D., Snow Hill, Va., —— ——, æ. 29. He attended his first course of lectures at the University of Virginia, his second at the university in Philadelphia, Penn., where he graduated. He commenced the practice of medicine at Snow Hill, the county seat of Green Co., where he was building up an enviable reputation in his profession.

SCHENCK, Daniel I., Pleasant Valley, Monmouth Co., N. J., Oct. 23, æ. 80. His name will long be cherished with respect and affection by numerous friends, by the church of Christ, and by the entire community in which he was known. He belonged to a class of men who, by their solid judgment, their invincible integrity, their uniform kindness, and their large benevolence, command the general confidence, and gain extensive influence without noise, without effort, and almost without knowing it themselves. The church was eminently dear to him, and for her welfare his prayers, his labors, and his contributions went together. Although others, not of his own denomination, shared largely in his liberality, he cherished a special regard towards his own beloved church. In her institutions he took a lively interest. He stood conspicuous among that noble band of men in Monmouth to whose liberality these institutions are so largely indebted. Within a short period before his death he contributed $500 to the college, and a like sum of $500 to the seminary. His last will and testament reveals still further the character of his musings on the question of doing good. Besides an affectionate remembrance of his beloved pastor, he bequeathed the sum of $1000 to be employed for the benefit of the feeble churches of the classis of Michigan, and $3000 to the seminary.

SCHLEY, Hon. Wm., Richmond Co., Ga., —— ——, æ. 72. He was born in Frederick, Maryland, Dec. 10, 1786, and was educated in the academies at Louisville and Augusta, and admitted to practise law in 1812. He held important relations to the people of Georgia. In 1825 he was elected, by the legislature, judge of the Superior Court of the middle circuit, and held that position until 1828.

In 1830 he represented Richmond Co. in the legislature. In 1832 he was elected to Congress, and served during the sessions of 1833, '34, and '35; and in 1835 he was elected governor of the state, and filled the office until 1837. " In his first message to the legislature of Georgia, he strongly recommended the construction of the Western and Atlantic Railroad. To this work he devoted all the time he could possibly spare from the discharge of the duties of the executive office, and had the honor of signing the law authorizing the construction of this road." He was president of the Medical College of Georgia at the time of his death. He was an able counsellor, an upright citizen, an affable gentleman, and a devoted husband and parent. The Richmond Co. bar award him this high praise. William Schley was distinguished at the bar for assiduity, energy, and ability in the conduct of causes committed to his care; on the bench, for extensive legal lore, for dignity, impartiality, and firmness; in the legislative halls of Georgia, and of the Union, for uncompromising devotion to the interests of his immediate constituents, and a catholic patriotism that recognized all rightful claims upon his statesmanship; in the executive chair of our state, for "*wisdom, justice, and moderation,*" and in all the relations of life, for public spirit and integrity unquestioned and unquestionable.

SCOTT, Matthew S., Esq., Lexington, Ky., Aug. 20, æ. 73. He was born in Western Pennsylvania, and emigrated to Kentucky more than half a century ago. He has been for more than a quarter century connected with the Northern Bank, and was universally respected. For many years he was a member of the Presbyterian church, and died in the communion of the McChord Church of Lexington.

SCOTT, Joel, Dedham, Mass., May 5, æ. 46. He was a native of Newburyport, Mass., and at the time of his death was president of the Alliance Insurance Company, of Boston. For several years he held the office of deputy collector in the Boston custom house. As a man of business, he was remarked for his singular fidelity and ability, and he ever displayed the highest integrity in all business transactions. Unflinching in will, he submitted to nothing wrong; gentlemanly and courteous, he was forbearing to others As a friend, he was true as steel, knowing neither sunshine nor shade in his familiar intercourse; and this, owing to a slight eccentricity of character, was confined to a very few acquaintances. He was never married, but devoted his time and money to the comfort and support of an aged mother and a widowed sister, who survive him.

SCOTT, James S., Columbia, S. C., ——, ——, w. ——, president of the Exchange Bank, Columbia. The directors of the bank, at a meeting of the board, in a resolution say, " The members of this board, so long and so intimately associated with Mr. S., knew him well, and his excellence and worth had secured their highest confidence and esteem, for he was no ordinary man; with firm integrity and a strong and vigorous intellect which would have made him a conspicuous character in any vocation of life, it was with feelings of pride and satisfaction we looked upon him as the chief representative of our bank. In the discharge of his duties as president of this institution, he was faithful and unremitting in zeal and energy. As an officer, his talents commanded our respect, but as a friend, we loved him, for the fervor and decision of his character, tempered by amiability and gentleness, with simplicity of manners, imparted peculiar social qualifications which endeared him to us, and rendered him attractive to all who came in contact with him."

SCRANTON, Rev. Simeon, Clinton, Conn., Nov. 5, æ. 64. He had been a local preacher about 35 years, and was ordained deacon by Bishop Waugh, in the city of Brooklyn, in 1837. As a preacher, he was plain, practical, and generally very acceptable and useful with the people.

SCRANTON, Joel, Cleveland, O., April 9, æ. 65. He was the son of Stephen and Asenath Scranton, and was born in Belchertown, Mass., April 5, 1792. At an early age he removed, first, to Delaware Co., and afterwards to Cooperstown, Otsego Co., N. Y., where he engaged in business, and became associated with the Averell family, who resided there, and who were at that time largely engaged in those business operations which have since extended over much space and have resulted most successfully. Though young and inexperienced, he was commissioned by them to take charge of and manage a " trading venture," which they proposed to send out to what was then called the Ohio Country, with a view, if the skill and honesty of the agent, and the business prospects of the country, warranted it, to make a permanent location in the then small village of Cleveland. In the spring of 1823, with his stock of goods, Mr. Scranton made his way into this, to him, unknown region. He landed from a small schooner, and found only a few hundred inhabitants and a scattered village, where is now the hurry and bustle of a city of 60,000 inhabitants. Before the evening of the first day, he had made up his mind to make Cleveland his future dwelling place, and had engaged a room for his goods, and the next day he was a citizen of a new country, and was diligently employed in carrying out the instructions and the wishes of the employers who had put so much trust in him. With prudence, economy, and diligence, he attended to the interests of his distant employers, and by the middle of the first winter he had disposed of all their goods, and had the proceeds carefully laid by in specie. There was, at that period, no regular winter communication between Cleveland and the east. The roads were nearly impassable, the country was sparsely settled, and it was a journey at that time which can hardly be imagined by those who roll in a day, in a well-cushioned rail-car, through the same region of country which lay between young Scranton and those who had placed in him the trusts of which he was now so anxious to render his account. With his specie in one end of a common meal bag, and a few clothes in the other, he started on foot, a journey of 500 miles, to render an account of his stewardship, and place the money in the hand of its owners. In these days of ease, fraud, and default, this may seem strange and scarcely credible. At length, with surprise and pleasure, the travel-worn young man was welcomed by the Averells, when he walked in, unannounced, on a blustering evening in March, and dropping his bag upon the floor, exclaimed, "I have sold your goods, and there is the money." The judgment, prudence, honesty, economy, and perseverance, which Mr. S. had shown in this transaction, led the Averells at once to propose to him an equal partnership. The writings were immediately drawn, executed, and in a few days Mr. S. was on his way to N. Y., with the necessary means to procure goods for a permanent establishment at Cleveland.

From that time forth he retained the confidence of his partners, and continued to act as agent and partner until his death. The gains of business he invested in land in and about the city of Cleveland, until he accumulated a large estate, which always stood as the partnership property of Scranton & Averell. In June, 1828, he married Miss Irene P. Hickox, of Durham, N. Y. She was educated at Litchfield, Conn., and at an early age removed to Ohio, where she spent some years teaching young ladies. She was a woman of great good sense, and of superior education and judgment. She was one of the twelve members of the first organized Presbyterian church in Cleveland, and by her daily walk through life, illustrated the beauty of holiness. She possessed great energy and decision of character, and never swerved from duty, or wearied in doing good. She died March 15, 1858. Only one of their five children survive — Mrs. William Bradford, of Elyria, O.

SEARLE, George, Esq., Brookline, Mass., Jan. 2, æ. 69. He was a son of George and Mary Russell Searle, and was born at Newburyport, Mass., Dec., 1788. His father was a merchant, and died when his son was but seven years old. At the early age of 13 he went to Boston as apprentice to Messrs. Stephen and Henry Higginson. By his intelligence, faithfulness, and industry, he gained the confidence of his employers, and, by their generous aid, was soon enabled to contribute to the comfort of his mother and family at home. He engaged in business in Boston as a partner with Mr. Lewis Tappan as soon he was of age, and went to England for the purpose of gaining correspondents, forming business connections, &c. It was a period of commercial prosperity; and Mr. S.'s intelligence, his manly and honorable qualities, were rewarded by a fair portion of worldly success. Having removed his mother and family to Boston, he formed a new partnership with his only brother, seven years younger than himself, who had, under his care and at his expense, received a thorough mercantile education. In 1818 Mr. S. revisited Europe, enlarging his knowledge of men and things by travelling on the continent, as well as by a short residence in England and Scotland. In 1825 — a season of great disaster to merchants

— the house failed; but there was no failure of the regard and esteem entertained for the brothers by those who understood their fair and honorable course. A few years afterwards, notwithstanding a previous full discharge from their creditors, they paid the whole outstanding balance against them, having labored unceasingly and strenuously to obtain the means of doing so. Mr. S. was associated afterwards with Mr. Henry Upham in commission business, and again suffered in the great crash of 1837. Still he worked on, bating no jot of heart or hope." He devoted himself with the same faithful and untiring energy to the business of a broker in later life that he had manifested at an earlier period in his concerns as the head of an importing house. He was again so far successful as to acquire a competency, and free his estate at Brookline from mortgage. He had removed to that place in 1825, and had become greatly attached to the place, enjoying his garden with its fruits and flowers, the beauty of the surrounding country, and the society of his family and a few chosen friends. Mr. S. was twice married. He lost his first wife after one year of happy union, and subsequently his only child when only two years old. In 1834 he married a second time, but survived his beloved wife, who was taken from him in 1842. The last years of Mr. S.'s life were passed with his sisters and the two orphan sons of his brother, to whom he became as a father, making their interests as truly his own as if they had been indeed his children. Mr. S. was characterized by a high sense of honor, a certain nobleness and elevation which made itself felt by all who were associated with him, and by great disinterestedness, amounting to an absolute self-forgetfulness but rarely witnessed. He had a sanguine and earnest temperament, loved work, did every thing with life and energy, " doing with his might whatever his hands found to do." He had keen perceptions and fine taste for the beautiful in nature and in human character, an instinctive aversion from every thing low or mean, amounting sometimes to what seemed fastidiousness and impatience. He was impulsive and somewhat nervously excitable, not always bearing lesser trials and vexations with equanimity, but meeting the great afflictions of his life with fortitude and resignation to the divine will. He was a wide and general reader of English literature, always finding pleasure and occupation in books in those leisure hours which sometimes occur even in the busiest life.

SEAVER, Rev. Horace, New York city, April —, æ. 67, senior agent of the American and Foreign Bible Society. Mr. S. was widely known and highly esteemed as a faithful minister, and an indefatigable agent of the society which he served for many years.

SELLEA, James, Saco, Me., March 14, æ. 74. He was one of the soldiers of 1812, under Col. Boyd. He was at the battles of Chippewa and Bridgewater: his right hand man was shot by his side. According to his certificate, he had an honorable discharge by his commanding officer. At the time of Gen. Scott's visit here, some 18 or 20 years since, he was remembered by the old veteran, who recognized him in the crowd that surrounded him at that time, and received him with marks of pleasure.

SHAFROD, Geo. W., Lancaster, Wis., March 9, æ. 31. Mr. S. was a member of the Ohio bar.

SHALL, Mrs. Patsy, New Orleans, La., Nov. 12, æ. 64. Her residence of a quarter of a century in New Orleans has been an epitome of constant industry for her family, with the most indefatigable kindness and charity for others. For twenty years from the time she first landed at our levee, there was no more devoted disciple to the cause of suffering humanity than the late Mrs. S. For nearly 15 years after she arrived here, in 1833, she was busily engaged in conducting, first, a large boarding house, and then the city hotel, supporting a family at the same time, and yet with these multifarious duties, and trials, and responsibilities, to be met by her single self, she was ever ready to answer the call of the sick and afflicted. During the epidemics which the city was visited with in those long years, she never faltered or shrank from her duties; and hundreds on hundreds are those whose hours of sickness were carefully and tenderly watched by her, with a mother's solicitude and never-failing vigilance, while her experience as a nurse saved many and many a life. In fact, in this department of charitable service, she was known throughout the country, and many a person in the wide west and south will feel a throb of regret at her death, whose brow she soothed, whose pain she assuaged, whose death she prevented. So remarkable, indeed, were her labors during one fatal season, that one of our municipal bodies voted her a service of plate as a testimonial of their admiration for such disinterested and rare conduct.

SHARER, Mrs. Elizabeth, Paris, Ky., July 3, æ. 104. She was a native of Washington Co., Md., and emigrated to Paris in 1793, in company with her husband, Peter Sharer, and their children. At that time there were only three houses in this vicinity. Two of her sons, Philip and Jacob, were soldiers in the war of 1812. The former was an officer in the regular army, and was killed at the disastrous battle of the River Raisin. He was a lawyer by profession. Mrs. S. was the oldest member of the Presbyterian church of Paris, and lived and died a sincere Christian.

SHARP, John M., Comminsville, O., ——, æ. —, general western agent of the Baltimore and Ohio Railroad Co. At a meeting of the friends of Mr. S., at the Tremont House, Chicago, the following resolutions were passed unanimously:

"*Resolved*, that in the death of John M. Sharp, the active and most popular agent of the Baltimore and Ohio Railroad Co., we deplore the loss of a most accomplished officer, a noble, generous gentleman, a devoted friend, and an honorable and exemplary citizen.

"*Resolved*, that during several years of a personal intercourse with him as an editor, as a publisher, and as a railroad officer and agent, we always found him to be honest, faithful, steadfast, and true, in all relations of life.

"*Resolved*, that in Mr. S., while living, we recognized a gentleman and officer whose association was worthy the ambition of all his fellow-men; so in death exemplary virtues will be cherished while time exists for us."

SHATTUCK, Mrs. Sarah E., Concord, Mass., Aug. 30, æ. 64, wife of Hon. Daniel Shattuck.

SHATTUCK, Lemuel, Boston, Mass., Jan. 17, æ. 65. He was born at Ashby, Mass., Oct. 15, 1793, and was a son of John and Betsey (Miles) Shattuck. His parents removed to New Ipswich, N. H., when he was in his first year. Here and in the adjoining towns he resided during his minority, and until 1815, as a farmer, manufacturer, and school teacher. In 1817 he resided in Troy and Albany N. Y., and in 1818 to 1822 in Detroit, Mich., as a teacher; in 1823 to 1833 in Concord, Mass., as a merchant, in 1834 in Cambridge, as a bookseller; and after 1834 in Boston, as a publisher and bookseller, until his retirement from regular business. While at Detroit in 1818, he organized there the first Sabbath school opened in Michigan. In 1844 he was one of five persons, of whom Charles Ewer, Samuel G. Drake, William H. Montague, and J. Wingate Thornton were the others, who projected and organized the New England Historic-Genealogical Society. He was chosen its first vice president, which office he held for five years. He was also a member of the American Statistical Association, (of which he was also one of the founders,) of the American Antiquarian and Massachusetts Historical Societies, as well as of various literary and benevolent associations. He published a History of Concord, Mass., and Memorials of the Descendants of William Shattuck, a most thorough genealogical work. He was a member of the common council of Boston from 1838 to 1841, and for several years a representative from Boston to the Massachusetts General Court.

SHAW, Rev. John Knox, Newark, N. J., Oct. 4, æ. 58. He preached on various circuits, and was at one time presiding elder. Mr. S. was a man of generous sympathies, which he manifested by special kindness to the poor and suffering, not in word only, but also in deed. As a husband and father he was thoughtful and affectionate. As a Christian he was experimental and practical. His piety was deep and controlling. He was a good minister of Jesus Christ, nourished up in the words of faith and of good doctrine. Before he entered the itinerant field he had committed to memory the whole of the New Testament, and during the whole of his ministerial life he followed the directions of Paul to Timothy: "Be thou an example of the believers, in word, in conversation, in charity, in spirit, in faith, in purity. Give attention to reading, to exhortation, to doctrine."

SHEAFE, Mrs. Lucy Cushing, Boston, Ms., Mar. 14, æ. 78, widow of Maj. Henry Sheafe, formerly of Portsmouth, N. H.

SHEPARD, Samuel, Panton, Addison

Co., Vt., Dec. 29, æ. 90. His life is an instructive commentary upon the genius and spirit of our institutions and people, and a worthy example for our youth to emulate. He was born in the town of Granby, Hartford Co., Conn., May 29, 1768. When but a lad, he, with his father, emigrated to Panton, Vt., while the country was yet an unbroken wilderness, the town being entirely uninhabited, except that a few families had settled near the shore of Lake Champlain. At the age of nineteen he located himself upon the farm upon which he resided during the remainder of his life. He was ever an active, busy man, and prominent in the accomplishment of every plan for promoting the general welfare, advancing public morality, and attaining any human and philanthropic end. A favorite charity with him was the taking of orphan and homeless children into his family, and rearing and educating them. This he did in many instances, and his proteges have become useful and respected citizens. Two, especially, are now among the most wealthy and respectable inhabitants of the west. He was often called by the suffrages of his fellow-citizens to fill various positions of trust and responsibility. He was a justice of the peace for more than 40 years, and was at different periods selectman of the town, and county judge. He was for 11 years a member of the state legislature, besides holding other offices, both civil and military. In the family circle, as a husband and father, none knew better than he how to secure home happiness. With his children, the man never forgot that he had been a child, nor yet became oblivious that he was a man. He was playful, affectionate, and dignified. He never failed to secure both love and obedience. He taught his children virtue by example as well as precept, and in both exhibited it, not as a marble statue, fair, but cold and formal, but rather as a living reality, beautiful, warm, winning, and attractive. He was one of the constituent members of the first Baptist church formed in Panton some 60 years ago, and was always one of its most zealous and efficient members and supporters, as well as its largest contributor. He was the latest survivor of the little band who organized that church.

SHEPPARD, Leander U., M. D., South Bend, M. T., April 23, æ. 30.

SHERMAN, Mrs. Nancy, Canton, Mass., Dec. 7, æ. 96, widow of Capt. John Sherman, of the revolutionary army, who was the eldest son of Hon. Roger Sherman, signer of the Declaration of Independence. She was born at Milton, Sept. 27, 1762, and was one of the 11 children of Mr. Joseph Tucker, of that town, who died about 1781, aged 73. She enjoyed a pension of $600 per annum on account of the services of her husband in the revolutionary army. Her husband died at Canton in August, 1802.

SHERMAN, Thaddeus, New Haven, Ct., Sept. 23, æ. 84, an old resident of New Haven, formerly a merchant in New York. He was a native of Hamden, Ct., and was a nephew of Roger Sherman, one of the signers of the Declaration of Independence.

SHERWOOD, Samuel B., Newark, Licking Co., O., Dec. 1, æ. —. He was born in Connecticut, but was reared and educated in Newark. Having high social qualities, his relations with its leading men were always close and intimate, and his death will make a wide hiatus in these social relations. He was educated to the law, but his tastes and inclinations led him more into the walks of literature; and his culture and genius naturally attached him particularly to social life. The poetic effusions of his early days will be remembered by a large circle of friends, and will be cherished the more now that the author has departed.

SHIPHERD, Mrs. Elizabeth, Ballston, N. Y., May 22, æ. 84, widow of Judge Shipherd, of Vermont.

SHIRK, Rev. Joseph, Edgar Co., Ill., Sept. 19, æ. 65.

SHUTE, Moses, Esq., Concord, N. H., æ. 68, a lineal descendant, in the fourth generation, of Jacob Shute, one of the original settlers of Concord.

SIBLEY, Col. Samuel S., Savannah, Ga., Nov. 19. He was a citizen of Savannah during the past ten years, and was for a time connected with the Savannah Georgian as one of its editors and proprietors. In public and in private life he bore the character of a high-toned, honorable gentleman. He was a native of New Jersey, but removed to Florida some twenty years ago, where he was for several years proprietor and editor of the Tallahassee Floridian.

SIGUR, Laurent J., Pass Christian,

Miss., —— —, æ. 41. He was a graduate of Georgetown College, D. C. The early years of his manhood were spent in Europe, where he stored his mind with the rich treasures of the literature of Italy, Spain, France, and England. On his return home he was elected by the citizens of New Orleans to represent that city in the state Senate; and in that body he at once attained the high position which his talents never failed to command. He filled several prominent offices under the state and federal governments; and the duties imposed upon him were discharged with ability and fidelity. In politics he was a southern state-rights democrat, and rendered most effective service in the cause. He had an invincible contempt for those politicians who are always ready to sacrifice principle to expediency. In the language of the New Orleans Delta, "No man contributed so much as he to form and direct the peculiar tendencies of the south-west — tendencies that look so hopefully and so unceasingly to expansion, to growth, to development, to the silent and effectual working out of our 'manifest destiny' through the spontaneous energy, enterprise, and daring of the people, without waiting upon the circumlocution of diplomacy or the tardiness, wrangling, and partisan fury of congresses." In the social walks of life, in the councils of the state, in the political arena, in the profession of journalism, and at the bar, he ever occupied a foremost position. The people of Louisiana were proud of him; for he was the embodiment of that high-toned chivalry, that amenity of manners, and that boldness of oratory which popularize and endear man to his fellow-man. A warm and constant friend, his hand was ever ready to soothe and assist; as a journalist, no menaces could deter, no blandishments betray him from the path which duty had marked out for his guidance. "An integrity as incorruptible as that of Cato was the characteristic of the man." Few men have gone to the grave more deeply regretted than Laurent J. Sigur. Louisianians feel that they have lost a most gifted brother — one whose intellectual superior scarcely anywhere survives. The south has lost a warm and devoted friend, and our constitution one of its boldest defenders.

SIMMONS, B. F., Esq., Leavenworth, K. T., March —. The assembled bar of Leavenworth say, "In the person of our departed friend and brother we ever found the manly virtues of sobriety, urbanity of manners, a strict, unflinching probity in all his intercourse; though firm in principle, conservative in feeling; bland, without deception; kind in all his greetings, without hypocrisy; untiring in his industry and energy, and true to all his obligations in life; the warm friend, the social companion, and the modest, retiring, plain, and unpretending gentleman."

SIMONS, Cyrus G., Esq., Jonesboro', Ill., Sept. 28, æ. 40. Mr. S. graduated at a college in Montreal, C. W., read law in Rochester, N. Y., and opened an office in 1845 in Jonesboro'. No one ever struggled against adversity with more zeal and energy, or submitted to the hardships and privations of a pioneer life in the "far west" with better grace; and few, if any, have ever so soon succeeded in having their efforts crowned with success by gaining a large and lucrative practice in the profession of his choice, and by drawing around him a large circle of admiring friends, who are now left to mourn his departure from their midst. In 1849 Mr. S. was elected to a seat in the representative branch of the state legislature, and for two years filled that station with credit and honor to himself, and satisfaction to his constituency. In 1852 he was employed by the Illinois Central Railroad Company as their attorney; and about the same time he received the appointment of counsellor to the Cairo City Company; and, although the duties of either station were arduous in the extreme, yet he, with untiring industry and persevering effort, discharged all of his duties, including those of a large private practice at the bar, with ability, zeal, and energy. The bar of the county say, "We cherish the highest respect for his professional learning, untiring perseverance, and integrity displayed by him throughout his short but brilliant career on earth; and the bar will ever cherish the remembrance of their departed brother."

SINCLAIR, Purser William, New York city, May 23, æ. 69, for 59 years in the naval service of the United States.

SINCLAIR, James, M. D., New Orleans, La., Sept. —, æ. —. He was born in Dublin, and graduated with honors as a physician. He came to this country about 30 years ago. He was a surgeon in the United States army, under Gen. Z. Taylor, and was present at the battle of Monterey, and in the division of Gen. Worth at the storming of the bishop's palace, and was the man who handed the colors to be planted on the walls. He was then with those brave hearts that revelled in the halls of the Montezumas, and served with distinction in the army in the battles around the city of Mexico, and was wounded in saving the life of one of his brother soldiers. His own wounds did not prevent him from attending to his brother soldiers. Afterwards he followed his profession in Steubenville, O., St. Louis, Mo., and the neighboring country around. He was always ready with his purse and services to relieve the sick and needy, and was in every instance a friend to the widow and orphan.

SING, William, Sing Sing, N. Y., July 9, æ. 96. He was born of highly respectable parentage, June 4, 1762, in Bridgenorth, Shropshire, England. He emigrated to America contrary to the wishes of his parents, preferring the republican to the monarchical form of government; and during his whole life he was an ardent admirer of American institutions. A man of studious habit and of a well-cultivated mind, he was an ornament to the society in which he moved. In his manners he was a gentleman, hospitable, and beloved by all who knew him. Mr. S. united with the Baptist church in Eagle Street, London, in 1790. He occupied places of honor and trust from time to time up to extreme old age. He was associated with Mr. Elijah Hunter and others in the care of the Mount Pleasant Academy, originally established by the church to provide education for the ministry. For more than 50 years he resided in the village of Sing Sing; and up to the time of his death few men were more extensively known, and fewer still more beloved by all grades of civil and religious society. He was kind, sociable, affable to all, cheerful in his disposition, and strictly punctual to all his engagements. He literally died of old age, in the full possession of all his faculties. Three children only, out of a large family, remain to mourn his loss.

Of these Charles B. Sing, formerly of the United States army, is now a minister connected with the New York Methodist Episcopal conference, and Mary wife of Rev. D. Holmes, of Sing Sing.

SIZER, Abel Tryon, M. D., New London, Conn., March 24, æ. 58.

SIZER, James, M. D., Richmond, Va., Dec. 27, æ. —.

SKILTON, Avery J., M. D., Troy, N. Y., March 20, æ. 56, second son of James and Chloe (Steele) Skilton, born in Watertown, Ct. His early education was obtained in the common school, the academy, the quiet Christian New England home, and the town library. He studied medicine in the office of Dr. Catlin, of Bethlehem, Ct., and attended lectures at Yale Medical College. He commenced the practice of medicine in Troy in the year 1827, and continued it until Dec. 10, 1857, when his last illness prostrated him. During these 30 years he accomplished the work of a much longer life, giving himself no rest so long as the sick under his care needed attention. As a medical man he was obstinate and persevering in the combat with disease. Keeping well up with the improvements of his profession, but examining new theories with a clear, scientific eye, and with sound morality, he refused to accept any popular system which did not commend itself to his medical judgment. In all the responsibilities of life he was eminently a man of duty, and he never felt satisfied with himself or others until its stern dictates were complied with. Almost his only amusement, and recreation from the labors of his profession was the equally laborious, though to him enthusiastic and delightful study of the natural sciences — mineralogy, geology, botany, conchology, and paleonotlogy; and during his later years he gave his attention to philology and genealogy. The result of a portion of his efforts in the latter field have been published since his death in the "Genealogy of the Steele Family," under the direction of Daniel Steele Durrie, Esq., of Madison, Wisconsin, who was associated with him in the preparation. In summing up his character he might be said to have possessed great kindness of heart, great modesty, great strength of will, great devotion to duty and right, and perfect acquiescence in the dispensations of an overruling Providence.

SKINNER, Hon. Aaron N., New Haven,

Ct., Oct. 25, æ. 58. He was born in Woodstock, Vt., and was noted as an eminent teacher.

SKINNER, Hon. Elias, Cape Cod, Mass., ——, æ. 59, citizen of Ypsilanti, Mich., and late a prominent lawyer of Washtenaw Co., Mich. Judge S. had resided in Ypsilanti nearly 30 years, and was a member of the last constitutional convention of Michigan.

SKINNER, Rev. S. P., Philadelphia, Pa., Aug. 19, æ. —, a noted Universalist clergyman, brother of Rev. Otis A. Skinner, of Boston, Mass.

SLACK, Ruggles, Esq., Chelsea, Mass., April 20, æ. 65. He was the out-door financial agent and collector of the Boston Post for 25 years. His ecclesiastical connection was with the Episcopal church. He received his early religious impressions under the ministry of the late Dr. Morse, of Charlestown. He fully believed the peculiar doctrines of the Bible, and they sustained him on his dying bed.

SLAGLE, Mrs. Martha, St. Louis, Mo., May 15, æ. 65.

SLATER, Perry C., M. D., Springfield, Ill., March 12, æ. 33.

SLINGERLAND, Col. Peter, Ann Arbor, Mich., July 6, æ. 49. He was of Dutch descent, son of Albert E. Slingerland, of Maryland, and married Mary Ann D. Emmett, of Amsterdam, Nov. 4, 1829. He early settled in Ann Arbor, and held various offices of trust — city marshal, treasurer, alderman, and sheriff. His wife and four children survive him. One son is a member of the California legislature.

SMALL, Mrs. Ann Keziah P., Newburyport, Mass., ——, æ. —. She was one of the survivors of the ill-fated Central America, that foundered in the Atlantic last September. It will be remembered that Mrs. S. was then returning home, after having buried her husband at Panama, in the care of Capt. Herndon. Capt. Small had intrusted a package of papers to his wife, to be delivered to Eben Wheelwright, Esq., owner of the ship in which he had sailed. Just before the steamer went down, when the boat was leaving the steamer, and she was invited on board, she declined to go till she had secured that package of papers committed to her keeping by the dying husband, and against the remonstrance of the passengers, she waded through the water that filled the cabin, and obtained her trust, and then left. She was sick at the time of the sinking of the steamer, but amid all the terrors of that occasion she was calm and collected, and while brave men perished, she was saved for a short season, and has now followed them upon that long voyage from which none return.

SMALLCORN, Capt. John, Barrington, N. H., Sept. 28, æ. 86.

SMALLEY, Rev. Elam, D. D., Troy, N. Y., July 30, æ. 54. He graduated at Brown University in 1827, in the class with Gov. Clifford, Rev. Dr. Thompson of Salem, Judge Colby, and Hon. C. Thurber and P. C. Bacon, Esq., of Worcester, Mass. In 1829, he was settled as associate pastor with the venerable Dr. Emmons, of Franklin, where he remained till he was called to the pastorate of the Union Church in Worcester, over which he was installed Sept. 19, 1838. In the spring of 1854 he received a call from the Sixth Street Congregational Church in Troy, and, after due consideration, and with the advice of his friends, accepted the call, and was settled there. He remained the pastor of the church till the connection was severed by death. He possessed a strong and cultivated mind, and was a man of mark in his profession. As a Christian, he was earnest, devout, and sincere, and, although very decided in his own peculiar religious views, he had none of that bigotry which would exclude from his Christian love and fellowship those who, differing from him in opinion, yet gave evidence that they "loved the Lord." His last years were years of trial and suffering, calling forth the sympathy of the wide circle of friends who were so warmly attached to him.

SMEAD, Capt. Benjamin, Bath, Steuben Co., N. Y., Aug. 8, æ. 83, at the residence of his grandson. He was born in Greenfield, Franklin Co., Mass., May 3, 1775. His father, David Smead, was a farmer of high respectability, for 40 years a deacon of the Presbyterian church, for 19 years a representative in the state Assembly, and for many years previous to his death a justice of sessions. Benjamin was the youngest of a family of 12 children. In 1791 the first printing press of the county was established by Thomas Dyckman. At the age of 17 Mr. S. became his apprentice, and served at his trade until he became of age. After attaining his majority he worked as a journeyman in Boston for some months, and then entered into partnership with his former master, in the publication of the Federal Galaxy, a small sheet, 10 by 17 inches, four columns wide, printed in the old-style Roman-faced type, and upon paper which printers of the present day would reject as wholly unfit for use. The partnership continued for six months, at which time Mr. Dyckman withdrew, and Mr. S. became the sole proprietor of the Galaxy. In 1803 he sold out his paper, and removed to Bennington, Vt., where, in partnership with a gentleman by the name of Haswell, he published the Vermont Gazette. In 1808 this partnership was dissolved, and the Gazette establishment was purchased by a company of wealthy citizens. The paper was continued under Mr. S., as editor and publisher, until 1812. On the breaking out of the war with Great Britain Mr. S. received a lieutenant's commission, and left his printing office for the army. In Aug., 1813, he was promoted to the rank of captain, in which capacity he served till Jan. 8, 1815, the close of the war. In a letter to a friend, of about that date, he says, "On the receipt of the news of peace great hilarity reigned in the camp. Great was the rejoicing throughout the whole army. In our cantonment every soldier seemed to think that the necessity for discipline was over, and that there was nothing left to do but to hurrah, and shout, and be merry. In the evening the camp was illuminated by thousands of candles stuck in the snow. Rockets went whizzing up into the cold heavens; cannons boomed, waking the frozen echoes of the mountains; the different companies of the regiment paraded, and were put through their evolutions with torches in their hands; and gladness and joy seemed to reign supreme." In 1816 he received an invitation signed by Daniel Cruger, Dugald Cameron, George W. Taylor, William B. Rochester, and Gen. George McClure, to establish a democratic paper in the village of Bath, Steuben Co., N. Y. In answer to their invitation, Mr. S., in the fall of 1816, commenced the publication of the Steuben Patriot. In 1818 the name of his paper was changed to that of the Steuben and Alleghany Patriot, under which it was published until 1823, when it was again changed to that of the Steuben Farmer's Advocate. In 1837 he was elected a member of the legislature from Steuben Co., and occupied a high position, while serving in that capacity, for his practical sense and business capacity. In all his career as an editor Mr. S. advocated what he regarded as the right, always. While a close adherent to democratic principles, and a firm supporter of the democratic party, he was the tool of no faction, the follower of no mere leader. What he thought he wrote, and was ready to abide by the consequences. Party affinities were never suffered by him to shield political corruption; and allegiance to the constitution and the laws, allegiance to justice and the right, were with him paramount to mere allegiance to party. He was an honest editor and politician, as well as an honest man; and as such he was respected alike by political friends and foes. He was a terse, pleasant writer, maintaining his personal dignity, and that of his paper, under all circumstances. Mr. S. had five sons, all of whom served an apprenticeship as printers. One of his sons, B. F. Smead, died some years since at Manhattan, O., at which place he edited a paper, having secured a wide-spread fame as the author of several of the most popular campaign songs, and as one of the most pungent and facetious political writers of his day. He was buried with Masonic honors, all the craft in that region being in attendance at his funeral.

SMITH, A. D., M. D., Holden, Mass., Oct. 26, æ. —. Dr. S. pursued his medical studies in Lowell, Mass. He was having an extensive practice in Holden, was greatly respected by its inhabitants, and his sudden death in the prime of his usefulness is a severe loss, not only to his family and relatives, but to the community generally where he resided.

SMITH, Anthony W., M. D., Mecklenburg Co., Va., July 30, æ. 62, of Lunenburg Co., Va. In each relation of life, as a Christian, as a father, as a husband, and as a master, the deceased left behind him the most holy and endearing reminiscences.

SMITH, Bartholomew, Esq., Boston, Mass., Aug. 11, æ. 57. He was a man of strong intellect and much general information. He represented his native town five years in succession in the state legislature, and many subsequent years; held many other important offices, the duties of which he faithfully and efficiently discharged.

SMITH, Rev. Benjamin, Litchfield, Me., Aug. 31, æ. 33.

SMITH, Mrs. Betsey G., De Kalb, Ill., Sept. 7, æ. 53, wife of Dr. Dudley Smith. She was daughter of Josiah Davis, and was born in New Ipswich, N. H. Her mother was daughter of Rev. Cornelius Waters, for many years pastor of the Congregational church in Ashby, Mass. Mrs. S. was the oldest of four children. Her only brother is the Rev. J. G. Davis, of Amherst, N. H.; and one sister is the wife of Rev. Alvan Bond, D. D., of Norwich, Ct. Mrs. S., from her admission to the church in 1827, manifested striking Christian virtues, and was devoted and unwearied in her efforts to do good.

SMITH, George, Esq., Limestone township, Montour Co., Pa., April 6, æ. 60, formerly collector at Beach Haven.

SMITH, Isaac, M. D., North East, N.Y., March 26, æ. 42.

SMITH, Rev. Isaac B., Wilson, N. Y., June 5, æ. 78, a preacher over fifty years.

SMITH, Capt. Joab, Fairfield, Vt., Jan. 26, æ. 84. He was born in Oakham, Worcester Co., Mass., in 1774, and removed to Fairfield, Vt., in 1794, where he continued to reside until the day of his death. He was married May 5, 1808, to Sarah Merrill, who, with their three married daughters, survives him, and lives at or near the old homestead. He held several important civil and military offices for an unprecedented length of time. He was elected chief selectman of Fairfield for nine successive terms, and was town treasurer for many years, holding that office at the time of his decease. He was chosen justice of the peace for 49 successive years, and was 11 times elected to represent the town of Fairfield in the General Assembly. In the discharge of the many trusts which devolved upon him by reason of his intelligence and probity he was eminently prudent and faithful, always guarding the interests and welfare of the town with more jealousy, if possible, than his own.

SMITH, Hon. John, St. Albans, Vt., Nov. 20, æ. 69. The Burlington Times says. "Mr. S. has long been one of the public men of Vermont. Like Gov. Paine and Judge Follett, he was identified with the great railroad interests of the state from the beginning; and it is scarcely too much to say that his life, like theirs, was devoted and *sacrificed* to those interests. The most successfully managed railroad in Vermont, the Vermont and Canada, owes its position mainly to the sagacious foresight of Mr. S. We almost think he *never* made a mistake in his judgment of men or measures. For several years Mr. S. was the representative of St. Albans in the legislature, and for the sessions of 1831, '32, and '33 was chosen speaker of the House. In the Congress of 1839-41 he was the representative of his congressional district. He was afterwards candidate for governor of the state. In 1846 he was actively engaged in securing a grant to bridge Lake Champlain, which he, with his friends, accomplished in 1847. Subsequent to that time he was identified with the railroad interests of the state, as president, director, and trustee of the Vermont Central and Vermont and Canada Railroad. In these and all public trusts he was a true man — true no less to his own convictions than to the interests of his constituency. Vermont never had an honester or more intelligent representative than John Smith, of St. Albans. His politics, however objectionable to the prevailing sentiment of the state, never interfered with the just performance of his duty. He was a Vermonter, without fear and without reproach."

SMITH, John F., Philadelphia, Pa., June 24, æ. 73. He served as a surgeon in the war of 1812, and for 42 years was engaged at the Girard Bank.

SMITH, Col. John L., New York city, Sept. 13, æ. 70. He entered the army during the last war with Great Britain, as a second lieutenant. His first commission was dated Oct. 16, 1813. He rose to his majority, by the ordinary steps of gradation, July 7, 1838, and, for gallantry in the Mexican war, was brevetted colonel Aug. 20, 1847. Col. S. has been for some time the only officer in the corps of engineers who was not graduated at West Point. In the course of a long service in the corps of engineers he was distinguished for the ability and zeal with which he discharged the duties of his office, and for his professional and literary attainments. Society, as well as the army, has sustained a great loss in the death of this gallant officer and accomplished gentleman.

SMITH, James Madison, Clinton, Miss., April 6, æ. 53. He was born in Calvert Co., Md., and emigrated to Mississippi in 1824, and settled as a merchant at Rodney. By his business capacity, industry, and fidelity he amassed a large estate. No man was ever more eminent than he was for good faith and integrity.

GEN. PERSIFER FRAZER SMITH,

Fort Leavenworth, Kansas, May 17, æ. 59, of the United States army, and commander of the expedition to Utah. Gen. S. was a worthy son of Pennsylvania. He was born in Philadelphia, in Nov., 1798. He was a son of Jonathan Smith, former cashier of the Bank of Pennsylvania, and afterwards cashier of the Bank of the United States. Jonathan Smith, whose father held an important public office in Chester Co. under the colonial government, came to Philadelphia during the last century. The maternal grandfather of Gen. S. was Persifer Frazer, who was a lieutenant colonel in the revolutionary army.

After going through a collegiate course and graduating at Princeton, he studied law under the late Charles Chauncey, Esq. Upon his admission to practice he removed to New Orleans, where he resided, engaged in the duties of his profession, until the period of the Florida war, when he volunteered for service there, and served gallantly during two campaigns under Gen. Gaines. It was here that his military talent was brought to the knowledge of Gen. Taylor; and it was upon his recommendation that the governor of Louisiana gave to him the command of the Louisiana volunteers for service in the war with Mexico. He served under Gen. Taylor in the campaign of the Rio Grande.

In May, 1846, while in Mexico, he was appointed colonel of the rifle regiment, that was raised for the war; and for his services at the siege and capture of Monterey he was brevetted brigadier general. He was subsequently ordered to join Gen. Scott, and commanded a brigade on the memorable march from Vera Cruz to the city of Mexico, taking a prominent part in the most important battles.

At Contreras he rendered efficient service, Gen. Scott, in his official report, stating that he "closely directed the whole attack in front with his habitual coolness and ability." At Chapultepec also he was prominently engaged, as also in the final struggle at the city gates. Gen. Scott, in his reference to the Belen Gate affair, describes Gen. Smith as "cool, unembarrassed, and ready;" and these were distinguishing traits of his military character.

After the war was over Gen. S., who had been promoted to the rank of major general by brevet for his services at Contreras, was ordered to California, to the command of that military department. Subsequently he held a similar command in Texas. In 1856 he was ordered to Kansas, where he remained in command until quite recently, when he was appointed to the command of the expedition to Utah.

Gen. S. was superior to the majority of our military men in reach and force of intellect, and remarkable for his calm courage and activity. His personal appearance was soldierly and impressive. He was of middle height, stoutly built, and quick in his movements. His hair was light, and his eyes sparkled with intelligence. In the decease of such a man we mourn the loss of a brave and skilful soldier, and a faithful and patriotic public servant.

He leaves a widow, but only one son — Dr. Howard Smith, of New Orleans, the child of his first marriage. A brother and other relatives reside in Philadelphia. The country loses an able and gallant officer.

His remains were consigned to their final resting place at Laurel Hill, with every demonstration of honor and respect. It was a proper tribute from Philadelphia to one of her illustrious sons. The military display on the occasion was large, striking, and impressive. The public authorities in the city united in the last tribute. The remains arrived at Philadelphia via Pittsburg, under charge of an escort of the Duquesne Grays. The funeral took place from Mr. Beaton Smith's, in Walnut Street. There were present, besides the relatives and immediate friends of the deceased, Gen. Winfield Scott, with a number of military and naval officers, and several clergymen of the Presbyterian church. Among the latter were Rev. Albert Barnes, of the First Church, Rev. Thomas Brainerd, D. D., of the Pine Street Church, Rev. John Chambers, of the Independent Church, Broad and George Streets, and Rev. George Duffield, Jr., of the Coates Street Church.

SMITH, Gen. Peter Sken, Springfield, Mass., May 6, æ. 63. He was born in Utica, N. Y., June 6, 1795. His father was the extensive landholder, Peter Smith. His brother, Gerrit Smith, of Peterboro', N. Y., is the sole survivor of Peter Smith's family. Gen. S. was twice married. By his first wife, Ann, daughter of Rev. Joseph Prentiss, of Catskill, N. Y., he had two children — Cornelia (now Mrs. Lieut. A. Baird) and Gerrit Henry Smith. His second wife, Anna E. Cumming, of Augusta, Ga., has no children. This very intelligent and excellent lady survives her husband. Gen. S. was a gentleman of brilliant talents and warm heart. His friends were strongly attached to him; and they were very numerous; for to become acquainted with him was to become his friend.

SMITH, Mrs. Phebe, Waterloo, N. Y., Sept. 19, æ. 19, a pioneer settler of Waterloo, and a most excellent Christian.

SMITH, Hon. R. H., Perry, Wyoming Co., N. Y., Aug. 2, æ. 67. Judge S. was a native of Whitesboro', Oneida Co. His father, Nathan, was one of the earliest settlers of that county, having moved into it before its organization. He was one of its first representatives in the legislature of the state, and in connection with Peter Smith, the father of the well-known Gerrit Smith, operated extensively in public lands. The father of Nathan, David, was highly esteemed by the Seneca Indians, to whom he acted a friendly part, and was rewarded by them with the gift of 400 acres of fertile land in the vicinity of Geneva. He was extensively engaged in a great variety of occupations. Unlike most men, he did not give up one branch of business for another, but added the new to the old, and prosecuted all together with energy and success. His mills, and farms, and store, and bank, and extensive building operations, and various official duties, left him but few leisure moments in the closing years of his life; and yet such were his industrious habits and his characteristic energy, that care was welcome, and business a pleasure. He was elected four successive years supervisor of the town. For several years he was postmaster. Gov. Marcy appointed him associate judge of Genesee Co. In 1844 he was one of the state electors, and aided to cast the vote of New York for Polk and Dallas. Judge S. possessed the entire confidence of the community, as a business man who combined caution with energy; a spirit of accommodation with a proper regard for his own interests; rare skill to plan, suavity to conciliate, and efficiency to execute, — all united to unbending integrity. He was eminently successful in his business operations, accumulated a large property, and did much to cause his memory to be long and signally cherished by the community in which he lived and died. A resolution adopted by the board of trustees of the Perry Academy: "That by the death of Judge Smith, president of this board, we have been deprived of the counsels of a wise and prudent adviser, an ardent friend of learning, and a liberal supporter of this institution, for the prosperity and support of which he was always ready to expend time and means not surpassed by any of its friends."

SMITH, Rev. Samuel W., Mount Vernon, N. Y., March 16, æ. 45, pastor of the Methodist Episcopal church.

SMITH, Stephen H., ———, R. I., July —, æ. —. For a long time Mr. S. was one of the leading pomologists of his native state. He was one of the founders of the R. I. Horticultural Society, and its first president. A well-written notice of his death in the Homestead, says, "Horticulture was with him a speciality, and no man in the state has given so much time and attention to it, or devoted himself with more zeal and enthusiasm. Though unacquainted with botany as a science, he was a remarkably close observer of any product of the vegetable kingdom, and procured a vast fund of information respecting indigenous plants, and a respectable knowledge of cultivated species. Fruits, however, were his special favorites, and it was conceded by his fellow-members of the Horticultural Society that no man in the state was his equal in respect to a knowledge of all our cultivated fruits. He was for a quarter of a century the pioneer in horticulture in his state, and stood nearly alone during that period in his efforts, which were untiring and most enthusiastic, to diffuse a knowledge and promote the extension of that beautiful branch of human industry. It was not until within 15 years that his labors began to be appreciated or felt; and when the Horticultural Society was established, he found himself surrounded by a considerable number of co-laborers, who sympathized with his feelings and taste, and partook of his zeal. He was the animating spirit of that society for a long time, and its prosperity and success are due, in a greater measure than to any other source, to his large experience and ceaseless efforts." Mr. S. was intimately acquainted with all the eastern varieties of apples, and contributed much valuable information in Mr. Kenrick's American Orchardist, published 25 years ago. It was through him that most of the Rhode Island fruits were made known to our cultivators. Mr. S. lived and died in the parish where he was born. He was pastor of a church of which his father was deacon, and a very large proportion of whose members were kindred according to the flesh. A prophet preëminently in honor in his own country, among his own kin, and in his own house, universal confidence was placed in him by those who watched him from childhood, oy those who were associated with him in school days, and in college, and by all to whom he ministered. This confidence was manifested by the unanimity with which the Litchfield Academy was placed under his charge, for some five years after he graduated at Bowdoin College, in 1841, by the entire unanimity of the Congregational church and community in Litchfield, in electing him to be their pastor, and by the very large vote of the town in electing him to represent them in the legislature of Maine, in the winter of 1857-58. He was a most amiable and estimable man in all the relations of life which he sustained. As a preacher of the gospel, he was rich and varied in his subjects, clear and practical in his illustrations, pointed, forcible, faithful in his application. He loved the cause of Christ, the church, the Sabbath school, the poor and oppressed, and labored faithfully to do them all good; his record is on high; his works do follow him.

SMITH, Wm. C., M. D., Wilcox Co., Ala., Aug. 17, æ. 31, a graduate of East Tennessee.

SMITH, William, Watertown, N. Y., Nov. 24, æ. 82. Mr. S. was born in New Haven, Conn., in 1777. His early childhood and youth were spent upon a farm, where he acquired such habits of application and industry as qualified him for his place afterwards amidst the rugged realities of pioneer life. He early evinced an aptitude for mechanics, by the skill and tact with which he made any thing that could be constructed with his jackknife, and such other simple tools as were accessible to farmers' boys, so that at an age of 12 years he was somewhat noted for his ability to whittle. He went early to the State of New York, and was largely engaged in public business and enterprises. He took part in the battle of Sacketts Harbor, May 29, 1813, by heading a body of militia, and conducting them in the fight with skill and manly bearing. He built cotton mills, was treasurer of his county, laid out the grounds for Madison Barracks at Sacketts Harbor, and exhibited to the secretary of the navy the best plan to cover the 120 gun ship which was left upon the stocks at the close of the war of 1812. He was receiver in chancery of the large estate of La Farge and Schuyler. He was more than any other man the projector and promoter of the Central Railroad. During all this time, from the earliest inception of the project, in 1833, to the proud date of its triumph, in 1852, he was one of the earliest, most constant, and self-sacrificing friends of the project, and probably did more, by personal and direct application to the people at their own firesides, towards eliciting the stock for the road, than any other man. He was in the front rank of that class of men whom Providence had prepared on the rock-bound shores of our Atlantic sea coast, to step in here, at the proper time, and help to mould and fashion such crude elements as are to be found in new countries. Men of Mr. S.'s varied mechanical acquirements are valuable any where and in any age; and we have seen how it was that young, energetic men came here and "made their

26*

mark" as soon as they were needed; and now we see "the man for the times," a whittler from his youth, and who was equally at home in the cooper shop, on the mason's staging, behind the merchant's counter, at the joiner's bench, or in the iron foundery. With brain enough to invent, and skill enough to execute, whatever appliances were needed, and as fast as they were needed, to supply the necessities of a thriving, growing community, it may be truly said of him, that among all the schemes which have been devised from time to time, for a period of 56 years, having the general prosperity of the people of the county of Jefferson in view, none of them have lacked his cheerful, timely, and efficient aid and sympathy; while it may be also asserted, with equal truth and propriety, that some of the most important and vital projects might have failed but for his untiring, consistent, and sometimes unrequited energies.

SNELL, Rev. Thomas, Wethersfield, Ill., Jan. 25, æ. 41.

SNELLING, N. G., Esq., Boston, Mass., Sept. 9, æ. 74, late president of the Massachusetts Fire and Marine Insurance Company. He received the Franklin medal at the North School in 1798.

SORBETT, Hon. Judge J. H., Little Rock, Ark., Nov. 30, æ. —, member of the Arkansas legislature from Scott Co.

SOUTHWORTH, Nathaniel, Dorchester, Mass., on the way to Hingham from Boston, April 25, æ. 52. He was born in Scituate, Mass., in 1806. His father, Thomas Southworth, was a master mariner, who died many years ago. He had exhibited a talent for drawing, and had made good progress therein, mainly by his own unaided efforts; and soon after attaining his majority he began to use the pencil, and in a few years was established in Boston as a miniature painter. He ranked as one of the best in this department of the art; his works were good likenesses, and characterized by accuracy in drawing and great delicacy in execution. He resided in Boston till 1848, when he visited Europe, remaining there a year. After his return he practised his profession for a few years in New York and Philadelphia; but now his health began to fail, and during the remainder of his life he was doomed to struggle more or less constantly against the languor and depression of disease. Mr. S. was of medium height, slender in figure, and erect in bearing, with a countenance which in form and color was rather Italian than New England. Of simple nature and retiring manners, he was endeared to his friends by his purity of character, gentle temper, and affectionate heart. He was an excellent and conscientious artist; his eye and hand were equally accurate; a want of proportion was every where immediately detected by him. He was not less unerring in his discrimination of character. His truth of eye and hand were manifested in a way hardly to be expected in a man of so gentle a spirit, and of such delicacy of sentiment in his art.

SPALDING, James, M. D., Montpelier, Vt., March 15, æ. 66. Dr. S. was born in Sharon, Vt., March 20, 1792. His father, Dea. Reuben Spalding, was one of the early settlers of the state; and his life was not more remarkable for the toil and privations of a pioneer in a new country than for its unbending integrity and the best qualities of the old New England Puritanism. His father's family was very large, numbering 12 children, who all reached maturity; and consequently his early education was limited to the instruction of the common school. Aspiring to greater attainments than could be made in such a position, he left home at the age of 17, for Alstead, N. H., where he remained four years, studying medicine with Dr. Eben Carpenter, and attending, in the mean while, the medical lectures at Hanover, at the time when Dr. Nathan Smith was the most noted surgical operator and lecturer in the country. From his teacher the doctor acquired a taste for that particular department of practice; and he ultimately attained great skill and reputation in his professional career, and was especially noted in that region for his successful surgery. After graduating at Hanover, he commenced his professional life in Claremont, but was induced by the solicitations of his friends to remove to Montpelier. He went to that place in Sept., 1814, and had remained there ever since, in full and deserved possession of the public confidence as a physician and as a Christian gentleman. He united with the Congregational church in 1816, at the same time with the late Hon. Samuel Prentiss; and their relations were always of the most friendly and cordial character. The doctor, during his long residence in Montpelier, always identified himself with its leading moral and religious interests. With a wide and engrossing practice, he yet never failed in his duties as a Christian man or citizen. Ever prompt to attend his patients, he also rarely failed, by a careful prearrangement of his business engagements, to find time for the active discharge of his responsibilities to the church and the community. He was one of the foremost advocates of the temperance cause in the state; and, while he consistently and faithfully sustained the State Temperance Society to the end of his life, he yet never swerved from sound principles, nor sought to build the temperance movement on any other than scriptural and Christian foundations. He held to the duty of temperance on the ground of right and justice; to total abstinence on the ground of brotherly kindness. Dr. S. was interested and active in every effort for the moral, religious, educational, and physical good of the community. He was a most untiring reader and student. For years he was a trustee of the academy, and one of its prudential committee. He was a member of the Board of Fellows of the Vermont Academy of Medicine, an officer for a long period of the State Medical Society, and a frequent contributor to medical journals. An excellent physician, a warm-hearted citizen, a just, honest, and generous man, a sincere, reliable, and active Christian, he lived among us without reproach, he died honored and lamented by all.

SPALDING, Mrs. Lucretia S., Cleveland, O., Feb. 21, æ. 56, wife of Hon. Rufus P. Spalding, and daughter of the late Chief Justice Swift, of Connecticut.

SPANN, H. R., Esq., ——, Texas, May —, a citizen of Edgefield, S. C., and a prominent lawyer.

SPEAR, Hiram A., Esq., Laconia, N. H., March 4, 1858, æ. about 32. Mr. S. was born in West Braintree, Vt.; read law with J. P. Kidder, Esq., of that state. In 1852 he opened an office at Meredith, N. H., where he remained until his death, except a portion of 1854 and 1855, when he was absent in California. He was appointed register of probate for Belknap, July 11, 1856, and held the office at the time of his death.

SPENCER, Rev. Robert O., Athens, O., Sept. 6, æ. 52. He entered upon his ministerial career at the age of 18, and officiated in the pulpit over 30 years — 10 years beyond the average period allotted this arduous profession. He had the happy faculty of winning and attaching to him whomsoever he chose to be his friend; and but few men have the good fortune to rejoice in the possession of so many devoted to him by strong social ties. He left a family and numerous other relatives — two brothers, Judge O. M. and Hon. Henry E. Spencer — to mourn their loss. One son, Oliver M., who is a talented young man, is principal of the Female Institute at Xenia.

SPENCER, Elihu, Middletown, Ct., Oct. —, æ. 38. He graduated at the Wesleyan University, in Connecticut, in the class of 1838, and subsequently studied law with Judge Storrs, and commenced practice at Middletown, Ct. He held many offices of honor and trust, had been clerk of the courts, judge of probate, &c. He was a prominent member of the House of Representatives in 1855. Having about that time separated from the democratic party, he was chosen presidential elector in 1856 on the Fremont ticket, and was nominated in 1857 by the republicans for the office of lieutenant governor, but declined. His father, Elihu Spencer, Esq., was a lawyer by profession, of strong mind and spotless integrity, was editor of the Western Reserve Chronicle in company with Samuel Quinby, Esq., in 1816, and died in 1819, of pulmonary disease, at Warren, O.

SPOTSWOOD, Norbonne B., M. D., Columbia, Mo., July 30, æ. 69. He was the great-grandson of Alexander Spotswood, an early and most distinguished governor of Virginia. His father was Maj. John Spotswood, who served with distinction under Washington in the revolution, and was severely wounded at the battle of Germantown. The subject of this sketch served himself as assistant surgeon in the war of 1812. No man, perhaps, filled a warmer place in the esteem and affections of his friends than Dr. S., and none will find a greener spot in their memories. In all the relations of life he bore himself well. As a husband and father he was devoted, kind, and indulgent; as a neighbor he was generous and obliging; as a friend, disinterested and true.

SPRING, Col. John, Saco, Me., Aug. 17, æ. 76, sheriff of the county in 1830.

STAMBAUGH, Rev. John, Marshall, Ill., May 16, æ. —, a minister of long standing of the United Brethren persuasion.

STAMBAUGH, Mrs. Mary, Lancaster, Pa., Jan. 29, æ. 88. She was a Miller on the paternal and a Carpenter on the maternal side — two of the oldest and largest families in the old county of Lancaster; and she was the last of the last generation. She was remarkable, until late in the winter of life, for her accurate memory of incidents occurring at the close of the revolutionary war; and very few of either sex were better acquainted with the political history of the country through all our national administrations, from Washington's to the close of Andrew Jackson's, (who was her "model president,") or more competent, in strength of intellectual capacity, to discuss the different questions connected with them. In all the varied relations of life she sustained a reputation which classed her with the pure, upright, and dignified of her sex, with an eye and a voice always raised in supplication to her God in heaven.

STANDLEY, William M., M. D., Newnansville, Fla., July 19, æ. 22, youngest son of John and Nancy Standley, of Randolph Co., Ga. He was a young man of fine promise, and beloved by all who knew him.

STANLEY, J. C., M. D., Lancaster, Pa., Nov. 18, æ. 52.

STANLEY, Col. Salma, Geneva, N. Y., Jan. 1, æ. 78. He was born in New Britain, Ct., and went to Ontario with his father, Dea. Seth Stanley, in 1796, locating in Geneva, at what is now known as Stanley's Corners. At the commencement of the war of 1812 he marched to the Niagara frontier, in command of a company of detached militia, armed with rifles for a six months' service, forming part of the 20th regiment, under command of Lieut. Col. Peter Allen, in Gen. W. Wadsworth's brigade. At the battle of Queenstown, Oct. 13, 1812, Capt. S. crossed the river, and gallantly performed his part in that bloody conflict, in which the American arms were at first victorious, but afterwards sustained a defeat for lack of a small reënforcement. During the action Capt. S. received a musket ball on his left hip, striking the edge of his sword, battering it up, and causing a contusion on his person, but producing no serious consequences. That sword was presented to the state about three years ago, and is now in the public library, where it will be preserved as a relic of the war. In what constitute the social relations Col. S. was universally esteemed, by all who knew him, as a man and a Christian — happy in life, and happy in death.

STANLY, James Green, Esq., Newbern, N. C., May 1, æ. 74. His *alma mater*, Princeton College, has had more ambitious alumni, and his state and town have known sons whose fame is more trumpeted abroad; but where shall we find one so thoroughly and engagingly the Christian and gentleman, the scholar and lawyer, the friend and neighbor?· In 1809, by the vote of the entire bench of magistrates, who had then the appointing power, Mr. S. was elected clerk of Pleas and Quarter Sessions for Craven Co. Abandoning his law circuits, he labored in the clerkship for 51 years, and made it a model office, such as perhaps never before, nor since, has been seen; and he here so faithfully toiled, though doubtless to the impairment of his strength and the abridgment of his useful life, as to win, even in these times of change, universal admiration and regard.

STARBIRD, Charles N., Chester, Ill., March 6, æ. 34, a lawyer. He was born in Boston, Mass., and was a graduate of the college at Burlington, Vt.

STARK, William T., Xenia, O., ——, æ. 68, for 12 years postmaster of Xenia. He was a native of Virginia, and a descendant of Gen. Stark, of revolutionary memory.

STARK, Hon. Judge James H., Griffin, Ga., Feb. 23, æ. —. He was a lawyer of eminence and ability seldom surpassed, and in his course through life was called on to fill several important offices, the duties of which he always performed to the satisfaction of his constituency, and with honor to himself. For two successive terms he filled the bench of the Superior Courts of the Flint Circuit, and when he quitted it of his own accord, by resignation, his determination to do so was regretted by a large portion of the bar and many warm personal friends.

STARKWEATHER, Robert, M. D., Chesterfield, Mass., May 8, æ. 92.

STEARNS, Alfred, M. D., Vandalia, Ill., Dec. 11, æ. 38, son of Alfred Stearns, Esq., formerly principal of Westfield Academy.

STEARNS, Mrs. Abigail, Bedford, Mass., Dec. 21, æ. 83, widow of the late Rev. Samuel Stearns, of that place. The death of this excellent lady is regarded and felt as a great loss, not only by her numerous descendants, and a large circle of relatives and friends, but by the inhabitants of Bedford generally, among whom she had resided above 60 years. She was the eldest daughter of Rev. Jonathan French, for many years pastor of the South Church in Andover, and of Madam Abigail (Richards) French, his wife; was born at Andover, May 29, 1776; married to Rev. Mr. Stearns, pastor of the church in Bedford, May 9, 1797; and lived happily with the husband of her youth till he was removed by death, Dec. 26, 1834. Favored with the counsels, example, and prayers of pious parents, Mrs. S. became early impressed with a sense of the importance of religion and virtue; and giving evidence of a change of heart by the influence of the divine Spirit, she was received into the church, over which her father presided, at the early age of 13 years. Through the whole of her subsequent life, wherever she dwelt, and under every variety of circumstances, she uniformly adorned the doctrine of God her Saviour by a pious and Christian life. Being educated in the belief of the Assembly's Catechism, once almost universally used in the families and in the schools of New England, she ever adhered with firmness to the doctrines taught in that little manual. She had informed herself well respecting them. She believed them, upon examination, to accord with the divine standard, the word of God. And hence she cordially received them, was found abundantly able to defend them when attacked in her presence, and made it her great concern to manifest the reality of her faith in them by a life consistent with the spirit and precepts they enjoined. Yet her religion was without parade, cant, or affectation, but exhibited with all simplicity and with all humility in her habitual care to walk in all the commandments and ordinances of the Lord blameless. She was a very devout woman, and cherished habitually a spirit of prayer; loved especially to wait upon God in the morning and evening devotions of the family; and after the death of her beloved husband, was wont to lead in the exercises herself, with great regularity and exemplary constancy, till within live or six days of her death. She was a very benevolent woman, one that loved always, and by all means, to be doing good. For many years she was the president of a benevolent society in Bedford, and did much by her zeal in the cause to animate her associates, and to excite them to active exertion. Many a scheme did she set on foot, in her quiet way, for helping the poor, for imparting knowledge to the ignorant, and reclaiming the vicious and degraded. Mrs. S. was eminent for her wisdom and faithfulness. Her husband was greatly encouraged in his professional studies and toils by her kindness and advice. She was his main stay in the severe trials which befell him in his latter years, and by her tender sympathy, and by her willing, unwearied, watchful attentions, soothed and comforted him in the pains and weakness of his declining days. She presided over her household with great dignity, ordered all its affairs with discretion, and kept her children in willing subjection. Of her eleven children who attained to mature age, Abigail French, the eldest, (wife of Mr. Jonas Monroe, of Bedford,) is not; Charlotte Esther (wife of Rev. Jonathan Leavitt, D. D., of Providence, R. I.) is not; and Samuel Horatio (the beloved, hopeful pastor of the Old South Church, Boston) was early taken away from his family, his people, and the world, by disease and death. Eight yet remain, viz., — Sarah Caroline, wife of Rev. Forrest Jefferds, missionary in Boston; William Augustus, D. D., the reverend president of Amherst College; Maria Holyoke; Jonathan French, D. D., pastor of the First Presbyterian Church, Newark, N. J.; Elizabeth Williams, wife of Dea. Charles James, of East Boston; Josiah Atherton, principal of the Lawrence School, Boston; Anne Catharine; Eben Sperry, principal of the Young Ladies' Academy at Albany.

STEPHENS, Peter, Palestine, Cooper Co., Mo., Feb. 10, æ. 73. Mr. S. was among the first settlers in Central Missouri. He emigrated from Kentucky, and settled, in the winter of 1818, in what was afterwards made the county of Cooper, and resided there continuously up to the time of his death. He was a soldier in the war of 1812, and was among the number who fought the memorable battle of New Orleans, Jan. 8, 1815.

STEPHENS, Mrs. H. M., East Hampden, Me., —— —, æ. 35. She appeared upon the stage, under the name of "Miss Rosalie Somers," where she remained until 1851, since which time she has been well known by the contributions of her pen under the signatures of "Marion Ward" and "H. M. S." She was the authoress of one novel, Hagar the Martyr, and of a great variety of tales, sketches, and poems, a collection of which was published, with the title of Home Scenes and Home Sounds.

STERRETT, Alex. McDonald, Parkersburg, Va., Jan. 31, æ. —. He was born in Shenandoah Co., Va., in the year 1821. After graduating at Dickinson College, Pa., he selected Parkersburg as his place of residence, studied law, and obtained license to practise. His health, however, became too feeble for the labors incident to the profession of his choice, and he was forced to abandon it. Having cultivated a fondness for literary pursuits, and endowed as he was with a brilliant intellect, which had been improved by a liberal education, he was eminently qualified for the position he afterwards assumed, as editor of the Parkersburg Gazette. In private and public discourse he bore the prestige of scholarship, and the emanations from his pen were ever noted for literary excellence. In the circle of social life, few persons were more considerate of the feelings of others, or more studious not to wound them. Kind and affable in his intercourse with the world, he gained that warmth of friendship on the part of others which he felt himself: and.if he had an enemy, he has lived and died unconscious of the fact.

STEVENS, Rev. William, Bridgewater, Pa., March 1, æ. 80, an aged and respected minister of the gospel.

STEVENS, Dea. Wm., Milford, N. Y., Dec. 25, æ. 87. Mr. S. was probably the last survivor of the "Wyoming prisoners." His father died, near the fort, just before the approach of the enemy, and William, then in his 7th year, was taken into the fort. He had a distinct recollection of the events which transpired at its capture. Mr. S. was for 70 years a resident of Otsego, 60 of which were spent in Milford. He first came to Richfield, from Sheffield, Mass., where he was born in 1771.

STEVENS, Col. Simeon, Newbury, Vt., May 14, æ. 91. He was born in Newbury, and was one of the first white children born in the Connecticut valley.

STEVENS, Mrs. Mary H., West Acton, Mass., May 28, æ. 42, daughter of Ebenezer Hayward, of Boxboro'. She has left behind husband and children, parents, brothers and sisters, and a numerous circle of friends, to lament the loss they have sustained in her death.

STEVENS, Hon. Judge, Indianapolis, Ind., April —, æ. —, one of the oldest residents of Indianapolis, and brother of Hon. Thaddeus Stevens, of Pennsylvania.

STEVENS, Eben, M. D., Hopkinton, N. H., Jan. 25, æ. 66, formerly of South Boston, Mass.

STEVENSON, Warner S., M. D., Christiansburg, Ky., March 6, æ. 31. He was the eldest son of the late Dr. D. S. Stevenson, of Cannonsburg, Pa. After completing his literary studies at Jefferson College, he came to Kentucky, and studied medicine in Louisville. In the spring of 1854 Dr. S. located as a practising physician in Christiansburg. Skill and unwearied attention to his patients soon secured him an extensive practice. Studious in his habits, affable in his address, frank and generous in his intercourse with men, a bright future seemed to open before him.

STEWARD, Hon. Daniel, North Anson, Me., May 7, æ. 75.

STEWART, James, Brushvalley township, Pa., Jan. 8, æ. 68. He was in the war of 1812, under Gen. Harrison, and was stationed at Fort Meigs. He lived the life of a Christian, and died peaceful and happy.

STICKNEY, Capt. Amos, Auburn, N.H., Jan. 17, æ. 68. Capt. S. was born in Beverly, Mass., in Jan., 1789, where he resided until he was 24 years of age, when he removed to Salem. For several years he was master of different merchant vessels in foreign trade. In 1813, while in command of the Levant, he was taken prisoner by an English frigate, and carried to New Providence; from thence he was taken to England, and incarcerated in the Dartmoor prison, where he was confined for nearly two years. In July, 1815, he, with others of our brave countrymen, was liberated, and returned once more to his country and his home. He was married in March, 1823, to Elizabeth Hoyt, of Chester, N. H., (now Auburn,) who died in 1842, leaving three children. In 1845 or 1846 Capt. S. was married to Sarah C. Goodwin, of Exeter, N. H., his second wife. He was a man of great enterprise and firmness, a good neighbor, mild, social, and benevolent, esteemed by all his acquaintance.

STICKNEY, Joseph Hale, at Williams College, Mass., Nov. 9, æ. 17, only son of Samuel W. Stickney, Esq., Lowell, Mass., president of the Railroad Bank. The sensation produced at college and at Lowell by the death of this young man was of such marked character as to leave a general impression that a youth of uncommon worth and promise had passed away. It did not grow out of the circumstances of his death, his age, or social relations. There are boys of mark as well as men — those whose personal accomplishments, mental acquisitions, and purity of life place them as far above their fellows as the most distinguished men are above theirs. Young Stickney was a representative youth; a happy example of all that class of early-developed mind, of unstained morals, of lovely manners, of pious motive, of parental, filial, and social affections, which now and then meet in one individual, not only to gladden a domestic circle, but to stand in contrast to the masses, and to hold up to admiring gaze the real standard of human excellence and youthful ambition. The feeling manifested by his classmates at college; by the pupils of the high school at Lowell, from whom he had so lately withdrawn after several years' acquaintance; the interest of teachers, pastor, and people — were in homage of his virtues and promise. Rev. Mr. Foster, in his address at the funeral, said, "No event of human history is more painfully solemn and more deeply mysterious than the death of a youthful scholar — the principles of his character established, the aims of his life adopted, the faculties of his mind developed, going forth from the quiet shelter where parental love, with sleepless anxiety, had watched over him, prepared, by discipline and toil, to enter, with more independent steps, upon a career of higher study and larger accomplishment. We cannot suppress our startled surprise and grief when such an event occurs. To human view it is a life unfinished; it is a 'high endowment lost; it is a grand preparation thrown away; it is the withering of hopes and joys just blossoming into richest beauty, with no probability nor possibility of a harvest to be reached, in this life, from the gentle and blessed spring. It is a dark and insoluble problem, until, with the Psalmist, we go into the sanctuary of God and consult the divine revelation. Then may we truly say there is no event of human history more indicative of the infinite wisdom and benignant love of God than the death of a scholarly and Christian youth. It is not a life finished, but a life begun. It is not a death, but a transfer. It is not the cutting down of hopes, and plans, and joys, more beautiful than spring flowers: they strike a deeper root in a kindlier soil; they will bear richer fruit in a heavenly clime.... We desire to express our profound gratitude to God, because he has given to our sons such a companion, counsellor, and friend. His was an example of excellence not to be forgotten by them. This day, this scene, the lessons of that coffin, will never fade from their minds. The blessed and cherished memories of his life will never fade. We would be devoutly thankful that such a pattern of intellectual and moral beauty and of high attainment has been presented to the contemplation of the youth of this city. For the maturity and wisdom of his thought, for the depth and self-denial of his affection, for the comprehensiveness and accuracy of his scholarship, for his Christian hopes, we thank the Lord." Rev. Dr. Blanchard, his pastor, said, "A moral thoughtfulness beyond his years beautifully tempered each childish grace. It appeared in the family and at school, in his sports and studies. It made him flexible in disposition and firm in principle. Under its influence, his strenuous application to books came of a generous love of excellence that needed no help from appeals to the low feeling of selfish competition. His instructors and schoolmates unite in ascribing to him a deportment in school as near to faultless as it is given to any one to exhibit. These habits, added to his brilliant intellectual powers, placed him among the foremost in our high school, where he had no superior. His teachers and classmates in college testify that even within the brief fortnight of his attending recitations he gave promise of maintaining the same high position there. A nameless grace and charm of manners, in connection with his habits of prayer and of the daily reading of the Scriptures, indicated this excellence to be of no wholly native growth. It had its roots in practical religious feeling." Mr. Chase, principal of the high school, said in another place, " So deeply have the sympathies of the community been moved by the death of this beloved young man, and in so many minds has he left a precious memory, that, as his principal teacher for the last four years, I shall be pardoned for adding, to what has already been said, another tribute of respect and love. Upon entering the high school, young Stickney, though then but a small boy, was immediately recognized as one of the leading scholars in his class. Such was the clearness of his mind, the elegance of his manners, the amiableness of his temper, and the refinement of his moral sensibilities, that he very early elicited both our affection and our pride. I do not recall a single departure, in his intercourse with me, from that kindness and courtesy for which he was uniformly distinguished."

STIRRAT, Rev. James A., Kingston, O., Nov. 28, æ. 40. Mr. S. graduated at the Ohio University in 1844, spent several years in teaching in Marysville, O., and in Mount Pleasant Academy, located in Kingston, O. During this time he was ordained by the presbytery of Marion as an evangelist. As a teacher he was always popular and successful, because he succeeded in infusing much of his own energy and enthusiasm into his pupils. As a friend he was warm-hearted, generous, and confiding. As a Christian his views were clear, scriptural, and discriminating; but he said little of his own feelings. As a preacher he was sound, instructive, and at times impressive.

STOBER, James C., M. D., Shelby, Richland Co., O., Dec. 27, æ. 28.

STOCKING, G. W., M. D., Montezuma, N. Y., Feb. 13, æ. 39. Dr. S. was highly esteemed during life for his universal kindness and ardent devotion to his darling profession. His life was full of self-sacrifice in performing the duties of his calling. Highly as he was esteemed in the circle in which he moved, his truest life was found in the sanctities of home, in which he stood a being around whom clustered the dearest affections of his household.

STOCKING, Rev. Davis, Sing Sing, N. Y., Dec. 11, æ. 48.

STOCKTON, Col. David C., Lebanon, Tenn., Oct. 13, æ. 56, at the residence of D. Cook, Esq. He was the eldest son of the late Rev. Joseph Stockton, of Pittsburg.

STODDARD, William, New Haven, Ct., March 16, æ. 39, an accomplished scholar, distinguished in his profession for more than ordinary success and abilities, with a fine and sensitive temperament, uniting those qualities of heart which rivet esteem and regard in the daily intercourse of life.

STONE, Nathan, Dana, Mass., Nov. 26, æ. 82. He was one or more years a representative in the General Court, was a farmer, and lived on the same farm 60 years.

STONE, Joseph C., Rochester, N. Y., April 12, æ. 43. Mr. S. was born at Montpelier, Vt. He was a merchant in one or more places of his native state for some years after he attained his majority, and married at Wallingford, in 1840, a daughter of Joseph Packer. He removed to Rochester in 1841, and engaged in the grocery and dry goods trade on State Street, in Frankfort. He subsequently took an interest in the wooden flour mills near the foot of Brown's Race. Something more than two years since the firm of J. C. Stone & Co. was formed, Mr. W. W. Carr becoming a partner. Mr. S. was a gentleman of pleasing deportment, was mild in his manners, and by his frank and social way readily won and held the confidence and esteem of all with whom he had intercourse. He was a business man, and best known in business circles.

STONE, D. G., M. D., Henderson, Ky., ———, æ. 39.

STONE, Dan, Westfield, N. J., Nov. —, æ. 49, formerly a member of the Cincinnati bar.

STOY, Henry W., M. D., Harrison

Co., Va., Feb. 2, æ. 73. Dr. S. was born in Lebanon, Pa., Sept. 7, 1784. He studied medicine with Prof. Baker, of Lancaster, Pa. From that place he came to Brownsville, Fayette Co., Pa., in 1807. He resided a short time in Westmoreland Co., Pa., in the year 1849. He, however, returned to Virginia, where he had his residence for some years past. He practised medicine with remarkable acceptability and success up to within three months of his death. He died full of honors, and with an unimpeached reputation for probity and unblemished integrity. As a citizen he was active and ever striving to be useful to his fellow men. He was a member of the German Reformed church.

STREET, Gustavus, Esq., New Orleans, Nov. 21, a citizen of Charleston, S. C. Liberally educated, the influences of a fine culture and elevated tastes made their impress upon all with whom he came into association. He will be long remembered among the merchants of New Orleans for the nice and high-toned standard of right and honorable dealing which eminently marked his commercial career.

STREIT, Rev. Lawrence, Sunville, Venango Co., Pa., Aug. 15, æ. 57. He was a graduate of Jefferson College, was licensed to preach by the Presbytery of Erie in 1838, and in June of the following year was ordained and installed pastor of the church of Wattsburg, Erie Co., Pa. In the year 1846 he took charge of the church at Sunville, and continued his labors with that people until his death. Mr. S. was a faithful, laborious, devoted servant of Christ.

STRINGFIELD, Rev. Thomas, Strawberry Plains, Tenn., June —, æ. —. This aged Methodist preacher was well known in East Tennessee. He occupied for many years a prominent place in his denomination, and more than once was connected with the editorial corps of his church. The Western American, reaching from 1823 to 1826, of which Mr. S. was associate editor, contains his controversies with Rev. Mr. Gallaher of the Presbyterian church, reviews of Dr. Anderson, and other controversial pieces. He was afterwards, for a time, editor of the Nashville Christian Advocate. He was generally esteemed by his brethren, had acknowledged ability, and had been useful to his church.

STRONG, Capt. Martin, Summit Township, Pa., March 24, æ. 88. He was born in Windsor, Ct., in Nov., 1770, and was among the first settlers of Erie Co., having located on the farm on which he died, in the spring of 1795. Vigorous in intellect, quick of perception, energetic in action, kind and courteous in intercourse with his fellow-men, he was extensively known and highly esteemed, and his memory will be embalmed in the hearts of all who knew him.

STRONG, Geo. W., Esq., Rutland, Vt., Oct. 25, æ. 40. Mr. S. was a son of the late Hon. Moses Strong, of R. He graduated at Middlebury College in 1837, and immediately thereafter commenced the study of law, to the practice of which he was subsequently admitted. His health requiring a more active employment than the duties of that profession afforded, he engaged in other pursuits.

STROPES, Lieut. Adam, Green Co., Ind., April —, æ. 68. He went through the Indian wars with Gen. Jackson, and was first lieutenant under Capt. Lovell H. Rousseau, in Mexico, and did gallant service at Buena Vista.

STUART, Hon. James, Mansfield, O., Feb. 18, æ. —, late president judge of the judicial subdivision composed of the counties of Ashland, Richland, and Morrow, which post he occupied for the term of five years.

STUART, Mrs. Eleanor, Staunton, Va., Oct. 24, æ. 90. She was the daughter of Col. Gerard Briscoe, and was born in Montgomery Co., Md., Sept. 2, 1768. Col. Gerard Briscoe, whose family were originally from St. Mary's Co., Md., removed from Montgomery Co. about the year 1777, and settled on his estate, called "Cloverdale," about three miles from Winchester. Eleanor Briscoe was married in May, 1791, to Archibald Stuart, of Staunton, and from that time to her death, more than sixty-seven years, she resided in the town of Staunton. Judge Stuart died in the year 1832, and from that time Mrs. Stuart led a quiet and retired life, devoted chiefly to reading and to kindly intercourse with a large circle of descendants and relatives. Those who were privileged to enjoy her society and friendship will all concur in the remark that she was an extraordinary woman. Her appearance was in the highest degree striking and majestic, and she retained to within a few months of her death the erect carriage and active step of middle age. Her manners, full of the dignified courtesy of the olden time, commanded respectful deference, and yet were engaging and attractive alike to old and young. During her whole life she was accustomed to the society and conversation of clever men, and she was personally acquainted with most of the distinguished men of Virginia in the early days of the republic. She retained freshly and actively that kindly and affectionate interest in all around her which had ever distinguished her. She lost none of her sympathies with the joys or sorrows of her friends and neighbors, and she continued, while life lasted, the exercise of that unobtrusive charity and benevolence for which she will long be affectionately remembered.

STUBBLEFIELD, Col. John S., Charles City Co., Va. The Charles City Co. bar "resolved, that by the death of Col. John S. Stubblefield, this community has lost one of its most estimable, deserving, and useful citizens, and his family and friends have sustained an irreparable loss."

STURDIVANT, Isaac, Esq., Exeter, N. H., æ. 75, died at the residence of his son-in-law, Mr. Joseph Drowne. He was born at Yarmouth, in that part of the town which was set off to Cumberland, March 4, 1784. In early life he took to the sea, and eventually became a ship owner, as well as ship master. He had accumulated a very large estate, both real and personal, in Portland, owning more real estate and more bank stock than any other person in Maine.

STURGES, S. S., M. D., Wellsville, Alleghany Co., N. Y., June 12, æ. 34. The death of Dr. S. is an event of no ordinary moment. He had been a resident of Wellsville six or eight years, and one of its earliest settlers, after the impulse given by the completion of the Erie Railroad. As a man he was exemplary in deportment, and remarkably correct in his habits, a most worthy citizen, and had a large number of warm personal friends. As a physician he was most useful, and highly esteemed from his uniform sympathy and kindness towards the sick and afflicted.

SUMMONS, Capt. J. Blair, Cincinnati, O., Feb. 27, æ. 65. The deceased was widely known as a pioneer boatman on the western waters. He was born near the banks of the Alleghany, in Western New York, 65 years since, and commenced his boating career on rafts, keel-boats, flat-boats, and barges, before the introduction of steam. In 1812 he assisted in conveying supplies in barges to Gen. Wayne's troops, quartered in Leughery Creek, 30 miles below this city. He was one of the pioneers and oldest commanders in the Louisville mail line, in active service, having remained in the trade since 1826, 32 years. In his career as a boatman he was very fortunate. He never met with a serious accident to any boat while in his charge. He commenced his career a poor, penniless lad, in the capacity of deck hand, and steadily progressed, filling the stations of mate and pilot, and was commander of the proudest steamer (the Jacob Strader) that floats on the western waters.

SUTHERLAND, Hon. Judge J. K., Steubenville, O., May 29, æ. 47.

SWAIM, Rev. Jeremiah R., Randolph Co., Ga., June 22, æ. 79, known as "Father Swaim." He was born in North Carolina, where he lived till he became a man and was married. He settled in Columbia Co. when he first went to Georgia. After making two or three moves he settled in Randolph Co., where he resided till his death, some 21 years. He was a plain, straightforward, zealous minister, faithful in the discharge of duty, beloved by all who knew him in the various relations of life.

SWAIN, Wm. U., New Bedford, Mass., Sept. 20, æ. —. As the proprietor of Naushon, one of the Elizabeth Islands, (formerly the property of Gov. Bowdoin, of Boston,) Mr. S. was widely known abroad for the liberal hospitality, which, during the summer months, he so long maintained at that delightful retreat, and where it was his happiness to assemble around him the great and good men who have contributed to the moral and political advancement of the state and of the nation. His memory will long be cherished by a numerous circle, to whom he was endeared by his private virtues and public benefactions. We learn that Mr. S., by his last will and testament, bequeathed several inconsiderable legacies, amounting in the aggregate to about $20,000; and the income of the residue of the property (about $57,000) to the support of the widow, and eventually to be applied to the establishment of a Female Educational Seminary, to be founded upon the homestead estate, on County Street. Hon. John H. Clifford and Lincoln F. Brigham, Esq., are the executors named in the will.

SWENEY, George, Esq., Mooresburg, Pa., Dec. 1, æ. 75. For many years Mr. S. printed the Danville Watchman, then the only newspaper issued in Columbia Co., Pa.

SWENEY, D. G., M. D., Mansfield, O., Feb. 5, æ. —.

SWIFT, Rev. Ephraim G., Buffalo, N. Y., Aug. 28, æ. 76. He was born at Williamstown, Mass., Aug. 14, 1782. His father, Rev. Seth Swift, graduated at Yale College in 1774, and was ordained pastor of the church in Williamstown in 1779, where he continued his labors until his death in 1807. His mother was Lucy Elliot, of Killingworth, descended from the same ancestry as Eliot the Indian Apostle. He graduated at Williams College, in 1804, and soon after commenced the studies for the ministry with Dr. Stephen West, of Stockbridge, with whom he was afterwards settled as colleague, and where he continued for nine years, until the dismission of Dr. West. After leaving Stockbridge he supplied several pulpits until 1833, when he was settled over the Congregational church in Killingworth. Here he continued in the most harmonious relations to an affectionate and appreciative people for nearly 20 years, until the infirmities of age compelled him to seek a release from his pastoral charge, to the universal regret of the parish and the ministerial association with which he was connected. Here his ministry was laborious and successful, as attested by several revivals of religion, some of them being seasons of deep and extensive interest, and a large proportion of the present membership of that church are the fruits of his labors. During the last six years, until a short time previous to his death, he had resided in Chester, where he was universally respected and beloved.

SWIFT, Rev. Seth F., Oswego, N. Y., Oct. 12, æ. 72, for many years pastor of the Unitarian church in Nantucket. He was born in Sandwich, Mass., Oct. 25, 1786, and graduated at Harvard College in 1807, in the same class with Hon. David Sears, the late Rev. Dr. Francis Parkman, the late Hon. James C. Merrill, of Boston, and the late Hon. John Glen King, of Salem. In the spring of 1809, Mr. S. went to Nantucket, where he taught a school for a short time. During that year the Unitarians of the island erected a church, which was dedicated in November following, and they invited Mr. S. to become pastor, which invitation he accepted, and was ordained April 27, 1810. He continued his ministerial labors with great fidelity until 1833, when his pastoral relation was dissolved, and he removed to Oswego, where he passed the remainder of his life, having relinquished the clerical profession, and engaged in other pursuits. Shortly after his removal he became blind, and remained so until his death.

SWIFT, Mrs. Sarah A., Andover, Mass., Sept. 11, æ. 75, widow of Dr. Nathaniel Swift.

T.

TABER, Azor, Albany, N. Y., Aug. 10, æ. —. Mr. T. pursued a long and honorable career at the bar, and ranked for many years among the ablest lawyers of the state, discharging the duties of a very large legal practice with a fidelity and capacity which commanded universal approbation. His chosen profession was his almost exclusive pursuit, from which he was rarely tempted to turn aside. He was senator from Albany district in 1852 and 1853. His life was that of an honest, earnest, able man, and he leaves a memory upon which rests no stain.

TAFT, Edmund Morse, A. B., Whitinsville, Mass., Oct. 25, æ. 24, a graduate at Yale College at the last commencement. During his academic and college life, he was especially faithful in his private religious duties. His instructors have uniformly borne testimony to his conscientiousness and his elevated standard of Christian action. Few, if any, were more active in the late revival at Yale; and many have reason to thank God for his pious labors in their behalf. In his sickness he frequently spoke of his classmates with the kindest feelings, and with the deepest regard for their spiritual interest, expressing the hope that they might meet an unbroken class in heaven.

TALLMAN, Andrew J., Seneca Falls, N. Y., May 21, æ. 72. He was one of the pioneers in the improvement of Western New York, long and widely known as a prominent business man.

TANNEHILL, Wilkins, Esq., near Nashville, Tenn., June 2, æ. 71. Mr. T. was well known as a journalist and literary writer. For several years he has been suffering from blindness, and of late from slight mental affliction.

TANNER, James F., M. D., Wheeling, Va., Dec. 27, æ. 62. The deceased was one of the old residents of the city, having immigrated, with his father's family, over 40 years ago, from the city of Baltimore. He was favorably known as a practising physician, and was always ready to minister relief to the poor and needy. He was well known as a decided politician, being elected last winter mayor of the city on the democratic ticket, but discharged the duties of that position with great impartiality.

TAPPAN, Mrs. Ann Maria, Boston, Mass., Dec. 31, æ. 69, wife of Charles Tappan, Esq., of Boston.

TAYLOR, Alexander II., M. D., Faribault, Wake Co., N. C., March 30, æ. 54. He was born in Yorktown, Va., and was educated chiefly by that accomplished physician and gentleman, Dr. William V. Taylor, formerly of Oxford, N. C., now of Memphis, Tenn. In society he was frank, in business transactions upright and conscientious.

TAYLOR, Asa P., Esq., Jersey City, N. J., Jan. 12, æ. 36, at the house of his brother, T. L. Taylor. Mr. T. was the son of the late Thomas S. Taylor, Esq., of Kingston, R. I. He graduated at Brown University in 1841, and after studying law in the office of Hon. Henry Nicoll, of New York city, was admitted to the bar there. He shortly after returned to Kingston, and practised law with a good prospect of success. His kindness of heart and social disposition had endeared him to a large circle of friends.

TAYLOR, Daniel, Boston, Mass., ——, æ. 60, formerly a citizen of Portsmouth, N. H. He came from Sanbornton, N. H., to Portsmouth more than 40 years ago, and some years later than his senior townsman, George W. Crockett, of Boston. After serving his minority in the grocery business, he opened a store in Market Street, and continued in that business several years, when he formed a copartnership with the late Mr. Stephen Patten in the crockery-ware business. This connection continued until Mr. Patten retired and removed to Dover. Mr. T. then formed a business connection, in the same line, with his brother-in-law, Mr. Samuel W. Waldron. They continued for several years to be extensively and successfully engaged in the importing of crockery ware in Portsmouth. About a quarter of a century ago Taylor & Waldron removed to Boston, where they continued their business to within a recent period. Mr. T. retired about four years ago. Like most of the successful business men of New England, Mr. T. was the artificer of his own fortunes. Educated in the New Hampshire schools, he early learned to depend upon himself. He carried into his business that energy, perseverance, and care which usually command success; and he was a successful and fortunate man. In his social relations he was genial and always cheerful; his attachments were strong and enduring. Mr. T. had a happy life, left a large circle of attached friends, and a stainless character.

TAYLOR, John E., Cleveland, O., Oct. 30, æ. 39. Mr. T. was well known to our business men as of the late firm of John E. Taylor & Co., lumber dealers, and occupied that position his integrity, his promptness, and his scrupulous sense of honor justly entitled him to. Mr. T. graduated with credit at Union College. He practised law in the city of Troy, and for a number of years so devoted himself to his profession, so faithfully served his clients, and so ably represented their interests before the court of New York, as to attain an eminence at the bar seldom accorded to a man of his years, and opened to human eyes a future not only of profit. but of marked distinction in his profession. Ill health forced Mr. T. to abandon the law; and he came west some eight years since, hoping an active business and change of climate would restore his health; they undoubtedly prolonged his life.

TAYLOR, Joshua, M. D., Norridgewock, Me., Dec. 5, æ. 64.

REV. N. W. TAYLOR, D. D.,

New Haven, Ct., March 10, æ. 71. He was, and had been for 36 years, Dwight professor of didactic theology in Yale College. An associate, who had long known and loved him, says, —
"Although it has been known for some days that a great and good man was passing away from the midst of us, the tidings of Dr. Taylor's death will be received with no ordinary feelings by a large part of the community. There are few, comparatively, who can remember the time when he came to live among us. To nearly the whole of our active population he has always been here, known of all as a man of preëminent abilities, justly regarded as one of the most powerful preachers of the age, sought out by the churches of his denomination as a wise counsellor in their difficulties, revered and loved by his pupils for the clearness, and depth, and solidity of his instructions. Those who knew him in private life will naturally recur to his admirable social qualities, the frankness of his disposition, the generosity of his sentiments, the largeness of his views, his extraordinary conversational powers, his perfect independence, and yet courtesy in differing from others, his richness and originality of thought, and his admirable talent of giving lightness and variety to a discussion, by passing ' from grave to gay, from lively to severe.' Those who enjoyed his friendship will dwell with deeper emotion on the warmth and constancy of his affections, the ready sympathy he extended to those around him in their trials and sufferings, and the strength they derived from his counsels and prayers. All will unite in saying, 'A great man has this day fallen among us.'

"He was born at New Milford, Ct., in the year 1786, and graduated at Yale College in 1807. After residing for about two years in the family of Dr. Dwight as his favorite amanuensis, he entered on the ministry, and was ordained pastor of the First Congregational Church in New Haven, in April, 1812. How faithfully he discharged the duties of this office can be testified by some who remain among us, and is witnessed by the veneration and love with which he was regarded by the children and the children's children of multitudes who once sat under his ministry. His preaching was marked by extraordinary clearness, force, and pungency of application. He had great confidence, under divine grace, in the power of truth. Hence he dealt with the hearts of men chiefly through their understandings; he enforced the claims of the gospel, not by mere strength of assertion, but by vivid and luminous trains of reasoning; he turned the whole at last into an appeal to conscience; and the leading characteristic of his preaching was happily described by an eminent divine of Massachusetts: 'He makes every thing appear great — God, man, time, eternity!' His ministry was eminently successful. There were, in repeated instances, powerful and long-continued revivals of religion among his people; and these seasons of extraordinary interest were conducted with so much judgment and care to avoid every kind of excess, that the whole community around saw and acknowledged that they were no mere ebullitions of excited feeling, but were marked by the peculiar presence of the converting grace of God.

"When the theological department of Yale College was founded, in the year 1822, he was appointed Dwight professor of didactic theology. But in accepting this office, he never thought for a moment of relinquishing the duties of the ministry. On the contrary, while preparing young men for the sacred office, he continued to preach in the churches of our city or neighborhood, with his accustomed fervor and success. For nearly a year (in 1825–26) he acted as the regular supply of one of the societies in Hartford, which was destitute of a pastor. As new Congregational churches have branched out from the two original societies on the Green, his counsels and aid have been called in for the furtherance of each successive enterprise.

"'Also, in the revivals of religion which have occurred in college, he was exceedingly active and useful. During the revival here in 1831, he preached to the students twice every week, besides holding a meeting for inquirers. There is a large number of ministers among our graduates, together with many in other professions, who date their conversion from interviews with him. His quick discernment of the mental condition of those who applied to him for guidance, which it is often so hard for themselves to express, was only equalled by the ready wisdom and the parental kindness with which he pointed out the path of duty, the narrow way which leadeth unto life.'

"As a teacher in theology, it was his great object to make his pupils think for themselves. It required no ordinary effort to follow him through one of his lectures. They abounded in profound principles and far-reaching views, which, to a reflecting mind, were eminently 'the seeds of thought.' A gentleman who exchanged the bar for the pulpit once remarked, that never in the severest contests of the forum had he felt such a tension of his faculties, such a bracing and invigorating effect upon his mind, as in listening to the lectures of Dr. Taylor. Nearly 700 young men have enjoyed the benefit of his instructions. They are scattered throughout the United States; and they will all testify that the great end at which he aimed, in his theological system, was 'to exalt God, to humble man, and to bring all to the cross of Christ.'

"'The central peculiarity of Dr. T.'s theological system may be described thus: He so represented the divine side and the human side of religion, as to make them harmonize — as to render theology consistent with itself and with all known truth. While he admitted that in so profound and comprehensive a subject as theology, the science of God and his government, there are mysteries, or things above and beyond our understanding, he abhorred and scouted the idea that there are in theology contradictions and absurdities — things which we see and know to be contradictory or absurd. While he maintained firmly the doctrines of human depravity, or sinfulness, and that by nature, of God's foreknowledge and forcordination of all events, of his electing grace, of the sovereignty of his Spirit, and of the perseverance of his saints, he so presented them as that they did not contradict the equally true and scriptural doctrines of human freedom and just accountability. That doctrine of human freedom, which he justly defined, not merely and only as liberty to do as we will, but also as liberty to will, power to will either way, he illustrated, and fortified, and defended, and carried through all parts of his system of morals and theology.'

"He held with his whole heart, and taught from the pulpit, and from his chair in the seminary, the fundamental articles of the evangelical faith, which gave life to the Protestant reformation, and form the substantial contents of the gospel. A symmetrical system, compact and complete, ascending from the first axiom of mental science to the topmost doctrines of revelation, he constructed. Its main outlines were sketched by him when a young man. He is the author of a theodicy — a justification of the ways of God to men. The agency of God in the existence of sin and holiness — the relation of the decrees and providence of God to human responsibility — the grand question which the New England divines have debated for a hundred years, was the theme of his discussions. Whatever difference of opinion may exist in respect to his conclusions, pertaining, as they do, to the most profound and mysterious problems which have ever engaged the human mind, — however critics may dissent from his views, extending, as they do, over so vast a range of topics, candid men will admire his ability and appreciate the integrity and devotedness of his character.

"Dr. T. loved discussion; his mind rushed to an argument like a war-horse to the battle; he rejoiced in the well-guarded statement and strenuous defence of truth; his intellectual nature exulted in the discovery of a latent inaccuracy; he had an instinctive and ineradicable confidence in the power of logic to convince; but controversy, with its personal alienations, its exasperating imputations, and its too frequent appeals to prejudice and passion, was what his soul abhorred. In the earnestness of debate he might charge an opponent with absurdity and nonsense, but it was not his wont to charge a brother with denying the faith, or to represent an unguarded statement, or an inconclusive argument, as identical with heresy.

"Dr. T. died of no specific disease. He was simply worn out by hard study. About two months ago, he was no longer able to meet his class; and from that time he daily committed to one of their number a lecture to be read and discussed at their daily meetings. He told them his course was ended; and with a quiet and child-like submission to the will of God, he resigned himself to the prospect of a speedy death. To one of his friends he remarked, 'My only hope is in the atonement of Christ; and my wish is to die with the words of the martyr Stephen on my lips, 'Lord Jesus, receive my spirit.'

"To his best earthly friend he said, 'When the time comes for me to die, I want you to be perfectly calm, and when I am called to go, I want you to let me go; and the widow's God will be your God.'"

TAYLOR, Capt. Oliver H. P., killed in Oregon in a battle with Indians, —— ——, æ. 30. He graduated at West Point, and was in the Mexican war. His service during that war was chiefly on the upper waters of the Rio Grande, where he was engaged in a series of actions, in all of which he bore himself so gallantly, and with such energy and good judgment, that he was brevetted to a captaincy by the government. At a very early period, responsible duties and commands were confided to him, and from the time he left West Point to the time of his death, he had been almost constantly employed in the Indian country. Perhaps no officer of his age was more experienced in Indian warfare. He considered the savages "more sinned against than sinning," and remarked, when he was last here, that almost every " Indian outrage" was the recoil of some real outrage inflicted on them by the whites. Capt. T., when he fell, had just completed his thirtieth year. He was a native of Newport, R. I., and a son of the late Capt. William V. Taylor, of the navy, one of the heroes of Lake Erie, and a brother of Commander Wm. R. Taylor. Full of manly vigor, of high professional and moral qualities, independent and self-relying, and abounding in the most attaching personal traits, a long and happy future seemed before him. His premature loss will be deplored by the army, and by a large circle of devoted friends. He leaves a wife and two children.

TAYLOR, Parran, M. D., Denton, Md., March 10, æ. 33.

TAYLOR, Rev. Reuben, Freedom, O., Dec. 6, æ. 81. He was ordained a minister of the gospel in Connecticut in 1810, and for 48 years preached the gospel east and west. Since his residence in the west he had been a member of the Presbytery of Cleveland. He was remarkable for his clear, consecutive views of the doctrines and practices of Christianity as constituting, together, the great system and plan of man's redemption and salvation.

TAYLOR, Dea. Samuel, Yates, N. Y., Dec. 13, æ. 77. Dea. T. was born in NewLondon, Ct., whence he removed, first to Delaware Co., then to Yates, Orleans Co., N. Y. In the war of 1812 he served as an officer in his country's defence, till honorably discharged, and subsequently he held, at various times, the highest offices within the gift of his townsmen.

TAYLOR, Rev. Timothy Alden, Slatersville, R. I., March 2, æ. 48. Mr. T. was born in the town of Hawley, Mass., Sept. 7, 1809. He was the second of four sons of Jeremiah and Martha Taylor. He graduated with honor at Amherst College in 1835. In 1838 he completed his studies at Andover Theological Seminary, and in the autumn of the same year received a "call" to Slatersville, where he was ordained Jan. 23, 1839. This was his only settlement — a pastorate of more than 19 years uninterrupted, when death ended his work, and he was called to his reward. We think it may be truly said that there appeared in him an unusual number of excellences of the Christian pastor. His standard of spiritual attainment was high. In his tastes and sympathies he was puritanic, and, where truth and duty were involved, uncompromising. He used to say that it was in the Sabbath and Bible that there was any hope of the world, and that it was in preaching Christ and living for Christ that we could be of much, if any, service here. His general type of theology was Edwardian, and eminently spiritual and practical, as his success in winning souls to Christ bears unmistakable testimony. He excelled in pastoral labor. He was a sympathizing friend, a wise counsellor, a tender shepherd, a watchful keeper and guide of a flock, over which he felt the Holy Ghost had made him overseer. He came to them in their infancy and weakness; he left them in vigor and strength, and with the Spirit of the Lord resting upon them. He acquired great influence in this region; and one secret of it was, that people believed him to be a *good* man. A sweet savor with them will ever linger around his memory. In him the various benevolent objects of the day have lost an earnest and prayerful friend. As the Spirit of God was being poured out in Uxbridge and Whitinsville, he heeded the Macedonian call for "help," and preached on Tuesday evening, just one week previous to his death, at the former place. Returning home on Wednesday, he attended two funerals, with considerable exposure. On Thursday evening he preached at Whitinsville, from Is. xlii. 8, with unusual richness and power. This was his last work. On Friday he came home sick, and, as it proved, to die. The disease, "acute pleurisy," was painful, but divine grace sustained him even unto the end. "Live for Christ!" was the message left by this dying saint to his friends. On Tuesday evening following, about 9 o'clock, he prayerfully breathed out his soul to God.

TAYLOR, Capt. Wm. V., U. S. navy, Feb. —, æ. 70. He was conspicuous in the battle of Lake Erie, in which he navigated the Lawrence, Perry's flag-ship, into and during the action. His last sea service was in command of the Ohio seventy-four on a cruise to the Pacific.

TAYLOR, Wm. C., New York city, Feb. 22, æ.—, an eminent New York merchant.

TEBBS, Mrs. Hannah, Grassland, Loudon Co., Va., Dec. 23, æ. 50, wife of Col. Samuel Tebbs.

TENNEY, David, Palmer, Mass., March 2, æ. 46. He joined Dr. Stowe's church in Boston in 1842, and subsequently the Baptist church in Three Rivers. He was an earnest Christian and useful citizen.

TENNEY, Moses, Georgetown, Mass., Jan. 18, æ. 82, father of Hon. Moses Tenney, state treasurer of Massachusetts.

TENNY, Hon. Rufus, Milford, Mich., July 15, æ. 64. He was one of the early settlers of the township of Highland, and represented Oakland Co. in the legislature of 1841. He lived and died an honest man, respected by all that knew him.

TEWKSBERRY, Mrs. S. F., Lawrence, Mass., — —, æ. 57, wife of Dr. Isaac Tewksberry.

THACHER, Mrs. Elizabeth Day, New Haven, Ct., May 18, æ. 37, wife of Prof. Thomas A. Thacher, and daughter of Rev. President Day.

THATCHER, Hon. George M., Boston,

Mass., — —, æ. —, a distinguished merchant. He had held various offices. Several years ago he received the appointment of Danish consul for the States of Massachusetts, Maine, New Hampshire, and Rhode Island, residing in Boston; and subsequently the honor of knighthood was conferred upon him by the King of Denmark.

THAXTER, Adam Wallace, Boston, Mass., Dec. 15, æ. 79. He was a native of Hingham, and in his culture and fortune was a self-made man, and indebted to his own efforts for his social position. When quite young he went to Machias, Me., and worked in a tanyard five years. He then came to Boston, and served a seven years' apprenticeship as a house carpenter. He next went into copartnership with Elijah Loring, afterwards a well-known merchant on Long Wharf. In Nov., 1803, he was appointed inspector in the custom house, and held the office until 1810, when he was appointed deputy marshal, in which station he served until 1817, when he was made a marker and prover. That office was filled by him twelve years. In 1829 he was removed therefrom by a change in the reigning political power, as he was a national republican. He next kept a wood wharf two years, and then travelled two years, visiting Europe twice during that period. In 1836 the Mechanics' Mutual Fire Insurance Company in Boston was incorporated, and he was unanimously chosen its president, which office he retained till 1855, when he retired from business. He always had a great affection for his birthplace, and some years since gave the town of Hingham a large and valuable tract of land as a cemetery. Those who have seen this beautiful rural spot will recall it as inferior in size alone to Mount Auburn or Greenwood. He was a devout, liberal Christian, whose influence and example may well be emulated by the young who knew him. His long, eventful, and useful life, his pleasant and serene old age, the respect and esteem which his probity secured, are surely worthy to be remembered.

THAYER, Miss Charlotte, Dorchester, Mass., Feb. 5, æ. 79. She was a daughter of the late Arodi Thayer, Esq., (born Feb. 19, 1743, died May 5, 1831,) marshal of the Admiralty Court, Boston, under His Majesty George III., at the time of the American revolution. It will be remembered that Mr. Thayer, in virtue of said office, arrested John Hancock, owner of the sloop Liberty, Nov. 3, 1768. His commission and badge of office are in the keeping of the Dorchester Antiquarian and Historical Society. According to Thayer's Family Memorial, Arodi was the son of Gideon, the son of Richard, who was great-grandson of Richard, of Boston, the first of the name in New England.

THAYER, Ebenezer Francis, Avignon, France, ———, æ. 20. He was the grandson of Ebenezer Francis, Esq., of Boston, and the last survivor of the family of the late John E. Thayer by his first marriage. He was a young man of amiable qualities and unblemished character. He was a member of the Sophomore class of Harvard College, and had gone abroad in good health to travel during the summer term and vacation. The prospects of this young man for a useful and valuable life were in the highest degree favorable. From his father he inherited great wealth; and in the natural course of events he would in no long time have been heir to a still larger fortune. He left Paris for Avignon, in the south of France, 380 miles from Paris, only two days before his death; and a telegraphic despatch to Paris announced his sudden death almost immediately upon his arrival at Avignon.

THAYER, Nathaniel, East Kingston, N. H., June 4, æ. 75, eldest son of the late Rev. Dr. Elihu Thayer, formerly pastor of the Congregational church and society in Kingston.

THOM, Samuel, Esq., Conway, N. H., ———, æ. 54. He was one of the most successful business men in all that section of New Hampshire.

THOMAS, Gabriel D., M. D., Altoona, Blair Co., Pa., Oct. 26, æ. 42.

THOMAS, George, Washington, D. C., Sept. 29, æ. 67. Mr. T. was a citizen of Washington for upwards of 40 years, part of which time he was cashier of the Bank of the Metropolis.

THOMAS, John Pegre, M. D., Fairfield District, S. C., Jan. 1, æ. 59.

THOMAS, Gen. J. Addison, Paris, France, April —, æ. —. During the latter part of Mr. Pierce's administration Gen. T. filled the post of assistant secretary of state with great credit to himself and usefulness to the country. He had been previously appointed by President Pierce attorney on the part of the United States to the commission which had been created by treaty for the settlement of claims between the United States and Great Britain. The arduous, responsible duties growing out of this important position were discharged with distinguished ability and eminent success. He remained but a short time in the state department after Mr. Buchanan's inauguration. He resigned for the purpose of revisiting the shores of the old world, both to recuperate his health and to educate his children.

THOMAS, Seth, Plymouth Hollow, Ct., Jan. 29, æ. 75. Mr. T. was one of the earliest manufacturers of clocks in Connecticut. He had amassed a fortune, but was always accustomed to employ himself at the work bench.

THOMPSON, Benoni, Esq., Buffalo, N. Y., Nov. —, æ. —. He came to Buffalo about 1837, and engaged in the practice of the law. He held various offices of honor and trust, among them those of Member of Assembly and of Canal collector. In all of these, as well as in his daily walk of like, he maintained an enviable reputation for scrupulous integrity.

THOMPSON, David, M. D., Fall Creek, Tenn., March 18, æ. —.

THOMPSON, Eli, Waterbury, Conn., May —, æ. 81. He was formerly postmaster of the town, a man of influence in town affairs, and a prominent member of the Congregational church.

THOMPSON, Mrs. Mary, Middlesex Co., Pa., Oct. 23, æ. 87. The family emigrated to Butler Co. in 1797. She was the mother of the Hon. James Thompson, a member of the Supreme Court of Pennsylvania.

THOMPSON, Moses, Middleboro', Mass., Dec. 2, æ. 96. Mr. T. was born in Halifax, Mass., July 1, 1762, and was the last great-grandchild of Lieut. John Thompson, who was born in Wales in 1616, and arrived at Plymouth in the third ship, May 1, 1622, being then in the sixth year of his age, and of the first family of the name of Thompson that came to this country. He enlisted in the army as a soldier in 1778, and served his country nearly two years in the war of the revolution. He was married July 20, 1782, to Abigail Sampson, daughter of Capt. Thomas Sampson, of Plympton. In 1803 he removed to Middleboro', and lived in the same house and upon the same farm which he then bought till his death. He lived with his wife 75 years and 1 day, she dying July 21, 1857, æ. 91. No death occurred in any house where they lived after their marriage until two months before her death. He was the oldest man and the last revolutionary soldier of the town at the time of his death. He was known and respected as an upright man.

THOMPSON, Robert, Esq., Philadelphia, Pa., Oct. 19, æ. —, of the late firm of W. R. Thompson & Co., for over 40 years one of the most extensive wholesale houses of Philadelphia. Mr. T. was a man of the highest sense of honor and sterling integrity; a good Christian, both in feeling and action; and one of the few who are now passing away who gave tone and character to the circle to which he belonged.

THOMPSON, Samuel M., Esq., Augusta, Ga., Nov. 8, æ. 50. He had been connected with the press of Georgia 25 years — a longer period, with perhaps one or two exceptions, than any among the editorial corps of the state, and for the accuracy of his commercial reports, and general efficiency as a writer and journalist, had acquired a reputation seldom attained in his profession. In his relations with the fraternity, as well as in private life, those higher qualities of fidelity, generosity, and kindness were always observable. He ever sought to avoid offence, and to promote the interest and happiness of those around him.

THORNBURG, C. Bayly, Hickman, Ky., July 10, æ. —. He was editor and proprietor of the Hickman Argus.

THORNDIKE, Hon. A., Beverly, Mass., May 14, æ. 56. In the death of Mr. T. the people of Beverly and of Essex Co. experienced a serious loss. In former years he represented his town in the House of Representatives, and his county in the Senate. He was president of the Beverly Bank, and for a number of years a director and president of the Eastern Railroad; he was a deacon of Rev. Mr. Thayer's church, and superintendent of the Sabbath school for many years. Emphatically a good and useful man, his death will be sincerely regretted, not only by his immediate neighbors, but by many in the state.

THORNDIKE, Augustus, Boston, Mass.,
July 8, æ. 61. He was the son of Hon. Israel and Anna (Dodge) Thorndike, and was born in Beverly, Mass., July 8, 1797. His father was a man of great ability and energy. It has been justly remarked that "few individuals, endowed with such mental powers, appear in a generation; and when their influence is united, as was his, with high moral powers, and exerted during a long life on the side of virtue, and in promoting the best interests of society, it is enduring, and serves to give a character to the age in which they live." Mr. T. graduated at Harvard in 1816, and gave the college $20,000. After leaving college he went to Gottingen, and there took up his residence in company with Mr. Joseph G. Coggswell, (H. U. 1806.) After remaining a considerable time at Gottingen, he, with Mr. Coggswell, made an extensive tour, and visited various parts of Europe. In due time he returned to the United States. He married, about the year 1824, Henrietta Steuart, daughter of Dr. James Steuart, formerly of Annapolis, Md., and afterwards of Baltimore. The children of this marriage are four, two sons and two daughters. Their names are Rebecca, (now the wife of Lieut. H. C. Marin, of the navy,) James Steuart, Charles, and Henrietta Augusta. James Steuart graduated at Harvard College, 1848, and Charles in 1854. Mr. T. possessed much intellectual power and vigor. His mind was highly cultivated. He was a good classical scholar. He was a great reader of ancient and modern history. He had visited the most interesting portions of Europe. He had seen much, and had an excellent opportunity to make discriminating observations upon men and manners. He possessed a large fund of accurate information in relation to European society, and was familiar with its prevailing manners, customs, and usages. He possessed colloquial powers of a high order, and could make his conversation exceedingly pleasant and interesting. His bearing was that of a gentleman. His manners indicated good breeding, and a perfect knowledge of the forms and civilities belonging to the best society. In his opinions and feelings he was always conservative. He was early taught to respect and venerate the principles of Theophilus Parsons, Nathan Dane, Geo. Cabot, and other Essex statesmen. He was, during the greater part of his life,

on terms of intimacy and friendship with many distinguished noblemen in England and Scotland.

THORNTON, Samuel, M. D., Moorestown, Burlington Co., N. J., March 19, æ. 60. He was the son of Joseph and Mary Thornton, and was born Jan. 14, 1791, near Newtown, Bucks Co., Pa. He studied medicine under Dr. John Wilson, a noted practitioner of Bucks Co., and graduated at the University of Pennsylvania, in the year 1816. He removed from Pennsylvania to Moorestown, Sept., 1818, and devoted more than 40 years to an extensive and laborious country practice. During the whole of this period, to all classes of his patients he was equally a sincere friend and beloved physician. In his family he was a true husband and father.

THORP, Elder Jacob, Chicago, Ill., Oct. 26, æ. 82. About the year 1800, he removed to the State of Ohio, where, for more than half a century, in various portions of the state, he successfully labored to build up the kingdom of Christ.

THRASHER, Martin E., M. D., Fort Wayne, Ind., Nov. 1, æ. 25, youngest son of the late Ephraim Thrasher, Esq., of Weathersfield. Dr. Thrasher had been in the practice of his profession the last year in New York, and was absent from the city on business at the time of his death. He assisted the professor of anatomy, as demonstrator, during the last term of lectures in the Medical College of New York, and was spoken of in high commendation. From early life he had sustained an unblemished reputation.

THURBER, Reuben, Seekonk, Mass., Nov. 25, æ. 89. He was the son of Leonard, the son of John, the son of James, the son of John, who came to this country in 1671, and settled at New Meadow Neck, then in Rehoboth.

TICKNOR, Benajah, M. D., surgeon in the U. S. navy, Ann Arbor, Mich., Sept. 20, æ. 72. Dr. T. was a native of Vermont, but his family early removed to Salisbury, Mich. In 1814, he was commissioned assistant surgeon in the U. S. navy, and in 1824 as surgeon, which appointment he held to his death. During this period he was employed about 15 years at sea, mostly in large cruisers, as surgeon and assistant surgeon. Thus he saw more important and varied scenes than almost any person now living. He was also stationed about 10 years at the navy yards at Brooklyn and Charlestown, and other places of rendezvous. He received from Yale College, several years since, the honorary degree of M. D., and was also elected honorary member of the American Medical Society, and received several honorary notices from other sources. He was emphatically a self-made man, who, deprived of the advantages of instruction in a common school, attained an eminence in scholarship and varied learning, which gave him a rank among the most learned men of the age. He read the modern languages with fluency, and Hebrew, Greek, and Latin as his daily exercises. As a writer he possessed much merit, and contributed many able papers on various topics. His observations on the treatment of diseases in tropical climates, with cases which came under his observation, were eagerly sought after by the medical journals, and well received by the profession. In his intercourse with the world he was modest and unassuming, dignified and manly in his bearing, faithful in his friendship, and withal a consistent Christian, ardently devoted to the worship and ritual of the Episcopal church. His liberal salary, and prudent management of his pecuniary affairs, enabled him to make large donations to the active and useful benevolent objects of the day, the notice of which was seldom published in his name, as he made it a principle not to "let his left hand know what his right hand did."

TILLINGHAST, Mrs. Amelia M., Boston, Mass., March 13, æ. 24.

TILLINGHAST, Geo. H., Providence, R. I., Aug. 28, æ. 63. He graduated at Brown University, class of 1814.

TILLOTSON, Hon. Ira, Bellevieu, Eaton Co., Mich., April 10, æ. 77.

TILTON, Mrs. Abigail S. F., Sanbornton, N. H., June 3, æ. 38. She was the wife of Jer. D. Tilton, Esq.

TINKHAM, John Worthington, Esq., New Orleans, La., April 28, æ. 25. He was an only son of Mr. Franklin Tinkham, of Portland, Me., and a graduate of Bowdoin College (1855). He studied law, and opened an office in Chicago, Ill., in 1857. He was soon prostrated by a fever, and sought a milder climate as means of restoration, but passed rapidly away in consumption. He was a young man of high promise, fine talents, and noble principles.

TITUS, John, Moriah, N. Y., March 4,

æ. 96. He was born in Rehoboth, Mass., in 1761, where he lived until he was about 16 years old, when he entered the American army, and engaged in the contest for freedom. During the war of the revolution, he was out in various campaigns, and fought under various distinguished generals, sharing largely in the toils and sufferings of those who bled in freedom's cause. He was at Horseneck, the scene of Putnam's daring exploit; at West Point, where the treacherous Arnold sold his country for British gold. When Royalton was burned, he occupied a post of danger near that exciting scene. In the war of 1812 he again took the field, being then 50 years old. After being in various engagements with the British and Indians, while with the army stationed in Northern New York, he was wounded in an engagement with the enemy near Ogdensburg, on account of which he has since drawn a pension. Soon after receiving this wound, his oldest son was killed at the battle of Chippewa. At the last presidential election, Mr. T. went to the polls, and after depositing his vote, remarked, that he voted for George Washington, the first president of the United States, and had voted at every presidential election since.

TOBEY, Rev. Zalmon, Canaan, Ct., Sept. 17, æ. 66, while on a visit to his friends. He graduated at Brown University, in 1817. He was a Baptist clergyman, and was settled first in Bristol, afterwards in Providence and in Pawtuxet, and during the later years of his life resided in Warren. Though never an eminent preacher, he was a good scholar, and a useful and estimable man.

TODD, Patrick, M. D., Laurensville, S. C., Aug. 5, æ. 26. A graduate of the Medical College at Augusta, Ga.

TODD, Samuel P., Brooklyn, N. Y., May 10, æ. —, purser in the U. S. navy.

TOMLINSON, Rev. Thomas, Southport, Chemung Co., N. Y., Sept. 15, æ. 53. He was born in Cheshire, Eng., Nov. 17, 1805, and had been a preacher of the gospel for 40 years. He was ordained to the Christian ministry by the Rochester conference of the Wesleyan Methodist Connection, in 1845, and filled with acceptance several appointments in that and the New York conference.

TOMPKINS, Hon. Christopher, Glasgow, Ky., Sept. 9, æ. 78. At an early age he entered the office and the family of the late John Breckinridge, which he only left when ready to begin the practice of law. Passing through such hands for eight or ten years, it is not strange that he came out a good lawyer. His success at the bar was answerable to his natural adaptation to that great profession, and to his honest labor in preparation for its work. Not many years of practice brought him to the bench, on which he took his seat by appointment of the governor, in 1811, at the age of about 30, where he sat with much credit to himself, and equal advantage to the people, for more than a dozen years, and whence he retired at the earnest call of his friends, who desired to elevate him to the chief magistracy of the state. He became the candidate of the Old Court party of that day, but failed of his election, the majority of the people just then favoring the other party. It is hazarding nothing, however, to add, that, although he was not in office, the weight of his character, and the influence of his opinions, helped to change the public sentiment, and to bring his side into power. A few years more saw him in the Congress of the United States, to which he was twice chosen over strong competitors. He served the country in this capacity with the same signal ability and incorruptible fidelity which had already gained him his high position. He then returned to the bench by appointment of Governor ——, and held the office for ten years or more, filling it with rare distinction, as before. He retired from it on account of failing health, having nearly reached his seventieth year. He had fairly won the right, by his long and faithful public service, to become a private citizen. In early life he had cultivated, with much success, his thirst for general knowledge and a true love of letters. These followed him to the end, and made him an uncommonly accomplished and well-read scholar, especially in the more elegant literature of history and the English classics. And when he finally withdrew from public life, — out of choice, and not from necessity, — it was to enjoy the society of his children that remained to him, of his friends, and his books, with no longing for higher distinction than he had easily attained, and no grasping after a larger estate than his ample competency. His retirement was the simple and real *otium cum dignitate* of the scholar and gentleman. He was a true lover of his country, and an honest public servant. He received the trusts that were committed to him, and fulfilled them well, out of a desire to promote the general good, and for no sordid or selfish ends. He was a lover of good men, and himself a pattern of the best virtues. While in the private station, and especially among his intimate friends, and in the circle of his family, as a husband, a father, and a master, the noble simplicity of his manners, and the chaste purity of his character, shone with peculiar beauty. These things made him one of the first citizens of the commonwealth while he lived, and now that he is dead, they gather upon his name the homage of the people.

TONEY, Robert P., M. D., Franklin Co., N. C., Dec. 21, æ. 30. The deceased was a native of Powhatan Co., Va., and went to North Carolina in his 15th year. After going to school a while, he acted in the capacity of clerk in a store for two or three years, when he commenced the study of medicine, and graduated in Richmond in the spring of 1851. He soon after entered upon the practice of his profession, and was not long in establishing a reputation as a physician; for he was diligent in his efforts to extend his medical knowledge, industrious and punctual in his attentions to the sick, and skilful and sympathizing in his management of the many ills of suffering humanity.

TOOMER, Henry V., M. D., Charleston, S. C., Nov. 2, æ. 45. The epidemic of the present season severely taxed his energies. With kindness to the distressed, ay, with injustice to himself, he tried to mitigate the pains of others. Whilst thus usefully employed, disease attacked him, and although science did her utmost, her efforts were futile.

TOULMIN, Mrs. Martha, near Mobile, Ala., Aug. 26, æ. 87. In recording the death of this venerable lady, what a flock of events crowd the mind! Her life was a history. She came to the United States from England, her native place, in the latter part of the last century; her family were republicans — hence their removal here. After a few years' residence in Kentucky, she was married to Judge Toulmin. Her life was passed in doing good. She came to this portion of the country at the beginning of the last war with England. She made her home to blossom in the wilderness. It was from her hand many a poor soldier received relief. It was to her house the traveller would seek for safety; and to her and her distinguished husband did the noble and gallant officers of our army owe a welcome that softened the hard and stern realities of their duties on this outpost. Mrs. Toulmin lived and died a Unitarian, the faith of her fathers, the faith of her husband; but she loved all who were Christians, and all alike loved her. The whole bearings of her life presented the broad view of love. With a clear intellect and self-governing spirit, she caught at a glimpse the duty of life, and she fulfilled that duty.

TOWLE, Gen. Joseph, Epping, N. H., Sept. 9, æ. 69. Gen. Towle was one of the prominent men of Rockingham Co. In the war of 1812 he commanded for six months a company stationed for the defence of Portsmouth. He subsequently, and when the position was one of distinction, became major general of his division of N. H. militia. Later in life he filled for five years the office of high sheriff of Rockingham Co. He was a faithful and efficient public officer, and an honorable, benevolent, and upright man.

TOWNSEND, Elisha, M. D., Philadelphia, Pa., Oct. 13, æ. —.

TOWNSEND, Larman, Waterbury, Ct., May —, æ. —. Though a native of New Haven, he removed at an early age to Middlebury, where he engaged in mercantile pursuits, in which he continued either alone or in connection with one of his sons for upwards of 40 years. On the organization of the town in 1807, he was chosen town clerk and town treasurer, to which office he was annually reëlected for 39 years, till his resignation in 1846. He was postmaster for upwards of 20 years, was for several years a justice of the peace, had represented the town in the state legislature, and filled various minor offices of responsibility and trust, which were unsought, and accepted at the earnest solicitation of his fellow-citizens. More than all that, he was a sincere and devoted Christian, a communicant, and often a lay reader in the Episcopal church.

TOWNSEND, Capt. Solomon, Providence, R. I., Nov. 18, æ. 79. He was born in Providence, and at an early age embraced the nautical profession; endured all the hardships, privations, &c.,

incident thereto, in those times more severe than in these latter days; rose gradually, in regular promotion, to a post of honor, and while yet a young man reached the highest, in the course he had chosen, not only as commander, but commercial agent of his employers. He continued a sea-faring life for a period of about 30 years; never lost a vessel, except by capture, the first part of the war with England, 1812–14; he was then on his passage from the East Indies to the United States, and was considered the richest prize to the British during that war; was carried to Rio Janerio, and when a vessel was procured by the American minister at that court, for a cartel, he was appointed commander, and came home, with 60 other Americans, prisoners of war, who had been brought to Rio. After leaving the sea service he engaged with a brother in manufacturing, but found his chief pleasure in his garden and his home. He was an affectionate husband, good father, kind neighbor. He possessed a cheerful disposition; had great conversational powers; read a great deal, and remembered what he read; moved in society of his friends to recount the many interesting and amusing incidents and anecdotes of his past, and particularly early life; was benevolent, charitable, and universally esteemed at home and abroad. He married Amelia Sandford, (daughter of John Hubbard, of Newport, R. I.,) March 4, 1812, and leaves 3 children, 16 grandchildren, and 2 great grandchildren.

TOWSLEY, Eli, M. D., Lowville, Lewis Co., N. Y., March 15, æ. 63. He was born in Sharon, Ct., studied medicine and took his degree. After practising in Trenton, N. Y., and in Jefferson Co., he removed to Lowville, and spent 20 years in the practice of his profession, making more than 40 years of professional life. He was unwearied, faithful, and skilful; kind to the poor; social and religious.

TRASK, Charles G., M. D., Amite Co., Miss., April 13, æ. 45. Dr. T. was born at Windsor, Vt.; graduated in medicine, at Cincinnati, in the year 1837, and removed shortly after to Miss., where, until within a few years of his death, he continued the laborious practice of his profession. He was highly esteemed, not only for his skill as a physician, but equally as much also for his tender solicitude and sympathizing manner at the bedside of the sick and suffering. His patients loved him, because he seemed to participate, as it were, in the pains and griefs which it was his business to soothe and relieve.

TRASK, Charles B., Springfield, Mass., June 30, æ. 28, eldest son of Lieutenant Governor Trask. He was a young man of general accomplishments, public spirit, and pure character, much beloved, and respected by all who knew him. He was a member of the city council of S.

TRAVIS, Rev. Joseph, Memphis, Tenn., Sept. 16, æ. 72. This venerable man of God, and father in Israel, was a superannuated member of the Memphis Annual Conference. His useful life and abundant labors in the ministry are known and read of by hundreds and thousands, both north and south. He is embalmed in the hearts and memories of thousands on earth, and his record, for more than half a century, has been, from year to year, going up to Heaven in the character of the saved, who will to all eternity acknowledge him as the honored instrument of their salvation.

TREADWELL, Mrs. Dorothy, Salem, Mass., Jan. —, æ. —, widow of the late Dr. J. G. Treadwell. She left, among other bequests, one to the Barton Square Church of $4000.

TREMBLY, Daniel, Valparaiso, Chili, Jan. 5, æ. 45, a member of the Brooklyn bar.

TREMLETT, Thomas, Dorchester, Mass., Sept. 13, æ. 62. In recording the death of Mr. Thomas Tremlett, it is fit that something more than a passing notice should be given to his memory. Mr. Tremlett was born in St. John's, Newfoundland, where his early youth was passed. He removed to Boston in 1821, and there established himself as a merchant. He soon acquired the confidence of those with whom he had dealings by his strict honesty and his mild and courteous deportment. In social life he was beloved for his genial manners, his friendly sympathy, and his manly virtues. Mr. Tremlett was a religious man in the largest sense of the word; for he practised all the Christian virtues. He was singularly quiet and unostentatious in all his intercourse with men; but his hand was ever open to relieve the wants of the poor; and he was always active in co-operating with others in every thing which tended to promote the best interests of society. Mr. Tremlett was not only a good merchant, but he was a good citizen. He was instinctively gentle, and had therefore nothing to learn to qualify him for the highest social position in life. He was fond of rural pursuits, and when he removed to Dorchester in 1828, where he resided until his decease, he had ample scope to indulge his favorite tastes. He was a true lover of nature; he loved the trees which he planted, the flowers and shrubs which adorned his grounds, and the very birds which sang among their branches. Those who recollect him as he passed along his favorite walks on a spring or summer morning, will sigh to think that his manly and familiar form has passed away forever. Mr. Tremlett was an affectionate husband and a kind and indulgent father. His loss will be severely felt by them; and while we may not enter the sacred precincts of home to speak of his many virtues there, — how well he loved, and how much he was beloved, — we may be permitted to sympathize with his afflicted family, and earnestly to commend them to the care and blessing of Him who is the Father of the fatherless and the widow's God.

TRINCHARD, John B., Esq., Mobile, Ala., Nov. —, æ. —, commercial editor of the Mobile Register.

TRIPP, J. L., M. D., Shallotte, N. C., April 8, æ. 29, formerly of York Co., Me.

TROWBRIDGE, Mrs. Anna, Newton Corner, Mass., May 28, æ. 76, widow of Col. Wm. Trowbridge.

TROWBRIDGE, Capt. John T., near Racine, Wis., April 3, æ. 77.

TRUNDY, Meshach B., Esq., Portsmouth, N. H., Sept. 30, æ. 71, for many years a noted merchant of Portsmouth.

TUCK, Mrs. Margaretta, Chelmsford, Mass., Jan. 19, æ. 75.

TUCKER, Rev. Anson, Monmouth, Ill., ———, æ. —, a former citizen of Coldwater, Mich.

TUCKER, Mrs. C. C., Memphis, Tenn., May 17, æ. 42, daughter of the late Col. James Trezevant, and widow of Dr. W. W. Tucker.

TUCKER, Hon. John A., Dawson, Terrell Co., Ga., ———, æ. —, a state senator from Stewart Co.

TUCKER, Stephen, Boston, Mass., Dec. 31, æ. 57, a native of Plaistow, N. H.

Mr. Tucker was an intelligent, practical man, and took an active interest in municipal affairs, and justly enjoyed the respect and confidence of his fellow-citizens in ward 11. He was often called upon to serve in strictly ward offices, and for a long time was a member of the primary school board under the old organization. He was a member of the common council during the years 1846, '47, and '48, and subsequently, for five years, was superintendent of public lands. He was afterwards employed by the board of land commissioners to oversee the filling up of the new lands east of Harrison Avenue, so as to secure a faithful observance of the contract. In all the public trusts conferred upon him, he proved a watchful and judicious guardian of the interests of the city, while he at all times, in his official action, respected the legal and equitable rights of individuals. By his immediate neighbors he was regarded as a just, substantial, and kindly man, whose large information on local matters and sound judgment were always at their service and could be confidently relied on.

TUCKERMAN, John, Portsmouth, N. H., Aug. 23, æ. 75.

TUKEY, Wm., Portland, Me., Mar. —, æ. 93. He was born in Portland, Dec. 2, 1765, and was the oldest native resident in that city. He was the son of John Tukey, who had fourteen children, of whom the deceased was the tenth. He was in service in Portland in the revolutionary war, and was intimate with Talleyrand when he made his visit to that city. Mr. T. was a mason by trade, and built the first brick house erected in Portland, that on Congress Street, owned by the late Stephen Longfellow, Esq. He was a man of high moral worth, and much respected.

TULLOCK, John L., Princetown, N. Y., June 24, æ. —, postmaster of the town.

TUNNICLIFF, John W., Richfield Springs, N. Y., May 6, æ. 74. He was born in Columbia Co., N. Y., in the year 1784, when the Mohawk valley teemed with the aborigines. His grandfather came over from England before the revolution, and in John's early childhood the family settled in Richfield, in Otsego County. He would point with humor and with pride to a certain spot where the house of his father stood at the close of the last century — a house the door of which was so low as to make it necessary to assume a quadruped form in order to enter it. In that cabin a considerable family rejoiced in plenty and in independence. The country was slowly and painfully cleared; until, for many years before Mr. T.'s death, Richfield had become known as a highly cultivated and most lovely section of country. Indeed, for some years Mr. T. would entertain those who came from cities in quest of health and pleasure with the rich stores of his memory, crowded as it was with incidents in the more memorable passages of the nation's history, and would dwell upon the stricter attention, in earlier days, of heads of families to religious observances. He was a man of genial temper. He always met his friends with a smile, and had vivacity enough to make his society delightful to the young. He lived and died in the communion of the Protestant Episcopal church.

TURMAN, Hon. Judge S., Tampa, Fla., Oct. 31, æ. 60. He was a native of Ohio, but went to Indiana when twelve years of age, his father being one of the pioneers who settled in the wilderness in 1811, and who gave name to a fort, prairie, creek, and township in Sullivan Co. Judge Turman removed thirty years ago, and settled in Florida in 1843. Twenty years ago he was a member of the Indiana Senate. At the time of his death he was probate judge of Hillsboro' Co., Fla., which office he had held for thirteen years. He was in an eminent degree a kind-hearted man. While the yellow fever was raging in Tampa, and others left, he remained to take care of the sick, and died in the good work. He was a Christian.

TURNBULL, Col. William, Wilmington, Del., Jan. —, æ. —, of the corps of topographical engineers. He was chief of his corps under Gen. Scott, in Mexico, in 1848, and was twice brevetted for gallant and meritorious conduct — first in the battle of Contreras and Cherubusco, and secondly in the battle of Chepultepec. Col. T. was a graduate of West Point, and at the time of his lamented decease had been in the military service 40 years.

TURNER, Caleb B., North Adams, Mass., Dec. 19, æ. 69. He was formerly an extensive manufacturer in South Adams, having operated the first power loom and printed the first calico in the county. He built the Gould Mill and the Union Print Works, and was the first president of the Adams Bank, from its incorporation in 1832 until 1837. For the last two years he has lived retired from business. Mr. T. was an excellent man in domestic life, a popular employer, and a sympathizing and generous friend to the unfortunate.

TURNER, John R., Portsmouth, O., Oct. 15, æ. 71. He was born in Virginia, 1787; and from 1810 to 1855 he held the office of clerk of the Court of Common Pleas of Scioto Co. Perhaps no other man in the state could exhibit so long an incumbency of that or any other station. In 1855 he was elected mayor of Portsmouth, and served two years.

TURNER, William, M. D., New York city, March —, æ. —. Dr. T. was well known as the son of the late venerable John Turner, formerly one of the proprietors and editors of the New York Gazette. Some years ago Dr. T. was the health officer of this city. He adopted the chrono-thermal theory of medicine advanced by Dr. Dickson, of London, and was quite enthusiastic in his belief of its truth. He published a work on the subject which had an extensive sale and diffused a knowledge of his mode of practice; but the medical profession generally rejected it. As a man Dr. T. had many estimable qualities; and he leaves a large circle of friends, who will sincerely mourn his death. He was an active member of the old whig party, and was a long time a prominent member of the general committee.

TURNER, Capt. William, Warren, R. I., Feb. 21, æ. 90, father of Lieut. Gov. Turner, of Rhode Island.

TUTTLE, Niles A., Paris, France, Oct. 25, æ. —, a citizen of Hartford, Ct. He bequeathed $1000 each to the Domestic and Foreign Missionary Society of the Episcopal Church and the Hartford Hospital, and $500 each to the Retreat for the Insane and to Trinity College at Hartford.

TUTTLE, Norman, Troy, N. Y., ——, æ. 72, an old printer, who formerly worked on the Albany Argus, in 1820, when that paper was under the management of Jesse Buel. He was one of the oldest publishers in the country. Among the newspapers published by him alone, or in connection with others, were two Dailies — the Sentinel, started in 1826, and Mail, started in 1837. He was an excellent job printer in his day; and his taste, accuracy, and promptness in the despatch of business enabled him for many years to keep down competition. He had been a member of St. Paul's Church for 50 years.

TUXBURY, Dea. Moses M., Lowell, Mass., Dec. 8, æ. 70. Mr. T. came early from Amesbury, Mass., to Lowell, and contributed conservative influence in establishing all the institutions of the city. He had been for many years a member of a Baptist church.

REV. BENNETT TYLER, D. D., East Windsor Hill, Ct., May 14, æ. 75. Dr. T. was born at Middlebury, then a part of Woodbury, Ct., July 6, 1783. He graduated at Yale College in 1804, and, having studied theology under the instruction of Rev. Asahel Hooker, was licensed to preach in 1806, and was ordained in June, 1808, over the church in South Britain, Ct. During the 14 years of his pastorate the utmost harmony subsisted between him and his people; and repeated revivals, preceded by thorough discipline and the earnest inculcation of the distinctive truths of the gospel, largely increased the permanent strength and fruitfulness of the church. In 1822 he was chosen president of Dartmouth College. The urbanity and unaffected dignity of his manners, his energy and decision, his practical wisdom and warm piety, qualified him in no common degree for such a post. During the six years of his connection with the college its funds were considerably increased, and a large number of its pupils became the subjects of a sound and saving conversion, and are now laboring in the service of the great Master. Although his relations to the trustees, faculty, and students are believed to have been marked by great cordiality, such was his yearning for the work of a parish minister that he yielded to an overture from the Second Church in Portland, and became the successor of Dr. Payson in Sept., 1828. In that large and intelligent congregation all his gifts and acquisitions found delightful employment. A united and affectionate people continued to testify their confidence and esteem, and to many of them his preaching was a savor of life unto life.

Shortly after it was decided to establish a theological seminary at East Windsor Hill, the trustees appointed Dr. T. president, and professor of didactic theology. His happy relations at Portland, his aversion to controversy, and the trials attending the new enterprise, strongly dissuaded him from accepting the office. The question was not hastily determined. Holding his personal interests in subordination to the will of Christ, and seeking counsel of such men as Drs. Griffin, Humphrey, Porter, Woods, and Gov. J. C. Smith, of Connecticut, it appeared plain to him, at length, that the sacrifices involved in the establishment of the Theological Institute were demanded by loyalty to Him who came into the world to bear witness to the truth. He accordingly accepted the appointment, and was inducted into office May 13, 1834.

It was no party or sectarian zeal that urged Dr. T. into connection with the Theological Institute. Its creed embodies the doctrines set forth in the Westminster Confession and Assembly's Catechism, and taught in the private theological schools of Backus, Hooker, and Dwight 50 years ago. Perhaps the time has not yet come for a dispassionate history of the discussions in which the subject of this sketch bore a part; but it cannot be unseasonable, in this brief memorial, to record his solemn conviction that, unless decided measures were taken to stem the rising flood of error, he would be held in a measure responsible for imperilled truth and spurious revivals. With what clearness and force he taught the system of truth with which the religious prosperity of New England has long been identified successive classes of grateful pupils can attest.

In the community best acquainted with his daily life the name of Bennett Tyler will always be associated with integrity, benevolence, unaffected humility, and benignant cheerfulness. Very seldom was he known to offend in word. One whose personal and official relations to him had been most intimate could not forbear saying at his obsequies that during the last 24 years he never heard from his lips an expression of resentment or unkindness, although he had been with him when pierced by the "sharp arrows of the mighty." His

28 *

genial smile and instructive conversation, mingled with well-timed pleasantry, made him a favorite with young and old in the social circle.

On the occasion of resigning his office, July 15, 1857, he delivered an address to the alumni of the Institute, fraught with such reminiscences and counsels, and pronounced with such pathos and self-possession, as rendered it a fitting close of his public career.

When dying he was asked if it was a pleasant thought that he would soon be free from sin. "It is the pleasantest thought I have," was his reply, and shortly after he fell asleep. His widow, Mrs. Esther Tyler, died May 25, æ. 72.

TYLER, Charles C., East Boston, Mass., Oct. 20, æ. 37, one of the proprietors of the East Boston Ledger. Mr. T. was former publisher of the Eastport Sentinel.

TYLER, Hon. Marcus M., Eddyville, Ky., Oct. 27, æ. —, a distinguished Freemason, at the time of his death Grand Master Mason of Kentucky.

TYNG, Rev. Dudley Atkyns, Brookfield, near Philadelphia, Pa., April 19, æ. 34. He was the son of the well-known clergyman of the same name, and, like him, belonged to the Low Church wing of the Episcopal church. He was eminent for his piety and ability, and favorably known as a lecturer on religious and secular subjects. "Stand up for Christ!" was his dying exhortation. His death was the result of an accident, and caused a great sensation.

TYSON, Hon. Job R., Montgomery Co., Pa., June 27, æ. 54. Mr. T. was born in Montgomery Co., and was a descendant of Job Roberts, distinguished in the former history of Eastern Pennsylvania. At an early age he came to Philadelphia to embark in the study of the law, and was called to the bar under circumstances favorable to subsequent success. From the outset of his legal career he had been largely engaged in public affairs, and had participated in more than the usual share of public duties. He was a member of the select branch of councils for two or three terms, and in that position interested himself in various measures of public importance with which his name is associated as author or prominent advocate. Mr. T. occupied himself in matters of state policy, and assisted in inaugurating the plan of publishing the valuable manuscripts and early documents bearing upon the history of the state and its colonial times. The series of volumes published as Pennsylvania Archives was thus begun when the brother of Mr. T. was in the legislature, and himself an earnest student of our history. During his whole life Mr. T. mingled actively in the political and public events of the day. In 1854 he was elected to Congress as one of the representatives from Philadelphia; and his name is connected with many measures of public interest for the term. He was particularly active in what related to the commerce of Philadelphia, and to the restoration of the ascendency it formerly enjoyed as an importing city. Various essays and letters on this subject had been given to the public by Mr. T. within a recent period.

U. & V.

UNDERWOOD, Rev. Alvan, West Woodstock, Ct., April 4, æ. 78. He was born at Woodstock, Sept. 8, 1779, graduated at Brown University in 1798, studied theology with Rev. Dr. Sanger, Bridgewater, Mass., and was ordained pastor of the church in the west parish in his native town, May 27, 1801, succeeding the first pastor, Rev. Stephen Williams. This connection was terminated after a ministry of nearly 32 years, by his dismission, at his own request, March 30, 1833, after which time Mr. U. spent some ten years in supplying churches in the vicinity, especially in Westford and South Killingly. For a few years he resided in Oxford, Mass., but in 1852 returned to his old home, where he died after a short illness, the oldest member of the association of Windham Co. The pastor of a retired rural parish, he labored, not without success, for its prosperity, enjoying during his ministry several seasons of revival among his people. Originally Arminian in his doctrinal views, he embraced afterwards the system of the Westminster divines. He published a sermon on the death of two children of Philip Hayward, Esq., a discourse on the war of 1812, and another on the 50th anniversary of his ordination, with some small tracts and articles in various periodicals.

VAN CAMP, Lieut., borders of Texas, Camanche country, Oct. —, æ. —. He was killed in a battle with the Camanche Indians; he was the only son of Alderman John C. Van Camp, of Lancaster, Penn. He graduated at the West Point Military Academy in 1855, with the highest honors of his class, and since that time has been in active service in the army.

VANCE, ——, M. D., Texas, July —, æ. — , a distinguished physician and citizen of New Orleans, La.

VAN DORAN, Garrett, M. D., New York city, April 4, æ. 75, of East Millstone, N. Y.

VAN FOSSEN, Gen., Ypsilanti, Mich., ——, æ. —. He was one of the earliest settlers in Mich., and for many years occupied a prominent position among leading men and statesmen. As long ago as 1840, he was commissioner of internal improvements, and several times occupied a seat in the state legislature. He had a mind well stored with information relating to both national and state politics.

VAN OLINDA, Rev. Dow, Fonda, N. Y., June 19, æ. —. He was for many years pastor of the Reformed Dutch church in that village.

VAN SANDTVOORD, Capt. Abraham, New York, N. Y., —— —, æ. —, a pioneer in the steam navigation of the Hudson River.

VAN TINE, Daniel C., Racine, Wis., Sept. 27, æ. 72. He was formerly an active, well-known business man in Cleveland. He settled on the west side, then Ohio City, in about 1833, and was a member of the firm of Beebe, Van Tine & Co., whose business house was on the river, east side. He also entered largely into real estate operations of the west side during the inflated period which culminated about 1836, and was extensively interested in the first railroad enterprise of the lakes, the Ohio Railroad, being at one time president of the company. The railroad company failed, and with it their bank and president. He removed to Milwaukie about 1844, and has since resided in Wisconsin. He was an old school whig, business man, gentleman, and Christian.

VANTUYL, David B., M. D., South Bend, Ind., Feb. 18, æ. 43. He was formerly of Dayton, but for the last five years, with the exception of eight or nine months, he was a prominent member of the medical profession in South Bend, Ind. He was also a member of good standing in the Baptist church, and always was foremost in any measure which he thought would promote the public good.

VAN WAGENEN, Gerritt G., Utica, N. Y., Sept. 27, æ. 57. The death of this well-known and universally esteemed churchman makes a sad gap in the working corps of many of our church institutions, and will fill the hearts of all his numerous friends with grief. He was treasurer of the corporation for the Relief of Widows and Children of deceased Clergymen; a member of the standing committee of the diocese; a trustee of the Fund for Aged and Infirm Clergy; and also of the Society for the promotion of Religion and Learning; a member of the vestry of Grace Church, New York; besides filling various other public and private trusts, both in the church and out of it.

MRS. LÆTITIA VAN WYCK,

Fishkill Village, N. Y., May 22, æ. 92. Many of the leading incidents in the life of the subject of this biographical sketch are connected either immediately or remotely with not a few highly interesting reminiscences of bygone years. As probably few readers of the present day have taken much pains to ascertain the state of our country during ante-revolutionary times, it will not be out of place to observe, that some scores of years before the American struggle for independence, New Amsterdam, now New York, consisting then comparatively of but a few houses and stores, and but a small settlement of Hollanders, being as yet located at Rensselaerwick, the counties of Dutchess and Orange, together with almost the whole of our present national territory, were an unbroken forest. Here and there a solitary pioneer might be seen pressing his way into the valley of Fishkill, and in the shadow of the overhanging trees constructing his rude dwelling near the watercourse. His table was supplied in part from the finny shoals that sported in the stream, but principally from the fallow deer and wild fowl which lodged about his dwelling. Soon, however, under the well-directed force of his brawny arm, the tall trees in the vicinity one by one were falling. And when a field had been cleared and subjected to the plough, and the iron share used in upturning the virgin soil had become blunt from the operation, at early dawn he slung it over the back of his steed, and pursued his way on the narrow path which stretched along the east bank of the Hudson, towards the vicinity of Wiltwick, now Kingston, Newburg and Poughkeepsie being at that time nonentities. On his arrival at Wiltwick, if successful in making his rhetoric effective with the blacksmith, he obtained the mending of his implement by the dim light of the forge during the hours allotted to repose, and at the approach of morning remounted his beast with the expectation of reaching home at the close of the second day.

As years rolled on, the sturdy sons of Holland penetrated farther into the interior. At various localities the forest yielded to the woodman's axe. Comfortable dwellings sprang up, and fields waved with the rich fruits of industry. About this time, a widow lady of Long Island, by the name of Adriance, purchased a tract of land, and located two or three of her sons at Hopewell. One of these, Isaac Adriance, had assigned to him the farm now in possession of his great-grandson, Thomas S. Adriance. Near a large oak, which is still standing as a silent witness of the past, lifting its foliage to the clouds, and extending its massive boughs far around, he erected his family dwelling. It was in this house, Feb. 5, 1766, ten years before the declaration of our national independence, that Lætitia Adriance, afterwards Mrs. Cornelius C. Van Wyck, was born. She was the youngest in the family, and the only child of her mother, Ida Schenck, her father having been previously married to Lætitia Van Wyck, daughter of Theodorus Van Wyck, Jr., whose farm was purchased, in 1736,* of Madam Brett, and is now in possession of his grandson, General Abraham Van Wyck, who has already numbered 84 years. Like herself, the children of the first marriage lived to a very advanced age.

All intercourse with the family of her maternal grandfather, Ralph Schenck, of Long Island, was for a while entirely interrupted. Ralph and his sons were stanch whigs of the revolution; one of whom being afterwards for nearly 20 years in succession a member of the New York legislature. And when the British had gotten possession of Long Island, their officers thought it no robbery to tax the old gentleman with their board and lodging during the continuance of hostilities, but not without exercising the courtesy of liberally complimenting him for his magnanimity.

In one instance, however, Mrs. Van Wyck's mother managed, with a flag of truce, under the protection of Col. Harry Wyckoff, by permission of Gen. Sir Henry Clinton, to make a visit to her father, when she received her patrimony in gold, till then secreted behind a rafter, which she so well concealed about her person as effectually to elude British vigilance, and convey it in safety to Dutchess Co.

One of Mrs. Van Wyck's greatest blessings in life was the moral and religious character of her parents. Her mother, Ida Schenck, was not only eminently pious, but almost morbidly conscientious; and her domestic and religious duties to her daughter and stepchildren were discharged with the most tender and scrupulous fidelity. The instructions and prayers of this mother were not lost on Mrs. Van Wyck. The heart of her father, Isaac Adriance, was similarly interested in the cause of religion. His house was a second home to Dominie Rysdyck, whither he often resorted for ecclesiastical counsel and support, and not unfrequently for sympathy under the burden of his domestic sorrows.

The population of the county being at that time sparse, Mr. Rysdyck apportioned his labors among the four congregations of Poughkeepsie, Fishkill, Hopewell, and New Hackensack. Consequently, the great distance to the places where religious meetings were held, together with the then customary length of Sabbath services, made attendance on public worship not a little trying to children; but notwithstanding this, Mrs. Van Wyck, from very early years, commonly accom-

---

* The deeds given at this period are written on parchment, and contain not only the year of the Christian era, but also that of "the reign of the Sovereign Lord George the Second of Great Britain, France, and Ireland, King, and Defender of the Faith."

panied her parents. And it was at that tender age that she became a subject, if not of intelligent and evangelical repentance, yet of deep conviction and very humble contrition for sin, the impression of which was not obliterated from the tablet of her heart at the last hour of life.

In the progress of the revolutionary struggle, an event occurred, which, in its consequences, afforded her and many others of her age an opportunity for obtaining a thorough English education. The occupation of the city of New York by the British army, in 1776, broke up and dispersed the parochial school of the Collegiate Reformed Dutch church. Its pious and accomplished teacher, Mr. Van Steenbergh, together with many others, fled; and finding refuge at Hopewell, soon reorganized a flourishing school. He was one of those who attached much importance to a thorough knowledge of the Heidelberg Catechism, and required his pupils to recite the contents of one "Lord Day" every Monday morning. In addition to this, Mrs. Van Wyck translated it from the Dutch into the English language. A manuscript thus executed by her at school is still in the possession of the family; it is in the form of double columns, containing the Dutch on the left, and a literal translation on the right. If Dutchess Co. has any reason to boast of her intelligence, civil courtesy, and moral and religious excellence, it must be credited in part to Mr. Van Steenbergh's school. It was not only a seminary of learning, but it was also the handmaid of morality and religion. Its place, in point of usefulness, was next to the pulpit. The city of New York, with its vicinity, for half a century afterwards, still felt its happy effects; not a few of its leading merchants, and influential and honorable citizens having been here educated.

Some two or three years after peace was established, the subject of this sketch was, May 3, 1786, and in the 21st year of her age, united in marriage to Cornelius C. Van Wyck, of Fishkill. This happy union, spared from death for 46 years, Mrs. Van Wyck ever loved to recognize as one of the greatest of the many temporal blessings with which the Lord had crowned her life; and her mind often recurred to it, with apparently growing interest, to within a few days of her death; her own life was prolonged 26 years after the death of her husband, until she had attained the unusual age of 92 years and four months.

Under the ministry of the Rev. Mr. Van Vranken, the father of the venerable theological professor, Dr. Samuel Van Vranken, and at the age of about 28, she made a public profession of her faith in Christ; and through the divine blessing on the labors of the same estimable pastor, she had the happiness of seeing her husband follow her to the table of the Lord. When receiving her into membership, Mr. Van Vranken was so much pleased with the statement of her religious experience, that he made it a subject of remark after his return home.

Soon after marriage, they took possession of the real estate of her husband, whose father, Cornelius, had died in early life, the estate having been recently vacated by that division of the American army which was stationed at the foot of the Fishkill Mountains to guard the entrance through the Highlands; and until the present family dwelling was erected, which was in 1791, they resided in the barracks which had been occupied by the American officers, and which, being then of no further use to the United States, were left to the owner of the soil.* The plain occupied by the barracks and other buildings, in the service of the army, located between the mountains and Fishkill Creek, was purchased from Madam Catharyna Brett in 1733,† by Cornelius Van Wyck, the grandfather of the late Cornelius C. Van Wyck. And the first mansion on the plain was in that year erected, which has ever since been in the family, and is now owned by Sydney E. Van Wyck, the great-great-grandson of Cornelius Van Wyck. This mansion is, in Lossing's Pictorial Field Book of the Revolution, incorrectly called "The Wharton House."

* It was in these barracks, during their occupation by the American officers, that the late excellent John D. Kees, of New York, son of Major Kees, was born.

† Catharyna Brett, commonly called Madam Brett, was sole heiress to the "Rombout Precinct," which was bounded by the Hudson on the west, and the mountains on the south, extending sixteen miles in each direction. Margaret Van Wyck, the eldest daughter of the first Cornelius Van Wyck here named, married Francis Brett, one of Madam Brett's sons; some of her descendants are still in possession of a part of their hereditary domain. Theodorus Van Wyck, the ancestor of Theodorus Van Wyck, Jr., and Cornelius, emigrated from Holland, and soon after his arrival in this country made Long Island his permanent residence.

Receiving in the course of years the responsible trust of a very large family of children, Mrs. Van Wyck found under her own roof a moral field of the highest importance, for the faithful keeping of which, through labors and prayers, she was richly rewarded in the abundant fruits of filial love and evangelical piety. She had a benevolent heart, and an uncommonly vigorous and well-balanced mind, both of which were constantly brought to bear on the task of shaping the moral and religious character of her family. She was a fluent epistolary writer, and had a happy gift for it. When some of her children were called to leave the paternal roof and occupy posts of usefulness abroad, she kept up her intercourse with them by correspondence. These letters are strongly marked by deep-toned piety and force of thought; and many of them bear a greater resemblance to those of John Newton than to any other now occurring to the mind of the writer.

Mrs. Van Wyck was fond of the society of her Christian friends, especially of her children, and numerous grand and great-grandchildren, in all seventy-four, some of whom are deceased; and she was seldom more delighted than when her parlors were filled with them. Taking a lively interest in their affairs, and participating with them in their juvenile pleasures, she thus seemed to live over again the happy days of her own childhood and youth.

She sympathized with the cause of evangelization in general, but felt a special interest in the American and Foreign Christian Union, and the Seaman's Friend Society. God's honor and worship lay near her heart. She loved the solemnities of his house, and, so long as circumstances allowed, was a constant attendant.

The pastors under whose edifying ministry she attained her fulness of Christian stature, were Revs. Rysdyck, Blauvelt, and Van Vranken, and Drs. Westbrook, Fisher, and Kip, most of whom, through her protracted course, she either saw falling on the field or retiring and going to their reward.

Of the large family she reared, the greater part are still living. Her first-born, Isaac C. Van Wyck, of Fishkill Landing, (of whom she sometimes spoke as her earliest object of idolatrous affection,) a man of inflexible integrity, and a heart formed for friendship, after having, many years previously, publicly avouched the Lord to be his God, fell asleep in humble reliance on his Redeemer, just five weeks before the death of his aged mother; and when the intelligence of his decease was announced to her, she feelingly remarked, "Now my first idol is gone; I thought I should have passed before him."

If in the matter of real comfort her experience in life admitted of any distinction, the balance would be in favor of her latter years. With the exception of a growing dulness of the ear, a dimness of the eye, and an abatement of physical force, she was exempt from infirmity. Not an aching limb, not even a suffering muscle, disturbed her gentle slumbers. To her, life had not lost its charm. Having as much of the things of this world as she desired, receiving continually the gratifying attentions of valued friends, and possessing a heart overflowing with a grateful sense of the Lord's goodness to her in providence and grace, how could it be otherwise? With a lively perception of this goodness during her last indisposition, she remarked to her beloved pastor that the whole of her life had been one line of Ebenezers. While she was thus happy in being continued in the flesh, she was living in the closest intimacy with God, and in daily readiness for her departure, sometimes wondering why her chariot was so long in coming. Yet its delay was never tedious. Amid the tender assiduities of a devoted family, there was so much to interest and gladden the heart, that her declining years, like the gentle flow of a silvery stream, passed almost imperceptibly away. And when her final sickness came, it was neither very severe nor of long continuance. Already the forces of life were nearly expended. Of the work of dying, there was but little left to be done. A slight cold, a gentle fever, and a general prostration of bodily strength, prepared the way for dissolution. The intellect remained bright and the voice clear to the last. Considering the possibility that her end might be approaching, she observed, but a few hours before the event, "If it be the design of my Saviour to take me to heaven now, I am willing to go; I believe he will accept me;" adding, "I hope he will take me gradually to himself." A little before death, there being no apparent increase of suffering, she inquired the hour of the night; after which, a few minutes having elapsed, her head was gently raised by the tender hand of watchful solicitude, when, in the twinkling of an eye, she went to her Saviour, leaving scarcely the visible motion of a muscle in her countenance, which, like the symmetry of her Christian character in life, was remarkably beautiful in death. "Mark the perfect man, and behold the upright, for the end of that man is peace."

VAN ZANDT, John, Albany, N. Y., April 28, æ. 91. This venerable, well-known, upright, and amiable citizen was born in Albany, and was rarely ever out of sight of the city. In 1804 he entered the old Bank of Albany as a clerk. In 1814 he was appointed its cashier, which office he held until 1833, when he resigned.

VASEY, Wilson P., M. D., Philadelphia, Pa., Dec. 26, æ. 31.

VERPLANCK, Gen. Abraham, Brooklyn, N. Y., Nov. 23, æ. 65. Gen. V. represented Albany County in the Assembly of 1837.

VINCENT, Joseph, Salem, Mass., May 25, æ. 90. He was born in Kittery, Me., Nov. 25, 1767. From early youth till he was 70 years old, he was engaged in a manufacturing business, and found in his pursuit a field for exercising untiring industry, and an integrity as a business man that was spotless in word and deed. He was one of those good old American mechanics whose profession is their pride; and in his day there were few or none his superior, as a practical and economical mechanic, in the country. But his mind was comprehensive on general subjects; and though of an aspiring and adventurous disposition, he marked out for himself and adhered to a modest course, and was unostentatious both in civil and social life.

VINTON, Rev. Justus H., Rangoon, Burmah, March 31, æ. —, the well-known missionary to the Karens in Burmah. Mr. V. had been in the missionary service over 23 years. He was appointed in 1832, and first sailed from Boston, July 2, 1834, in company with Mr. and Mrs. Wade, who were returning from a visit to this country, and Messrs. Howard, Dean, Comstock, and Osgood, with their wives, and Miss A. P. Gardner, (afterwards Mrs. Abbott.) He was a man of iron constitution, great energy, and indomitable will, and was thoroughly devoted to the work of missions. He was generally esteemed one of the most effective missionaries ever sent out by the society. Thousands of converted Karens rise up to call him blessed. During the past ten years, difficulties have existed between him and the executive of the Union, which resulted, a year or two since, in his withdrawal from connection with the society. Whatever may have been his faults, his virtues were great, as were also his zeal, his labors, and his success. His name will occupy an honorable place in the roll of those who have devoted their lives to the work of giving the gospel of salvation to the millions of Burmah.

VIRGIN, Eli, Fort Wayne, Ind., Aug. 3, æ. —, killed accidentally on the Great Western Railroad. He was a young man of remarkable business attainments, and the firm of Alexander & Virgin was reputed to be the heaviest in the United States. Some 18 months since, Mr. V. purchased from Jacob Strawn, at one sale, lands amounting to $99,000, while, during the same year, his investments in cattle exceeded that of any previous year of his transactions. The loss of a citizen of such universal esteem, and of such remarkable business capacity, falls heavily upon the farming community of Central Illinois.

VOSBURG, Charles, a few miles below Natchez, Miss., June 13, æ. —, killed by the bursting of the steamboat engine. He was a citizen of Vicksburg, Miss. Mr. V. went to Jackson, Miss., in 1845. His father was a respected physician, in Erie, Pa., of which place the son was a native, and from which he brought with him the clear judgment, prudence, and steady principles of his mother state. He resided, and read law, with Hon. Daniel Mayes, but, although licensed, did not engage in the practice of his profession. Preferring an out-door life, and possessing a mind cast in a mathematic mould, he gave his energies to the practical study of surveying and civil engineering. His busy life was varied and embellished by pursuits of another nature and a higher range. He manifested an early taste and aptitude for the natural sciences, which drew to him the fostering regard of men of cultivation and research. For geology he contracted an especial fondness, viewing it with earnest interest, from its bearings on the Mosaic record, and the use sought to be made of it by infidels as a lever against the truth. He was an active and efficient correspondent of, and a valued contributor to, the New Orleans Academy of Sciences; sending it, from time to time, minerals and fossils, and, a few weeks before his death, adding to its collection a complete set of sections of the forest growth of Lauderdale Co., Miss., which presented in itself a fair view of the state. His observant and intelligent interest gave him a high place in the opinion and regard of this enlightened body. In his pursuits among men, he was a tried man, a true citizen, and an earnest Christian.

W.

WADE, Col. John, Woburn, Mass., July 9, æ. 78. He was born in Woburn, April 3, 1780, and was the son of Ebenezer and Elizabeth (Leath) Wade. He married Polly Dorcas, daughter of Dr. John Page, Feb. 26, 1806, (Mrs. Wade died Jan., 1826,) by whom he had one son, John, born in 1810. His son graduated at Amherst College, entered the profession of law, and married Miss Annie E. Warfield. He died in 1851, leaving no issue. Col. W. commenced business as a country trader, in Woburn, in 1802, upon a capital of $170. He leased a shop of Mr. Joshua Reed, situated on the land now owned and occupied by J. J. Pippy, Esq.; but before the expiration of three years, he purchased the land where A. E. Thompson's store now stands, and erected a building thereon. He afterwards purchased the rest of the land, situated on Main and Park Streets, for the sum of $1500, and erected all the buildings thereon. At the time Col. W. commenced business there were but three stores in town — one at what was then called "Black Horse," now Winchester, kept by Paul Wyman; one at New Bridge, kept by Maj. Abijah Thompson; and one in the centre of the town, kept by Mr. Zebadiah Wyman. He continued in business until 1825, when he sold out to the Hon. Bowen Buckman. Since he sold his interest to Mr. Buckman he has been more or less engaged in the shipping business, and taking care of the property which he had honestly accumulated by his prudence, sagacity, and industry. In his business relations his integrity has never been questioned. He was a trader of the old school, and with him fair dealing was a matter of course. In his political sentiments he was a democrat, and has been fortunate in retaining the confidence of his fellow-citizens, having received more offices at their hands than any other man in town — sometimes elected almost unanimously, at others with a strong and bitter opposition. He was elected chairman of the board of selectmen 14 years, town treasurer 12 years, representative to the General Court 19 years, and a delegate to the Constitutional Convention of 1820, with but one opposing vote. He was also chosen moderator of nearly every town meeting from 1814 to 1830, state senator in 1824 and 1825, and appointed justice of the peace by Gov. Sullivan, and postmaster under President Madison in 1811. In military life he passed through the various grades of captain, major, and colonel. All the official trusts committed to him he has discharged with honesty and ability, and with reference to the best interests of his constituents. As a townsman he has done much to adorn and embellish his native place by the erection of good and substantial buildings. As a friend, there are those who bear witness to his kindly assistance and wise counsels — who feel that he has ever been to them a sincere friend, assisting them in their hour of need, and counselling them wisely in their hour of danger. Thus passed one who filled a larger space in the history of the town than any other man. Of a strong and comprehensive mind, he was eminently fitted to influence his fellow-men. He was the man of his time, and his influence will long be felt.

WADE, Benjamin, Natchez, Miss., May 9, æ. 67. He was born in Milford, N. H., in Sept., 1790. At a very early age he was sent by his parents to Boston, Mass., where, under his uncles, he was instructed in mercantile business. In 1816, at the age of 21, he went to Mississippi, where a brother, a physician, had preceded him, and commenced active life in Natchez as a merchant. In 1821 he married the wife who now laments his decease. By his ability and energy he rapidly advanced in prosperity, which never was interrupted in all the calamities that have passed over this commercial community since his beginning in business. His qualities as a business man were integrity, knowledge, skill, and promptness — the pillars which erect and sustain success. At one period he gave up business, and confined himself to his planting interests; but he found these insufficient for his mental employment, and he again returned to business, and continued to the last his success as both planter and merchant. In 1825 he was elected a member of the board of selectmen of Natchez, and served, at different periods, for five years in that body. In later years he was the efficient president, for many terms of service, of the board of police of the county, and in that capacity he gave full satisfaction to its citizens.

WADSWORTH, Hon. John, Albany, N. Y., æ. 90. He was an elector of president and vice president in 1800, and was appointed a judge of the Supreme Court of the state in 1819.

WAIT, Thomas, East Rodman, N. Y., Jan. 16, æ. 49. He held the office of judge of the county court, supervisor of the town, and postmaster, acceptably to the people, and with credit and honor to himself. He was a high-minded, honorable merchant, a kind and affectionate husband, father, friend, and neighbor.

WALDRON, Rev. Luke, Newport, Jan. 10, æ. 59.

WALES, Hon. S. A., Columbus, Ga., Oct. 4, æ. 59, a distinguished citizen. He was born in Connecticut, and moved from that state to Georgia at an early age. He was admitted to the bar, and practised law in Middle Georgia 40 years ago. He represented Habersham Co. in the Georgia legislature when a young man, and Jasper and Putnam counties in the year 1847. In 1855 he was the senator from Muscogee Co.; in 1857 he was elected one of the judges of the inferior court of this county, which position he held at the time of his death.

As a man, Col. W. was known for his integrity and honor; as a citizen, for his public spirit; as a neighbor, for his hospitality; as a friend, for his devotion.

WALKER, Hon. Wm. P., Lenox, Mass., ——, ——, æ. 80, judge of probate of Berkshire Co. His father was his predecessor, and the first judge of the court, while the late Judge Walker was succeeded by Judge Dewey. Judge W.'s personal appearance and manners were striking and dignified. As a judge he was courteous, patient, dispassionate, and intelligent; and he discharged all the trusts and duties of his office with ability and impartiality. As a citizen he was mild, candid, and remarkably free from violence of partisan feeling and expression. In all the relations of domestic and private life, he was exemplary, affectionate, and faithful. Honorable sentiments, unquestioned integrity, and genial and pleasant manners made him a popular citizen, and a highly satisfactory judge; and during the active years of his life, he held an enviable position in the affections and confidence of the people of Berkshire Co. Among a wide circle of relatives and intimate friends is Hon. Julius Rockwell, of Pittsfield, whose wife was Judge Walker's daughter.

WALKER, Lieut. Theodorick L., at sea, March 17, æ. —, attached to the African squadron. He was buried at Porta Praya, Cape de Verd Islands.

WALKER, John D., M.D., Manchester, N. H., ——, ——, æ. 49, assistant surgeon in the Mexican war.

WALKER, Isaac C., Esq., Buffalo, N. Y., May 31, æ. —. The Chicago Board of Trade "Resolved, that in the death of Isaac C. Walker, we have lost one who, as a business associate, had commanded the confidence and esteem of all, and as a friend had endeared himself to us by his many virtues."

WALL, Enoch, Carlinville, Ill., Aug. 22, æ. 46. He was born in Baltimore, Md., but removed to Carlinville, where he was elected justice of the peace, and acted as deputy in various county offices till about 1844, when he was elected recorder. When the new constitution was adopted, and the office of county clerk created, Mr. Wall was elected to that office, which he filled to his death, to the entire satisfaction and approbation of the whole county. Kind, obliging, and attentive, he had, by his numberless acts of friendly courtesy, won a place in the hearts of the entire people. A true Christian, of noble and lofty sentiments, strict and unswerving integrity in all his intercourse with men, the social circle, the church, the Masonic fraternity, and the people of Macoupin Co. have lost one of their brightest and most useful men, and his loss leaves a vacuum no man can adequately fill.

WALLACE, John P., M. D., Union District, S. C., Aug. 24, æ. 43, a citizen of Panola Co., Miss., a man of much skill and many virtues.

WARD, Charles M., M. D., Galveston, Texas, Sept. 30, æ. 33. Although a young man, Dr. Ward had attained an eminence in his profession that few arrive at, and had by his gentlemanly bearing and amiable disposition secured the favor and esteem of all who knew him.

WARD, Capt. James N., St. Anthony's Falls, Min., Dec. 12, æ. —, an officer of the United States army. He took a distinguished part in the Mexican war, and subsequently rendered valuable services to the government in the settlement of New Mexico.

WARD, Rev. Stephen D., Agawam, Mass., June 11, æ. 57, the only pastor in actual service in the state who died within the year. He was a native of New Jersey; graduated at Nassau Hall in 1819, studied theology at New Haven, and was employed there a few years in teaching. He was pastor of the church in Machias, Me., from 1834 to 1844, and after preaching in various places in New Jersey and Virginia, came to Agawam, and was installed in October, 1853. Mr. Ward was sound in doctrine, discreet, quiet, and unobtrusive in his manners. He was a good scholar, and his sermons were finished and scholarly. His voice was rather feeble, and he sought the quiet of a retired and small parish. Having no small children, and being possessed of some means of his own, he could live upon a small salary. The church at Agawam have therefore had the services of a minister who was qualified to fill a place where he could have obtained a salary twice as large as they were able to pay. He died peacefully, choosing to "depart and be with Christ."

WARD, Thomas W., Boston, Mass.,

March 3, æ. 71. Mr. W. was the son of Capt. Wm. Ward, and was born in Salem in the year 1787. In early life he for several years followed the business of a mariner, and became first officer of a ship of which his father was commander, in which profession he proved himself so efficient, active, and energetic, that, at the age of 19, he was placed in command of an Indiaman, belonging to the Hon. Wm. Gray. About the year 1810, he removed to Boston, where he established himself in business, and became one of the most enterprising and successful merchants of that time. He continued in business by himself until 1816, when he became a partner in the house of William and Hardy Ropes, under the style of Ropes & Ward. This partnership was continued about nine years, when Mr. Ward withdrew, having been appointed agent in this city for the house of Messrs. Baring Brothers, of London, a post of great responsibility, the duties of which he discharged with much ability and fidelity until recently, when ill health compelled him to relinquish it. He has been for many years a prominent and influential citizen, and has held various offices of great trust and responsibility. From 1830 to 1842, he was treasurer of Harvard College, and in 1843 the college conferred upon him the honorary degree of master of arts. He was also for many years treasurer of the Boston Athenæum, and was a trustee of the Massachusetts General Hospital. He was a man of strict integrity, of great enterprise, and uncommon business capacity, and much respected in the community.

WARDWELL, Rev. Granville, Westminster, Vt., June 24, æ. 38. He was born in Nelson, N. H., entered on his fitting course at Meriden, N. H., after he was 21, graduated at Dartmouth College in 1849, went immediately to Lane Seminary, after one year to Andover, Mass., where he finished his theological course in 1853, in the mean time teaching two years in Phillips Ac⸺ Andover, for the purpos⸺ paying debts incurred for in order that he might ent⸺ try unembarrassed, which ... the autumn of '53 he was c⸺ an evangelist at Sullivan, N. his aged and afflicted mothe⸺ ... resides. In a few weeks he went to Kalamazoo, Mich., and was installed pastor of the Congregational church there the following summer. After a short pastorate he returned again to Phillips Academy, in the autumn of 1853, and continued to teach there, preaching in the mean time almost constantly till November, 1857, when he felt that he could no longer be denied the privilege of giving himself wholly to the ministry. In Jan., 1858, Mr. W. entered on an engagement to preach in Kennebunk, Me., one year. Here, as everywhere else, he was fast becoming endeared to all who knew him.

WARE, John J., M. D., Galveston, Texas, Sept. 29, æ. 24.

WARREN, Freder'k, Worcester, Mass., ——, —, æ. 49, city marshal of Worcester, accidentally shot. In his office of marshal he was a prompt and efficient officer. And although his fulfilment of the Maine law gave but little satisfaction to the temperance community, yet, in all other respects, he proved himself a faithful and a popular officer.

WARREN, Dea. Benjamin, Augusta, Me., Oct. 26, æ. 90. Deacon W. settled in Augusta in 1795, and built the third log cabin ever erected within the township. On the same farm on which he then located he lived ever afterwards, and on it he died, and was buried beside his wife and several children.

WARROCK, John, Esq., Richmond, Va., Mar. 7, æ. 84. He was regularly elected printer to the Senate of Virginia for the last thirty-five or forty years, which office he held at the time of his death, having discharged the duties thereof with a zeal and efficiency worthy of all praise. For more than thirty years he published that very useful and popular work, "Warrock's Almanac." He was a good citizen, amiable in his deportment, of unpretending manners, and esteemed by all who knew him.

WASHBURN, Daniel, M. D., Stowe, Vt., Dec. 16, æ. 83.

WASHINGTON, Prof. Henry A., of William and Mary College, Md., Mar. —, æ. —. The Faculty of William and Mary College, at a meeting, say, "Intelligence having been received of the sudden and accidental death of Henry A. Washington, for the last nine years the professor of history, political economy, and constitutional law in this institution, —

"*Resolved*, that in the death of Mr. Washington, the impartial and dignified professor, the clear and convincing lecturer, the just and upright man, the Faculty have been deprived of a zealous and distinguished member, and the college has lost an ardent and active supporter."

WATERS, Rev. J. H., Apelousas, La., Feb. 22, æ. —. He was a young man of piety, of sound mind, and full of promise for usefulness in the ministry.

WATERSTON, Miss Helen R., Naples, Italy, July 25, æ. 17, the beloved and only daughter of the Rev. Robert C. and Anna Waterston, of Boston. She was the granddaughter of the Hon. Josiah Quincy, Senior, and a young lady of rare native gifts and accomplishments.

WATKINS, Rev. Nicholas J., Annapolis, Md., Aug. 1, æ. —, a minister of the Methodist Episcopal Church for upwards of 50 years. He was "an Israelite indeed."

WATSON, Hon. Shelton, El Dorado, Union Co., Ark. Jan. —, æ. —. He served as a prominent member of the last legislature of this state, and by his strong, practical good sense, his experience and wisdom, and the acknowledged rectitude of his intentions, accomplished, as he had sought, much for the public good. The voters of the sixth judicial circuit twice honored him with the seat upon their bench, and he was at the time of his death the incumbent of that office by a large majority of the circuit. As a judge he discharged his duties with ability, fidelity, and impartiality; and perhaps at no period of his life were his qualifications for that important office more highly appreciated than at the time of his death. Truly the state, in the death of Judge Watson, has lost one of her first and best citizens.

WATSON, G., M. D., Phil., Pa., Oct. 28, æ. —. Dr. W. was a Scotchman by birth, but had resided in Philadelphia for several years, and was favorably known to the medical profession, as also to the scientific world. He was connected with the city medical associations, the Academy of Natural Sciences, &c. He never aspired to prominence as a practitioner among his medical brethren, but was much esteemed on account of his social qualities, and his quiet, unobtrusive manners.

WATSON, George, Springfield, Ill., Aug. 15, æ. 33. Mr. W. was a native of Canaan, Conn. He went to the west about twelve years ago. Within the last seven or eight years he has been extensively engaged in constructing railways, among others the Illinois Central. Though quite young, he proved himself a man of great energy and business capacity. Every thing he undertook proved successful, and he very soon acquired fame and prominence in the circle of railway men. Nearly two years ago he was appointed superintendent of the Great Western Railway; and it is admitted by all that his peculiar talents and unceasing industry were of great value to the fortunes of the road. The railroad board of officers and employees, at a meeting, passed this resolution:

"*Resolved*, that in the death of Mr. Watson, the railroad community have lost one of its most valuable and able advisers, and the community at large a valuable and public servant, and his career among us gave unmistakable evidence of great financial ability, as well as external knowledge of the wants and requirements of the travelling community."

WATTERS, Gen. Henry H., Brunswick Co., N. C., June 14, æ. 47. At an early period of life the deceased was admitted to the navy of the United States, and after spending several years in that branch of the national service, during which time he visited many portions of the globe in the discharge of his duties, he resigned, and became a rice planter in his native county. It was natural that a man of his mental and moral worth should be appreciated by his county-men, and accordingly he was elected, in the year 1844, to represent his county in the House of Commons, and was repeatedly afterwards elected to the same position. He exhibited the same estimable virtues of the head and heart which he had previously done in private life,—practical sense, sound judgment, and sterling integrity of character,—qualifications which gave him the confidence of the House, and which made him a useful and influential member of that body.

WAUGH, Andrew, Esq., Roane Co., Va., June 12, æ. —, attorney for the commonwealth for that county.

WAUGH, Bishop Beverly, Baltimore, Md., Feb. 9, æ. 69, senior bishop of the Methodist Episcopal church. He was elected to the Episcopal office in 1836, and was universally respected for his character and ability.

WAYLAND, Wm., M. D., Batavia, O, Oct. 6, æ. 74. He was born in Madison Co., Va., June 20, 1783, and by his unaided exertions acquired a liberal education, and was particularly distinguished for the proficiency he had made in mechanical philosophy. His medical education was of a high order, the best his times could afford. In 1814 he commenced the practice of his profession at Circleville, and during that year served for a short time as a surgeon in the U. S. army, in the war with Great Britain. In 1815, after the death of the late Dr. Rogers, Dr. Wayland located at Bethel, where he soon acquired the confidence of the community, and obtained a large practice in his profession, which he continued to enjoy until 1826, when he removed to Batavia, where he continued the practice of his profession for about 20 years with great success. In 1829 Dr. W. was chosen to represent his county in the Senate of Ohio. In 1842 he united with the M. E. church at Batavia, of which he continued a worthy member till his death, leaving satisfactory evidence that his end was peace.

WAYNE, Hon. Henry C., Savannah, Ga., June 28, æ. 55. Dr. Wayne was a native of Savannah. He was a son of Richard Wayne, a highly esteemed merchant and citizen, and was born on the 25th of April, 1804. He was educated at Union College, Schenectady, N. Y., and subsequently graduated, with the degree of M. D., at the Medical College in Philadelphia. He soon after received the appointment of surgeon in the U. S. army, and in this capacity was stationed at Oglethorpe cantonment, Savannah. He was highly esteemed by the troops for his kindness and attention, especially when they removed from their barracks to Effingham Co. for their health. During the troubles between South Carolina and the general government, he was transferred to Charleston and stationed with the garrison at Fort Moultrie. Upon the departure of the troops from that station, he resigned his commission in the army, and settled in Savannah, where he pursued his profession with untiring zeal to the time of his death. Dr. Wayne filled many important posts of trust and honor at the hands of the people, and the ardor with which they generally came to his support evinced the strong hold he had upon their esteem and confidence.

He represented Chatham Co. in the Lower House of the legislature for one or two sessions. He was elected an alderman of the city in 1828, 1842, and again the year following. He was first elected mayor of the city in 1844, and served six terms in that important post, which he held at the time of his death. Dr. W. left a widow and three daughters, to whom he was every thing that is summed up in the endearing words husband, father, friend. He was a man of strong attachments, generous charity, and with but little of selfishness in his nature. These qualities attached to him a large circle of devoted friends, whom he was ever ready to serve at any cost to himself.

WEBB, Hon. E. H., Carmi, White Co., Ill., Oct. 13, æ. —. Mr. W. was one of the most prominent men in Southern Illinois, an able lawyer, a distinguished politician, an accomplished gentleman, and an honest man.

WEBB, Capt. Henry, Austinburg, O., Jan. 21, æ. 71. He was not one of the first pioneers to Austinburg, yet he emigrated from Stamford, Ct., at an early day, when Ashtabula Co. was comparatively a wilderness, the abode of savage beasts and savage men, and for more than 40 years enjoyed the blessings of a home and the fruits of his labor upon a farm, which his industrious hands had transformed from a wilderness into beautiful and highly-cultivated fields. He was connected with the war of 1812, and the vessel which he then commanded was the first captured by that struggle.

WEBER, Wm., St. Louis, Mo., March 13, æ. —, one of the oldest German citizens of that city. At the time of his decease he was a justice of the peace. Mr. W. was a man of fine talents, and was regarded as a remarkably vigorous and forcible writer. He was the original publisher and editor of the *Anzeiger*, which he founded, we believe, in 1833, and which he continued to edit until 1848.

WEBSTER, Jonathan P., Salisbury, N. H., Oct. 29, æ. 76. More than 50 years ago, Capt. W. was widely known as an honest trader in the adjoining town of Boscawen, and for more than 40 years he had been in business where he died; and every where, and by every body, he was esteemed a good citizen, an affectionate husband, an indulgent father, a kind neighbor, and an honest

man. In the whole state there is not to be found another man who has passed so many pleasant hours in business with neighbors in his store, spring, summer, autumn, and winter, as did the deceased, for the last half of a century. Every evening his books, his business, his whole earthly affairs, were well arranged, either for continued action or for a final closing up. Emphatically was he one of that number of the race whose actions tend to make the world the better for their having lived in it.

WEBSTER, Dea. Moses, Haverhill, Mass., Sept. 20, æ. 76. He belonged to a generation of Christians who had known trials, and were willing to suffer for the truth's sake. Kind, sympathizing, unostentatious in his deeds of charity, and conciliating towards all, so far as principle would allow, he still was ready to endure any sacrifice, rather than that the doctrines of the gospel should in the least be compromised. He was eminently a Bible Christian. He sought to become acquainted with all its teachings. He loved its precepts, and endeavored to square his whole life by them.

WEED, Mrs. Thurlow, Albany, N. Y., July 3, æ. —. Mrs. Weed possessed a vigorous intellect and extraordinary energy of character, combined with uncompromising honesty and sincerity, and a spirit eminently benevolent. Through that severe struggle for independence and position, incident to so many in our country, and which, to the gratification of an extensive acquaintance, was early crowned with distinguished success, she performed the duties devolving upon her with courage, fidelity, judgment, and assiduity, which won the respect and esteem of all observers. Auspicious change of circumstances worked no change in her modesty of manner, or in her sincerity of life and conversation. She only became more widely known to the affluent by hospitalities always as unpretending as they were munificent, and to the poor by more widely extended charities.

WELBORN, Maj. Carlton, Houston Co., Ga., Aug. 18, æ. 73. He was born in Wilkes Co., Ga.; was with Gen. Jackson in the war of 1812; was elected surveyor general in 1826; moved to Houston Co. in 1828, and has represented that county in the legislature more than once. He was a member of the M. E. church for more than 30 years, and class-leader most of that time. He was strictly an honest man and a faithful Christian.

WELCH, Rev. J. C., Providence, R. I., Feb. 13, æ. 66.

WELCH, Gen. Rufus, Philadelphia, Pa., ———— —, æ. —. Gen. W. was well and favorably known to the citizens of Philadelphia. For many years he made that city his residence and centre of business, and contributed more than any other man to the innocent amusements and instructive pastimes of its people. To accomplish these objects he spared neither time, labor, money nor health. It was his ambition to excel in and lead the particular kind of exhibitions to which he had devoted himself, not so much for pecuniary ends as popular approval. He sought fame, not money. He desired to be considered a generous and public-spirited manager. He opened new studies for those fond of natural history, and contributed more to the advancement of science, by his introduction into this country, after immense toil and at vast expense, from the burning sands of Africa, animals known to us only through the pen of the traveller, some of which were looked upon as fabulous. He was the pioneer in such enterprises. He took pride, too, in the city of his adoption, and sought to give her a standing above her sisters, by introducing and establishing there those games and amusements which are considered great features in European capitals. This prompted him to attempt the Hippodrome, which, for a time, drew thousands to its exhibitions.

WELCKER, Hon. James M., Knoxville, Tenn., Sept. 19, æ. —, judge of the third Judicial Court. In all the relations of life, as a citizen, member of the bar, and judge, he eminently deserved and obtained the high respect and esteem of all who knew him. He was a native of Roane Co., Tenn., but obtained his collegiate and legal education in this county, and continued to reside here until his death. A little less than a year ago, at a youthful age for so distinguished an honor, by the voice of the people he was transferred to the bench of this circuit. He was patient in the investigation of causes, courteous in his demeanor to the members of the bar, and in society, and possessing an acute sense of justice, gave promise, in a longer life and greater experience, to exercise no ordinary influence in the community where he lived, as one of its most useful and intelligent members. By general consent he deserved the title of the honorable counsellor. Fair, candid, and liberal in his practice, he scorned and avoided the low acts of chicane, seeking to present his cause upon the facts and the law, without turning aside into tortuous or indirect paths, to reach or to evade the measure of justice due to his clients. While he remained at the bar, he added much to its dignity and power. He sat upon the bench barely long enough to secure a full appreciation of his sound judgment and his impartial feeling. As a judge, his career had but just opened, the folds of the judicial ermine had gracefully draped his manly form, only to be laid aside forever. His death, though not instantaneous, was sudden and unexpected. A few days before his last illness, in conversation with one of his most intimate friends who congratulated him on his robust and healthful appearance, he remarked that he never enjoyed better health, and attributed it to his relief from the cares and anxiety of the practice of the law, a labor which only the members of the profession can appreciate. In less than two weeks from the time of this conversation, his earthly existence terminated, and he was numbered with the dead. His was, indeed, an untimely death. He went down to the grave from the very hill top of life, from the high table land, which those of us who have attained it hope to traverse yet not a few years, before reaching the declivity that leads to the tomb. His sun was in the brightness of its meridian, and went to its setting while it was yet noon. By the whole community, to which he was so well and so favorably known, his death will be felt long and sadly.

WELLES, Eben B., M. D., Waterville, N. Y., June 3, æ. 43. He was formerly, for several years, warden and vestryman in the parish of Trinity Church, Watertown, whence he removed, in 1855, to Waterville, where he was a member of the vestry of Grace Church, in that village. He was a man eminently genial and kind in his good works; and the universal sorrow at his death is a testimony how widely his merits and usefulness had become known, and how generally his loss is felt.

WELLS, Hon. E. N., Milwaukie, Wis., Aug. —, æ. 51. Mr. W. was a prominent member of the bar, and in 1839 was elected to represent the Territory of Wisconsin in Congress.

WELLS, John B., Esq., Boston, Mass., March 18, æ. 75. He had filled many offices of honor and trust in Boston, his native city, having been an alderman, representative, and senator in our state legislature. For many years, also, he held the office of inspector general of beef and pork, and was also for many years an active member and officer of the Charitable Mechanic Association. In all these situations he faithfully discharged his trusts. That genial disposition which made his home so delightful he carried into his daily walk in life. He possessed a heart open as day to melting charity. Many a poor widow and orphan will miss his kind assistance and advice. To his children and friends he leaves the example of an honest and useful life.

WELLS, Rev. Nathaniel, Deerfield, N. H., Dec. 31, æ. 84. He was the eldest son of Hon. Nathaniel Wells, of Wells, Me., for many years chief justice of the court of Common Pleas in York Co. He was born in July, 1774. The influence of a pious mother gave a serious turn to his mind at the first dawning of intelligence. At the age of 17, just before entering college, he made a public profession of religion, having, a few months previous, indulged a hope that he had passed from death unto life. He graduated at Dartmouth College in 1795, taking a high stand as a scholar. Dr. Snell, of North Brookfield, Mass., Rev. Josiah Prentice, late of Northwood, and the late Samuel Worcester, D. D., were classmates. His own inclination would have led him to enter the ministry as soon as practicable after leaving college; it was only in compliance with the earnest wishes of his father that he decided to remain at home and form a partnership with his only brother in mercantile business and navigation. About this time he married Eunice, daughter of Rev. Moses Hemmenway, D. D., for more than 50 years pastor of the First Congregational church in Wells, and who took a prominent part in the Hopkinsian controversy of those days. At the suggestion of Dr. Hemmenway, his father-in-law, and some neighboring ministers, he again turned his attention to the ministry, to which his heart had always inclined. He studied theology under the direction of his father-in-law, and in 1811 was licensed to preach by the association of ministers in York Co., Me. In July, 1812, after having preached as a candidate four months, he was ordained over the Congregational church and society in Deerfield, N. H. Here he remained till he closed his mortal life. His pastorate was a happy one. He had not great popular power as a preacher, but had other qualities which greatly endeared him to the people of his charge. In the pulpit and in all his private intercourse there was an air of sincerity and good will to all, which never failed to inspire confidence. He made no pretension to elegance either in diction or delivery. He thought the plainest statement of the truth the best. But though he took no pains to cultivate the graces of style and elocution, there was an earnestness and clearness and strong conviction of the truths he uttered which often made his preaching effective upon the conscience. His character was perfectly transparent; but while he was unusually frank he was remarkably prudent. He exercised great charity in judging of others; was inclined to think no evil of men, to hope all things, and believe all things. He was a diligent student of the Bible all through life, reading the Greek Testament with as great facility as the English translation. He made the Bible his sole guide in theological study, usually making his doctrinal statements in scriptural phraseology. He was dismissed in Sept., 1851, the society giving him the parsonage where he lived, worth about $1000, as a token of their regard. After his dismission he was a good parishioner, giving his hearty coöperation to the acting pastor, and always striving for the things which make for peace. During his last illness, which continued about four weeks, he was peaceful and happy, with the exception of a few intervals of severe physical suffering. Though he expressed a deep sense of unworthiness, his hope of heaven was firm. In his intercourse with his family, he was remarkably genial and affectionate; this made his home a happy one to all its members. He had twelve children. Of these, four died young; eight are still living, viz.: Maria, wife of T. M. White, Esq., of Deerfield, born July, 1798; David Wells, M. D., a physician of Lowell, Mass., born

Nov., 1803; Nathaniel Wells, Esq.. of Somersworth, N. H., born Feb. 28, 1805; Rev. Theodore Wells, of Barrington, N. H., born Feb. 21, 1807; Rev. Moses H. Wells, of Hinsdale, N. H., born Aug. 27, 1814; Elizabeth J., born Oct. 24, 1816, wife of John T. Humphrey, of Winchester, N. H.; Abby T. Wells, a teacher in Packer Institute, Brooklyn, N. Y., born June, 1819; and Alexander Wells, of Deerfield, born in the summer of 1821.

WENTWORTH, Mrs. Thomas, Antwerp, O., June 5, æ. 66, wife of Hon. Thomas Wentworth, formerly of Buxton, Me.

WESSELHOEFT, Wm., M. D., Boston, Mass., Sept. 15, æ. 65, homœopathic physician, and Ex-President of the Mass. Homœopathic Medical Society, a native of Chemnitz, Saxony. He was a skilful physician, and a kind-hearted man.

WESTBROOK, Cornelius D., M. D., Kingston, N. Y., March 23, æ. 76.

WETMORE, Mrs. Susan M., Bergen Hill, N. J., June 26, æ. 60, relict of the late Commander William C. Wetmore, U. S. N.

WHALL, Joseph B., Boston, Mass., Nov. 11, æ. 39. He was widely known and universally respected in the business community. Few men of his age have attained to a more honorable and useful position in the community by the exercise of their own abilities than Mr. W. The mind naturally reverts to the many excellences which marked his character — his great devotion to his mother and his family, his quick sympathies, elevated tastes, frankness, noble and generous impulses, combined with rare qualities of manliness, which made him a man of mark among his fellows, and gave him much influence in all circles.

WHALLON, Hon. Samuel S., Mayville, N. Y., July 6, æ. 54. He was the architect of his own fortunes. No adventitious aid of friends and fortune was his. Our common schools, without the appendages of modern libraries, or the accomplished instructors now generally secured, were the only academies accessible to him. But the advantages he had he improved to their utmost capacity; and underlying all, as the foundation for the superstructure, was plain, practical common sense, combined with untiring energy and unrelaxing perseverance. At an early period he filled several town offices creditably and satisfactorily. His mercantile career he commenced as a clerk, and, continuing some years in that position, became a partner and at length sole owner of the establishment in which he first engaged, and prosecuted a long, extensive, and successful business upon his own account. In the county he held several positions of trust and confidence, and represented his Assembly district in the legislature of 1855. In the fall of 1856 he was nominated and elected canal commissioner, and held that position at the time of his death. It is conceded that the duties of the office were discharged with ability, and with much independence and firmness. He sought not to evade responsibilities when imposed by duty. Seeking no conflict with any, yet, when the public interests intrusted to his charge seemed to demand it, contracts were annulled without hesitation, and the work of the contractor performed by the hands of the state. In the spontaneous tributes of respect which the news of his death has everywhere called forth is evinced the deep hold he had on the public heart. But few of our public men have fallen whose death created a greater sensation, or whose loss was more sincerely deplored. As a husband, father, brother, friend, his life practically illustrated the duties of each, and won in return the almost idolized affections of those sustaining towards him these respective relations.

WHEELER, Charles, Philadelphia, Pa., June —, æ. —. The Philadelphia bar "*Resolved*, that we have received with sentiments of painful regret the announcement of the decease of our respected fellow-member of the Philadelphia bar, Charles Wheeler, who furnished, during the course of a long life, an admirable example, both to the young and to the old, of learning, honesty, and fidelity as a lawyer, of simplicity, frankness, and purity of character as a citizen, and of sincerity, modesty, and devoted piety as a Christian.

"*Resolved*, that we deeply deplore the loss which this bereavement has occasioned to his estimable family, to the profession of which he was a worthy member, and to the community whose confidence and affectionate regard he had so long and so deservedly enjoyed."

WHEELER, Lieut. George L., Savannah, Ga., Oct. 27, æ. —, formerly of the Japan expedition, and recently attached to the revenue cutter Aiken. He was a native of Pennsylvania.

WHEELER, Moses, Claremont, N. H., Sept. 3, æ. 72, a member of the legislature for three consecutive years.

WHETSTONE, John A., M. D., Moorhouse Parish, La., Dec. 30, æ. 56, formerly of Antauga Co., Ala.

WHIDDEN, Samuel, Portsmouth, N.H., Oct. 22, æ. 79, formerly publisher of the Intelligencer, a newspaper printed in Portsmouth for about 12 years, ending in 1817.

WHITAKER, Cary, M. D., Weldon, N. C., June 12, æ. —. He was a graduate of Chapel Hill in 1802, and soon after commenced the study of medicine, which profession he practised for many years, with credit to himself, and usefulness to the community in which he was born and resided.

WHITE, A. J., M. D., St. Anthony's Falls, Minn., —— —, æ. —. Dr. W. was a native of Lincoln Co., Me., and in 1851 received the degree of M. D. at Bowdoin College. Possessing a strong, highly-cultivated, and vigorous intellect, which was adorned by the study of long years and a heart imbued with the highest virtues which belong to the living, by his good deeds, his unbidden charities, his domestic affections, which clustered so steadily and fondly around his young and trusting family, he exerted an almost mesmeric power over those who clung to him with the fervor of true and devoted friendship.

WHITE, Capt. James, Northfield, Mass., Nov. 5, æ. 76. Capt. W. had represented Franklin Co. in the state Senate, and was a highly-respected and influential citizen of Northfield.

WHITE, Rev. Henry, Garland, Vt., Dec. 7, æ. 67, formerly of Longmeadow, Mass.

WHITE, Rev. L. R., Brighton, Iowa, March 20, æ. 42. In addition to the ordinary labors of the ministry he devoted much time to the planning and general oversight of the work on the house of worship just completed at Brighton. His own hands were ready to assist in any part of the work; he wrought with the trowel and hammer on the foundation; and his last manual labor was in painting the pulpit. At the first meeting in that house his funeral services were performed; and his mortal remains were the first laid upon the table, made after a plan which he drew and gave to the mechanic, with special instruction to make it strong enough to support the remains of the dead on funeral occasions. That house of worship, also the one at Le Claire, remain monuments of his skill and energy. His work was truly pioneer in its character — a labor often unappreciated, but, after all, in some respects the most important part of the work to be done in the new fields of the west. As a preacher Mr. W. was instructive, earnest, and faithful; as a theologian, decidedly Calvinistic, yet tolerant; as a Christian, conscientious; and as a man, courteous and highly esteemed.

WHITE, Menzo, M. D., Cherry Valley, N. Y., Jan. 16, æ. —.

WHITING, Miss Susan, Copenhagen, N. Y., June 13, æ. 38. Miss W. was one of the oldest school teachers in the county, having taught nearly thirty terms. She was a reformer in her profession, and added to an excellent private character a womanly dignity well befitting the position she so long and usefully occupied. In her decease the educational cause has lost one of its most honored sympathizers, and the community an intelligent and worthy member.

WHITMAN, David, Lewiston, Me., Aug. 30, æ. 59. Mr. W. was born in Warwick in 1799. He had no advantages of early education, and owed nothing of his distinction to adventitious circumstances. He was placed in a cotton mill when quite young, and soon began to develop those remarkable mechanical talents which have given him such a wide-spread and enduring reputation. He worked his way up through all the gradations of a factory to the superintendency and agency of the largest establishments. During the few prosperous years which succeeded 1842 he was engaged with two gentlemen of Providence in the manufacture of cotton. In that time he accumulated a moderate fortune, which satisfied all his desires; and he retired to his farm in Cranston, determined to spend the remainder of his days in its improvement and embellishment. But he was not allowed to remain in this comparative repose. Almost every body engaged in the construction of new mills, or in the reparation of old ones, sought his services. Not only at home was he known and appreciated, but in every part of New England; and all over the country, where there is a cotton mill, he was soon recognized and acknowledged as the very best cotton spinner in the United States. With every part of the business — from the excavation of the first foot of earth for the edifice, to the last finish upon the fabric before exposed for sale — he was as familiar as with the alphabet. Many other men undoubtedly equalled him in theoretical knowledge; but he could produce — and this was his distinguishing characteristic, and which made his services and labors of such great value to manufacturers and capitalists — the very best article at the very lowest possible cost. Many of the most profitable establishments in Rhode Island and other states owe their success entirely to his ability and skill. He has spent most of the last five years in Maine, principally in planning, building, and arranging those gigantic and perfect structures which have been reared in the new manufacturing town of Lewiston.

WHITNEY, Asa Hammond, Vicksburg, Miss., Oct. 8, æ. 40, a graduate of Harvard, class of 1838.

WHITNEY, Jackson D., Oshkosh, Wis., May —, æ. 35 or 40. He was a lawyer of uncommon ability; was once a pupil of Judge Douglas, at Springfield, Ill., and afterwards entered the office of Ex-Senator Wilson, of Milwaukie, as a law student, and eventually succeeded to a partnership with that gentleman. He went to Oshkosh about eight years ago, and commenced the practice of law. His superior ability and eminent success as a lawyer soon secured him an extensive business. He was respected as a lawyer, loved as a companion, neighbor, and friend, ever ready to administer aid and comfort to the destitute, scorning a mean action, and alike faithful to friends and clients.

WHITON, Capt. E., Boston, Mass., Aug. 30, æ. 61, for more than thirty years agent for the New York line of packets. Capt. W. was a man of unflinching integrity, and had the entire confidence and esteem of merchants.

WHITTIER, Reuben, Palermo, Me., March 9, æ. 66. He was one of the oldest and most esteemed citizens of Palermo, respected for his personal worth, and his qualities as a citizen and a neighbor, by all who knew him.

WHITTLESEY, Elisha M., Washington, D. C., Dec. 7, æ. —. Mr. W. has for many years past occupied the position of a principal clerk in the treasury department at Washington, and was regarded as an able and efficient officer; and by his gentlemanly deportment, and kind and affable manners, won the esteem of all those with whom he was associated. Wherever he was known he enjoyed the respect of his fellow-citizens. His remains were conveyed to Canfield — the residence of his father, and the place of his nativity — for interment.

WHITTLESEY, Mrs. A. G., Colchester, Ct., July 18, æ. 70. Mrs. W. was for some time preceptress in the Deaf and Dumb Asylum of Hartford, Ct.; and afterwards, for several years, was editress of the Mother's Magazine, of New York city.

WIGGINS, Mrs. Irene H., wife of Dr. A. J. Wiggins, of Goshen, Ind., while on a visit at her mother's, æ. 27. She was a native of Palmyra, N. Y. At an early age she, with her parents, removed to Michigan, where she grew up and enjoyed the pleasure of a large acquaintance of warm and true friends. She was married in 1852, when she removed to Goshen, and for the last year was a resident of that place, where she leaves many acquaintances, together with her husband, to mourn her untimely loss. Peace to her memory.

WIGGINS, Nehemiah H., M. D., Rusk, Texas, Dec. 2, æ. 28. He was a native of Oxford, N. C.; received his education at Caldwell Institute, N. C., and Hampden Sidney, Va., with the ministry in view, but turned his attention to medicine, and graduated at Augusta, Ga., in 1853. In October, 1852, he was married to Clara C., daughter of Dr. Lovick Pierce, and sister of Bishop Pierce, of Georgia. He practised medicine for some time, with great success, in Georgia. In 1858 he removed to Rusk, Texas, where he had made many warm friends.

WILDER, Mrs. Mary, Boston, Mass., June 15, æ. 75, wife of Thomas Wilder, Esq., and sister of the late Rev. Dr. Leonard Woods, of Andover.

WILLEY, Hon. Calvin, Stafford, Ct., Aug. 23, æ. 82. He was born at East Haddam, Ct., Sept. 15, 1776; commenced the study of law at Hebron, in June, 1795, with John Thomson Peters, late a judge of the Supreme Court. In 1798 he was admitted to the bar in Tolland Co., and commenced the practice of law the same year. While he lived in Stafford he twice represented that town in the General Assembly of his state; and in 1806 was appointed the first postmaster at Stafford Springs, which office he held till he removed to Tolland, in 1808. While he resided in Tolland he was eight years postmaster in that place, and seven years judge of probate for Stafford District. He was an elector for President and Vice President of the United States in 1824, seven times represented the town in the General Assembly, was two years a member of the state Senate, and six years a member of the Senate of the United States, which time expired March, 1836. Since that time he held no public office save that of justice of the peace, but pursued with assiduity his profession.

WILLIAMS, Mrs. Harriet H., Mosul, Dec. 25, æ. —, wife of Rev. W. F. Williams, missionary to Mosul. She had just reached her field of labor.

WILLIAMS, Hon. Gardner, Saginaw City, Mich., Dec. 11, æ. 56. He was the eldest son of the very large family of Oliver Williams, and Polly, his wife, who resided at Concord, Mass. The father emigrated to Detroit in 1811, though the family did not follow him until some years after. They resided at Detroit for some years, and about the year 1818 removed to what is now the township of Waterford, Oakland Co., three miles west of Pontiac. There the father and sons erected a house and barn, which are still standing upon the bank of Silver Lake. The family consisted of Gardner, Ephraim, Alfred, Benjamin, Alpheus, and James, sons, and three daughters, one of whom is now deceased, the wife of Rufus W. Stevens, of Flint; a second, widow of the late Schuyler Hodges, of Pontiac; and the third, wife of Geo. W. Rogers, of Pontiac. The widowed mother, a hale and intelligent lady of nearly 90, a fine specimen of the old New England stock, still survives, living with her sons Alfred and Benjamin, at Owasso, Shiawassee Co. The deceased went early into the Indian trade, and soon became, and for many years remained, an agent of the American Fur Company. Perhaps no man understood the language of the Indians of Michigan, in its different dialects, better than he, or used it with greater effect. His power over them was complete, owing to his dignity, his strength of will, and his taciturn, self-collected manner. In personal character, he was honorable, upright, liberal, and, like the entire family, temperate. The deceased exercised a wide personal influence, through the nature and extent of his business, and from the number looking to him. He held many public offices at different times during his life, both under the federal government and the state government, in all of which, as well as those of a more local character above named, he acquitted himself with honor. He had, at different times, held the office of Indian farmer, and of Indian interpreter, for the duties of which he was unusually well fitted, and, if we are not mistaken, filled one of these up to the day of his death. The deceased was a commissioner of the first Board of Internal Improvements, appointed March 21, 1837; was county judge of Saginaw Co. for several years, was elected senator from the sixth district in Nov., 1844, and received the office of circuit court commissioner of Saginaw Co. during the same year.

WILLIAMS, Elihu, San Augustine, Texas, Oct. 13, æ. 21. Mr. W. removed in Dec., 1856, when about 20 years old, from Talladega Co., Ala., to San Augustine, Texas, where he read law, was admitted to the bar, and continued the practice of his profession till his death. By the noble impulses of his heart he had secured the confidence and esteem of all who knew him; and in 1856 was elected to the representative branch of that state legislature.

WILLIAMS, Rev. Eleazar, Hogansburg, St. Regis, N. Y., ——, æ. —. Mr. W. must have been between 70 and 80 years old when he died, as he was quite conspicuous in the war of 1812, as a bold and skilful leader of the St. Regis Rangers, under Gen. Dearborn, especially about the time of the investment of Plattsburg by the British; and there is good reason for the opinion that the precipitate raising of the siege and flight of the enemy was in consequence of an admirable ruse, well conceived and skilfully carried into effect, by Mr. W. In this service he received a severe wound, the effects of which annoyed him during life. Letters from Gen. Dearborn, and also from Gen. Moores, who was in command of the New York militia, to the secretary of war, speak of his moral character and gallant and efficient conduct in terms of very high commendation. Mr. W.'s father, Thomas Williams, was, if I mistake not, of a Massachusetts family, and though a white man, became the principal chief of the St. Regis Indians, then inhabitants of Canada; but on the invitation of Mr. Jefferson to the tribe in 1805, and afterwards of Gen. Dearborn and others, about the beginning of the war of 1812, a band, with this Williams family at their head, since distinguished from those who remained as the American party, abandoned their comfortable homes and property, and settled in the United States. The young men organized themselves as a band of rangers, which proved an efficient auxiliary to the American forces on that frontier. Thomas Williams abandoned a valuable property in Canada, remuneration for which was promised by the United States authorities; but that promise has never been fulfilled, and for the want of which the highly meritorious subject of this memoir had to endure, in his old age and a protracted illness, the griping hand of poverty. The writer of this was well acquainted with Mr. W. for more than 30 years, and this he thinks will justify the expression of his opinion that, notwithstanding Mr. W.'s defective education, he was a man of extraordinary ability. He need not say he was a pious man; his long and excellent standing in the church to which he belonged is proof of that fact; but he will add, that in all his intercourse with him, he always found him bland and courteous in his deportment, honest and honorable; in short, a man of the strictest probity, and withal a man of boundless benevolence in his disposition. Had this principle been weaker, and his self-love stronger, he might, and probably would, have died rich instead of poor. For a long time Mr. W. was the sole agent and chief of the American party of the St. Regis Indians, and it is believed that to the day of his death they reposed unlimited confidence in him.

Soon after the war of 1812 Mr. W. projected the enterprise for the New York Indians to purchase a large tract of land on Green Bay and the Fox River for their future home. With great perseverance and expense, and under the auspices of the executive of the United States, and after several long and fatiguing journeys, the object was effected. By treaties with the Menominee and Winnebago Indians a very large tract was acquired, which, a few years ago, was exchanged with the United States for a tract in Kansas equal to 320 acres for each of the New York Indians, and being less than one third of the quantity given for it in Wisconsin. These Kansas lands are the same which the executive, during the last session of Congress, asked for authority to sell for the use of the United States, and for which a bill was reported, and perhaps passed the Senate; it did not pass the other house. Of Mr. W.'s claim, if we may so call it, to being the son of Louis XVI., or dauphin of France, I have nothing to say, excepting that I always found him reserved on that question; and when urged to speak of it he did so with the utmost modesty, simply remarking that the testimony was before the public, and they must form their own opinions. Few persons, it is believed, can read that testimony, as arranged and published by the Rev. Mr. Hanson in a volume entitled "The Lost Prince," without feeling amazed and confounded. Able lawyers of extensive practice have declared that they have rarely seen made out, in any adjudicated case in court, a chain of evidence more complete. But he is gone where to have been a faithful servant of Him to whose service he devoted his life is infinitely higher regarded than royal birth and dominion. He died as he had lived, looking steadfastly to the author and finisher of his faith. His last words were, "Lord Jesus, have mercy on me, and receive my spirit."

WILLIAMS, Mrs. Amanda G., New London, Ct., Oct. 12, æ. —. Mrs. W. was endeared to a large circle of friends and acquaintances. Many will miss her numerous charities, and keep her memory green. She was a most estimable lady, and her decease will be very generally lamented. Mrs. W. was a daughter of Henry B. Gibson, Esq., of Canandaigua, and sister of Mrs. Watts Sherman, of New York.

WILLIAMS, Miss Charlotte E., Rutland, Vt., Oct. 7, æ. —, daughter of the late Chief Justice Williams, of that state.

WILLIAMS, Edwin M., Brownsville, Prairie Co., Ark., Sept. 18, æ. 33. At the age of 21 he was elected clerk of Prairie Co., upon its organization in 1847, which office he held for eight successive years. In 1854 he was elected by his fellow-citizens as their representative in the lower house of the General Assembly, and served his constituents in that body during the session of 1854-5, at the close of which he commenced the practice of law, and continued therein until his death.

WILLIAMS, D. O., M. D., Camden, Ark., Sept. 30, æ. —. He was an estimable and upright man, and a good citizen, whose loss will be deeply felt and deplored, as well by the community at large as by his immediate relations and friends. He formerly resided in Mississippi, where he had filled several responsible public positions, and was at one time a member of the Senate in that state. He possessed enlarged financial capacity, combined with great prudence and economy, and had accumulated a very large estate, part of which lies in Arkansas, and part in Mississippi.

WILLIAMSON, Col. John, Newton Co., Miss., May 19, æ. 48. Col. W. was born in Orangeburg District, S. C., Dec. 1, 1810, and moved to Newton Co. in 1844. For the greater part of the period since, he filled the office of sheriff in the county of his residence, and, in the discharge of his official and other duties as a citizen, deported himself with such amenity, justice, and kindness as to secure and retain the confidence and friendship of all who knew him.

WILLIAMSON, George T., London, England, Dec. 25, æ. 55, a citizen of Cincinnati, O. Mr. W. was born in Cincinnati, May 10, 1804. Since the organization of the Pioneer Association he had been its corresponding secretary, and probably did more than any other man to collect and preserve interesting facts and reminiscences connected with the early settlement of Ohio and Cincinnati. In him the association has lost one of its most useful and efficient members. He was a man of warm social qualities, of high and honorable impulses, an excellent member of society, and possessed more than ordinary abilities.

WILLIAMSON, Robert, Lincolnton, N. C., Dec. 21, æ. 45, clerk of the Superior Court of Lincoln Co.

WILLING, Richard, Philadelphia, May 18, æ. 82, one of the oldest representatives of one of the oldest and most distinguished Philadelphia families. He was a son of Thomas Willing, former president of the old United States Bank. He was born at the old family mansion, (demolished a year or two ago,) at the corner of Third Street and Willing's Alley, Dec. 25, 1775. Mr. W., having inherited great wealth, never engaged actively in business, though in his younger days he made several voyages to India and to Europe as supercargo of vessels belonging to the firm of Willing and Francis. In 1814 he was elected captain of the State Fencibles, who were ordered to Camp Dupont in anticipation of a British invasion. But he declined the office, and, indeed, throughout his whole life he avoided public situations of all kinds. He was married in 1804 to Eliza, daughter of Thomas Lloyd Moore. Four daughters and one son survive him. One of the daughters is married to John Ridgeway, Esq., and resides in Paris. The son has been abroad, but soon to return. He was connected also with other distinguished families in this country and in Europe. A niece of his was the wife of the late Lord Ashburton. He has always been regarded as an intelligent, upright, and honorable man, and a worthy representative of the class of courtly gentlemen of the past generation.

WILLIS, Rev. John M., Hampton, Va., March 26, æ. 67. For more than 34 years he was a resident of Hampton, and during that long period it was his fortune to occupy various responsible posts of federal, state, and local trust. As postmaster under the administration of Mr. Adams; as trustee of the Hampton Academy, which office was subsequently merged into the presidency of the board of school commissioners; as presiding officer of the town council; as presiding justice of the county court; and as a minister of the gospel, — he displayed traits of character which will embalm his memory in the minds and hearts of all who knew him.

WILLITS, Allison J., Mount Vernon, Iowa, April 22, æ. 47.

WILLSON, William B., M. D., Frederick City, Md., May 1, æ. 59.

WILSON, Sergeant, Fort McHenry, near Baltimore, Md., Sept. 28, æ. 45, of the ordnance arm of the U. S. army. The last 20 years of his life were spent in the army. He was with the American army under Gen. Z. Taylor, in Mexico, and fought in the battles of Monterey, Vera Cruz, Cerro Gordo, and most of the bloody engagements in the valley of Mexico. He was remarked for his bravery; and the late Gen. Persifer F. Smith mentioned him by name in his general despatches to the government at Washington; and at the conclusion of the war he was presented with a certificate of merit.

WILSON, John, Talladega, Ala., Aug. 23, æ. 40. Mr. W. was born and reared in Botetourt Co., Va. He resided for a short time in Athens, O., where he was professor in the university, returned and taught successfully in his native county, visited Texas, was for two years the principal of the Presbyterian Institute, in Talladega, and then the founder and proprietor of Southwood. He was a man remarkable for energy, industry, and punctuality, a good scholar, a fine writer, and most laborious teacher. In the discipline of his school, which was rapidly rising in popular favor, he was strict and close, watching over the morals and conduct of his pupils with untiring vigilance. As a father he was eminently judicious and faithful, and as a husband provident, kind, and devoted. In early manhood he became pious, and was, at the time of his death, a ruling elder of the Presbyterian church.

WINCHESTER, Rev. Thomas W., Phœnixville, Pa., Feb. 6, æ. —.

WINSLOW, Edward, Harvard, Mass., Sept. 23, æ. 62. Mr. W. was born at Middleboro', Mass. He acquired, early in life, a practical knowledge of machinery, in that town, and was for many years connected with the cotton manufactory established there. He afterwards moved to Dedham, and entered with zeal upon an invention which has conferred incalculable benefit upon our woollen manufacturers. This was the condenser, a machine which was at once adopted in all the mills in the country, and, so perfect did he do his work, it still continues to be used. Like many other really valuable inventions, however, it was seized upon at the time by the woollen manufacturers, and appropriated to their use without any acknowledgment to the man who originated and perfected it, so that he lost the pecuniary benefit which rightfully belonged to him. In after years, a sense of justice compelled many of the manufacturers to acknowledge his claim, and they made him a small compensation. This was one of those cases where the benefits are counted by millions, and the reward by tens and hundreds. But Mr. W. had acquired a celebrity, and was called to Nashua, N. H., where he took charge of the machine shop on the Indian Head Corporation, and aided in planning an extensive woollen mill. The crisis of 1828 was too severe a trial for the Indian Head Co., and the manufacture of woollens at Nashua ceased. The next year Mr. W. went to Lowell, where his reputation had preceded him, and when the Lawrences came in possession of the Hurd mill, now known as the Middlesex, he took charge of the machinery, both in building and running it. In his intercourse with men he was retiring and unobtrusive almost to a fault, but to his acquaintance he was social and warm-hearted. He had a strong religious and holy hope, and through life bore the character of an honest and upright man.

WINSLOW, Jeremiah, Havre, France, ———, æ. 77, brother of Isaac Winslow, of Philadelphia. Mr. W. was a native of Westbrook, Me., but for nearly half a century resided at Havre, where he accumulated a large fortune, chiefly in a successful management of the whale fishery. Previous to his residence in Havre, he resided temporarily in New Bedford, Mass., and is familiarly remembered by many who enjoyed his society at that time, and subsequently during his frequent visits here, and in their business relations with him. As an upright merchant he was esteemed, and as an accomplished gentleman and warm-hearted and sincere friend he was beloved by all who knew him. His brother, Isaac Winslow, of Philadelphia, was with him at the time of his death.

WINTHROP, Mrs. Elizabeth A., Maumee City, O., Aug. 30, æ. —, sister of the Rev. John A. Andras, principal of Blackheath college, London, and wife of the Rev. Edward Winthrop, rector of St.

Paul's Church, Maumee City, and formerly rector of St. Paul's, Norwalk, O. The deceased was a native of the city of Bath, Somersetshire, England, and came to America in 1832. She was married in 1839, at Lexington, Ky., at the residence of Capt. Henry Johnson, brother of Col. Richard M. Johnson, formerly vice president of the United States, to the Rev. Edward Winthrop, then professor of sacred literature in the Protestant Episcopal Theological Seminary of Kentucky. Modest and unobtrusive in her deportment, earnest and warm-hearted in her piety, indefatigable in her efforts for the good of others, it was the delight and glory of her strong and highly-cultivated intellect to lay all her trophies at the feet of Jesus; and she departed hence with a cordial and loving trust in that dear Saviour whom she had so cheerfully and strenuously served from her early youth. Much of her life had been spent in the work of Christian education. She was most loved by those who knew her best, and she left many friends to deplore their loss.

WITBECK, Martin, West Troy, N. Y., ———, æ. 52. As a citizen, he was highly esteemed for his integrity and ability. He had several times been elected to the presidency of the village. He held a very important position in the U. S. arsenal until the time of his decease, which he had sustained with credit to himself and profit to the government for 30 years. He was a ruling elder in the Reformed Dutch church, in which office he had often served with great faithfulness.

WITHY, Samuel J.; M. D., Philadelphia, Pa., June 23, æ. 65.

WOFFORD, Gen. W. B., Habersham Co., Ga., June 10, æ. 67. He was born in Franklin Co., Ga., May 13, 1791. Few men who possessed so few advantages in youth have acquired the eminence of Gen. W. All the days that it was his fortune to spend within the school room would not exceed six months. His father removed from Carolina, and was one of the first white settlers in that portion of Georgia. The settlers were compelled to build a fort, to protect themselves from the depredations of the Indians, who at that time also inhabited the same settlement. Any one can well imagine the advantages that country afforded for education, society, or any of the other ennobling and refining associations that are so essential to youth. William's youthful years were spent in the ordinary occupations that are incident to country life — looking after the affairs of his father's farm, and working upon it with his own hands. In the course of time schools came in, the Indians were driven off, and a new county was organized from that portion of Franklin and later purchases from the Indians, called Habersham; and he became the first sheriff, while yet quite a young man. He held that office one term only, having been elected to the state legislature, and successively for 14 years. His useful and varied services during that time cannot be enumerated. He was elevated to the position of speaker of the House, which has never been considered a questionable honor, as some of Georgia's brightest sons have looked to it as a position of no small moment. Having been a volunteer in the United States service in the war of 1812, he was promoted by the governor of Georgia from major through different grades to that of major general in command of the Georgia militia. At the expiration of his service in the legislature he was elected president of the Branch Bank at Dahlonega, and resided there several years. His duties as a banker, like all others intrusted to him, were discharged to the satisfaction as well as the profit of those concerned. He was subsequently sent by his constituents of Habersham to the state Senate, and twice elected president of that body. He was elector of the state at large for President Polk in 1844, and also for Gen. Pierce. In 1854 Gov. Johnson appointed him treasurer of the Western and Atlantic Railroad of Georgia, an institution that belongs to the state — an arduous and responsible position, which he held four years, and discharged the duties to the satisfaction of all parties. A few months after his retirement from this place he died at his residence in Habersham Co.; and his bones now rest under the sod where he was born. He was a benevolent, generous, and honest man. The beggar never went from his door empty. Few men of his means (and he had plenty) have contributed more to alleviate the suffering, appease the hungry, or bring out the latent virtues of those whom fortune did not favor, than Gen. W.

WOLF, John, M. D., Mohecanville, O., Feb. 17, æ. 30. He was born in Shippensburg, Cumberland Co., Pa., prosecuted his classical studies for some time at Pennsylvania College, and graduated at Cannonsburg, Pa., after which he completed his medical studies at one of the medical institutions of Philadelphia. As a successful practitioner he had few equals, and perhaps none superior of his age.

WOOD, Hon. George T., Trinity River, Texas, Sept. 5, æ. —. He was colonel of a regiment of Texas volunteers at the storming of Monterey, and distinguished himself by the coolness and courage of his bearing. He had been previously a representative in the Congress of Texas, and in 1847 was elected governor of the state.

WOOD, James A., M. D., Barre Centre, N. Y., Jan. 1, æ. 35. He graduated at Geneva, N. Y., and settled in Barre as a physician soon after. His practice had already gained him a good degree of eminence in his profession, and his intellectual force was of a high order. As a husband and father he was earnestly beloved, and is deeply lamented; as a neighbor and citizen he was very generally esteemed.

WOODBURY, Prof. Isaac B., Columbia, S. C., Oct. 26, æ. 39. He was born in Beverly, Mass., in 1819. He lost his father when only eight years of age; but this, as might be expected, drew forth the redoubled care of an affectionate mother. At the close of his 13th year he was placed at school in Boston, or, rather, he was removed to that city for the purpose; but, being himself intrusted with the necessary funds, he devoted his time and means to the all-absorbing object — music. To our distinguished countryman, Lowell Mason, Mr. W. owes his thanks for his first employment in Boston, it being through his influence that he was engaged as teacher in the public schools of that city. From this time he cast loose from the pecuniary aid of friends; and at the age of 19 such had been the success attendant upon his industry and frugality that he was enabled to visit Europe for study. A year was passed in London and Paris, under such instructors as Bishop, Phillips, Panseron, and Auber, while every moment, husbanded with a miser's care, was devoted to the theory and practice of music. On his return to Boston he at once took a high stand as a teacher, and for six years was thus fully occupied. Turning his attention towards New York, he at this time accepted the charge of the music at Rutgers Street Church, where he remained until severe application compelled him, in the autumn of 1851, to visit Europe for his health. Prior to leaving Boston Mr. W. had put forth several minor works, which had been well received, and gave evidence of no ordinary talent; and the autumn of 1850 was marked by the appearance of his great work — the Dulcimer. Critics condemned, but the people received it with admiration and delight; and a success before unheard of has attended it from the first. As a composer and compiler of many of the most popular musical works of the day, as one of the most devoted friends of sacred music and church psalmody, as a Christian poet of unsurpassed sweetness, and as a writer of rare ability and winning tenderness, such as touched and moved the heart, we do not propose to speak; we leave that for others who knew him better in those departments, and who have plucked garlands with him in the fields of that much-loved science, to which he devoted his life, and to which he has fallen a martyr. We prefer to allude to him as a man of great worth, as a citizen of a generous, noble nature, as a Christian gentleman in the highest sense of the word. The Musical Review was first issued in Jan., 1850, Mr. W. being its sole editor; and, without an effort on the part of the publishers, it commanded at once a wide circulation, simply from the charm imparted to its pages by its editor. To Mr. W.'s efforts the public are indebted for the great change in the *morale* of American songs for the piano-forte. Previous to the appearance of his compositions, all, with hardly an exception, were, to say the least, of doubtful moral tendency. The first song of Mr. W. — "He doeth all things well" — has acquired a world-wide reputation. Others of later date — such as "Be kind to the loved ones," "Strike the harp gently," "Mother dear, pray for me" — are also popular. He returned from Europe in the summer of 1852, with a good store of musical treasures, and fresh impressions of the music of the old world, and renewed health and vigor. During the summer of 1855 he purchased of Judge Butler that beautiful table of upland on Prospect Hill, so delightfully overlooking the two villages of Norwalk and South Norwalk, the waters of the Sound, the Norwalk Islands, and the picturesque and romantic country far interior to the north and east, the west and southwest, for a home. But, his health having again failed, he travelled largely abroad and at home, and was at the south when his strength rapidly gave out, and he expired with the consoling words upon his lips — " I am prepared ; God's will be done ; I have not deferred my preparation to this time."

WOODBURY, Rev. John, Hastings, Minn., Aug. 27, æ. 55, a citizen of Lynn, Mass.

WOODFORD, Mrs. Pauline A., Grasshopper Falls, K. T., Jan. 26, æ. 27, wife of Rev. O. L. Woodford, home missionary at that place. For two years and a half she was principal of the Cherokee Female Seminary, for the higher education of young ladies. While among that tribe in the far west, to a great extent through her instrumentality, the seminary was visited by a precious work of grace in which many of the pupils were hopefully converted to God. Her short life was not barren of these most glorious fruits. As a wife she was an example of perfectness. Her good sense, her amiable disposition, and her Christian character won at once upon the esteem of the community, and made her death, less than eight months after her location among them, felt as a public calamity.

WOODRUFF, Rev. Horace, Huntington, L. I., Feb. 8, æ. 54.

WOODS, Robert E., Bardstown, Ky., May —, æ. 32, educated at St. Joseph's College, Ky., at one time treasurer of San Francisco.

WOODWARD, Hon. Apollos, Williamsport, Pa., June —, æ. —, associate judge of Lycoming Co.

WOODWARD, Rev. W. H., St. Louis, Mo., March —, æ. —, rector of Grace church. A meeting of the clergy of St. Louis say, " Resolved, that we have lost a brother, amiable and sincere, accomplished as a scholar, and much esteemed as a preacher."

WOODWORTH, Hon. John, Albany,

N. Y., June 1, æ. 88. He had resided in Albany nearly half a century. He established himself at Troy, in the practice of the law, more than 60 years ago, when the present city of Troy was a straggling village quite overshadowed by Lansingburg. He was a member of Assembly from Rensselaer Co. in 1803, and an elector of president and vice president in 1800. He was associated, at an early day, with John V. N. Yates in a revision of the laws of this state. In March, 1819, he was appointed by Gov. Clinton a judge of the Supreme Court in the place of the late Chief Justice Spencer, whose constitutional term of service then expired, and remained on the bench till 1823, when, though in the full vigor of mind and body, it was assumed that he had reached the period in life when the constitution interposed a disqualification. Judge Woodworth's active habits, and his correct, temperate mode of life, contributed to his good health, cheerfulness, and longevity.

WORTH, Edmund, Kennebunk, Me., Feb. 5, æ. 84, a citizen of West Newbury, Mass., and a member of the Baptist church.

WORTHAM, Elbert H., M. D., Mount Pleasant, Tenn., Jan. 2, æ. 26. He was son of Augustine W. Wortham, and was born Dec. 13, 1831. He read his profession with Dr. W. J. Hunter, of Mount Pleasant, and graduated at the Medical College in Louisville, Ky., in 1853. He married Miss Edmond Vanhorn, and practised two years in Mount P., when he removed to Santa Fe, in Maury Co., and there pursued his profession with great success and satisfaction. He was kind and attentive to his patients, affectionate to friends, and possessed great good will to all.

WRIGHT, Hon. Nathaniel, Lowell, Mass., Nov. 5, æ. 73. He was the oldest son of Hon. Thomas and Eunice (Osgood) Wright, and was born in Sterling, Mass., Feb. 13, 1785. He was fitted for college by Rev. Reuben Holcomb, of Sterling, (Y. C. 1774.) He held a very respectable rank in his class, and graduated with distinction at H. U. in 1808. He pursued the study of law in the office of Hon. Asahel Stearns, of Chelmsford, Mass., (H. U. 1797;) was admitted to the bar in 1814, and opened an office in Dracut, Mass. In 1816 Mr. Stearns was elected university professor of law in Harvard College, and removed to Cambridge the following year. Mr. W. succeeded to Mr. Stearns's office, and to much of his professional business; and subsequently purchased his (Mr. S.'s) residence, which he occupied during the remainder of his life. He attained to a high rank in his profession as an able and well-read lawyer. For forensic display he had little taste, and made no pretension, but when an emergency required a sound, reliable, and disinterested opinion, he was the dependence of his community for many years. Singularly simple and almost blunt in his manners, and sparing of words, there was an honesty and independence about him which won confidence and secured respect. On the organization of the town of Lowell, Mr. W.'s judgment, counsel, and legal knowledge were under great and constant requisition. He performed an important part in the preliminary purchase of land by the founders of the town, and in setting it off from Chelmsford he was an efficient agent. When Lowell was incorporated as a town in 1826, he was elected its first representative in the legislature, and was reëlected the two following years. He was also chosen chairman of the first board of selectmen. In 1834 he was elected to the state Senate from Middlesex district. In 1836 Lowell was incorporated as a city, and Mr. W. was elected its mayor in 1841 and 1842. On the organization of the Lowell Bank in 1828, he was elected first president, an office which he held uninterruptedly for more than 30 years, resigning it only on the 22d of October, 1858, just two weeks before his death. In all the positions which he filled he gave entire satisfaction to those whose interests were intrusted to his care. He married, March 5, 1820, Laura Hoar. They had five children, four sons and one daughter, viz., Nathaniel, Thomas, William Henry Prentice, Emery, and Laura Grace. Two of his sons, Nathaniel and Thomas, graduated at Harvard College in 1838 and 1842 respectively. Nathaniel was a lawyer in Lowell, and died Sept. 18, 1847, æ. 27. The others are still living. Thomas is a lawyer in Lawrence, Mass. Mr. W.'s wife died Jan. 21, 1857, æ. 62.

WRIGHT, Matthew B., Rome, N. Y., Dec. 3, æ. 28, at the residence of his father, William B. Wright. He was grandson of Deacon Allen Wright, who died Aug. 19, 1855, æ. 82, whose parents emigrated to R., then called Fort Stanwix, as early as 1788. Mr. W. had been engaged in constructing various railroads in Illinois and Iowa. A few years more only were wanting to have placed him in the front rank of the many talented members of the useful yet arduous profession to which he had devoted himself.

WRIGHT, Samuel, M. D., York District, S. C., Sept. 12, æ. 55. His reputation as a physician gave him an extensive practice; and, although for some years in very feeble health, he never refused to go where he thought he could be of service in relieving the miseries of his fellow-man.

WRIGHT, Rev. Luther, Woburn, Mass., June 21, æ. 88. He was born April 19, 1770, in Acton, Mass. He was the son of Samuel and Rachel Wright. His parents were professors of religion, and much respected. Early developing an active and vigorous intellect and a fondness for study, he entered upon his studies preparatory for college, under the tuition of his pastor, Rev. Mr. Adams, of Acton. He graduated at Harvard College, with good reputation as a scholar, in 1796, in the class with Leonard Woods, D. D., John Pickering, LL. D., James Jackson, M. D., and others of distinguished reputation. Of fine social powers and moral habits, and much respected as a scholar, he was immediately after his graduation engaged as the teacher of a select school in Cambridge. In the mean time he pursued a course of theological study with Rev. Dr. Tappan, professor of divinity in the college. On being licensed to preach, he was well received, and soon had a call to settle in the ministry in Medway, and was ordained there June 13, 1798. December 23, 1798, he was married to Miss Anna Bridge, daughter of Rev. Josiah Bridge, of East Sudbury. At the time of his ordination, his views of theology were of the Arminian type, but subsequently he believed and faithfully preached the Calvinistic system, and in his last days cherished it as his only foundation of consolation and of hope. He remained at Medway 17 years, with good acceptance as a preacher and pastor, and during his ministry there many were added to the church. While there he instructed a considerable number of young men in their studies, preparatory for college. He was dismissed from his pastoral charge in Medway in Sept., 1815, with the unanimous recommendation of the council, as an able and successful pastor. In January, 1817, he was settled in Barrington, R. I., where he remained four and a half years, and where his labors were attended with signal success. From Barrington he went to Carver, where he remained about three years. Here, also, he enjoyed a precious revival of religion. After this he went to Tiverton, R. I., where also his labors were greatly blessed. He loved the precious doctrines of the gospel, and preached them with plainness and earnestness, and with such skill and practical adaptation to his hearers, as gave them a lodgment in the mind, until by a divine blessing they became the power of God and the wisdom of God to the salvation of many. His devotional services were peculiarly appropriate and fervent. No Christian could listen to his prayers without feeling that he was near the throne of grace. He was very happy in his visits to the sick and afflicted. His directions to the inquiring, his exhortations in meetings for conference and prayer, and his instructions to young converts, were always edifying, happy, and useful. He was scrupulously careful and upright in all his dealings with his fellow-men. Nor was he without interest in the benevolent movements of the day. He gave more in charity than was known except to his intimate friends, and some years since, by his last will and testament, he made disposal of his property mostly to charitable and religious objects, amounting to several thousand dollars. He was careful and prudent as a steward of the Lord's bounty, that he might be able to leave something to promote the interests of Zion.

WURTS, Wm., Carbondale, Penn., July 15, æ. 47. He was born in Morris Co., N. J., was a graduate of Amherst College, and about the year 1830 removed to Carbondale, where he commenced the practice of law. In 1836 he was married, and removed to Wilkesbarre, where he continued the practice of his profession for about 10 years, when he returned to Carbondale. While residing in Wilkesbarre, about the year 1839, he united with the Presbyterian church, and was for many years superintendent of the Sabbath school connected with the Wilkesbarre church, and was a diligent, punctual, and faithful officer. Upon his return to Carbondale, he united immediately with the church there, and was shortly after installed as elder.

Y.

YEOMAN, Samuel F., Washington, O., July 7, æ. 65. The deceased served a term in the war of 1812, after which he went to Fayette Co., where he was a citizen a greater part of the time. He was an editor two years, held the office of magistrate, postmaster, county commissioner, judge of the Court of Common Pleas, and representative in the state legislature, the duties of all which he discharged to general satisfaction.

YOUNG, Rev. David, Zanesville, O., Nov. —, æ. —. At his death he was a superannuated minister of the Ohio conference. He made a bequest for building a new house for the Second Street Methodist Episcopal Church in Zanesville, the seats or pews of which must be free forever, $12,000; to the Ohio Wesleyan University, at Delaware, $1,000; to the Bible Society, $1,000; to the Missionary Society of the Meth. Episcopal Church, $1,000; the residue of his estate, after providing a few small legacies, to go toward building a Methodist church in the third ward of Zanesville. It is estimated that this will amount to from $5,000 to $10,000. His library, which was valuable, was given for the benefit of the preacher in the Second Street charge. To the colored man raised in his family he gave a life estate in four acres of ground, the cottage house just east of his own residence for life, an annuity of $200, and a quantity of personal property necessary to establish him in life. The bequests in this quarter were nearly equivalent to a donation of $5,000.

YOUNG, Henry B., M. D., Zanesville, O., Oct. 12, æ. 36. He possessed a happy combination of intellectual and moral qualities which recommended him to the community in which he lived. A man of exemplary modesty and humility, free from self-importance and dogmatism, and deservedly admired for his uncommon self-control, sterling intelligence, and Christian decision.

PROF. IRA YOUNG,

Dartmouth College, Hanover, N. H., Sept. 13, æ. 57. He was born in Lebanon, N. H., and spent his minority with his father as a house carpenter. He then fitted for college, and graduated at Dartmouth in 1828. "For 28 years," says Prof. Brown, "he has been connected with Dartmouth College as an officer, having been appointed tutor in 1830, and professor in 1833. During that long period of service nearly 1500 students have received his instruction, of whom it would be difficult to find one who does not remember him with great respect, and who will not hear of his death with heart-felt sorrow.

"Prof. Young had some qualities which fitted him eminently for his position. He was, in the first place, thoroughly master of the science and literature of his own department. Distinguished while in college for mathematical attainments, he never relaxed in careful and constant study of those branches to which he particularly directed his attention. His mind was thoroughly disciplined for patient investigation according to sound philosophical principles. He sought for truth, and not for victory; and thus he was ready to test his attainments by the most thorough methods. As he was thorough with himself, so he was with his pupils; trying them with doubtful questions, which the studious might answer with ease, but which the ignorant could not evade. Yet he was never harsh, nor captious, nor irritating, though quick and ingenious in exposing the mistakes and follies of the student. Besides his ample knowledge, he possessed remarkably the power of clear and complete statement. It was the habit of his mind to reduce his facts to principles, and to present these in their simplest forms. Few instructors could have excelled him in the facility with which he could disentangle and elucidate a complicated problem, whether for the satisfaction of his own mind, or the instruction of another. And he was as patient as he was acute. He was of a quiet temperament, not easily roused, nor rendered impatient at the dulness or want of perspicacity in another, unless this resulted from a moral rather than an intellectual weakness. He was truly modest; tolerant of others who differed from him; not over-confident of his own opinions; nor arrogant of the claims of the sciences which he loved; nor obtrusive of his views upon any subject. His friends, knowing his ability, regretted that he gave too little of himself to them and to the world; while he, aiming to be just with himself as with others, and unambitious of distinction, was contented with abundantly fulfilling the duties of his station, seconding, according to his opportunity, every good work that was presented, and willing that others should win the laurels and wear them. Another cause probably restrained him from very active exertion. The disorder which led to the last fatal result had been growing upon him for years, though he knew it not, and by many symptoms, not aggravated, but constant, was inviting him to quiet.

"In all the relations of life Prof. Young was most friendly and genial. In the midst of whatever differences of opinion might naturally arise between associates, there was never even a momentary interruption among them of sincere respect and regard, and unrestrained familiarity of intercourse. His kindliness of nature attached to him, by bands delicate but strong, all who came into connection with him. But the true exaltation of his life was in its moral and religious beauty. Not indifferent to the good opinion of others, he did not make their opinion the guide of his life, but rested with simple, unostentatious faith on the word of God. On that he reposed with a confidence which nothing could shake, and which was sufficient for the severe trials of his last days.

"A few years since, Prof. Young went to Europe, mainly in behalf of the college, selecting and purchasing the instruments for the Shattuck Observatory, and purchasing several thousand volumes for the library.

"His associates have in him lost a brother whose aid was always ready, and whose counsels were always wise; the church a faithful member; and the college a learned and judicious officer, whose place cannot soon be filled." Said President Lord, "Prof. Young was a consummate teacher. During his college course he taught school every successive winter, as he had done for years preceding; and earned nearly enough to pay the expenses of his course, for he had high wages, and never wasted them on his clothes or pleasures. That discipline settled in his mind the elements of knowledge. The principles of all true knowledge were already laid — first, when he was born; and, secondly, when he was born again. He had, of course, tools to work with, and facility to use them for the good of others, enlarging all the while his own fabric, till he became the man of science that he was for his successive trusts. He loved, as few men ever love, to teach, and as no man can love who begins not early and makes not teaching his profession. He was never more at home, or more at ease, than with his class. He loved to enrich them out of his own stores, and thereby draw out and sharpen their independent faculties. He was not disconcerted when he sometimes drew to little purpose; though sure, by set remonstrance, or by his peculiar, quaint, dry, and caustic humor, to rebuke indifference and neglect, or expose the artifice of a bold, shrewd, or sly pretender. He was sure of what he knew, and never gave way without a reason. Yet he would never persist when he saw no foothold. He was set, but not dogmatic, or no more so than a sincere man must be when he believes what he teaches and is in earnest. He would never defend before his class a theory because it was new, or because it was learned, or because it was his own, or because it was popular, or because he would otherwise be ruled out of the synagogue, till he had made it sure by calculation, or probable by analogy. When convinced that an hypothesis could not be verified in the present state of knowledge, or never in logical consistency with established facts or moral certainties, he abandoned it like an honest man. But where he had his ground he stood, and would have it understood. Of course his teaching was effectual. Those who would be made scholars, he made sound and good ones. He gave a strong character to his departments, and his departments were an honor to the college."

YOUNG, Rev. G. W. F., Baltimore, Md., July 12, æ. 33.

EXTRACTS FROM LETTERS.

From Hon. Edward Everett, LL. D., Boston, Mass.

"I have much pleasure in expressing a very favorable opinion of your work, both as to design and execution. If the succeeding volumes are prepared with the same diligence in collecting the materials, and the same skill and judgment in digesting them, as the specimen volume which has already appeared, the work will possess far more than a temporary interest; it will become a valuable historical compend."

From Joseph Palmer, M. D., Boston, Mass. (Harvard Necrologist.)

"Your Annual Obituary Notices of persons who died in 1857, which I have examined again and again with increased interest, is a work of great value to every community, as it places upon record, in a permanent form, memorials of friends and relatives who have passed away, and who would otherwise, in a short time, be forgotten by the world at large. As a book of reference it is invaluable to the historian. The amount of information you have collected is truly surprising, and the labor and skill you have exhibited are such as few would or could have displayed. *Haud inexpertus loquor,* for I have had no inconsiderable experience in writing and compiling biographies, and I can well appreciate the value of your labors in that department. I am much gratified to learn that you intend to continue your enterprise."

From Rev. Dr. Blanchard, Lowell, Mass.

"I have been surprised and delighted at the amount of valuable reading in your volume of 'Notices' for 1857, and in that portion of the volume for 1858 which I have had the privilege of examining. It was a happy suggestion which led to the collecting and arranging, in a form convenient for reference of these memorials of many who might not have found a place in our biographical dictionaries; but whose names, characters, and services, private affection could not, and public spirit should not, forget. I feel myself personally indebted for information respecting various important facts and dates, and for the means of acquiring it as occasion may demand."

From Rev. Dr. Cleaveland, Lowell, Mass.

"So far as I know, it is perfectly original with yourself, in its conception, — the only attempted work of the kind. Other registers in abundance there are, and registers of annual mortality; but they are mere registers. They are not repositories of 'Annual Obituary Notices.' The record of character and service is not in them.

"Your work has the somewhat rare merit of being exactly what it claims to be, — nor less, nor more. You propose to publish, in compact and permanent form, such obituary notices as the passing year had published in scattered, isolated, and transient forms. The authors of the *originals* published what their tastes, or more frequently their feelings, dictated at the time, and you have garnered up in your book the fruits of such isolated labor. You have done your task with exemplary diligence and fidelity. The over-minuteness of some of these notices, and the extreme meagreness of others, are no fault of yours. You have *gathered,* not *written* them.

"No one has any right to complain that his departed friends are not sufficiently noticed, for that should have been attended to when their original obituaries were composed. You do not profess to give the actual or comparative merits of the deceased, but to let the world see what friends and contemporaries were pleased to say concerning them. Viewed only in this light, your book I would unhesitatingly pronounce worth three times its cost.

"It is as a book for reference hereafter, as a contribution to yet unwritten, but invaluable history, that is to vindicate its real, intrinsic, and rare value. Ten, twenty, thirty years hence, hundreds will wish they owned it."

From Rev. O. Street, Lowell, Mass.

"I have derived an unexpected pleasure from a three hours' acquaintance with your book. One would hardly think of going to an obituary catalogue for entertainment. Our first thought is, that we should go through it as we walk through a cemetery, caring to notice only here and there a monument, and that, not for the sake of the epitaph, but from respect to the memory of the buried one. But I find it quite otherwise. I have made a list of between fifty and sixty names, for future reference, with a view to their historic associations alone. There is to me the full value of the book in two or three of the notices it contains. I shall greet the successive volumes of the work with the deepest interest. May Heaven prosper you in this good work of rescuing precious memorials from oblivion."

"I thank you for the privilege of reading the advance sheets of your forthcoming volume [Vol. II.] of obituary notices. I congratulate you on your success in condensing your material without a loss of interest. You are engaged in a great and good work. If others read your sketches with a tithe of the interest with which I have read them, they will reap a blessing from this converse with the great and good who have passed away."

From Rev. Jos. R. Page, Perry, N. Y.

"The idea of your work is an admirable one, and so far, well executed. The great wonder is, that such a work was not commenced years ago. How much knowledge of great importance and deep interest would, in that case, have been rescued from oblivion!"

From Judge Bell, of New Hampshire.

"The plan of the work is good, and its design meritorious. It will preserve many valuable notices of the eminent men who are passing away, which must otherwise, for all practical purposes, be soon lost. Its execution, both literary and mechanical, is highly creditable to yourself and your publishers."

From Rev. Prof. Rood, of Hartland, Vermont.

"I have read it with unexpected and unabated interest. It is an original conception, a new book on a new plan. It is just the thing needed in every library and every intelligent family. I am surprised that you could have obtained such an amount of interesting biographical notices, so ably written, and filled with so many thrilling incidents, in a single year. It contains some of the most classic writing, and some of the most poetic and refined outbursts of feeling, to be found in our language. Any one who will read the notice of the Hon. James Bell, of N. H., or that of the Hon. Andrew Pickens Butler, of S. C., with the addresses made in the U. S. Senate on the announcement of their death, will understand what I mean. I think your book, humble as its pretensions are, is an onward and upward step in biographical literature, and you have my hearty wish for your success."

From Thomas N. Stanford, Esq., Perth Amboy, N. J.

"Its examination and perusal has afforded me very great satisfaction and interest. Many of the individuals who have been thus noticed by you were among my most intimate friends, and I am glad to possess the volume on their account."

From Rev. Stephen G. Bulfinch, Dorchester, Mass.

"I am surprised to find, upon a very cursory examination, how much of interesting information has been collected. The notices of such men as Governor Marcy, Judge Parris, Langdon Cheves, Judge Wilde, Senators Bell, Butler, and Tappan, Lieut. Herndon and Dr. Kane, make your volume a work of national importance. Of its interest to individuals, as conveying intelligence respecting those they have known, I can judge from the fact, that among the first names I noticed in it, was that of a venerable friend in a distant part of the country, who died last July, but of whose decease I had not before heard."

From Hon. Robert C. Winthrop, of Boston, Mass.

"I have examined it with great interest, and hope it may prove the commencement of a valuable series. When our call shall come, none of us can wish any thing better on this side of the grave than to be honorably mentioned in so permanent a register."

From Rev. William Horton, D. D., Newburyport, Mass.

"We were pleased to see the memorial of our dear Anna, and my wife's honored father. It must be valuable to all whose friends are noticed in it, and certainly you have got it up in the very best style."

From Charles Stoddard, Esq., Boston, Mass.

"You do a great service to the country by thus preserving notices of good men and women, and I hope you will persevere."

From Henry Austin Martin, M. D., Roxbury, Mass.

"It places upon permanent record memorials of multitudes of men who would otherwise be forgotten, but who have exercised important influences, more or less general, on the civilization and development of their time. Necessarily mingled with these biographical notices must often be introduced anecdotes and incidents of much historical interest. Men and events have soon been forgotten, or their memory obscured in the onward rush which characterizes the marvellous growth of this country. I must allude to the pleasure I have enjoyed in looking over the numerous notices of deceased physicians, and a particular satisfaction in reading the notice of the admirable life of Dr. William Yates, whose claim to having been the first to introduce vaccination into America, though quite new to me, is ably vindicated, and seems undoubted."

From Hon. Edward S. Rand, Newburyport, Mass.

"I am much pleased with the work. It will be found a very useful book, and should find a place in all good libraries, and I believe will meet with a most favorable and deserving reception."

EXTRACTS FROM NEWSPAPER NOTICES.

From the Lowell Courier.

"Every year removes by death many persons eminent in their profession or business, or distinguished for their attainments, their achievements, or moral worth. Their merits are often duly recorded in the ephemeral columns of a newspaper, but beyond this they have no lasting memorial. Yet it is desirable that by some means a record may be made of their virtues and distinguishing characteristics, in a permanent form. Such a desideratum Judge Cresby has undertaken to supply, and in the volume before us we have the result. The obituaries evince great care and research, and comprise a large number of names."

From the Citizen and News, Lowell.

"Many of the notices are very valuable in an historical point of view, and many others throw much light on genealogical points. It has been said, 'There is no history; it is all *biography*.' If this is so, the careful compilation of a work of this kind from the evanescent issues of the newspaper press, both preserving the historical and personal facts and daguerreotyping the ever-changing expressions and opinions of the times, is a valuable service, and one deserving of strong encouragement."

From the Boston Journal.

"In the rapid succession of events, great and small, which crowd our swift-speeding lines, the dead are quickly forgotten, are fairly jostled from thought and memory." "The present volume is the result of a happy thought. The brevity of the notices fit them for the general eye, and even those who peruse them with a sigh and tear, would equally feel the inadequacy of a finished sketch, while they cannot fail to be soothed by the comparative durability of the record."

From the Boston Traveller.

"This is the first volume of a work that must be found very useful, and which, we think we can venture to say, is destined to meet with success of the most marked character. Judge Crosby's aim is to bring together the obituaries of the distinguished people of the country, including women, and the wives and widows of eminent and professional men." "We know of no work of this kind which has struck us more favorably than that of Crosby's, and we are convinced that the public will extend to it that reception which it so eminently deserves, and which shall at the same time do justice to its own taste and intelligence, while solidly rewarding the deserving author. The publishers, let us add, have brought their usual skill to bear upon the work, which therefore must be, merely in point of beauty, a welcome addition to all good libraries. Works that are to increase and endure should always be handsomely printed; and such is the case with this new candidate for favor."

From the Boston Courier.

"Judge Crosby is entirely competent to make the work all that is needed; indeed, the book as we now have it is a good and useful book; we only venture to offer a suggestion (more of suppression and compression) which may increase its value and utility."

From the Congregational Journal.

"Within a few years, a new interest has been awakened with reference to the preservation of memorials and records of the eminent dead. The names of the great and good are annually enrolled in the bills of mortality. In many instances, this is their only memorial. Brief obituary notices are, perhaps, prepared by friends, which meet the eye of here and there one, and their very names are soon forgotten. In after years, when dates and deeds are called for where they have been prominent actors, no living man can furnish the requisite information. The history of our state and nation, the local histories of towns, colleges, schools, and churches, are intimately blended with the biographies of public men and benefactors. If history is not written by contemporaries and by eye-witnesses, it must necessarily be marred by mistakes. Nothing is so soon forgotten as dates. The biographies of useful and benevolent citizens who have contributed to the establishment and development of good institutions are little prized by those who succeed them and enjoy the fruits of their toil." "Now, every effort to rescue from oblivion the history of the prominent actors in life's drama, ought to be encouraged. Judge Crosby, of Lowell, Mass., has originated a noble enterprise in the right direction and in the right way." "It is to be hoped that the compiler will find sufficient encouragement in his labors to continue the work from year to year, as he proposes, and thus furnish a fund of useful material for future historians and biographers."

From the New York Observer.

"A volume of great interest and value. In its preparation the compiler has made use of a vast amount of printed and manuscript materials, availing himself largely of the newspapers of the day."

From the Vermont Standard.

"He was induced to undertake the herculean work of publishing a series of such publications, in the hope of supplying a permanent record of the virtues and distinguishing characteristics of deceased persons, whose death is oftentimes too meagrely noticed in village newspapers. We have examined this work, and have derived pleasure and profit from this obituary catalogue." "The work is one which not only ought to be in the library of those relatives whose friends are noticed in it, but it is needed in every intelligent family. Its arrangement is excellent, and its literary and mechanical execution such as to commend it to the favorable reception and cordial welcome of the public."

From the Boston Recorder.

"This handsome octavo is the first instalment of a series of volumes, which, if life and health are spared, the competent and diligent author contemplates giving to the public from year to year. The design and utility of such a work any one can see at a glance. Such a record in an individual case will not interest all readers, but there are very few who can look through an annual volume of Obituary Notices without finding many names that will awaken recollections of interest, and some that will deeply affect the feelings." "The beginning is a good one, and the author has our best wishes for his success in like labor through many years to come."

There is a notice of Gov. Marcy in the volume for 1857. As the steel plate likeness of him was not obtained in season for that volume, it is now used for this.

N. C.

www.ingramcontent.com/pod-product-compliance
Lightning Source LLC
Chambersburg PA
CBHW030745250426
43672CB00028B/482